TEACHING MACHINES AND PROGRAMED LEARNING, II

Data and Directions

Edited by

ROBERT GLASER

Professor of Education and Psychology
Director of Research, Learning Research and
Development Center, University of Pittsburgh

TEACHING MACHINES AND
PROGRAMED LEARNING, II

Data and Directions

DEPARTMENT OF AUDIOVISUAL INSTRUCTION
NATIONAL EDUCATION ASSOCIATION
OF THE UNITED STATES

Contents

Preface   vii

Foreword   xi

I. Perspectives and Technology

1. Reflections on a Decade of Teaching Machines—
   B. F. Skinner   5
2. The Analysis of Instructional Objectives for the Design of
   Instruction—Robert M. Gagné   21
3. Research on Programing Variables—James G. Holland   66
4. An Analysis of Programing Techniques—David J. Klaus   118
5. Teaching Machines and Computer-Based Systems—
   Lawrence M. Stolurow and Daniel Davis   162
6. The Theory and Practice of Adaptive Teaching Systems—
   Brian N. Lewis and Gordon Pask   213
7. Assessing the Effectiveness of Instructional Programs—
   A. A. Lumsdaine   267
8. Programing Classroom Instruction—Bert Y. Kersh   321

II. Technology and Subject Matter

9. Programing in Mathematics and Logic—*James L. Evans*   371
10. Science Education and Behavioral Technology—
    Francis Mechner   441
11. Reading and Related Verbal Learning—*Harry F. Silberman*   508
12. Programed Instruction in English—*Susan Meyer Markle*   546
13. Programed Learning of a Second Language—*Harlan Lane*   584

III. Implementation

14. School Use of Programed Instruction—*Lincoln F. Hanson
    and P. Kenneth Komoski*   647
15. The Use of Programed Instruction in Industry—
    H. A. Shoemaker and H. O. Holt   685
16. Use of Programed Instructional Materials in Federal
    Government Agencies—*Glenn L. Bryan and John A. Nagay*   743

IV. Directions

17. Toward a Behavioral Science Base for Instructional Design—
    Robert Glaser   771

Subject Index   810
Author Index   821

Preface

A few years ago, I was greatly concerned that the uncritical rapid acceptance and too-ready use of programed instruction would accomplish two things: that high expectations coupled with awkward usage would result in disappointing outcomes and that the rush toward immediate practicality would pull the field away from its loose ties with the scientific study of behavior. As is usually the case, things were neither as good nor as bad as expectations. There were disappointments, but there were more successes, and nowadays one hears educators planning the use of programed instructional materials in future courses of study. The interest of behavioral scientists and subject matter scholars in education has multiplied with gratifying rapidity, but the demand is still much greater than the supply. The words "teaching machines and programed learning" are heard less and less, and one hears more about "behavioral science research relevant to education" and "educational and teaching technology." This is as it should be, because the present techniques of programed learning represent only instances of the ways in which behavioral science might contribute to educational practice. The coordination of scientists and educators is still a fledgling enterprise which requires constant nourishment, and it is to this end that the papers in this book are presented. The authors represent individuals who consider teaching machines and programed learning as essentially an endeavor in which behavioral science and modern subject matter knowledge provide necessary fundamental bases for education. The authors, in general, are not committed to any method of programed instruction, but are committed to teaching methods which are developed on the basis of behavorial theory and experimental evidence. It is as a possible contribution to the strengthening ties between behavioral science and the process of education that this book is put together.

As indicated in Lumsdaine's Foreword, this book had its beginning when I chaired a three-day national symposium on research in programed instruction convened by the National Education Association in 1963. The symposium was opened by William G. Carr, executive secretary of NEA, who emphasized its theme by stressing the significance of a meeting of behavioral scientists in the halls of the National Education Association. At this meeting, most of the authors of this book presented preliminary papers for discussion; other authors served as discussants and were invited later to prepare papers. Subsequent to the symposium, the chapter by Lewis and Pask was requested. For the symposium, Edward J. Green was requested to prepare a paper on college level and professional education; this excellent paper was not included in this volume because of the relative dearth of programed instruction in higher education and because experiments carried out with college and professional students were reported as appropriate parts of other chapters.

A significant source of stimulation at the symposium was the participation of invited discussants. These people were: C. Ray Carpenter, Donald Cook, Norman A. Crowder, Jack A. Easley, James D. Finn, John C. Flanagan, Thomas F. Gilbert, Lloyd E. Homme, John L. Hughes, David R. Krathwohl, Phil C. Lange, J. C. R. Licklider, C. Mauritz Lindvall, Wesley C. Meierhenry, Omar K. Moore, Ross L. Morgan, Gabriel D. Ofiesh, Jay Orear, Douglas Porter, James H. Reynolds, Wade C. Robinson, Ernst Z. Rothkopf, Stanley M. Sapon, Wilbur Schramm, Warren D. Shepler, and George Spooner.

The symposium and the preparation of this book were made possible by a grant from the Carnegie Corporation of New York to the National

Education Association. This assistance is keenly appreciated. The continuing active interest of the NEA, and particularly its department of Audiovisual Instruction, in the technological aspects of instruction has made them a significant force for dissemination in the field. Appreciation is due to Anna L. Hyer, executive secretary of DAVI, and to Robert C. Snider, assistant executive secretary of DAVI, who is as delightful and helpful a publisher as one could wish. Special appreciation is due to Janet Leban, editor for DAVI, for all details of final editing. Margaret Fullick, technical assistant at the University of Pittsburgh, acted as editorial associate from initial notions through final product; her suggestions, rewritings, and editorial work were constantly helpful.

My work on this book was done at the Learning Research and Development Center at the University of Pittsburgh. This Center is one of the national research and development centers sponsored by the U.S. Office of Education and provides the appropriate climate for thinking about and working on educational innovation.

ROBERT GLASER

Pittsburgh, Pennsylvania
May 1965

Foreword

The status of any scientific and professional field can be gauged in large part by the publications that represent it. This is especially true of the benchmarks that are provided by a few key papers. In the present field such key papers have been represented particularly by Skinner's 1954 and 1958 articles, by Pressey's initial articles in the late twenties, and, it may turn out, by a few of the more recent papers.

Another kind of benchmark in a developing field is provided by major compilations that bring together or integrate a host of individually less comprehensive reports. Such volumes may take the form of a sourcebook such as the initial publication of *Teaching Machines and Programmed Learning* (TMPL-I); alternatively, they may constitute more integrative reference works such as the present volume (TMPL-II) or, in a broader and more mature field, the *Handbook of Experimental Psychology*.

In introducing TMPL-II, I have no intention of attempting to delineate the major perspectives of the rapidly developing and still quite young field which it represents. Glaser and I earlier tried to do something like that, as of 1960, in our concluding remarks to TMPL-I. But the job was easier then, even though the major points of view we tried to outline then still seem (to me at least) to stand up rather well after five years of further and somewhat riotous growth of the field. In any case, the fitting perspective for an evolving field is primarily one that looks forward to the future rather than backward to the past or intro-spectively to the fleeting present. Such a mainly future-oriented per-spective comes appropriately at the conclusion rather than at the out-set of such a volume as this and has been ably supplied by Glaser in his concluding chapter to the present one. It would be a gratuitous task to endeavor to preview either the book itself, the field it currently represents, or the trends to which its contributors and editor have point-ed. The rest of these brief introductory remarks will, rather, mainly be confined to some comments about the evolution of the book itself, par-ticularly as it relates to its predecessor volume, TMPL-I.

Sometime around late 1958 or early 1959, Glaser and I decided that a useful service to researchers in the then infant field of educational technology would be performed by putting together in a single, com-prehensive sourcebook the theretofore scattered and already sizable, though as yet still manageable, literature dealing more or less directly with "teaching machines and program(m)ed learning." This seemed like an easy as well as useful thing to do—the work of a few weekends, perhaps, we told ourselves. About a year and a half later, after James Finn (then president of the NEA's Department of Audiovisual Instruc-tion) had induced that organization to sponsor and publish the book—and after Glaser and I had spent most of our weekends and other spare time for over a full year at the seemingly simple job—*Teaching Ma-chines and Programmed Learning* (I) finally went to press—724 pages of it.

At that time, with the exception of Galanter's slender and somewhat fragmentary collection of some symposium papers and abstracts, TMPL-I was the only published volume in its field. Our initial concep-tion of the usefulness and demand for such a volume seems to have been as much an underestimate as was our notion of the amount of time and effort needed to produce it. Though conceived originally as a reference work primarily for research workers, the book turned out to have a much wider popular audience. After an initial impression of a paltry 3,000 copies, the book quickly ran (by May 1962) into some five printings and to date (not counting its Japanese translation) has sold around 15,000 copies—one of the most profitable (and most bulky) works ever issued by the NEA, I am told. This phenomenal best-seller record was, presumably, due more to the hunger of the educational profession for *any* comprehensive source delineating the programed learning field than to any editorial merits of TMPL-I as such. The book's timing coincided with an almost frightening avidity for enlightenment in the field—an appetite that had been sparked largely by Skinner's papers and their numerous subsequent paraphrases by disciples and other followers.

However, by mid 1961 or thereabouts, TMPL-I was already far from up to date as a sourcebook, due to the rapidly accumulating literature of research reports and other substantive papers that had appeared since it went to press. Without fully foreseeing the number of other compendia in which various samplings of more recent as well as earlier papers would presently be collected, DAVI began to talk, not long thereafter, about the need for one or more successor volumes to supplement and update number I. At the time that Glaser and I agreed to take on a second volume, the temporally optimistic assumption was, as I recall, of biannual and possibly annual supplements.

When I later begged off on the plea of intolerable pressures of other commitments, Glaser, younger and more venturesome, bravely agreed to persevere. The volume was to comprise a set of individually authored review chapters, to fit the appropriately altered conception required by the times for a successor volume of integrative reviews—rather than a further sourcebook of basic papers. It was realized that a second volume, given an anticipated surge of other publications preempting part of the overly wide market that had latched onto TMPL-I, might require some subsidy. Appropriate funding, providing the necessary incentive for the authors as well as relieving DAVI of speculation as to whether TMPL-II would be as good a risk venture as TMPL-I, was happily forthcoming as a grant from the Carnegie Corporation. With this backing, drafts of most of the papers here included were prepared and read at a meeting of the National Education Association in the Spring of 1963. However, the time required to revise and expand these drafts ran to nearly another two years. Thus, the present volume will see the light of day after a perhaps, after all, more suitable interval of five years rather than the originally contemplated couple of years after the initial volume.

During its lengthy gestation period, some of TMPL-II's intended functions were partly anticipated, though in partial and compressed form, by several other publications that surveyed the field (a notable example is the thoughtful little volume prepared by Wilbur Schramm for the Ford Foundation in 1962) and by several reviews of the programed instruction and related instructional-media research literature (e.g., the one recently published by Lumsdaine and May in the 1965 *Annual Review of Psychology*). Prior to the present volume none of these, however, has approached the comprehensiveness in simultaneous scope and depth needed for a true handbook of the field to complement TMPL-I.

As a sourcebook with the conscious aim of collecting and presenting or abstracting for ready availability virtually all of the then available literature in the field, TMPL-I was of necessity loaded with considerable redundancy—as at least one reviewer later complained. TMPL-II, by contrast, has a much higher rate of content summarized to pages expended, and, accordingly, a much lower (though not zero) rate of redundancy. This fact reflects its different purpose and function of summarizing the state of the art and practice in a series of integrating papers, written *ad hoc*, rather than of collecting original papers for convenient availability.

The necessity as well as desirability of the shift in purpose and scope is a consequence of the quite different, vastly more massive literature which had appeared by 1964-65 as compared with 1959-60. To reprint all of the now-extant research papers (even excluding interim secondary compilations, reviews, and an undeterminable as well as interminable number of popular summaries and interpretations of the field) would surely by now require a 5-foot shelf rather than a single even if bulky volume. The total number of papers cited by the authors of the chapters of TMPL-II runs to well over a thousand. Making allowance for the surprisingly small number of these that are cited in more than one chapter still leaves a small library of original publications, only a few of them of the ancillary sort that are tangential (even thought relevant) to the book's central purpose. The size and at the same time diversification of this by now rather vast (for education) technical literature is surely indicative not only of the productivity of TMPL workers but also of the differentiation and increase in compass that marks a maturing field.

The wide sale of TMPL-I reflected the lack at the outset of the 1960's of other, less compendious works suitable for the enlightenment of the merely curious or for the guidance of those seriously interested in applying the techniques, devices, and materials of the new "technological revolution" in instructional method. This void was not long in being filled almost to overflowing, however; TMPL-I, with a head start of only a year or so, was followed by several other less comprehensive, if more selective and partly more up-to-date, collections of papers, by a rash of how-to-program papers and subsequent textbooks, and by a swelling number of published programs (of which hardly a single one was available when TMPL-I first appeared). The programs themselves —representing a wide range of apparent quality (at least as predicted in terms of input effort expended in preparing them) and a narrower range of diversity and ingenuity in style and technique—by now would require *several* 5-foot shelves to contain. This remarkable outpouring is indicative of the prodigality if not always perspicacity of the publishing industry in supporting the efforts of writers hoping to contribute to the new technology of instruction (and to accrue the divers rewards anticipated therefrom).

The growing diversification of the instructional technology field at the level of application has been complemented by some sharpening focus and sophistication on certain conceptual and methodological perspectives that cut across subject matters, disciplines, and fields of application. This centralization of focus on common conceptual and pervasive methodological problems is mainly embodied in Part I of the present volume. Some overlap is inevitable, of course, between some of these initial chapters (e.g., Holland's on programing variables) and the later treatment of instructional variables as they enter into, and are appropriately dealt with, in relation to particular subject matter fields (in Part II). To a lesser extent, the same is true in areas of application with which the Part III papers are concerned.

The conceptual and methodological frameworks on which the authors have to draw are, to be sure, still in immature stages of evolution, and both development and research on instruction still afford, as yet, only a promise of what the future should hold. Hopefully, by the time when a TMPL-III might be appropriate, a few years hence, sufficient validation of at least some internal criteria of program quality will have been accomplished to permit nontrivial prediction of effectiveness for alternative program styles on at least a reasonably confident probabilistic basis.

As a former collaborator in editing the initial TMPL volume, it is difficult not to feel some godfatherly pride in the publication of this more-than-worthy successor. It is interesting to speculate whether changes with the times will, indeed, result in a somewhat lesser volume of sales than for TMPL-I. If so, and this is anybody's guess, it will reflect the altered status of the field and correspondingly greater specialization of audience rather than any lesser worth of the new volume. Glaser is to be congratulated for his contribution in "doing it again" (with some differences) by getting out *Teaching Machines and Programed Learning, II: Data and Directions*—one "m" shorter in the title, but many milestones ahead in the work it represents by its editor, its contributing authors, and the many others on whose work the latter have drawn to supply the grist for the book.

A. A. LUMSDAINE

Los Angeles, California
April 1965

TEACHING MACHINES AND PROGRAMED LEARNING, II

Data and Directions

Perspectives and Technology

B. F. SKINNER
Harvard University

Reflections on a Decade of
Teaching Machines

To the general public, and to many educators as well, the nature and scope of teaching machines are by no means clear. There is an extraordinary need for more and better teaching, and any enterprise which may help to meet it will not be left to develop normally. The demand for information about teaching machines has been excessive. Articles and books have been published and lectures given; symposia have been arranged; conferences and workshops have been held and courses taught. Those who have had anything useful to say have said it far too often, and those who have had nothing to say have been no more reticent.

Education is big business. Teaching machines were soon heralded as a growth industry, and fantastic predictions of the sales of programed texts were circulated. Devices have been sold as teaching machines which were not well built or designed with any understanding of their function or the practical exigencies of their use. No author was ever more warmly received by a publisher than the author of a programed text. Many programs, to be used either with machines or in textbook form, have been marketed without adequate evaluation.

The "mechanizing of education" has been taken literally in the sense of doing by machine what was formerly done by people. Some of the so-called computer-based teaching machines are designed simply to duplicate the behavior of teachers. To automate education with mechanical teachers is like automating banking with mechanical tellers and bookkeepers. What is needed in both cases is an analysis of the functions to be served, followed by the design of appropriate equipment. Nothing we now know about the learning process calls for instrumentation as complex as computer technology.

Educational specialists have added to the confusion by trying to assimilate the principles upon which teaching machines are based to older theories of learning and teaching.

A Technology of Teaching

In the broadest sense, teaching machines are simply devices which make it possible to apply technical knowledge of human behavior to the practical field of education (11). Teaching is the expediting of learning. Students learn without teaching, but the teacher arranges conditions under which they learn more rapidly and effectively. In recent years the experimental analysis of behavior has revealed many new facts about relevant conditions. The growing effectiveness of an experimental analysis is still not widely recognized, even within the behavioral sciences themselves, but the implications of some of its achievements for education can no longer be ignored.

An important condition is the relation between behavior and its consequences; learning occurs when behavior is "reinforced." The power of reinforcement is not easily appreciated by those who have not had firsthand experience in its use or have not at least seen some sort of experimental demonstration. Extensive changes in behavior can be brought about by arranging so-called contingencies of reinforcement. Various kinds of contingencies are concealed in the teacher's discussions with his students, in the books he gives them to read, in the charts and other materials he shows them, in the questions he asks them, and in the comments he makes on their answers. An experimental analysis clarifies these contingencies and suggests many improvements.

An important contribution has been the so-called "programing" of knowledge and skills—the construction of carefully arranged sequences of contingencies leading to the terminal performances which are the object of education. The teacher begins with whatever behavior the student brings to the instructional situation; by selective reinforcement he changes that behavior so that a given terminal performance is more and more closely approximated. Even with lower organisms, quite complex behaviors can be "shaped" in this way with surprising speed; the human organism is presumably far more sensitive. So important is the principle of programing that it is often regarded as the main contribution of the teaching machine movement, but the experimental analysis of behavior has much more to contribute to a technology of education.

The direct contact which often exists between teacher and student favors the construction of programed sequences, and the teacher who understands the process can profit from the opportunity to improvise programs as he goes. Programs can be constructed in advance, however, which will successfully shape the behavior of most students without local modifications, and many of them can conveniently be mediated by mechanical devices. Laboratory studies have shown that contingencies emphasizing subtle properties of behavior can often be arranged *only* through instrumentation (10). There are potentially as many different kinds of teaching machines as there are kinds of contingencies of reinforcement.

Teaching machines which present material to the student and differentially reinforce his responses in well-constructed programs differ in several ways from self-testing devices and self-scoring test forms, as well as from the training devices which have long been used by industry and the armed services. As Pressey pointed out many years ago (8), a student will learn while taking a multiple-choice test if he is told immediately whether his answers are right or wrong. He learns not to give wrong answers again, and his right answers are strengthened. But testing traditionally has been distinguished from teaching for good reason. Before using a self-testing device, the student must already have studied the subject and, presumably, learned most of what he is to learn about it. Tests usually occupy only a small part of his time. Their main effect is motivational: a poor score induces him to study harder and possibly more effectively. Materials designed to be used in self-testing devices have recently been programed, but the contingencies which prevail during a test are not favorable to the shaping and maintaining of behavior.

Conventional training devices arrange conditions under which students learn, usually by simulating the conditions under which they eventually perform. Their original purpose was to prevent injury or waste during early stages of learning, but attention has recently been given to programing the behaviors they are designed to teach. To the extent that they expedite learning, they are teaching machines. Terminal performances have usually been selected for practical reasons, but a more promising possibility is the analysis and programing of basic motor and perceptual skills, often called aptitudes—a goal which should have an important place in any statement of educational policy.

In arranging contingencies of reinforcement, machines do many of the things teachers do, and in that sense they teach. The resulting instruction is not impersonal, however. A machine presents a program designed by someone who knew what was to be taught and could prepare an appropriate series of contingencies. It is most effective if used by a teacher who knows the student, has followed his progress, and can adapt available machines and materials to his needs. Instrumentation simply makes it possible for programer and teacher to provide conditions which maximally expedite learning. Instrumentation is thus secondary, but it is nevertheless inevitable if what is now known about behavior is to be used in an effective technology.

The New Pedagogy

Any practical application of basic knowledge about teaching and learning is, of course, pedagogy. In the United States, at least, the term is now discredited, but by emphasizing an analysis of learning processes, teaching machines and programed instruction have been responsible for some improvement in its status. The significance of the teaching machine movement can be indicated by noting the astonishing lack of interest which other proposals for the improvement of education show in the teaching process.

Find Better Teachers

In his *Talks to Teachers*, William James insisted that there was nothing wrong with the American school system which could not be corrected by "impregnating it with geniuses" (7). It is an old formula: if you cannot solve a problem, find someone who can. If you do not know how to teach, find someone who knows or can find out for himself.

But geniuses are in short supply, and good teachers do not come ready-made. Education would no doubt be improved if good teachers who know and like the subjects they teach could be attracted and retained, as Conant has repeatedly pointed out (3). But something more is needed. It is not true that "the two essentials of a good teacher are (i) enthusiasm and (ii) thorough knowledge of and interest in his subject" (5). A third essential is knowing how to teach.

Emulate Model Schools

Rickover's criticism of the present American school system is well known (9). His only important positive suggestion is to set up model schools, staffed by model teachers. The implication is that we already have, or at least can have for the asking, schools which need no improvement and whose methods can be widely copied. This is a dangerous assumption if it discourages further inquiry into instruction.

Simplify What Is To Be Learned

Unsuccessful instruction is often blamed on refractory subject matters. Difficulties in teaching the verbal arts are often attributed to the inconsistencies and unnecessary complexities of a language. The pupil is taught manuscript handwriting because it more closely resembles printed forms. He is taught to spell only those words he is likely to use. Phonetic alphabets are devised to help him learn to read. It may be easier to teach such materials, but teaching itself is not thereby improved. Effective teaching would correct these pessimistic estimates of available instructional power.

Reorganize What Is To Be Learned

The proper structuring of a subject matter is perhaps a part of pedagogy, but it can also serve as a mode of escape. Proposals for improving education by reorganizing what is to be learned usually contain an implicit assumption that students will automatically perceive and remember anything which has "good form"—a doctrine probably traceable to Gestalt psychology. Current revisions of high school curricula often seem to lean heavily on the belief that if what the student is to be taught has been "structured," he cannot help understanding and remembering it (1). Other purposes of such revisions cannot be questioned: materials should be up-to-date and well organized. But a high school presentation acceptable to a current physicist is no more easily taught or easily remembered than the out-of-date and erroneous material to be found in texts of a decade or more ago. Similarly, the accent of a native speaker encountered in a language laboratory is no more easily learned than a bad accent. No matter how well structured a subject matter may be, it must still be taught.

Improve Presentation

Pedagogy can also be avoided if what is to be learned can be made memorable. Audiovisual devices are often recommended for this purpose. Many of their other purposes are easily defended. It is not always easy to bring the student into contact with the things he is to learn about. Words are easily imported into the classroom, and books, lectures, and discussions are therefore staples of education, but this is often an unfortunate bias. Audiovisual devices can enlarge the student's nonverbal experience. They can also serve to present material clearly and conveniently. However, their use in attracting and holding the student's attention and in dramatizing a subject matter in such a way that it is almost automatically remembered must be questioned. It is especially tempting to turn to them for these purposes when the teacher does not use punitive methods to "make students study." But the result is not the same. When a student observes or attends to something in order to see it more clearly or remember it more effectively, his behavior must have been shaped and maintained by reinforcement. The temporal order was important. Certain reinforcing events must have occurred *after* the student looked at, read, and perhaps tested himself on the material. But when colored displays, attractive objects, filmed episodes, and other potentially reinforcing materials are used to attract attention, they must occur *before* the student engages in these activities. Nothing can reinforce a student for *paying* attention if it has already been used to *attract* his attention. Material which attracts attention fails to prepare the student to attend to material which is not interesting on its face, and material which is naturally memorable fails to prepare him to study and recall things which are not, in themselves, unforgettable. A well-prepared instructional film may appear to be successful in arousing interest in a given subject, and parts of it may be remembered without effort, but it has not taught the student that a subject may *become* interesting when more closely examined or that intensive study of something which is likely to be overlooked may have reinforcing consequences.

Multiply Contacts Between Teacher and Students

Audiovisual devices, particularly when adapted to television, are also used to improve education by bringing one teacher into contact with an indefinitely large number of students. This can be done, of course, without analyzing how the teacher teaches, and it emphasizes a mode of communication which has two serious disadvantages: the teacher cannot see the effect he is having on his students, and large numbers of students must proceed at the same pace. Contributions to pedagogy may be made in designing programs for educational television, but the mere multiplication of contacts is not itself an improvement in teaching.

Expand the Educational System

Inadequate education may be corrected by building more schools and recruiting more teachers so that the total quantity of education is increased, even though there is no change in efficiency.

Raise Standards

Least effective in improving teaching are demands for higher standards. We may agree that students will be better educated when they learn more, but how are they to be induced to do so? Demands for higher standards usually come from critics who have least to offer in improving teaching itself.

The movement symbolized by the teaching machine differs from other proposals in two ways. It emphasizes the improvement of teaching, on the principle that no enterprise can improve itself to the fullest extent without examining its basic processes. In the second place it emphasizes the implementation of basic knowledge. If instructional practices violate many basic principles, it is only in part because these principles are not widely known. The teacher cannot put what he knows into practice in the classroom. Teaching machines and programed instruction constitute a direct attack on the problem of implementation. With appropriate administrative changes, they may bridge the gap between an effective pedagogical theory and actual practice.

The Goals of Education

An effective technology of teaching calls for a reexamination of educational objectives. What is the teacher's actual assignment? Educational policy is usually stated in traditional terms: the teacher is to "impart knowledge," "improve skills," "develop rational faculties," and so on. That education is best, says Dr. Hutchens (6), which develops "intellectual power." The task of the teacher is to change certain inner processes or states. He is to improve the mind.

The role of the teacher in fostering mental prowess has a certain prestige. It has always been held superior to the role of the trainer of motor skills. And it has the great advantage of being almost invulnerable to criticism. In reply to the complaint that he has not produced observable results, the teacher of the mind can lay claim to invisible achievements. His students may not be able to read, but he has only been trying to make sure they wanted to learn. They may not be able to solve problems, but he has been teaching them simply to think creatively. They may be ignorant of specific facts, but he has been primarily concerned with their general interest in a field.

Traditional specifications of the goals of education have never told the teacher what to do upon a given occasion. No one knows how to alter a mental process or strengthen a mental power, and no one can be sure that he has done so when he has tried. There have been many good teachers who have supposed themselves to be working on the minds of their students, but their actual practices and the results of those practices can be analyzed in other ways. The well-educated student is distinguished by certain characteristics. What are they, and how can they be produced? Perhaps this can be answered by redefining traditional goals: instead of imparting knowledge, one could undertake to bring about those changes in behavior which are said to be the conspicuous manifestations of knowledge, or one could set up the behavior which is the mark of a man possessing well-developed rational power. But mentalistic formulations are warped by irrelevant historical accidents. The behavior of the educated student is much more effectively analyzed directly as such.

Contrary to frequent assertions, a behavioristic formulation of human behavior is not a crude positivism which rejects mental processes because they are not accessible to the scientific public (13). It does not emphasize the rote learning of verbal responses. It does not neglect the complex systems of verbal behavior which are said to show that a student has had an idea, or developed a concept, or entertained a proposition. It does not ignore the behavior involved in the intellectual and ethical problem solving called "thinking." It does not overlook the value judgments said to be invoked when one thing is taught rather than another or when the time and effort given to education is defended. It is merely an effective formulation of those activities of teacher and student which have always been the concern of educational specialists (12).

Not all behavioristic theories of learning are relevant, however. A distinction is commonly drawn between learning and performance. Learning is said to be a change in some special part of the organism, possibly the nervous system, of which behavior is merely the external and often erratic sign. Performance is the observed, and usually much less orderly, effect of learning on behavior. With modern techniques, however, behavior can be much more successfully studied and manipulated than any inner system, even when inferences about the latter are drawn from the behavior with the help of sophisticated statistics. An analysis of learning which concentrates on the behavior applies most directly to a technology, for the task of the teacher is to bring about changes in the student's behavior. His methods are equally conspicuous: he makes changes in the environment. A teaching method is simply a way of arranging an environment which expedites learning.

Such a formulation is not easily assimilated to the traditional psychology of learning. The teacher may arrange contingencies of reinforcement to set up new *forms* of response, as in teaching handwriting and speech or nonverbal forms of behavior in the arts, crafts, and sports. He may arrange contingencies to bring responses under new kinds of *stimulus control,* as in teaching the student to read or draw from copy or to behave effectively upon other kinds of occasions. Current instructional programs designed to fulfill such assignments are mainly verbal, but comparable contingencies generate nonverbal behavior, including perceptual and motor skills and various kinds of intellectual and ethical self-management.

A second kind of programing maintains the student's behavior in strength. The form of the response and the stimulus control may not change; the student is simply more likely to respond. Some relevant methods are discussed traditionally under the heading of motivation.

For example, behavior can be strengthened by introducing new rein-forcers or making old ones more effective, as in giving the student bet-ter reasons for getting an education. The experimental analysis of be-havior suggests another important possibility: schedule available re-inforcers more effectively. Appropriate terminal schedules of reinforce-ment will maintain the student's interest, make him industrious and persevering, stimulate his curiosity, and so on, but less demanding schedules, carefully designed to maintain the behavior at every stage, must come first. The programing of schedules of reinforcement is a promising alternative to the aversive control which, in spite of repeated reforms, still prevails in educational practice.

In neglecting programing, teaching methods have merely followed the lead of the experimental psychology of learning, where the almost universal practice has been to submit an organism immediately to ter-minal contingencies of reinforcement (14). A maze or a discrimination problem, for example, is learned only if the subject acquires appro-priate behavior before the behavior he brings to the experiment has extinguished. The intermediate contingencies are largely accidental. The differences in behavior and in rate of learning which appear under these conditions are often attributed to inherited differences in ability.

In maximizing the student's success, programed instruction differs from so-called trial-and-error learning where the student is said to learn from his mistakes. At best he learns not to make mistakes again. A suc-cessful response may survive, but trial-and-error teaching makes little provision for actually strengthening it. The method seems inevitably committed to aversive control. For the same reason, programed instruc-tion does not closely resemble teaching patterned on everyday commu-nication. It is usually not enough simply to tell the student something or induce him to read a book; he must be told or must read and then be questioned. In this "tell-and-test" pattern, the test is not given to measure what he has learned, but to show him what he has not learned and thus induce him to listen and read more carefully in the future. A similar basically aversive pattern is widespread at the college level, where the instructor assigns material and then examines on it. The stu-dent may learn to read carefully, to make notes, to discover for himself how to study, and so on, because in doing so he avoids aversive con-sequences, but he has not necessarily been taught. Assigning and test-ing is not teaching. The aversive by-products, familiar to everyone in the field of education, can be avoided through the use of programed positive reinforcement.

Many facts and principles derived from the experimental analysis of behavior are relevant to the construction of effective programs leading to terminal contingencies. The facts and principles are often difficult, but they comprise an indispensable armamentarium of the effective teacher and educational specialist. The point has long since been passed at which basic knowledge of human behavior can be applied to education through the use of a few general principles.

The difference between general principles and an effective technology can be seen in certain efforts to assimilate the principles of programed instruction to earlier theories. Programed instruction, for example, has been called "Socratic." It is true that Socrates proceeded by small steps and often led his students through an argument with a series of verbal prompts, but the example often cited to illustrate his method suggests that he was unaware of an important detail—namely, that prompts must eventually be "vanished" in order to put the student on his own. In the famous scene in the *Meno*, Socrates demonstrates his theory that learning is simply recollection by leading an uneducated slave boy through the theorem of doubling the square. The boy responds with the hesitant compliance to be expected under the circumstances and never without help. Although Socrates himself and some of those among his listeners who were already familiar with the theorem may have understood the proof better at the end of the scene, there is no evidence whatsoever that the boy understood it or could reconstruct it. In this example of Socratic instruction, at least, the student almost certainly learned nothing. The program of the *Meno* episode constructed by Cohen (2) is an improvement in that the student responds with less prompting.

A seventeenth-century anticipation of programed instruction has also been found in the work of Comenius who advocated teaching in small steps, no step being too great for the student who was about to take it. Programing is sometimes described simply as breaking material into a large number of small pieces, arranged in a plausible genetic order. But small steps are not enough. Something must happen to help the student take each step, and something must happen as he takes it. An effective program is usually composed of small steps, but the whole story is not to be found in Comenius' philosophy of education.

Another venerable principle is that the student should not proceed until he has fully understood what he is to learn at a given stage. Several writers have quoted Thorndike, who wrote in 1912 (16): "If, by a miracle of mechanical ingenuity, a book could be so arranged that only to him who had done what was directed on page one would page two become visible, and so on, much that now requires personal instruction could be managed by print." In commenting on this passage, James D. Finn and Donald G. Perrin (4) have written: "Here are the insights of a genius. History can very often teach us a lesson in humility—and it does here. The interesting question is: why couldn't we see it then?" It might also be asked, why couldn't Thorndike see it then? He remained active in education for at least 30 years, but he turned from this extraordinarily promising principle to another and—as it proved—less profitable approach to educational psychology.

It is always tempting to argue that earlier ideas would have been effective if people had only paid attention to them. But a good idea must be more than right: it must command attention; it must make its own way because of what it does. Education does not need principles which will improve education as soon as people observe them; it needs a technology so powerful that it cannot be ignored. No matter how insightful the anticipation of modern principles in earlier writers may seem to have been, something was lacking—or education would be much further advanced. We are on the threshold of a technology which will be not only right but effective (15).

Educational Research

A science of behavior makes its principal contribution to a technology of education through the analysis of useful contingencies of reinforcement. It also suggests a new kind of educational research. Thorndike never realized the potentialities of his early work on learning because he turned to the measurement of mental abilities and to matched-group comparisons of teaching practices. He pioneered in a kind of research which, with the encouragement offered by promising new statistical techniques, was to dominate educational psychology for decades. It led to a serious neglect of the process of instruction.

There are practical reasons for knowing whether a given method of instruction is successful or whether it is more successful than another.

It may be desirable to know what changes it brings about in the student, possibly in addition to those it was designed to effect. The more reliable the answers to such questions, the better. But reliability is not enough. Correlations between test scores and significant differences between group means tell less about the behavior of the student in the act of learning than results obtained when the investigator can manipulate variables and assess their effects in a manner characteristic of laboratory research. The practices evaluated in studies on groups of students have usually not been suggested by earlier research of a similar nature, but have been drawn from tradition, from the improvisations of skillful teachers, from suggestions made by theorists working intuitively, or from facts obtained in laboratory research on the behavior of individual organisms. No matter how much they may have stimulated the insightful or inventive researcher, the evaluations have seldom led directly to the design of improved practices.

The contrast between statistical evaluation and the experimental analysis of teaching has an illuminating parallel in the field of medicine. Various drugs, regimens, surgical procedures, and so on must be examined with respect to a very practical question: does the health of the patient improve? Techniques for measuring improvement and comparing different procedures are therefore valuable. But "health" is only a very general description of certain specific physiological processes, and "improvement" is, so to speak, merely a by-product of the changes in these processes induced by a given treatment. Medicine has reached the point where research on specific processes is a much more fertile source of new kinds of therapy than evaluations in terms of improvement in health. Similarly, in education, no matter how important improvement in the student's performance may be, it remains a by-product of specific changes in behavior resulting from the specific changes in the environment wrought by the teacher. Educational research patterned on an experimental analysis of behavior leads to a much better understanding of these basic processes. Research directed toward the behavior of the individual student has, of course, a long history, but it can still profit greatly from the support supplied by an experimental analysis of behavior.

The distinction explains why those concerned with an experimental analysis of learning are not likely to take matched-group evaluations of teaching machines and programed instruction very seriously. It is not possible, of course, to evaluate either machines or programs *in general*, since only specific instances can be tested, and available examples by no means represent all the possibilities; but even the evaluation of a given machine or program in the traditional manner may not give an accurate account of its effects. For example, those who are concerned with improvement are likely to test the student's capacity to give right answers. Being right, of course, has practical importance, but it is only one result of instruction. It is a doubtful measure of "knowledge" in any useful sense. It can be said that a student "knows the answer" if he can select it from an array of choices, but this does not mean that he could have given it without help. The right answer to one question does not imply right answers to all questions said to show the "possession of the same fact." Instructional programs are often criticized as repetitious or redundant when they are actually designed to put the student in possession of a number of different responses "expressing the same proposition." Whether such instruction is successful is not shown by any one right answer.

A preoccupation with right answers had led to a common misunderstanding of programed materials. Since a sentence with a blank to be filled in by the student resembles a test item, it is often supposed that the response demanded by the blank is what is learned. In that case a student could not be learning much, since he may respond correctly in 19 out of 20 frames and must therefore already have known 95 percent of the answers. The instruction which occurs as he completes an item comes from having responded to other parts of it. The extent of this instruction cannot be estimated from the fact that he is right 19 out of 20 times, either while pursuing a program *or on a subsequent test*. Nor will this statistic tell whether other conditions are important. Is it most profitable for the student to execute the response by writing it out, by speaking it aloud, by speaking it silently, or by reading it in some other way? These procedures may or may not have different effects on a selected "right-answer" statistic, but no one statistic will cover all their effects. The actual results of instruction are too subtle, diverse, and as yet undefined to make group comparisons very helpful.

Research in teaching, of course, must not lose sight of its main objective: to make education more effective. But improvement as such is a questionable dimension of the behavior of either teacher or student. Dimensions which are much more intimately related to the conditions the teacher arranges to expedite learning must be studied, even though they do not contribute to improvement or contribute to it in a way which is not immediately obvious.

The changes in the behavior of the individual student brought about by manipulating the environment are usually immediate and specific; the results of statistical comparisons of group performances usually are not. From this study of the behavior of the individual student, the investigator gains a special kind of confidence. He usually knows what he has done to get one effect and what he must do to get another.

Confidence in education is another possible result of an effective technology of teaching. Competition between the various cultures of the world, warlike or friendly, is now an accepted fact, and the role played by education in strengthening and perpetuating a given way of life is clear. No field is in greater need of man's most powerful intellectual resources. An effective educational technology based upon an experimental analysis will bring it support commensurate with its importance in the world today.

References

1. Bruner, J. S. *The Process of Education.* Cambridge, Mass.: Harvard University Press, 1960. 97 pp.
2. Cohen, I. S. "Programed Learning and the Socratic Dialogue." *American Psychologist* 17: 772-75; November 1962.
3. Conant, J. B. *The American High School Today.* Cambridge, Mass.: Harvard University Press, 1959. 140 pp.
4. Finn, J. D., and Perrin, D. G. *Teaching Machines and Programed Learning: A Survey of the Industry, 1962.* Washington, D.C.: U.S. Department of Health, Education, and Welfare, Office of Education, 1962.
5. Helwig, J. "Training of College Teachers." *Science* 132: 845; September 1960.
6. Hutchens, R. M. *On Education.* Santa Barbara, Calif.: Center for the Study of Democratic Institutions, 1963. 20 pp.
7. James, W. *Talks to Teachers.* New York: Henry Holt and Co., 1899. 301 pp.
8. Pressey, S. L. "Educational Research and Statistics." *School and Society* 33: 373; March 1926.
9. Rickover, H. G. *Education and Freedom.* New York: E. P. Dutton Co., 1959. 256 pp.
10. Skinner, B. F. *Science and Human Behavior.* New York: Macmillan Co., 1953. Chapter 6.

11. Skinner, B. F. "The Science of Learning and the Art of Teaching." *Harvard Educational Review* 24: 86-97; Spring 1954.
12. Skinner, B. F. "Why We Need Teaching Machines." *Harvard Educational Review* 31: 377-98; Fall 1961.
13. Skinner, B. F. "Behaviorism at 50." *Science* 140: 951-58; May 1963.
14. Skinner, B. F. "Operant Behavior." *American Psychologist* 18: 503-15; August 1963.
15. Skinner, B. F. *The Technology of Teaching.* (In preparation)
16. Thorndike, E. L. *Education.* New York: Macmillan Co., 1912. 292 pp.

ROBERT M. GAGNÉ
American Institutes for Research

The Analysis of Instructional Objectives
for the Design of Instruction*

The techniques of auto-instructional programing have brought about a number of changes in ways of viewing the process of instruction. One of these changes pertains to an emphasis on *defining instructional objectives*, which has come to be considered a matter of critical importance in the design of effective instruction.

Virtually all writers who have attempted to describe the factors to be taken into account in designing instructional programs have paid some attention to the defining of objectives. Skinner (63), for example, describes this as a first step in the design of programs and in another paper (64) considers a variety of objectives which might be intended in the programing of verbal knowledge. Discussions of programing techniques which contain emphases upon defining objectives as an initial step include those of Cook and Mechner (9), Evans, Homme, and Glaser (16), Gagné and Paradise (31), Goldberg (39), Green (40), Mager (47), and Klaus (43). Stolurow (65, pp. 85-102) devotes considerable attention to this subject in his review of concepts and techniques. The mathetics technique, as described by Gilbert (35), is based upon the operation of "prescribing a mastery repertory," a phrase

* The preparation of this chapter in its final form has been aided by helpful comments by several people, particularly David R. Krathwohl, who commented on the original seminar paper on which the chapter is based.

21

which may well be considered to add precision to the more widely used "stating instructional objectives."

Several authors in the field of research on auto-instructional methods have given more extensive consideration to the problem of defining the objectives of instruction. Mager's book (48) is a most convincing and useful essay on the subject, prepared in the form of an intrinsic program, which should be of great value to teachers and to designers of instructional programs of any type. Taber, Glaser, and Schaefer (66) have contributed a critical discussion of a number of ways of viewing the problem, as well as its relation to the question of sequencing the instructional material and to the broader problem of developing a taxonomy of performance objectives. Coulson (11) considers a number of characteristics of the performance for which instruction is intended, including analysis, synthesis, and other types of integration of response elements, and shows that these require specific decisions affecting the design of instructional programs.

It is of some importance to note that besides the teaching machine movement per se, there are at least two other historical roots to the specification of instructional objectives as a practical technique and as a research problem. One of these centers upon an interest in the measurement of achievement in education and is the culmination of many years of effort in this area, beginning at the University of Chicago and later spreading to other universities in the Midwest. The responsibility for devising university-wide examinations in a variety of subjects forced the examiners, together with the faculty, to face squarely the hard fact that achievement measures cannot be sensibly designed until the course instructor states the objectives of his course. Furthermore, such statements need to be made in terms which imply some specific type of observable behavior, in order for measures to be constructed. The point of view which developed from this continued effort is presented by Tyler (68, 69). The taxonomy of objectives which was developed in this setting is discussed with examples by Bloom (4), and recent experiences with this system of specifying college examinations have been reported in books by Dressel (13, 14).

The second source of research and development emphasis on the description of objectives as an initial step in instructional design comes from programs of research on military training, particularly the training of Air Force technicians. This is evident in reviews of research oriented to the training of military personnel, such as those of Gagné and Bolles (28) and Briggs (5), and in a review of the problem of deriving requirements for training by the Training Psychology Branch, Aerospace Medical Laboratory (67). Defining objectives is specifically referred to in such studies of training effectiveness as those of Briggs and Besnard (6) and French (18). In the earlier writings of Miller (50) and Gagné (21), the specification of training objectives is conceived to be accomplished by means of a technique of broad usefulness in the development of personnel subsystems for man-machine systems, namely, by *task analysis*. The use of this technique results in the statement of training objectives in behavioral terms.

The Reasons for Specifying Objectives

Why is it considered an important step in the design of instruction to describe and analyze instructional objectives? Many writers have simply stated that this must be done before a program can be constructed—and left it at that. Some, however, either clearly state their reasons for considering this an essential step or else imply them in more or less unmistakable fashion.

Revealing the Nature of the Terminal Behavior

There is virtually unanimous agreement that an important reason for specifying objectives is so that the terminal behavior which is aimed for can be known to the instructional designer. To have a hope of success, the designer must know the nature of what must be learned. As Mager (48) points out, a statement of an objective like "knowing how an amplifier works" is quite insufficient to provide this information, since the word "know" is ambiguous. (It might mean drawing a picture of an amplifier, or building an amplifier, or describing the purpose of components in an amplifier, or several other things.) Additional examples of the ambiguity of commonly used phrases in conveying the true meaning of an objective are given by Taber, Glaser, and Schaefer (66) and by Stolurow (65), among others.

At the very least, the reason for knowing the nature of the terminal behavior is so that the instructional designer can plan properly the final sequences of his program. While much learning may have taken place in an instructional program, there will be no proof of this unless

the designer and the user are agreed upon what the learner will be
able to do after he has been through the instruction. "What the learner
is expected to be able to do" is the key phrase. The latter parts of a
program can be designed to go in any of several directions, i.e., to aim
at any of several forms of terminal behavior. Accordingly, they can be
designed to establish in the learner some particular capability which
is agreed upon as an instructional objective. Since the designer wants
to choose the acceptable course for arriving at this terminal behavior,
he must have a statement about the sort of human performance which
is overtly observable.

Besides determining the terminal sequence of the program, the behaviorally defined objective has another related function. Because of
its unambiguous nature, it can constitute a basis from which inferences
can be made by the instructional designer about the kinds of behavior
modification required throughout the program, not only within its final
portion. Further attention will be devoted to this function in a later
section.

Specifying Postlearning Behavior for Measurement

An equally good reason for the specification of instructional objectives in terms of observable human performance, concerning which
there is again widespread agreement, is to meet the requirements of
measurement. An instructional program has the aim of establishing
the capability for certain kinds of behavior; the learner must be able to
do something after completing the instruction that he could not do beforehand. To know whether a program has fulfilled such an aim, it must
be possible to observe, or in a more refined sense to measure, this postlearning behavior. Here also, then, is a reason why the objectives of
the instruction must be specified in terms which imply reliable observ-
ability. Whatever capability of the learner cannot be specified in such
terms cannot be measured. Mager (48) emphasizes, in addition, the
need for including in the objective statement an indication of minimally
acceptable performance, in order that measurement can include considerations of "how well" or "how much."

Meeting the requirements of postlearning measurement is naturally
given much prominence in the discussions of objectives contributed by
those who have been primarily concerned with the design of tests to
measure student achievement. When the intentions of many college

teachers were put into the concrete form of test items, often after lengthy discussion, it was found that they reflected a great variety of objectives which Bloom (4) describes under the general headings of knowledge, comprehension, application, analysis, synthesis, and evaluation. These category names themselves, however, appear to have little operational meaning and in that sense contrast markedly with the many particular examples of actual test items which Bloom provides. For example, the objective called "comprehension" is used to classify a variety of kinds of test items, some of which are as concretely described as the following single example: "The ability to distinguish consequences which are only relatively probable from those for which there is a high degree of probability" (4). Although the language used in this work does not always meet the criterion of reliable identification of observable behavior, there can be little doubt that this movement in educational measurement has actually accomplished a great deal in the effort of specifying instructional objectives.

Distinguishing the Varieties of Behavior Which Can Be Modified by Instruction

A third reason for defining objectives which has often been mentioned is that of drawing distinctions among the different classes of behavior to be established, as a basis for inferences concerning how modification of preexisting behavior can be undertaken. Actually, this may turn out to be the most important reason for describing objectives, although it has not always been stated clearly. What is intended is nothing less than the definition of certain classes of terminal behavior (such as discriminations, chains, etc.) each of which, regardless of its specific content, carries a particular set of implications for the conditions of learning required for its establishment. For example, if it is known that the learner must be able to *discriminate* among 10 printed foreign words when instruction has been completed, this has a certain implication for the conditions of learning as they are built into an instructional sequence. Furthermore, it is quite a different implication than is the case for the establishment of a capability to reproduce orally a particular *chain* or *sequence* of 10 foreign words.

The attempt to distinguish classes of terminal behavior having different implications for the design of instruction has led to a great variety of schemes for suggested categorization. Tyler (68) states the problem as one of relating objectives to the types of learning experiences provided by the curriculum, but proceeds only to suggest, rather than specify, what these learning experiences may be. Perhaps the most thoroughgoing elaborations of this basic idea have been developed in the setting of military technical training, as reflected in the writings of Miller (51, 52, 53), Gagné (23), Glaser and Glanzer (36), and others (67). In connection with programed instruction, Stolurow (65) discusses the distinguishing characteristics of tasks which were originally proposed by Cotterman (10). The mathetics approach of Gilbert (35) places emphasis upon three major categories of behavior for which differential treatment is to be prescribed: chains (including mediating chains), multiple discriminations, and generalizations. Evans (15) distinguishes two major categories for which different learning techniques can be developed, "classes of discrimination" and "functional relationships between these classes." The existence of these various approaches makes desirable a further analysis of their common and distinctive features, which will be undertaken in a later section. It should already be evident, though, that from these various sources, there is general agreement that the specification of objectives can and should have a definite effect upon the design of sequences for auto-instruction.

Defining the Reinforcement Situation for the Learner

Some authors have stated that there is still a further reason for defining objectives: to make them known to the learner, in order that he can carry out the matching procedure involved in reinforcement. In particular, this suggestion is to be found in the writings of Gagné (24), who proposed defining objectives and subobjectives for the learner throughout all instructional sequences, and of Mager and McCann (49), who relate the notion more broadly to the idea of providing the learner with the capability of programing his own activities.

Most investigators of learning are agreed that some set of conditions which either follow or are coincident with the newly acquired behavioral act serves the function of raising the probability that this act will occur again when the situation calls for it. This set of conditions is called *reinforcement*, and there is still no generally accepted definition of exactly what it is, in a fundamental sense. Nevertheless, as used in connection with programed instruction, the procedure of bringing this important set of conditions to bear upon learning is fairly standard. The learner is required to supply a missing word, character, or phrase which will serve to complete a statement containing a blank. Having done this, he is asked to look at a printed representation of this response, in order to see whether he has performed correctly. (He "checks the correctness" of his response.) Evidently, what reinforcement means in programed instruction is that the learner matches a response production of his own to one he is told (or already knows) is correct.

Since this matching procedure is an integral part of the learning process, it does not seem unreasonable to suppose that giving the learner prior knowledge which enables him to circumscribe, or bracket, the variety of responses which is expected of him may have the effect of controlling the reinforcement and thus improving the efficacy of the learning which occurs. For example, in undertaking a multiple discrimination sequence, if the learner *knows beforehand* that he must distinguish the foreign words *fin, femme, faim,* and *fine,* this may enable him to make the kind of match to printed reproductions of each of these words which is highly effective in a reinforcement sense. If he does not know this beforehand, he might tend to match *fin* with *fine,* and thus be receiving incorrect reinforcement. The frequent occasions in programed instruction in which physically exact matches cannot be used to define correctness of response serve to emphasize the importance of this possibility.

Effect of Specifying Instructional Objectives

Given the generally accepted importance of defining objectives, for whatever reasons, one might reasonably expect a fair amount of evidence for the efficacy of the procedure. In a sense, it may be said that every demonstration of effectiveness of an instructional program constitutes such evidence, since the attainment of objectives in such a program means that they must have been well defined, as a necessary but not sufficient condition. But besides this, it is necessary to seek out findings which show the effectiveness of specifying objectives in a rather direct fashion. Evidence of this sort is varied both in nature and in source.

An Example from Higher Education

The procedures of defining objectives described by Bloom (4) have been tried out in a variety of colleges in connection with achievement testing and evaluation programs. A volume by Dressel (13) summarizes the experience of 13 different institutions of higher learning with the use of these techniques in a variety of different courses. Although quantitative data are not reported, one is impressed with the repeated occurrence of a similar sequence of events reported in many of these chapters, as expressed by Bloom (3). Initially, the faculty were interested in improving the construction of achievement tests themselves. As they became better acquainted with the method, however, they began to realize the full import of Tyler's (68) statement to the effect that examining has to be conceived as part of the total educational process.

The results of this realization were manifold and striking, it is reported. The faculty began to recognize the fundamental purpose of an educational program as one of changing the behaviors of students. They became increasingly skilled in relating their hopes for teaching outcomes to definable objectives. They began to question their own methods of teaching and proceeded to try out new ones. As for the students, they too became aware of objectives and recognized a need for evidence about the extent of their progress toward these objectives. In all of these changes, one is ready to infer that teachers must have been improved, instruction must have been improved, students must have exhibited heightened achievement. Perhaps it is unfortunate that the "evaluation" carried out by means of these procedures has not itself been evaluated in some controlled fashion. One is left, nevertheless, with the strong impression of instructional improvement.

An Example from Military Training

French (18) reports an experimental study of the training of electronic maintenance personnel in troubleshooting. Forty apprentice mechanics for the K-system (an airborne bombing navigational system), graduates of a regular course of instruction, were given additional instruction in tracing the flow of information through the system, as exemplified in a number of equipment "problems." Half of the group received this type of instruction on an actual layout of the system, half on a training device called the MAC trainer. As measured on a test of system functioning, both groups showed a significant and marked increase in proficiency after seven and one-half days of instruction.

To gain the full import of this finding of improved performance, certain other facts need to be stated. First, the subjects in this experiment were considered to have been fully trained, as a result of having completed a standard course of many weeks in length. However, an analysis of objectives, carried out prior to the experiment (19), revealed that despite much instruction in "theory," the objective of capably performing troubleshooting on this system was not adequately represented in the standard instruction. The additional instruction, making use of the MAC trainer, was specifically designed to establish student skill in making the decisions and carrying out the procedures involved in diagnosing malfunctions of the K-system. The results show that this instruction was effective in improving the performance of graduates of the standard course. They therefore demonstrate in a specific sense the importance of carefully defined objectives to the accomplishment of desired training outcomes.

Another example of improved performance resulting from instruction based upon a detailed specification of objectives, pertaining to a somewhat different type of Air Force maintenance training, is reported by Briggs and Besnard (6). In this case, two different training devices were employed in the establishment of identification responses, on the one hand, and checkout procedures, on the other, these having been identified as separate job-relevant objectives on the basis of a preceding analysis. Some additional examples deriving from military training are briefly described by Mager (48).

Examples from Research on Programed Instruction
Certain experimental studies of variables in programed instruction pointedly demonstrate the importance of defined objectives to the effectiveness of the instructional enterprise. Falling in this category is the work of Gagné and his collaborators (24, 30, 31). As this method has developed, it has emphasized not only the specification of the terminal performance, but the analysis of this performance into entire hierarchies of supporting "subordinate knowledges," which of course are also performance objectives.

In this series of studies on various tasks of mathematics, it has been shown that the attainment of each of these "subordinate" objectives by the learner is an event which makes a highly dependable prediction of the next highest related performance in the hierarchy. If a learner attains the objectives subordinate to a higher objective, his probability of learning the latter has been shown to be very high; if he misses one or more of the subordinate objectives, his probability of learning the higher one drops to near zero. In this view, the entire sequence of objectives, one building upon another until the terminal performance is reached, is considered to be the most important set of variables in the instructional process, outweighing as a critical factor more familiar variables like step size, response mode, and others. According to these results, failing to achieve a subordinate objective means that the learner effectively "drops out" of the learning at that point and is unable to acquire the higher-level knowledges. The implication is that when one sets out to design instruction having this hierarchical character, the specification of an entire sequence of objectives is essential to insure an effective learning program.

Another approach to the study of the effects of specifying objectives on learning is represented by a study of Mager and McCann (49). Groups of engineers were trained in a number of different tasks pertaining to their jobs. In the initial group, the instructor controlled the sequence of content presented. In a second group, the students were permitted to select the content in accordance with an importance and a sequence they themselves assigned. In still a third group, the students were initially given a detailed statement of training objectives, illustrated by the kinds of questions they were to be expected to answer; in addition, they were permitted to instruct themselves in any order or by any means they wished, reporting to the instructor when they believed they were ready to demonstrate achievement of objectives selected by themselves. The results of this study showed that time required for training could be reduced markedly (as much as 65 percent in the third group) without loss of proficiency. Although this experiment does not incorporate the careful control of conditions possible in a laboratory, its findings are too striking to be dismissed lightly. Clearly, these results pose the question: How much of learning (particularly by adults) can be accomplished simply by making the learner aware of learning objectives? If one were to set out to construct a self-instructional program containing a full set of stated objectives (terminal and subordinate), what else would be needed? These are challenging questions for those interested in understanding learning efficiency.

Identifying Objectives—Task Description

If objectives are to have this widely acclaimed importance in the technology of instruction, they must be clearly specified. But where do such specifications come from? What exactly is being described, and on what observations does this description depend?

Perhaps the clearest and most consistent tradition of beginning to plan instruction with a specification of objectives derives from research on military training, particularly the training of electronic technicians. In this tradition, the initial step has been called *task description*, and it seems reasonable to use this terminology here.

In describing what a man does in furthering the goals of any system, it is customary to describe these events as accomplishments (sometimes called "operations"), such as "putting a radar set into operation" or "computing amount of wind drift." The smallest convenient units of these accomplishments, such as "setting knob to zero" or "looking up the tangent of angle A," are designated as *tasks*. In theory, one can reconstruct conceptually the entire set of operations to be carried out by any system, without errors or misconceptions, by reading a properly prepared description which is given in terms of tasks listed in the correct order. It is evident, then, that descriptions of tasks must be *complete, unambiguous*, internally *consistent*, and *reliable* (in the sense that two readers would make the same prediction from them), in order to fulfill this function. Descriptions of tasks do not depict "raw behavior"; they do not, in a psychological sense, inform the reader what the human operator is "doing." Instead, they state only the *accomplishment* or *outcome* of the behavior, which is usually called performance.

Tasks descriptions of this variety bear a close relationship to statements of instructional objectives. The latter are also descriptions of performance: one wants to know what the student will be able to accomplish after learning; not how he will accomplish it, but what. Similarly, it is desirable that statements of instructional objectives be complete (one wants to know *all* that the student will be able to accomplish) and unambiguous (there should be no misunderstanding of the denotations of the words employed). The description must be internally

consistent; for example, the stated requirements for speed of performance must not conflict with those for accuracy. And above all, such
objectives should be reliable, in the sense previously used: two readers
should have no disagreement about the kind of performance expected
of the learner. It may in fact be said that "describing instructional objectives" can be considered in all respects equivalent to "describing the
(terminal) tasks" expected of the learner.

What characteristics must objectives, or terminal tasks, have in order
to meet these criteria? A number of attempts have been made to formulate an answer to this question.

Probably no one has written more extensively on the topic of task
analysis than has Miller (50, 51, 53, 54, 57). According to a recent
formulation (55), the following elements are required in such a description:

1. An *indicator* (or indication), which is the signal for the beginning
   of the action. (Example: a light has come on.)
2. An *action word*, usually a verb and its qualifiers. (Example: push
   to right.)
3. A *control*, a physical object which the individual manipulates or
   otherwise acts upon. (Example: a toggle switch.)
4. An *indication of response adequacy*, another signal which tells the
   individual when his action is correctly completed. (Example: the
   click of the switch.)

Evidently, a complete and reliable task description, using the examples
given, would be: "When light comes on, push toggle switch to right
until click is heard."

Can such a set of criteria be applied to the kinds of tasks which are
more familiar in an educational framework? It is quite apparent that
they can, and the exercise of doing so may be quite instructive. Suppose
one tried to state whatever is suggested by "adding integers" as a task
in Miller's terms. The result would be somewhat as follows: "Given the
printed instruction 'add' and two integers (indicator), writes (action
word) the symbol representing their sum (indication of response adequacy)." Of course, the use of a pencil (the control) is simply understood in this statement. Otherwise, it seems to be a perfectly good
statement of an instructional objective! Consider another example, from
the field of language: "recognizing similes in poetry." This might be

expressed as follows: "Given lines of poetry such as 'As a fond mother when the day is o'er. . .' (indicator), identifies (action word) in oral speech (the control) the essential items compared as a simile, in the form, 'as ——, so ——' (indication of response adequacy)." It seems evident from these examples that no important conflict arises in applying Miller's method of task description to the definition of instructional objectives.

It is of considerable interest to compare Miller's method and criteria for task descriptions with Mager's (48) approach to the preparation of instructional objectives. Presumably, although each of these authors has faced a common problem of how to describe human performance, the backgrounds from which they approach the problem are somewhat different. According to Mager, the characteristics of a good objective description are as follows:

1. Specification of the kind of behavior which will be accepted as evidence that the learner has achieved the objective.
2. Description of the imporant conditions under which the behavior will be expected to occur.
3. Description of how well the learner must perform to have his behavior considered acceptable.

One does not have to alter the words in these statements to any great degree to be able to observe a considerable resemblance between these and the requirements stated by Miller. The first of Mager's points pertains to an "action word," externally observable. The second relates to the "indicator," and perhaps also to the "control," as conditions under which the behavior occurs. The third clearly identifies the "indication of response adequacy." It should be mentioned, however, that Mager gives an additional type of emphasis to the third of these points, namely, a quantitative one. For example, he considers that this criterion would be met by such a statement as "spelling correctly 80 percent of the words called out to him during an examination period." But it is evident that he also accepts a meaning of "performance accuracy" which resembles the Miller notion more closely, as in "weighing materials accurately to the nearest milligram."

The fact that these two writers independently have arrived at criteria for task (or objective) descriptions which are so closely similar leads one to believe that they must both be right and that the technique of description must be a straightforward and unassailable one. Summarizing their technique, it may be said that instructional objectives can be described as tasks, the outcomes of human behavior. Such descriptions are designed to be understandable and reliable, so that different individuals are able from a reading of them to agree fully on a set of events which would constitute an example of each task. They contain the following kinds of terms:

1. Words denoting the stimulus situation which initiates the performance ("given two numerals connected by the sign $+$").
2. An action word or verb which denotes observable behavior ("states").
3. A word denoting the object acted upon (which sometimes is simply implied, as in "orally").
4. A phrase which indicates the characteristics of the performance that determine its correctness ("the name of the numeral which is the sum of the two").

A final word may be added to the effect that there is general agreement that "action words" must be observable activities. This of course is important to the criterion of reliability, as defined here. To "know," to "understand," to "appreciate" are perfectly good words, but they do not yield agreement on the exemplification of tasks. On the other hand, if suitably defined, words such as to "write," to "identify," to "list," do lead to reliable descriptions. There is nothing at all obscure about this distinction: it is simply one of a difference between actions which can be identified with agreement by several observers and actions which cannot be so identified. Acts which are overt are in the former category, without obvious exception.

Identifying Implications for Learning—Task Analysis

It appears from the preceding discussion that the technique of describing instructional objectives is fairly well agreed upon. But the next step, which is called *task analysis*, has neither been so fully developed nor so precisely specified. There are, in fact, various approaches to this problem.

The aim of task analysis (or the analysis of objectives) seems to be fairly clear, although this is not always apparent in the writings of those who have described such a technique. Once the performance expected at the termination of learning has been reliably specified, one needs to be able to draw some inferences concerning how these performances can be established most effectively. As Gilbert (35) puts it, what is needed is to "prescribe a repertory of behavior structures." Involved in this aim must be the *identification of classes of behavior which differ in respect to the conditions most effective for their learning.* The optimal strategy for the attainment of a generalization, for example, is presumably not the same as the optimal strategy for the establishment of a multiple discrimination.

Approaches to Task Analysis from the Background of Military Training

Miller (53) undertakes to draw the differential training implications of several categories of tasks. It should be borne in mind that this work was done before teaching machines and their programing requirements had had their impact on such analyses. Miller classifies behavior into the main categories of perceiving, recalling procedures, recalling nomenclature, interpreting, making logical inferences, and performing manual operations. Some of these categories, according to Miller's analysis, can be taught by means of demonstrations, while others require verbal presentations, and still others are best learned by periods of practice on actual equipment. Obviously, this is a line of thinking which points in the direction of increasingly precise differentiation of categories of behavior having implications which can be distinguished as optimal conditions for learning. In a more recent formulation, Miller (56) discusses the training implications of these and other categories derived from task descriptions in the following terms:

1. *Goal orientation.* The learner must be informed of the conditions and time of initiation of the task, as well as of the criteria of performance.
2. *Reception of task information.* The learner must acquire responses which permit him to *detect* relevant cues, *identify* nomenclatures and actions, and *filter* signals through "noise."
3. *Retention.* Conditions need to be prescribed for the use of *short-term retention*, and practice will be needed for *long-term retention* of *procedures* and *codes.*

4. *Interpretation and problem solving.* This kind of activity requires the learning of a variety of mediating activities, including *classes of response options, response implications, goal priorities,* and *rules for selecting responses.*
5. *Motor responses.* Practice sequences may be specifically designed to eliminate likely human errors, to avoid negative transfer, and to group responses into performance units.

Developing approaches to the problem of behavior categorization can also be seen in the writings of Gagné concerning task analysis (21). Gagné and Bolles (28) proposed five major categories of behavior as training objectives, based upon an analysis of Air Force jobs. These are (a) identifying, (b) knowing principles or relationships, (c) following procedures, (d) making decisions about courses of action, and (e) performing skilled perceptual-motor acts. Each of these categories is conceived as having different training implications, not all of which can as yet be fully specified. Lumsdaine (44) has undertaken to relate these same categories to the potentialities for training of various training devices and self-instructional devices.

In a recent formulation of behavior categories, Gagné (23) includes these formerly described classes in three major ones, *sensing, identifying,* and *interpreting.* As represented in human tasks, each of these categories is conceived to generate a different set of requirements for its performance. These requirements apply not only to the conditions of learning but also to the conditions immediately accompanying the performance itself, such as the stimuli displayed at the time of performance and the verbal instructions which may be given to determine the conditions of "filtering" and "shunting" for the human performer (that is, the conditions under which the behavior will be expected to occur, cf., Mager [48]). These categories and their differential implications may be briefly summarized as follows:

1. *Sensing,* or indicating, the presence or absence of a difference in physical energies. This behavior is not directly influenced by learning, but the capabilities of "filtering" may be learned and the accuracy of reporting thereby improved.
2. *Identifying.* Basically, this category may be described as making a number of different responses to a number of different classes of

stimulation. This class of behavior is considered to be mediated by learned *models* (percepts and concepts), which also include the *sequences of action* occurring in procedures and in motor skills.

3. *Interpreting.* In this class of behavior, the individual identifies inputs in terms of their consequences. Accordingly, the primary mediators which must be learned are *rules* or *principles*. In the most complex forms of interpreting, such as problem solving, filtering rules (sometimes called strategies) also may need to be acquired.

Approaches to Task Analysis from the Background of Programed Instruction

Stolurow (65) and Cotterman (10) have formulated an answer to the problem of task analysis as a part of the principles of instructional programing. Their point of view, as recently summarized (65), clearly identifies as a criterion of task classification the question of whether a task characteristic produces an interaction effect with a practice (or teaching) variable. Accordingly, they identify a set of "critical learning task characteristics" which apply to the content of what is to be learned, where this is conceived as a variety of relationships between an S and an R. These dimensions of variation are considered to generate differential implications for the method of teaching (or programing) which may be summarized as follows:

1. *Number and sequence.* The number of S-R's to be established strongly affects the ease of learning, according to previous evidence. So also does the length of the sequence of S-R's and whether the sequence to be established is an invariant one.
2. *Limits of S and R.* The extent to which variations are permitted in the stimuli and responses that define the task, as well as the similarity of these components, will affect the ease of learning.
3. *Meaning.* The orderability, the number of associations, and the associative significance of the responses are factors which may be expected to affect the learning of a task. There are many instances in which the learning of mediating associations facilitates the acquisition of the required responses.
4. *S-R linkage pattern.* The nature of the linkage to be established by learning may be one-to-one (pairing object and name), one-to-

many (genus-species relationship), many-to-one (species-genus), or many-many (a number of symptoms-a number of causes).

5. *S-R homogeneity and compatibility.* Both S's and R's may be derived from a homogeneous class (such as English words), or they may not be. In addition, they may be compatible in the sense of increasing and decreasing at the same time, or not. Studies indicate that heterogeneity aids learning and that compatibility does also.

It is evident that these categories of critical factors in learning are not at all to be considered "behavior categories" of the sort attempted by other writers. According to this approach, there are many varieties of behaviors; and in order to derive the specific implications each has for learning, one needs to consider the five sets of characteristics that each may possess. Stolurow's further discussion points out some of the relationships of learning conditions to these characteristics and emphasizes the problems which remain to be illuminated by research.

Gilbert's (35) discussion of the problem of analyzing objectives again reflects the approach of identifying categories of behavior which imply different optimal teaching sequences. These categories are constituted by different sequencing of what Gilbert calls "the basic exercise model." This model is the minimal essential set of events which must occur for a new operant to be established. These are considered to be (a) an observing response, which leads to identification of (b) the S^D, the stimulus situation to be associated with the response; (c) another stimulus (S^I), which is able to call out the desired response; and (d) reinforcement provided by recognition of the end product. With this as a basis, it is considered that three major categories of prescription for teaching may be made, each of which is independent of specific content.

1. *Chains* of behavior are best established by "retrogression through the basic exercise model"; in other words, by means of a sequence which works backward from a terminal response to the observing S-R which begins the chain.

2. *Multiple discriminations* are exemplified by instances in which different responses have to be made to an equal number of different stimuli. This kind of behavior is particularly subject to competition (interference), which may be overcome by judicious use of *induction* (the facilitation of similarity) and by *mediation* (a process of chaining, utilizing an existing verbal operant of high strength).

Gilbert argues that a multiple discrimination is best established in one exercise.

3. *Generalizations* occur when classes of responses (like the positions in an alphabetical file) must come under control of classes of stimuli (like the letters in names to be filed). Generalization teaching is required whenever it can be estimated that two separate instances of the stimulus, as different from each other as possible, would not serve as direct substitutes for each other in controlling the desired response.

Task Analysis from the Standpoint of Education

Tyler (68) states the second step in curriculum construction as selecting "learning experiences that are likely to attain the chosen objectives." Such selection, he says, should be in terms of the probable usefulness of the learning experiences in reaching the desired goals, as guided by studies of learning conducted in the psychological laboratories and in schools.

Following the leads suggested by Tyler's writings, a committee of College and University Examiners of the University of Chicago undertook to describe a taxonomy of educational objectives, and these are collected in the volume edited by Bloom (4). Six major categories of objectives, each containing a variety of subcategories, are described. The six taken together are considered to constitute a hierarchy, in which the objectives in the later classes are likely to make use of (or build upon) those in the earlier ones. A summary of these categories is as follows:

1. *Knowledge.* This category is measured by tests requiring the recall of specific and universal facts, methods and processes, patterns, structure, or settings. The examples indicate that the class includes the recall of specific identities, of verbal statements, and of abstract concepts.

2. *Comprehension.* This class includes translation (supplying equivalent responses for previously acquired identifications), interpretation (formulating a statement representing a set of events), and extrapolation (predicting consequences of courses of action).

3. *Application.* Applying general principles and abstract concepts to specific novel situations.

4. *Analysis.* Distinguishing the kinds of elements in a communication, such as facts and hypotheses; recognizing the facts and assumptions essential to a major thesis and distinguishing relevant from irrelevant statements; identifying general form, pattern, purpose, or other organizing principle.
5. *Synthesis.* Producing a total communication, plan, or set of operations, given the essential components.
6. *Evaluation.* Making reasonably accurate judgments of value, accuracy, consistency, or correspondence with certain criteria.

On the whole, the categories described by the Bloom committee provide a highly informative picture of the variety of kinds of human performances which reasonably may be expected in an educational setting. They therefore represent a genuine challenge to those who wish to define the objectives of instructional programs and apply them to education at all levels. It is also quite apparent that these statements fail to meet the criteria of task description described by Miller and Mager. In particular, they provide inadequate information about what Mager calls "the important conditions under which behavior will be expected to occur." For example, what does "recall of specific facts" mean? Can it, or can it not, be phrased as "supplying a word or phrase which will correctly complete a verbal statement"? Many other examples of this sort, exhibiting equal or greater degrees of ambiguity, can be identified readily in this work. It appears possible that a first step in improving the usefulness of these statements would be to "translate" them into other statements which satisfy the criteria previously discussed.

As categories of behavior, the classes described by the Bloom committee likewise are not entirely adequate. For one reason, some of the subordinate classes described are distinct from each other only in terms of their specific content rather than in terms of formal characteristics which affect their learning conditions. "Knowledge of terminology," for example, may not be formally distinct from "knowledge of classifications and categories"; similarly, "knowledge of conventions" appears to be highly similar in a formal sense to "knowledge of principles." Unfortunately, too, it is not clear that these similarities of formal characteristics do not apply even across major categories, as when "knowledge of generalizations" is distinguished from "interpretation" (comprehension) and both of these in turn from "comprehending the interrelationships of ideas" (analysis). The test items used to illustrate each type of statement are indeed valuable in providing objective meanings for these phrases. But the objectives described here cannot be successfully employed, as they stand, for the derivation of distinct classes of behaviors for which optimal learning strategies can be specified. As suggested previously, a reformulation of these objectives, using the test items as a basis, might yield an extremely valuable product.

The Design of Optimal Conditions of Instruction

The problem to be faced after the definition of objectives has been achieved is one of drawing inferences about the conditions of instruction needed to establish them. Since each objective is quite specific, it would be possible to conclude that there are as many conditions of learning to be specified as there are statements of objectives themselves. Insofar as the particular content of the learning materials is concerned, this is true. But what various authors have attempted to show, as the previous discussion indicates, is that there seem to be classes of behavior, the members of which have a *formal identity*, irrespective of their particular content. These classes of behavior can be described as performances (that is, as objectives) and distinguished from each other. The question can then be asked, with respect to each of them, what conditions are necessary to bring about their learning?

The approaches to this question, as previously summarized, exhibit several differences and also striking similarities. To consider the latter in detail would perhaps not be the most fruitful exercise to engage in for the purposes of the present chapter. Therefore, the attempt will be made instead to make another formulation of *behavior categories*, which is hopefully comprehensive and which can be related at every point to the suggestions of previous writers. In the case of each category, the question to be addressed is, what are the conditions which specify (so far as is known) optimal conditions for learning the tasks that involve this kind of behavior?

It may be noted that this account does not begin with the simple conditioned response, whether classical, operant, or some other form. It is a fundamental fact of learning that such stimulus-response relationships do get established. But there are differing views concerning the conditions necessary for the acquisition of these signal-response acts, which makes the task of describing them as objectives a very difficult one. In addition, without questioning the involvement of conditioned responses in the learning process in some fundamental sense, there is room for considerable doubt that such simple, uncomplicated responses to signals often occur as objectives of instruction. Accordingly, the following account simply assumes that conditioned responses occur and proceeds to describe some of the categories of learned behavior which are presumably built upon them.

Response Differentiation

A basic form of learning, which appears to be prerequisite for other forms, has been called *response learning* or *response differentiation*. According to Skinner (62), the simplest case in which verbal behavior comes under the control of verbal stimuli is to be found in echoic behavior, in which the response generates a sound pattern similar to that of the stimulus. When a young child learns to say "daddy" to the stimulus supplied by a parent "Say daddy!" the child's response produces a sound which occasions reinforcement. The stimulus "daddy" is of course a discriminated stimulus, since the child learns not to make this same response in the presence of other stimuli like "Say mama!" Furthermore, the sound produced by the child himself now becomes a discriminated stimulus for the response, as evidenced in babbling. One can then speak of this response (or more precisely, this act) as having become *differentiated*, since a given stimulus is dependably followed by a response that sounds like the stimulus, whereas other stimuli do not have this outcome.

While verbal responses may be the most frequently occurring type involved in the learning of echoic behavior in human beings, *response learning* is also exhibited in other kinds of motor acts. In nonverbal behavior, discriminated stimuli may come to control responses other than verbal ones in just as dependable a fashion, and these too can become the basic links in the learning of other kinds of behavior. Learning to write the characters of shorthand is an example from the educational sphere.

As an instructional objective, the outcome of response differentiation learning may be defined as follows: *Upon presentation of a stimulus definable within narrow physical limits, and no other stimulus, makes a response which produces a copy of the stimulus, and no other response.*

It is of interest to note that response learning, while usually too simple a form of behavior to be treated separately as an objective of instruction, is often mentioned as a *prerequisite* to other learning. Gilbert (35) states that the basic operant on which any chain is established must be a "strong" one in order that another act can be linked to it in what he calls the basic exercise. Modern methods of teaching foreign languages also frequently make use of response differentiation of the sounds of the unfamiliar language as a first step in the establishment of speaking and comprehension skills. Additional discussion of this point is contained in Chapter 13 by Lane. The work of Underwood and Schulz (73) demonstrates the great importance of "response availability," "familiarity," and "pronunciability" to the learning of verbal paired associates. Studies by Saltz (61) and McGuire (46) suggest that response familiarity is probably a matter of response differentiation. Mowrer's (58) discussion of the acquisition of speech by animals also includes the idea that speech sounds must be discriminated as sounds before being associated with other signals. Again, in human language training, the learning of correct speech has been shown to depend critically upon the discrimination of speech sounds as stimuli (42). All these lines of evidence show the importance of response learning as a precondition of other forms and further suggest that response availability is brought about when the response-produced stimuli arising from the response become an S^D for the response itself.

Assuming reinforcement to be the basic condition for all learning, there is only one other condition which appears to be required for response learning. This is *contiguity*, in the sense that the R must occur within a few seconds after the S. As has been said, the stimulus "Say daddy!" must be followed closely in time by the response "daddy" on the part of the learner. It is possible that a single repetition involving contiguity of this sort will accomplish the learning that is sought. In any case, the long-continued controversy about the continuous or noncontinuous nature of learning cannot be reviewed here.

Associations
There are many human tasks whose acquisition requires the learning of what has traditionally been called an *association*. In using the term

here, there is no intention of naming a mechanism, neural or otherwise, but simply to describe the observation that a stimulus (S) comes to be "associated" with an individual's response (R) in such a way that the occurrence of S is followed by R predictably with a high probability. When a child acquires a new word naming an object, he has acquired an association; and the same is true for an adult, if the object is a new and unfamiliar one. Acquiring new technical words, or new words in a foreign language, are other well-known examples. Of course, responses other than verbal ones may be involved in associations, as when an individual learns to press a new button on the dashboard of an unfamiliar automobile. Instructional programs are often concerned with the teaching of new words, new *associations*. In its simplest form, the objective of instruction which represents the outcome of association learning is this: *Upon presentation of a stimulus definable within narrow physical limits, and no other stimulus, makes a response other than a copying response which identifies (names, codes) the stimulus, and no other response.*

It is important to mention that what must be learned is often more complicated than a simple association. In particular, one thinks of the situation in which the individual must not only learn to say *le bras* to the stimulus "arm" but also *la jambe* to the stimulus "leg" and *la main* to the stimulus "hand." As soon as the possibility of confusion exists among stimuli, the behavior becomes that of *multiple discrimination*, which is to be discussed in the next section. But one must consider first the simplest situation, in which such possibilities of confusion do not exist. In addition, it is apparent that the simple association *hand—la main* must itself be learned, regardless of whether or not it is later found to exhibit confusion with some other association. Many foreign words may be acquired under conditions in which little confusion is evident, as for example, *cheese—le fromage.*

Although association learning was for many years treated as though it involved a single S-R event, it is now widely accepted that three separate parts make up an association, each of which can be subjected to different learning conditions (46). What this means, actually, is that an association is a three-member *chain*, a form of behavior to be described more extensively in a subsequent section. For an association to be established most readily, there must first be discrimination of the S from the surrounding situation in which it is embedded. In other words, the S must become an S^D. Gilbert (35) points out that this condition is a prerequisite for the "basic exercise." Typically, a stimulus is used as a part of verbal instructions to call out an observing response (R^O), which leads the learner to locate and respond to the S^D.

The second condition is one of response availability, occasioned by preceding response learning, as previously described. When a new word is being taught, one should insure that the echoic behavior $S^D{}_{fromage}$ ——$R_{fromage}$ is well established before attempting the association $S^D{}_{cheese}$ ——$R_{fromage}$. The relevance of the findings of Underwood and Schulz (73) to this point has previously been mentioned.

The third condition pertains to the preexistence (or previous learning) of a "coding" response, usually not exhibited in overt behavior, which becomes a link between the response occasioned by the initial stimulus and the following stimulus that controls the desired response. In other words, the "code" is the central member in the paradigm:

$$S_{RED}\text{——}r_{rose}: s_{rose}\text{——}r_{flower}: s_{flower}\text{——}R_{FLOWER}.$$

There is considerable evidence that the stronger this "word association" act has been made by previous learning, the more rapidly the learning of the desired association will take place (12).

In its purest form, then, association learning requires the previous acquisition of (a) a discriminated stimulus, (b) a differentiated response, and (c) a coding act which can become the middle part of the chain. When these conditions are met, the learning of an association appears to be a very simple matter involving contiguity of the S^D, the coding link, and the R. An association like *chérie—dear* can be assumed for practical purposes to be learnable when the contiguous S-R events occur on a single occasion.

Multiple Discrimination

This form of behavior, which Gagné (23), among others, calls *identification*, requires that the individual make several different responses to an equal number of stimuli. In the language of task description, he "distinguishes" or "differentially identifies" two or more physically different stimuli. As an example, one may take the task described by Gilbert (35) of identifying the 10 different colors of resistor bands with the numerals zero through nine. Many other examples come to mind immediately: the identification of unfamiliar words, the acquiring of a foreign language vocabulary, the distinguishing of locations and names of instruments on a panel. As a learning objective, the outcome of multiple discrimination learning may be stated as follows: *Upon presentation of two or more potentially confusable stimuli (physically defined), makes an equal number of different responses which differentially identify these stimuli, and no other responses.*

It is evident that the individual acts which constitute multiple-discrimination behavior are associations and must therefore basically depend upon the conditions already described for the establishment of these. If a single identification is to be acquired, which is already distinctive and which generates no confusion with other activities, the behavior is simple association. But since there are few enough instances of this sort in real life, special pains must be taken to select such instances for experimental study. More usually, the possibilities of confusion abound. One must not only associate *faim* with "hunger," but also *femme* with "woman," and the two stimuli sound very much alike when received aurally.

For many years it has been recognized that the event which most clearly governs the learning of multiple discriminations is *interference*, that is, the tendency for the individual associations involved in identification behavior to get "mixed up," so that the stimulus for one tends to call out the response for another, and vice versa. The basic rationale has been described by Gibson (33), and has in general withstood the test of time and much experimentation (cf., 71). From the standpoint of an optimal learning prescription, the various findings may be summarized as follows: *make the stimuli as distinctive as possible.* The evidence is clear from paired-associate studies that the rapidity of acquiring multiple discriminations increases directly with the degree of distinctiveness (lack of confusability) of the members of the set being learned (70).

How does one go about making the stimuli of a task more distinctive? Three main methods have been used: (a) The first involves adding distinctive cues to stimuli during learning, which are later "faded" and "vanished" (2). (b) A second method, and an extremely effective one in many situations, is to use mediation (35). A stimulus like the color brown may be linked to a response like "penny," already at high strength. This in turn is associated with "one," the required response.

At the same time, the stimulus "black" may be linked to "nothingness," which in turn is associated with "zero." As Gilbert shows, this procedure can be effectively applied to all 10 resistor colors. (c) A third method is to group stimuli which are highly similar and whose responses possess elements in common, thus capitalizing upon induction (or stimulus generalization, as it is often called).

Should the responses in multiple-discrimination behavior also be made distinctive? The answer to this question is yes, if what is meant is making the responses highly available by differentiating them as stimuli for echoic acts, as previously discussed. In many cases of multiple discrimination, the responses may be assumed to be highly available, as is the case with the numerals zero through nine in Gilbert's example. No purpose would be served by attempting to differentiate them further. However, if *new* words are being learned (as is the case, for example, in paired-associate studies using nonsense words), there can be little doubt that prediscrimination learning of these responses represented as stimuli would have a facilitating effect on learning (cf., 32, 33). In terms of the present discussion, response availability is assumed as a *precondition* of multiple-discrimination learning.

If there are, say, 10 associations to be differentiated in a multiple discrimination, the question of *sequence of presentation* obviously arises. Should they be presented in instruction one at a time, two at a time, or even all at the same time? Gilbert (35) argues for the effectiveness of an "all at once" presentation, using mediation. With 10 or fewer differentiations to be learned, this method often may be practically useful. However, a general answer to the question of sequence must certainly consider the problem of more than 10 individual associations. There does not appear to be clear evidence which would make possible a general prescription at the present time. Two additional possibilities should be given serious consideration in research on this question of learning sequence for multiple-discrimination learning. One is the advantage of various part-whole arrangements (45, pp. 499-507), and another is the effects of grouping of similar and dissimilar stimuli (20, 60).

Multiple-discrimination learning, then, requires that two or more individual S-R associations be distinguished and freed from interference. Optimal conditions for such learning begin with the assumption of (a) response availability (differentiation) and (b) association of the individual S-R's, as prerequisites. The tactics to be employed are concerned with making the stimuli of the task as distinctive as possible. Methods of accomplishing this include the use of mediating responses, addition of cues for stimuli which are then progressively "vanished," and grouping of stimuli to enhance the effects of stimulus generalization (induction). Sequence of presentation of the individual associations may also have an important effect on the interference generated in such learning.

Behavior Chains

Another way in which single associations may be put together is as behavior chains. Gilbert (35) discusses chains and subchains at some length. Gagné (23) calls them *sequences* and notes that they often occur within tasks commonly identified as *procedures*. Certainly behavior chains are very common; examples are computational procedures of mathematics or of accounting. Adding fractions, for example, is an activity which may be described as a sequence including (a) finding the lowest common denominator; (b) multiplying individual fractions by a factor; (c) adding numerators; and (d) dividing numerator and denominator by a common factor. However, in designing instruction for this activity chain, one might well need to break these steps into smaller ones, in order to insure that each step is within what Gilbert calls the "operant span." As an instructional objective, a behavior chain has the following description: *Upon presentation of a specific stimulus, makes a series of two or more responses in a particular order, using no other order and no other responses.*

In the pure case, the learning of a behavior chain is a matter of putting together in prescribed order a set of previously learned individual associations. One would expect in this instance to find many results having applicability to this problem from studies of serial verbal learning (45). For a number of reasons, however, this does not appear to be the case. It is now fairly generally recognized that serial verbal learning represents a mixture of several different kinds of behaviors, including response learning (72), association learning (59, 74), and the learning of order. It is therefore difficult to separate the influence of independent variables on these behaviors in terms of the measurements of learning employed. What the results do emphasize is simply this: the determination of optimal conditions of learning an *order* of things must depend upon the assumption that these "things" have already been individually learned. This means, as the previous discussion implies, that the establishment of behavior chains (in its optimal form) requires the prelearning of (a) the individual associations that make up the chain and (b) any multiple discriminations that may be required to prevent interference among the stimuli in the chain (which tend to make otherwise correct responses occur in the wrong order).

The prescription of establishing chains retrogressively, described by Gilbert (35), apparently has no clear precursor in the literature on serial verbal learning, despite the long history of such research. It is based on animal learning, particularly the chaining of operants (17), and upon the concept of reinforcement. According to Gilbert's statement of this idea (35, p. 21), if the consequence of a response is reinforcing, the occasion for this response will be reinforcing, and any operant which produces that occasion will be strengthened. Accordingly, if one sets out to establish a chain in an optimal fashion, he would begin with a final (reinforcing) act and then proceed to associate it with the next preceding act in the chain. Once this has been done, the new act itself acquires reinforcing properties; it may then be associated with another new occasion and so on back to the beginning of the chain. This method has a definite intuitive appeal as a programing technique. Further exploration of the conditions under which it may operate with greatest effectiveness would be valuable. In addition, consideration might be given to investigating the relation between "backwards chaining" and the "forward-looking objective" proposed as an initial frame in instructional sequences (24).

Class Concepts

It is generally recognized that many responses made by a human being serve to identify, not specifically denotable objects (such as a particular switch or a particular French word), but classes of objects or events, the stimulus characteristics of which may vary widely. Such classes include not only categories whose physical features seem to have a "prototype" identity, like chairs, birds, automobiles, etc., but also those categories whose membership may be infinitely variable, like "the upper one," "the middle one," "the odd one," "a space," and many others. Obviously, it is not a difficult task for a human being to "choose the odd one"; for a monkey, it is initially quite difficult (41). The objective applicable to this kind of behavior may be stated as follows: *Upon presentation of stimuli which differ widely in their physical appearance, makes a response which identifies them as instances of a class and which distinguishes them from instances belonging to other classes.*

Systematic research on how such concepts are learned by human beings has struggled for years against the difficulty of formulating the problem, as well as how to go about studying it (cf., 22). In all probability, the best clues to the understanding of this kind of learning will come from studies of children who do not yet know what a word like "odd" or "upper" means. In the case of adult human beings, however, it is usually clear that they *do* know what such words mean and that the problem of "concept acquisition" is not for them a problem of learning, but merely one of reinstatement. Accordingly, the basic operation involved in instruction which establishes a class concept is in fact *instructions* such as the sentence, "Choose the odd one."

Beyond this, it may also be noted that a possible meaning for "learning a concept" in an adult is "learning the limits of generalization of a concept." A concept like *cell* has a meaning in biology which has more or less specific limits. Some things observed through a microscope are not cells, while others, although widely different in physical appearance, *are* cells. One would like a biology student to be able to identify a cell correctly throughout a very considerable range of variation in physical appearance of these objects. Accordingly, learning the concept "cell" may be seen to be a matter of learning to generalize the correct identification among a suitable variety of stimulus situations containing instances of the class. So far as is known, the best prescription for such instruction is to establish such multiple discriminations (in the manner described in a previous section) in a representative variety of situations. Gilbert's (35) discussion of the problem of generalization learning is consistent with this account.

As is true with other forms of behavior, the learning of class concepts can be seen to have some preconditions. The response itself (such as "cell" or an unfamiliar one, like "nucleolus") must be differentiated. And at least one association must be established before generalization learning can proceed. Following this, multiple-discrimination learning can be undertaken with each stimulus sample selected, in order to establish the concept fully.

Principles

The acquisition of "principles" or "rules" is perhaps the most common form of learning undertaken by means of an instructional program. Principles are involved in learning to spell ("*i* before *e* except after *c*"); to handle sentence structure ("the pronoun agrees with the noun subject"); to perform numerical operations ("ab + ac = a[b + c]"); to determine the date of federal elections ("first Tuesday following the first Monday in November"); and, in fact, in almost every conceivable subject to be taught. It has occurred to some scholars that perhaps principles are the *only* things which reasonably can be programed in instruction. But this is not so, as previous paragraphs have shown. In addition, such a view runs the danger of overlooking the fact that the learning of principles is based upon simpler forms of learning and that the latter may therefore be required to be directly involved in any particular instructional sequence.

Formally described, a principle is a chain of two concepts (25). Actually, a chain may be longer than that in the sense that it contains some subchains; but it is convenient to consider the essential aspects of a principle as exhibiting two links. In common language, a principle can be stated in the form "If *a*, then *b*," where *a* and *b* are two concepts. Examples are the following: if (a) the temperature of water is above 212 degrees, then (b) boiling occurs; if (a) two integers have the same sign, then (b) they are summed as whole numbers in the same direction; if (a) a diphthong is composed of *i* and *e*, then (b) the second letter is pronounced. Defined as a learning objective, the act of using a principle may be stated as follows: *Upon presentation of a situation containing stimuli classifiable as concept a, and instructions to produce concept b, performs the sequence a→b.*

Are principles inevitably verbal? Certainly not. It is not intended here to suggest that in order to pronounce the diphthong "*ie*" the individual must say to himself verbally, "When *i* and *e* occur in a diphthong, pronounce the second letter." The exact composition of what the individual "says to himself" need not be known, perhaps cannot be known. All one needs to know is that the task can be performed and that it can be done with any letters of the class *i* and *e* and in any context of surrounding stimulation. One does not know exactly what the mediation of such tasks is, and whatever it is undoubtedly varies among individuals.

In order to describe and communicate what the individual is doing, however, it is completely inadequate to say that the individual "makes the response $\bar{e}$ to the stimulus *ie*." (It is not denied that the individual *may conceivably* be doing only this, but in that case, it is an inadequate objective for learning.) In performing a task according to a principle, the individual is reacting to instances of the *class* of "*i* and *e* combinations" by pronouncing instances of the *class* of "second letters." As a matter of convenience, one can describe these classes and their chained relationship in a verbal phrase of the form "If *a*, then *b*." This is the way a principle is described, but not necessarily the way it is learned.

There are, however, some very important preconditions for the learning of principles. Outstanding among these is the condition that the concepts which make up the principle must be previously acquired, in order for learning to occur most readily. Gilbert's example of a principle (35, p. 54) provides a good illustration of this point. The principle pertains to the operation of filing, and is as follows: "All spaces between 'filing reference names' count as one alphabetic position weighted less than A." As Gilbert's discussion implies, such a principle cannot be learned unless the individual has learned the generalized meanings (i.e., the concepts) of "filing reference names" and of "alphabetic position," as well as of "weight less than A." While it is possible, of course, to teach the two parts of a principle all at the same time, such a procedure does not permit the separation of "concept learning" from "principle learning" and accordingly does not make possible the specification of optimal conditions for the latter as is attempted here.

If one assumes that both parts of a principle have been previously learned as concepts, it is a fairly easy matter to bring about the acquisition of the principle. It may be desirable, before actually suggesting the order of events in the chain, to insure that each concept is highly "available" and can be recalled readily. A frame devoted to review may be used to accomplish this purpose (cf., 24). Following this, it is a matter of getting one link of the chain to become the occasion for the other, so that the sequence becomes established. In all probability, it is of particular importance in this situation to encourage the learner to make a "constructed" rather than a "copying" response.

Strategies

Are there forms of behavior which are more complex than principles? First of all, it may be noted that rules themselves can get pretty complicated, without departing in any important way from the basic structure already described. There may even be "higher-order rules," which are composed of two or more "simpler rules" (25). But some authors have emphasized the importance of strategies with which an individual approaches a task or solves a problem (cf., 7). The existence of such strategies, in fact, appears to be well established (8). It seems reasonable to consider that strategies are *mediating principles* which do not appear in the performance of the task itself, but which may nevertheless affect the speed or excellence of that performance. If this be so, then obviously one has to use rather special methods to uncover these strategies. But it is also possible to conceive of them as having principle-like qualities and of being made up essentially of a chain of concepts. Such strategies as "choose the odd except when the light is on the left," or "choose the alternate keys in order," or "alternate every third choice" are, after all, principles which can be readily analyzed into their component concepts. As a learning objective, a strategy may be described as follows: *In discovering content principles applicable to a series of novel situations, performs a mediating sequence a'→b' in which a' is a class of concepts to be attended to selectively, and b' is a class of responses intermediate to those required for completing the action.*

If strategies are really principles, then obviously they can be learned as principles, and no new specifications for their learning are needed. It may be well to emphasize again, however, that strategies (considered as principles) imply the learning of their concepts as a prerequisite condition. Bruner, Goodnow, and Austin (8), for example, studied the discovery of "conjunctive" and "disjunctive" principles in classifying a set of cards containing figures which could be conceptualized in terms of a number of stimulus attributes. Faced with such a problem, an individual might, it was found, try a strategy such as "Continue matching on the basis of shape until a negative instance is found, then switch to matching borders." If one is going to be able to learn such a strategy, he must already have mastered the concepts "shape," "borders," "match," and "continue," among others. If he has learned these, the learning and use of a strategy will be easy. If he has not, then it is difficult to say what is happening, since one individual may have to learn the concepts while another may not, while both will need to acquire the strategy.

There is considerable interest in the learning of strategies in connection with education in science, since scientific methods may themselves be viewed as containing strategies. Science educators frequently emphasize the importance of the learning of "processes" (such as observation, classification, inference, model building) to instruction in the sciences. A full discussion of this question cannot be undertaken in this chapter (cf., 26). The view of strategies described here, however, implies that they are derived under conditions which include the prior learning of concepts and principles pertaining directly to content.

Recapitulation—Behavior Categories

The preceding discussion has attempted to identify six main categories of behavior which exhibit formal differences among themselves with respect to the conditions required for their most rapid acquisition, but irrespective of their content. Such differences in learning conditions have an obvious relation to the tactics used in designing instructional programs of greatest effectiveness. It has been emphasized that one large and important class of "learning conditions" includes those called *preconditions* of the learner, that is, they must be assumed as previously established behaviors of the learner ("entering behaviors"). The other major class comprises those conditions which obtain within the confines of any particular instructional sequence. These ideas are summarized in Table 1.

Viewing the process of instruction from the standpoint of this table, one is inclined to emphasize several implications:

1. Designing optimal instruction is a matter of choosing the proper tactics for each of six categories of behavior implied by the formal (noncontent) characteristics of instructional objectives (tasks).

TABLE 1

Categories of Behavior Differing in Formal Characteristics Relating to Ease of Learning, Including Preconditions of the Learner and Conditions of the Instructional Situation

Behavior Category	Behavior Description	Preconditions of the Learner	Conditions of Instructional Situation
Response Differentiation	Response controlled by discriminated stimulus (most frequently, echoic)		Contiguity of S^D and R
Association	Specific stimulus related by coding to a particular response	Discrimination of stimulus by observing response; differentiation of response: a prelearned coding	Contiguity of S^D, coding stimulus, and R
Multiple Discrimination (Identification)	Two or more specific stimuli call out an equal number of different responses	Individual associations; differentiation of responses	Make the stimuli highly distinctive
Behavior Chains (Sequences)	Two or more acts to be completed in a specific order	Individual associations; multiple discriminations among members of the chain	Begin with high-strength acts, associate these with low-strength acts in order
Class Concepts	Responses made to stimuli of a class, differing in appearance	Individual associations; multiple discriminations as necessary	Present sufficient variety of stimuli to insure generalization
Principles	Chaining of at least two concepts: if a, then b	Concepts	Insure availability of concepts, encourage constructed responses
Strategies	Chaining of concepts	Concepts which determine selective attention and mediate responses	Insure availability of concepts, encourage constructed responses

2. Any set of instructional objectives may require one or more, or any combination, of these tactics to insure that learning occurs most effectively. An excellent description of this problem and its complexities is given by Gilbert (35).
3. For each type of behavior shown, the process of learning in its pure form is exceedingly quick and depends mainly upon the contiguous occurrence of certain stimulus and response events.
4. The impurities in learning, which occasion slowness and difficulty, are largely attributable to insufficient preconditioning of the learner, so that more than one kind of behavior has to be acquired at one and the same time. Since optimal conditions for learning are different for each type, this results in ineffective tactics.

Conditions of the Learner: It is also evident from this discussion that in the design of instruction, one needs to give full consideration to the individual capabilities and dispositions of the learner when describing the "conditions of learning" as a whole. The course of learning for any individual is importantly affected by the capabilities he brings to the instructional situation. This is of course true of certain basic innate capacities which are recognized by all investigators as imposing certain limits on the rapidity of learning and on the levels of performance attained. It is also true of the specifically acquired capabilities listed in Table 1 as "preconditions of the learner." And in a larger sense, it applies to other kinds of dispositions, also previously acquired, but which are not dealt with in this chapter, such as attitudes, interests, and motivations.

The Objectives of Retention and Transfer

It is not uncommon for descriptions of instructional objectives to include aims such as retention of performance over a specified period of time and transfer or "application" of the behavior that has been learned to new situations. It may be recalled that indications of concern with these kinds of events have already been noted in the categories proposed by Miller (54), one of which is "recall," and even more prominently in those described by Bloom (4) which include "application" as a major class. It is worthwhile to consider here whether these two kinds of objectives imply any different or additional tactics for the design of optimal instruction.

Retention: The results of studies which have undertaken to measure retention of programed instructional materials are remarkably similar in some respects. First of all, they tend to show high amounts of retention over periods of weeks and months (1, 27, 29, 38). Second, they report high degrees of correlation between achievement measured immediately following learning and after a longer retention interval. Of some relevance to the question of instructional objectives is the fact that few relationships have been demonstrated between independent variables in effect during the learning period and the later retention scores. Thus, Alter (1) finds no significant differences in retention related to differences in initial achievement or in rate of retention as affected by intelligence scores or rate of program completion. Glaser and Reynolds (38) report no differences in retention associated with a number of variations in amount of repetition and the spacing of reviews. Gagné and Bassler's (27) results fail to reveal differences in retention associated with amount of repetition of subtask examples, or of a time separation between the completion of one subtask and the introduction of the next.

Thus these results provide few hints as to the possible differential effects of task differences on the retention of materials acquired by programed instructional methods. Nevertheless, one cannot dismiss lightly the possibility that such differences may be found, if direct attempts are made to study them. From the point of view of the present discussion, the important question is, can differences in retention be found for the various behavior categories of association, multiple discrimination, behavior chains, class concepts, principles, and strategies? The answer to such a question requires the conduct of experimental studies which deliberately set out to deal with the acquisition (and retention) of relatively "pure" forms of each of these behaviors in isolation from others. This form of experimentation has not as yet been carried out within the tradition of programed learning. Previous findings in verbal learning (45) probably have some relevance, insofar as they reveal differences in retention for paired nonsense syllables (multiple discrimination), verbal sequences (behavior chains), and logically connected ideas (principles).

Transfer: In a manner similar to retention, one can ask whether there are differences in transferability of the behaviors of association, multiple discrimination, chains, concepts, and principles. However, it is at once apparent that instructional objectives enter into the question in a definitional sense.

In the case of association and the two forms of behavior which represent direct elaborations of it, multiple discrimination and behavior chains, the objectives of instruction are opposite to those of transferability. In each of these instances, the aim of instruction is to produce mastery of tasks which require specific response outcomes to stimuli having specific physical identities. In stating the required outcome of an association such as boy-happy, for example, the response "joyful" would be considered incorrect by the experimenter; similarly, the response "happy" would be called an error if made to the stimulus "youth." Multiple discriminations also have this characteristic, since their learning is undertaken primarily to *overcome* the tendencies to generalization which may occur among members of the set of stimuli to be discriminated. Accordingly, it may be said that the criterion of transferability is a negative one, so far as the objectives represented by these forms of behavior are concerned.

But the situation is quite different for class concepts and principles. As has been pointed out previously, these forms of behavior are established by conditions which foster generalizability. Furthermore, it is necessary to state the objectives of instruction for these behaviors in terms which will clearly distinguish them from simpler forms such as associations and multiple discriminations. This is the reason for using the word *class* in task descriptions comprising the former kinds of behaviors. The learner acquires responses to stimuli of the *class* "left," "right," "opposite," "noun," "fraction," or whatever. Or he acquires a principle which chains the class "subject" with the class "sentence"; the class "numerator" with the class "fraction." In such instances, transferability is a part of the instructional objective, rather than being specifically excluded from it.

There is, then, an immediately apparent difference in objectives of instruction between the "simpler" forms of behavior, i.e., association, multiple discrimination, and behavior chains, and the more "complex" forms, i.e., concepts, principles, and strategies. The former imply an absence of transferability (generalizability), whereas the latter require its presence. Beyond this, there are some intriguing research questions which remain to be investigated. For example, the extent of generalization which should be used in instruction on concepts and principles, in order to insure transferability, has not yet received a clear specification (cf., 35, p. 54). There is also the important question of what implications for subsequent learning may result from the inadequate transferability of concepts and principles, which may have been acquired under conditions of inadequate generalization in the first place. Answers to these and other related questions will add much to knowledge of how to specify tasks to be learned.

Transfer and the Measurement of Objectives: Certain disparities between the definitions of instructional objectives proposed by investigators of learning and those which grow out of the achievement testing tradition have already been pointed out. It is possible that these differences arise because the learning investigator is mainly interested in obtaining an indication of *mastery of what has been taught*, whereas the achievement tester, responding to the often highly general aims of an educational effort, seeks a measure of *transferability of what has been taught.* The former is asking the question, "Did the learner meet the criterion of performance stated by the objective?" The latter is inquiring, "To what degree is whatever has been learned useful?" As previous quotations from Bloom (4) have indicated, the achievement tester is interested in "interpreting," "extrapolating," "applying to novel situations," "analyzing," "synthesizing a new plan." In attempting to meet these *transfer objectives*, he in fact cannot specify all of the situations to which transfer can be expected to occur. By his measures, he is trying to predict the amount of transferability to be expected to a variety of situations, some of which have not yet been thought of.

It appears that the *measurement of attainment* and the *measurement of transferability* are both important goals of an educational program (cf., 37). While this chapter has concentrated chiefly on *attainment objectives*, it has not had the intention of denying the importance of measurement in terms of *transfer objectives.* However, it is noteworthy that educational measurement often appears to be exclusively concerned with the latter kind of measurement. Attention to the measurement of attainment objectives may turn out to be a desirable undertaking for those interested in achievement measurement. If no other reason can be adduced, the logic of behavioral measurement would seem to require it. The typical achievement test (of transfer objectives) makes no distinction between those individuals who have fully attained the principles on which it is based and those who have not. The score which such a test yields is therefore to some degree uninterpretable and may even be less highly predictive of transfer than it should be. Both attainment scores and transferability scores have their separate uses in educational measurement; together, it is possible that their systematic use could lead to a model of behavior measurement superior to that now employed.

Summary—Objectives and the Design of Instruction

This chapter has presented the point of view that the defining of instructional objectives has a number of purposes, perhaps the most important of which is the design of instruction. Unambiguous and complete statements of tasks to be performed when instruction is finished make possible the identification of certain categories of behavior to be learned. These categories have been described as response differentiation, association, multiple discrimination, behavior sequences, class concepts, principles, and strategies.

Each of these forms of behavior carries a different implication regarding the conditions of learning needed for its establishment. Depending on what the objective is at any point in its total sequence, therefore, a learning program needs to make a particular set of provisions in order for learning to occur in an optimal fashion. At the present time the evidence does not permit us to state these conditions with a great deal of precision. Differential reinforcement and contiguity are two factors which appear to have general applicability.

Perhaps the most important condition for the learning of each type of behavior objective, however, is the apparent fact that each depends upon the preestablishment of a lower-order behavior in the individual learner. This has two important implications for instructional design. First, it means that the sequence of instruction, to be most effective, must proceed from associations to discriminations to concepts to principles, and not vice versa. Second, it implies that the learner's previously acquired capabilities are of critical importance to the effectiveness of instruction and must surely be known if the instructional program is to "take hold."

As terminal objectives of an instructional program, each of the categories of behavior identified may be measured as *attainment*. It is also recognized that objectives of instruction in a larger sense may include those of retention and, most significantly, of *transferability*. The latter kind of objective appears to be the aim of achievement measurement as typically employed and is emphasized in the writings of those who have applied these techniques to educational measurement and evaluation. It is suggested that both forms of measurement are important for a full understanding of the changes in behavior effected by learning.

References

1. Alter, M. *Retention in Programed Instruction.* Technical Report 620917. New York: Center for Programed Instruction, 1962.
2. Angell, D., and Lumsdaine, A. A. *Research on Cueing Factors Related to Programed Instruction.* Research Report AIR-C14-9/62-TR2. Pittsburgh: American Institute for Research, 1962.
3. Bloom, B. S. "Changing Conceptions of Examining at the University of Chicago." *Evaluation in General Education.* (Edited by P. L. Dressel.) Dubuque, Iowa: William C. Brown Co., 1954. pp. 297-321.
4. Bloom, B. S., editor. *Taxonomy of Educational Objectives.* New York: Longmans, Green, 1956.
5. Briggs, L. J. "Teaching Machines for Training of Military Personnel in Maintenance of Electronic Equipment." *Automatic Teaching: The State of the Art.* (Edited by E. Galanter.) New York: John Wiley & Sons, 1959.
6. Briggs, L. J., and Besnard, G. G. "Experimental Procedures for Increasing Reinforced Practice in Training Air Force Mechanics for an Electronic System." *Air Force Human Engineering, Personnel, and Training Research.* (Edited by G. Finch and F. Cameron.) Washington, D.C.: National Academy of Sciences—National Research Council, 1956.
7. Bruner, J. S. "The Act of Discovery." *Harvard Educational Review* 31: 21-32; Winter 1961.
8. Bruner, J. S.; Goodnow, J. J.; and Austin, G. A. *A Study of Thinking.* New York: John Wiley & Sons, 1956.
9. Cook, D., and Mechner, F. "Fundamentals of Programed Instruction." *Applied Programed Instruction.* (Edited by S. Margulies and L. D. Eigen.) New York: John Wiley & Sons, 1962.
10. Cotterman, T. E. *Task Classification: An Approach to Partially Ordering Information on Human Learning.* Technical Note 58-374. Wright Patterson Air Force Base, Ohio: Wright Air Development Center, 1959.

11. Coulson, J. E. "Combining Educational Techniques for Specific Students and Tasks: A Concern for Research." *Prospectives in Programing.* (Edited by R. Filep.) New York: Macmillan Co., 1963.

12. Deese, J. "From the Isolated Verbal Unit to Connected Discourse." *Verbal Learning and Verbal Behavior.* (Edited by C. N. Cofer.) New York: McGraw-Hill Book Co., 1961, pp. 11-31,

13. Dressel, P. L., editor. *Evaluation in General Education.* Dubuque, Iowa: William C. Brown Co., 1954.

14. Dressel, P. L. *Evaluation in Higher Education.* Boston: Houghton Mifflin Co., 1961.

15. Evans, J. *Programmers, Experts, and the Analysis of Knowledge.* Paper delivered at the Symposium on Teaching Machines and Mathematics Programs, American Association for the Advancement of Science, Denver, Colorado, December 29, 1961.

16. Evans, J. L.; Homme, L. E.; and Glaser, R. "The Ruleg System for the Construction of Programmed Verbal Learning Sequences." *Journal of Educational Research* 55: 515-20; June-July 1962.

17. Findley, J. D. "An Experimental Outline for Building and Exploring Multi-Operant Behavior Repertoires." *Journal of the Experimental Analysis of Behavior* 5: 113-66; January 1962.

18. French, R. S. "Evaluation of a K-System Trouble-Shooting Trainer." *Air Force Human Engineering, Personnel, and Training Research.* (Edited by G. Finch and F. Cameron.) Washington, D.C.: National Academy of Sciences—National Research Council, 1956.

19. French, R. S. *The K-System MAC-1 Trouble-Shooting Trainer: II. Derivation of Training Characteristics.* Technical Memorandum ASPRL-TM-56-9. Lackland Air Force Base, Tex.: Air Force Personnel and Training Research Center, 1956.

20. Gagné, R. M. "The Effects of Sequence of Presentation of Similar Items on the Learning of Paired Associates." *Journal of Experimental Psychology* 40: 61-73; February 1950.

21. Gagné, R. M. "Methods of Forecasting Maintenance Job Requirements." *Symposium on Electronic Maintenance.* Washington, D.C.: Advisory Panel on Personnel and Training Research, Office of Assistant Secretary of Defense, Research, and Development, 1955.

22. Gagné, R. M. "Problem Solving and Thinking." *Annual Review of Psychology* 10: 147-72; 1959.

23. Gagné, R. M. "Human Functions in Systems." *Psychological Principles in System Development.* (Edited by R. M. Gagné.) New York: Holt, Rinehart & Winston, 1962.

24. Gagné, R. M. "The Acquisition of Knowledge." *Psychological Review* 69: 355-65; July 1962.

25. Gagné, R. M. "Problem Solving." *Categories of Human Learning.* (Edited by A. W. Melton.) New York: Academic Press, 1964.

26. Gagné, R. M. "The Learning Requirements for Enquiry." *Journal of Research in Science Teaching* 2: 144-54; June 1964.
27. Gagné, R. M., and Bassler, O. C. "A Study of Retention of Some Topics of Elementary Non-Metric Geometry." *Journal of Educational Psychology* 54: 23-31; June 1963.
28. Gagné, R. M., and Bolles, R. C. "A Review of Factors in Learning Efficiency." *Automatic Teaching: The State of the Art.* (Edited by E. Galanter.) New York: John Wiley & Sons, 1959.
29. Gagné, R. M., and Dick, W. "Learning Measures in a Self-Instructional Program in Solving Equations." *Psychological Reports* 10: 131-46; February 1962.
30. Gagné, R. M., and others. "Factors in Acquiring Knowledge of a Mathematical Task." *Psychological Monographs* 76: 1-21; Whole No. 526, 1962.
31. Gagné, R. M., and Paradise, N. E. "Abilities and Learning Sets in Knowledge Acquisition." *Psychological Monographs* 75: 1-23; Whole No. 518, 1961.
32. Gannon, D. R., and Noble, C. E. "Familiarization (n) as a Stimulus Factor in Paired-Associate Verbal Learning." *Journal of Experimental Psychology* 62: 14-23; July 1961.
33. Gibson, E. J. "A Systematic Application of the Concepts of Generalization and Differentiation to Verbal Learning." *Psychological Review* 47: 196-229; May 1940.
34. Gibson, E. J. "Intra-List Generalization as a Factor in Verbal Learning." *Journal of Experimental Psychology* 30: 185-200; March 1942.
35. Gilbert, Thomas F. "Mathetics: The Technology of Education." *Journal of Mathetics* 1: 7-73; January 1962.
36. Glaser, R., and Glanzer, M. *Training and Training Research.* Pittsburgh: American Institute for Research, 1958.
37. Glaser, R., and Klaus, D. J. "Proficiency Measurement: Assessing Human Performance." *Psychological Principles in System Development.* (Edited by R. M. Gagné.) New York: Holt, Rinehart & Winston, 1962. pp. 419-74.
38. Glaser, R., and Reynolds, J. H. *Investigations of Learning Variables in Programmed Instruction.* Pittsburgh: Department of Psychology, University of Pittsburgh, 1962.
39. Goldberg, I. "An Introduction to Programed Instruction." *Applied Programed Instruction.* (Edited by S. Margulies and L. D. Eigen.) New York: John Wiley & Sons, 1962. pp. 15-20.
40. Green, E. J. *The Learning Process and Programmed Instruction.* New York: Holt, Rinehart & Winston, 1962.
41. Harlow, H. F. "The Formation of Learning Sets." *Psychological Review* 56: 51-65; January 1949.

42. Holland, A. L., and Matthews, J. "Application of Teaching Machine Concepts to Speech Pathology and Audiology." *Asha* 5: 474-82; January 1963.

43. Klaus, D. J. "The Art of Auto-Instructional Programming." *Programmed Learning: Theory and Research.* (Edited by W. I. Smith and J. W. Moore.) Princeton, N.J.: D. Van Nostrand Co., 1962.

44. Lumsdaine, A. A. "Design of Training Aids and Devices." *Human Factors Methods for System Design.* (Edited by J. D. Folley.) Pittsburgh: American Institute for Research, 1960.

45. McGeoch, J. S., and Irion, A. L. *The Psychology of Human Learning.* New York: Longmans, 1952.

46. McGuire, W. J. "A Multiprocess Model for Paired-Associate Learning." *Journal of Experimental Psychology* 62: 335-47; October 1961.

47. Mager, R. F. "A Method for Preparing Auto-Instructional Programs." *I.R.E. Transactions on Education.* Palo Alto, Calif.: Varian Associates, 1961.

48. Mager, R. F. *Preparing Objectives for Programmed Instruction.* San Francisco: Fearon Publishers, 1962.

49. Mager, R. F., and McCann, J. *Learner-Controlled Instruction.* Palo Alto, Calif: Varian Associates, 1961.

50. Miller, R. B. *A Method for Man-Machine Task Analysis.* Technical Report 53-137. Wright-Patterson Air Force Base, Ohio: Wright Air Development Center, 1953.

51. Miller, R. B. *Handbook on Training and Training Equipment Design.* Technical Report 53-136. Wright-Patterson Air Force Base, Ohio: Wright Air Development Center, 1953.

52. Miller, R. B. *Psychological Considerations in the Design of Training Equipment.* Technical Report 54-563. Wright-Patterson Air Force Base, Ohio: Wright Air Development Center, 1954.

53. Miller, R. B. *A Suggested Guide to Functional Characteristics of Training and Training Equipment.* Technical Memorandum ML-TM-56-14. Lackland Air Force Base, Tex.: Air Force Personnel and Training Research Center, 1956.

54. Miller, R. B. *A Suggested Guide to Position-Task Description.* Technical Memorandum ASPRL-TM-56-6. Lackland Air Force Base, Tex.: Air Force Personnel and Training Research Center, 1956.

55. Miller, R. B. "The Newer Roles of the Industrial Psychologist." *Industrial Psychology.* (Edited by B. von H. Gilmer.) New York: McGraw-Hill Book Co., 1961. pp. 353-80.

56. Miller, R. B. "Task Description and Analysis." *Psychological Principles in System Development.* (Edited by R. M. Gagné.) New York: Holt, Rinehart & Winston, 1962. pp. 187-228.

57. Miller, R. B., and Van Cott, H. P. "The Determination of Knowledge Content for Complex Man-Machine Jobs." Technical Report AIR-A93-55-FR-115. Pittsburgh: American Institute for Research, 1955.

58. Mowrer, O. H. *Learning Theory and Behavior.* New York: John Wiley & Sons, 1960.
59. Primoff, E. "Backward and Forward Association as an Organizing Art in Serial and in Paired Associate Learning." *Journal of Psychology* 5: 375-95; March 1938.
60. Rotberg, I. C., and Woolman, M. "Verbal Paired-Associate Learning as a Function of Grouping Similar Stimuli or Responses." *Journal of Experimental Psychology* 65: 47-51; January 1963.
61. Saltz, E. "Response Pretraining: Differentiation or Availability?" *Journal of Experimental Psychology* 62: 583-87; December 1961.
62. Skinner, B. F. *Verbal Behavior.* New York: Appleton-Century-Crofts, 1957.
63. Skinner, B. F. "Teaching Machines." *Science* 128: 969-77; October 1958.
64. Skinner, B. F. "The Programming of Verbal Knowledge." *Automatic Teaching: The State of the Art.* (Edited by E. Galanter.) New York: John Wiley & Sons, 1959. pp. 63-68.
65. Stolurow, L. M. *Teaching by Machine.* Washington, D.C.: U.S. Department of Health, Education, and Welfare, Office of Education, 1961.
66. Taber, J. I.; Glaser, R.; and Schaefer, H. H. *Learning and Programmed Instruction.* Reading, Mass.: Addison-Wesley, 1965.
67. Training Psychology Branch, Behavioral Sciences Laboratory, Aerospace Medical Laboratory. *Uses of Task Analysis in Deriving Training and Training Equipment Requirements.* Technical Report 60-593. Wright-Patterson Air Force Base, Ohio: Wright Air Development Center, 1960.
68. Tyler, R. W. "Achievement Testing and Curriculum Construction." *Trends in Student Personnel Work.* (Edited by G. Williamson.) Minneapolis: University of Minnesota Press, 1949. pp. 391-407.
69. Tyler, R. W. "The Functions of Measurement in Improving Instruction." *Educational Measurement.* (Edited by E. F. Lindquist.) Washington, D.C.: American Council on Education, 1950.
70. Underwood, B. J. "Studies of Distributed Practice: VIII. Learning and Retention of Paired Nonsense Syllables as a Function of Intra-List Similarity." *Journal of Experimental Psychology* 45: 133-42; March 1953.
71. Underwood, B. J. "An Evaluation of the Gibson Theory of Verbal Learning." *Verbal Learning and Verbal Behavior.* (Edited by C. N. Cofer.) New York: McGraw-Hill Book Co., 1961.
72. Underwood, B. J., and Postman, L. "Extraexperimental Sources of Interference in Forgetting." *Psychological Review* 67: 73-95; March 1960.
73. Underwood, B. J., and Schulz, R. W. *Meaningfulness and Verbal Learning.* Chicago: J. B. Lippincott Co., 1960.
74. Young, R. K. "A Comparison of Two Methods of Learning Serial Associations." *American Journal of Psychology* 72: 554-59; December 1959.

JAMES G. HOLLAND
Harvard University

Research on Programing Variables [*]

Ten years ago a few of the most general discoveries from the learning laboratories enabled the initial description of a rationale for a behavioral technology of education. Among the principles discussed were some which collectively constitute programing. The statements descriptive of programing were culled from laboratory experience and experimentation and have served successfully as a guide for the development of many useful teaching machine programs. Upon examination, however, the principles often are too general and too prone to be misunderstood. They need a clear, concise definition which results from direct experimentation. Such experimental definition should be quantitative to permit one to indicate for any program how large its steps are, how sequentially dependent the material is, and how response-contingent reinforcements, or correct answers, may be.

This chapter is a critical review of experimental research on variables in programing. The criterion for inclusion or evaluation is that the research deal with fundamental variables which apply to all programs, or at least a specifically delineated class of programs, rather than answer only problems peculiar to a specific case. The chapter attempts to designate findings which are valid and general in their significance for programed instruction.

[*] Much of the time for preparation of this chapter was made possible by the Harvard Committee on Programmed Instruction, which is supported by a grant from the Carnegie Corporation.

To review all research having implications for programing would be impractical, as it would go back through many years of productive basic research; instead, the chapter covers only applied research on variables in programing. A strict definition of the term *programing* further delineates the range. Programing is taken to mean "the construction of carefully arranged sequences of contingencies leading to the terminal performances which are the object of education" (91, p. 169; see Chapter 1 of this volume). Research on "adjunct programing," therefore, is excluded. The reader who is interested in adjunct programing will find many worthwhile papers by Pressey and his associates in Part II of Lumsdaine and Glaser (68). In addition, a recent book edited by Lumsdaine (65) contains examples of the adjunct questioning of students viewing films. In general, classical rote-learning studies are also excluded, except for a few which use paired associates specifically to investigate programing parameters.

The attempt is made to examine the appropriate research in depth, to summarize what has been learned thus far, to point up the methodological problems confronting the research, and, hopefully, to reveal new research questions.

Parametric Studies of Program Design

Research on the techniques of programing largely has been the demonstration of the principles discussed in Skinner's early papers which elucidate the rationale for teaching machines and the guiding principles for preparation of programs. The experimenter attempting a quantitative demonstration of the principles must somehow isolate pure instances of each variable. He must translate into an experimental setting variations of a single variable unconfounded by other variables. This is a difficult task, especially for programs which necessarily vary throughout their length, and has not often been done with success. It is important that the few successes be examined and methodological problems clarified, because the creation of a vital behavioral technology serving education must rest upon such research.

Progressive Raising of Response Contingencies:
Gradual Progression and Fading

A program usually establishes a desired ultimate behavior as a result of nearly errorless performance on a sequence of tasks which gradually increase the demands placed on the subject. This principle is illustrated in program after program, and each program is a study in the feasibility of one or more techniques of progression. The finished program and the data collected in its development illustrate and verify the techniques of progression used within it, although the particular technique is not necessarily the only, or even the best, method. The distinction between research and program development is therefore somewhat arbitrary, since a finished program is usually the product of experimentation; but because other chapters in the book deal with a variety of programs, only demonstrations which are explicitly presented as such will be included here.

There are several types of learning tasks, each with somewhat different forms of gradual progression: (a) a program may teach a factual, verbal content consisting of hierarchies of interrelated elements; (b) a program may shape a difficult response form or topography, as in training pronunciation or handwriting; (c) a program may train subtle discrimination among stimuli; or (d) a program may establish a large number of single, unrelated associations.

Teaching Components of a Hierarchical Subject Matter: The most frequent and best known form of gradual progression is found in programs which teach verbal knowledge. Such material builds hierarchies of verbal behavior from components. The validity of this principle was demonstrated by Gavurin and Donahue (31). They compared the original sequenced order of a short, 29-item section of *The Analysis of Behavior* (48) program with a scrambled-order version as to (a) the number of repetitions required until one errorless trial and (b) the number of errors in reaching the criterion. For either measure, the sequenced order was superior. On a retention test there was no difference between the conditions, but a difference would not have been expected since both groups had originally repeated the material until they reached the same criterion.

However, a study by Levin and Baker (64) using a geometry program with second-grade children failed to show a significant effect of scrambling 60 items, but apparently the subjects did not come under the control of the program items. A 10-item sample in the report contained 8 items needing only a "yes" or "no" answer, thereby providing a 50 percent chance level for correct responding. In the unit of the normal program used in the study, error rate was a high 26 percent. Moreover, the 10 items did not seem to build much on one another. The authors assert that "probably the most important limitation of the present study was the failure of the program to teach the material presented thoroughly to most of the subjects, as indicated in posttest performance. It seems likely that a more effective program would have been made less effective when scrambled" (64, p. 143).

Roe, Case, and Roe (83), with 71 items of a statistics program, found no difference between scrambled order and the normal ordered sequence on posttest scores. Despite the willingness of these authors to accept the null hypothesis, it is noteworthy that program error rate for the two forms did not differ, suggesting that the items were not highly interdependent even in the "sequenced" case, either because of the nature of the concepts taught or because of overcueing. Moreover, a subsequent experiment by Roe (81) using a slightly longer (93 items) segment of this *same* program revealed a significant advantage for the ordered sequence in score on posttests, errors on the program, and time to complete the program. The conclusion of this first study should therefore be set aside; ordering seems to be important in this program as well.

Although the studies are few and to an extent conflicting, the need for sequenced material is supported, at least if the frames are interdependent and not severely overcued. What is needed now is not more studies of scrambled versus ordered sequences, but constructive and creative research which will indicate when, how much, and in what way items may be sequenced. A few such functional studies have been attempted. After an analysis of programed mathematics material into hierarchies of tasks, data from student use demonstrated that mastery of the higher order tasks could usually be achieved only if the subordinate tasks were mastered (29, 30).

Wolfe (107) investigated the differences between "discovery" and the "expository" sequences in a mathematics program. In the "discovery" method, a frame teaching each rule was presented after a series of frames giving examples. In the "expository" method, the frame teaching the rule preceded the same series of examples. The experiment revealed no differences between the two procedures, but this issue should not be considered closed.

Reynolds and Glaser (78) evaluated the placement of spaced review items within a general science program. A 7,000-item general science program without review covered each of 10 independent topics completely before moving to the next topic, while a spaced review condition of the program rotated among the topics to facilitate adding review items. In the spaced review condition, each of the 10 topics was broken into components and arranged so that the student worked through the easiest part of each topic before moving ahead to the next level of difficulty. For each topic, specially prepared review items were placed just before the next difficulty level; there were a total of 3,000 such review items. When the use of the program was limited to daily 40-minute class periods over 17 weeks, no one finished all of the program, and consequently those in the nonreview condition did substantially better on a posttest because they covered more new material. In a second study in which all subjects were given time to complete the programs, the review group showed greater gain over pretest scores, lending support to the hypothetical advantage of programed review. Unfortunately, there was a group difference on the pretest, as Reynolds and Glaser indicated, which could account for the greater gain by the review group. A subsequent series of studies (79), using a smaller section of the general science program, clearly demonstrated improved retention after spaced review material while revealing no advantage for unspaced repetition. With portions of this same program (77), it was demonstrated that more errors are made early in working through a program rather than later. Relative difficulty was controlled by reversing the order of topics for one group of subjects.

Unlike the demonstrations of a gross principle, as in comparing "ordered" and "scrambled" programs, the studies by Gagné and his associates, by Wolfe, and by Reynolds and Glaser explore variables which could lead to refinements of programing techniques. Future research should also pursue this goal.

Shaping Response Topography: When a response is especially difficult or has an especially low probability of occurrence, extremely crude approximations can be reinforced at first; on subsequent occasions the criterion for differential reinforcement can be increased gradually until the skilled response is shaped. Such gradual shifting of the criterion for differential reinforcement has been demonstrated repeatedly in animal research by the shaping of difficult schedule performances, as in shaping long interresponse delays (differential reinforcement of low rates) or large numbers of responses at high rates for infrequent reinforcement (large, fixed, or variable ratio schedules of reinforcement) and by shaping difficult or unusual response topographies. Although such shaping procedures resemble those used by athletic coaches and others who shape subtle skills, deliberate adoption of the principles has been rare. The clearest demonstration of the shaping of response topography is the procedure developed for establishing rhythmic skill in children (93). The subject strikes the key in synchrony with a series of auditory stimuli; a bell sounds or a light flashes when the key is struck close enough in time to the sound. At first, the response is reinforced even if the beat is poorly matched; gradually, closer and closer correspondence between the response and the stimuli is required until a nearly perfect matching is obtained.

Shaping Discrimination: In the pure form of discrimination training, a simple response already in the organism's repertoire is brought under the control of a new and often subtle stimulus property. In this case, gradual progression may occur in moving from gross to subtle differences among stimuli, or progression might consist of pairing a new stimulus with one which already controls the response and gradually removing the old stimulus.

Clear prototypes of the two favored techniques are provided in the basic research using animals (102). A simple discrimination without errors was established in a pigeon by first reinforcing responses on a variable-interval schedule of reinforcement with a red key color; then, at appropriate times the key light was turned off for brief periods. The duration of periods with the key "dark" gradually increased, and a dim green light soon replaced the light off as the negative stimulus. The duration and brightness of the green key gradually increased. The changes were so gradual that some pigeons never emitted a response to the negative stimulus, although they continued to respond during the red light or discriminative stimulus. Thus, a discrimination was formed without extinction of responses under the negative stimulus. In the next phase, Terrace (103) was able to establish still another discrimination without error by "stimulus transfer." The same response was brought under the control of a new stimulus by pairing the established discriminative stimulus with the new discriminative stimulus and the established negative stimulus with a new negative stimulus, then gradually fading out the old stimuli. The new discrimination was between horizontal and vertical lines. Vertical lines were presented when the key light was red (the old discriminative stimulus), and the horizontal lines were presented when the key light was green (the old negative stimulus). Gradually the key colors were desaturated until the horizontal or vertical lines appeared against a white field. Again, pigeons learned this with few, if any, errors.

A similar procedure was successful (101) in teaching first-grade students to read color names. The children already had accomplished the first step: the color already controlled the spoken color name. Taber and Glaser proceeded much as Terrace subsequently did by pairing the color with its printed name in a series of stimuli to which a spoken color name was the appropriate response. Colored lines were gradually shortened to dots, dots decreased in number, colored letters were introduced, and the colored letters were gradually replaced by black letters until all were black. What began as color naming ended as reading names of colors. In a similar ingenious example of transferring stimulus control, Csanyi (18) taught the pronunciation of Spanish words from printed stimuli by using intersecting printed English words, printed vertically on the page, which intersected horizontally printed Spanish words at the point of a common phoneme. Initial control for the sound in a new context and, occasionally, a new grapheme was provided by the English word.

A variation in the technique is found when the stimulus to be faded is also new, but less subtle than the stimulus to which control is transferred. Kindergarten children learned the concepts of equipollence (equal number of objects in two sets) when equipollent sets were initially colored red and nonequipollent sets were initially colored yellow (99). Beginning on the thirteenth trial the colors were gradually fused until, after 48 trials, they were indiscriminable. Performance on the next 60 trials with black objects proved this procedure to be better than either having 60 preceding trials on the criterion task or shifting suddenly after 60 trials with unfaded correlated color cues. In fact, only the group with the fading procedure performed better than chance on the criterion trials. Similarly, six-year-old children were able to master a "matching-to-sample" problem within 120 trials when a combination of cues (placing the sample above the correct match and using a desaturated, nonmatching stimulus) were gradually faded (39). Without fading there was no evidence of learning in 600 trials.

Two additional examples of shaping fine discriminations (23, 40) also illustrate the role of discrimination learning in developing continuous minimal repertoires. Evans (23) found that after training in discrimination of letter forms, children who had been unable to copy letters were able to draw fair, if imperfect, letters. In Holland and Matthews' (40) study the most effective of three programs shaped the discrimination by using several different discrimination tasks in different phases of the program. The child first discriminated isolated [s] from other sounds; then indicated which of two spoken words had an [s]; next identified the position of the sound (initial, medial, or final) with words containing the sound; and, finally, indicated which two utterances of the same word had the correct [s]. In addition to progression of tasks, the items within each task progressed from easy to difficult. After the program, [s] discrimination was nearly perfect; moreover, [s] articulation showed immediate improvement even though no formal articulation training intervened. Two other programs, equal in length to the first, were relatively ineffective. One was a long version of the isolated sound phase of the successful program, and the other was a long version of the "criterion" phase of the successful program in which correct and incorrect articulations were discriminated. Therefore, it is important both to sample the complete context in which a stimulus will later occur and to include a variety of tasks that shape attentive behavior. In a follow-up study one year later (7), the group differences persisted, and the group with the adequate program had correct [s] articulation after the intervening time provided opportunity for "automatic" shaping.

The greatest significance of these studies is the confirmation they provide for Skinner's (91) analysis of continuous repertoires. In a continuous repertoire, small variation in a set of responses produces a corresponding variation in a set of stimuli. Small differences in hand and arm movements produce different lines on paper in the case of writing, and small differences in vocal action produce different speech sounds. The stimuli resulting from such responses are capable of reinforcing the responses differentially only to the extent that the stimulus differences are discriminable. Practice at trying to sing middle C is useful only to the extent that the singer can hear the difference between middle C and an off key C. If he can, shaping automatically proceeds.

Shaping stimulus control has proven to be a specially fruitful research area yielding not only excellent practical techniques but making basic contributions to understanding discrimination learning without errors, transfer of stimulus control, and continuous repertoires.

Establishing Single Associations: In the fourth type of learning situation the stimuli are easily discriminable, and the responses are well differentiated. Only the stimulus-response associations must be learned. If unconfounded by stimulus discrimination or response differentiation, this is classical paired-associate learning. Such associations are simple when only one stimulus-response pair must be learned; they are difficult, however, when several must be learned at once. It is within such tasks that much of the research on gradual progression and fading has occurred. This choice is apparently influenced by the heritage of laboratory rote-learning work, since only a few educational tasks involve pure rote learning.

In the process of vanishing or fading, a prompt in the form of a response term is gradually removed in successive cycles. In exploring several methods of fading partial prompts in paired-associate learning (3, 4, 37), fading was compared with unfaded complete prompts and with the classical unprompted anticipation method. In partial prompting the stimulus is presented, the subject attempts to recall, and, if successful, is usually shown the response term for confirmation; but when unaided recall does not occur, formal prompts are presented until the subject responds correctly. In the condition using a complete prompt, the subject is shown the response term (often with the stimulus term) just before he must respond to the stimulus alone.

A series of seven studies (2) investigated partial prompting with city names as stimuli and with standard airline code names as the response terms. The code names consisted of three consonants similar to consonant nonsense syllables in having no apparent associative strength. In the partial prompt condition, the city name was presented, and if recall was not possible, a partial prompt was provided by presenting one or two of the letters or by presenting the response term under conditions of lowered visibility either by tachistoscopic presentation or by adjusted illumination. None of the experiments found an unequivocal advantage for partial cueing over the standard anticipation method, though slight nonsignficant differences were common. The studies taken as a whole suggest a slight advantage for partial prompting over the anticipation method. Even this hint of a difference, however, might result from response term learning, since it was noticed that occasionally one or two letters could be recalled when the whole term could not be recalled.

The belief that partial prompting should help assumes that intermediate associative strengths exist before unaided recall is possible. Conventional measures are "all or none" since the response either does or does not occur, but it is usually assumed that associative strength increases with trials even before actual recall is possible. Israel (53, 54) used a prompting technique to measure the strength of association even when no recall occurred. German stimulus words were presented one at a time on a screen, and to each stimulus word the subject tried to name the English equivalent. When the English term could not be recalled, the subject closed a switch causing a motor-driven screen to move toward its focal point bringing the projected image of the response term (the English word) gradually into focus. Control words were interspersed which had no stimulus term and measured only the subject's ability to read defocused words. For the experimental (paired-associate) words, the distance from the focal point at the moment the subject was able to say the response was the measure of combined contributions of the prompt and the strength of association. Since there was no associated stimulus for the control words, the distance of the screen from the focal point resulted entirely from the prompt. Therefore, the difference in the distance from the focal point between experimental and control words was a measure of intermediate strength of association. Results of Israel's three experiments are summarized in Figure 1. The black solid lines are in all cases the control words. Experiments 1 and 2 (the first two sets of curves) indicate some intermediate associative strength on paired associates as seen in the differences between experimental and control words. There are, however, two troublesome problems: (a) repeated trials beyond the second trial did not increase the difference, as would be the case if associative strength increased with trials, and (b) there was a rapidly changing baseline as subjects became more proficient at reading defocused words. The third experiment was designed to obtain a more stable base-

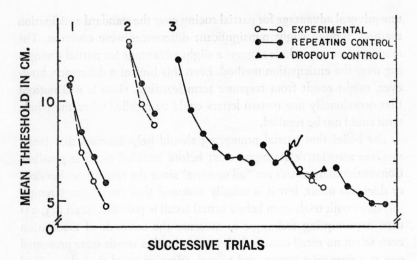

SUCCESSIVE TRIALS

FIGURE 1. *Mean thresholds for three experiments indicated by numerals. Broken lines indicate experimental words having paired-associate stimulus terms in view. Solid lines indicate control words (adapted from Israel [53]).*

line by pretraining on all of the words to be used. Therefore, in the initial phase, pretraining was carried out until the thresholds had leveled off, as shown in Figure 1 by the first nine trials of Experiment 3. The German stimulus words were introduced on Trial 10 (indicated by the arrow) for the experimental words. There was no difference on the second trial, and, in fact, no reliable differences throughout. (The difference in the fourth trial is unreliable because most pairs are recalled without prompting.) Although some evidence is found for intermediate associative strength in Israel's first two studies, the third and better controlled experiment raises doubts of the existence of intermediate associative strengths and strengthens Rock's (80) much debated theory that paired-associate rote learning is all-or-none.

With the very existence of intermediate associate strengths in paired-associate learning in doubt, the difficulty in finding advantages of partial prompting is reasonable. If there is little or no intermediate associative strength, the subject might as well be told the answer if he does not know it. The problem is far from closed, and additional research might well alter this conclusion.

A different type of progression, therefore, should be sought. One which might be promising rests on the fact that short paired-associate lists are quickly learned. One or two pairs could be introduced and established at a time while gradually expanding the total collection. Each new pair should at first be fully prompted, but unprompted on later cycles. On successive cycles only one or two new pairs would be added while old terms are drilled. Schaefer (85, 86, see also 32) has demonstrated a technique somewhat similar to this in teaching German reading vocabulary by beginning with passages of English prose and gradually replacing English words with German words in later passages. New words were heavily prompted by the context of English and already-established German words. The rate of introducing new words was slow enough to prevent interference among new pairs. Although final conclusions regarding partial prompting await further research, attention should also be given to gradually increasing the number of rote paired-associate items, retaining the old and introducing the new in successive pyramiding cycles. This technique may prove the more useful one for those few situations in which rote material must be taught.

Prompting Versus Confirmation: Except for the above research on fading, all basic research on classical paired-associate learning would have been excluded from this chapter if a few investigators had not viewed it as a prototype of programed instruction and set off "prompting" and "confirmation" as opposing principles. In paired associates, prompting means that the response term is shown before there is an opportunity for an overt response; whereas in the anticipation method (called the confirmation method in these studies), the response term is shown after the chance to respond.

Several studies (8, 12, 14, 15, 57, 58, 89, 96, 100) found significant advantages of prompting as compared with the classical anticipation method. However, Angell and Lumsdaine (4) found no significant difference between these procedures and quite reasonably attributed the difference found in other studies to the difficult nature of the response and the need for response learning; in their own studies, already familiar numerals were the response terms. Although the explanation has merit, it does not explain the results of Swets and others (100) who also used numerals.

Despite the supposition by one author (13) that these experiments provide a crucial argument refuting Skinner's view of programed instruction, the procedures seem largely unrelated to programed instruction (45), and the effort by Cook to equate the anticipation method with recommended programing practice is perplexing. To be sure, overt responses are required, and immediate confirmation given; the parallel, however, ends there. Paired associates are unrelated to one another and do not build in a progression. Beginning performance is necessarily poor, and the subject is left to learn for himself with initial responses almost completely undetermined. Indeed, this seems to be the very reason that they have been used in the laboratory to study learning, though even there they seem more appropriate for studies of habit interference since the only difficulty arises from the long lists used. Moreover, it is only in the paired-associate case that "prompting" and "confirmation" have been described as alternatives to one another. In the rare instances in which sheer rote material must be taught, the programer would be better advised to increase the length of his list gradually than to use either of the above two procedures as a model.

Causing Appropriate Behavior

The answer required of the subject should be one he can give if, and only if, appropriate percursory behavior has occurred. Such behavior is usually "covert" in the form of silent reading or problem solving. Answering correctly should be possible only after the total desired response sequence has taken place. Learning is only assured for the behavior upon which attainment of the correct answer is contingent. Often the response contingency is nothing more than reading a statement of a principle (25), although in other cases the contingency may involve solving a problem, carefully observing some graphs, or even physically manipulating laboratory materials or models.

Most other principles presuppose that correct answers cannot be attained unless appropriate precursory behavior has taken place. Arranging a progressive sequence assumes that the items in that sequence are each designed to assure mastery of its materials. Designing programs for low error rate is reasonable only if by correctly answering, something of consequence has had to occur. A common misinterpretation in programing is the assumption that the one-word response is itself the thing taught. The nature of the response is critical, but only in its dependence upon (and assurance of) appropriate preceding behavior.

To demonstrate the principle, the original contingent relationship between the principal content and the answers was destroyed for 377 items of *The Analysis of Behavior* program (41, 46). This altered version differed from the normal version only in the choice of the word that the subject was asked to provide; the subject could supply the missing word without carefully reading the complete item or performing other tasks being taught. The new answers had little relation to the critical content, and answering correctly was no longer contingent on mastering the content but was, instead, only contingent on noticing trivial cues. Consider, for example, the following altered item taken from a point shortly after the concept "extinction" was first introduced:

> If a previously reinforced response is no
> longer ——————, it soon occurs less
> often. This is called extinction.

The syntax of the opening phrase is sufficient to evoke the response "reinforced" even though the phrase, "it soon occurs less often," and the entire sentence, "This is called extinction," may be ignored. In the normal or "correct" version, this same item is:

> If a previously reinforced response is no
> longer reinforced, it soon occurs
> (1) —————— frequently. This is
> called (2) ——————.

The first response, "less," while not a technical word, can be provided with certainty only if the student notices that we are concerned with a previously reinforced response and that this response is "no longer reinforced."

The results of a posttest are shown in Figure 2. Condition A is the normal program; Condition B is the form of the program with answers possible through the use of trivial cues. The difference in percentage of errors on the posttest is substantial. Condition D in Figure 2 represents posttest errors for subjects who read completed statements and had no overt responses. Conditions B and D are quite close in error scores on the test, but D is significantly inferior to A. Conventional reading with neither blanks nor overt responses is comparable in posttest performance to giving answers dependent only on trivial cues, and either of these conditions is inferior to giving answers to "programed" items which have answers contingent upon attention to the important content.

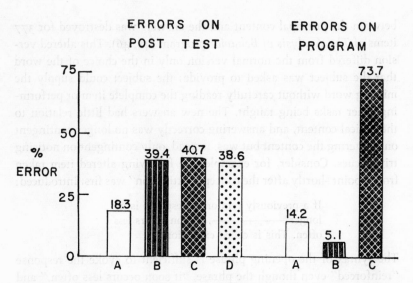

FIGURE 2. *Percent error on posttest and in the program for four experimental versions. Program A is the normal program, with response determined and dependent upon critical content; Program B has responses determined, but answers relatively unrelated to critical content; Program C has responses relatively undetermined, but dependent upon critical content; and Program D has only complete statements with no responses (46).*

Additional tentative evidence is found in an exploratory study (76) in which extraneous material, in so far as the answers were concerned, was added to items. For example, the direct portion of an item was as follows:

> Removal from office comes only ———
> (before/after) the President has been con-
> victed.

To this direct portion was added:

> In fact, no President has ever been re-
> moved from office.

The direct portion resulted in higher posttest scores than did the appended material. The fact of different test items for the two types of material weakens the evidence even though there was no pretest difference between the two tests. The results, nevertheless, are consistent with the proposition that the critical portion of the item should be necessary for the answer.

Eigen and Margulies (22) also demonstrated the importance of the relation of the response to the material in the frame using two sets of seven nonsense syllables and one set of seven three-letter meaningful words. The three sets varied as to "difficulty" in that they represented different information levels. The items teaching each of the sets required the subject to respond to only three of the seven words, and in repetitions of the material the same three words were used; the other four were unrelated to the response. A sample of their items of intermediate difficulty follows:

Item 1	Learn these nonsense words: RIZ TUV RUD TIB KIG COJ YOL Fill in the missing nonsense words: RIZ TUV —— —— —— COJ YOL
Confirmation for Item 1	RIZ TUV *RUD TIB KIG* COJ YOL
Form of Items 2-4	RIZ TUV *** *** *** COJ YOL
	The missing nonsense words are ——, ——, and ——.
Confirmation for Items 2-4	RIZ TUV *RUD TIB KIG* COJ YOL

The posttest required that all seven words in each of the three sets be supplied. At all levels of difficulty, the material relevant to the response was recalled more frequently than the material incidental to the response (see Figure 3). At every level of difficulty, the difference in posttest performance between relevant and incidental responses was substantial, with the differences ranging from 15 to 45 percentage points.

In summary, behavior which must occur in order to reach an answer is considerably more likely to be learned than behavior not so controlled by the design of the item. This conclusion is surprising only because of the very high frequency with which the principle is violated, even in published programs. Discussion of "prompting" to assure correct answers and low error rate has led to prompts that often render important content irrelevant for attaining the correct answer. This "overprompting" is often subtle, involving syntax or common phrases. There are also many gross types of "overprompting." Long series of

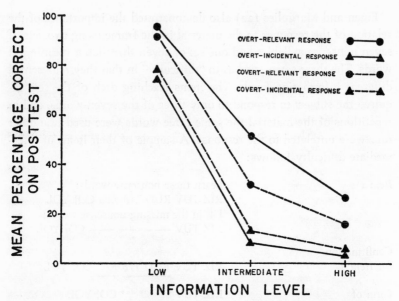

FIGURE 3. *Posttest performance for three sets of material at different information levels. Separate functions indicate performance on material relevant to program response and incidental to program response for subjects who responded overtly and subjects asked to respond covertly (22).*

items may have the same answer (a procedure which is receiving some sanction due to the proposal of a "density ratio," [36] defined as the ratio of new answers to total answers). Moreover, programs are common which regularly supply the first letter of the answer or in which a few high association words are found near the blanks.

In practice, low error rate is found in some programs that almost never require appropriate behavior of the student. This has been illustrated in a specially deficient program by marking out with black crayon pencil all parts of the item not needed for answering correctly (44). Table 1 shows a series of items as they appear in the program and as they appear when the material which would not need to be used to answer the question is "blacked out." All that remains in the blacked-out version is material which, if removed, would increase the error rate. Column 1 reveals material full of important information; however, most of this information is actually not programed because it bears no contingent relationship to the subject's answer. If the subject is to learn the difference between a check and an ordinary draft in

TABLE 1*

Normal and Blacked-Out Items from Monetary Program

Column I — (Normal)	Column II — (Blacked-Out)
18. To distinguish between domestic trade and international trade the word "*Draft*" (Sometimes spelled "Draught") was created to identify ——— of *Exchange* used in domestic trade.	18. ▮▮▮▮▮▮▮ to identify ——— of *Exchange* ▮▮
19. The *Bill* of *E* ——————— is the forerunner of the modern *Check*.	19. ▮ *Bill* of *E* ——————— ▮
20. A *C* — — — *k* is a demand *Draft* drawn on a bank.	20. ▮ *C* — — — *k* ▮
21. The only difference between a *Check* and an ordinary *Draft* is that the custodian of the money in case of a *Check* must be a b — — —.	21. ▮▮▮ the custodian of the money in case of a *Check* must be a b — — —.
22. A *B* — — — of *Exchange* (*Draft*) is convenient for the payment of debts.	22. ▮ *B* — — — of *Exchange* (*Draft*) ▮
23. The seller of merchandise by sending a *Bill* of *E* ——————— drawn on the buyer and attaching the shipping documents to a bank for collection can be assured that the merchandise will not be delivered to the buyer until the buyer pays for it.	23. ▮▮▮ *Bill* of *E* ——————— ▮

* Material covered in blacked-out version can be omitted without influencing the subject's ability to answer correctly. Item 18 can be answered because of previous item.

Item 21, he will do so only incidentally (as he would in a textbook where the material is not even alleged to be programed). The principal content is extraneous or nonprogramed as far as the answer is concerned. A 140-item banking program was blacked out as indicated in Table 1. It proved possible to obliterate 68 percent of the words in this manner. The material was then presented by teaching machine to a group of 15 subjects whose performance was compared with that of another group of 15 subjects who had gone through the original program. The normal error rate was 11.4 percent; after 69 percent of the program had been obliterated, the error rate was still only 12.9 percent. (This difference is not statistically significant.) Thus only a third of this material was programed because only a third served as a basis for answers. This technique could provide a quantitative index of response contingencies in any verbal program.

A major difference between programed and nonprogramed material is that programed material increases the probability of a correct answer, while nonprogramed material in normal textbooks or in pseudoprograms is not directly related to an answer by the student, either because no answer is required or because the material is extraneous as far as the response is concerned. Material can vary in the degree to which the content is programed; quantitative measures of these differences are possible, and more highly programed material has been demonstrated to be more effective.

Assuring the Correct Answer

Since the answer is designed to assure occurrence of the appropriate behavior, it is important that the correct answer can be given only after meeting the intended contingency; it is equally important that the contingency be met and the correct answer given. This is largely the reason for the low error rate requirement. In the high error rate item, students who are unable to reach the correct answer have failed to engage in the intended precursory behavior. This principle of response determination has been demonstrated by a condition in the study discussed above and summarized in Figure 2. A third distorted version of the program was prepared with the blanks undetermined and therefore quite difficult to answer. Although the words omitted were highly related to the critical content of the item, they were insufficiently prompted by the content, causing a high error rate. The following illustrates an undetermined item:

> The technical term for "reward" is
> (1) ————————.
> To "reward" an organism with food is to
> (2) ———————— it with food.
> Answers: (1) reinforcement
> (2) reinforce

There was no basis in this item for answering because this was the first time "reinforcement" was introduced. In this instance the item might have been acceptable later in the program, but early in the program the answers were undetermined and a high error rate resulted. In contrast, the comparable item in the normal program was:

> A technical term for "reward" is reinforcement. To "reward" an organism with food is to —————— it with food.

Condition C in Figure 2 shows that posttest performance following use of the 377 items which were distorted so as to make the responses indeterminate and the error rate high was considerably worse than posttest performance following the normal program and not significantly different from that following simply reading completed statements.

The response should be determined; thus, the error rate should be low. However, the independent variable is response determination, *not* error rate. It has frequently been suggested that error rate should be experimentally determined and the optimum error rate discovered, but the suggestion misidentifies the independent variable. Error rate is necessarily a dependent variable—an effect—and not an independent variable. Error rate can be changed only by changing some other variable. Subjects may be selected or items altered, but these variables are themselves the independent ones which influence not only posttest but rate as well. It is tempting to interpret the results in Figure 2 as indicating an optimal error rate. As seen in the figure, the best posttest performance was for the program with the intermediate error rate. However, error rate was not the independent variable, but was rather dependent upon the variables manipulated, response determination, and answer-to-content dependency. There are, however, empirical (46) as well as rational grounds against interpreting this as a U-shaped function for relating error rate and posttest performance. The above experiment was conducted with an earlier version of the program; subsequent revision of this program was designed to further determine the responses (decrease error rate) and to increase the relevance of the answers to the critical content. As a result of this revision, the error rate on this portion of the program was lowered to 7 percent, while error rate on the posttest was lowered to 8 percent.

Learning from Errors: Number of Alternative Responses: When errors are made in a program, not only has the appropriate precursory behavior failed to occur, but other inappropriate behavior probably has occurred, and that inappropriate behavior could be established. This possibility has been offered as a criticism of multiple-choice items in programs: "Effective multiple-choice material must contain plausible wrong responses which are out of place in the delicate process of 'shaping' behavior because they strengthen unwanted forms" (92, p. 970). The opposite claim (74) is that multiple-choice items are better *because* errors occur, permitting elimination of inappropriate behavior. Therefore, it is claimed that multiple-choice material should be written so that the wrong answer represents "those errors occurring often enough that they seemed to need dealing with" (74, p. 501).

A well-conceived and carefully executed study (55) provides data on the effects of the number of alternates and other resulting errors, or, as the authors prefer, "negative knowledge" in multiple-choice material. They manipulated the amount of negative knowledge by using, with a Pressey punchboard, 30 multiple-choice items teaching psychology vocabulary. Different groups of subjects had five, four, three, two, or one choice on their first trial with the material. (An additional five-choice group had no confirmation on Trial 1.) On the subsequent four trials, all subjects used the five-choice form with confirmation. Positive knowledge was held constant, since the correct choice eventually was made before advancing to the next item. The results are shown in Figure 4. Performance on Trials 2-5 is the measure of the effects of the number of choices (and number of resulting erroneous responses). Errors on Trial 2 and subsequent trials are directly related to the number of choices on Trial 1. Although these differences are most apparent on the second trial, the difference resulting from one or five alternatives during the first trial alternatives persists through the fifth and last trial. Having only one possible answer, and thus no chance of error, was superior to all other conditions. An analysis of the nature of the errors on Trial 2 revealed that "negative information increases the probability that S will repeat his error" (55, p. 15). The unambiguous outcome of this study indicates that in multiple-choice items, incorrect alternatives will be learned and, therefore, the degree of mastery is *inversely* related to the number of difficult alternatives.

Abstraction and "Size of Step": Education seldom seeks to establish control by concrete, specific stimuli; instead, it establishes concepts or

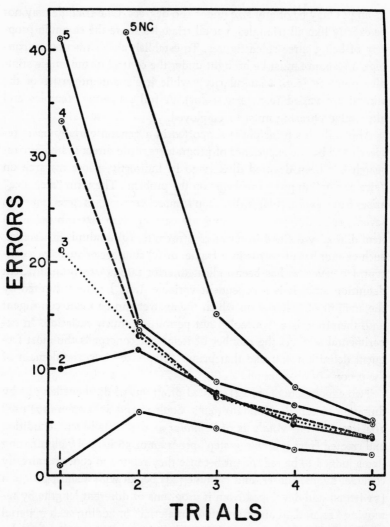

FIGURE 4. *Mean errors made on punchboard by groups having one to five alternatives available on Trial 1. The label for each curve indicates the number of choices on Trial 1. Condition "5NC" had five choices without confirmation on Trial 1. Items for Trials 2-5 had five choices with confirmation for all groups (55).*

abstractions. In an abstraction, a response is under the control of a single property of a stimulus or a set of stimuli. Consider the concept of triangularity. A triangle may be of any size or of any color, and its angles may be of any size under 180 degrees. One triangle may not be exactly like all triangles, yet all triangles share the common property of being three-sided figures. To establish an abstraction or concept, a response must be brought under the control of the single stimulus property (e.g., triangularity), while irrelevant properties of the stimuli are varied (e.g., size, color). A full range of examples and alternative phrasing must be employed.

Although this principle is supported in a general way by basic research and by the experience of programers, little direct systematic research has been devoted directly to it. Indirectly, some research on "size of step" in programs bears on the problem. The term "step size" arises from a vernacular rather than from science and, as a consequence, several quite different definitions are current. Step size can mean (a) item difficulty defined in terms of error rate, (b) amount of material, such as number of words in a frame, or (c) number of items per concept. However, as has been indicated, error rate is hardly a sufficient definition since it is a dependent variable. Item length is limited by the amount of material on which the answer can be made contingent and, therefore, is a "variable" not permitting much variation. In experimental settings the number of items per concept is the most frequent definition and one that brings "step size" into the domain of the process of abstraction.

Two experiments (17, 24) created programs of different lengths by dropping so-called redundant items. Coulson and Silberman (17) used 104 items of *The Analysis of Behavior* as the "small-step" condition and created from it a "large-step" program of 56 items by eliminating items judged to be redundant because they related to concepts already covered. Evans, Glaser, and Homme (24) began with a short program (51 items) and developed from it programs of different lengths by removing "redundant and transitional material" or adding such material to obtain programs of 30, 40, 51, and 68 items. Both studies found a posttest advantage for longer, or small-step, versions. The extra items in the small-step programs seem to be additional examples and syntactic arrangements needed to form abstract responses.

One experiment (94) using a spelling program failed to attain a difference among programs of 1,008, 838, and 596 frames in length. Since not even program error rate differed, all versions may have had more than a sufficient number of items per word. The alternative is that the extra items in the longer program might have been ineffective as indicated, for example, by the low gain score of 11.23 words out of a possible gain of 26.58 words. Almost doubling the number of exposures to the words provided *no* help in mastering the remaining words. Before accepting the null hypothesis, one might prefer to obtain a program that—in at least one version—teaches more effectively.

Gagné and Bassler (28) investigated the role of variety in examples using a program on set theory. Retention after nine weeks was over 100 percent for groups having examples which were high or intermediate in variety, but a group with a minimum of variety in their examples showed significantly lower retention. This minimum variety condition was even worse in retention than a no-example condition. If further research confirms the detrimental effect of low variety in examples, it will be an important consideration in programing.

A sufficient number of varied items for each concept seems to be necessary, but more research is needed. Simple demonstration of this variable is not enough; parametric studies would be more useful, and for these studies a measure of item similarity needs to be developed. Given such a measure, future research should explore the type and degree of item redundancies which are effective.

Reinforcement and Confirmation

All of the experiments discussed above deal with reinforcement; more specifically, they deal with the contingent relationship between responses and the events which will establish these responses. Beyond the question of reinforcement *contingencies,* however, there are unsolved problems of the nature of the reinforcer itself: What are reinforcers? What are the effects of changing the magnitude of reinforcement? And what are the side effects of reinforcement or nonreinforcement?

Confirmation: In the usual program, after the subject has written his answer, it is "confirmed" by the presentation of the correct answer. Many studies which have compared such confirmation with no confirmation (26, 41, 51, 69, 72, 73) have failed to show a difference in posttest performance as a function of confirmation. Again, caution is required in interpreting studies reporting negative results. One of the studies (26) had nine different conditions and was unable to show a significant difference among any of them, thereby raising questions regarding the sensitivity of the procedures used.

However, Meyer (71) found a clear advantage for confirmation as measured by both posttest performance and errors within a program. Also, Angell (5) and Kaess and Zeaman (55), using Pressey-type multiple-choice test items, found significant advantage for confirmation. Kaess and Zeaman found that a group which had no confirmation on the first trial did just as poorly on the second trial as the comparable confirmation group had done on its first trial, and, of course, strikingly worse than the confirmation group had done on its second trial (see Figure 4). The entire curve for the group having no confirmation on the first trial is shifted one unit as if the trial without confirmation had no effect at all. In addition to simple confirmation, a study by Suppes and Ginsberg (98) suggests that an overt correction response after confirmation may result in faster learning. When children using two-alternative multiple-choice material were required to pick the other alternative after an error, they learned faster than if they were only told they were wrong. This finding is similar to that found in comparison studies on "corrective" and "noncorrective" procedures in animal discriminative learning and may result from decreasing the likelihood of learning incorrect alternatives.

Confirmation is effective in at least some situations, and a corrective response appears to have additional benefits. The six experiments which found no difference among confirmation and nonconfirmation had in common the use of programs with low error rates. Consequently, the subjects may have had little doubt of the correctness of their answers, even without confirmation. Most of the studies showing an advantage for confirmation or correction used multiple-choice items with high error rates; confidence in the answer would not be great for such items. Meyer's study is the exception in that she used a constructed response program with a moderate (14 percent) error rate. Her program introduces another possibly important difference. It is a program which builds vocabulary by useful prefixes and suffixes; the responses often consist of spelling newly discovered words (e.g., circumspect), and this correct spelling is necessary for the response to be scored as correct. Perhaps, when the *form* of the constructed response is itself important, "self-evaluation" of answers is more difficult, and confirmation is more advantageous (20).

The relation between item difficulty and relative effectiveness of confirmation may be indicative of the nature of the reinforcer in the program. The reinforcer may be an answer known by the subject to be correct either because he is told it is correct or because he was already confident of his answer. With difficult, high-error-rate programs, confirmation might be necessary; whereas with easy, low-error-rate programs, confirmation might be unimportant. Future research on the interaction of confirmation with error rate and response topography should further clarify the nature of reinforcement in programed instruction.

Intermittent Confirmation: Two experiments (62, 87) investigated various schedules of confirmation by omitting confirmation either after fixed numbers of items, such as after every third item, every second item, every fourth item, or after variable numbers of items. There is a strong (but nonsignificant) trend favoring confirmation on every item in Scharf's data, and Krumboltz and Weisman found that error rate on the program increased as the size of ratio increased.

Both studies owe their rationale to the literature on intermittent reinforcement. As interesting as intermittent confirmation might be in itself, it should be clear, however, that the situation is *not* analogous to intermittent reinforcement and, consequently, that there is no basis for expecting similar results. In intermittent reinforcement the reinforcer follows repeated instances of a single response; in a program responses are not generally repeated. A program is a sequence of items, none of which are alike and few of which have the same answer. The findings of these studies are quite consistent with others comparing confirmation with nonconfirmation; there is enough suggestion of small differences so that the importance of confirmation cannot be discounted. The effect, however, is not pronounced.

Disruption by Errors: The aversive side effects of frequent erroneous responses is another reason that low error rate is considered desirable. Melaragno (70) conducted an ingenious study using 50 multiple-choice items with very easy alternatives and five with quite ambiguous alternatives. Punishment consisted of telling the subject that any answer he made to the five ambiguous items was incorrect. Punishment had no effect when the five punished items were equally spaced among the other items, but when the punished items were grouped at the center of the set, posttest performance was worse for material covered just before and just after the punished items.

Summary

Investigations of the variables of program design, in general, have lent support to the earlier proposed general principles of program design. Contingencies must be arranged for the material being taught, material must be designed so that the contingencies can be met, a progression of items is usually necessary, and to create abstract responses, a range of instances of each new "term" is necessary. However, research has not yet improved upon the principles because the studies have been limited to gross comparisons. The "vs." in the titles of many studies suggests the comparison of crude dichotomies without indication of where the two cases fall on the dimension they represent or even how this distance could be measured. Consequently, a generalization of results is difficult since magnitudes of differences in important variables cannot be specified for either experimental material or programs.

Future work should be more constructive in two ways:

1. The means should be developed for measuring, or otherwise more exactly specifying, the variables in programed materials, as in measuring the degree of contingency between the answer and the rest of the item or items by the "blackout" procedure.
2. Research should be directed toward improving existing techniques or developing new ones, as in the studies of Terrace (102, 103) and of Taber and Glaser (101) in transferring stimulus control.

Instrumentation and Procedural Variables

Much of the research has been concerned with secondary variables: response mode, presentation mode, and branching. The effects of these variables, while of interest, depend largely on interactions with fundamental variables of program design. The conclusions of such studies should be prefaced with "given material of such and such characteristics, then . . ." because the effects depend upon the nature of the program used in the study.

Overt Responses

The question of whether an overt response is necessary has been a popular one for research studies. Overt responding in the form of writing answers, speaking answers, or indicating alternatives in a multiple-choice question has been compared with program use in which subjects were instructed to "think" the answer or with simply reading the program, either with no blanks or with correct multiple-choice alternatives indicated. The importance of the subject's answer, as seen in the previous sections, is in its relationship to the critical material being taught. In truly programed material the answer assures attentive reading of material, or assures critical steps in problem solving, or assures other mediating behaviors; in unprogramed material it does not. Skinner (92) suggests that the response should be public because when no overt, public response is made, covert responding often ceases (42). The reason for a public answer is not theoretical, but practical. What begins as private answering often may change to private omissions as the subject continues work in a longer program. All aspects of programed instruction presuppose that performance of the task being taught is essential to the subject's correct answer. Therefore, misuse of a program by not answering at all circumvents the characteristics which make it a program.

The rationale for overt responses implies that three conditions must be met for a difference between overt and covert responding to appear: (a) programed material must be designed so that the subject can answer correctly; (b) the material must be designed so that he can answer correctly only after engaging in the appropriate mediating behavior; and (c) the program must be long enough for subjects in the covert condition to become careless since, under controlled conditions, they may respond consistently for awhile.

In a study discussed earlier and summarized in Figure 2, the normal program, written to insure that correct responses could be made only after careful reading of the items, and in which the response was determined, resulted in posttest performance that was superior to posttest performance following the simple reading of completed statements. The results for the normal version of this same program were confirmed (105) by using a shorter (192-item) segment as review for subjects who had already completed a psychology course. Williams found that either an overt constructed response or an overt choice between two alternatives yielded better posttest scores than reading the completed statements with or without critical material underlined. However, as seen in Figure 2, the distorted versions of the programs, in which blanks were either not related to the critical material in the items or in which the responses were undetermined, showed a high error rate. The posttest scores following completion of these programs were not different from those which followed reading of the completed items (46); thus, when the answers are not contingent on the important content or when correct answers are rare, overt responding may not be effective. When these two prime rules of programing are met, these studies indicate a posttest advantage for overt responding.

The interaction of response mode and relevance of content to answer is also demonstrated in the study by Eigen and Margulies (22) discussed above. They compared overt responding with "thinking" answers and found no difference at any level of "difficulty" for those parts of their specially constructed items that were irrelevant to the answer, but the parts that were relevant showed a substantial superiority for overt responding for high and middle levels of difficulty (see Figure 3). Although no difference between overt and covert responding was found at the lowest level of difficulty, the test performance was very nearly perfect for the covert response; hence, the overt case had no opportunity to show superiority.

The above three studies, then, confirm the principle that overt responding is important when the items are designed so that the response assures mastery of the material. However, if the material is not programed in the sense that response and major content are independent, no difference is found between overt and covert responding.

It has been suggested (20) that overt responding might be of special importance when the answer is one in which the response topography is itself a major part of the task being taught. "Thinking" answers was compared with written answers in a 119-item program which contained some items with the usual verbal answers and other items which required the drawing of examples of myocardiographic tracings. The posttest permitted separate measurement of the effects of these two types of items. Posttest performance was better for the overt responses than for the covert responses in the case of both types of material, but the overt-covert difference was especially striking for the items which demanded drawn answers. Their hypothesis also gains support from a comparison of overt and covert responding in teaching the phonetic alphabet (19). Subjects who read aloud the phonetic symbols in the program did better on a delayed posttest that required articulation in response to printed phonetic symbols than did subjects instructed to read silently, but a multiple-choice delayed posttest showed the advantage for overt responding was not statistically significant. (There was, however, a strong trend favoring overt responding.) On an immediate posttest similar to the delayed test, the same trends were apparent, but were not sufficient to meet the experimenters' statistical requirements. The delayed test, nevertheless, indicated that overt responding in the program was especially important if the criterion behavior was production of this sound. This variable deserves more attention in the overt response question as well as the constructed response and confirmation areas. If response topography is to be learned, it is probably especially inappropriate to ask the subject to think of the response, to choose alternatives, or to respond without confirmation.

In addition to the five studies with unequivocal evidence that overt responding is necessary, there are two studies which lend somewhat equivocal support. Overt responding proved superior to "thinking" the answer or reading completed statements in a 177-frame statistics program on a retention test two weeks after use of the program, but this difference was not statistically significant on the immediate posttest (61). An advantage was found for overt responses with elementary school children with IQ's of below 120, but not for children with higher IQ's (106). One year later on a retention test this interaction was no longer statistically significant.

Despite the differences shown in the above studies, 12 other studies failed to reveal posttest differences between overt and some no-response condition, but the sheer number of these "no-difference" studies should not be given undue emphasis. These experiments must individually meet the three requirements forming the rationale for overt responses, and, given that, they must show sufficient experimental rigor to give compelling evidence that the study would have been able to reveal differences—if such differences exist. To determine whether or not the material meets the above criteria for a program is made difficult because unpublished programs often are used, and samples are occasionally omitted in the published reports. An examination of all available samples of programs from many of the "no-difference" studies, however, is revealing. One such study (82) with no difference for overt responding also failed to find a difference comparing multiple-choice and constructed answers, programed lectures, programed texts, and machines. Since all these variables hinge on the correct design of the material, examination of the program is especially critical. The program used a 192-item sequence teaching elementary probability which, while not as long as one might want for such a study, is nevertheless no shorter than the sequence used in four of the seven studies giving positive results. Fortunately, sample program items were published. A typical item from the sample is subjected to blackout procedure in the top row of Table 2. Column II shows an item as it appeared in the program, and Column III shows the same item after material unrelated to the answer has been blacked out. It is easy to answer the blacked-out version; therefore, all the obliterated material was not programed. The response to the item has little to do with most of the content of the item. Regardless of the experimental group, the response should have little to do with learning the content. It is, therefore, not surprising that no differences resulted on criterion performance after thinking the answer, writing the answer, choosing one of three possible alternative answers, or, for that matter, not answering at all. Positive results would have been more surprising.

Two studies by Goldbeck and Campbell (34) fail to support the advantages of overt responding. In one experiment they used 35 independent, unsequenced items. From these they created three versions by adding cues of differing difficulty levels. The degree of response determination can be inferred from the high error rates on the program (18 percent, 42 percent, and 79 percent), indicating that at least for two difficulty levels, they did not adequately meet the requirement that the subject be able to respond correctly. If items cannot be answered anyway, it should make little difference whether the failure to answer is in writing or in thought.

In their second study (35), a very short program (32 frames) was again used, but in this case a segment of a sequential program was used that might have been adequate in its original form. However, the experimenters altered it: "Some frames were deleted; some direct prompts within a frame were moved to earlier frames; other direct prompts were replaced by less direct cues; some response terms were changed

TABLE 2*

Normal and Blacked-Out Items from Three Studies of Role of an Overt Response

Study	Normal	Blacked-Out

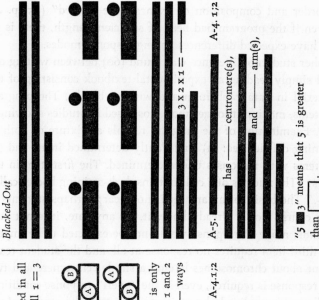

Study

Roe, A., Massey, Mildred, Welman, G., & Leeds, D. Automated teaching methods using linear programs.

Item 128, p. 20

Normal

This illustration shows Cells 1 and 2 filled in all the possible ways they can be filled. Cell 1 = 3 ways, Cell 2 = 2 ways.

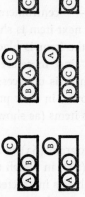

We can see in this illustration that there is only *one* way (ball) left to fill cell 3 when cells 1 and 2 are filled. Thus, there are $3 \times 2 \times 1 =$ —— ways in which 3 balls can fill 3 cells.

Study

Kormondy, E. J., & Van Atta, E. L. Experiment in self-instruction in general biology.

Item A-5, p. 6

Normal

A-5. Each of the *46 chromosomes* in a human cell has —— centromere(s), which is (are) related to chromosomal movements in mitosis, and —— arm(s), which is (are) believed to contain the hereditary material.

Study

Lambert, P., Miller, D. M., & Wiley, D. E. Experimental folklore and experimentation: The study of programmed learning in the Wauwatosa public schools.

Book II, S-283 and S-284

Normal

"5 > 3" means that 5 is greater than _____ .

"6 > 4" means that 6 is greater than _____ .

Blacked-Out

A-4. 1;2

A-5. —— has —— centromere(s), —— and —— arm(s).

A-4. 1;2

"5 ▮ 3" means that 5 is greater than _____ .

"6 ▮ 4" means that 6 is greater than _____ .

* Material covered in the blacked-out version can be omitted without influencing the subject's ability to answer correctly.

and the order and composition of frames were revised" (35, p. 4). Again, even if the program had been of sufficient length, there is no reason to have expected differences among response modes.

In another study no difference was found (60) between writing answers and simply reading an experimental textbook consisting of the same material in paragraph form and without blanks. The program had 461 items, making it longer than most used in studies showing a difference. Examination of the program reveals a mixture of both of the remaining deficiencies: (a) irrelevantly determined items and (b) test-like items with responses underdetermined. The *first* item in the program is: "The nucleus of a cell contains dark-staining bodies called ————." The basis for an answer is not clear; perhaps students in a genetics course would already know it. At any rate, it is not programed; thus, mode of response would not be expected to be important. The third item requires no response at all, and the student reads a statement about chromosomes having a single centromere and two arms. No response is required, even in the "overt" response condition. This is followed immediately by an item which *tests* the content of the previous item: "Each chromosome has ——— centromere(s) and ——— arm(s), of equal or unequal length." The next item is shown with the blackout treatment in Table 2. Most of the item is blacked out. The student could answer "1" and "2" easily, since these are the same answers as the answers to the previous item. It is unnecessary to notice the remaining content of the item. Moreover, in their programed text format, the correct answer to the previous items (as shown in Table 2) is located directly beside the item.

Another case of a relatively longer program (63) is an 843-frame program, *Sets, Relations, and Functions* (21), in which the investigators failed to find a difference between subjects instructed to write answers in an answer booklet and those instructed not to write answers. Examination of this material indicates two ways students could answer without performing the task intended. The programs were printed on light paper with answers on the reverse side of each leaf. The paper was sufficiently thin so that answers easily could be seen through the page. The present author asked a subject to answer the 329 items in Book II of this program under instructions to give no attention to the items, but to try to read the answers through the page, and when this failed, to lift the leaf a fraction of an inch and try again. He was able to read answers correctly to 201 items with the page flat and another 71 items when the page was lifted just enough to avoid obstruction from the following item. Only 57 answers could not be read through the page; therefore, this subject "missed" only 17 percent of the items, even when trying to ignore them.

The second problem was the design of the items themselves. For example, in Table 2, the item "5 > 3 means that 5 is greater than ———" can be answered easily by subjects when the all-important "greater than" sign is blacked out. Not all of the items have this problem, but many do; and combined with the ease of reading the correct answer through the page, the validity of the experiment is brought into question.

Hartman, Morrison, and Carlson (38) found no posttest difference between constructed response and reading completed sentences using, for different classes, four different sections of a program varying in length from 251 to 682 frames. The low error rate of 4 to 6 percent for different sections demonstrates that the responses were sufficiently determined, but there seemed to be a problem of irrelevantly cued answers. One example is as follows:

> The numbers printed along the 10 numeric positions on your IBM card are, in order from top to bottom, 0, 1, 2, 3, ———, ———, ———, ———, ———, and ——— (52, p. 8).

Their programed text format provides an even greater source of inappropriate cueing. The subjects confirmed responses by looking in the back of the book where successive answers were neatly arranged in columns, enabling easy viewing of the answers to the next several questions. Again, with subjects' answers controlled by cues other than the content being taught, there was no reason to expect a difference in response modes.

Keislar and McNeil (56) used a 432-item multiple-choice program in a Videosonic teaching machine. The overt response group pressed a button for one of two or three alternative answers until correct. The nonovert response group used the same device, but was asked not to press the buttons; instead, for the nonovert group, a green light automatically turned on in front of the correct answer after five seconds. Although the green light was needed to assure feedback for the covert group, it is here contended that it confounded the experiment by converting the "covert" group into a single alternative group. With the exception of the five-second pause, this condition is like the one-alternative condition in Kaess and Zeaman's study of number of alternatives which indicated that one alternative was superior to either two or three alternatives (see Figure 4). Therefore, the parametric data on the function of number of alternatives in multiple-choice items are capable of accounting for these results without regard to whether responses were overt or covert. Had more alternatives or more difficult alternatives been used, the data in Figure 4 suggest that the "overt" multiple alternative response group might have been substantially worse than the "covert" *single* alternate response group—not because of response mode differences, but because of differences in number of alternatives.

Many studies with no obvious deficiencies in the design of items have failed to indicate differences in response modes (1, 25, 97, 104, 108). These studies, however, all used relatively short programs. Alter and Silverman (1), using an 87-item program on basic electricity, found no significant differences among reading complete statements, thinking answers, speaking answers, writing answers, or writing and speaking answers. Their second study with the same program compared written responses and reading under both paced and unpaced conditions, and again showed no significant difference. In the third study the same investigators used a 90-frame program in binary numbers, but again failed to find a significant difference between writing answers and reading completed statements. With this same binary number program Tobias and Weiner (104) compared writing answers, thinking answers, and reading completed statements; they also failed to obtain significant differences. Stolurow and Walker (97) found no difference between subjects instructed to think answers and those writing answers in a 78-item segment of a descriptive statistics program. Evans, Homme, and Glaser (25), with a 72-item program in symbolic logic, found no difference between subjects writing their answers and subjects having the answer in view below each item. While these several studies used programs which on examination reveal no obvious lack in item design, all were done with programs so short that the user, particularly under controlled experimental conditions, might not yet have moved from covert responding to not responding.

Overt-covert response studies have been analyzed above in terms of how well they have met the rationale underlying the expected response mode differences. Many of the studies were also deficient in ordinary matters of experimental technique. Usually, programed texts were used rather than machines, and they were used in environments which gave little assurance of correct use of the material; glancing ahead, copying answers, and moving back and forth in the sequence were often possible. Testing classes of subjects at the same time is a common practice, and when conditions are sufficiently controlled, it is probably acceptable. But some reported studies raise questions concerning the adequacy of their control. For example, Lambert, Miller, and Wiley (63) used all of the ninth-grade mathematics classes in a school system, and the teachers who normally conducted these classes were responsible for distributing and collecting the material—pretest, program, and posttest —as well as keeping records and, presumably, insuring that all students followed the experimental procedures. No mention is made of special monitoring of students or special training of the teachers, nor even of analysis of student answers in the program. Can one even be sure that the overt response group wrote answers? The most casual collection of data is illustrated by Kormondy and Van Atta (60), who asked students to use the programed text at their own convenience in places of their own choosing with *no* supervision.

Criterion tests are usually of unknown sensitivity; moreover, there is occasional internal evidence that a test is too insensitive to measure any but the most gross effects. For example, in one of Alter and Silverman's (1) experiments, one of the subtests failed to yield a posttest difference between three of the experimental groups and a no-treatment group, which received no training at all. On a second subtest there was no difference between the no-treatment group and two of the five experimental groups. When the two measures were combined, the no-treatment group was different from any of the other five, but the largest of the differences was only 5 points out of a possible 15, suggesting that the test sensitivity left little chance for differences to appear. Similarly, the Feldhusen and Birt (26) experiment found no differences among any of nine experimental variations, suggesting either problems of experimental procedures or test sensitivity.

The requirement for an overt response seems adequately supported by evidence when the items are designed properly and the programs are long enough. Studies failing to reveal this effect are largely explained by failures in meeting the rationale for overt responding and by poor experimental procedures. However, these studies undoubtedly raise enough doubts for some investigators to insure that still more research on the need for overt responses will be conducted at the expense of more fundamental variables of program design.

Time and Efficiency: All investigators report that overt responding takes longer than covert responding. This finding seems clear, unequivocal, and most reasonable. It requires a finite time to write an answer, and over a whole program this writing time accumulates to an easily measured amount. Most programers have given only secondary consideration to time requirements as compared with comprehension. Since thousands of students use successful programs, it is important to think of even relatively small savings in time when such savings are possible. Methods should be devised for overt responding which take less time, such as speaking into a microphone or using special systems of abbreviation or shorthand.

Some investigators (34, 105) have attempted to put comprehension and time together in a single efficiency index by dividing test scores by learning time to give a measure of the amount learned per unit time. However, this practice is deceptive and violates principles of measurement (95). To perform this operation, one treats test scores as though they formed a ratio scale when, in fact, they form only an ordinal scale. Comprehension tests (and ordinal scales generally) permit only statements of greater or less; that is, rank ordering among conditions or subjects. Such measures do not provide valid statements regarding the magnitude of difference, and, further, there is no absolute zero. A subject in a typical comprehension examination who answers 5 questions correctly cannot be said to know exactly half as much as one who answers 10 questions correctly. Depending on the difficulty and sampling of the items, he may be almost as knowledgeable or almost completely ignorant. An "efficiency" index could easily be shifted by changing the level of difficulty on even a few items on the test.

Another, less fundamental, problem of the efficiency score is the use of posttest performance rather than a gain score (34, 105). This practice makes a no-treatment condition the most efficient since this condition would yield an infinitely large efficiency score. Williams' (105) efficiency index may serve as an example. She reported sizable differences in learning efficiency among several groups; however, a group which did not use the program scored 8.8 on a 29-point test which should require using gain scores rather than raw posttest scores. When the 8.8 is subtracted from the group posttest means before calculating a new efficiency index, the differences are greatly attenuated and would not likely be significant. Indeed, had pretest scores been larger, the differences might even have been reversed. This problem is not limited to adjusting for pretest performance. Consider, for example, the effect on the index of deciding to exclude (or, for that matter, include) several nondiscriminating items in the posttest.

Constructed Response Versus Multiple Choice

A number of studies (9, 25, 50, 75, 82, 105) have directly compared constructed response and multiple-choice response in rather standard verbal programs and failed to find posttest differences. However, many are inconclusive. For example, Roe and others (82) used the statistics programs discussed above and illustrated in Table 2, in which the answer is largely unrelated to the content of the item. There is little reason to expect response mode to be important in such a program.

Similarly, Burton and Goldbeck (9) compared a sequence of 35 independent items with difficult alternatives, easy alternatives, and constructed responses. The sample item in their report has the same problem as in Roe's experiment and renders their lack of a difference inconsequential. The item is: "Valuable for its use in making coonskin caps, the strictly nocturnal animal that washes its food in water before eating it is the————." The difficult alternatives were: "fox," "wolf," "squirrel," "raccoon," "muskrat"; the easy alternatives were: "ostrich," "dog," "llama," "raccoon," "canary." The test question related to this item was: "What nocturnal animal washes its food in water before eating it?" (9, pp. 3-4). It should be apparent that the program item can be answered on the basis of the "coonskin cap," without reference to the information important for the test. Whatever is learned about the cleanliness or sleeping habits of raccoons would be through incidental learning, which would make responses of any mode irrelevant. The relationship between the response and the critical material in the item is probably as important here as in the overt-covert response question.

Williams' (105) finding of no difference between constructed response and multiple choice merits greater credence than the other "no-difference" studies. Because she did find both to be significantly better than covert responding, her program test and experimental procedures were demonstrated to be capable of detecting effects. A slight, although not significant, difference favored the constructed response condition, but when the test items requiring a technical term were analyzed separately, the constructed response program proved significantly better than the multiple choice and, on these items, the multiple-choice form was not better than reading completed statements.

Similarly, Coulson and Silberman (17), using a different segment of the same program as Williams, also found no over-all posttest difference, but did find that on the constructed response portion of the posttest the constructed response program provided better performance. Both studies, therefore, suggest that the constructed response might have special advantages for certain types of learning tasks as, for example, having to recall (as distinct from recognizing) a new technical term. This interpretation is also supported in an experiment (27) comparing constructed response and multiple choice in learning Spanish equivalents of English words. When the posttest required writing the Spanish word, the constructed response program was better, but when the posttest required choosing the Spanish equivalent from among several alternatives, no differences were apparent between the conditions. Writing the new Spanish word helped the person to reproduce it later, but it was unnecessary for choosing it later from among alternatives.

The sketchy pattern which emerges is that the nature of the learning task determines the preferred response form. When the criterion performance includes a precise response topography (even a simple one such as writing a new Spanish word), constructed response seems to be the better form; whereas if mere recognition is desired, the response form in the program is probably unimportant. Although there is no relevant data as yet, perhaps when a fine stimulus discrimination is to be trained, alternative responses are preferable. Most verbal knowledge programs do not shape precise topographies, but they do tend more often toward a verbal repertoire than toward simple recognition. Moreover, the Kaess and Zeaman (55) study indicates that difficult multiple-choice alternatives have clear dangers.

Adjusting for Individual Differences

There is face validity in the proposition that differences in individuals' past histories and innate abilities are best accommodated by programs which adjust to the performance of the individual. Therefore, different branching methods have been described by which responses on items determine what material will be presented next, either by moving well ahead in the program, looping back for review, or presenting special remedial frames. Some programers make branching their principal tool. Other programers suggest that branching is rarely necessary, and, when necessary, it consists of very large branches within whole segments of courses. The issue has become a red herring with debates regarding "branching versus fixed sequence," ignoring the need for analysis of difference among tasks and the related problems of diagnosing differences among subjects.

Curiously, even though advantages for branching are self-evident, at least for extreme individual differences, most studies find no advantage for branching (6, 10, 11, 33, 81, 90). Some of these, however, are inconclusive for reasons similar to those explaining inconclusive negative results in response mode studies. Roe compared a fixed sequence with moving backward after errors and with skipping ahead after correct responses. Skipping ahead required less time, but the three procedures were not different in criterion performance. The program used, however, was the one discussed earlier in which the response is little related to the rest of the item. The value of such items for diagnosing achievement is probably as low as their value in teaching. Campbell (10, 11), in 11 different experiments, compared a short form of a program and a form with forward loops through remedial material, but found a significant difference in comprehension favoring branching in only 1 of the 11 studies, and it proved unreplicable. In all cases the condition resulting in fewer items required less time. Similarly, Glaser, Reynolds, and Harakas (33) created a branching program from a small-step nonbranching program by combining items and requiring a single answer which when incorrect required use of the small-step component items from which the larger one was constructed. They found no posttest difference between a group using the branching program and one using the small-step linear program.

A study using 411 multiple-choice items in a logic program (90)

introduced a particularly important control condition in which subjects were randomly paired, and the control member of the pair received
the same sequence as the "branched" member of the pair, except that
the sequence was not adjusted to his errors but to his match-mates'
errors. The study found no differences, but the new "yoked" control
should become standard for research in branching programs.

There are two studies, however, which indicate at least a little advantage for adjusting the sequence to individual differences. Skinner's
(92) original write-in machine branched in a small way by automatically repeating incorrectly answered items at the end of each 29-item set.
Even in a low error-rate program, this repetition of missed items improved posttest performance as compared with use of the machine without repeating missed items (47). A posttest advantage of an adjusting
sequence over a fixed sequence was found in a more extensive use of
branching (16). The branching group's sequence was controlled by
performance on diagnostic items, errors in the instructional items, and
the subject's own evaluation of his readiness to advance. Out of a population of 345 items, the branched group used an average of 213.5
items, while the fixed-sequence group used a 233-item program that
had been prepared by a programer who chose from among the original
345 items. Unfortunately, there is no way to know whether useful
items had been excluded or unnecessary items included in the fixed-
sequence version. An additional "yoked" control group is necessary
before concluding that the difference results from adjusting to individual differences or simply use of different sequences.

Despite the predominantly negative results regarding adjustment of
programs to individual differences, such adjustment must be effective
at least when wide differences in achievement or capacity are found in
the subject population. The practical question is whether the degree of
selection imposed by the normal processes which segregate students
into grade levels, if supplemented by prerequisite testing, leaves a useful role for sequences that adjust to individual differences. The difficulty is finding effects of branching points toward a qualified negative
answer. Stronger evidence is reported by Shay (88) who investigated
the hypothesis that different programs might be preferable for different
ability levels. He specially designed parallel programs having 103, 150,
and 199 items, using data from subjects of high, medium, or low intelligence, respectively. After each of the three programs was perfected

for subjects of a specific intelligence level, all three programs were used by subjects in all three difficulty levels in a 3 x 3 factorial design. No significant interaction resulted between intelligence and program, thereby lending credence to the claim that within broad limits, persons of different abilities do not require different programs.

Gross Evaluative Comparisons

A great many studies have compared programed instruction with conventional methods, or compared programed texts with teaching machine presentation, or compared educational "media" one with the other. Despite their prevalence such studies lack validity in the sense that they do not permit generalization of the results beyond the particular instances used in the study. No teaching-machine program and no "conventional" method represent their whole class; nor do the two differ in only a single dimension; they differ, instead, in an indefinite number of ways. The adequacy of any "method" can be changed considerably by manipulating often subtle variables. The case has been well stated by Lumsdaine:

Experimental measurement of the effects of a single instrument apply only to that particular instrument, and generalizations of the results of such an evaluative experiment to other instruments of the media it represents have, at most, the status of untested hypotheses. Similar limitations apply when a comparison is made between the attainments effected by a particular instrument and those obtained by some alternative form of instruction often characterized as "conventional" or "currently used" instruction. The restrictions on interpretation of such a comparison arise from the lack of specificity of the instruction with which the instrument in question is compared. Similar restrictions apply in general to the overall comparison of alternative "media" (66, p. 251).

Practical decisions, of course, must be made as to whether or not to adopt a program. It is perhaps comforting that comparison studies almost always show large advantages for programed instruction, but such pseudoexperiments do not serve as a justified basis for decision, except for the rare occasions involving the very program and "other method" used in such a study. Nevertheless, valid evaluation is possible by other means (42, 67, 84), and the attainments of a particular program can be quantitatively stated. In this volume, program evaluation is discussed in Chapter 7 by Lumsdaine. Studies which are exclusively gross comparisons are not reviewed here because of their lack of generality.

Summary

Dependent Variable

Research in programing is severely handicapped by poor measures. The dependent variable of greatest interest is number of errors on tests or on terminal frames. But for purposes of evaluating subtle differences in experimental variables, this often is unsatisfactory. As an ordinal scale it permits only a rank ordering of conditions and does not indicate the size of differences. However, this dependence of the score on the characteristics of each test item is usually overlooked. Many test items either may always be missed or never be missed, leaving few items to reveal effects of even potent variables. This lack of sensitivity is obvious in the occasional "ceiling effects" when test performances are near perfect for all conditions. Problems of test sensitivity, program adequacy, or experimental procedures seem likely in the several cases of programs and associated posttests which have been used repeatedly in a variety of experiments without ever revealing a significant effect.

Control of Experimental Conditions

With a few exceptions the data are collected under poorly controlled conditions. Programed books are often used, and these offer little protection from a variety of distortions of the data including outright cheating by the subjects. Often, the work is done in open classes of 20 or 30 students, in many cases, without the supervision of a trained experimentalist. Occasionally, control is made worse by having students work at home without supervision. In one instance retention data were gathered by mail. Not only were these tests unsupervised and uncontrolled, but dunning letters and phone calls were used to get complete returns, and these late returns were plotted as longer retention periods, thereby leaving both the independent and dependent variables open to error. More frequent and more dangerous are the instances of poor control that are not easily discovered in the written report, such as subjects following the wrong sequence in a programed text, looking ahead at answers, looking back at previous items, or even reading answers through the page. Holz and Robinson (49) have demonstrated such pitfalls comparing error rates in a published vertical format program (using a mask) with a teaching-machine presentation of the same material. In the programed text the error rate was a low 4.6 percent, comparable to the publisher's claims, while in the machine the error rate was 22.2 percent, presumably because the subjects could not misuse the material in the machine. It is unlikely that even the original programer was aware of the true error rate, much less the unsuspecting research investigator using such a programed text. Regardless of the pros and cons of machines for ordinary classroom use, in conducting experiments, proper instrumentation is essential.

Results

Most experiments have been limited to simple dichotomous tests of the general principles of programing. The results, in general, support the original principles:

1. A contingent relation between answer and content is important.
2. The ability for the contingency to be met (low error rate) has received support.
3. Sequencing is important at least for material that builds progressively. Principles of progression have been demonstrated in teaching verbal knowledge, shaping skillful response topographies, and establishing or transferring stimulus control. Fading of formal prompts in teaching isolated stimulus-response associations has not been demonstrated.
4. A range of examples is probably necessary for full comprehension.
5. For long programs, a public, overt response is necessary, provided the material meets the above criteria of a program.

Results are equivocal regarding branching and multiple-choice vs. constructed responses, but if many errors are made, the evidence indicates that erroneous alternatives will interfere with subsequent learning.

Future Research Needs

The need is for constructive research which clarifies, defines, and quantifies the parameters of programs. The frequent use of "versus" in the titles of studies is symptomatic of an inability to measure variables even approximately. How sequenced is a program in a study comparing "sequenced vs. nonsequenced" arrangement of items? When one can, at least roughly, identify in a program the magnitude of each of several dimensions, the technology of programing will be much further along, and "versus" studies will be things of the past.

References

1. Alter, Millicent, and Silverman, R. "The Response in Programed Instruction." *Journal of Programed Instruction* 1: 55-78; January 1962.
2. Angell, D., and Lumsdaine, A. A. *A Study of Subject-Controlled Partial Cueing in Paired-Associate Learning.* AFOSR 1342 Research Report. San Mateo, Calif.: American Institute for Research, 1961. 13 pp.
3. Angell, D., and Lumsdaine, A. A. "Prompted Plus Unprompted Trials Versus Prompted Trials Alone in Paired-Associate Learning." *Student Response in Programmed Instruction: A Symposium.* (Edited by A. A. Lumsdaine.) Washington, D.C.: National Academy of Sciences —National Research Council, 1961.
4. Angell, D., and Lumsdaine, A. A. *The Effects of Prompting Trials and Partial-Correction Procedures on Learning by Anticipation.* AFOSR 1343 Research Report. San Mateo, Calif.: American Institute for Research, 1961. 47 pp.
5. Angell, G. W. "The Effect of Immediate Knowledge of Quiz Results and Final Examination Scores in Freshman Chemistry." *Journal of Educational Research* 42: 391-94; January 1949.
6. Beane, D. G. *A Comparison of Linear and Branching Techniques of Programed Instruction in Plane Geometry.* Technical Report No. 1. Urbana: University of Illinois, 1962. 115 pp.
7. Bloom, L. A. *Evaluation of Teaching-Machine Processes with Children with Articulation Disorder One Year After Application.* Master's thesis. Pittsburgh: University of Pittsburgh, 1963. (Typewritten)
8. Briggs, L. J. "Prompting and Confirmation Conditions for Three Learning Tasks Employing the Subject-Matter Trainer." *Student Response in Programmed Instruction: A Symposium.* (Edited by A. A. Lumsdaine.) Washington, D.C.: National Academy of Sciences—National Research Council, 1961. pp. 375-87.
9. Burton, B. B., and Goldbeck, R. A. *The Effect of Response Characteristics and Multiple-Choice Alternatives on Learning During Programed Instruction.* Technical Report No. 4. San Mateo, Calif.: American Institute for Research, 1962. 16 pp.
10. Campbell, V. N. *Adjusting Self-Instruction Programs to Individual Differences: Studies of Cueing, Responding and Bypassing.* San Mateo, Calif.: American Institute for Research, 1961. 56 pp.
11. Campbell, V. N. *Studies of Bypassing as a Way of Adapting Self-Instruction Programs to Individual Differences.* San Mateo: American Institute for Research, 1962. 68 pp.

12. Cook, J. O. "Supplementary Report: Processes Underlying Learning a Single Paired-Associate Item." *Journal of Experimental Psychology* 56: 455; November 1958.

13. Cook, J. O. " 'Superstition' in the Skinnerian." *American Psychologist* 18: 516-18; August 1963.

14. Cook, J. O., and Kendler, T. S. "A Theoretical Model To Explain Some Paired-Associate Learning Data." *Symposium on Air Force Human Engineering, Personnel and Training Research.* (Edited by Glen Finch and F. Cameron.) Washington, D.C.: National Research Council, 1956. pp. 90-98.

15. Cook, J. O., and Spitzer, M. E. "Supplementary Report: Prompting Versus Confirmation in Paired Associate Learning." *Journal of Experimental Psychology* 59: 275-76; April 1960.

16. Coulson, J. E., and others. "Effects of Branching in a Computer-Controlled Auto-Instructional Device." *Journal of Applied Psychology* 46: 389-92; December 1962.

17. Coulson, J. E., and Silberman, H. F. "Effects of Three Variables in a Teaching Machine." *Journal of Educational Psychology* 51: 135-43; June 1960.

18. Csanyi, A. P. "An Investigation of Visual Versus Auditory Programming in Teaching Foreign Language Pronunciation." *Investigations of the Characteristics of Programmed Learning Sequences.* (Edited by R. Glaser and J. I. Taber.) Cooperative Research Project No. 691. Pittsburgh: Programmed Learning Laboratory, University of Pittsburgh, 1961.

19. Csanyi, A. P.; Glaser, R.; and Reynolds, J. H. "Programming Method and Response Mode in a Visual-Oral Response Task." *Investigations of Learning Variables in Programmed Instruction.* Pittsburgh: Programmed Learning Laboratory, University of Pittsburgh, 1962.

20. Cummings, Allana Q., and Goldstein, L. S. *The Effect of Overt and Covert Responding on Two Kinds of Learning Tasks.* Technical Report. New York: Center for Programed Instruction, 1962.

21. Eigen, L. D. *Sets, Relations, and Functions.* New York: Center for Programed Instruction, 1961.

22. Eigen, L. D., and Margulies, S. "Response Characteristics as a Function of Information Level." *Journal of Programed Instruction* 2: 45-54; Spring 1963.

23. Evans, J. L. *Multiple-Choice Discrimination Programming.* Paper read at American Psychological Association Convention, New York, September 1961.

24. Evans, J. L.; Glaser, R.; and Homme, L. E. "An Investigation of 'Teaching Machine' Variables Using Learning Programs in Symbolic Logic." *Journal of Educational Research* 55: 433-52; June-July 1962.

25. Evans, J. L.; Homme, L. E.; and Glaser, R. "The Ruleg System for the Construction of Programmed Verbal Learning Sequences." *Journal of Educational Research* 55: 513-18; June-July 1962.

26. Feldhusen, J. F., and Birt, A. "A Study of Nine Methods of Presentation of Programmed Learning Material." *Journal of Educational Research* 55: 461-66; June-July 1962.

27. Fry, E. B. "A Study of Teaching-Machine Response Modes." *Teaching Machines and Programmed Learning*. (Edited by A. A. Lumsdaine and R. Glaser.) Washington, D.C.: National Education Association, 1960. pp. 469-74.

28. Gagné, R. M., and Bassler, O. C. "Study of Retention of Some Topics of Elementary Nonmetric Geometry." *Journal of Educational Psychology* 54: 123-31; June 1963.

29. Gagné, R. M., and others. "Factors in Acquiring Knowledge of a Mathematical Task." *Psychological Monographs* 76: 1-21; Whole No. 526, 1962.

30. Gagné, R. M., and Paradise, N. E. "Abilities and Learning Sets in Knowledge Acquisition." *Psychological Monographs* 75: 1-23; Whole No. 518, 1961.

31. Gavurin, E. I., and Donahue, Virginia M. *Logical Sequence and Random Sequence Teaching-Machine Programs*. Burlington, Mass.: RCA, 1960. 16 pp.

32. Glaser, R. "Some Research Problems in Automated Instruction: Instructional Programming and Subject Matter Structure." *Programmed Learning and Computer-Based Instruction*. (Edited by J. E. Coulson.) New York: John Wiley & Sons, 1962. pp. 76-85.

33. Glaser, R.; Reynolds, J. H.; and Harakas, T. *An Experimental Comparison of a Small-Step Single Track Program with a Large-Step Multi-Track (Branching) Program*. Pittsburgh: Programmed Learning Laboratory, University of Pittsburgh, 1962.

34. Goldbeck, R. A., and Campbell, V. N. "The Effects of Response Mode and Response Difficulty in Programed Learning." *Journal of Educational Psychology* 53: 110-18; June 1962.

35. Goldbeck, R. A.; Campbell, V. N.; and Llewellyn, Joan E. *Further Experimental Evidence on Response Modes in Automated Instruction*. Technical Report No. 3. Santa Barbara, Calif.: American Institute for Research, 1960. 24 pp.

36. Green, E. J. *The Learning Process and Programmed Instruction*. New York: Holt, Rinehart & Winston, 1962.

37. Guthrie, P. M., and Lumsdaine, A. A. *Some Effects of Graduated Partial Cueing on the Learning of Paired Associates*. Research Report 1341. San Mateo, Calif.: American Institute for Research, 1961. 34 pp.

38. Hartman, T. F.; Morrison, B. A.; and Carlson, M. E. "Active Responding in Programmed Learning Materials." *Journal of Applied Psychology* 47: 343-47; October 1963.

39. Hively, Wells. "Programming Stimuli in Matching to Sample." *Journal of the Experimental Analysis of Behavior* 5: 279-98; July 1962.
40. Holland, Audrey L., and Matthews, J. "Application of Teaching-Machine Concepts to Speech Pathology and Audiology." *Asha* 5: 474-82; January 1963.
41. Holland, J. G. *Design and Use of a Teaching-Machine Program.* Paper read at American Psychological Association Convention, Chicago, September 1960.
42. Holland, J. G. "Evaluating Teaching Machines and Programs." *Teachers College Record* 63: 56-65; October 1961.
43. Holland, J. G. "New Directions in Teaching-Machine Research." *Programmed Learning and Computer-Based Instruction.* (Edited by J. E. Coulson.) New York: John Wiley & Sons, 1961.
44. Holland, J. G. *Sorting Response Contingencies in Teaching-Machine Programs.* Paper read at Eastern Psychological Association Convention, Philadelphia, 1964.
45. Holland, J. G. "Cook's Tour de Farce." *American Psychologist* 19: 683-84; August 1964.
46. Holland, J. G. "Response Contingencies in Teaching-Machine Programs." *Journal of Programed Instruction.* (In press)
47. Holland, J. G., and Porter, D. "The Influence of Repetition of Incorrectly-Answered Items in a Teaching-Machine Program." *Journal of the Experimental Analysis of Behavior* 4: 305-307; October 1961.
48. Holland, J. G., and Skinner, B. F. *The Analysis of Behavior.* New York: McGraw-Hill Book Co., 1961.
49. Holz, W. C., and Robinson, J. "A Note on Machines in a Technology of Education." *Journal of Programed Instruction* 2: 31-33; Fall 1963.
50. Hough, J. B. "An Analysis of the Efficiency and Effectiveness of Selected Aspects of Machine Instruction." *Journal of Educational Research* 55: 467-71; June-July 1962.
51. Hough, J. B., and Revsin, B. "Programmed Instruction at the College Level: A Study of Several Factors Influencing Learning." *Phi Delta Kappan* 44: 286-91; March 1963.
52. IBM Research Psychology Staff. *Introductory Program: The IBM Punched Card.* Yorktown Heights, N.Y.: Thomas J. Watson Research Center, 1961.
53. Israel, M. L. *Variably Blurred Prompting in the Analysis of Paired-Associate Learning.* Doctor's thesis. Cambridge, Mass.: Harvard University, 1960. (Typewritten)
54. Israel, M. L. "Variably Blurred Prompting: I. Methodology and Application to the Analysis of Paired-Associate Learning." *Journal of Psychology* 50: 43-52; July 1960.
55. Kaess, W., and Zeaman, D. "Positive and Negative Knowledge of Results on a Pressey-Type Punchboard." *Journal of Experimental Psychology* 60: 12-17; July 1960.

56. Keislar, E. R., and McNeil, J. D. "A Comparison of Two Response Modes in an Auto-Instructional Program with Children in the Primary Grades." *Journal of Educational Psychology* 53: 127-31; June 1962.
57. Kopstein, F. F., and Roshal, S. M. "Methods of Presenting Word Pairs as a Factor in Foreign Vocabulary Learning." *American Psychologist* 10: 354; August 1955. (Abstract)
58. Kopstein, F. F., and Roshal, S. M. "Verbal Learning Efficiency as Influenced by the Manipulation of Representational Response Processes: Pictorial-Verbal and Temporal Contiguity Factors." *Student Response in Programmed Instruction*. (Edited by A. A. Lumsdaine.) Washington, D.C.: National Academy of Sciences—National Research Council, 1961. pp. 335-50.
59. Kormondy, E. J. *Introduction to Genetics*. New York: McGraw-Hill Book Co., 1964.
60. Kormondy, E. J., and Van Atta, E. L. "Experiment in Self-Instruction in General Biology." *Ohio Journal of Science* 4: 4-10; January 1962.
61. Krumboltz, J. D., and Weisman, R. G. "The Effect of Overt vs. Covert Responding to Programed Instruction on Immediate and Delayed Retention." *Journal of Educational Psychology* 53: 89-92; April 1962.
62. Krumboltz, J. D., and Weisman, R. G. "The Effect of Intermittent Confirmation in Programed Instruction." *Journal of Educational Psychology* 53: 250-53; December 1962.
63. Lambert, P.; Miller, D. M.; and Wiley, D. E. "Experimental Folklore and Experimentation: The Study of Programmed Learning in the Wauwatosa Public Schools." *Journal of Educational Research* 55: 485-94; June-July 1962.
64. Levin, G. R., and Baker, B. L. "Item Scrambling in a Self-Instructional Program." *Journal of Educational Psychology* 54: 138-43; June 1963.
65. Lumsdaine, A. A., editor. *Student Response in Programmed Instruction: A Symposium*. Washington, D.C.: National Academy of Sciences —National Research Council, 1961.
66. Lumsdaine, A. A. "Instructional Materials and Devices." *Training Research and Education*. (Edited by R. Glaser.) Pittsburgh: University of Pittsburgh Press, 1962.
67. Lumsdaine, A. A. "Assessing the Effectiveness of Instructional Programs." *Teaching Machines and Programed Learning, II: Data and Directions*. (Edited by R. Glaser.) Washington, D.C.: National Education Association, 1965.
68. Lumsdaine, A. A., and Glaser, R., editors. *Teaching Machines and Programmed Learning*. Washington, D.C.: National Education Association, 1960.
69. McDonald, F. J., and Allen, D. "An Investigation of Presentation Response and Correction Factors in Programmed Instruction." *Journal of Educational Research* 55: 502-507; June-July 1962.

70. Melaragno, R. J. "Effect of Negative Reinforcement in an Automated Teaching Setting." *Psychological Reports* 7: 381-84; October 1960.

71. Meyer, Susan R. "Report on the Initial Test of a Junior High School Vocabulary Program." *Teaching Machines and Programmed Learning.* (Edited by A. A. Lumsdaine and R. Glaser.) Washington, D.C.: National Education Association, 1960. pp. 229-46.

72. Moore, J. W., and Smith, W. I. "Knowledge of Results of Self-Teaching Spelling." *Psychological Reports* 9: 717-26; December 1961.

73. Moore, J. W., and Smith, W. I. "A Comparison of Several Types of 'Immediate Reinforcement.' " *Programed Learning.* (Edited by W. Smith and J. Moore.) New York: D. Van Nostrand, 1962, pp. 192-201.

74. Pressey, S. L. "Some Perspectives and Major Problems Regarding 'Teaching Machines.' " *Teaching Machines and Programmed Learning.* (Edited by A. A. Lumsdaine and R. Glaser.) Washington, D.C.: National Education Association, 1960. pp. 497-506.

75. Price, J. E. *A Comparison of Automated Teaching Programs with Conventional Teaching Methods as Applied to Mentally Retarded Students.* Tuscaloosa, Ala.: Partlow State School and Hospital, 1962.

76. Resnick, Lauren B., and Ellis, A. B. *Stimulus Control in a Self-Instructional Program: The Effect of Material to Which No Direct Response Is Made.* Cambridge, Mass.: Committee on Programmed Instruction, Harvard University, 1962. (Mimeo.)

77. Reynolds, J. H., and Glaser, R. "Learning Set Formation." *Investigations of Learning Variables in Programmed Instruction.* Pittsburgh: Programmed Learning Laboratory, University of Pittsburgh, 1962.

78. Reynolds, J. H., and Glaser, R. "Repetition and Spaced Review Variables." *Investigations of Learning Variables in Programmed Instruction.* Pittsburgh: Programmed Learning Laboratory, University of Pittsburgh, 1962.

79. Reynolds, J. H., and Glaser, R. "Effects of Repetition and Spaced Review upon Retention of a Complex Learning Task." *Journal of Educational Psychology* 55: 297-308; October 1964.

80. Rock, I. "Repetition and Learning." *Scientific American* 199: 68-72; August 1958.

81. Roe, A. "A Comparison of Branching Methods for Programmed Learning." *Journal of Educational Research* 55: 407-16; June-July 1962.

82. Roe, A., and others. *Automated Teaching Methods Using Linear Programs.* No. 60-105. Los Angeles: Automated Learning Research Project, University of California, 1960. 57 pp.

83. Roe, Kiki V.; Case, H. W.; and Roe, A. "Scrambled vs. Ordered Sequence in Auto-Instructional Programs." *Journal of Educational Psychology* 53: 101-104; April 1962.

84. Rothkopf, E. Z. "Criteria for the Acceptance of Self-Instructional Programs." *Improving the Efficiency and Quality of Learning.* Washington, D.C.: American Council on Education, 1962.

85. Schaefer, H. H. "A Vocabulary Program Using 'Language' Redundancy." *Investigations of the Characteristics of Programmed Learning Sequences.* (Edited by R. Glaser and J. I. Taber.) Pittsburgh: Programmed Learning Laboratory, University of Pittsburgh, 1961.

86. Schaefer, H. H. "E. A. Poe as a Reinforcer." *Psychological Reports* 8: 398; June 1961.

87. Scharf, Eugenia S. "A Study of the Effects of Partial Reinforcement on Behavior in a Programmed Learning Situation." *Investigations of the Characteristics of Programmed Learning Sequences.* (Edited by R. Glaser and J. I. Taber.) Cooperative Research Project No. 691. Pittsburgh: Programmed Learning Laboratory, University of Pittsburgh, 1961.

88. Shay, C. B. "Relationship of Intelligence to Step Size on a Teaching-Machine Program." *Journal of Educational Psychology* 52: 98-103; April 1961.

89. Sidowski, J. B., and others. "Prompting and Confirmation Variables in Verbal Learning." *Psychological Reports* 8: 401-406; June 1961.

90. Silberman, H. F., and others. "Fixed Sequence vs. Branching Auto-Instructional Methods." *Journal of Educational Psychology* 52: 166-72; June 1961.

91. Skinner, B. F. *Science and Human Behavior.* New York: Macmillan Co., 1953.

92. Skinner, B. F. "Teaching Machines." *Science* 128: 969-77; October 1958.

93. Skinner, B. F. "Teaching Machines." *Scientific American* 205: 91-102; November 1961.

94. Smith, W., and Moore, J. W. "Size-of-Step and Achievement in Programmed Spelling." *Psychological Reports* 10: 287-94; February 1962.

95. Stevens, S. S. "Mathematics, Measurement and Psychophysics." *Handbook of Experimental Psychology.* (Edited by S. S. Stevens.) New York: John Wiley & Sons, 1951.

96. Stolurow, L. M., and Lippert, H. *Prompting, Confirmation and Vanishing in the Teaching of a Sight Vocabulary.* Urbana: Training Research Laboratory, University of Illinois, 1963. (Mimeo.)

97. Stolurow, L. M., and Walker, C. C. "A Comparison of Overt and Covert Response in Programmed Learning." *Journal of Educational Research* 55: 421-29; June-July 1962.

98. Suppes, P., and Ginsberg, Rose. "Application of a Stimulus Sampling Model to Children's Concept Formation with and Without Overt Correction Response." *Journal of Experimental Psychology* 63: 330-36; April 1962.

99. Suppes, P., and Ginsberg, Rose. "Experimental Studies of Mathematical Concept Formation in Young Children." *Science Education* 46: 230-40; April 1962.

100. Swets, J. A., and others. "Learning To Identify Nonverbal Sounds: An Application of a Computer as a Teaching Machine." *Journal of the Acoustical Society of America* 34: 928-35; July 1962.

101. Taber, J. I., and Glaser, R. "An Exploratory Evaluation of a Discriminative Transfer Learning Program Using Literal Prompts." *Journal of Educational Research* 55: 508-512; June-July 1962.

102. Terrace, H. S. "Discrimination Learning with and Without 'Errors.'" *Journal of the Experimental Analysis of Behavior* 6: 1-27; January 1963.

103. Terrace, H. S. "Errorless Transfer of a Discrimination Across Two Continua." *Journal of the Experimental Analysis of Behavior* 6: 223-32; April 1963.

104. Tobias, S., and Weiner, M. "Effect of Response Mode on Immediate and Delayed Recall from Programmed Material." *Journal of Programed Instruction* 2: 9-13; Spring 1963.

105. Williams, Joanna P. "A Comparison of Several Response Modes in a Review Program." *Journal of Educational Psychology* 54: 253-60; October 1963.

106. Wittrock, M. C. "Response Mode in the Programming of Kinetic Molecular Theory Concepts." *Journal of Educational Psychology* 54: 89-93; April 1963.

107. Wolfe, M. *Effects of Expository Instruction in Mathematics on Students Accustomed to Discovery Methods.* Doctor's thesis. Urbana: University of Illinois, 1963. (Typewritten)

108. Zuckerman, C. B.; Marshall, G. R.; and Groesberg, S. *Research in the Automation of Teaching.* Port Washington, N.Y.: U.S. Naval Training Device Center, 1961.

DAVID J. KLAUS
American Institutes for Research

An Analysis of Programing Techniques

Trying to describe the techniques used to prepare programed materials is much like trying to count the number of angels perched on the head of a pin. The outcome in either case depends not so much on what there is to see as it does on what is assumed to be relevant. The uniformity with which almost any written material can promote learning is inescapable. The writers of programs, textbooks, and even advertising all owe their livelihood to changes in performance which are produced by their materials with at least modest regularity. However, few behavioral scientists would care to regard all instructional materials as *programs*, regardless of this outcome and even if the more traditional lessons were consigned to the less effective end of the spectrum. The criterion that learning results from their use, then, does not establish particular materials as programs and even may exclude some materials which might be regarded as programs despite their ineffectiveness.

Other definitions of programs similarly risk errors of inclusion or exclusion. For example, Dolmatch (12, p. 13) defines a program as "a sequence of items, steps, or frames which present material to the learner. Each frame contains new information and/or a recapitulation of information, combined with some material requiring a response." According to Markle (43), "The distinguishing characteristic of programed materials is the testing procedure to which they are subjected. Empirical evidence of the effectiveness of each teaching sequence is obtainable from the performance records of students." Ofiesh (46, p. 5) says programed instruction is "an effort to package for the student the essential aspects of the tutorial method of instruction." The Epsteins (13, p. 1) define a program as "lessons prepared in a special way, so that the student can scarcely fail to learn," and Glaser (22, p. 9) characterizes programing as "the process of constructing sequences of instructional material in a way that maximizes the rate of acquisition and retention, and enhances the motivation of the student."

Lumsdaine and Klaus (40) describe three characteristics of programed materials. The first is that programs are potentially *autonomous*, in that they "contain the features felt to be essential for dependably producing learning of a given subject matter or repertoire on the part of the student—without his necessarily receiving additional instructional assistance." The second is that programs are *autogenous*, in the sense that "the student's responses to preliminary versions of a program sequence themselves are instrumental in generating the subsequent development of the material." And, third, is that programs are amenable to *automation*, since they "lend themselves, where desired, to presentation in some form of device which may have a considerable range of automatic or semi-automatic control features governing the sequence of presentation, the scoring or discrimination of correct and incorrect responses, etc." In other words, any form of instruction which is self-contained, is repeatedly tried out and corrected, and is replicable with regard to controlling the learning process may be regarded as a program.

As can be seen from these examples, most efforts to define programs result in a series of specifications which reflect their superficial appearance, the methodology used in their preparation, their theoretical or historical antecedents, or their emphasis on uniformly high levels of achievement. This includes a host of possibilities with respect to styles, approaches, methodologies, and features, but there is no reason for expecting a greater uniformity among the products of programers than there exists among theories of learning, philosophies of education, or the content of courses. When considering the specific techniques used in preparing a program, on the other hand, the definition can be pragmatic. The programer, as he develops his materials, is concerned with facilitating learning in every possible way. To this end he tries out his materials at various stages so as to detect and correct any inadequacies. Even more important, he does everything possible before attempting tryouts to insure the effectiveness of the instruction. It is during the initial planning and drafting of a program, then, that the programer employs the techniques which will determine the general characteristics of his materials even after they have been subjected to repeated tryouts and revisions.

In this sense, *an instructional program is an effort to anticipate and overcome probable learner difficulties.* Of all the characteristics which may be felt to be peculiar to programing, this emphasis on the learner instead of the content may be the most outstanding. Tryouts of instructional materials are not particularly unique to programing. Not only are textbooks often "use tested" by their authors, but the use of student responses as a basis for revisions has been applied successfully in the past to training films (see 37), to educational television (see 25), and to other instructional materials. What features seem to be original with programing are the systematic steps taken first to minimize and then to correct defects in the effectiveness of instruction on the basis of what is known about the learning process. The techniques used for this purpose comprise the nucleus of programed instruction and, along with their origins and features, are going to be the emphasis of this discussion. How effective any of these techniques may be empirically is an issue discussed in the chapter on research (see the chapter by Holland). The analysis in this chapter is based primarily on theoretical grounds. First, a framework will be offered which attempts to characterize programing techniques in terms of a sometimes explicit but often implicit parallelism between particular techniques and fundamental learning-theory positions. Next, several dominant issues in programed instruction will be considered in light of how contrasting theoretical positions have been implemented in the development of programs. Finally, several individual systems of programing methodology will be described to recapitulate specific techniques within their appropriate settings.

Programed Instruction and Theories of Learning

Programing techniques do not readily lend themselves to categorization. The type of cueing used, the kind of response required of the learner, the method of sequencing, and so forth often are regarded as stable characteristics. Yet, they frequently reflect the topic being programed, the attributes of the learner population, the limitations of the presentation format, and the chance effects of tryout-based revisions. A general consistency seems evident in the approach a programer is inclined to use, however. The techniques he employs to diminish the effects of anticipated learner problems are expressions of the programer's conceptualization of the learning process. Thus, a full range of learning-theory positions can be reflected in the programing process as subtle influences on program characteristics. Programed instruction is a uniquely limited instance of learning control. Except in the most broadly conceived sense, it is concerned only with human verbal behavior of one form or another. Programs have been prepared to teach motor skills, sensory discriminations, and symbolic problem solving; even in most of these cases, however, the control exerted over the learner's responses is largely verbal. Furthermore, very few programs develop responses of the kind studied in the typical learning laboratory or make use of the techniques, such as deprivation-assisted motivation, usually employed in these situations. Within the scope of variables appropriate for modifying those behaviors which are dealt with by programs, there is nevertheless ample opportunity for the development of very diverse approaches.

Response-Centered and Stimulus-Centered Programs

On the one hand, many programers—perhaps the majority at the present time—tend to emphasize the response aspects of learning from their programs. An extremely *response-centered program* might not consist of anything more than repetitive opportunities for practicing approximations of the desired terminal response until mastery has been achieved. The model for such a program is simple trial-and-error learning, akin to the learning which occurs when a child first begins to draw with crayons and paper. On the other hand, there are numerous program writers who tend to emphasize the stimulus aspects of learning in preparing their programs. These *stimulus-centered programs*, in their purest form, might be limited completely to the presentation of information to the learner. The model for this kind of program is cognitive or field-theory learning of the kind that might occur when a child first relates a drawing to the object illustrated. These divergent approaches, which Hebb (27, p. 58) calls "connectionist" and "configurationist" theories, respectively, long have represented antagonistic positions in psychology. It is not surprising to find that these each have become a rallying point in programing technology about which individual program writers tend to group themselves.

A response-centered programer is concerned, primarily, with the effects and conditions of practice. This emphasis of the response-centered position has been expressed succinctly by Holland (29, p. 219) as a fundamental postulate: "Behavior is learned only when it is emitted and reinforced." No learning can be expected in the absence of performance nor will practice be beneficial unless appropriately punctuated by the necessary reinforcement. A stimulus-centered programer, in contrast, is particularly concerned with the perceptual organization of the stimulus material. He views learning as the acquisition of information and assumes that learning occurs somewhat independently of performance. Hatch (26), for example, was speaking largely for the stimulus-centered position when he stated, "Learning is presumed to take place at the point of information dissemination, prior to the response." Many of the contrasts between these two positions are readily apparent. Not only do they represent conflicting views as to the locus of learning, but they reflect wide differences as to the conditions that are essential for learning as well.

Connectionist and Configurationist Positions

Both the approaches just described can claim a foundation in psychological science and a well-documented history: the connectionist's position in Thorndike's *Fundamentals of Learning* (65) and the configurationist's position in Tolman's *Purposive Behavior in Animals and Men* (66). However, the vast amount of experimental research accomplished since these two volumes were published has resulted in little, if any, assistance to a programer in choosing his fundamental approach since the basic issues never have been fully resolved. As in the selection of a learning theory to guide the conduct of research, the developer of a program must first, in the absence of conclusive evidence, select the approach which has impressed him as potentially the most fruitful. It is his approach which then guides him in identifying relevant variables and in isolating promising relationships. Only after the approach has been selected do conclusions from laboratory research have practical implications for program development.

In other words, the specific programing techniques employed by a program writer seem to reflect his position with respect to existing theories of learning. In particular, the programer may lean toward a connectionist position with the result that his approach is response-centered, or he may lean toward a configurationist position with the result that his approach is stimulus-centered. In selecting the techniques he will use, the programer tries to overcome anticipated learner difficulties by concentrating on variables which are consistent with his position and which represent principles which can be implemented within the scope of his approach. Thus, response-centered and stimulus-centered programers are not necessarily concerned with the same issues nor are they likely to find research based upon contrasting styles either of interest or of value. Because specific programing techniques necessarily are related to the general conceptual position adopted and these, in turn, reflect the bias of connectionist or configurationist theory, a quick look at these theories may be of assistance in constructing a framework within which individual programing techniques can be located. At the risk of oversimplification, then, the connectionist position of Thorndike and Skinner and the configurationist position of Tolman and Lewin will be examined in an effort to identify some features of them which can be found reflected in response-centered and stimulus-centered programing approaches and techniques. A fuller statement of these positions can be found in several reference sources (such as 14, 28, 36) and in many textbooks on learning.

The connectionist position, as noted, is response oriented. Learning occurs gradually as the probability of certain responses is increased through repeated instances in which a reinforcement or reward follows the occurrence of the response. Since learning can take place only when opportunities for reinforcement exist, the learner must be performing the desired response actively; and, since many instances of the response must occur for any degree of learning permanence to be achieved, numerous trials are required. Complex responses are assembled, again by reinforcement, from single units by establishing a behavioral chain in which one part of the complex response leads to the next. The stimulus environment in which learning occurs is critical primarily to the extent that the tendency for the newly learned response to occur in other situations will depend on the degree of stimulus correspondence between the two situations. To get the response to occur only under specific circumstances, responses are reinforced when they occur in these circumstances but not in others. Similarly, to improve the quality of a response, reinforcement is applied differentially to gradually "shape" the response to the desired degree of proficiency. Motivation is regarded as those conditions which permit reinforcement, e.g., water deprivation will permit the use of water as a reinforcement. There need be no logical relationship between the kind of response being strengthened and the kind of reinforcement used; a reinforcing state of affairs effective for one response ought to be equally effective for all others. Most connectionist theorists feel the learning process is mechanistic; unobservable intervention, if it occurs, does not affect the course of learning. Thus, all that is required to promote response acquisition is a responding organism which is properly reinforced when instances of the desired behavior occur.

The configurationist position is stimulus oriented. It assumes that learning consists of the formation of associations which, unlike the mechanistic stimulus-response relationships described by the connectionists, are essentially cognitive phenomena. Stimuli in the organism's environment are perceived in an organized and structured manner; which stimuli and in what organization are dependent upon the characteristics of the stimuli themselves and the previous experiences of the learner. The associations formed among these stimuli are a consequence of the dynamics of perceptual organization and reorganization, a process which may continue long after the original stimuli have disappeared. As a result, a pattern of readinesses and expectancies are formed which the learner then can use to obtain desirable goals. Performance is not essential to learning; rather, it is a product of learning in the sense that learning permits goal-directed, problem-solving behavior to occur under the proper motivating conditions. Learning itself occurs when perceived stimuli become related to each other, either spatially, temporally, or conceptually in the form of a symbolic representation. Not all stimuli are perceived, however, nor do all those which are perceived become incorporated in the relational pattern. Thus, in order to insure that the desired learning will occur, the learner's attention must be directed at the relevant aspects of his environment, and these must be arranged in such a way as to facilitate the formation of new cognitive relationships. Insight and ideation are important determiners of postlearning performance and must therefore be promoted by the instructional process. Most configurationist theorists believe that learning is cognitive and that the outcome may or may not be reflected in later performance independently of the success of learning. Thus, it is what to do, not doing, which is learned and later applied when conditions are appropriate for performance.

Approaches to Program Construction

The basic approaches to the preparation of programed materials which can be derived from each of these positions cannot be contrasted easily. As is apparent from these brief descriptions of the connectionist and configurationist theories, the distinction between them is not so much one of opposing methods but, rather, one of conflicting emphases. The cognitive aspects of the configurationist position are as difficult and foreign to the connectionist as his mechanistic principles are to the configurationist. While the connectionist is attempting to condition responses, the configurationist is attempting to generate insights; while the configurationist is providing the learner with purpose, the connectionist is providing the learner with practice. Unfortunately, this disparity in emphasis frequently has been disregarded by those who seize upon one variable for an empirical investigation designed to resolve some major issue in programing technique. Comparing an isolated feature of one approach with its apparent counterpart in the other frequently is an injustice to both positions regardless of the outcome of the investigation. There may be considerable value, on the other hand, in describing how the techniques stemming from each broad approach are used to overcome specific types of anticipated learner difficulties. These issues will be explored following an overview of the approach taken by response-centered and stimulus-centered programers.

The approach of a response-centered programer is quite consistent with connectionist theory. To insure a response will be learned, each occurrence of it is followed by a reinforcement and, to insure it will be retained, there must be numerous instances when the desired response is reinforced. The need for a large number of reinforcement opportunities is reflected in the gradually increasing complexity and difficulty of a response within a given sequence, which heightens the likelihood of a correct response at each step, and in the practice of using relatively short frames. The stimulus characteristics of the material presented to the learner are particularly significant only when a discrimination is being formed or unless the initial occurrences of a desired response can be made more probable by using discriminative stimuli known to be previously effective in evoking that response. Because he assumes learning is a direct result of reinforced practice and only that which is practiced will be learned, the response-centered programer is likely to insist that the behavior represented by the level of proficiency aimed for be required as part of the program-controlled learning process. To the response-centered programer, objectives such as understanding, appreciation, and judgment are achieved through a progression of instances in which the discriminations necessary for later correct responding are learned. Finally, the approach used by the response-centered programer is organized around the types of performance to be mastered rather than the subject matter content to be taught; the strategies employed generally are felt to be applicable to any topic so long as the response topographies are comparable.

A stimulus-centered programer is likely to stress configurationist principles in his approach. To begin with, requiring a response on the part of the learner is not to insure practice but to test the adequacy of learning. Thus, to control the course of learning, effort is directed at improving the quality of the presentation. To accomplish this, the material to be learned is organized and structured in a logical and familiar context with particular concern for the intensity, coherence, and meaningfulness of new information. Because his goal is intelligent learning, the stimulus-centered programer is likely to provide the learner with a clear sense of purpose and direction. He is apt to avoid fragmenting material into steps so small that the main ideas are lost and the development of creative insights is made difficult or impossible. The composition of the program is designed to encourage cognitive mediation, to make the learner think about what is being taught so that the new relationships necessary for proficiency can be acquired. The learner's motivation is an important concern of the stimulus-centered programer, and therefore he takes special pains to give the learner a clear understanding of his progress and the usefulness of his accomplishments. Stimulating the imagination of the learner is more likely to be regarded as a goal of the program than the mastery of specific details. In this respect, the stimulus-centered programer sees his approach as being particularly well suited to providing intelligent learners with instruction on the complex abstractions that are the objectives of modern education, and, as a result, the strategies he is likely to use will tend to reflect the unique properties of the subject matter being taught.

Techniques Used in Program Development

Within these two broad approaches, there are a variety of techniques employed in hopes of overcoming anticipated learner difficulties. Furthermore, a considerable number of program writers seem to be combining the best, or worst, of these two approaches in the materials they produce. There is a fairly smooth continuum of programing technique, then, between the stimulus-centered and response-centered extremes. Regardless of which approach is selected, certain learner problems must be dealt with, and, because they are independent of the approach, these problems provide a convenient way of looking at the specific techniques which have evolved from each approach. As will be seen, the techniques used by response-centered programers often tend to be stated more explicitly than those used by stimulus-centered programers, possibly because response-centered programers exist in greater numbers or possibly because their approach is less familiar to the educators and training specialists who develop, use, or evaluate their materials. In some instances, therefore, less detail can be provided concerning the stimulus-centered approach since it simply has never been specified. In other cases, the problem has been explored from many points of view, some of which are neither stimulus centered nor response centered, but which represent some sort of middle ground. Finally, it will become apparent that not all that is preached is practiced. Many individual programers who would tend to identify themselves with one approach create materials which better reflect the other. Such inconsistencies are apt to be fruitful hypotheses for research, however, in the sense that there is still much to be learned about learning.

Response Requirement

The response requirement is perhaps the first aspect of learning a programer must consider when beginning a program. The options available to him include overt, covert, and reading modes, as well as constructed and selected response formats. He can require either long or short constructed responses or any number of options for selected responses or mix overt and covert modes. The response can serve to provide practice to the learner, assessment of the learner's progress, or the means for keeping the learner active, and presumably attentive, in the learning situation. The response-centered programer is quite likely to replicate the procedures used in the behavior laboratory. There, reinforcement is provided to the learner only when the desired behavior or some predetermined component of it occurs. As a consequence, the response-centered programer will strive for constructed responses of gradually increasing scope and complexity which eventually correspond to the desired level of mastery. The stimulus-centered programer is more likely to regard the response feature of programs as a means of evaluating learning than as an opportunity for practice. Since he would not regard responding per se as a necessary condition for learning, he has no need for constructed responses, particularly those which are lengthy and time consuming. The stimulus-centered programer is likely to feel that, as a means of measuring student progress, selected responses to well-written multiple-choice questions are fully adequate and, in addition, are quite amenable to automation. Neither approach would be firmly opposed to covert responding provided there was some assurance that the learner did make the response, even if recorded evidence was collected only periodically. Activity for its own sake would not be consistent with either approach; both the stimulus-centered and response-centered programer would argue that if a response were required, it would have to be pertinent to the objectives of the lesson. Reading would not be considered a mode of responding to either kind of programer. The response-centered writer would feel that reading what otherwise would belong as responses in the blanks afforded little control over the learner's practice, while the stimulus-centered writer would not find it necessary or valuable to consider reading as responding at all.

Even though it is apparent that the response requirement adopted is a characteristic and not a critical test of the approach used, many descriptions of programing technique emphasize the response as an important determiner of program effectiveness. For example, Skinner (61, p. 95) states:

The student should compose his response rather than select it from a set of alternatives, as he would in a multiple-choice scheme. One reason for this is that we want him to recall rather than merely recognize—to make a response as well as see that it is right. An equally important reason is that effective multiple-choice material must contain plausible wrong answers, which are out of place in the delicate process of shaping behavior because they strengthen unwanted responses. Our ability to remember wrong facts because we recall having read them somewhere is notorious.

Deterline (11) "favors constructed response programs whenever the aimed-at terminal behavior is the ability to verbalize conceptual material, and for multiple-choice programs only when the terminal behavior consists only of the ability to recognize, select or discriminate between the correct and incorrect choices." Crowder (10, pp. 150-51) is fairly definite on the role of the response in stimulus-centered programing when he states:

As I have indicated, I believe the practice consideration is irrelevant, particularly in intrinsic programs. We use multiple-choice questions for the purely practical reason that we think of the questions as primarily serving a diagnostic or testing function, for which the multiple-choice question is directly useful while the open-ended question is not. . . . We expect the student to give the right answer to a question because he has understood the material he has just read on the point in question, not because he has given the response in question more often than he has given another response.

Pressey (50, p. 32), in criticizing programs with constructed responses, points out that "some half-dozen experiments seem to agree that, in a given time, no more learning may actually result than if that same material were organized in continuous discourse (questions and their answers turned into declarative sentences) and simply read!" Finally, Fry (17, p. 151) compromises, "We may well expect to find that sometimes overt responses will be better and sometimes covert responses will be better, depending upon various factors involved in the particular learning situation."

Although the response-centered approach favors overt, constructed responses, alternate techniques could insure that the necessary practice occurs without undue effort on the part of the learner. For example, the blanks in a program could be responded to covertly except for random instances where an overt, recorded response is required. Cook (3, p. 122) suggests that this type of response requirement "will be effective in establishing habits of clear and explicit thinking," since it establishes the conditions under which complex covert verbal behavior can be reinforced. Evans (15), Morton (45), and others have emphasized the role of discrimination in the acquisition of complex skills; the strategy suggested by their work is that the production of many kinds of responses can be facilitated substantially if practice in making the response is preceded by instruction leading to accuracy in choosing a correct example of that response from among a set of alternatives. In these cases, multiple-choice responding adequately develops the necessary discrimination skill needed for maintaining one's own responses since the learning involved is largely perceptual. Rothkopf (54) approaches programing from the position of verbal learning research. He suggests that the primary purpose of responding is to control "inspection behaviors" and thus insure that the entire frame is carefully read. Not all stimulus-centered programers favor multiple-choice responding. Kay (31) reports on the use of constructed responses as a means of assessing learning from textual material. After the learner completes his response, he exposes the correct answer and compares the two; then either he proceeds or he requests a further explanation depending on whether he regards his response as adequate. The incongruity inherent in equating constructed responses with relevant practice has been noted many times, particularly with respect to such topics as arithmetic, where far more is being learned than is evidenced by the learner legibly writing a particular digit in response to a given problem. To complicate matters further, the Skinner passage quoted above points to the "notorious" ability to remember wrong facts that have been read and not expressly practiced. That learning can occur without observable rehearsal is obvious, but whether this involves cognition or simply covert responding is not obvious.

Stimulus Content

The stimulus content presented to the learner is another programing aspect which must be considered. Although the options available to the program writer for manipulating stimulus content are not as clearly defined as they are for response requirements, the stimulus-centered and response-centered approaches differ substantially on the criteria used for selecting stimulus content and on the amount of material which should be presented to the learner at any one time. A response-centered program is likely to contain three types of stimulus material (33): cue, context, and enrichment. Cueing is that part of a frame which assists the learner by insuring that the correct response is evoked. Context is the new setting in which the response is to occur. Enrichment consists of information, such as might be used for motivational purposes, which the learner is expected to respond to but not master. A writer using a response-centered approach will likely decrease the extent of cueing and increase the complexity of context within any sequence of frames. This gradual "weaning" is designed so that the learner will practice making the desired criterion responses without assistance by the end of the sequence. Enrichment in a response-centered program probably is more of a reflection of writing style than programing approach.

A stimulus-centered program contains two kinds of stimulus content (8): a unit of material to be read, usually a paragraph, and a question designed to assess whether the expected learning took place. The content of the text material is prepared so that the information contained in it is communicated to the learner as effectively as possible. This means not only that the passage must be clear and unambiguous, but that the student must be properly motivated and oriented as well. If the program employs branching, as many stimulus-centered programs do, the passage also must reflect the reason why it is being presented to the learner at that point. Thus, the text associated with an immediately preceding correct answer will include a repeated or reworded statement of the correct answer, transition introducing the new topic in relation to what already has been learned, and a single new idea succinctly stated and explained. The text following a wrong answer repeats the incorrect alternative, describes why it is the wrong answer, and then provides the learner with the additional explanation he needs to then get the correct answer on the next attempt. The question part of a frame in a stimulus-centered program is designed to diagnose the reasons for learner errors as well as assess his progress. All incorrect alternatives should reflect realistic possibilities of misunderstanding; preferably, they should be derived empirically from the responses obtained from learners during program development.

The techniques used to prepare the stimulus content of programs representing both approaches is quite varied. Lumsdaine (38), Meyer (44), Fry (17), and others have listed numerous varieties of cueing that have been or could be employed. Broadly, these can be divided into two groups, denotative prompts and connotative cues. The former includes the use of physical controls such as underscoring or italic

type, indicating the first few letters of the desired response and desig-
nating the number of words or letters in the desired response and the
use of prompt words which are partially obscured by overprinting or
some other method. The latter includes the use of sentence structure,
relational words, induction from instances, opposites, rhyming, and
other forms of adjusting the wording of the frame. Pictures and diagrams can be used as connotative cues also. Schaefer (55) uses the normal redundancy of written passages to cue the meaning of unfamiliar
foreign words. Techniques for insuring the adequacy of context have
been specified still less carefully and systematically. Although there is
general agreement that the terminal frames in a program should be
comparable in difficulty to the "test" situation and without cueing,
little work has been done within the field of programing to define the
conditions which will insure adequate transfer of training from the instruction contained in the program. As for enrichment, the only suggestions seem to be to keep it minimal. In describing the preparation of the
text passages for stimulus-centered programs, Tucker (67) notes that
the concept of learning used "is a primitive but compelling communication theory. . . . Errors in communication are reduced by presenting subject matter in small (but not necessarily atomistic) units, that are pains-
takingly prepared so as to reduce the likelihood of misunderstanding
(transmission error)." Pressey (51, p. 3) suggests that "the initial presentation might most often best be a very well organized and well
written substantial statement much like a chapter in a good textbook!"
He continues, "Problems may be explicated in autoinstructional matter
supplementary to the text; and there, or perhaps every three or four
pages in the book, clusters of autoexplicating queries may keep check
on understanding. But a book's structured coherence and orderliness
of presentation, and its convenience for overview, review, and reference, can be kept." As to the nature of the questions used in a stimulus-
centered program, Crowder (9, p. 122) indicates they should "a) Determine whether the student has learned the material just presented.
b) Select appropriate corrective material if the student has not learned.
c) Provide desirable practice with the concept involved. d) Serve to keep
the student actively working at the material. e) Presumably, if the student gets the question right, serve a desirable motivational purpose."

   It is apparent that program writers, particularly those favoring the
response-centered approach, have not been able to derive principles

and techniques for the preparation of stimulus content from their respective positions with anywhere near the explicitness applied to the response requirement. There have been some noteworthy exceptions, however. For example, Stolurow (63) emphasizes the relationship between the stimulus content of an instructional sequence and the response requirements associated with it. One suggestion he makes (p. 91) is that progressive changes in stimuli and responses over items should be asynchronous, defined as "cue-stimulus change accompanied by no change in response or no change in cue-stimulus accompanied by change in response." Another attempt to identify the appropriate stimulus content of program frames is the "ruleg" system developed by Evans, Homme, and Glaser (16). Using this technique, a matrix of "rules" is prepared which yields all the permutations of rules or principles to be taught in a program sequence. The cells of the matrix then are filled with appropriate examples (or "e.g.'s"). The programer then has available to him a set of stimulus content to choose from when preparing his program. Several authors (see 63) specifically suggest the use of a logic model in the development of a program, the liberal use of examples, and beginning with content that is familiar to the learner. Gilbert (21) suggests the use of interim cues or "mediators" which will help evoke the correct response in criterion situations. In his very effective sequence for teaching electrical resistor color codes (see 47, p. 301), Gilbert prompts existing responses already at high strength in the learner's repertoire, such as "one brown penny," to maintain the response "one" to the stimulus "brown." Response-centered programers as a group tend to avoid explanations as part of the stimulus content of their frames. This keeps them brief which, in turn, provides ample opportunities for reinforcing learner responses but, also, often leads to frames which routinely employ copying to cue the desired response. Copy cues are difficult to "fade" or "vanish," and frames containing copy cues are not particularly interesting to read. A widely recommended alternative is the use of cues which are as subtle as possible, but yet effectively control the response. One technique for devising subtle cues is to use familiar word associations, whether they are logical or not. For instance, "Because they find uncles indigestible, aardvarks eat —————" provides the desired response without explanation or a cue so direct that subsequent frames would be required to withdraw it.

Confirmation Characteristics

The next general category of programing issues dealt with by techniques having contrasting theoretical bases concerns confirmation characteristics. Superficially, at least, the opposition between approaches is clear on this point; the stimulus-centered programers consider the confirmation as "feedback" which provides the learner with information, while the response-centered programers view confirmation as "reinforcement" which heightens the probability that the response will occur again at a later time. Thus, Uttal (68, p. 172) states, "The success of teaching machines will depend largely, I believe, on the degree to which they provide feedback to the student and are responsive to the student's learning needs. The desired relationship between student and teaching machine may be termed 'conversational interaction,' by analogy with the relationship between a student and a human tutor." Glaser (22, p. 10) takes the opposite view when he states: "A central process for the acquisition of behavior is reinforcement. Behavior is acquired as a result of a contingent relationship between the response of an organism and a consequent event. . . . Reinforcement must follow the occurrence of the behavior being taught." From the point of view of a stimulus-centered programer, the confirmation following a learning trial must be informative not only as to the correctness of the response in terms of some standard or criterion, but as to the degree and type of error, if it occurred, as well. As Crowder (7, p. 26) points out:

The criterion for whether a particular topic is programmable (in the branching technique) is whether there is anything that can be usefully said to a student who has made an error. If we can say to the student who has erred: a) your answer is wrong; b) this is *what* is wrong with your answer; c) this is *why* this feature of your answer is wrong; d) this is *how* you go about figuring out what the right answer is; and e) now go back and try again, then we are dealing with programmable material.

To the response-centered programer, the appearance of the correct response typically has been used as the confirmation, although not all of these programers would concur with Goldberg (24, p. 16) that "desired learning is automatically 'reinforced' with programed instruction by immediate confirmation of each correct response that the learner makes. The learner's self-awareness of successful responding is inherently rewarding."

The role of confirmation in stimulus-centered and response-centered programs tends to be differentiated on the basis of the correctness of the learner's response. In a stimulus-centered program, emphasis usually is given to instances where the learner was wrong. For instance, Annett (1, p. 284) suggests that "tentative responses in the problem solving/learning situation are not necessarily attempts at *the right* answer or response. They can be attempts to extract information from the environment. A wrong response can be just as informative as a right response." In a response-centered program, the appearance of a correct answer serves as a reinforcement only when the response was correct; otherwise, the trial is wasted. This leads Kay (31, p. 12) to the conclusion that "since the system can only cope with correct responses (they alone are reinforced), it is essential that students should make the minimum of errors." Later, he continues (p. 29), "The consensus of opinion is that when knowledge of results confirms that a response is correct it does act as a reinforcer, but where the response is wrong it does not. Hence the accent in linear programmes is upon being correct." There is an obvious paradox in how correct responses are dealt with in a stimulus-centered program and in how incorrect responses are dealt with in a response-centered program. A learner who does select a correct answer in a stimulus-centered program is not given further explanation on that point; instead, he is informed that he is correct, often shown a positive statement of the desired answer, and introduced to new material. This seems to be precisely the technique used by response-centered programers to reinforce a correct response. Similarly, when a learner provides an incorrect response in a response-centered program, he is shown the correct answer. But, simple substitutes, such as the statement "You are correct," should prove equally effective as a confirmation of the correct answer if the purpose of the correct answer is solely to provide reinforcement and not information. There is ample reason to believe with Cook and Mechner (4, p. 4) that "although knowledge of results is the most usual form of reinforcement in programed instruction, other varieties are possible. Advancing to the next frame of the program can be reinforcing in its own right because it indicates mastery of the previous step and an opportunity to enlarge a skill. The number of frames successfully completed can be tallied, with some extrinsic incentive made contingent upon this total."

The theoretical problem posed by the response-centered programer's use of information-containing reinforcement to the connectionist learning-theory position has been explored by Lumsdaine (39). In suggesting the use of a temporal contiguity model, especially the one formulated by Guthrie, instead of a reinforcement model as a basis for programed instruction, Lumsdaine (39, p. 143) notes the relative emphasis given to cueing and prompting, as opposed to reinforcement: ". . . when adequate prompting is provided variations in the kind of confirmation or feedback given are much less important than when less prompting is provided." He continues (p. 143):

Similarly, a number of observers of programmed learning behavior have noted informally that in a well-cued program students may tend to ignore or bypass the confirmation or correction subframe. . . . the correction panel affords a cue or prompt for a further response, generally at an implicit or covert level, rather than merely strengthening the practice effect of the response already made. This fact is of particular importance when the student's first response has been in error; he can now supersede his incorrect response with the correct one.

There is growing support, also, that reinforcement can be defined as an event which occasions a preemptive response, i.e., allows a response at higher strength to occur (48). Thus, it would be consistent with the response-centered position to suppose that exposing the subsequent step in the program would be as reinforcing as a confirmation panel. This approach would be somewhat similar to what Barlow (2) calls "conversational chaining"; in using this technique, the programer incorporates the answer to each frame in the stimulus content of the frame that follows it. Not only does this tend to reduce the bulk of a program but it also provides a degree of smoothness often found lacking in very short frames.

Error Control

The confirmation aspect of programed instruction is tied closely to the issue of error control. Whether or not the occurrence of errors during learning affects achievement is perhaps not as crucial a problem as whether the occurrence of errors affects the efficiency of instruction. A response-centered programer is likely to emphasize that learner errors should be minimal. Not only is it undesirable to have a student practice making the wrong response, but the consequences of being

wrong could prove aversive and, in addition, an opportunity to reinforce a correct response has not been utilized. A stimulus-centered
programer is concerned with learner errors, but tends to believe that
error rate is not optimally zero when considered in terms of instructional efficiency or the variability among learners. The difference in
viewpoint is particularly pronounced with respect to the consequence
of an error: whether it can be ignored, must be overcome, or actually
contributes to learning. In part, the first two possibilities relate to the
separate problem of adaptive sequencing which presupposes that errors
are not desirable per se and that they must be dealt with by the program. There is not universal agreement that errors are harmful, however. Configurationist theory does not concede that errors impair learning and, in fact, several stimulus-centered programers suggest that
errors may be integral or at least beneficial to the learning process.
For example, Pressey (51, p. 4) suggests that the items he would have
follow the initial presentation of a lesson should consist of "multiple-
choice questions with only such wrong alternatives as express common misunderstandings and a right answer notably clear. There is
evidence that contrary to theoretical inference, students do, after auto-
instruction with such items, *less* often make the so-labeled mistakes,
more often get things right, and transfer or generalize so that the
gains appear on recall and yet other types of end tests." In another
paper, Pressey (52, p. 6) makes a similar point: "It seems to be taken
as axiomatic that wrong answers in a multiple-choice item mislead and
that the task of discrimination does not aid recall. The writer has seen
no satisfactory evidence that any unfortunate results follow from a
wrong choice in an autoinstructional item dealing with meaningful
matter, if the wrong is at once shown to be wrong and the right to be
correct. Instead, the presence of wrong choices can clarify meanings."

Cram (5, p. 34) suggests that the apparent effect of errors in multiple-
choice programs is not as clear as is often implied. He identifies two
factors which may diminish the effects that errors might have on
achievement: "A. The law of frequency: The student may sometimes
get a wrong answer, but in each frame he ultimately gets a correct
answer. By chance he will get more correct than incorrect answers.
B. The law of recency: No matter how many wrong answers a student
may try in response to a question, the correct answer is always the last
one and is more likely to be remembered because it comes closest to

the reinforcement." Also to be considered is the contention of Crowder (7, p. 25) and others that some error is important with respect to motivation: "I think I should mention, in connection with the motivational function served by the questions in the material, that I have never been an advocate of questions so easy that the learner rarely, if ever, makes an error. I believe that the questions should be of sufficient level of difficulty that the student has the feeling of earning the satisfaction that he receives from getting an answer correct, and I think experience is accumulating that shows that if the questions asked are too easy the student loses motivation after a while." On the other hand, and also for the purpose of maintaining student interest, Holland (29, p. 219) insists, "Not only is reinforcement needed for learning, a high density of correct items is necessary because material which generates errors is punishing. . . . In our experience with teaching machines we have also observed that students stop work when the material is so difficult that they make many errors. Furthermore, they become irritated, almost aggressive, when errors are made."

Individual Differences

Whether they have been planned for or not, some number of errors are likely to be made by learners during the course of the program. What is done in anticipation of them concerns the problem of individual differences. In the typical response-centered program, revisions of the materials are continued, usually, until a minimum error rate is achieved. Even though the goal may be zero errors, however, Senter's Law (56) prevails: "Senter's Law states that it is impossible to write an item so simple that no student will miss it." The technique used in response-centered programs for overcoming the effects of the errors that do occur, while not explicitly stated, seems to be based on the use of sufficient redundancy in response opportunities to insure that reinforcement for the correct response will occur with high probability. The errors that are successfully overcome by this approach are very likely spurious errors, however—errors not made consistently by individual learners. They do not account for differences in ability nor differences in prior attainment. Spurious errors are similarly ignored in most stimulus-centered programs. The adaptive sequencing typical of many stimulus-centered programs is based on a limited range of previously established alternatives, generally presented in the form of a multiple-choice question. Errors which might otherwise have been made by individual learners are concealed in that corresponding response alternatives do not exist. The probable effects of these spurious, or idiosyncratic, errors are apt to be more of a concern to response-centered than stimulus-centered programers. The configurationist, as noted previously, might even regard occasional errors as facilitating, either as an aid to the development of concepts or as a means of maintaining the attention of the learner. The connectionist might regard the spurious error as equivalent to irrelevant activity in the operant conditioning situation which eventually is diminished in frequency as the rate of desirable responses is increased with regular reinforcement. The small number of trials devoted to each response in a program may result in spurious errors affecting achievement, however, since this would limit opportunities for further correct practice. Finally, it is likely that the incidence of spurious errors in responding to a program will be reflected in a similar incidence of unrelated errors during the criterion examination which would make it difficult to establish any causal relationship between program and examination errors.

Systematic sources of response error can be dealt with by various kinds of corrective and adaptive sequencing. The two basic techniques used for these purposes might be described as "looping" and "tracking." A loop is a corrective sequence of frames which can be inserted into the normal sequence; a track is an alternate sequence of frames which replaces a segment of the normal sequence. Which is used depends on some fundamental assumptions regarding the learning process. By and large, the connectionist position assumes that the circumstances which are optimal for one learner will be equally optimal for all similar learners. Thus, most response-centered programers feel that learners may vary in the rate at which they learn and in what they must learn considering their previous attainment, but do not vary in how they learn best. On the other hand, the configurationist is not likely to make this assumption; one learner may learn best by one method, and a second by another (see 30). On the basis of this assumption, several different paths might be employed in a stimulus-centered program to achieve the same objective. In practice, of course, the amount of adaptability that can be built into a program is limited. However, multiple tracks which reflect patterns of individual differences, just as loops reflect the effects of these differences, would be consistent with the theory underlying stimulus-centered programs. Whether or not differences in mode of learning among individuals are considered, two further problems remain which can be dealt with using adaptive sequencing. The first concerns the difference in previous preparation of the learners with respect to the subject matter being taught. Stating the assumed prerequisites of a program does not eliminate the need to consider variability among learners with respect to these prerequisites or to the objectives of the program. Some learners will fail to have the skills and knowledge they need as background to acquire new skills and knowledge from at least some sequences in the program. Similarly, a few learners already may have mastered some of the topics included in the program and would not need to be exposed to the corresponding sequences of frames. In these cases, loops can be provided, either in the form of sections to be omitted if a test or "gate" item is answered correctly or in the form of corrective instruction designed to remedy particular defects. Interestingly, the response-centered programer tends to emphasize "bypassing" or the omission of material pertinent to an already existing level of attainment, while a stimulus-centered programer is more likely to emphasize "branching" or the inclusion of material pertinent to an observed deficiency. The second problem concerns the size of increments between steps, the amount of new learning which can be expected during a single step, and the amount of review or repetition needed for mastery and acceptable retention. Here, either loops or alternate tracks could be used as long as the sequence of frames was adapted to the differential requirements of the learners. One version would have more, and presumably shallower, steps than another, thus providing smaller increments and greater opportunities for review. Various techniques for implementing looping and tracking have been discussed by Shettel (57).

One last aspect of individual differences which often is considered is the ability of the learner to acquire new knowledge. As Klaus (34) has suggested, it is possible to use the distinction between "mental age" and "intelligence quotient" as two separate predictors of the performance of an individual learner using a program. How much the learner already knows or already can do is what is directly assessed by an intelligence test. This score is reported as a mental age based on comparisons of the learner's performance with that of normative groups. To the extent that success in using a program depends upon these skills, mental age is a reasonable measure of whether the learner has the requisite skills to enable him to learn from the program. His vocabulary, mathematical skills, use of visual materials, awareness of relationships, and so forth must be at some minimum level inherently established by the program writer in preparing his material, and some requisite mental age score—or its equivalent, depending on the program—could be established for this purpose. On the other hand, an intelligence quotient compares mental age with chronological age to yield a measure of that individual's rate of previous learning. A child of ten with a mental age of eight has taken ten years to acquire what the average child acquires in eight years; he is a slow learner. This child also might be expected to be a slow learner from a program for the same reasons he learned slowly from previous experiences. Thus, while intelligence quotient should not be predictive of what will be attained from the program, it should be predictive of the rate of learning. The self-pacing aspect of programed instruction can accommodate individual differences in rate of learning; however, it cannot accommodate learner differences in entering performance without redundancy, adaptive sequencing, or recycling through segments of the program.

Program Organization

A remaining issue which most programers are likely to consider is program organization. Both the learning experiences offered by the program and the content can be organized in hopes of minimizing learner difficulties. The stimulus-centered programer can be expected to be particularly sensitive to the problem of program organization. For example, in discussing the best way to present material to be learned, Pressey (51, p. 3) suggests that "programmers have been cutting it into little pieces each responded to, but now recognize that one may learn from reading without responding. Then how big may the piece be? The writer has stressed that the bigger piece may have structure which should be made evident, and that first consideration as well as review or selective use may make it desirable that the learner can move about freely in the material." The response-centered programer is almost equally concerned about the sequence of instruction. For instance, Fry

(17, p. 3) notes: "Because the subject matter is broken into small bits, the author must think carefully about the learning steps involved, and the result is a much better sequence of presentation. Careful sequence also embodies the notion of shaping or gradually leading the student toward the desired goals by rewarding him for activity that more and more closely approximates those goals." The concept of shaping expressed by Fry has been suggested by many authors as the model for organizing a response-centered program. This term, frequently found in discussions of operant conditioning, refers to the gradual development of a skilled response through successively narrowing the criterion used to determine when a reinforcement will be provided. However, there is a substantial difference between the shaping of a skilled response and the transfer of a response already at high levels of strength so that it will occur under new stimulus conditions, which is the objective of most verbal programs. Thus, it has been suggested that the model for a response-centered program is more consistent with the paradigm of classical conditioning (69), contiguity learning (39), human verbal learning (54), or transfer of training (32) than it is with the paradigm of operant conditioning. Each of these alternate paradigms might have different implications for the ordering of content and learning experiences within a response-centered program.

On a practical level, several schemes have been proposed for the organization of content in a program. Mager (42) has proposed that the sequence of topics in a program might be initially learner determined; that is, the sequence of topics should be in the order selected by the learner and not by the instructor. This is very much in contrast with letting the "inner logic" of the content (41) determine the arrangement of material. If several objectives are being programed together, it is possible to teach one thoroughly before proceeding to the next, to try to present all possibly conflicting steps in as close proximity as possible (20), or to gradually spiral through the material (23). A quite elaborate procedure for the organization of program content which is based on the ruleg system has been proposed by Thomas and others (64). Stolurow (63) devotes considerable attention to the optimum organization of learning experiences, suggesting, for example, that the content of a program be ordered according to rules of logic. Some attempts, too, have been made to consider the sequence of instruction from the standpoint of program effectiveness. Klaus (35), for example, suggests that a learner first should be taught to discriminate a correct from an incorrect answer, then to edit answers, and finally to produce his own answers completely. This approach has the advantage of allowing the learner to make unique, constructed responses during instruction on skills, such as argumentation or technical writing, when the confirmation panels in the program could not anticipate all acceptable learner responses. Gilbert (20) proposes that whenever "behavioral chains" are to be learned, instruction should begin with the end of the chain and gradually proceed backward. This approach insures that procedural skills will be practiced extensively and as a unit during instruction. Gagné (18) approaches the problem of sequencing from the point of view of a hierarchy of learning sets, identified from a progressive analysis of final and interim objectives. As each successive subordinate objective is defined, it is further analyzed with respect to what the learner would have to be able to do to accomplish the performance specified by that objective, given only direct instructions.

The categories which have been used in contrasting stimulus-centered and response-centered programing approaches were chosen not because of their dominance in experimental literature on programed instruction, but because they appeared to reflect those issues which are likely to be paramount in any theory of instructional technology. This list, which includes response requirements, stimulus content, confirmation characteristics, error control, individual differences, and program organization, far from exhausts the entire list of variables which should be manipulated so as to enhance learning from a program. For example, step size, intermittent reinforcement, program format, meaningfulness of material, and reading difficulty could be modified experimentally with probably enlightening and profitable results. However, these latter variables tend to be determined by, rather than themselves determine, the basic characteristics of the approach selected by the programer. The issues which have been described also cannot be considered as the consequences of any one programer's diligence or ingenuity; instead, they are the issues which are pertinent to all methods of instruction. As noted previously, existing programs tend to deal with only a limited spectrum of human learning and tend to employ only a narrow range of controls over learning experiences, and new advances in instructional technology are not likely to occur within this framework. Programed instruction is an outgrowth of learning research; aside from its obviously greater practical value, it is no different conceptually from the maze, the pigeon box, or the nonsense syllable. The issues which can and will be investigated using programed instruction as a paradigm more than likely reflect the dominant issues of current learning theory, at least as it might be applied within the constraints of existing instructional practices. In this sense, programed instruction follows rather than leads new advances in understanding how learning occurs.

Integrated Styles of Programing

Within each of the basic approaches, considerable latitude exists both in which issues are emphasized and in what strategies are employed to deal with them. On the other hand, specific techniques cannot be applied in isolation. For better or for worse, certain patterns of techniques have evolved which often are cited as fundamental styles attributable to the efforts and influence of particular individuals. Two of these styles, those of Pressey and Crowder, are basically stimulus centered while two others, those of Skinner and Gilbert, are basically response centered. A quick review of each of these styles will give some idea of the way in which various techniques can be organized into a functional system. The diversity which still exists among styles even after a fundamental approach has been selected also may illustrate the extent to which further efforts are required before programed instruction turns from an art into a technology.

Pressey

One of the pioneers in the development of programed instruction was Sidney L. Pressey. During the 1920's Pressey became aware of the inefficiencies which occurred when teachers called upon individual students to recite their lessons in class. Only one student could recite at any one time; and, while he was reciting, the remaining students in the class became bored and listless, lost their eagerness after trying to obtain the teacher's attention time and time again, failed to get feedback and correction from the teacher, and sooner or later sat passively being exposed to information rather than actively participating in the classroom situation.

As is well known, Pressey felt considerable improvement would result if it were possible to automate the recitation aspect of the instructional process.

The procedures in mastery of drill and informational material were in many instances simple and definite enough to permit handling of much routine teaching by mechanical means. The average teacher is woefully burdened by such routine of drill and information-fixing. It would seem highly desirable to lift from her shoulders as much as possible of this burden and make her freer for those inspirational and thought-stimulating activities which are, presumably, the real function of the teacher (49, p. 35).

Pressey reasoned that if every student in the class could be asked questions at the same time, and receive an indication whether or not he was correct, all students would experience active responding and have immediate confirmation of the correctness of each response. Pressey proposed the use of the same kind of quizzes or examinations teachers typically used in the classroom, but which were inefficient as instructional devices because the student typically completed the entire test and then had to wait two or three days before finding out whether he was correct. The technique Pressey developed was to expose a question to the student and permit him to answer by pressing a key, by inserting his pencil tip in a punchboard, or by means of chemically treated paper. Because the primary purpose of the materials was to indicate to the student whether or not he was learning what he was supposed to learn, multiple-choice responding was used.

The impact of these early efforts to automate instruction was limited, however, and it was not until the recent surge of interest in programed instruction that Pressey elaborated on this basic formulation. His present position is that the animal laboratory research of the past few years has tended to dominate programed instruction and that the approach which is now considered orthodox by many programers should be given close, critical inspection.

The archvillain, leading so many people astray, is declared to be learning theory! No less a charge is made than that the whole trend of American research and theory as regards learning has been based on a false premise—that the important features of human learning are to be found in animals. Instead, the all-important fact is that human has transcended animal learning. Language, number, such skills as silent reading, make possible facilitations of learning, and kinds of learning, impossible even for the apes. Autoinstruction should enhance such potentials. Instead, current animal derived procedures in autoinstruction destroy meaningful structure to present fragments serially in programs, and replace processes of cognitive clarification with largely rote reinforcings of bit learnings (51, p. 5).

Pressey's current approach, which he terms "adjunct autoinstruction," he feels, "keeps, makes use of, and enhances meaningful structure, the autoinstruction serving to clarify and extend meaningfulness" (51, p. 5). In essence, the learner would first be exposed to a substantial and organized unit of instruction such as a textbook chapter, a field trip, or some other learning experience. With respect to this initial presentation, Pressey feels:

[the] study of a complex and structured subject seems better begun by an overview of reading matter to display the structure and order the complexity. A good book will show its structure in the table of contents and catalog its contents in the index; with such aids the learner can easily move about in its numbered pages with only the flick of a finger, using page headings and subheads in the text to guide him. He may turn back and forth from table or graph to related text, skip something already known, review selectively for major and difficult points. In the writer's opinion, only after such first contact with a complex structured topic should a student turn to autoinstruction for review and differentiation of major points in material just read (50, p. 32).

Following the presentation would be a series of questions designed "to enhance the clarity and stability of cognitive structure by correcting misconceptions and deferring the instruction of new matter until there had been such clarification and elucidation" (51, p. 3). These questions would not necessarily cover everything in the initial lesson and might well jump back and forth from one point to another. The purpose of these questions is to help the student determine whether or not his learning had progressed satisfactorily so that he could return to the initial lesson to review the information presented there or, if necessary, seek additional help. The questions themselves are prepared in multiple-choice form with wrong alternatives selected from among common misunderstandings. In this way, the auto-instruction follows the presentation of what is to be learned and deals only with issues which need further clarification or emphasis. At the end of each series of questions, which would appear every three or four pages in the presentation, both the learner and the instructor could note the distribution of errors to determine what topics needed to be reviewed by each learner and which should be emphasized for the entire class with corrective discussion.

Pressey feels it is possible, if the material "had been programmed, the learning would have been more. But such adjunct auto-elucidative matter can be prepared relatively easily on any textbook, military or industrial training manual, or other matter" (53, p. 12). Thus, the advantages to adjunct programing are that this form of instruction is easily prepared, maintains the coherent structure of the subject matter, and accomplishes the dual purpose of testing the student and identifying areas of difficulty which require further instruction.

Crowder

The approach developed by Norman A. Crowder is somewhat similar, although it is much more specific as to the consequences of a wrong choice on the part of the learner. Crowder conceives of his "intrinsic" style of programing as a parallel to the process of private tutoring. During the years when he was associated with the U.S. Air Force, Crowder conducted research on training troubleshooters to find malfunctions in complex electronic equipment. The method being used was the "coach and pupil" method, and, since a sufficient number of skilled tutors was not available, some means had to be found for replicating that type of instructional situation without requiring a tutor for each student. Crowder identified three activities central to what an individual tutor does when working with a student: "(a) presented new information to the student; (b) required the student to use this new information, usually to answer questions; and (c) took appropriate action on the basis of what the student did, either going on to new information if the student performed correctly, or going back and reviewing or representing the old material, perhaps in a more thorough or simplified fashion, if the student did not demonstrate mastery of each piece of information" (7, p. 23).

The programing technique which Crowder developed to meet these functions consists of steps each containing a limited amount of information, usually less than one page, and a question presented at the same time. The question is in multiple-choice form. The learner chooses whichever answer he thinks is correct after reading the passage, and he then proceeds to the step indicated by that choice. If he has chosen the correct answer, that next step will give him new information and another question. If an incorrect answer had been chosen, that step will contain information specifically written to overcome the mistake; the student then is told to return to the step on which the error was made and to try to answer the question again. The program thus simulates a tutor by performing the functions of presenting material, examining the student, and providing corrective instruction or advancement to new information based upon the learner's performance. Crowder explains:

To predictably achieve a desired result, one must either have an infallible process to bring about the result or one must have a means of determining whether the result has been achieved and of taking appropriate action on the basis of that determination. This latter capability is the basis of the intrinsic programming, or automatic tutoring, technique. The automatic tutoring devices require the student to respond to the material presented, and the devices, in turn, modify their behavior (exposing new and different material to the student) until the desired result is obtained. The primary purpose is to determine whether the communication was successful, in order that corrective steps may be taken by the machine if the communication process has failed (6, pp. 287-88).

Since it is likely that each student might have different difficulties in learning, there are often several alternate corrective passages for each topic. Each student is referred to the appropriate corrective passage in terms of the specific error he has made. This method of programing is designed primarily to account for individual differences in learning. The bright student who is having no difficulty proceeds rapidly through the topics in their planned order without ever experiencing the need for corrective material. Students who have difficulty, however, are given the additional help they need. In some cases, in fact, a student might proceed through several different corrective passages for each topic of material until his difficulty is thoroughly overcome. The technique of directing a student to corrective material based on his own particular difficulties is termed "branching." The over-all technique, then, "is actually quite conventional in its details. We confront the student with symbolic material; we expect that, in some unspecified way, reading this material will equip the student with the ability to answer a question on the material he has read; we test the student immediately to see if he did, in fact, learn the material presented; and, finally, we either advance to the next point, or return and re-teach the present point, as indicated by the test result" (7, pp. 23-24).

The rationale for Crowder's style of programing instruction is not theoretically oriented.

Intrinsic programming assumes that the basic learning takes place during the student's exposure to the new material. The multiple-choice question is asked to find out whether the student has learned; it is not necessarily regarded as playing an active part in the primary learning process. The view of the learning process itself is essentially naturalistic, or, if you will, naive. We do not pretend to know in any very useful detail exactly why students are able to learn from exposure to symbolic material, but we postulate with great confidence that such learning does occur. This underlies virtually all formal communication between human beings (8, p. 3).

However, Crowder does have some definite ideas on how learning can best be facilitated, particularly with respect to instructional efficiency and the effects of learner errors.

Certainly no one would propose to write materials systematically designed to lead the student into errors, and anyone would prefer programs on which no student made an error *if this could be achieved without other undesirable results*. To see what undesirable results we must concern ourselves with, consider how we would proceed to write a program on which no student will make an error. We can produce virtually error-free programs if we are careful never to assume knowledge that the most poorly prepared student does not have, never to give more information per step than the slowest can absorb, and never to require reasoning beyond the capacity of the dullest. The inevitable result of such programs is that the time of the average and better than average student is wasted, and what is more important, the subject matter itself, no matter how dignified and characteristically human are its antecedents, must be reduced to fragments appropriate to the conditioning model of learning (10, pp. 149-50).

Crowder feels:

In an optimally arranged program in some circumstances there might be a ratio of as high as 20 to 1 between the number of right answer frames seen by the poor student and the number seen by the student who missed no questions. In cases where the questions and subsequences were used to select out students who needed remedial instruction in some aspect of the subject or in some prerequisite for the subject, the ratio might run quite a bit higher, of course. Even on material that was completely new to all students, we might see situations in which some students might require twenty times as many steps as the brightest student (7, p. 25).

Crowder's intrinsic programing is designed to meet training problems involving complex problem solving, preferably when the subject matter has a coherent, logical basis or structure which systematically can be developed step by step. He considers it particularly useful when dealing with ranges of individual differences among learners, wherever material automatically adapted to each learner's needs is required. Crowder is not convinced that programed instruction, as he envisions it, will turn out students all at the same level of competency. There will be fairly striking differences in the time required by slow and fast learners to complete a program. The opportunities afforded by intrinsic programs to keep a student working and learning at the maximum practical rate is perhaps its most emphasized characteristic. As Crowder expresses it:

While there are many practical problems to be worked out in educational economics, there is one fundamental fact that we must not lose sight of. This fundamental fact is that the basic educational resource that cannot be increased by any administrative procedure, and which must be conserved at the expense of other aspects of the system if necessary, is the learning time available to the individual student. We must use the student's time efficiently (7, p. 27).

Skinner

Perhaps the most widely adopted style of programing has been the one first described by B. F. Skinner. Because it is so widely used, there also are many publications on specific techniques falling within this style. These helpfully exist to round out those details omitted from Skinner's own presentations. The approach which Skinner designed is based almost exclusively on the extensive work on learning he and his colleagues have done under the carefully controlled conditions of the animal laboratory. As to the applicability of this research, he has pointed out, "The advances which have recently been made in our control of the learning process suggest a thorough revision of classroom practices, and, fortunately, they tell us how the revision can be brought about. This is not, of course, the first time that the results of an experimental science have been brought to bear upon the practical problems of education. The modern classroom does not, however, offer much evidence that research in the field of learning has been respected or used" (58, p. 107).

The heart of Skinner's approach might be described as the careful use of available reinforcements which are made contingent upon the learner's behavior. To do this, the instructional method used must accomplish two tasks, "The first task is to shape up these responses— to get the child to pronounce and to write responses correctly, but the principal task is to bring this behavior under many sorts of stimulus control" (58, p. 103). These outcomes are brought about by exerting control over when reinforcements occur, preferably by the use of a mechanical device.

In the experimental study of learning it has been found that the contingencies of reinforcement which are most efficient in controlling the organism cannot be arranged through the personal mediation of the experimenter. An organism is affected by subtle details of contingencies which are beyond the capacity of the human organism to arrange. Mechanical and electrical devices must be used. Mechanical help is also demanded by the sheer number of contingencies which may be used efficiently in a single experimental session. We have recorded many millions of responses from a single organism during thousands of experimental hours. Personal arrangement of the contingencies and personal observation of the results are quite unthinkable. Now, the human organism is, if anything, more sensitive to precise contingencies than the other organisms we have studied. We have every reason to expect, therefore, that the most effective control of human learning will require instrumental aid (58, p. 109).

The variables which Skinner has felt important are that the contingencies which occur following a response must be reinforcing and not aversive, that these reinforcements must be immediate, and that there must be many of them. Very small steps are used, therefore, to insure that a reinforcement can be made to follow each instance of relevant behavior and to insure that the frequency of reinforcement is raised to a maximum while the possibly aversive consequences of being wrong are reduced to a minimum. Each step in the program is designed on the basis of the programer's having specified the objectives of the instruction, his assessment of previous knowledge, and his formulation of a sequence which progresses from the knowledge initially assumed to the specified final repertoire. Once this is accomplished, the individual steps can be written. "With rare exceptions, frames are statements with words missing, the missing word being supplied by the student" (62, pp. 164-65). Thus, the responses of the learner are composed rather than selected from a set of alternatives.

Neither the vigorous correction of wrong choices nor the confirmation of the right choice will free the student of the verbal and non-verbal associations generated by reading the wrong items. . . . If he chooses that item and is corrected by the machine, we may say that he has "learned that it is wrong," but this vague characterization tells us very little about his subsequent behavior. It cannot mean that the sentence will never occur to him again. And if he is unlucky enough to select the right answer first, his reading of the plausible but erroneous answer is corrected only "by implication" —an equally vague and presumably even less effective process. . . . In solving an equation, reporting a fact of history, restating the meaning of a sentence, or engaging in almost any of the other behavior which is the main concern of education, his task is to *generate responses*. It is true that he may generate and reject, but only rarely will he generate a set of responses from which he then makes a choice. Instruction furthers the *origination* of behavior. Exposing the student to ingenious alternatives, few of which he would himself originate, adds nothing to his capacity to emit the correct response (60, pp. 63-64).

Getting new responses to occur without unnecessary errors is particularly important. "Learning can be accelerated by making successful responses more probable. When material in a program is carefully graded, both sub-human and human subjects can learn complex discriminative or matching behavior with very few errors. Although we learn something from our mistakes—for example, how to avoid them —this is not essential to the acquisition of successful behavior" (60, p. 62). To control the probability of errors, Skinner suggested various kinds of cueing techniques designated as either "echoic and textual behavior and formal prompts" which include the use of panels, the introduction of a new word so that it must be carefully observed, and formal prompts such as rhyming; or as "thematic prompts" which include the use of phrases having a high association value and categories such as opposites (62, pp. 165-66). Once produced, the response then must be practiced in the context of a variety of examples and reviewed periodically to maintain it at high strength. Two other features of programing have been employed by Skinner. First, "In acquiring complex behavior, the student must pass through a carefully designed sequence of steps, often of considerable length. Each step must be so small that it can always be taken, yet in taking it the student moves somewhat closer to fully competent behavior. The machine must make sure that these steps are taken in a carefully prescribed order" (59, p. 141). Second, "A program designed for the slowest student in the school system will probably not seriously delay the fast student, who will be free to progress at his own speed. (He may profit from the full coverage by filling in unsuspected gaps in his repertoire.) If this does not prove to be the case, programs can be constructed at two or more levels, and students can be shifted from one to the other as performances dictate" (59, p. 157). These two aspects of his approach have resulted in most Skinnerian programs being "linear," or prepared so that all reasonably similar learners proceed through an identical sequence of frames.

The use of small steps has not deterred Skinner from exploring some very complex forms of behavior. As examples, he has devised strategies which he feels are appropriate to teach not only fairly simple skills such as spelling or arithmetic, but reading, rhythm, and inductive reasoning (61) and attitudes as well (60, p. 76). The precise techniques which might be used to develop these and other skills are never clearly stated by Skinner. However, the model of instruction he has generated has resulted in a narrowing of the gap between educational practices and educational potential.

We are on the threshold of an exciting and revolutionary period, in which the scientific study of man will be put to work in man's best interests. Education must play its part. It must accept the fact that a sweeping revision of educational practices is possible and inevitable. When it has done this, we may look forward with confidence to a school system which is aware of the nature of its tasks, secure in its methods, and generously supported by the informed and effective citizens whom education itself will create (58, p. 113).

Gilbert

Not all response-centered styles of programing follow the approach advocated by Skinner. One of the most outstanding of those which do not is the style originated by Thomas F. Gilbert. This approach, which Gilbert calls "mathetics," is characterized, largely, by its concern over using the largest response units possible as the beginning point of instruction and by its concern with the criteria of mastery. Says Gilbert,

All teaching exercises have in common a limited and specific aim, which is to educe from the student a new behavior combination and to relate it to the other components of mastery. Our student is not a master of the subject because he cannot make the mastery responses on the right occasions, not because he is unable to make those responses at all. . . . The responses of mastery are there; we have to induce the student to make them on the proper occasions—in response to the proper stimuli. To accomplish this, an exercise has to train the student (1) under the proper stimulus, (2) to make the proper response, and (3) in consequence of this, to determine what responses he should follow through with (21, p. 8).

The procedure in writing a mathetics program begins with the development of a "prescription," a detailed analysis of all the stimuli and responses involved between the initiation of the task and its completion. The "prescription" then is revised to reduce the number of stimulus-response units to the minimum possible number based on what units the student can be assumed already to have in his repertoire. A "characterization" then is prepared which identifies possible competitive responses or stimulus situations and specifies ways in which these might be dealt with during the preparation of the program. The next step involves the preparation of a "lesson plan," in which a strategy is developed for teaching each portion of the chain of responses which are required for task completion. In the lesson plan, the instructional sequence for procedural skills is ordered from the last response in the chain to the first so that the student experiences completing the task during each step of instruction. The actual lesson is then developed. Every response is first "demonstrated" to the student by means of text and illustrations, then "prompted" by having the student perform the response with assistance, and then "released" so that the student performs the response without assistance.

An important feature of mathetical programing is that it assumes all necessary responses are already in the repertoire of the student, and it is only necessary that these responses must be manipulated in terms of the circumstances and the order in which they occur. Gilbert has observed:

. . . a subject matter is a class of behaviors and . . . everyone has some behavior which approximates that behavior class. It is easy to forget that the behaviors one goes through to master the subject matter may be different from the actual subject matter behaviors. The failure to grasp fully the implications of this rule has been, in my experience, the biggest single stumbling block for people learning to program education. The natural tendency is to begin by breaking the subject matter down into small, concise units. While this is valuable for describing the repertory you wish to build, these behavior units usually are not the ones which will actually build that repertory. They are test items, not teaching guides (19, pp. 478-79).

To aid the learner in making the transition between instruction and performance, several specific techniques are employed. As examples, discriminations among potentially confusing stimuli are all taught simultaneously; mnemonics are used liberally as mediators, and motivation is enhanced by having the completion of the task—with its normally occurring results—conclude each step in the program. Wherever possible, the stimuli which will be present in the performance situation are simulated in the preparation of a mathetics program. The cues used generally are very direct; during the demonstration step in each exercise, the attention of the learner is specifically directed at the relevant aspects of the stimulus situation, and he is given explicit instructions as to what he is to do. These cues are diminished considerably during the subsequent prompt step and are eliminated entirely from the release step which follows. Routinely, tryouts of the materials are not conducted until after the lesson is complete even though the insistence on steps which initially are as large as possible can lead to the need for extensive revisions. Finally, the style and characteristics of the program are not decided until the very last, after the aims, sequence, and features of instruction already have been determined. This is felt to result in more efficient programs than otherwise would be possible.

Summary

In summary, it is possible to describe two basically different approaches which can be used to prepare programed materials. These two approaches each represent significant but conflicting points of view regarding the learning process. The views of connectionist and configurationist theories have been differentiated by Stolurow (63, p. 51) in terms of the assumptions: "(a) That the learner is a receptive mechanism for whom associative connections become formed so as to mirror experience; (b) that the learner is a selective self-organizing mechanism who selects and extracts information from the environment."

The consequences of these opposing assumptions are reflected in the techniques selected by an individual programer to overcome anticipated learner difficulties. The stimulus-centered programer views learning as essentially a cognitive phenomenon and emphasizes techniques which are likely to enhance the postulated underlying perceptual and associative events. The response-centered programer considers learning as a change in behavior which occurs as the result of the conditions under which practice occurs; in preparing programed materials, he focuses his attention on the learner's responses and how these may be carefully controlled and differentially strengthened. Many of the controversial issues which have evolved in the design of programed materials have been reflections of these two basic learning-theory positions rather than reflections of simple questions regarding technique. The descriptive terms frequently applied to programs often have failed to differentiate between styles because they tend to point selectively to only one dimension of programing technique rather than to any composite pattern. Although differences do exist within styles and although there undoubtedly are many programers who fail to be at all consistent in their application of learning principles, there is likely to be greater value in identifying programs as *stimulus-centered* or *response-centered* than attempting to classify them according to the techniques utilized in their preparation —for example, "linear" or "branching."

As to how differences in technique might be dealt with, programed instruction is a relatively new paradigm in which to conduct learning research, and it is overoptimistic to assume that the basic issues which currently exist in learning theory will be resolved simply as the result of a new kind of laboratory apparatus—the teaching machine. Yet, both of the two approaches to programed instruction that have been described have been able to meet on common ground, in that they apply systematic control to relevant, human learning problems. It is not inconceivable that this in itself might lead to advances, if not solutions, toward a more complete understanding of the learning process. Certainly, if nothing else, the divergence of current programing techniques will lead to experimentation which cannot fail to be of value to those offering and those receiving instruction.

References

1. Annett, J. "The Role of Knowledge of Results in Learning: A Survey." *Educational Technology.* (Edited by J. P. DeCecco.) New York: Holt, Rinehart & Winston, 1964. pp. 279-85.

2. Barlow, J. A. "Conversational Chaining in Teaching Machine Programs." *Psychological Reports* 7: 187-93; June 1960.

3. Cook, D. A. "Behavior Theory and the Automation of Instruction." *Programmed Learning and Computer-Based Instruction.* (Edited by J. E. Coulson.) New York: John Wiley & Sons, 1961, pp. 120-28.

4. Cook, D., and Mechner, F. "Fundamentals of Programed Instruction." *Applied Programed Instruction.* (Edited by S. Margulies and L. D. Eigen.) New York: John Wiley & Sons, 1962. pp. 2-14.

5. Cram, D. *Explaining "Teaching Machines" and Programming.* San Francisco: Fearon Publishers, 1961.

6. Crowder, N. A. "Automatic Tutoring by Intrinsic Programming." *Teaching Machines and Programmed Learning.* (Edited by A. A. Lumsdaine and R. Glaser.) Washington, D.C.: National Education Association, 1960. pp. 286-98.

7. Crowder, N. A. "Characteristics of Branching Programs." *The University of Kansas Conference on Programmed Learning.* (Edited by O. M. Haugh.) Lawrence: University of Kansas Publications, 1961. Vol. II, No. 2, pp. 22-27.

8. Crowder, N. A. "The Rationale of Intrinsic Programing." *Programed Instruction* 1: 3-6; April 1962.

9. Crowder, N. A. "Simple Ways To Use the Student Response for Program Control." *Applied Programed Instruction.* (Edited by S. Margulies and L. D. Eigen.) New York: John Wiley & Sons, 1962. pp. 120-28.

10. Crowder, N. A. "On the Differences Between Linear and Intrinsic Programming." *Educational Technology.* (Edited by J. P. DeCecco.) New York: Holt, Rinehart & Winston, 1964. pp. 142-51.

11. Deterline, W. A. "Response Mode: Different Effect or Different Purpose?" *AID* 1: 47-48; September 1961.

12. Dolmatch, T. B.; Marting, Elizabeth; and Finley, R. E., editors. *Revolution in Training: Programmed Instruction in Industry.* New York: American Management Association, 1962.

13. Epstein, S., and Epstein, Beryl. *The First Book of Teaching Machines.* New York: Franklin Watts, 1961.

14. Estes, W. K., and others. *Modern Learning Theory.* New York: Appleton-Century-Crofts, 1954.

15. Evans, J. L. *Multiple-Choice Discrimination Programing.* Paper presented at the American Psychological Association Convention, New York, September 1961.

16. Evans, J. L.; Homme, L. E.; and Glaser, R. "The Ruleg System for the Construction of Programmed Verbal Learning Sequences." *Journal of Educational Research* 55: 513-18; June-July 1962.

17. Fry, E. *Teaching Machines and Programmed Instruction.* New York: McGraw-Hill Book Co., 1963.

18. Gagné, R. M. "The Acquisition of Knowledge." *Psychological Review* 69: 355-65; July 1962.
19. Gilbert, T. F. "On the Relevance of Laboratory Investigation of Learning to Self-Instructional Programming." *Teaching Machines and Programmed Learning.* (Edited by A. A. Lumsdaine and R. Glaser.) Washington, D.C.: National Education Association, 1960. pp. 475-85.
20. Gilbert, T. F. "Mathetics: The Technology of Education." *Journal of Mathetics* 1: 7-73; January 1962.
21. Gilbert, T. F. "Mathetics: II. The Design of Teaching Exercises." *Journal of Mathetics* 1: 7-56; April 1962.
22. Glaser, R. "Principles of Programming." *Programmed Learning: Evolving Principles and Industrial Applications.* (Edited by J. P. Lysaught.) Ann Arbor, Mich.: Foundation for Research on Human Behavior, 1961. pp. 7-20.
23. Glaser, R. "Some Research Problems in Automated Instruction: Instructional Programming and Subject-Matter Structure." *Programmed Learning and Computer-Based Instruction.* (Edited by J. E. Coulson.) New York: John Wiley & Sons, 1962. pp. 67-85.
24. Goldberg, I. A. "An Introduction to Programed Instruction." *Applied Programed Instruction.* (Edited by S. Margulies and L. D. Eigen.) New York: John Wiley & Sons, 1962. pp. 15-20.
25. Gropper, G. L. "What Should Be Programmed for Television?" *Trends in Programmed Instruction.* (Edited by G. D. Ofiesh and W. C. Meierhenry.) Washington, D.C.: National Education Association and National Society for Programmed Instruction, 1964. pp. 263-66.
26. Hatch, R. S. "More on the Response Mode Controversy." *AID* 1: 76-77; December 1961.
27. Hebb, D. O. *The Organization of Behavior.* New York: John Wiley & Sons, 1949.
28. Hilgard, E. R. *Theories of Learning.* Second edition. New York: Appleton-Century-Crofts, 1956.
29. Holland, J. G. "Teaching Machines: An Application of Principles from the Laboratory." *Teaching Machines and Programmed Learning.* (Edited by A. A. Lumsdaine and R. Glaser.) Washington, D.C.: National Education Association, 1960. pp. 215-28.
30. Jensen, A. R. "Teaching Machines and Individual Differences." *Automated Teaching Bulletin* 1: 12-17; Summer 1960.
31. Kay, H. "General Introduction to Teaching Machine Procedures." *Teaching Machines and Programming.* (Edited by K. Austwick.) New York: Macmillan Co., 1964. pp. 1-42.
32. Kendler, H. H. "Teaching Machines and Psychological Theory." *Automatic Teaching: The State of the Art.* (Edited by E. Galanter.) New York: John Wiley & Sons, 1959. pp. 177-86.
33. Klaus, D. J. "Programming: A Re-Emphasis on the Tutorial Approach." *Audiovisual Instruction* 6: 130-32; April 1961.

34. Klaus, D. J. *Assessment and Planning of Programmed Instruction in a Large Scale System.* Paper presented as part of a symposium on Problems in Adopting Programmed Instruction for Large Training Systems at the meetings of the American Psychological Association, St. Louis, September 5, 1962.
35. Klaus, D. J. "Programming the Impossible." *Trends in Programmed Instruction.* (Edited by G. D. Ofiesh and W. C. Meierhenry.) Washington, D.C.: National Education Association and National Society for Programmed Instruction, 1964. pp. 19-23.
36. Koch, S., editor. *Psychology: A Study of a Science. General Systematic Formulations, Learning, and Special Processes.* New York: McGraw-Hill Book Co., 1959. Vol. II.
37. Lumsdaine, A. A., editor. *Student Response in Programmed Instruction.* Washington, D.C.: National Academy of Sciences—National Research Council, 1961.
38. Lumsdaine, A. A. "The Development of Teaching Machines and Programmed Self-Instruction." *New Teaching Aids for the American Classroom.* Washington, D.C.: Department of Health, Education, and Welfare, 1962. pp. 136-73.
39. Lumsdaine, A. A. "Some Theoretical and Practical Problems in Programmed Instruction." *Programmed Learning and Computer-Based Instruction.* (Edited by J. E. Coulson.) New York: John Wiley & Sons, 1962. pp. 134-51.
40. Lumsdaine, A. A., and Klaus, D. J. "What's in a Name? A Problem of Terminology." *AV Communication Review* 9: 208-211; November-December 1961.
41. Lysaught, J. P., and Williams, C. M. *A Guide to Programmed Instruction.* New York: John Wiley & Sons, 1963.
42. Mager, R. F. "On Sequencing of Instructional Content." *Psychological Reports* 9: 405-413; August 1961.
43. Markle, Susan M. "The Changing Role of the Audiovisual Process in Education: A Definition and a Glossary of Related Terms." *AV Communication Review* 11: 64; January-February 1963.
44. Meyer, Markle, Susan R. "Report on the Initial Test of a Junior High-School Vocabulary Program." *Teaching Machines and Programmed Learning.* (Edited by A. A. Lumsdaine and R. Glaser.) Washington, D.C.: National Education Association, 1960. pp. 229-46.
45. Morton, F. R. "The Language Laboratory as a Teaching Machine." *International Journal of American Linguistics* 26: 113-66; October 1960.
46. Ofiesh, G. D. "The Emergence of Instructional Technology." *Trends in Programmed Instruction.* (Edited by G. D. Ofiesh and W. C. Meierhenry.) Washington, D.C.: National Education Association and National Society for Programmed Instruction, 1964. pp. 7-10.
47. Pennington, D. F., and Slack, C. W. "The Mathetical Design of Effective

Lessons." *Applied Programed Instruction.* (Edited by S. Margulies and L. D. Eigen.) New York: John Wiley & Sons, 1962. pp. 298-310.

48. Premack, D. "Toward Empirical Behavior Laws: I. Positive Reinforcement." *Psychological Review* 66: 219-33; July 1959.

49. Pressey, S. L. "A Simple Apparatus Which Gives Tests and Scores— and Teaches." *Teaching Machines and Programmed Learning.* (Edited by A. A. Lumsdaine and R. Glaser.) Washington, D.C.: National Education Association, 1960. pp. 35-41.

50. Pressey, S. L. "Basic Unresolved Teaching-Machine Problems." *Theory into Practice* 1: 30-27; February 1962.

51. Pressey, S. L. "Teaching Machine (and Learning Theory) Crisis." *Journal of Applied Psychology* 47: 1-6; February 1963.

52. Pressey, S. L. "Autopresentation vs. Autoelucidation." *Programed Instruction* 2: 6-7; April 1963.

53. Pressey, S. L. "Auto Elucidation Without Programming." *NSPI Journal* 3: 12-13; August 1964.

54. Rothkopf, E. Z. "Evaluation and Research with Self-Instructional Programs at Bell Telephone Laboratories." *Programmierter Unterricht und Lehrmaschinen.* Berlin: Pädagogische Arbeitsstelle Sekretariat Pädagogisches Zentrum, 1964. pp. 455-61.

55. Schaefer, H. H. "A Vocabulary Program Using 'Language Redundancy.' " *Journal of Programed Instruction* 2: 9-16; Fall 1963.

56. Seeman, W. "Phenomenon." *American Psychologist* 19: 772; November 1964.

57. Shettel, H. H. *Individual Differences in Subject Matter Knowledge and Programmed Instructional Format.* Pittsburgh: American Institute for Research, 1963.

58. Skinner, B. F. "The Science of Learning and the Art of Teaching." *Teaching Machines and Programmed Learning.* (Edited by A. A. Lumsdaine and R. Glaser.) Washington, D.C.: National Education Association, 1960. pp. 99-113.

59. Skinner, B. J. "Teaching Machines." *Teaching Machines and Programmed Learning.* (Edited by A. A. Lumsdaine and R. Glaser.) Washington, D.C.: National Education Association, 1960. pp. 137-58.

60. Skinner, B. F. "Learning Theory and Future Research." *Programmed Learning: Evolving Principles and Industrial Applications.* (Edited by J. P. Lysaught.) Ann Arbor, Mich.: Foundation for Research on Human Behavior, 1961. pp. 59-66.

61. Skinner, B. F. "Teaching Machines." *Scientific American* 205: 90-102; November 1961.

62. Skinner, B. F., and Holland, J. G. "The Use of Teaching Machines in College Instruction." *Teaching Machines and Programmed Learning.* (Edited by A. A. Lumsdaine and R. Glaser.) Washington, D.C.: National Education Association, 1960. pp. 159-72.

63. Stolurow, L. M. *Teaching by Machine.* Washington, D.C.: Department of Health, Education, and Welfare, 1961.
64. Thomas, C. A., and others. *Programmed Learning in Perspective: A Guide to Programme Writing.* Barking, Essex, England: Adelphi Press, 1963.
65. Thorndike, E. L. *The Fundamentals of Learning.* New York: Teachers College, Columbia University, 1932.
66. Tolman, E. C. *Purposive Behavior in Animals and Men.* New York: Century, 1932.
67. Tucker, J. A. "Intrinsic Programming: A Simulation Technique." *Psychological Reports* 9: 713-16; October 1961.
68. Uttal, W. R. "On Conversational Interaction." *Programmed Learning and Computer-Based Instruction.* (Edited by J. E. Coulson.) New York: John Wiley & Sons, 1961. pp. 171-90.
69. Zeaman, D. "Skinner's Theory of Teaching Machines." *Automatic Teaching: The State of the Art.* (Edited by E. Galanter.) New York: John Wiley & Sons, 1959. pp. 167-76.

LAWRENCE M. STOLUROW
DANIEL DAVIS*
University of Illinois

Teaching Machines and
Computer-Based Systems**

The purpose of this paper is to develop a general model of the teaching process as accomplished by an adaptive teaching machine system. In doing this, definitions and distinctions will be made in an effort to provide clarity. No attempt will be made to completely inventory existing equipment or to describe particular machines in great detail. There are many reasons for this, one of which is that an inventory would be incomplete at best. Another is that it would be obsolete before this paper was in print. Furthermore, judging from past efforts to provide such an inventory, many of the items it would contain would be unavailable (25, 58). Consequently, it seems most useful to examine a general model rather than the machines themselves. Hopefully, in doing this the horse will be put before the cart—the teaching machine concept before the machine itself.

Through the development of a proper and complete model of the teaching machine process, several advantages could accrue. For example, specific machines could be evaluated in terms of the basic func-

* The authors are grateful to the following people for their editorial comments and suggestions: John Kearns, Henry Lippert, and Mrs. Valerie Anderson.
** This chapter was made possible in part by funds provided by the U.S. Office of Education, Title VII, Educational Media Branch, Contract 2-20-003, and the Office of Naval Research, Contract 3985(04). Reproduction in whole or in part is permitted for any purpose of the U.S. government.

tions they perform, and new designs could be developed with a clear perception of the criteria they should meet. Thus, a general and formal model provides criteria both for design and evaluation. Furthermore, it focuses attention on a real and important problem long in need of serious scientific study, the nature of teaching itself. Hopefully, an existing and developing interest in teaching machines will permit a look at the teaching process with the same sincerity and scientific purpose as in the past, but with a new purpose, namely, freedom to consider the process as accomplished by a device. This new synthetic approach is both challenging and intriguing, for, in general, scientific progress is made when one is freed from subjective thinking. The ability to consider the hitherto personal activity of teaching in a thoroughly impersonal and objective manner should provide a basis for the development of a better understanding of the process.

Background of Thinking About Teaching Machines

Contrary to popular belief, the development of teaching machines has been a long-term process. As early as 1866, Halcyon Skinner (39) developed and patented a spelling machine which was conceived as an aid to a teacher, and about 1873 a machine was developed with generated solutions to logical problems which were presented symbolically (33). In 1915, a teaching machine of the type that is so common today was developed (45). It is interesting that none of these early devices for automating particular teaching functions struck a very responsive chord.[1]

The original Pressey teaching machine and that of Ordahl and Ordahl (40) were neither simpler nor less glamorous than the later devices of Skinner which did spark interest. All did just three things: displayed stimulus materials, accommodated a response, and provided reinforcement. The last of these three functions, reinforcement, was considered

[1] Somewhat earlier, Thorndike (62) had suggested the idea of a response-dependent display device, but the reinforcement function per se was not made an explicit factor. However, in this statement, Thorndike did specify "... only to him who had done what was directed on page one would page two become visible, and so on. . . ." Consequently, reinforcement was implied through the different consequences attendant on right and wrong responses. In retrospect, Thorndike's conception reads like a blueprint of today's printed devices, yet he neither solved the problem he posed nor did he ignite either the interest of educators or the imagination of researchers.

the most important and critical for a teaching machine by both Pressey and Skinner.

Pressey had set for himself the task of designing a machine that both "tested and taught." In order to test, the machine had to display materials and accommodate a student's response; to teach, it also had to tell the student whether or not he made a correct response. Thus, the feedback in terms of automatic reinforcement or knowledge of results took on a special definitive significance. It was seen as critical for a machine that taught. While memory drums did this, they did not do it automatically. A teaching machine needs to provide the student automatically with reinforcement, and to do this, it uses the student's own response.[2]

Since the early Pressey and English teaching machines, a variety of other simple devices designed to deliver automatic reinforcement have been developed, tried out, and found to be effective (45). Thus, Pressey first demonstrated, through research, an effective and deliberate transplant from the learning laboratory to the classroom. Furthermore, in doing this, he used an automatic mechanism (45).

During World War II (see 66, 67) an extensive set of printed devices was developed to teach skills by individualized self-instructional methods without the intermediation of a teacher. These devices, called phase checks, served to both teach and test. Each step of a skill, such as the disassembly-assembly of a piece of equipment (e.g., a machine gun or turret), was organized in the sequence required for successful performance of the terminal behavior, and an overt, constructed response was required. This was a linear program in which the student's task was to accomplish the steps rather than write a response, since he was being taught a manual skilll. After practicing by himself until he was proficient, the phase check was administered by an instructor. This means that the student performed the same steps, but now he did them without the program. The instructor now used the program (phase check) as a test and recorded each of the student's responses as either a success or a failure. In effect, the phase check procedure also provided

[2] H. B. English (24) invented a device used in 1918 to help train soldiers to squeeze a rifle trigger. It provided visual feedback through the use of a manometer, which revealed to the soldier a change in the height of a liquid column. If he squeezed the trigger smoothly or spasmodically, the mercury column would rise correspondingly and provide visual feedback.

a vanishing condition, since the verbal cues were removed and the trainee had to perform the steps without them. In fact, vanishing was carried even one step further when the trainee was blindfolded and required to perform the skill (e.g., disassemble a machine gun) without seeing the parts. Here, feedback was automatically provided by the accomplishment of each step with the actual equipment. The student either removed the part (e.g., the back plate) or he did not. There was no need for externally provided knowledge of results. Feedback was provided for each step, and every step had to be performed correctly before the next one could be done. Students progressed at their own rate and were scored on the phase check in terms of both errors and time. There was no external test since the objective of the program was to teach as terminal behaviors the very skill that was practiced and on which the trainee was checked. Thus, the basic concepts of automatic feedback, providing both knowledge of results and reinforcement, and the use of sequentially ordered steps anticipated the subsequent labeling of the device and explication of the conception by Skinner (52).

Some 30 years after Pressey's first published description of his teaching machine (45), when there was no depression, surplus of teachers, or war, interest in the possibilities and potentialities of automated instruction was sparked by Skinner (51, 52). The idea of automating the classroom was long overdue relative to other areas. In fact, instruction seemed to be the last frontier for the application of cybernetic notions (29, 68). It was well established that learning required feedback, and a simple extension of this clearly revealed the necessity and advantage of controlling the learning by mechanisms which automatically provided feedback to the student.

In reviving and redirecting thinking about automated instruction, Skinner, like Pressey before him, focused attention on the "teaching machine," the hardware; but unlike Pressey, he gave greater prominence to the "program." In fact, Skinner emphasized the symbolic significance of the stimulus materials and used them rather than the "machine" to provide the feedback. He also related his thinking about operant conditioning to programed instruction through the notion of "shaping," which can be accomplished only if the material is organized (50, 53). The organization of the verbal material (the steps of a program) becomes especially important when one thinks, as Skinner does, in terms of the program and machine doing all the teaching. It is this departure from Pressey's conception of the machine as an adjunctive device used in combination with other instruction that raised questions of strategy that are so prominent today. For Skinner, the machine was an instrument that taught independently of other means of instruction; it was not merely a testing device. This represents an important dimension of the problems of teaching and in particular suggests that these problems should be observed with a broader view.

The Current Conception of Teaching Machines

The dominant current conception of the "teaching machine" and of its value relative to that of the "program" is an obvious switch from that expressed earlier by Pressey and Skinner. The current conception is a turnabout resulting in the dismissal of the machine as an important instrument in programed learning. Instead of the machine being the great hope of the future, it now is either tolerated or thought unnecessary, and programed instruction is seen as achieving its effectiveness through the functions performed by the "program."

The software in automated instruction now is perceived as being more important than the hardware (28, 56). The distinction between software and hardware has evolved intuitively to mean program and machine, respectively. However, the distinction between a program and a machine does not rest upon physical characteristics, but rather upon psychological characteristics, if this distinction is to be made at all. It is quite clear that there are things called programs and other things called machines. However, a so-called machine is obviously an insufficient mechanism for teaching, although it may be a necessary element in the set of things required for teaching. It has become a cliché to say that a machine does not teach, that it needs a program to do so. This is an explicit recognition of the unsubstantial nature of the distinction between machine and program. The set of functions that needs to be performed in order to teach can be accomplished in a variety of ways. When these are all accomplished by means of printed materials, it has become conventional to refer to them as a program. However, when some of the same functions are accomplished by a piece of hardware, that set of functions has come to be referred to as a machine. This is obviously an arbitrary and probably unnecessary distinction and, in fact, leads to confusion when automated instruction is viewed more broadly.

Unfortunately, the current conception of teaching machines has focused on only a limited set of functions involved in instruction rather than upon the broader set. This has led to the development of simple devices which are not representative of possible automated teaching systems. There are two substantial arguments for a monistic view of the teaching process as a single set of functions in contrast with the prevailing dualism fostered and encouraged by the early pronunciamentos of the apostles of the new educational technology. The first is the unnecessary distinction between machine and program which, at best, relates to a separation of functions based on convenience of implementation rather than on necessity. In fact, the set of functions allotted to a machine is known to be insufficient. The second argument is that the distinctions applied to simple machines do not also apply to computer teaching machine systems, thus they do not always correspond to the hardware-software distinction.

This dualistic view seems to have resulted from the common, but unfortunate, separation of the functions now associated with the software (paper or film) from those associated with the hardware. The simple nature of most teaching machines currently available allows both the content and logic (decision functions) to be kept together on paper or film. Therefore, the paper or film (the so-called program) appears to be the essential item, while the device in which it is placed for display (the machine) is merely auxiliary. The position taken here is that this simple division of functions is ill-advised and inadequate. Although it describes most simple teaching machines, it cannot be extended to more adaptive and complex machines where the content and logic are physically separated. With these more sophisticated systems, it is no longer possible to separate "machine" functions from "program" functions according to physical location. They both will be accomplished by a complex combination of display, switching, and computer operations.

Toward a General Conception of Teaching Machines

It should be realized that the concept of the teaching machine is not uniquely defined by any existing machine and that existing machines give a limited and biased view of the concept. Therefore, in considering what a machine is, one should not think of teaching functions that are now accomplished by a machine, but rather of functions that *can* be accomplished by a machine and which are suggested by an analysis of teaching. The fact that many conceive of the teaching machine in terms of its present capabilities indicates that the current concept of a teaching machine is poorly defined and in need of reformulation.

In most general terms, a teaching machine is an instructional mechanism used to produce systematic behavioral changes in a student whose responses to the material presented determine the further operation of the mechanism. Here "mechanism" is used in the abstract and general sense referring to a set of specific functions or transformations. Teaching machines that can be touched are exemplars of the general concept, and each of them implements a set of specific functions associated with teaching. No physical machine should be confused with the general teaching machine concept as just defined in this paragraph.

The specific way in which a machine is made to work is a separate question from that of the functions it performs. Not only does the former involve synthetic operations while the latter involves analytic ones, but also there is a one-to-many relationship between a function and the ways it can be accomplished. Therefore, when teaching functions for the purpose of machine design are considered, there are two fundamental problems. One is specifying the set of functions to be considered and the other is specifying the manner in which each is to be accomplished. Whereas the former is determined by an analysis of learning and the objectives of instruction, the latter is decided by such practical factors as cost, convenience, state of the art, etc.

Toward a General Concept of Teaching Programs

A teaching machine is any mechanism that uses response-dependent information to bring about systematic behavioral changes (e.g., rate or form of response and the contingency of a specified response upon a particular stimulus or set of stimuli). In short, it is a mechanism for accomplishing a set of functions the net effect of which is to build upon the student's entry behavior repertoire and to transform it. This transformation also requires for its accomplishment a set of elements and a related set of functions. The elements are the content set and consist of expository and interrogative materials divided into units called *frames*. The functions are collectively called a strategy, a set of decision rules relating to the responses students make to the content. It is important to notice that this definition of a teaching program says nothing about software or hardware. The physical location of either the content set or the strategy can vary from paper or film in the simple machines to magnetic tape or core storage in more complex systems.

On the basis of these definitions, it becomes clear that any comparison of machines and programs is meaningless. They are not comparable. Anything which uses response-dependent information to change the learner's performance is a teaching machine (whether it is a book or a computer-based system). Also, every teaching machine, no matter how simple or complex, uses some sort of teaching program to bring about the desired changes in behavior, even though the program itself may not be specified by the developer. In other words, there is a set of rules which can be formulated to describe the operation of any device, and these rules are part of the program. Each program has two basic dimensions: first, the set of rules used in sampling content (e.g., concepts, principles, facts) and, second, the set of rules describing the operation to be performed on this content in relation to a particular student for the purpose of accomplishing the stated objectives of instruction.

The Two Phases of Teaching Machine Operation

In order for a teaching machine to be maximally adaptive, it should have the following capabilities. First, for a given subject area it should have at its disposal a number of different teaching programs. It is clear that every instructional program has had failures. Some students either do not meet the minimum standards set for the program or do not perform at or above the expected level in terms of their ability. Therefore, it is clear that no single strategy will work for all students and that no single set of content elements is best for all.

Second, when specifying a program for each student, the teaching machine should make use of the student's past performance including ability or personality measures. This information is necessary if either the "best" or "optimum" teaching program is desired for each student.

Third, the teaching machine should have the capability of changing programs *during* the course of instruction. In other words, it should be capable of dynamic programing. Getting the "best" program for each student appears to involve a great deal of information about the student which may not always be possible in the time available. Therefore, if it is found that a program is not effective, then a new one should be used to correct the original decision so as to eliminate the difficulties which the old one could not handle.

These capabilities are imbedded in the model of the teaching process which is developed in the following sections. The model divides the teaching process into two phases. The first, the *pretutorial phase,* specifies a teaching program which can attain a desired outcome subject to the ability constraints of the student. The second, the *tutorial phase,* implements and monitors the program which was specified in the pretutorial phase. The monitoring process allows the teaching machine to change programs if the student exceeds certain limits (either upper or lower) in level of performance.

The Pretutorial Phase of Instruction

Variables

The pretutorial process can be described in terms of three basic sets of variables. The first set is made up of the *possible outcomes* of the teaching, and it contains a subset which consists of the *desired outcomes* or *objectives*—the desired minimum capabilities or behaviors we want to produce. It is necessary to have the minimum acceptable objectives clearly in mind when specifying a teaching program for each student.

The second set is made up of the possible *"entry behaviors"* (things the student knows when he starts), and the third contains the *teaching programs* which are available (the how-to-do-it information). Thus, the pretutorial process deals with relations between outcomes, entry behaviors, and teaching programs. The goal is to specify a teaching program which will accomplish a stated minimum objective for a given entry behavior.

Characteristics of the Outcomes: A closer look at what is meant by an outcome reveals three characteristics. It is a *level of performance* for a given *subject area* which is attained within a *given time.* Therefore, when one describes the desired minimum acceptable outcomes or objectives of teaching, it is necessary to specify three things: (a) the *subject area* or topic; (b) the final *level* of student performance that would be the *minimum* acceptable; and (c) the *maximum* time allowed to achieve the minimum level. A proper statement of objectives is readily translatable into training specifications, on the one hand, and into the requirements for performance scores of the student, on the other.

It is assumed that the achievement of an objective for a particular student requires a teaching program. Consequently, if any of the three characteristics (topic, level, or time) is changed, then the objective is changed, and a different program might be required to achieve most efficiently the new objective for the student with a particular level of aptitude (A_p) and entry behavior (P_e). To illustrate that this is a necessary outcome, consider the situation in which the minimum acceptable level of terminal performance is raised for some reason while the topic and time remain unchanged. If it is necessary to cover the topic in the same amount of time while the minimum acceptable level of terminal performance is raised, then a new program is required for students of a particular level of entry behavior. Another example would be one in which both the minimum acceptable terminal performance level was changed and the time increased somewhat, but the topic held constant. Here the program change might be to give the students more opportunity for practice. On the other hand, if the time available for teaching is reduced, but the topic and minimum acceptable level of final performance are not changed, a new program is necessary for students of a given entry level (e.g., the concepts might be organized differently).

Frequently, it is necessary to change deliberately a second characteristic of the objective when one characteristic has been changed (e.g., the school may change from a semester to a quarter system, or the amount of time allotted for training a particular group of technicians may be changed by fiat). If the amount of time available is reduced, then it may be the case that no known program can be found to achieve the specified final level of performance (P_f) with the given students. If this is so, then it may be necessary also to alter either the topic covered (T) or the time allotted (t) or both. By reducing the expectation with respect to the scope of the topic or by increasing the time, the new objective may be achievable with given students using an existing program developed originally for a different aptitude or achievement level. However, if this is not the case, then it may be decided to change *both* of the other two characteristics (P_t and t) to make possible the achievement of a different objective. The implication is clear. If one characteristic of the objective is changed, a change in another also may be required when the same program is to be used with students of a given entry level.

In many contexts when the word "objective" is used, it has a more limited meaning than the term is given here. For example, many teachers define their objectives simply in terms of the minimum level of performance they will accept. Consequently, they may say they get all their students to meet the same objective when they achieve a satisfactory score on a test. From the present point of view they do not do this. To indicate more specifically why this is so, consider the case where all students taught attain a minimum score on an achievement test. Among these students, the different ability levels will have used different amounts of time to complete the material. Consequently, they will have achieved different objectives. Also consider their terminal level of performance, assuming that they all achieved the minimum test score. It usually will be found that there are distinguishable final test score levels. If the objective is defined in terms of time required to achieve a particular minimum level of proficiency in a topic, then students who achieve at different rates are really achieving different objectives. To consider only the final minimum test score is to court confusion in thinking about the problem.

Characteristics of Entry Behaviors: There are two critical characteristics of the entry behavior (B_e) of the students with respect to cognitive factors. The first is their level of performance on the immediately preceding relevant task or on a pretest (P_e); the second is their aptitude level (A_p). Usually it is possible to specify these characteristics reliably and with acceptable precision. In order to determine the student's level of entry behavior, it is necessary to give him tests before he takes the instructional program. The scores obtained can be used to select the students for training. Usually, the level of entry behavior (B_e) varies among the students selected, but for any one student it is a fixed value at a particular time. Nevertheless, even for the individual student, it is potentially variable over time. Consequently, it is possible to alter a student's entry behavior before he takes a program. For example, this could be done by giving him review sequences or additional practice on the task just completed to increase his level of performance on the pre-test (P_e). It is more difficult to change the student's aptitude level, particularly as he gets older and as the available time is reduced. Aptitude is the more stable component of entry behavior.

In experimental studies, student entry behavior is typically an independent variable, and students are *grouped* in terms of selected levels. Then, one treatment is given them and differences in final performance observed. In the usual training situation, on the other hand, some screening procedure is used to *select* students in order to minimize failure or to maximize successful training in the allotted time with the training strategy constant. Therefore, both in research and in practice there is a recognition of individual differences in response to a treatment or procedure. When different levels of entry behavior are known to exist among a group of students, then choice is possible between the use of the same objectives for all of them or of *different* objectives for various entry levels. In the practical situation, there is associated with each of these alternatives a different requirement for the number of teaching programs, if it is desired that all students within a given range achieve the same objective. It should be noted that ability and performance measures are not the only input measures which will prove useful in specifying programs for the individual. There is evidence that motivationally related variables such as personality measures are also important, especially as regards the type of feedback (26) given the students.

Characteristics of Teaching Programs: The programs are the means used to transform the student's entry performance level (P_e) into a specific final level (P_f). Unfortunately, the state of the art is such that it is not uncommon for a program to be developed independently of a specification of entry behavior or final performance. Then it is tested to find the objectives which can be accomplished with it as revealed by the maximum time it takes a selected group of students to make a minimum satisfactory score on a test covering the topics taught.

The setting of objectives after the fact, while not a recommended procedure, appears to be common practice and, in fact, may be necessary in view of the current state of the art. In this way, normative data could be obtained with representative samples of subjects within the aptitude and achievement ranges that are anticipated. If, for example, the topic to be taught is 25 spelling words, and the sample of students completed the set of frames presented to them but failed to meet the minimum required P_t of 23 correct words, then they may be given the entire set of frames again or a selected subset and tested a second time. This process might have to be repeated in order for all of them to achieve the minimum P_t score. The distribution of total times taken by the students can then be used as a basis for setting the maximum time limit (t) which will be used in the future in making decisions about the use of the program with comparable students.

Not too long ago, when the technology for producing transistors was at a similar state of its development, the procedure used was akin to that described for the development of programs today. A large batch of transistors was produced, and then each was submitted to tests to determine its characteristics. Once characteristics were specified, the transistor was typed or classified. This *ad hoc* procedure was necessitated by lack of specification of the production procedures (programs) in relation to particular input-output relationships. In the design of an instructional program, there is not adequate data to permit specification of one program for a particular change in entry behavior to achieve selected objectives. However, the model, as formulated, specifies the conditions so that adequate data can be obtained for future use.

As was mentioned in a previous section, a program is made up of two interacting parts: the set of content units and the set of decision rules (strategy) which are defined for the content units. It is possible to change a program for a given topic by changing the type of content that is used, e.g., from a geometrical to an algebraic presentation in mathematics. Also, it is possible to change a program by specifying a new set of decision rules, e.g., change the number of responses used in making decisions or change the amount of remediation given for errors. Thus, a complex teaching machine would have at its disposal a number of different types of strategies which, when combined with different sets of content units, yield a wide variety of programs.

Pretutorial Decision Processes

The pretutorial decision process, which has as its goal the selection of a suitable program, is described as follows:

Step 1. Search for a program. As indicated, in order to identify a teaching program, it is necessary to know at least two things about every student (A_p and P_e) and three things about the objectives (T, P_t, and t). With this information as input (See Figure 1), the search for a program begins. The outcome of the search may be any one of three types:

a. *More than one may work.* If the search reveals that there is more than one available program which will transform the entry level to the desired final level, then these must be listed so they can be evaluated in terms of efficiency criteria.

b. *None may work.* If no available program works, then one or more of the objectives will have to be changed.

c. *One may work.* Only one of the available programs may be found to work, and, if so, it is identified.

Step 2. Evaluation. This step varies depending upon the outcome of Step 1 as indicated.

a. When more than one program will work, then there is a problem of deciding which to use. The educational decision maker has to provide the system with a set of external criteria to use when this situation occurs. Two types of criteria can be distinguished. One type relates to economic factors and the other to educational factors. An example of the first of these would be the use of time and/or cost. Using this criterion, the program that takes least time or costs least is the one used. Alternatively, educational factors may determine the criteria used. For example, the "best program" may be the one that can be used over the widest range of talent. In order that the system be capable of functioning when more than one program will work for a given set of objectives and students, it is necessary to have an auxiliary set of criteria to use.

b. When no available program will work, the problem is to decide what to change—inputs or objectives. The priority order in which

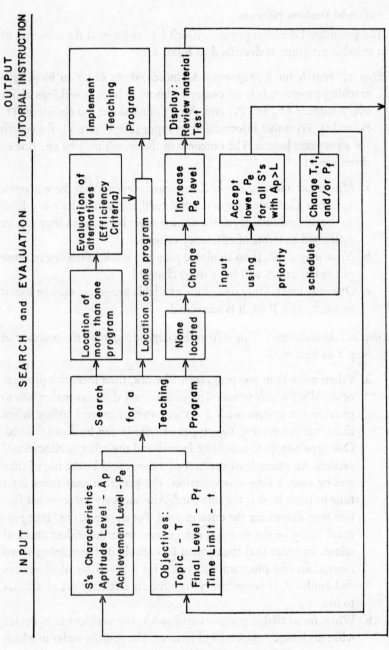

FIGURE 1. *The Pretutorial Decision Process.*

the changes will be considered will depend upon the particular situation. However, a general pattern can be described. The basic decision is between changing the students or the objectives. For example, if student changes are considered, a decision might be made to improve students who fall within a specified range of the minimum entry level (P_e). In other words, for all students whose entry performance (P_e) is less than P_x but above P_y, review exercises might be given to bring them to the minimum entry level of performance for starting the program. If time for review is excessive, an alternative, but risky, decision might be to accept a lower P_e for students who are very high in aptitude. In these cases, the value of student aptitude (A_p) is greater than some designated lower level (L). If, on the other hand, the objectives are changed, the most likely change is in the time allotted to the student. The second is the amount of content or definition of the subject area; the least likely characteristic to be changed is the minimum acceptable final performance level.

c. When only one program works, it is identified.

Step 3. Implementation. Once a program is specified it can be put to work. The decision process just described can be represented as a flow diagram and can serve to describe one basic set of things that a sophisticated teaching machine might be designed to do. This is illustrated in Figure 1. Relating this process to a machine suggests that the *input* to the machine would be information about the *entry behavior* of the students in the terms already indicated. Given this information and data on objectives to be achieved, the machine would carry out definite procedures to make appropriate decisions about the program to be used. Figure 1 represents a general model of the teaching process as accomplished by an adaptive teaching machine. It contains as its last step the implementation of a program as the tutorial decision process. This is discussed in detail in a subsequent section.

The Pretutorial Process as a Two-Person Game

It is possible to consider the set of relationships in teaching as a process involving a single student and a teacher in interaction. In doing this, the process is represented as a matrix using the sets of variables already described. This is done in Figure 2 with three elements per set—teacher's program (α, β, γ), student's entry levels (a, b, c), and possible outcomes (1, 2, 3).

| | | Teacher's Programs | | |
		a	β	γ
Student Entry Level	a	2	1	3
	b	1	3	2
	c	3	2	1

FIGURE 2. *A 3 x 3 Matrix Representing Instruction.*

In using this form of representation, for example, a particular objective (e.g., number 1) for a student (S) whose entry behavior is represented by *a* in the matrix can be selected. Having done this, the teaching program is determined and is β. If, however, S's status were *b*, rather than *a*, then the required teaching program to achieve objective 1 would be *a* rather than β.

It is apparent that it is necessary to know three things in order to set up a matrix representing instruction, as shown in Figure 2. The outcomes need to be specified (the numbers), the teaching programs must be known (α, β, or γ), and the entry behavior of the students must be determined (a, b, or c). Any one of the outcomes can be achieved by applying programs α, β, γ to students with a known level of entry behavior. With the example given in Figure 2, the teacher's position is ideal, for he can always achieve a stated objective by simply using one of the available programs. T (the teacher), in fact, has complete control over the outcome, for every row has at least one of the possible objectives in it.

Consider another example. Figure 3 presents a different matrix of the same general form. The difference is not just in size, as an examination in greater detail will show. For example, if S's status at the beginning of the program is c, then T has several ways of achieving outcome 1—by using program β, γ, or δ. If, however, outcome 2 were the objective instead of 1, then T could not always achieve his objective, for if S's entry status was b or c none of the programs available to T would work. Students with entry status b, for example, can only be made to accomplish objectives 1 and 4. The same is true for those whose entry status is c, but for those whose entry status is a, d, or e, objectives 1, 2,

		Teacher's Programs			
		a	β	γ	δ
Student Entry Level	a	2	4	1	1
	b	1	4	1	4
	c	4	1	1	1
	d	4	2	1	2
	e	4	1	2	4

FIGURE 3.   *A 4 x 5 Matrix Representing Instruction.*

or 4 can be achieved. This approach recognizes that it is not always possible to achieve every objective with a given set of programs.

It is apparent that different arrangements within the matrix and different numbers of programs and states available to T and S, respectively, can give rise to a variety of situations with respect to what T can do. In order to cope with the many possibilities that can arise, it is necessary to set some restrictions on the population of matrices, and in doing this to maintain sufficient complexity to be of interest. One type of matrix that does allow a good deal of variability and some measure of precision is the set in which no column contains a repeated outcome. Whenever this is the case, T must select a strategy which takes into account S's entry behavior in order to accomplish the stated objective. Every S requires a different program if a particular objective is to be accomplished. The relations between columns and rows are unrestricted in all respects so that for any r x c matrix there are a number of possible combinations leading to different outcomes. Under

		Teacher's Programs		
		a	β	γ
Student Entry Level	a	6	6	11
	b	11	5	6
	c	13	11	1
	d	2	2	2
	e	3	17	3
	f	8	8	13
	g	10	4	4
	h	1	16	9
	i	12	14	8

FIGURE 4.   *A 3 x 9 Matrix Representing Instruction.*

these conditions the teacher, or teaching machine, needs to be discriminating in specifying a program. Figure 4 is a 3 x 9 matrix of this type. Once an outcome is specified, T must decide which program will be used for each type of entry behavior (a through i). For instance, to achieve objective 11 for an S entering at level a, T should use program γ. When S's entry status is b, then T has to use program a, and when it is c, T must use program β.

Implications of This Analysis of Teaching

The program as a means of transformation uniquely specifies a minimum outcome for a student and a set of outcomes for students who differ in entry behavior. If, for example, only one of the programs (Figure 4) were used with Ss at different P_e levels, then every S would achieve a different score. The outcomes in the matrix might be levels of performance on a valid achievement test divided by the time the program takes.

If only one outcome is accepted as the objective, and the students differ in their entry behavior, then the teacher, or machine, must use a different program for every level of entry behavior. If more than one outcome is accepted, then many different programs still are required, but not as many are needed as when only one outcome is sought. In the example given in Figure 4, the best T can do is to use one of three programs (e.g., once for each of the first three Ss), and then he must repeat one of the programs for the fourth S. Obviously it is impossible to get all Ss to earn the same score unless T has available to him as many different programs as he has types of students in terms of their entry status. This implies the following: *if no two outcomes in the same column are equal, and if a set of outcomes is selected by T, one from each row, and if the table has r rows and c columns, then the number of different outcomes cannot be fewer than r/c.*[3] In the case of Figure 4, the minimum number of outcomes is nine divided by three.

Some Implications for Teaching Machine Design

One thing this analysis implies is that every machine that is limited to a single strategy and set of content units will produce as many out-

---

[3] This is based on the "Law of Requisite Variety" as presented by Ashby (2, Chapter 11).

comes as there are different types of entry status since r/c would reduce to r, with c equal to 1. This implication may seem unacceptable, for it might be asserted that a machine which accommodates only a linear program could be used with a variety of different Ss who might answer every question on the postprogram test. While this might sound like an empirical denial of the analysis, it is not. There are many things that are unspecified in the description which could make the example not fit the model. To get a purchase on the problem, reexamination of each class of events in relation to it is necessary. Since the program is specified, there is no ambiguity there. The other two classes of events, however, could present problems in fitting this model to the hypothetical data. If the achievement test is accepted as both a valid and sufficient index of the outcome, then the distinctions among Ss were invalid. All Ss actually must have been alike at the beginning, for a program transforms a given entry behavior into a single outcome. This says that different values should appear in the matrix for *each* combination of entry level and program. However, all scores were said to be the same, e.g., 100 percent.

With the hypothetical situation just described, the conclusion is that the entry behavior measures are either irrelevant or invalid. As long as the notion of individual difference in entry behavior is accepted, it follows that the outcome of a single teaching program will be the achievement of different outcomes. In other words, different values (representing outcomes) must appear in the rows of any one column, if the entry behavior measure is valid and the test used at the end of instruction is a valid measure of the outcome. While it is possible for students who achieve different aptitude and achievement test scores to attain the same terminal performance level on a valid test of the topics taught, if given a single program, they will not do this in the same amount of time. However, if different programs are given to the students at each of the entry behavior levels, then it is possible for all of them to achieve the same score within the minimum time.

If the number of different outcomes are not equal, at a minimum, to the number of valid classes of entry behavior, something is wrong in one of the following ways: The classes of individual differences are invalid; the test of attainment of objectives is insensitive and does not provide the degree of discrimination that is required; or the programs are not really different.

It is useful to distinguish between the objectives set for a group of students when the content on which they are working is held constant from the objectives set for a single student when content varies. The former are *group objectives* and the latter *individual objectives*. In teaching, the generally accepted goal is to minimize the number of outcomes which are accepted as group objectives. If this goal is used, then it follows that a large number of teaching programs is required if the entry behaviors vary over a broad range. It is generally desired to maximize the number of objectives which each individual student can achieve. Accepting this as a goal will also require a greater number of teaching programs when the number of entry levels is increased.

The implications of this analysis for the design of a teaching machine are clear. A machine must have the capability to handle program decisions if it is to teach students who vary widely in entry behavior. In fact, the broader the range of entry behavior to be taught, the larger the requirement for using different programs if all students are to achieve the same objective. This means one of two things. The first is that a battery of simple machines and linear programs can be used, one with each entry behavior level. The second is that a computer-based teaching system can be used to cope with a wide range of individual differences in entry behavior and in this sense replaces the battery of simple machines. Since the first alternative means that a great deal of program development would be required (a task not easily accomplished), the computer-based system seems to be the more promising alternative. Here, different strategies and sets of content units can be combined to generate a large variety of programs as needed.

Individual Differences: Ability and Methods Interactions

Examination of available data on the possible interactions between ability and method suggests that they do, in fact, occur. Little (37), for example, found that even with college students studying educational psychology, the immediacy of knowledge of results was more critical for the students in the lower half of the ability range than it was for the upper half. Porter (44), working with second- fourth- and sixth-grade children, found greater gains with students in the lower half of his IQ distribution when the use of programed instruction was compared with conventional instruction. McNeil (38), in a study of elementary reading skills requiring oral response, reported that children in lower IQ ranges benefited most. He also found that the boys learned significantly more than the girls from the program, but that when the group was switched to conventional instruction with a teacher the reverse was true. Eigen and others (23) also found an interaction effect between method and IQ (p<.10).

Not all studies that report interaction effects show this pattern, however. Gropper and Lumsdaine (30) and Reed and Hayman (48), for example, found that the better students were helped most with programing. Furthermore, Reed and Hayman report that low-ability students performed better following conventional instruction. These data suggest that while there are significant interactions between ability and method, the maximum benefit may not always involve the high-ability group.

Burton and Goldbeck (8) studied the effect of several factors on learning. Their results with ninth graders who learned about animals did not support Skinner's idea that constructed response was superior to multiple-choice response. However, they did find a significant interaction among learning methods, student aptitude, and the strength of the desired response in the student's repertoire. When easy multiple choice alternatives were used, they produced better learning of common responses by students who had high verbal reasoning aptitude. These data suggest that the difficulty of the material may be a determiner of the particular aptitudes that come into play. If this is correct, then one alternative to build into a monitoring program of a computer-based teaching system would be the capability of altering the difficulty level of the material. By changing the difficulty level (e.g., providing steps with more or less prompting), one should be able to adjust for the contributing aptitudes. Campbell (12) found that "bypassing" or branching was more effective than a linear program for students who scored about the 50th percentile on the DAT[4] numerical test. He further suggests that "bypassing" is most useful when the subject matter has a hierarchical structure. Angell and Lumsdaine (1), using eleventh and twelfth graders, found that a "partial cueing procedure" was more effective for slow learners who were learning hard items of the airline code names for cities. On the other hand, partial cueing procedures

---

[4] Differential Aptitude Test, published by the Psychological Corporation; see Bennett, Seashore, and Wesman (5).

which should make the items easier were found to be less effective for fast learners when they were learning easy items.

In developing strategies it is necessary to combine several procedures. One set of combinations studied by Angell and Lumsdaine (1) involved prompting and confirmation and different conditions of knowledge of results. They found that prompting was more effective than confirmation when partial correction was used to provide knowledge of results. In partial correction, the student was told that one, two, or more responses were correct, although he was not told which one in the set was correct. Prompting and confirmation were equivalent in effectiveness when full correction was used. It would appear from these findings that the process providing full correction has an additional function, namely to give the learner the opportunity to practice another response and in doing this to provide a prompting condition for that practice. Thus, the two procedures become more equivalent.

Aptitude and Achievement Test Correlation: Cartwright (14), Smith (55), and Dick (72), for example, all report evidence suggesting that different methods result in differential patterns of correlation between ability and performance on an achievement test following learning. These data suggest that the differential methods result in different rankings of the students. In other words, each method makes use of different abilities and compensates for others. The research required here is to find the match between ability test scores and strategy decisions.

Methods and Outcomes: It has been reported that methods differ in the outcomes they maximize. Therefore, when it is the case that method A maximizes learning and method B maximizes retention, it is necessary either to choose one or the other or to look for ways in which the outcomes can be optimized. Stolurow and Lippert (60) and Stolurow (57) found that in teaching a sight vocabulary to mentally retarded children, prompting maximized rate of learning and confirmation maximized retention when a high overlearning condition was used. The next step is to study the combinations of prompting and confirmation to see how they can be used together to optimize both rapid acquisition and high retention.

To date the results of studies in programed instruction reveal a larger proportion of differences in time than of differences in level of achievement. This suggests that the outcome to be considered as a dependent variable should involve time required to achieve a particular level of performance. The level of performance is defined by the achievement test administered after completion of the program. Beane (4), for example, used an efficiency index, the ratio of achievement to learning time, as a measure, and in these terms found a branching program more efficient than a linear program in teaching high school students the basic theorems of the geometry of parallel and perpendicular lines.

Coulson and Silberman (16) studied response mode and size of step using a program in psychology with college students. They found a small-step program significantly superior to a large-step program in the amount students learned. However, the small-step program required significantly more time. When students studied with a branch or linear program, they learned an equivalent amount, but with the branch program they took less time.

While Beane's results support those of Coulson and Silberman, his do add an additional finding that complicates the problem. Beane found that students preferred his linear program to his branch version, even though the latter was more efficient for them. If this is repeatedly found, then it suggests that it may be necessary to trade off some efficiency for some amount of positive attitude toward the learning experience. On the other hand, it also may be possible to change attitudes toward the two so that the more efficient procedure also is preferred.

Implications: These data indicate some of the variables that could be considered in the development of teaching strategies and in their selection for use with students in computer-based systems such as those described by Bushnell (9) and Licklider (36). If, for example, one were to decide to use a strategy that compensated for an ability on which students scored low, then the pretutorial decision would be different from that based upon a decision to make maximum use of the ability on which the student was deficient. Both of these pretutorial decisions can be implemented and compared. Consequently, it is not necessary to choose between them. In fact, it might be desirable to make maximum use of deficient aptitudes when the student is very young and to make minimum use (compensate) of deficient aptitudes when the student exceeds a particular age after which aptitude is relatively stable.

The Tutorial Phase of Instruction

Thus far this chapter has been concerned with the decision process required before the tutorial process is begun. Once a strategy and set of content units are selected for a student, the program is implemented in the tutorial phase of instruction. The tutorial process can be defined in terms of three sets of variables. The first set is made up of content units. The second set consists of response measures such as latencies or number of incorrect responses for a given set of content units. The third set consists of the *decision rules* which relate the response measures to the presentation of subsequent content units.[5] For a given program (set of decision rules and content units), the values of the response measures obtained from the student determine the instructional sequence. This can be illustrated by considering a branching program of the Crowder type (18). Here, one response measure is used which can take on a number of values: correct response, incorrect response-A, incorrect response-B, incorrect response-C, etc. The content units are divided into two sets: the main sequence units and the remedial units. Each main unit has associated with it a number of remedial units. The decision rule is as follows: for each main unit, look at the student's response; if it is correct, present the next main content unit; if it is incorrect-A, present remedial content unit-A; if it is incorrect-B, present remedial content unit-B; etc. Thus, the decision rule specifies the next frame on the basis of the student's response.

In computer-based systems, the decision rule can make use of more comprehensive, and, therefore, more reliable, response information (e.g., latencies, sets of past responses) and is able to specify a greater variety of instructional sequences on the basis of data of this kind and their derivatives (e.g., weighted averages, expected values). Rigney (49) reports some data indicating that if a frame is missed once, one cannot assume that it will or will not be missed again and that one cannot be certain that if it is not missed once, it will not be missed on a subsequent trial. Decisions at branch points, he suggests, probably should be based on performance on concepts rather than on individual frames. For a computer-based system, four requirements are to be

[5] In the model presented by Stolurow (59) which deals with the instructional system, a learning task is defined in terms of performance standard as related to input. The decision rules are the means by which performance standards are put to use.

considered in developing decision rules: (a) appropriateness of stimulus materials, (b) reliability of response measure, (c) validity of criteria for branching, and (d) availability of remedial or enrichment sequences.

The interaction of the program and the student as previously described is much like that of a teacher and a student. Therefore, to distinguish the implementation of a program from the monitoring of a program (which is discussed shortly), the former will be referred to as the *Teacher Function*. The Teacher Function, then, involves the use of a decision rule with particular frames to choose subsequent content frames or feedback statements on the basis of entry infomation so as to achieve a particular objective.

It is also possible to build into a teaching system the capability of learning about the student as he responds (41). On the basis of a monitoring process, changes in the program itself can be made (e.g., either content, strategy, or both) if the student's performance exceeds certain bounds. If it is found that the strategy being used is too demanding (e.g., the pace is too fast), then a strategy more suited to the student can be substituted while keeping the content fixed. On the other hand, it may be found that the content being used (e.g., theory) is not suited to the student, in which case a new set (e.g., application) is specified while the strategy remains fixed.

The monitoring of student's responses, the forecasting of future achievement from current response data, and the decision to continue or change the program depending upon the relationship of the forecast to the objective will be referred to as the *Professor Function*. A part of the computer core memory is allotted to each student, and both the responses and their latencies are stored. Sets of these are compared with standards to determine whether they are within the limits set. If they are, then the program will be continued. If not, then a different program will be used. The changes in strategy while the student is responding are called dynamic decisions. Each is a change in the program on the basis of student performance. The performance measures which are used in this case are more comprehensive than those used in the Teacher Function. In fact, in addition to ability and personality measures, responses to program materials may be used in a decision process similar to that employed in the pretutorial phase (Figure 1).

A diagram of the interaction of the student, Teacher, and Professor is illustrated in Figure 5. Here, there is two-way communication from the student to the Teacher and from the Teacher to the Professor, but only one-way communication from the student to the Professor. In other words, the Professor always communicates his decision through the Teacher to the student.

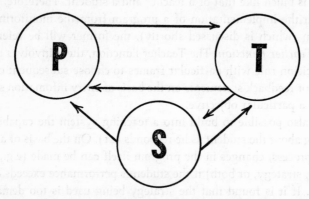

FIGURE 5. *Flow Diagram of Student-Teacher-Professor Interactions.*

The professor builds up an "image" or model of the way the student is learning. The model, therefore, is not known in advance of the student's performance on the program, but the kinds of information used to build it are known. Once certain information is determined about the student's behavior while he is learning, then the strategy or content set can be changed. For example, if latency of response is used initially and the student continues to respond at or above a specified rate over a set of steps, then the Professor may decide that use of response latency can be dropped out of later decisions. If student performance is within certain limits of accuracy, the Professor may change the tolerance limits used in giving the student knowledge of results. Thus, higher and higher levels of accuracy could be required at a rate determined by each student's own responses.

The Professor might use response rate as information about motivation level, and this might be derived from a comparison of the present student's rate with the average of other students on the same steps. Thus, the Professor may use records of a large number of different students in making a decision about one. Another basis for dynamic decision making might be a discrepancy between a predicted error rate based upon a correlation of aptitude and errors using a standardization sample of students and students' actual error rates. Correlation techniques might be used in computing the expected value, and then this would be used in accomplishing the transformation. If this were done, then performance that was better than expected might be transformed into an order from the Professor to the Teacher to skip particular sections of the content set or to reduce to a minimum all sets of review steps scheduled to appear later on, etc. If, on the other hand, the performance of the student were as expected, then the Teacher would continue with the program as originally planned. If, however, performance were lower than expected, the Professor might specify a change in strategy which might result in more remediation for each student error.

This description of the tutorial phase of instruction completes the functional analysis of teaching as accomplished by an adaptive teaching machine system. The process is accomplished in two phases: the pretutorial and tutorial decision processes. The pretutorial process involves the selection of a program for a particular student on the basis of his past ability and performance records. The tutorial process involves two interacting processes. In the first, the Teacher Function selects an instructional sequence on the basis of immediate student performance. In the second, the Professor Function makes changes in the process, and it is hoped that this analysis provides a start in that direction.

To those who are familiar with present-day teaching machines, this description may seem too elaborate. However, the development of complex computer-based systems requires a careful analysis of the teaching process, and it is hoped that this analysis provides a start in that direction.

In a subsequent section, a computer-based system which incorporates some of the ideas developed here is described. Prior to this description there is a detailed examination of the basic functions of a teaching system.

Functions Performed During the Implementation of a Program

In order to implement a program it is necessary to perform certain functions. Thus, if a machine is to make use of the student's responses in making decisions, it must somehow acquire the responses and put them in usable form for evaluation. The system component which accepts the student's responses (e.g., a typewriter) and displays the output of the computer (e.g., a printout on the typewriter) is called the interface unit. It acquires the student's responses and codes them in an unambiguous way and in a form that permits the computer to use them. This is the communication link between the student and the teaching machine. As such its design and operation depend on human engineering factors relating to man-machine compatibility and learning objectives.

Within the limits of machine capabilities it is desired to allow the communication of all information which is necessary for the program to work properly. Thus, depending on the teaching requirements, the interface unit might involve any combination of mechanical, oral, visual, written, or typewritten communication. Also, each mode of communication may be either one-way (only student to machine or only machine to student) or two-way (from student to machine and machine back to the student). An example of two-way communication is the case in which the student communicates with the machine via push buttons (mechanical), and the machine communicates with the student via a viewing screen (visual). Many systems which are used by blind, deaf, or paraplegic students will require specially designed interface equipment.

The problems which are encountered in this area are perhaps the most difficult within the field of teaching machine design. The reason for this is that the design of the interface unit is subject to technological constraints and human engineering factors (see 43) as well as educational factors. The educator, of course, must define the objectives of instruction in behavioral terms. Knowing his demands, the human engineer and technologist must devise a *workable* interface unit. In the final analysis, the design of a working system will depend on financial as well as technological factors.

Within the broad classification of *response accommodation, evaluation, selection,* and *display functions,* there are certain operations which must be performed by every teaching machine. While all of these are not always stated explicitly, each is nevertheless involved in every instance of tutorial instruction. Furthermore, depending upon the degree of automation, each of these functions is performed either by a device or a person. Consequently, a description of a teaching system's operation is a statement that considers each of these functions.

When the learner accomplishes one or more of these functions, he is, in fact, performing a teacher's function, not a learner's function. In other words, students can teach themselves, but this is just a special case of the general concept of teaching described here. In short, from a systems point of view it is not critical that any function be performed by either a machine or a person. Nor is it critical who the person is if it is not performed by a machine. The nature of the function is the same in any case.

In teaching machine operation, the actual transformations specified by each function determine the teaching strategy. When these are used in conjunction with a particular set of content units, the teaching program is determined. Thus, the output of the pretutorial decision process is implemented by specifying the particular transformation accomplished by each function on a set of content units or frames. For example, evaluation can be made in terms of any number of responses, and selection can be made from various subsets of the total content set. The remainder of this section is concerned with a description of various machine functions.[6]

Response Accommodation: The response function involves the communication of the student's response to the machine and the transformation of it into a form that is usable by a particular teaching machine system. The characteristics of the equipment used to perform this function depend on the response mode (written, typed, punched, etc.) indicated by a behavioral analysis of the task being taught and the form of the response information needed for purposes of evaluation. In a simple machine which incorporates a linear program, the response is written (constructed or selected) and stored on paper for later analysis. There is no need for the system to use the response for evaluation purposes, since there is no decision making involved.

In the case of computer-based systems their versatility has been greatly increased by using typewriter-like response units at the student stations (e.g., 6, 36, 64). With these devices the response is constructed and then transformed into a form which can be used for decision

---

[6] These are based on an earlier analysis of the critical requirements of teaching machines (27, pp. 129-32; 58).

making. Also, several response measures other than the correctness of the student's response can be used (e.g., latencies, electrocardiographic response, [3][7]) with the appropriate equipment.

Evaluation: Involved in the evaluation function is the *comparison* of the response measure with a standard. This is called the comparator function, and the component in a teaching machine system which serves this function is called a comparator. The input to a comparator may be either the same symbol system used in the display or a transformation of these symbols. Whichever is used must permit a comparison of the student's response with that which is correct—the standard. If a computer does the comparing for the student, as does PLATO (7, 70, 71) and SOCRATES (described later in this chapter), then the response has to be transformed into computer language so that it can be compared with the answer that is stored in the computer. In the simpler systems, however, the comparison function is accomplished by the student himself when he looks at his response and compares it with the correct one printed in a particulur place on the display material (e.g., Skinner's machines and those like them [25]).

While a student can perform this function, a machine such as a computer is required if the student is told he is wrong without also being told the right answer (e.g., PLATO). Furthermore, if response rate is part of the critical response information, then the comparison function is performed using response latency as well as correctness, and consequently the process is more complicated and the temporal constraints more severe. By providing the student with data on his response rate, he could compare his response latency to a standard, but requiring him to do this, particularly if he is young, might destroy the rhythm and continuity of his response sequence (e.g., in learning to play a musical instrument). In the automated teaching of Hollerith card punching (42), typewriting, or stenotyping (65), both the accuracy and the latency of response are compared to appropriate standards. For these purposes a computer-based system seems indicated. If the evaluation is to make use of past response information, then the machine must have

---

[7] Another report describing heart rate measures obtained during programed learning on PLATO is currently being prepared by J. Easley and will be issued as CSL Report No. R-186.

memory capabilities for the student's previous responses as well as for the performance standards used in the evaluation. If the evaluation is to be used to select subsequent content units for presentation, it is necessary to have a library of content units available and to have a means of choosing the way in which the units are presented. Also display functions are needed to present the selected content units and to give the student knowledge of results.

The output of a comparator must be arranged and stored in a form which permits its use in immediate or delayed decision making and in subsequent analysis. This is accomplished by the *collating* and *recording* functions which involve accumulation and arranging of information about the student's responses as the program progresses. Generally, it is desired that the individual responses be related to relevant steps of the program. This is useful for program revision and for individual diagnosis once a program has been developed. For individual diagnostic purposes the accumulated record of a student's responses to selected sets of steps (e.g., all steps relating to a concept) may be used in making dynamic decisions about the teaching program (Professor Function) that follows.

Selection: The information stored by the collator-recorder is used to select content units for presentation and/or to choose a particular pace for the student. The content units are in the *library* of the machine which is used for storage of material to display. Storage may be in the form of magnetic fields, perforated tape, punch cards, or printed as in film or on paper. The transformation differs depending upon the form of storage and the amount of memory used. Memory may be in more than one form and place, as when a computer stores the frame locations of steps in its core storage and uses these to select information for display which is stored on film in a projector. The two problems associated with this function are those of capacity and access time. Available systems differ in their limitations on storage, e.g., core storage of computers and film capacity of projectors, for PLATO (7, 70, 71), the IBM 1410 System developed by Uttal (63), and SOCRATES developed by Stolurow (74).

The input to the library is provided by a *selector*; the output is a particular set of frames and KR that is displayed to the student. The selector function is equivalent to the *teacher* in that it uses response-dependent information to choose content units or KR statements for subsequent display. Part of the selector function is the provision of knowledge of results (KR) in which the student is given feedback relating to his response. The separation of this function from the selection of content units is desirable if there is likely to be a delay in the display of the step providing new information due to the search time involved in locating the next step. If the student rather than the machine provides knowledge of results, then with the minimum level of selection represented by a linear style of program, the feedback is just as rapid for wrong as for right responses since the next frame provides the stimulus material which the student used in evaluating his own response. In general, it can be assumed that the student would recognize his errors as rapidly as he would his correct responses. However, this is not necessarily the case, and if it is not the case, the time interval between response and knowledge of results when he is right would not be equal to the time interval when he is wrong. With a branch style of program, a more complex level of selection, the times can be manipulated so that they are not necessarily the same. If a machine such as a computer is used to provide KR feedback, then the times can be equated, or not, dependent upon their relative effectiveness for teaching a student. At this level of selection, KR can be programed by a computer so that it is on a schedule which could provide anywhere from o to 100 percent reinforcement. In intrinsic programing (18, 19), information and KR are contingent upon the last response. Consequently, the selection rule in intrinsic programing involves a decision based on a one-step memory.

In idiomorphic programing, as used in the SOCRATES system, selection is contingent upon a more extensive response history than that used in intrinsic programing. For example, the selection rule may take into account aptitude data, initial knowledge, and information about a set of responses made during learning, but not necessarily those immediately preceding the responses to be made. This is similar to the description provided by Husky (32). In this case, correctness and latency may be used either separately or jointly. Idiomorphic programing also may use derived scores such as estimations of performance which are forecasts based on earlier responses and their relation to the criterion task.

Display: The display function represents a transformation of a designated sample of content into a set of conventional symbols with certain constraints. The symbols determine the modality (e.g., printed words —visual modality). The constraints imposed are those pertaining to the *form* of the display as a set of instructional steps and to the *duration* of its exposure to the student.[8] To illustrate the transformation, the program to be taught might be stored in the system as a perforated tape, but the display used by the student, which might be printed words on a TV screen, requires a fairly elaborate transformation process. The engineering details are much more complex than those of moving a printed page into view or of transporting a film and illuminating it to make it visible to the students (see 25 for examples of devices using these methods). In using these devices, the content is stored in the same form that it is seen by the student. Therefore, the transformation accomplished by display is trivial, e.g., the linear motion of a piece of paper. The function cannot be ignored, however, for obviously it is significant in the case of a computer-based teaching system.

An important part of the total display is knowledge of results. As discussed, the transformation that is required to display this information to the student may be independent of that involved in the display of content, but it is more common to achieve both by the same transformation, e.g., a new display may appear only if the response to the last one is correct, or knowledge of results may be given to all students when they go to the next frame as in a linear program. Obviously, a general model has to allow for the independence of these two transformations as well as for their complete dependence upon one another.

While all the above functions must be included in any teaching machine, examples were given which illustrated that the manner in which the functions are carried out varies widely. In the simplest or least adaptive machines, they are carried out by the learner himself. In more complex or adaptive machines, many are carried out automatically, and it is expected that in computer-based systems all teaching functions will be controlled by the computer and its peripheral equipment.

---

[8] Recently, Hickey and others (31) considered the problems of display in relation to a graphic teaching machine. They present a content analysis of graphics used in a high school textbook.

TABLE 1

Some Current Computer-Based Systems

	IBM[1] T. J. Watson Res. Center	U. of Ill. CSL[2] PLATO	U. of Ill. TRL[3] SOCRATES
# Input Stations	40	10	14
Input Equipment	Stenotype, IBM 1050 I/O type-writer, and matrix keyboard	Special keyboard	Modified Autotutor (Master Tutor) special keyboard
Library (Media)	Slides and audio tape	Randomly accessible slides	Randomly accessible 35mm filmstrip
Computer	IBM 1410/1440	CDC 1604	IBM 1620 IBM 1710 Control System
Programing Languages	Coursewriter	Codap, Fortran	Symbolic Programming System, Fortran
Display	Type-written text, pro-jected image, and audio input and output	Projected slide image on TV screen, electronic blackboard	Projected filmstrip image, message display

[1] See Koppitz, (34); Uttal, (63).
[2] Coordinated Science Laboratory. See Bitzer, Braunfeld, and Lichtenberger (7); Bitzer and Braunfeld (6); Bitzer (70); and Braunfeld (71).
[3] Training Research Laboratory, University of Illinois. See Stolurow (74).

TABLE 1 *(Continued)*
Some Current Computer-Based Systems

	System Development Corporation CLASS[4]	Bolt Beranek & Newman[5] Socratic System	Stanford University Stanford System[6]	Cybernetic[7] Dev. Ltd. Automated Classroom
# Input Stations	20	1	6	20
Input Equipment	Special keyboard	Typewriter or teletype	Keyboard, paper tape, light pen, microphone	Teleprinter or type-writer
Library (Media)	35mm filmstrip, individual sound tapes or printed material	Magnetic Drum	Random access microfilm and audio tape	Punched tape and/or coded cards
Computer	Philco 2000	PDP-1	PDP-1 (modified) IBM 7090 Backup	Adaptive controller
Programing Languages	JOVIAL	Special	DEC MARCO	Prewired Logic
Display	Type-written text, pro-jected slide image	Typewritten text	Slide image, audio message, character display	Typewritten cards and printed paper, tape, cue lamp, display

[4] See Coulson (15). Also in Bushnell and Cogswell (11); Bushnell (9, 10).
[5] See Licklider (36). See Feurzig (73).
[6] Personal communication.
[7] Teaches only teleprinter operation.

Some Computer-Based Systems

While a number of computer-based systems have been developed and are being used experimentally at the present time, their use in automated instruction is often less than it might be (15). Too frequently, they simply ape the simpler systems. There is little point in using a computer to simulate a Skinner-type machine, a programed text, or even a "Tutor Text" (e.g., 18).

Pask (42), on the other hand, originally described machines that use computers to do things which it would be impossible or impractical to accomplish by any other means. In addition, PLATO and SOCRATES perform functions involving a large number of decisions in extremely short periods of time, so short that no person could process the same data in the time available. It is quite apparent from the brief description given of the functions involved in tutorial instruction that there are many different ways in which each function can be accomplished. For example, the display function can be accomplished with paper, film, or tape, and the response function might be accomplished by a keyboard or a typewriter. The specification of a set of functions for eventual use in machine design has to be supplemented with an engineering description to achieve a workable system.

Table 1 is a very brief description of some of the major features of several computer-based systems currently being used. The descriptions do not reveal all that needs to be known in evaluating a system of this type for a particular purpose. It would be necessary to consult the references and the personnel involved to do this.

Description of SOCRATES

SOCRATES is a newly designed cybernetic instructional system. It was developed as an adaptive teaching machine system along the lines of the model presented earlier. It will be described here in order to illustrate the features of a modular system designed to conduct educational research of the kind described in the next section. The system gets its name from its description—System for Organizing Content To Review and Teach Educational Subjects. As in the case with even the simplest machines, the basic plan is a student, a machine, and a program in interaction.

The display unit for SOCRATES is a rear-view projection screen. The student's response is the selection of 1 of 15 buttons which is fed into a computer. The computer has stored in its memory the instructions that will tell it what to do with this information. One thing it does is to make a permanent record of the response in such a way that the response can be collated with the display that was shown at the time. Another thing it does immediately is tell the student that he is right or wrong through a separate KR circuit which turns on a green (right) or red (wrong) light in the display. This is done before the next frame is displayed. The computer also scans the library key stored in the core and selects from it a program step to be displayed next. The displayable library is a 35mm film containing as many as 1,500 frames on each of which can be stored anything that can be put on a printed page.

The flow diagram of SOCRATES is shown in Figure 6. The response acquisition and display functions, each of which is cable-connected to the multiplexer and terminal unit, are carried out at the student station (interface unit). The evaluation and selection functions are carried out by the Professor and Teacher. While the Teacher is involved with the implementation of the current program, the Professor searches for the new programs if the present one is not effective. The Administration controls the entire process, and a large-capacity remote computer may be used in cases where the on-line computer cannot handle the operations. Also, when a student leaves a station, a command is relayed to the administration (via the "recess" path), and action is taken to record the current status of the system (e.g., last frame presented, topic, strategy, content set) and the student's response record. When the student returns, this information is fed back into the system, and the status is restored so he can continue.

The actual equipment system is diagrammed in Figure 7. As indicated, the student stations, of which there are 14, can be different and could include at any time such devices as AutoTutors, Perceptoscope teaching machines, BINARY (Beginning Instruction for Normal and Retarded Youngsters), a typewriter, or any digital device.

Each student station has its location code or address. It is wired directly to the computer. The Professor rules and associated memory blocks are stored in the computer. The Teacher uses the rules specified in the pretutorial phase. The associated content set is chosen from the

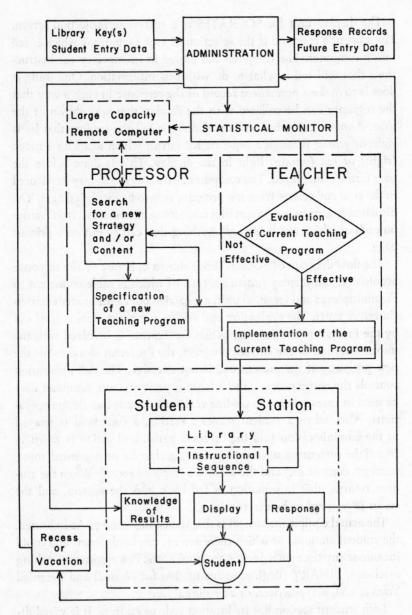

FIGURE 6. *Flow Diagram of SOCRATES System.*

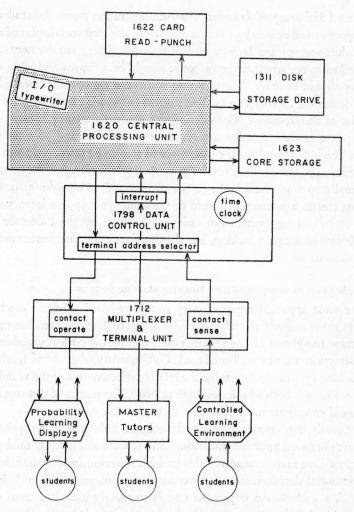

FIGURE 7. *Equipment Interconnections.*

displayable library. Not all students need to start at the same place, nor do they all have to study the same thing. Each of the 14 stations can have a different content.

Each time a student makes a response, an interrupt signal is generated. The Administration interrupts whatever it is doing (which may be just waiting for a student to respond) to identify the student who made the response and the response he made. Multiple responses are queued and accepted in order. The Administration stores the student's responses and determines the time at which the step was displayed and its duration, or the latency of the response. Pacer requirements are checked to see whether the response should be accepted and what display should be made. The response is checked against the library key to determine its correctness. The student is signaled knowledge of results of this response. Considering the student's latency history, his response history, and his test scores (e.g., aptitude and personality), the Teacher determines the instructional step to be displayed from the library key. The decision results in a signal which transfers the instructional step from the library to the display unit. The Administration then creates a permanent record of the student's response latency and instructional step which not only can be used by the Professor for subsequent decision making, but also is a part of the permanent record of the student.

Applications of Computer-Based Teaching Machine Systems

The most apparent application of computer-based teaching machine systems is to study the relative effectiveness of particular teaching programs. In spite of all the research on teaching, the critical variables in instruction are not well analyzed. Consequently, the use of teaching machine systems to determine the relative effectiveness of the variables in teaching is both a basic and high priority. The results of this research should contribute materially to a theory of teaching.

Equally important is the research designed to determine the optimum match between aptitude (individual differences) and instructional programs. One manifestation of this problem, previously identified, is the pretutorial decision, since it determines the program used initially to teach a student. An important task is to specify useful categories of individual differences among the Ss. One way to determine the utility of a set of distinctions is to use a single program with Ss whose test scores differ to see which Ss perform best. There should be at least as many different levels of outcome as there are meaningful distinctions (categories) among the Ss. The results of these studies would contribute to a theory of adaptive teaching, for the data would reveal the best combinations to use in teaching.

Basic research on learning is a third area of study to which the teaching machine system can be applied, e.g., paired associates learning

(36). In particular, a computer-based teaching machine system should provide a means for studying more complex experimental designs to determine the interactions of higher order that might be important in developing strategies (e.g., see 69). Furthermore, such a system would permit the more rapid conduct of these studies, reducing the time lags that now exist in basic research between hypothesis formation and its test and between research and application.

It would seem that the real future of programed instruction lies in the development of knowledge about the more complex strategy of instruction which cannot be implemented in any other way than by the use of the computer-based system. In brief, the variables comprising the Professor strategies, as well as Teacher strategies, need to be studied. Some specific variables that seem promising at this time, both in terms of educational implications and practicality, are correctness and latency patterns of response on frames selected because of their known relevance to the frame to which the student is currently responding. Associated with this is a requirement to specify the tolerance limits that define acceptable performance. Whenever these limits are exceeded, a decision should be made, and it would seem reasonable to expect that the decisions made would be when the values exceed the upper boundary and when they exceed the lower boundary.

Two Instructional Problems: Two similar and interrelated instructional problems seem to be undifferentiated in current thinking about the requirements for automated instruction. One of these, the more prominent of the two, is the preprogramed self-instruction (PSI) which has enjoyed widespread and increasing attention in recent years. In developing this form of instruction, a strategy is developed through pragmatic research and built into a set of instructional materials (a program). These materials are used uniformly for all students to whom the instruction is given. This has been referred to in this chapter as the Teacher strategy, and the familiar forms are linear and branch (or intrinsic) programs.

A second form of instruction has gone almost unnoticed. However, Licklider (35) has considered the situation in which the individual has passed the spoon-feeding stage and needs to learn how to direct and organize his own activities. For this pattern of learner-computer interaction, he has suggested the term "man-computer symbiosis." The computer becomes an inanimate assistant performing a variety of routine tasks including routine information, storage, and retrieval functions. At still another level of sophistication, an inanimate assistant can be envisioned that learns about the person being assisted and thereby increases the efficiency with which assistance is provided. Both of these levels of man-computer symbiosis can be considered as a variety of self-programed individualized education (SPIE). In this form of instruction, the learner is presumed to be more mature and knowledgeable than in PSI. For example, the learner may have acquired logic and mathematics skills and concepts, and the ability to use these, for example, to develop a proof. Here, the student may quiz the system in that he may formulate or select a step and ask if it is acceptable. The system affirms or denies the step depending upon whether or not it conforms to a set of rules. The PLATO group has been developing this approach (21). Here the general objective of the instruction is to teach the student a performance paradigm strategy, or skill in information processing, e.g., inquiry, logic of proof.

In another variation of this basic approach, it also is assumed that the student has acquired substantial amounts of information relating to general areas of knowledge, has acquired some self-instructional strategies, but has gaps in what he has already mastered. In other words, with SPIE, the learner has some knowledge and information processing skills and wants to complete his repertoire of information as it relates to a specified objective. He is presumed to be capable of defining for himself the gaps that he has in his knowledge and of making useful decisions about the sequence he wants to follow to fill in these gaps.

Under these conditions, the strategies or decisions about learning are taught or they were just turned over to the student. For the SPIE applications, the teaching system must be developed to provide appropriate and critical categories as the topical areas to be selected by the student. These would provide a kind of inventory of the available or possible programs. The student's task is to select (or construct) appropriate steps in a particular order that meets his own needs as he perceives them.

Finally, a computer-based teaching facility could provide data that would soon make it obsolete. The research on the problems mentioned also will provide data relating to the redesign of the system used, and these very data are what will permit even more substantial research at a later time.

Implications for Research

The question is often asked about the advantages of a teaching machine over a book format. This seems to be a relevant question on the surface, but, on analysis, turns out to be specious for two reasons. First, it is specious for the same reason that a comparison between automated instruction and live instruction is invalid. Any study that compares a program with a teacher is comparing two samples of a single case each. Furthermore, each sample (the program, the teacher, the program without a machine, or the program with it) is typically of unknown merit relative to other possible exemplars of its own universe. Thus, a subsequent study comparing two other exemplars drawn, respectively, from each of the two populations, could find opposite results.

Second, the question is wrong. The one that needs to be asked is, "How simple or how complex a machine should one use?" By simple and complex is meant the number of different teaching programs the machine can make available for use. The machine vs. book question cuts things differently from the question of having one vs. having many programs available for use. Consequently, the pertinent variable does not get manipulated when studies are conducted in which a group using a machine is compared with a group using a book. The results could come out differently in separate experiments depending upon the relative number of programs used by the machine compared to the number used by the book in coping with different levels of student entry behavior and their appropriateness for each category of student. The typical finding from the studies reported thus far (28) is that there is no difference in the effectiveness of a machine and a book. This result is to be expected since in these studies the number of teaching programs was equal for the two. As long as the number of different groups of Ss classified in terms of entry behavior was the same for those using the book as for those using the machine, the results should be the same in terms of the number of different classes of outcomes.

The implication, then, is that research should be conducted on the relationships between input behaviors (aptitude and performance), programs (strategies and content), and outcomes (time, final performance level, and topic covered). As a result, questions such as the following would be answered: For a given subject area and objective (or set of terminal behaviors), how many strategies and content sets should the system have in order to teach efficiently with a given range of student input? What are the characteristics of strategies and content units which work best for particular aptitudes? What are the natures of the limits which aptitude places on the outcomes that are achievable? Related is the notion of the aptitude span which a given strategy equates in terms of outcome; the strategy can be considered an operator which works with a set of aptitude scores. Some strategies do not work, so the distribution of individual differences and the mean remain unchanged. Others obviously do work and typically change the rank order of the students on the posttest, but do not alter the mean or variance (14, 55). Still other strategies produce different degrees of dispersion at different levels within a group of students. In fact, a potentially useful difference among strategies could be the range of ability scores over which equivalent posttest performance is achieved. For example, Detambel and Stolurow (20) used ACE[9] quintiles and compared them under two different strategies. With one strategy the lowest quintile performed as well as the highest, whereas with the other strategy these two levels were significantly different.

In the early stages of research, computer-based systems would be used to develop optimum decision rules in relation to the aptitude and personality characteristics of the students (17, 54). On the basis of this, tables such as those in Figures 2, 3, and 4 would be filled in, and a true technology of teaching would result. Computer-based systems would be used to find the best program for each student and to implement and monitor tutorial instruction given him.

Is a Computer-Based Teaching Machine Practical?

If this question means "Is a computer-based system something which only the most wealthy can afford?" then the answer is no. In fact, it may be just the reverse (6), for it has been estimated that with the PLATO system as many as 1,000 students could be taught up to eight different programs simultaneously, and the computer would be working only about one-third the time. Therefore, the computer could be used for other things, e.g., computing estimated scores for students or step difficulty values.

[9] ACE is the American Council of Education test.

In terms of cost per student hour of instruction, it is difficult to get a firm estimate; however, one recently computed by Bitzer and Braunfeld (6) suggests that the cost based upon the use of existing hardware could be brought down to 10 cents per hour per student. However, this does not include the cost of the system nor the cost of the programs used in it. Teager (61) has pointed out that time sharing and multiprograming can be an important mechanism for reducing total cost. Cost also can be reduced by using commercially available components as used with the SOCRATES system which also used an inexpensive computer. In estimating cost, it is important to include the cost of the equipment as well as that of operation. Consequently, the cost per hour of instruction would be greater than indicated; however, the real question is whether the system makes the cost of instruction competitive with the alternatives. Secondly, it is probably realistic to consider the possibility that many alternatives may not be as effective, and effectiveness needs to be put into the equation. Edwards (22) has presented a model for doing this. The available data (6) say that the computer-based teaching machine system is not only practical for research but for regular instruction as well. The problems in achieving widespread use are not those of economics; they are psychological and educational.

References

1. Angell, D., and Lumsdaine, A. A. *The Effects of Prompting Trials and Partial-Correction Procedures on Learning by Anticipation.* San Mateo, Calif.: American Institute for Research, 1961.
2. Ashby, W. R. *An Introduction to Cybernetics.* London: Chapman and Hall, 1962.
3. Avner, R. A. *Heart Rate Correlates of Insight.* CSL Report R-198. Urbana: Coordinated Science Laboratory, University of Illinois, April 1964.
4. Beane, D. G. *A Comparison of Linear and Branching Techniques of Programed Instruction in Plane Geometry.* USOE Title VII Project No. 711151.01. Technical Report No. 1. Urbana: Training Research Laboratory, University of Illinois, 1962.
5. Bennett, G. K.; Seashore, H. G.; and Wesman, A. G. *Differential Aptitude Test Manual.* Third edition. New York: Psychological Corporation, 1959.
6. Bitzer, D. L., and Braunfeld, P. G. "Description and Use of a Computer Controlled Teaching System." *Proceedings of the National Electronics*

Conference. Chicago: National Electronics Conference, 1962. Vol. 18, pp. 787-94.

7. Bitzer, D. L.; Braunfeld, P. G.; and Lichtenberger, W. W. "Plato II: A Multiple Student, Computer Controlled, Automatic Teaching Device." *Programmed Learning and Computer-Based Instruction.* (Edited by J. E. Coulson.) New York: John Wiley & Sons, 1962. pp. 205-16.

8. Burton, B. B., and Goldbeck, R. A. *The Effect of Response Characteristics and Multiple-Choice Alternatives on Learning During Programed Instruction.* San Mateo, Calif.: American Institute for Research, 1962.

9. Bushnell, D. D. "Computer-Based Teaching Machines." *Journal of Educational Research* 55: 528-31; June-July 1962.

10. Bushnell, D. D. "Computers in the Classroom." *Data Processing* 4, April 1962.

11. Bushnell, D. D., and Cogswell, J. F. A. "Computer-Based Laboratory for Automation in Systems." *AV Communication Review* 9: 173-85; July-August 1961.

12. Campbell, V. N. *Studies of Bypassing as a Way of Adapting Self-Instructional Programs to Individual Differences.* San Mateo, Calif.: American Institute for Research, 1962.

13. Carpenter, C. R., and others. *Comparative Research on Methods and Media for Presenting Programed Courses in Mathematics and English.* University Park: University Division of Instructional Services, Pennsylvania State University, 1963.

14. Cartwright, G. P. *Two Types of Programed Instruction for Mentally Retarded Adolescents.* Master's thesis. Urbana: University of Illinois, 1962. (Typewritten)

15. Coulson, J. E. "A Computer-Based Laboratory for Research and Development in Education." *Programmed Learning and Computer-Based Instruction.* (Edited by J. E. Coulson.) New York: John Wiley & Sons, 1962.

16. Coulson, J. E., and Silberman, H. F. "Effects of Three Variables in a Teaching Machine." *Journal of Educational Psychology* 51: 135-43; June 1960.

17. Cronbach, L. J., and Gleser, Goldene C. *Psychological Tests and Personnel Decisions.* Urbana: University of Illinois, 1964.

18. Crowder, N. A. "Automatic Tutoring by Intrinsic Programming. *Teaching Machines and Programmed Learning.* (Edited by A. A. Lumsdaine and R. Glaser.) Washington, D.C.: National Education Association, 1960.

19. Crowder, N. A. *The Arithmetic of Computers.* New York: Doubleday and Co., 1960.

20. Detambel, M. H., and Stolurow, L. M. "Stimulus Sequence and Concept Learning." *Journal of Experimental Psychology* 51: 34-40; January 1956.

21. Easley, J. A.; Gelder, H. M.; and Golden, W. M. *A PLATO Program for Instruction and Data Collection in Mathematical Problem Solving.* CSL Report R-185. Urbana, Ill.: Coordinated Science Laboratory, 1964.

22. Edwards, W. "The Use of Statistical Decision Functions in Making Practical Decisions." *Air Force Human Engineering Personnel and Training Research.* (Edited by G. Finch and F. Cameron.) Baltimore: ARDC, 1956. pp. 115-24.

23. Eigen, L. D., and others. *A Comparison of Three Modes of Presenting a Programed Instruction Sequence.* New York: Center for Programed Instruction, 1962. (Mimeo.)

24. English, H. B. "How Psychology Can Facilitate Military Training: A Concrete Example." *Journal of Applied Psychology* 26: 3-7; February 1942.

25. Finn, J. D., and Perrin, D. G. *Teaching Machines and Programed Learning, 1962: A Survey of the Industry.* Occasional Paper No. 3. Washington, D.C.: Technological Development Project, National Education Association, 1962.

26. Frase, L. T. *The Effect of Social Reinforcers in a Programed Learning Task.* ONR Contract Nonr 1834(36), Technical Report No. 11. Urbana: Training Research Laboratory, University of Illinois, September 1963.

27. Gage, N. L. "Paradigms for Research on Teaching." *Handbook of Research on Teaching.* Chicago: Rand McNally & Co., 1963. pp. 94-141.

28. Goldstein, L. S., and Gotkin, L. G. "A Review of Research: Teaching Machines vs. Programed Textbooks as Presentation Modes." *Journal of Programed Instruction* 1: 29-35; No. 1, 1962.

29. Goodman, R. *Programed Learning and Teaching Machines: An Introduction.* London: English University Press, 1962.

30. Gropper, G. L., and Lumsdaine, A. A. *An Experimental Comparison of a Conventional TV Lesson with Programed TV Lesson Requiring Active Student Response.* Studies in Televised Instruction, Report No. 2. Pittsburgh: Metropolitan Pittsburgh Educational Television Stations WQED-WDEX and American Institute for Research, 1961.

31. Hickey, A. E., and others. *Requirements for Graphic Teaching Machines.* USOE Grant No. 7-31-0570-161. Boston: Northeastern University, December 1962.

32. Husky, H. D. "Automatic Computers and Teaching Machines." *Programmed Learning and Computer-Based Instruction.* (Edited by J. E. Coulson.) New York: John Wiley & Sons, 1962. pp. 257-72.

33. Jevons, W. S. *The Principles of Science.* New York: Dover, 1958.

34. Koppitz, W. J. "The Computer and Programed Instruction." *Datamation* 9: 50-58; November 1963.

35. Licklider, J. C. R. "Man-Computer Symbiosis." *IRE Transactions on Human Factors in Electronics* 1: 4-11; March 1960.

36. Licklider, J. C. R. "Preliminary Experiments in Computer-Aided Teaching." *Programmed Learning and Computer-Based Instruction.* (Edited by J. E. Coulson.) New York: John Wiley & Sons, 1962. pp. 217-39.

37. Little, J. K. "Results of Use of Machines for Testing and for Drill upon Learning in Educational Psychology." *Journal of Experimental Psychology* 3: 45-59; September 1934.

38. McNeil, J. D. "Programed Instruction as a Research Tool in Reading: An Annotated Case." *Journal of Programed Instruction* 1: 37-42; No. 1, 1962.

39. Mellan, I. "Teaching and Educational Inventions." *Journal of Experimental Education* 4: 291-300; March 1936.

40. Ordahl, Louise E., and Ordahl, G. "Qualitative Differences Between Levels of Intelligence in Feeble-Minded Children." *Journal of Psycho-Asthenics* 1: 3-59; Monograph Supplement 1915.

41. Pask, G. "Adaptive Teaching with Adaptive Machines." *Teaching Machines and Programmed Learning.* (Edited by A. A. Lumsdaine and R. Glaser.) Washington, D.C.: National Education Association, 1960.

42. Pask, G. "Electronic Keyboard Teaching Machines." *Teaching Machines and Programmed Learning.* (Edited by A. A. Lumsdaine and R. Glaser.) Washington, D.C.: National Education Association, 1960.

43. Pollock, W. T., and Gildmer, G. G. *Study of Computer Manual Input Devices.* Technical Documentary Report No. ESD-TDR-63-545. Air Force Systems Command USAF, September 1963.

44. Porter, D. *An Application of Reinforcement Principles to Classroom Teaching.* Cambridge, Mass.: Laboratory for Research in Instruction, Graduate School of Education, Harvard University, 1961.

45. Pressey, S. L. "A Simple Apparatus Which Gives Tests and Scores— And Teaches." *School and Society* 23: 373-76; March 20, 1926.

46. Pressey, S. L. "Development and Appraisal of Devices Providing Immediate Automatic Scoring of Objective Tests and Concomitant Self-Instruction." *Journal of Psychology* 29: 417-47; April 1950.

47. Pressey, S. L. "Further Attempts To Develop a Mechanical Teacher." *American Psychologist* 15: 124-27; February 1960.

48. Reed, J. E., and Hayman, J. L., Jr. "An Experiment Involving Use of English 2600, An Automated Instruction Text." *Journal of Educational Research* 55: 476-85; June-July 1962.

49. Rigney, J. W. "Potential Uses of Computers as Teaching Machines." *Programmed Learning and Computer-Based Instruction.* (Edited by J. E. Coulson.) New York: John Wiley & Sons, 1962. pp. 155-70.

50. Skinner, B. F. *Verbal Behavior.* New York: Appleton-Century, 1957.

51. Skinner, B. F. "Teaching Machines." *Science* 128: 969-77; October 1958.

52. Skinner, B. F. "The Science of Learning and the Art of Teaching." *Teaching Machines and Programmed Learning.* (Edited by A. A. Lums-

daine and R. Glaser.) Washington, D.C.: National Education Association, 1960. pp. 99-113.

53. Skinner, B. F. "Why We Need Teaching Machines." *Harvard Educational Review* 31: 377-98; Fall 1961.

54. Smallwood, R. D. *A Decision Structure for Teaching Machines.* Cambridge, Mass.: Massachusetts Institute of Technology Press, 1962.

55. Smith, Leone M. *Programed Learning in Elementary School: An Experimental Study of Relationships Between Mental Abilities and Performance.* USOE Title VII Project No. 711151.01, Technical Report No. 2. Urbana: Training Research Laboratory, University of Illinois, August 1962.

56. Stake, R. E. "The Teaching Machine: Tool of the Future or Passing Fancy." *Phi Delta Kappan* 44: 247-49; March 1963.

57. Stolurow, L. M. "Prompting vs. Confirmation Sequences and Overlearning in the Automated Teaching of Sight Vocabulary." *The Fourteenth International Congress of Applied Psychology.* Copenhagen: Emil Kristensens Bogtrykkeri, 1961. (Abstract)

58. Stolurow, L. M. *Teaching by Machine.* Cooperative Research Monograph No. 6. Washington, D.C.: U.S. Office of Education, 1961.

59. Stolurow, L. M. *A Taxonomy of Learning Task Characteristics.* AF 33(616)-5965, Project No. 1710, Task No. 171003, AMRL-TDR-64-2. Wright-Patterson Air Force Base, Ohio: Behavioral Sciences Laboratory, January 1964.

60. Stolurow, L. M., and Lippert, H. "Prompting, Confirmation, and Vanishing in the Teaching of a Sight Vocabulary." *Educational Technology: Readings in Programed Instruction.* (Edited by John P. DeCecco.) New York: Holt, Rinehart and Winston, 1964. pp. 187-97.

61. Teager, H. M. "Systems Considerations in Real-Time Computer Usage." *Programmed Learning and Computer-Based Instruction.* (Edited by J. E. Coulson.) New York: John Wiley & Sons, 1962. pp. 273-80.

62. Thorndike, E. L. *Education.* New York: Macmillan Co., 1912. pp. 164-67.

63. Uttal, W. R. *My Teacher Has Three Arms!* IBM Research Report RC-788, September 15, 1962.

64. Uttal, W. R. "On Conversational Interaction." *Programmed Learning and Computer-Based Instruction.* (Edited by J. E. Coulson.) New York: John Wiley & Sons, 1962. pp. 171-90.

65. Uttal, W. F.; Charap, Marilyn; and Maher, Anna. *The Computer Tutoring of Stenotype: A Preliminary Report.* IBM Research Report RC-663, April 1962.

66. Valentine, J. A. "The Development and Use of Phase Checks." *Psychological Research on Flexible Gunnery Training.* (Edited by N. Hobbs.) Washington, D.C.: Government Printing Office, 1947. pp. 119-39.

67. Vallance, T. R., and Shrader, W. B. "The Evaluation of Training Devices

and Procedures." *Psychological Research on Flexible Gunnery Training.* (Edited by N. Hobbs.) Washington, D.C.: Government Printing Office, 1947. pp. 141-258.

68. Wiener, N. *Cybernetics.* New York: John Wiley & Sons, 1948.

69. Williams, A. P. O. *An Experimental Study of an Automated Teaching Machine and Keyboard Operation.* London: Department of Occupational Psychology, Birkbeck College, University of London, 1963.

Additional References

70. Bitzer, D. L. *PLATO: An Electronic Teaching Device.* Urbana: Coordinated Science Laboratory, University of Illinois, 1963.

71. Braunfeld, P. G. "Problems and Prospects of Teaching with a Computer." *Journal of Educational Psychology* 55: 201-11; August 1964.

72. Dick, W. "Experiment IV: Paired vs. Individual Study of Programed Instruction in Contemporary Algebra." *Comparative Research on Methods and Media for Presenting Programed Courses in Mathematics and English.* (Edited by C. R. Carpenter and L. P. Greenhill.) University Park: University Division of Instructional Services, Pennsylvania State University, 1963.

73. Feurzig, W. "Conversational Teaching Machines: Substitute for Socrates." *Datamation* 10: 38-42; June 1964.

74. Stolurow, L. M. *Model the Master Teacher or Master the Teaching Model.* Office of Naval Research Contract Nonr 3985(04), Technical Report No. 3. Urbana: Training Research Laboratory, University of Illinois, 1964.

75. Stolurow, L. M. *Some Educational Problems and Prospects of a Systems Approach to Instruction.* Office of Naval Research Contract Nonr 3985(04), Technical Report No. 2. Urbana: Training Research Laboratory, University of Illinois, 1964.

BRIAN N. LEWIS AND GORDON PASK
System Research Ltd.
Richmond, Surrey, England

The Theory and Practice of Adaptive Teaching Systems*

Within the last few years, programing methods have been strengthened by the addition of more and more objective rules of procedure. There are ruleg-type matrices (2) for insuring that the main concept areas of a subject matter are adequately covered and interrelated. There are flow charts for ordering frames into connected sequences and for insuring that different subsequences feed into one another with minimum discontinuity (4). There are graded cueing techniques for simplifying subject matter. And there are procedures for varying the grammatical form of sentences so that students are induced to give them a more thorough inspection than might otherwise be the case (39). Methods of this kind are important, and they undoubtedly work. But they have very little theoretical underpinning, and no attempt has been made to integrate them into a systematic *theory* of programing. Since they have a commonsense rather than a theoretical origin, and since commonsense ideas tend to be rather abundant, the desire to be explicit has led to a proliferation of "practical aids" to good programing. And as they proliferate, it becomes increasingly clear that they are often mutually incompatible.

In a recent discussion on the collection and organization of programed materials, for instance, Thomas and others (44) give five rules

* The work reported in this paper has been generally supported by the Wright Air Development Division of the Air Research and Development Command, U.S. Air Force, through its European Office, under Contract AF61 (052)—402.

that are likely to prove helpful in ordering such materials. Their advice is to proceed (a) from the known to the unknown, (b) from the simple to the complex, (c) from the concrete to the abstract, (d) from observations to reasoning, and (e) from a whole view to a more detailed analysis. These rules of sequence are not represented as anything more than guides to intuition. But even at this level it is difficult to think of a single subject matter for which all five rules could be satisfied at once. On any ordinary language interpretation, (e) implies a breaking down of unfamiliar ideas into simpler components, whereas (a) and (b) imply the opposite building up process. Conflicts of this kind cannot be resolved by the continual stockpiling of informal rules. Presumably it would be quite reasonable to propose that programs should proceed (f) from a qualitative to a quantitative treatment or (g) from a discursive account to a more precise account. But these additions would compound the confusion and would serve little purpose except, perhaps, to underline the desirability of a theory which would indicate precisely what was required. Moreover, they would not illuminate the many ancillary problems that arise in program construction, problems such as how to balance theory with practice, how to convey the wider implications of the subject matter, and how to introduce isolated facts or *exceptions* to rules.

Since different circumstances call for different procedures, it is clearly more pertinent to examine the conditions in which one type of procedure is likely to be preferred to another. And this leads directly to a consideration of the intrinsic structure of the subject matter and to a supplementary consideration of the kind of conceptual apparatus that the average student can be expected to bring to bear upon it.

To some extent the ruleg procedure indicates both the structure *and* a possible ordering of its subject matter. In general, cells which are easiest to assign examples to can be taken to indicate rules which are most closely and most often related. Such rules can be grouped accordingly into clusters or "concept areas" and ordered (within clusters) to give good continuity from one concept area to the next. This again is an informal procedure, and although it produces a high degree of connectedness between successive frame sequences, it leaves many important considerations out of account. Given four subject matter rules sequenced in the manner just described, it might well be the case that Rules 1 and 4 present one kind of conceptual difficulty, whereas Rules

2 and 3 present another. For example, the frame sequences for 1 and 4 might be expressed mainly in words, and the frame sequences for 2 and 3 might be expressed mainly in symbols. In such cases Rule 4 might be inserted profitably between Rules 1 and 2, notwithstanding the fact that this would increase the discontinuity existing between Rules 3 and 5.

The important point is that no subject matter can be analyzed and organized in complete disregard of the student's capabilities. To some extent this is recognized whenever the programer "tries out" his program in the early stages of construction. But the suggestion is that this is not early enough. Instead of ordering the instructional frames on the basis of the subject matter alone, and then shuffling them in the light of experience with actual students, it is desirable to order them *ab initio* with respect to the error factors that are likely to obstruct the learning process. In order to exemplify the use of error factors in a teaching situation, a subsequent section of this chapter will give a brief account of an experiment by Harlow (6) which may be already well known to readers of this book. But first it is necessary to say more about the theoretical orientations of the work to be described in this chapter.

A Special Model of Learning and Teaching Systems

To some extent, the initial work carried out at the System Research Laboratory was open to similar criticisms concerning its reliance upon intuitions, etc. Furthermore, the theoretical interests of the authors were different from those of the majority of workers in this field and stemmed from cybernetics rather than education.

In consequence, the teaching systems that were developed were adaptive systems with an application to teaching that was incidental rather than primary. Their main objective, in fact, was to investigate ways of maintaining stable interactions between men and machines. Now it happens that steady man-machine interaction cannot be maintained for very long unless the man gets some sense of satisfaction and achievement from the activity. The machine must hold the man's interest. It must provide him with things to do and to think about. Otherwise his attention wanders, and the machine cannot be guaranteed to achieve anything at all.

It follows that a stable interaction, between a man and a machine, is an interaction in which the man must of necessity be learning something of interest to him. Conversely, the machine must have at least some of the characteristics of a teacher. But the machine's teaching function need be of only secondary importance. For example, it could be designed chiefly to amuse or excite, or to act as an aid to performance, or to act as a research tool. In its latter capacity it might serve as an intelligence or aptitude tester, or it might pose problems that induce the man to reveal certain features of his thought processes.

Although these adaptive systems worked, in the sense that they did establish satisfactory and consistent man-machine interaction of a kind which was later found to satisfy the criteria of stability embedded in the present model, their design involved a great deal of intuition. This was an unsatisfactory state of affairs. Even the simplest machines had to be designed to a rather careful specification, and intuition was not a clear enough guide. The least that is needed in such circumstances is a model of learning and teaching that enables effective forms of teaching to be *designed*, rather than intuited.

Such a model has been devised and, in the sense that it leads to nontrivial and efficient designs, it has been validated. Two restrictions must be noted, however. First, the model *does* entail certain assumptions about a student. But these assumptions are of a very basic kind that underlie any psychological experiment or hypothesis. Secondly, the model can be directly applied only to a rather limited subset of those situations in which a man might properly be said to learn. More precisely, it applies only to those situations in which the skill or behavior being learned will satisfy the axiomatic requirements that render it a "structured skill" (31) and in which the man's environment is controlled either by an adaptive machine or by a strategy (instrumented by a real instructor) of a kind that could actually be embedded in a suitable adaptive machine.

Fortunately, this last restriction is not too serious. As will be seen in a subsequent section, a skill is a structured skill if (*inter alia*) it can be reduced to a collection of component subskills which are related to each other in a specifiable fashion and for which systematic simplification or "cueing" procedures are known. No attempt has yet been made to represent complex academic skills (like learning a foreign language) in this way, but it seems reasonable to conjecture that with effort, they could be so represented. Certainly, there are many smallish intellectual skills (like deriving simultaneous equations from word problems) that can be treated in this fashion, as well as all the more familiar perceptual motor skills. And it is always possible to specify experiments that will decide whether or not the skill to be taught is a structured skill.

The restrictions just described can therefore be regarded as fairly minimal. Nevertheless, they generate a rather elaborate theoretical structure which will be briefly outlined in the next two sections.

Assumptions and Specific Features of the Teaching Model

The assumption made about a student is that his behavior is a specially restricted kind of self-organizing system (27). This assumption can be expressed in psychological terms by asserting:

1. A student necessarily and continually learns about something, however trivial. (The general validity of this assumption becomes particularly evident in sensory deprivation experiments on man in isolation.) Hence teaching, regarded as the control of learning, is concerned with making a student learn about something relevant to the subject matter being instructed. A further implication is that an optimal teaching system must satisfy dynamic criteria, like maximizing the student's *rate of learning*, rather than static criteria, like achieving a given proficiency by such and such a stage.

2. Although learning can be approximated as goal-directed adaptation it can be shown that it is insufficient to require adaptation alone. A complete specification must entail the possibility of *creating*, as well as satisfying, goals (32).

3. A student has a finite decision-making capacity. Hence it makes sense to talk, at any instant, about a definite field of attention that the student contemplates and to speak of learning as a process which, among other things, reduces his uncertainty about choosing actions or responses that bear a given relationship to the stimuli in the field of attention. In other words the field of attention can be taken to designate a class of problems. The instructional situation is correspondingly defined in terms of problems that have a solution within a field of attention, and performance of the skill is conceived as the act of solving these problems. This approach

contrasts with the familiar construction in terms of stimuli that *denote* the problems concerned and responses that *denote* their solutions.

4. Because of the postulate that a student needs to maintain a certain rate of learning, it is possible to argue that two additional constraints must be satisfied by the data which occupy his field of attention. (In a realistic system, these data will constitute the items in a training routine.) First, the data must be intelligible. The student's decision-making capacity must not be exceeded. Secondly, the data must supply sufficient variety for the student to learn about. This latter condition, which resembles "neophylia" (22), can often be interpreted as a requirement for maintaining the student's interest or satisfying his "curiosity drive."

Given these assumptions, it can be shown that the learning and teaching process must be imaged at several different levels of discourse. The number of levels can be shown to depend upon the skill being instructed, but, except in trivial cases, more than one level of description is always needed. At the behavioral "S-R" level, for example, a skill and its instruction are described in terms of stimuli and responses and rules that designate certain pairs of these as correct outcomes. Stimulus and response probabilities may also form part of the behavioral description, and terminal or criterion behaviors are also describable in these terms.

But this account is not complete. If a skill is a "structured skill," it can be reduced to component subskills. Hence the stimuli will belong to different subsets, named by the subskill with which they are associated. (Members of a given subset will denote problems belonging to a given class.) Further, if the skill is a structured skill, it will be possible to specify procedures for each subskill (applicable to the corresponding subset of problems) which *simplify* these problems for the student, in the sense that they partially or completely solve them without destroying their logical form. Quite often, a simplifying procedure is tantamount to a cueing procedure. It partially solves the problems that are posed for solution when the student is required to perform the subskill concerned, and, since it can thus be regarded as carrying out problem-solving activity that the student would need to carry out in real life, it may also be viewed as a cooperative action. In machine-paced tuition, where there are difficulties involved in locating or applying the correct problem-solving methods, simplification might alternatively take the form of an increase in the interval allowed for responding. In anticipation of subsequent sections of this chapter, it suffices to note here that an effective simplification procedure involves the adjustment of as many variables as there are distinct "error factors" connected with the subskill concerned. Given these conditions, it is both possible and necessary to construct, for each subskill, a regular index of proximity to a correct outcome.

As a further complication, it must also be noted that the several subskills of a structured skill are related. Given subskills A and B, there may be only positive transfer of training between them. Or there may be some positive and some negative transfer of training effects. And there may be a precedence relationship in the sense that A must be learned before B, because A demonstrates some principle that is needed in order to perform B.

These additional considerations are important. They lead immediately to the point that the entire structure of simplification procedures and subskills and their relation is, in fact, defined at a higher level of discourse. Superimposed on the behavioral level of discourse is a level dealing with problems and their solutions and with methods of solution (i.e., with the problem-solving algorithms) used by the student. It is convenient to express this part of the model in the terms used to describe "artificial intelligence" programs (21, 24, 49). At this level, a start can be made on wedding together rules or principles (say from a ruleg analysis) and their behavioral concomitants. At this level, it is also possible to specify the kind of terminal repertoire discussed in the section on the concept of teminal behavior.

This by no means exhausts the number of levels that might be needed. For many skills it is necessary to consider not only the problem-solving procedures adopted by a student (which correspond to particular artificial intelligence computer programs) but also the methods of *constructing* these procedures. The latter, corresponding to computer programs that write other computer programs, are described at a still higher level of discourse. The language of artificial intelligence is particularly suitable for comprehending many of the complications involved, and the entire research effort reported in this chapter can be regarded as an attempt to wed behaviorism to the theory of artificial intelligence.

An Artificial Intelligence Representation of Learning and Teaching

Effective teaching implies an ability to take appropriate corrective action whenever the student runs into difficulties. Before this can be done, however, it is necessary to characterize in some detail the structure of the subject matter being taught. Moreover, this structure must be directly related to the difficulties that the student is likely to encounter. Otherwise there will be no basis on which to take the corrective action required.

The concept of a structured skill was devised to provide the kind of characterization needed. It was originally formulated within the framework of artificial intelligence theory. But it is equally consonant with the psychological models of learning implicit in the writings of Piaget (36) and Vygotsky (45). Given a slightly different interpretation, it also incorporates the main features of the TOTE model of Miller, Galanter, and Pribram (20) and the concept learning models of Hovland (8) and Hunt (9).

In each case mentation is conceived as an essentially hierarchical affair, in the sense that only certain hierarchies of concepts can arise as a result of learning. For example, the hierarchy of relationships involved in children's concepts has been well documented by Welch and Long (46) and by Flavell (3). In the field of artificial intelligence, the need for a hierarchy of data processing operations is reflected in the need to abstract and generalize (23). More discursively, there are academic subjects like jurisprudence in which conceptual hierarchies are indexed by the presence of abstract notions of "justice" which are used to systematize and evaluate specific rulings in courts of law.

The constraints upon the development of concepts can be variously imaged as a hierarchy of structures and groupings, as a linguistic structure restricting the patterns of communication that mediate learning, as a hierarchy of TOTE units (or units mediating recursive computation of which the TOTE unit is a special class), or as a hierarchy of classes. One way to represent these constraints is by a collection of artificial intelligence programs, the canonical form of which will be a hierarchy of problem-solving procedures such that if the lowest-level procedures solve problems from a domain with members denoted by stimuli, the next level procedures solve "problems" from a domain of the properties of (such as differences between) the lowest-level problem-solving procedures. Hence, in this canonical representation, learning appears as a hierarchy of problem solving.

Although the present model for the learning process is closely related to models advanced by the authors just cited, it was derived independently as the least structure in terms of which it is possible to carry out the form of control procedure normally credited with the name "teaching." Thus an adaptive control mechanism cannot be designed without some framework within which it can adapt to salient aspects of the student's performance ("chance-trial" adaptation is known to be hopelessly impracticable). Moreover, the framework must be carefully selected, for it must have a sufficient caliber to encompass the logic of the learning process.

If this learning process is reduced to the canonical form just proposed, it is not difficult to argue that a minimal descriptive structure will be a dual hierarchical organization (A, B) in which A consists of a hierarchy of models of procedures (or descriptive accounts of the learning process of the kind that might, in principle, be given by the student), symbolized as $A^0, A^1, \ldots A^m$, and in which B consists of a hierarchy of mechanisms $B^0, B^1, \ldots B^m$, that are in some sense *responsible* for the processes specified in A. Thus the B structure can be regarded as a hierarchy of *control mechanisms* that evolve in the medium of the student's brain as he learns to cope with the skill being taught. And the A structure can be regarded as a hierarchy of *descriptions* concerning the way in which the student solves the body of problems posed by the skill in question. The function of the B structure, therefore, is to explain the problem-solving process by providing a hierarchy of mechanisms that might plausibly underlie it. This means that for each Level A^i in the descriptive account, an analogous mechanism B^i (belonging to the same level) must be specified.

The A, B distinction reflects the requirement of demarcating an "algorithm" or a "procedure" (terms which belong to the A structure) from the "value" or "reinforcement" (terms which belong to the B structure) associated with its application or construction. The hierarchical form of each component, A and B, reflects the requirement that the organization is embedded in a stratified system of control which, in its most logically explicit form, is a stratification or hierarchy of logical types (37, 47). Hence its least complete description will be couched in a language of the kind used by Martin (17) to express genuine *intensions*, namely (apart from the object language), an open-ended metalanguage that embodies some theory of logical types. To avoid this usage, it is alternatively possible to characterize a description of the A or B component by a hierarchy of distinct meta-languages $L^1, L^2, \ldots$ L^m over the object language L^o that is needed to describe the problem solving manifest at the behavioral level A^o, B^o. In this case there are "construction rules," defined as legal expressions in L^o, that give rise (or could give rise) to correct response sequences. And there are legal expressions in L^1 that construct *methods* leading to correct response sequences. In this case, also, A^o and B^o respectively constitute the *extensive* and *intensive* definitions of L^o, and B^o can be said to provide the "meaning" or "connotation" of A^o. If L^o forms part of a mechanical language used in a data processing or artificial intelligence system, A^o can be defined as the set of strings of signs that are producible and permissible in L^o. B^o can be defined as the set of data processing and executive procedures that act upon L^o and its structural constraints.

For a more detailed account of these matters, the reader should consult Gorn (5) and Pask (30, 32). Here it must suffice to say that no lesser elaboration is possible for describing the stability of a joint system of learning {(Student), C} where component C is a hierarchically organized adaptive control mechanism. The minimal stable coupled system therefore has the form {(A, B), C} with (A, B) constituting a minimal specification of the student. By adjoining certain axioms concerning the evolution of the B^i in B, and by assuming that the various elements of (A, B) can be operationally defined, it does, however, become possible to assert a class of *weakly optimum* adaptive coupled learning systems {(A, B), C*} where C* is a specific adaptive control mechanism. (C* is weakly optimal in the sense that it is one of possibly many systems which belong to the optimum subset for a given data-processing capacity and which are subsystems of the given class of representation.) So far it has been possible to realize systems that are weakly optimum at the level of L^o. These systems are applicable when the skill and the terminal criteria can be defined in the behavioral terms of L^o; in other words, when the concept of a "terminal repertoire" *coincides* with a "terminal behavior."

The trick adopted in the axiom-strengthened construction is to define {(A, B), C} as stable if and only if it is a self-organizing system. Roughly speaking, this implies that for each level i, the rate of goal-directed adaptation in {A^i, B^i, C^i} is positive. Now this definition is empirically plausible. Further, given a bound of the form "A^i, B^i has a maximum (and, it can be shown, also a minimum) data-processing capacity," it is possible to design a C_j^i in C^* that will maximize this rate of goal-directed adaptation as well as *any* other adaptive control mechanism with the same limitations. It is thus a weakly optimum *stabilizing* device.

In psychological terms, the adaptive control mechanism will maintain the subject's interest and attention by presenting him with sufficiently difficult but intelligible problems for solution. But if stability is obtained by maximizing the rate of goal-directed adaptation for *all* values of i, the stable system can also be said to have a maximum rate of learning. C^* therefore becomes a weakly optimum *teaching* device.

To provide an operational definition for the elements of this model, it is necessary to introduce specific restrictions upon the skill being instructed. And to say that a skill is a structured skill implies that such a set of restrictions is satisfied. These restrictions can be briefly summarized as follows:

1. The skill must be reducible to a collection of subskills, each of which consists of solving problems of a single class.

2. For each subskill, there must be a simplification procedure which removes the effects of one or more "error factors" (7) by partially or completely solving problems belonging to the subskill in question. Simplification involves the adjustment of as many variables as there are error factors.

3. For each subskill, it must be possible to obtain a monotonic and additive statistical measure (θ, say) of performance over typical sequences of behavioral outcomes.

4. For any coherent and nontrivial skill, θ will normally prove to be superadditive over the outcomes of *combinations* of subskills. This could imply positive transfer of training between the subskills concerned, or it could imply the existence of interference (due to L^1 overload) whenever the student is required to perform two or more subskills at once. In the latter case the student finds difficulty in creating classes of algorithms that are applicable to several subskills jointly. Alternatively, he cannot apply such algorithms at a sufficient rate.

5. Whether or not there is interference, there may be precedence relations between the subskills because one must be learned before the other. This arises whenever the solutions of L^0 problems in one sub-

skill ostensively define either some algorithm applicable to the other subskill or some jointly applicable class of algorithms. (Since the ostensive definition by this L^0 problem-solving activity can often be replaced by instructional assertions that constitute expressions in L^1 or L^2, there is a possibility of teaching at different levels of discourse. Most academic materials consist of sequences of precedent subskills, and one class of adaptive teaching machine is concerned with discovering, for each individual student, whether an ostensive definition or an instructional assertion is preferable for a given set of classes of problems or of subskills.)

In general it is apparent that the adaptive teaching machine always adapts within a framework of constraints that must be inferred or experimentally determined. The adaptive activity is experimental insofar as it evaluates estimates of the undetermined descriptive parameter values, and it exercises control insofar as it uses these estimates to maximize an approximate rate of increase of θ. Furthermore, the machine has a hierarchical structure that closely reflects the hierarchical model considered for the learning process in the student. In the simplest case of a two-level skill, the machine can be reduced to a number of subcontrollers that are concerned with the adaptively controlled simplification of subskills in order to maximize $\Delta\theta$ and an over-all control mechanism that selects among the subcontrollers (and, consequently, among the subskills) in order to maximize the student's over-all rate of learning.

Adaptive systems of this kind differ from systems of the kind proposed by Smallwood (42). In the Smallwood method, relevant characteristics of a whole population of students are sampled by means of sequential experiments. The results for the population are then averaged to yield a branching or (in the limiting case) a linear program. The adaptive machines described in this chapter lay more emphasis on individual oddities. The statistical estimates made by these machines are necessarily cruder, but they suffice to provide a dynamic background or dynamic environment with which the student can indulge in partly competitive and partly cooperative interaction. This, rather than the accuracy of the statistical estimates, is the important feature.

The actual form of the student-machine interaction is empirically reflected in the construction of L^0 and L^1 forms of expression which are not legal, but which help the student to learn the skill because they allow him to change the characteristics of the teaching machine within the constraints imposed by the structure of the $\{(A, B), C^*\}$ model. Hence the models of Piaget and Vygotsky are applicable, and the adaptive process can be regarded as performing operations on a set of linguistic constraints embodied in the $\{(A, B), C^*\}$ model.

Like the language systems in society, the structure of these constraints is substantially invariant throughout the interval of individual maturation. But their presentation must be modified by some instruction if learning is to occur. In this sense, the operations of the adaptive teaching machine with reference to the student are akin to those of a parent with reference to a child. And the $\{(A, B), C^*\}$ model has the status, in this analogy, of the social-linguistic milieu.

By way of summary, it can be said that such machines differ from Smallwood's in two ways. Although the design of the teaching routine exploits as many population regularities as possible, it still makes rather more provision for individual oddities. Secondly, more emphasis is given to the need to maintain conversational interaction within specified dynamic limits of the dynamic environment. These are two all-important and recurring themes, and the remainder of the chapter will be devoted to illustrating their application.

A Paradigm Teaching Situation

A monkey crouches in a small wire cage with one arm protruding through a narrow opening hatch. A Klüver-type stimulus tray is slid on rails, toward the hatch, by an experimenter who faces the monkey from the opposite side of a one-way vision screen. Dispersed about the tray are three objects, two of which are identical and one different (say, two matchboxes and a cigarette end). If the monkey picks up the odd object, he is rewarded. Otherwise he is not. In any event the tray is then withdrawn, and a new set of three objects (e.g., two plates and a saucer or two buttons and a matchbox) is presented. This procedure may continue for several hundred trials, but eventually even the dumbest monkeys see the point. Apart from a few "exploratory" variations, they go straight for the odd object on every occasion and are accordingly credited with having attained the concept of *oddity* or *difference*.

There are, however, one or two difficulties to be negotiated along the way. Monkeys are not telepathic. If the experiment begins with the odd object in the middle or to the right-hand side of the stimulus tray, the monkey is not to know whether he is being rewarded for picking up an odd object or an object in a particular position (or, more subtly, an object in a particular spatial relationship with the other two objects). If the monkey misjudges the requirements of the task, he might come to regard certain positions as rewarding and will therefore select objects in these positions irrespective of whether or not they are odd. In the same way, a monkey rewarded for picking up a cigarette end might come to regard smallness or color or texture as the salient discriminative property. In the event of the odd object departing from these properties, the monkey might then make a probabilistic guess between the two identical objects. Thus a monkey who thought "smallness" was important would select, from two buttons and a matchbox, one of the buttons.

Confusions of this kind, which obstruct the learning process, have been described by Harlow (7) as "error factors." Strictly speaking, any mistake made by a learner (human or animal) can be ascribed to an error factor. But the only interesting error factors are those that generate whole classes of mistakes. These are interesting because they provide opportunities for clearing up, in a single operation, all mistakes having the same root cause. If it were not for the existence of underlying error factors, teaching would be inordinately long, since mistakes would have to be dealt with in isolation and one at a time. In the case of the monkey experiments, Harlow (7) identified several important error factors, some of which were rather general in nature and others which were more specific to the type of problem being learned. By a judicious arrangement of test problems he was, moreover, in a position to show (a) how the presence of error factors could be determined in individual cases, (b) the frequency of such error factors in the population of monkeys studied, and (c) the most likely order of their occurrence in the training routine.

Although Harlow apparently did not recognize the significance of his methods for teaching practice, it is clear that they enable highly efficient teaching routines to be constructed. If the "position" error is known to be important, the three objects must be distributed about the stimulus tray in ways that are especially designed to counteract the hypothesis that positional cues are relevant. If the "size" error is important, the experiment should not start with two matchboxes and a cigarette end and continue with two plates and a saucer because this could readily strengthen the belief that smallness rather than oddness is the critical property. Because of the limited conceptual abilities of rhesus monkeys, it is neither desirable nor possible to safeguard against all error factors at once. It is therefore necessary to begin by safeguarding against those errors which are known, from empirical investigation, to arise at an early stage. However, monkeys, like humans, do not always exhibit errors in the same order. It is therefore necessary to embed, in the sequence of problems presented, test problems which will enable the presence of other error factors (not currently being dealt with) to be detected.

Given an adequate detection procedure, combined with a remedial procedure for dealing with whatever error factors are detected, the teaching problem is solved. As a result of empirical investigation, it is possible to state quite precisely the main dimensions of error that obstruct the learning process. It is also possible to obtain partial orderings of these error factors in terms of (a) their frequency of occurrence and (b) their most probable position of occurrence (in a sequence of test trials). As a result of further empirical inquiries, it is also possible to specify procedures for detecting the presence of error factors in *individual cases* and for removing these whenever they occur. The teaching program will therefore commence with the best possible assumption, namely, that the monkey about to be taught is an "average" monkey. But the teaching system, whether man or machine, will have facilities for establishing the monkey's characteristics (in particular, his vulnerability to the principal error factors). The program will therefore branch to sequences which, by virtue of their special stimulus properties, will be expressly designed to get rid of those error factors which seem most prominent.

Automating the Teaching Situation

In order to automate the kind of teaching program just described, a hierarchical control mechanism is required.

1. At the bottom of the hierarchy is a set of registers which accumulate evidence about the presence or absence of particular error factors. At least one register must be provided for every error factor for which information needs to be acquired. If two or more error factors interact (so that the removal of one induces the occurrence of another), separate registers may also be needed to detect the presence of such interactions.

2. Each problem given to the monkey must be associated, in a quanti-
    fiable way, with one or more of the registers. In other words, each
    problem must contribute at least some information about the
    monkey's ability to overcome standard obstacles to learning. If the
    instructional sequence of problems involves mastery of, say, three
    or four distinct error factors, the machine will contain at least
    three or four separate registers, and problems will be correspond-
    ingly grouped into at least three or four classes. A problem intended
    to test the monkey's mastery of error factor 2 would then be coded
    (for the machine's benefit) to insure that only register 2 is activated
    by the monkey's response.

3. To save time, problems will often be designed to test for several
    error factors at once. If a particular problem is likely to involve
    error factors 1 and 3, a correct (or incorrect) response could readily
    be coded to produce a uniform increment (or decrement) in each
    of the registers 1 and 3. And if the problem involves error 1 to a
    greater extent than error 3, the code could be further adjusted to
    produce differential increments (or decrements) in these two regis-
    ters. Prior research, of course, must be carried out to establish how
    these test items should be coded. Given a judicious coding system,
    the registers can rapidly provide useful cumulative indices of the
    monkey's ability to handle different kinds of test problems. In
    effect, the registers index the monkey's progress in terms of the
    rate at which he overcomes those difficulties that most commonly
    frustrate learning.

4. To complete the system, the machine must embody a mechanism
    which can evaluate the information accumulating on these regis-
    ters and can cause the training program to vary in ways that seem
    most likely to meet the monkey's special requirements. This mech-
    anism has been described in the teaching machine literature as an
    "over-all control mechanism" (29). It examines all the registers
    that are active in order to see, for each in turn, the extent to which
    the monkey is falling short of some ideal criterion of efficiency.
    In the simplest case, this mechanism is a single comparator which
    matches the state of each register against some predetermined norm
    and secures an electrical readout of the discrepancy.

5. These readouts constitute measures, on an ordinal or interval scale,
    of the monkey's vulnerability to particular error factors. The over-
    all control mechanism accordingly has a double job to do. It must

secure readouts from each of the error registers, and it must also apply decision rules to them to determine what changes, if any, should be made to the teaching routine. Readouts showing above average discrepancies imply that the monkey needs assistance in overcoming the error factors concerned. Readouts showing below average discrepancies imply that the monkey has already avoided or overcome the error factors in question. The greater the discrepancies, the greater the need for action. In the former (above-average) case, the over-all control mechanism must select, from a set of possible test problems, problems which are likely to contribute most to the extinguishing of prevalent errors. In the latter (below-average) case, the over-all control mechanism might simply reduce the amount of rehearsal on test problems associated with error factors that are not giving trouble. There will be occasions, however, when the registers show the monkey as requiring more assistance than can be given at any one time. In such cases, the over-all control mechanism must be equipped with decision rules for determining some suitable compromise procedure.

6. The kinds of computation needed to establish this compromise are determined by decision rules that are programed into the machine at the time of its construction. Once again, they are based on empirical research, this time on research conducted into the "transfer of training characteristics" between one error-removing procedure and another, or on the precedence relationships existing between the different component subskills. It may be found, for instance, that the removal of error A incidentally helps to remove error B, but the removal of error B does very little to assist in the removal of error A. Discoveries of this kind add to one's knowledge of the structure of the skill being taught; they also determine an order of priorities for dealing with more than one error factor at a time. This order of priorities could very well be changed in the light of further experience (42). And the machine could even be programed to change its own rules if it found that certain procedures were not working effectively.

The Problem of Motivation

Experiments on the training of animals typically have the advantage that the animal is in some kind of deprivation state and is therefore motivated to participate in the learning activity. By way of contrast, humans usually have to be convinced by some form of rhetoric that it is in their interests to participate. Usually there are social pressures to remain in the teaching situation, but human students (unlike starved rats) are not likely to feel very threatened or deprived if the teaching session is terminated. If they have something more interesting to do, they may in fact feel rather pleased.

Since the motivational factor cannot be taken for granted, any comprehensive theory of teaching must strive to comprehend it. It is important to see, however, that motivational problems do not enter into the teaching situation *at the same level* as problems pertaining to the structure and content of the instructional materials delivered. It is rather the case that a three-level theory is required. At the lowest level there is a need for a theory which will predict how a student will learn, given that he attends to (i.e., processes) the materials presented to him. At the next level, there is a need for a theory which will specify the conditions under which a student will continue to attend, given that he has initially agreed to participate in the teaching activity. At the highest level, there is a need for a theory which will specify sufficient conditions for gaining the student's initial agreement. Finally, a metatheory is required to show how the three levels interact. And this can be provided via the neophyllic principle, already mentioned, that conscious man must always have something to decide about.

In the adaptive teaching machines constructed at System Research, special control procedures have been devised to keep the student motivated. As a first step it is, for example, essential to adjust the training program to a level that the student is likely to find congenial (11, 14). If the instructional materials are too simple, the student will get bored, and his attention will wander. If the instructional materials are too difficult he will get frustrated and, once again, his attention and enthusiasm will diminish. By moving into a region which is neither too simple nor too difficult, the machine can, however, give the student problems which he regards as challenging and, more importantly, as being within his immediate realm of competence. On either side of this "optimum" level of difficulty, there is a fairly narrow *region* of difficulty which also suffices to hold the student's interest. Toward the lower boundary of this region the instructional materials are almost too easy for the student's liking. And this is the area in which linear programs tend to operate. Toward the upper boundary instructional materials are almost too difficult for the student's liking. But there are special advantages to be gained by *occasionally* touching this boundary because the effect of reaching it is to (a) spur the student on to greater efforts and (b) reveal incipient weaknesses which might not otherwise have shown up. To locate this general region of difficulty, and to stay within it if it shifts, the machine must adjust the standard of difficulty of its instructional items in a manner determined by the student's own performance. And this can be done by reference to its internal registers. If these registers show that the student is making very few errors, the difficulty is stepped up until the error score starts to rise. At this point the machine continues to increase the difficulty, but at a reducing rate. Finally, at some empirically determined error rate, the machine relaxes its pressure by introducing some simplifying operations. By shifting its level of difficulty in this way, the machine guarantees that the student will receive a regular supply of challenging problems. In this respect the machine satisfies one of the most fundamental human needs—the need for new and stimulating experiences. Looked at another way, it can be said that the machine adopts a pressuring technique which endeavors to keep the student working as near as possible to the threshold of his ability. This is an ideal state of affairs because it means that the student cannot afford to let his attention wander from the job. In consequence, he tends to be highly amenable to the teaching process. At the same time the pressuring technique also tends to maximize the amount of useful information that the machine can gain about the student.

Perhaps it should be stressed that although the machine may succeed in temporarily pushing the student to the peak of his ability, it is up to the student to decide whether or not he wants to stay there. If he suddenly tires of working under pressure, he will inevitably start to make mistakes (e.g., by failing to answer a test item quickly enough), and the machine will promptly slacken its pace. As might be expected, this whole procedure tends to generate an extremely congenial relationship between the student and the machine, not unlike the relationship between a child and a novelty-producing toy. Once the student starts interacting with the machine, he tends to get permanently caught up in a stream of activity. And this is hardly surprising because the machine is deliberately engaging him in a sort of intellectual donkey

and carrot race. In the early stages of instruction he is offered inducements (in the form of hints and similar guidance) that enable him to
improve, but as he gets better the inducements are systematically withdrawn.

This situation can be summarized more formally by saying that the
machine engages the student in a partly cooperative, partly competitive game. By giving the student special hints and guidance, the machine clearly does some of the work that the student's brain is not yet
capable of doing. In this respect, the machine can be said to function
as a cooperative extension of the student's brain. But the machine is
a reluctant cooperator that refuses to spoon-feed the student. It repeatedly tries to withdraw its assistance, in a selective manner, so that
the student can stand on his own feet. And this is the competitive element in the game. It arises because both the student and the machine
have the same ultimate objective, namely, to reach a state of affairs
in which the student is able to handle all the most difficult problems
with the minimum of support.

The adaptive teaching machine can therefore be described as a device which forms a close and dynamic partnership with its student in
order to maximize some quantifiable measure of the student's efficiency.
To this end, the machine sometimes cooperates with the student by
helping him out of difficulty. And it sometimes competes with the student by putting new difficulties in his way. Both these strategies have
the common aim of keeping the student on the move. By withdrawing
its assistance at regular intervals, the machine finds out what the student is worth and endeavors to keep him working at high capacity.
In a very real sense, the machine minimizes its own efforts so that the
student must maximize his. But active support is always ready at hand
whenever the student shows signs of needing it.

The Concept of Error in Adaptive Teaching

The kind of teaching method just proposed is not likely to appeal to
the tough-minded operant conditioner. To the operant conditioner,
good teaching requires instructional sequences simplified to such a degree that the student hardly ever puts a foot wrong. By way of contrast,
the adaptive machine requires the student to reveal, by making some
sort of mistake, the kind of instruction that he should receive next.

This requirement not surprisingly conjures up an image of an aversive and threatening situation in which the student is repeatedly forced, by tricky test questions, to reveal his ignorance. This image is completely false. If the adaptive control procedure is competently designed, there is no reason why the revealing of weaknesses should have any adverse consequences at all. In fact there is often no need for the student even to *know* that he has revealed a weakness. He might, for instance, be given a multiple-choice question inviting him to give an opinion rather than a correct answer. In this case all the response alternatives might be designated correct, but the selection of any one of them would tell the machine all it wanted to know.

Alternatively, the teaching system might have all the appearances of an ordinary student-paced linear machine except that (unknown to the student) it measures the *time* that the student takes to respond to each test item presented. By noting that the student is getting slower, etc., the machine could simplify its instruction to maintain some empirically determined level of success. If there were grounds for believing that the often-quoted level of 90-95 percent successes was optimal, the machine would therefore adjust the content of its instructional and test items in order to hold the student within this range.

There is, of course, nothing sacrosanct about the 90-95 percent criterion. To some extent it is forced upon the linear programer because there are no remedial procedures for dealing with errors. The maintenance of a high success rate, moreover, can be guaranteed only by making test questions comparatively easy. And this inevitably creates the risk that the brighter student will be bored. To counteract this tendency, the adaptive machine could at least insure that between 1 in 10 and 1 in 20 questions *were* answered incorrectly. In other words the machine could make its test questions as difficult as possible, having regard to the 90-95 percent criterion laid down. In so doing, the machine would insure that the student gained the greatest possible sense of achievement compatible with the restriction imposed.

In all probability the maintenance of a high "reinforcement" rate is only one of several important conditions that an optimal teaching system has to maintain. The essential point to note about an adaptive teaching machine is that it can always maintain such conditions better than a nonadaptive device because it is capable of sensing individual differences in capabilities and interests. In order to sense these differ-

ences, the machine must admittedly test the student in a rather searching way. But the risk involved in the search process (e.g., of losing the
student's good will), in a well-designed machine, is quite minimal.
Certainly it is much smaller than the risk involved in presenting
intelligent students with lengthy strings of frames having only the
smallest intellectual bite.

If a situation arises in which mistakes are rather likely to occur, the
student's ego can often be protected by imposing some sort of pacing
function. In general, students are much less demoralized by making
mistakes if they can blame them on shortage of time. And there is in
fact a perfectly good distinction between mistakes that are made as a
result of applying the wrong method and mistakes that are made
through failing to complete a correct method. In the on-going excitement of the teaching situation, mistakes having the former cause can
often be attributed to the latter in order to avoid losing face. The introduction of pacing functions has other advantages. If a person is
put under time pressure, his range of behavior patterns will diminish.
He restricts himself to performing, without embellishments, only those
operations that seem to matter. Time pressure is therefore a way of
inducing him to distinguish between operations that are important and
operations that are not. A properly designed adaptive machine will
exploit this fact in order to discover what the student considers to be
the essentials of the situation.

Time pressure must of course be used with discretion. In the training of sensory-motor skills, it is useful because it induces the student
to group stimulus configurations into larger and larger "chunks" (19).
In the case of intellectual skills, too much time pressure is fatiguing
and may induce the student to go always for the "safe" method of
solution. In some subjects, such as geometry, there are problems which
are baffling because the customary methods of solution do not work.
It is therefore important that the student should be given the time and
opportunity to try out bizarre modes of solution. Continuous time pressure would be quite inappropriate in such cases. Instead, it might be
introduced occasionally just to liven up the teaching process and to
increase motivation. Alternatively, a weaker form of pacing might be
introduced in which additional and possibly unusual (i.e., thought-
provoking) cues are exhibited on a supplementary display after some
empirically determined time interval. In its simplest form, this pro-

cedure offers the quick student a chance to "beat the cue" by responding correctly before it appears.

Despite the richness of these possibilities, the whole method of tuition may still look suspect to the experienced linear programer. The
occurrence of mistakes and the corresponding concern with error factors might be criticized, for example, on the grounds that errors arise
only in the case of bad instruction. Underlying this criticism is the
suggestion that instead of inducing errors and then removing them,
the adaptive machine would do better to prevent errors from occurring
in the first place. There may also be the further implication that adaptive machines are highly elaborate devices for teaching in the wrong
way. The short answer to this objection is that the error factors referred to in this section are not created as a result of faulty instruction.
They are already there. Moreover, their presence is tacitly acknowledged by linear programers whenever they *cue* or *preadapt* (38) their
programs to suit the population of students to be taught. The point
about linear programs is that they remove error factors without allowing them to be manifested in the form of overt mistakes. But this procedure necessarily involves a working in the dark. The result is that
linear programs often make provision for far more error factors than
any one student is likely to have. By way of contrast, the adaptive machine can sense the error factors that need to be dealt with in particular cases and can tackle these directly.

One further point needs to be made. Despite the successes achieved
by error-minimizing linear programs, there are many unrepentant advocates of the view that students profit from making mistakes. Among
European educationalists, this belief is commonly argued out in the
context of disputes concerning the so-called "active" and "passive"
methods of teaching. When an Adlerian teacher like Spiel (43) extols
the virtues of the active method, he is not thinking in terms of the active responding that goes on in linear programs. He is referring, instead, to the desirability of students "discovering things for themselves" rather than passively accepting whatever they are told. In the
course of self-discovery the student will undoubtedly make mistakes
as a result of exploring blind alleys, but he will gain (so the argument
goes) a clearer understanding of the subject matter involved. If a student is told a fact, he often need do no more than store it in any way
that happens to be convenient. If a student discovers a fact for him-

self, he must at least construct a conceptual framework that is strong enough to enable the fact to be formulated. In the process of constructing such a framework, he may well come upon other facts that he might otherwise have regarded as unrelated. This is part of what is meant by being able to see "the deeper implications" of a particular subject matter. And a linear program which tells the students the facts must take care also to tell them how the concomitant conceptual framework can be established.

To some extent, linear programs can certainly teach students to discover facts and principles for themselves. But there is a basic incompatibility between inducing discoveries and minimizing error responses. If students are led (by a series of hints) to the very brink of a discovery, no doubt 90-95 percent of them can be relied upon to make it. But the intellectually satisfying discoveries are those which are *not* obvious from the data at the student's immediate disposal. Of necessity, there is more than a 5-10 percent risk that such discoveries will not be made. Direct attempts to induce them are therefore out of place in a teaching method which strives to protect students from the possibility of experiencing failure. Instead, recourse must be had to *showing* the student the discoveries that can be made (by showing, for example, how particular facts and principles can be derived from the information he has already received).

A special property of the adaptive machine is that it can vary the form of its instruction in ways that induce students, wherever possible, to discover the relevant facts and principles for themselves. This is a direct consequence of its strategy of giving the student no more assistance than is needed to sustain his active interest in the teaching activity. It can, moreover, diversify the problems it poses to the student in order to establish the student's mastery of his subject matter over a wide range of different conditions. As a result of this procedure, the student develops a well-integrated conceptual framework which enables him to interrelate all the essential facts of the subject matter and to know the exact range of circumstances over which they are applicable. In short, he becomes trained both in the *acquisition* and in the use of the knowledge imparted.

In principle it should be possible to obtain the same result by means of a linear program. But, if the high success level of 90-95 percent is to be insisted upon, an inordinately lengthy sequence of frames may be required. This will inevitably bore many of the students participating. Adaptive teaching systems do not suffer from this defect because they can sense the kinds of instruction that can be conveniently omitted in individual cases. They do not have to play safe by saying everything. In order to reduce the linear program to comparable dimensions, it is necessary to compromise either by (a) assuming that the student will evolve the appropriate conceptual structures on his own account or (b) settling for a more modest terminal behavior. In case (a), the student is hopefully relied upon to make those adaptations that the linear program, by its very nature, cannot help him to make (14). In case (b), there are reduced claims about what the program can achieve. In an algebra program on simultaneous equations, for example, there may be no pretense of training students to solve word problems of the form: "If Bill is twice as old as Jack was three years ago. . . ."

The Concept of Terminal Behavior

In its most naïve interpretation, the specification of a terminal behavior consists in listing a representative set of problems that the student is expected to be able to solve at the end of the program. The problems are of course intended to index the student's understanding of the subject matter worked through. But there are grounds for doubting whether they always do this successfully. Ultimately, all tests of understanding must be behavioral. But it is misleading to say that programs typically or ideally aim at a well-specified terminal *behavior*. It is rather the case that they aim at a terminal *repertoire of acceptable problem-solving methods*.

The need to refer to problem-solving methods arises because there are many subjects for which it is possible to get the right answer by an incorrect or inferior (e.g., devious) reasoning process. It is therefore particularly desirable to get good indices of understanding, such as the ability to alternate between different problem-solving methods or the ability to spot shortcut routes to a correct solution. Abilities of this kind signify the existence of higher-order abstractions which enable the student to think *about* his problem-solving procedures while he is actually working *with* them. An efficient program will accordingly embed these abilities in the student and will test, at regular intervals, for their presence. To give a student more insight into the structure of algebra, for example, the solving of simultaneous equations might be taught by the "multiplying up" method (to get rid of one variable at a time) and also by the method of determinants. A terminal specification would then consist in requiring the student to alternate freely from one method to the other and to select the method that yields the quicker results on each particular occasion. (To establish that the student was actually alternating in the manner required, it may be necessary, incidentally, to conduct an *adaptively controlled* test. In particular, it may be necessary to switch from one type of problem to another and to manipulate response-time allowances, in order to infer that the student really could use the most appropriate methods of solution.)

In more ambitious programs it might be desirable, if not necessary, to strive for higher-order objectives. Presumably it is possible to train a person to some criterion standard (e.g., to recite long poems), but to do so in a way which kills his enthusiasm for the subject for good. A higher-order terminal specification would therefore consist of insuring that the student maintained, or emerged with, a favorable attitude toward the subject matter as a whole. Other higher-order objectives might consist of getting the student to conceptualize a subject matter (like mathematical set theory) in abstract rather than in concrete or visual terms. And it could also be an explicit objective of the program to train students to retain their efficiency under conditions of stress.

Considerations of this kind make it clear that an optimal teaching system must frequently operate at several levels of discourse at once. And the model or theory which specifies the teaching routine accordingly must have the same multilevel structure. In a program on jurisprudence, for example, it might be convenient to start with a set of legal precedents that exemplify certain general legal concepts or principles. These principles might themselves cluster together to exemplify more abstract ideas of justice or "natural law." These may then be justified, at a still higher level of abstraction, in terms of deterrence, reformation, retribution, etc. And these justifying notions might themselves be evaluated with reference to some meta-ethic or generalization principle of the kind found in Singer (41). Since it is also necessary to give the student some idea of the uses and abuses to which legal rulings, etc., have been put, it is clear that the component ideas of the over-all subject matter strictly belong to different levels of a highly complex conceptual hierarchy.

In order to comprehend these complications, it may well be necessary to elaborate the ruleg procedure by constructing a hierarchy of inter-related matrices corresponding to the hierarchy of abstractions demanded by the subject matter. And these matrices might themselves need to be related (within levels and between levels) to a hierarchically ordered set of *error matrices* specifying the confusions and obstacles associated with different regions of the subject matter hierarchy. The appropriate teaching machine would then require a similar hierarchical structure in the sense that different levels of feedback and data processing would be required to monitor the growth, within the student, of the necessary conceptual levels.

The detailed requirements of such a procedure have still to be worked out. But until they are worked out, there is no way of being sure that a program will achieve what the students, teachers, and parents *hope* it will achieve. Despite Mager's (16) aversion to the concept of "really understanding," educationalists are right to insist that there is an important difference between really understanding a subject matter and being able to pass a terminal examination in it. In the training of pilots, for example, there are good grounds for requiring trainees to have an understanding of algebra in addition to being able to perform certain gambits on their control panels. This requirement reflects an entirely proper concern with the problem-solving methods that underlie (or *should* underlie) the gambits in question.

Anyone who has ever sat or set an examination must surely know that these tests can all too often be passed by means of short-term mnemonic systems, rule-of-thumb procedures which are committed to memory for specific circumstances and which are uncritically applied whenever similar-looking circumstances recur. Mnemonic systems are unacceptable because they substitute, partly or wholly, for the higher-order coordinating principles that would enable the student to handle his subject matter fluently. They enable the student to get by, at some strain to his memory, with the help of assorted mental props which may well be irrelevant and which he will probably forget or distort anyway. So while it is entirely proper to justify programed instruction in terms of the terminal behavior produced, the terminal behavior must *itself* be justified by showing that it cannot be achieved until the full conceptual structure has been developed.

At the present time, terminal behaviors are justified on an intuitive

basis. This may well be satisfactory in many cases, but it is a pity to
have to *rely* upon intuition. It is also regrettable that defects in existing
programs are sometimes obscured by redesigning school examinations
to fit them. If these matters are to be handled objectively, it will be
necessary to conduct subject matter analyses of the kind just described.
And there are several advantages to be gained from doing this. The
analyses, for example, might enable different subject matters to be
classified and compared. This could lead (with the help of error matrices
to define and interrelate the main dimensions of difficulty) to measures
of complexity being derived for the subject matters concerned and to
special tests for predicting student suitability, etc., for training. The
know-how for programing one type of subject matter might also be
transferable to other subject matters with considerable saving in time.
And it should also be possible to decide between program methods
which introduce just one topic or concept area at a time (for ease of
assimilation) and "spiral-type" programs (4) which simultaneously
cover several topics at a time (for breadth of understanding). It should
also be possible to devise "evolutionary" techniques for insuring that
the best elements of already-existing programs can be identified and
preserved for eventual recombination in more powerful programs. This
will at least obviate the necessity for using intuition afresh, whenever
a new program needs to be constructed. Finally it should be possible
to prescribe rules for programing those awkward subjects, rarely dealt
with in the literature, which are not "rule-dense."

All this is a doctrine of perfection. The System Research group so
far has made only small inroads into the many problems involved, but
progress *is* being made, and a testable theory of teaching is slowly
emerging (29). The more important aspects of the theory have in fact
already been tested on the machines described in the following section
and on the machines discussed in the section on research equipment
and experimental results. Admittedly, the task has been simplified by
the selection of skills for which a terminal repertoire is comparatively
easy to specify. And mnemonic systems of responding have been de-
feated mainly by diversifying the content of the problems presented
and by introducing pacing functions which *necessitate* the development
of the appropriate conceptual apparatus. But these are only short-term
expedients. In principle, there seems to be no difficulty in carrying

through the full research program and, when this is completed, there will exist a verifiable theory of teaching that will enable effective programs to be *designed* in the strict sense of the word.

Some Illustrative Machines

The adaptive teaching techniques described in this chapter are entirely general and can be applied to the instruction of any well-structured skill. Since 1953, more than 30 adaptive machines have been built and exhibited from the System Research Laboratory. About 10 more have been constructed for research purposes, to test different aspects of the theories of teaching and learning being developed. These devices are not particularly well known in educational circles because they have been concerned mostly with the teaching of skills found in commerce, industry, and the armed services. Typical examples are skills like card punching and continuous tracking, in which the trainee is required to make rapid motor responses (on some sort of keyboard or response panel) to an equally rapid sequence of visual or auditory signals.

Machines of this kind were particularly suitable for early illustrations of the adaptive method. Apart from being comparatively cheap and easy to program, they were easy for the casual observer to comprehend and operate. They gave, in a short space of time, an excellent idea of the kind of dynamic man-machine interaction that could be achieved, but they also gave a number of false impressions about the ultimate scope of the adaptive machine. Thus, the presence of the pacing factor (popularly associated with the training of high-speed manual skills) suggested that such machines were not particularly suitable for instruction of intellectual subjects. And the different display characteristics of each new model encouraged the belief that every skill required its own special-purpose machine.

The truth of the matter is that limited financial resources made it desirable to concentrate, initially, on the production of simple special-purpose devices that were likely to have immediate impact. These were accordingly made as diversified as possible in order to convince an unreceptive public of the generality of the methods advocated. The intention was to imply that adaptive teaching techniques could be taken dramatically further if necessary. And it has since become evident that adaptive machines can be built to instruct *any* subject matter that can be broken down into logically tractable stages.

While it is certainly true that adaptive machines sometimes require special-purpose displays, etc., so does any other realistic teaching method. To have any practical value, a course of instruction must always terminate with problems that the student is likely to encounter in real life. If the final objective is to make the student proficient in card punching, typewriting, Morse, radar watching, etc., the teaching machine, like the human instructor, must provide the appropriate keyboards and visual displays to practice with. But it does *not* follow that the adaptive computing facilities (connected to these displays) must be different for different skills. To prove this point, the authors are currently designing electronic "modules" that can be interconnected to form a wide variety of hierarchical control systems. In addition to their more direct applications to industrial control problems, sets of these modules should eventually be able to monitor the instruction of almost any well-defined skill.

Saki

Perhaps the best-known adaptive teaching machine is one devised by Pask for the training of card punch operators (25). The device is known as Saki (Self-Organizing Automatic Keyboard Instructor). Card punching is essentially a touch-typing skill, and the training system consists of (a) a near-vertical display panel which exhibits exercise materials; (b) a real-size keyboard which the trainee must learn to operate without actually looking at the keys; (c) a "cue information" display of lights which helps the trainee to locate particular keys without his having to look for them directly; and (d) an adaptive computer which senses the characteristics of the trainee and adjusts the training routine to suit his requirements.

Almost any type of keyboard skill can be taught by Saki-like devices (25). At the top of the near-vertical display panel is a transparent and removable exercise card on which are printed four exercise lines of 30 letters or numbers. The figures on this card are made visible by being back-illuminated, one at a time, from left to right. Each illuminated number poses a problem to which the trainee must respond by pressing, within a short time allowance, the appropriate key. To help him find this key without looking at the keyboard, a further display of "cue information" lights is provided immediately below the exercise card. This display duplicates the spatial layout of the keyboard being used, and a light appears in the appropriate position to tell the trainee where the correct key is located. If he presses this key, the problem light and cue light extinguish, and the next pair are illuminated immediately. Otherwise the machine waits until the expiration of the time allowance, clocks up an error against the trainee, and then moves on automatically to the next problem and cue light. During the early stages of learning the figures move on rather slowly, at approximately three-second intervals. But as the trainee gains in speed and accuracy, the waiting times become shorter and the cue lights diminish in intensity. This is done differentially, so that the machine continues to wait longer and to give cue information on those keys that persist in giving difficulty. Furthermore, it will slow down and restore cue information for any key on which the trainee suffers a sudden relapse.

Whereas the simpler "branching" machines take corrective action on the basis of just one response, Saki adjusts its program in accordance with an integrated performance measure (based on speed and accuracy) secured over a whole series of responses. The result is a continuous adjustment of difficulty and time pressure which keeps the trainee working always near the limit of his ability. Since some combinations of figures are harder to punch than others, the exercise cards (together with the programs associated with them) are changeable and graded in difficulty. Within each exercise card, the four exercise lines are likewise graded in difficulty. A trainee is therefore put through the same exercise line, over and over again, until he reaches criterion efficiency, whereupon Saki promotes him to the next line down.

The Typewriter Trainer

A prototype model of an adaptive typewriting instructor has recently been developed. It exposes exercise materials in the form of characters on a printed tape that moves one space leftward for every key that the trainee presses. These characters are exposed through an aperture of variable width, but which normally shows five characters at a time. The student's task is to press the key corresponding to the character appearing at the extreme left of the aperture, and a display of cue information lights (functioning in the Saki manner) is provided to help him do this. If the correct key is depressed, the tape moves one character space to the left, and the next cue light comes on. In any event, the student obtains immediate knowledge of results by seeing his response typed on a sheet running in parallel with the exercise tape. As an additional form of guidance, the "home" keys are fitted with vibrators to provide tactile information (a) about their location and (b) about the finger to be used for making the next response. Unlike Saki, the machine normally waits for the student to press the correct key, but it emits an indignant buzz if he falls short of his recent average response time. The machine adapts by comparing the student's response record against a code punched on the exercise tape. According to predetermined decision rules, it adjusts its visual and tactile cues together with the rapidity with which the buzzer is sounded. It can also direct the student to change to one of four different classes of exercise tape, each of which is especially designed to eliminate some error factor that the machine is programed to detect.

The whole device is more complicated than Saki because there are more difficulties to be overcome. Whereas the trained card punch operator must be prepared to press keys in all possible orders (since one ordering of numbers is just as likely as another), English is so constituted that certain letter sequences (e.g., *q* followed by *u*, or *t-h-e*) are more common than others. An efficient teaching device should allow for this by making the trainee typist most fluent on those letter and word combinations that recur most frequently. In addition to accumulating data on the efficiency with which individual keys are pressed, the machine must therefore compute speed and accuracy measures over many different combinations of keys, unless some special programing technique can be devised to insure, without elaborate computation, that the necessary practice is obtained. The machine just described appears to be the best compromise available, having regard to the enormous cost of multiple computation facilities. The technique, of course, can be equally well applied to instruction in teleprinting and related skills.

Other Keyboard Skills

Essentially the same methods have been successfully used in the training of Morse, ad-listing, and telephone dialing operations. An interesting skill not yet automated is piano-playing. The difficulty here resides in the fact that proficiency cannot be measured satisfactorily in terms of the speed and accuracy with which the student strikes particular keys. Instead, there are complex criteria of efficiency and "style" which could be handled by an adaptive machine, but only at prohibitive cost. At present nothing more elaborate exists than a simple adaptive device for teaching rhythmic finger movements, but the position may well change if the price of computer components continues to fall.

Perceptual Coding Skills

In industrial and military organizations there are many skills that depend, in one way or another, on the vigilance of the human operator. To show how adaptive machines can be used in this field, a radar training machine has been built that checks on alertness by repeatedly projecting false test signals onto the radar screen. The device actually introduces several kinds of false signals to allow for the possibility that different operators will tend to miss different kinds of perceptual events. In the early stages of training, the different test signals are presented in roughly equal proportions and at "medium" intensity. If the operator misses a particular signal, it is repeated shortly afterward with greater perceptual distinctness. Otherwise its reappearance is deferred and/or reduced in clarity. (This involves the adjustment of signal intensity and duration relative to the "background noise.") In effect, the machine learns about the kinds of signals that the trainee operator is likely to miss, and it brings him up to standard on these. Eventually a state of affairs is reached in which the operator is sensitive to a wide range of faint signals, presented at irregular intervals against a varying background of noise. If necessary, the device could form part of a real radar system to maintain the fully trained operator in a state of maximum vigilance throughout his watch. To allow for the remote possibility of false signals coinciding with real signals, ideally there should be at least two parallel recognition systems in which no false signals occur at the same time.

Given that a signal is detected, there may be complex problems (especially in air-to-air radar) of securing an optimal interception course. To cover this contingency, a machine has been made to simulate a target capable of taking different kinds of evasive action. This is an adaptive device that learns about the operator's weaknesses in tracking elusive objects and provides remedial experience to improve his efficiency. A simpler variation on the same theme is a two-coordinate tracking device in which the trainee is required to align a pair of needles by manipulating a set of relative velocity controls.

Yet another machine exists for training people to correlate visual information coming from two independent locations. This particular device consists of a display which simulates two cross-flows of road traffic. The problem is to relate one cross-flow to another in order to avoid collisions at particular road junctions. The trainee must therefore learn to make rapid predictions about the consequences of steering one way rather than another. His efficiency is accordingly indexed by the speed with which he takes particular kinds of anticipatory or avoidance action. Whereas the radar trainer helps to keep the operator awake when he is perceptually *under*loaded, this machine helps the operator to deal with a situation in which he is perceptually *over*loaded. These devices, of course, could be used as "continuous aids to performance" rather than as "teaching machines." In this case they would simply form a cooperative partnership with the operator in order to compensate, indefinitely, for whatever weaknesses he exhibits.

Maintenance Training Skills

Another important class of industrial and military skills is concerned with the servicing of electrical equipment. In order to train student electricians and electronic service engineers in the methods and logic of fault detection (troubleshooting), a special adaptive trainer has been constructed to simulate some of the defects that actually occur in the more common electrical systems. The main display unit here consists of three input lights leading, through an intermediate network, to three output lights. The student is presented with a sequence of defects that disrupts the normal patterns of correspondence between input and output lamps and which signify the presence of a "break" at some critical point in the intermediate circuit. At each of these critical points, there is a hole into which a spare test plug can be fitted. If the student inserts the plug in the right hole, he is deemed to have repaired the fault, and a new defect is introduced. If the student makes a wrong insertion, the machine analyzes the nature of the mistake and uses it, in conjunction with previous error information, to adjust its subsequent training routine. It is in fact equipped with an internal representation of the logical requirements of the task, and it relates these to the student's test plug manipulations by means of a variable interrogation procedure. The machine has facilities for pacing and for providing cue information in the form of lights which signify the presence or absence of power at certain key regions of the circuit. It can also introduce more than one defect at a time.

Special Purpose Intellectual Skills

Several special purpose devices exist for instruction in intellectual skills. One of the earliest was Pask's 1953 "Coordinate Transformation Trainer" (14). This device had a main display consisting of 12 letters arranged in a 3 x 4 block. The same letters were also arranged in random order around a circular clockface. All the student had to do was to press two buttons on a response panel, corresponding to the coordinates of any letter that happened to be back-illuminated in the circular display. To facilitate the teaching process, a vectorial simplifying operation was provided by signifying the row or column in which the problem letter was located. And the machine was programed to give the student additional practice on any row or column that appeared to be giving special difficulty.

Following this model was a series of machines that engaged the student in concept-forming games of the Lewis Carroll kind. In these cases the student was induced (by adaptive changes in the game situation) to acquire and apply concepts under conditions of increasing difficulty. For instance, it was possible to provide the student with unreliable or inadequate or confusing evidence on which to base his decisions. By introducing irregularities of this kind, the game was converted from a deductive into an inductive skill, and the student was repeatedly forced to work at higher levels of abstraction, because it was repeatedly necessary for him to reevaluate the game strategies he had been using previously.

Data Comprehension Skills

A machine that is suitable for a large number of comprehension skills is the General Comprehension Trainer now being developed by the present authors. This machine has facilities for back-illuminating two quarto-size (9 x 12) sheets of exercise materials printed on the back of a plastic sheet that the student clamps behind a transparent viewing frame. The left-hand quarto sheet is illuminated first, to reveal typescript, technical diagrams, pictures, etc. The sheet is illuminated for a preset interval of a few seconds, during which time the student must extract as much relevant information as possible. At the end of the time interval, the illumination of the left-hand sheet is terminated and replaced by an exposure of the right-hand quarto sheet which presents up to four multiple-choice comprehension questions on the material just presented. The machine then analyzes the four responses, awards a mark (or some similar knowledge of results), and tells the student which sheet to insert next. In the simplest case, the exercise materials are arranged in two piles, each of which is designed to eradicate a different dimension of error. If necessary, the four multiple-choice questions can be exhibited sequentially, so that just a quarter segment of the right-hand sheet is exposed at a time. In this case different segments can be made to incorporate cue information for segments still to be exposed. Further cue information can be provided by allowing the student another quick look at the left-hand sheet. As the student improves, the machine reduces the exposure times so that faster and faster comprehension is required.

With slight modification the device can be used to instruct students in the skill of speedreading, proofreading, and skimreading. By making the multiple-choice buttons register *opinions*, rather than correct responses, the device can also be effectively used to conduct attitude surveys of the market research kind.

Research Equipment and Experimental Results

In addition to the commercially sponsored machines just described, several research devices have been built to test particular aspects of the teaching theory being developed. One of these concerned the teaching of a keyboard skill in which various combinations of four keys (selected from an eight-key response panel) had to be pressed, within a five-second time allowance, in response to various combinations of four lights (selected from an eight-light display panel). The lights and keys were not in direct correspondence. Subjects therefore had to learn, for example, that the illumination of lights (1, 2, 5, and 6) required the depression of keys (2, 4, 7, and 5), and that the illumination of lights (1, 3, 7, and 8) required the depression of keys (2, 1, 8, and 6). Altogether, eight different combinations of four lights were used. These occurred with equal frequency, and subjects were required to achieve a terminal behavior criterion of 75 percent accuracy over 40 successive problems.

About nine subjects out of ten were unable to learn the skill unless simplification procedures were introduced. These took the form of a graded training routine in which rehearsal of the four-light problems was preceded by practice on one-light, two-light, and three-light problems. By means of cue lights, which could be made to exhibit the relevant patterns of light → key correspondence, it was in fact possible to obtain seven degrees of simplification. In order to reach criterion performance on the four-light problems, it was not necessary to spend too long on the simpler levels. The transfer of training characteristics, between one level and the next, was such that complete mastery of each level was not required. In fact, too much practice on the simpler levels produced "overlearning" of a kind that could temporarily inhibit learning of the four-light problems.

The machine was therefore equipped with two tally counters, X and Y, which recorded (respectively) the number of correct and incorrect responses given by a subject (S). For every m correct responses recorded on X, S was "promoted" to the next higher level of difficulty. For every n incorrect responses recorded on Y, S was "demoted" to the next lower level of difficulty. Table 1 shows some typical results for $m = 6$ or 12, and for $n = 6$ or 12. Subjects were required to proceed through the seven simplified levels to the eighth "unsimplified" level, in which four-light problems appeared without cues. This eighth level was the level at which 75 percent accuracy had to be achieved, and it can be seen from Table 1 that the number of trial problems required to reach this criterion is lowest in condition D, where $m = 6$ and $n = 12$.

Under condition D, it is twice as easy to be promoted as to be demoted. Provided the over-all proportion, p, of errors is less than two-thirds, subjects can in fact be sure of reaching the eighth level after not more than $84/(2 - 3p)$ trials.[2] In practice the over-all percentage error turned out to be about 52 percent, as indicated in the bottom right-hand corner of Table 1. Such a high proportion of errors runs

---

[2] Thus, if $p=0$, subjects reach the hardest level of difficulty after $84/2$ trials; and if $p=.52$ (for 52 percent error), subjects reach the eighth level after about 191 trials. In practice, they may of course fluctuate between levels 7 and 8 for a further 50-100 trials before reaching criterion efficiency at the eighth level.

TABLE I
Number of Errors Made at Each Level of Difficulty and the Number of Trials To Reach Criterion Performance for Four Conditions of "Promotion"

	Number of errors made at each of 8 levels, L_1—L_8, of difficulty								Total errors	Total trials to criterion	Percentage error	Over-all percentage
	L_1	L_2	L_3	L_4	L_5	L_6	L_7	L_8				
Condition A												
S_1	4	3	5	3	34	14	36	26	125	305	.41	
S_2	1	3	5	8	55	31	56	25	184	418	.44	
6 correct — level up S_3	2	1	7	4	27	20	72	61	194	440	.44	
6 incorrect — level down S_4	2	1	8	12	38	35	80	32	208	469	.44	
	9	8	25	27	154	100	244	144	711	1632	(.44)	44% error
Condition B												
S_5	3	1	9	1	17	4	34	23	92	270	.34	
S_6	7	4	11	5	15	9	28	14	93	274	.34	
12 correct — level up S_7	8	2	6	2	17	9	44	17	105	297	.35	
12 incorrect — level down S_8	3	2	7	10	18	10	36	38	124	344	.36	
	21	9	33	18	67	32	142	92	414	1185	(.35)	35% error
Condition C												
S_9	4	3	3	1	25	13	33	18	100	388	.26	
S_{10}	1	0	3	3	25	14	66	25	137	497	.28	
12 correct — level up S_{11}	5	3	3	4	27	29	59	31	161	569	.28	
6 incorrect — level down S_{12}	4	3	10	8	35	23	59	37	179	623	.29	
	14	9	19	16	112	79	217	111	577	2077	(.28)	28% error
Condition D												
S_{13}	9	2	6	7	17	14	26	20	101	203	.50	
S_{14}	3	1	5	3	22	23	39	26	122	240	.51	
6 correct — level up S_{15}	4	2	4	3	17	20	55	49	154	286	.54	
12 incorrect — level down S_{16}	2	0	1	4	25	18	40	67	157	301	.52	
	18	5	16	17	81	75	160	162	534	1030	(.52)	52% error

contrary to the spirit of Skinnerian-type training. It works in this particular case because subjects do best if they have only a slight acquaintance with the simpler levels. Moreover, the generation of over 50 percent mistakes tends to induce high concentration on the task, since S, in his dynamic interaction with the machine, is continually made aware of the latter's efforts to push him to a higher level of difficulty. Using the "trend test" of Jonckheere (10), it can be shown that condition D is better than either conditions A or B, and that conditions A and B are both better than condition C (for which the over-all error rate is lowest). These results all exceed the .5 percent level of significance.

It is worth remarking that if subjects are allowed to determine their own rate of progress through the eight levels, they typically spend much longer on the simpler levels in order to master them and to reduce their error scores to about a 20 percent maximum. Thirty subjects who were allowed to pace themselves took an average of 22 percent more trials (S.D. = 9 percent) to reach the same criterion efficiency, a result which on an analysis of variance well exceeded the .01 percent level of significance.

In a further series of experiments, the set-up just described was elaborated to comprise two partly conflicting subskills, a and β, involving two different rules (r_t and r_β) of correspondence between lights and keys. Thus in subskill a, the illumination of lights (1, 2, 5, and 6) still called for the depression of keys (2, 4, 7, and 5), but in subskill β the same lights called for the depression of keys (2, 4, 6, and 8). As before, there were seven degrees of simplification for each subskill, and subjects had to learn how to maintain 75 percent accuracy (on four light problems without cues) when they were being switched at frequent intervals from one subskill to the other.

Once again, subject-controlled rehearsal of the subskills proved grossly inefficient. If subjects were left to determine their own order of rehearsal of the subskills, they generally tried to master them one at a time. Thus they might concentrate exclusively on subskill a until they had achieved 75 percent accuracy. They would then concentrate exclusively on subskill β, only to find that, once they had mastered it, they could no longer perform the a subskill. Because of these interference effects, an adaptively controlled procedure was required to ensure that subskills a and β were tackled together. Details of several workable procedures can be found in Pask (33). In general they all

TABLE 2

Comparison of Three Training Conditions for Four-Light Keyboard Skill

Number of blocks of 25 trials
required to reach criterion performance
(16 subjects tested under each condition)

Condition A*	Condition B*	Condition C*
25	24	25
25	25	27
26	25	29
26	25	29
26	26	29
26	28	29
26	30	29
27	30	29
27	30	30
28	31	31
28	32	31
28	32	31
29	32	32
30	32	32
31	33	32
31	33	35
Means: 27.4	29.2	30.0

* The above data are taken from a series of experiments in which the subskills (a and β) were rehearsed in blocks of 25 trials at a time. Within each block, problems were always for the same subskill. At the end of each block, it was necessary to decide whether to continue with the same subskill (for a further block of 25 trials) or to change over to the other subskill.

In condition A, these end-of-block decisions were made solely by the adaptive teaching machine. In condition B, they were made by the machine if S was doing badly, and by S if S was doing well. In condition C, the decisions were made solely by S without any machine guidance.

A one-way analysis of variance on the above data shows that the three conditions differ significantly, due to the fact that condition A is markedly better than conditions B or C. Snedecor's F-ratio = 4.2, 2/45 d.f., $p < .025$.

have the property of switching S from one subskill to the other in order to maximize some plausible index of learning rate. From S's point of view, this was frequently perceived as a "balancing up" strategy which provided challenging problems on the subskill he was better at, mixed with easier problems on the subskill he was worse at. Because of individual differences, no single "linear" training routine is possible for this skill. The adaptive teaching machine produced different routines for different subjects and, on the whole, these were all significantly better than the routines that subjects produced for themselves (Table 2).

Given four keys to press in response to four lights, subjects are compelled to group the lights and keys in a manner analogous to that used in the Van der Veldt experiments reported by Woodworth (48). Responses are generally quickest if all four keys are pressed together, as a "quadruple" group. They tend to be slowest if they are pressed one after the other, as four distinct "singles." Intermediate cases consist in pressing three keys together (a "triple"), followed or preceded by one single, or two pairs of keys ("doubles") in succession, or one double and two singles in various orders. These different response patterns are worth investigating, because they indicate the existence of different modes of problem solving. They show that the same "terminal behavior" (75 percent accuracy on each of the α and β subskills) can be achieved by several, and possibly many, different *repertoires* of problem-solving methods.

Some typical distributions of response patterns are set out, for eight subjects, in Table 3. One way of learning the α and β subskills conjointly consists in developing high-order classification schemes that overcome the interference effects initially existing between them. If this method *is* adopted, then the distribution of response patterns should be similar for both the subskills in question. Table 3 shows that, given a machine-controlled rehearsal of α and β, large correlations between the α and β distributions do indeed occur. If the *subject* is allowed to control the order in which he rehearses the α and β subskills, however, the correlations are lower. This difference, for two groups of four subjects, exceeds the 5 percent level of significance. It suggests that although both groups can reach the 75 percent criterion demanded, the machine-controlled groups are using more powerful methods of solution.

The figures in Table 4 are taken from a prototype version of the experiment just described. In this case there were two subskills, α_1 and β_1, but only six lights and six response keys. Within each subskill there were six three-light problems, each of which called for the pressing of three keys. Just two levels of simplification were introduced, namely,

TABLE 3

Analysis of Response Patterns Exhibited by 8 Subjects During the Period in Which They Achieved (for Two Subskills α and β) an Over-All "Terminal Behavior" Criterion of 75% Accuracy

Condition A

Order of rehearsal of subskills α & β determined by adaptive machine

Percentage number of correct responses for each of α and β subskills:

Categorization of response patterns	S1 α	S1 β	S2 α	S2 β	S3 α	S3 β	S4 α	S4 β
1. quadruple	46	39	18	28	12.5	34	57	38
2. triple + single	40	42	74	44	62.5	62	36	22
3. two doubles	9	19	4	14	7.5	0	3.5	40
4. double + singles	2.5	0	0	7	5	0	0	0
5. four singles	2.5	0	4	7	12.5	4	3.5	0

Rank ordering of percentages under each category:

Categorization of response patterns	S1 α	S1 β	S2 α	S2 β	S3 α	S3 β	S4 α	S4 β
1. quadruple	5	4	4	4	3.5	4	5	4
2. triple + single	4	3	5	3	5	5	4	3
3. two doubles	3	5	2.5	2.5	2	1.5	2.5	5
4. double + singles	1.5	1.5	1	1.5	1	1.5	1	1.5
5. four singles	1.5	1.5	2.5	1.5	3.5	3	2.5	1.5

Spearman's rho: S1 = .90, S2 = .925, S3 = .95, S4 = .50

Condition B

Order of rehearsal of subskills α & β determined by the subject

Percentage number of correct responses for each of α and β subskills:

Categorization of response patterns	S5 α	S5 β	S6 α	S6 β	S7 α	S7 β	S8 α	S8 β
1. quadruple	16	34	28	40	22	37	21	14
2. triple + single	29	19	47	30	52	18	15	32
3. two doubles	24	31	0	15	14	18	0	19
4. double + singles	31	16	16	5	4	23	52	33
5. four singles	0	0	9	9	8	4	12	2

Rank ordering of percentages under each category:

Categorization of response patterns	S5 α	S5 β	S6 α	S6 β	S7 α	S7 β	S8 α	S8 β
1. quadruple	2	5	4	5	4	5	4	2
2. triple + single	4	3	5	4	5	2.5	3	4
3. two doubles	3	4	1	3	3	2.5	1	3
4. double + singles	5	2	3	1	1	4	5	5
5. four singles	1	1	2	2	2	1	2	1

Spearman's rho: S5 = .00, S6 = .50, S7 = .125, S8 = .50

The t-value for the difference between the condition A and the condition B coefficients of correlation is t = 3.2, 3 d.f., p < .05.

TABLE 4

Comparison of Three Training Conditions
for Three-Light Keyboard Skill

Number of trials required to reach criterion performance
(20 subjects tested under each condition)

Condition A* (fully adaptive)	Condition B* (partly adaptive)	Condition C* (nonadaptive)
150	180	130
170	210	140
190	220	150
190	230	190
220	250	240
220	270	290
250	310	320
260	330	320
260	350	360
270	350	390
290	370	430
290	370	430
290	370	450
300	390	470
310	410	490
310	420	500
330	440	510
360	460	510
380	460	530
440	470	570

Jonckheere's test of the null hypothesis, against the ordered a priori alternative of $C_A < C_B < C_C$, permits the null hypothesis to be rejected (in favor of the expected trend) at the .005 level of significance.

* See text for account of these conditions.

rehearsal on one-light and two-light problems that formed part of the final set of triples. The interest of the experiment lay in discovering how the subskills should be intermixed, and varied in difficulty, in order to produce 90 percent accuracy (on both a_1 and β_1) in the shortest possible time.

In the "fully adaptive" condition A, each subskill had its level of difficulty adjusted independently. Thus if S was better at a_1 than at β_1, he might at one time be handling three-light problems on a_1, mixed with two-light (or even one-light) problems on β_1. Further, the relative amounts of practice on the two subskills were varied, so that S received more problems on the subskill that he was less good at. In the "partly adaptive" condition B, the independent adjustment of difficulty levels was retained, but practice on the two subskills was equalized (i.e., α_1 and β_1 problems were always mixed in equal proportions). In the nonadaptive condition C, subjects were rehearsed to 90 percent criterion accuracy, first on one subskill, then on the other, and finally on the two subskills combined (in equal proportions, again). The two levels of simplification were omitted in this condition, so the trials all consisted solely of three-light problems. According to the views expressed in this chapter, there is an a priori expectation that condition A should be more effective than condition B and that B should be better than C. Jonckheere's (10) test of the null hypothesis, against the ordered alternative A > B > C, permits the null hypothesis to be rejected (in favor of the expected trend) at the .5 percent level of significance.

In Table 5, data are presented for a speedreading skill involving two different classes, X and Y, of reading materials. X consisted of scientific passages containing a great deal of quantitative facts and figures. Y consisted of nonscientific prose containing only qualitative information. A modified form of General Comprehension Trainer was used, so that each passage was followed by a comprehension test consisting of four multiple-choice questions. Sixteen passages were used, of which eight belonged to class X and eight to class Y. Once again, the problem was to achieve a satisfactory balance in the rehearsal of the X and Y materials and to reduce the reading time allowance in a way that would induce S to read faster and faster.

Table 5 shows some results for two of the experimental inquiries conducted. In series 1, an adaptive procedure for adjusting time allowances is compared with a nonadaptive "linear" routine. In series 2, an adaptive procedure for varying the order of presentation of the X and Y materials is compared with the nonadaptive procedure of alternating these materials in blocks of four. In both cases, the nonadaptive procedures were the best that could be found, but they proved to be significantly inferior.

The foregoing results constitute only a small sample of the data now being prepared for publication. Further results will not be produced here, because they have very little meaning without extensive

TABLE 5

Comparison of Conditions for Speedreading Skill

| Experimental Series 1 | | Experimental Series 2 | |
| Total Correct Responses per Session | | Mean Terminal Reading Time | |
Condition A (Adaptive)	Condition B (Nonadaptive)	Condition C (Adaptive)	Condition D (Nonadaptive)
21	17	29	28
23	18	29	32
27	18	31	34
28	19	32	34
30	22	33	35
30	22	34	37
31	24	34	39
32	26	34	39
33	26	35	39
34	27	36	40
34	27	36	41
34	27	36	41
36	29	36	43
37	32	38	43
38	35	38	44
39	35	39	45
41	37	40	47
41	38	40	47
42	38	43	49
44	41	45	49
Means = 33.75	27.9	35.9	40.3

For the above data, student's $t = 2.6$, 38 d.f., $p < .02$.

For the above data, student's $t = 2.7$, 38 d.f., $p < .01$.

Condition A (Adaptive):
Reading time increased or decreased according to score on previous comprehension tests.

Condition B (Nonadaptive):
Reading time systematically reduced by 2 seconds per trial to a terminal allowance, after 16 trials, of 36 seconds (36 seconds being the mean terminal allowance achieved in Condition A).

Condition C (Adaptive):
Two types of material presented in an order determined by subject's success on comprehension tests.

Condition D (Nonadaptive):
Two types of material presented in alternate blocks of four, irrespective of subject's performance score.

descriptions of the actual apparatus and experimental conditions used. They do, however, all tell the same story, namely, that adaptively controlled instruction gives significantly better results than fixed training sequences obtained from "averaging out" the requirements of a representative sample of students.

A Group Tuition System

The adaptive teaching methods outlined above can be extended to the case of controlling the learning of a *group* of persons. In the teaching machine literature, group learning is usually discussed in terms of computerized classrooms (1). With the aid of a centralized computer that is time-shared among a group of students, detailed records can be compiled of each student's progress. These can be evaluated and acted upon in many elaborate ways. However, insofar as the computer (rather than a human being) performs these operations, the classroom is necessarily run according to a predetermined scheme. If the scheme is comprehensive enough to cover all the more important contingencies and error factors, the instruction will in general be successful. But no teaching method can be guaranteed to be as comprehensive as this if its subject matter is conceptually complex or ill-defined. Even the most carefully designed courses of study defeat some students, and when a student runs into trouble, the nature of his difficulty can often be sensed by a human teacher in a way that is not (and probably never will be) open to the conventional digital computer. In recognition of this fact, computer-controlled classrooms characteristically provide "readouts" and visual displays which human supervisors can inspect to see if anything further needs to be done. This is tantamount to an admission that there usually *is* more to be done. As in the case of individual teaching machines, the specialist human supervisor has an indispensable role to play in ironing out problems that the machine proves unable to handle.

The ability of one human to understand the difficulties of another derives from the richly complex ways in which they are capable of sharing common dimensions of experience (18, 40). But this ability is not peculiar to the teacher-student relationship. Two students can have it equally well, and this raises the possibility of a computer-controlled system which *induces students to teach each other.*

Such a system has been constructed and tested by the present writers (12, 13, 15, 26, 34, 35). To exemplify the general principles involved a small group of only three students was used, but the method is generalizable to larger groups. Whereas the normal teaching machine assumes direct responsibility for instructing and testing students, and for resolving their difficulties, this particular system hands the bulk of these duties over to the students themselves so that each student's progress becomes the collective concern of his neighbors. Underlying this procedure is the assumption that humans potentially are still the best devices for interpreting complex information coming from other humans. Instead of using an expensive computer to evaluate and assist each student in turn, the system exploits the members' own data processing and learning capabilities to achieve similar objectives. It does this by feeding them with information and problems which they are then required to try out among themselves.

In effect, the total system provides an adaptively controlled environment in which students are invited and encouraged to develop interaction patterns that enable them to become their own best instructors. To facilitate this process, the automaton computes objective measures of the progress made by particular students (and combinations of students), and, on the basis of these computations, it adjusts their working conditions in ways that seem most likely to insure that progress will continue. For example, it regulates time constraints, availability of relevant information, and extraneous disturbances, so that the group's immediate objectives are neither too hard nor too easy; it increases the amount of information allowed to pass between students who seem to be working well together; it encourages the students to vary their approach in systematic ways, so as to broaden their outlook and to give effective modes of interaction a better chance of emerging; and it seeks, by various means, to induce the development of a common language so that the students can make themselves understood to each other. (Until a common language is established, students will rarely exert the kinds of influence over each other that their capabilities warrant.)

The system therefore applies to a group of students essentially the same kinds of pressuring techniques that could be applied, if desired, to one individual at a time. By allowing the students to assume different roles at different times, it gives each a chance to see the group activity from several points of view. In this way, it satisfies their needs for diversity and fair play, and it tends to keep them favorably motivated. To minimize unprofitable variations in behavior, the system does, however, restrict each student's control over his neighbors so that the greatest control always tends to reside with those students who teach the best.

Within the limits imposed by the foregoing considerations, the system can also strive for higher-order objectives. Thus it can handicap individual members so as to equalize their success scores. In consequence everyone feels on level terms, and group "cohesiveness" tends to go up. It is also worth noting that the system secures informational feedback from the group members at several different levels at once. In particular, it obtains information about the behavior to be controlled and about the students' preferences for particular communication patterns and game situations. (Interaction between the group and the adaptive control system therefore involves the kind of multilevel or "meta-linguistic" discourse mentioned in the earlier section on assumptions and specific features of the teaching model.)

Experimental data obtained from the group tuition system suggest that the collection of such information is essential for effective control over the group. And the actual control procedures, of course, must be applied at several different levels at once. Thus if the group's task is made harder, help must be given in the form of cues or channels for cooperation or a reduction in time pressure. Facilities also exist for concomitantly varying a displayed score and the rate at which this is accumulated by a successful student.

In some respects, the group tuition system adopts the "student teacher" method of the old-fashioned English country school. Instead of teaching directly, it selects students who are able to teach other students and places them in suitable tutorial relations to one another. Although it *could* impart knowledge, it tends to function as a catalyst, to bring out the resources of the students themselves. By systematically manipulating the conditions under which they work, it induces a wide variety of behavior patterns, so that it can detect and perpetuate those which are most likely to raise the over-all group standard. In so doing, the system gives each student experience in learning how to communicate with his fellow human beings. This is an experience which is all too often neglected in current educational practice.

TABLE 6

Three Comparisons of Group Performance Under Adaptive vs. Nonadaptive Training Conditions

	Control Sample (consisting of 25 groups in which assignment of duties was fixed by predetermined rota)	Experimental Sample (consisting of 25 groups in which assignment of duties was adaptively varied)
1. Mean number of games required to recover from the introduction of misinformation:	12.6	10.2
Standard deviation:	3.1	2.7
On the above data, student's t = 2.9, 48 d.f., p < .01.		
2. Mean number of items of evidence transmitted per game during 10 games following the introduction of misinformation:	7.6	6.2
Standard deviation:	2.1	1.4
On the above data, student's t = 2.7, 48 d.f., p < .01.		
3. Mean transmitting time (in seconds) per game during 10 games following the introduction of misinformation:	64	59
Standard deviation:	12.9	8.7
On the above data, Snedecor's F-ratio = 2.2, 24/24 d.f., p < .05.		

The adaptively controlled groups therefore recover from misinformation more rapidly than the nonadaptively controlled groups.

Following the introduction of misinformation, the adaptively controlled groups therefore need to transmit significantly fewer items of evidence. In this respect, the adaptively controlled groups are therefore less vulnerable to the presence of misinformation.

Following the introduction of misinformation, the adaptively controlled groups therefore show significantly less variation in the time required to transmit information. The Fisher-Behren's test does not yield a significant difference between means.

For further information and statistical data on this system, the reader is referred to Pask and Lewis (35). It is possible here to present only one illustrative table of the results obtained. Table 6 accordingly shows some typical gains achieved by using the adaptive control methods just described. Three comparisons are made. From comparison 1 it can be seen that groups which change roles according to some fixed rota scheme take longer to recover from disturbances (in the form of misinformation, etc.) than groups in which the assignment of roles is varied adaptively. In comparison 2, the further point is made that while they are actually recovering from disturbance, adaptively controlled groups also need fewer items of evidence in order to make themselves understood. Finally, comparison 3 shows that adaptively controlled groups exhibit less variation in the time they take to communicate to each other. In all three comparisons, the adaptively controlled groups therefore emerge as being more "flexible" and resilient to stress.

Conclusions

The work reported in this chapter constitutes what is believed to be the only sustained attempt to apply the notions of cybernetics and artificial intelligence to teaching machines and teaching theory. Inevitably, many of the concepts discussed in this chapter are likely to be unfamiliar to other workers in the field of programed instruction. To anyone unversed in the theory of artificial intelligence, the sections on this topic can hardly do more than give the general flavor of the approach. Nevertheless the approach is rich in possibilities and well deserving of further consideration.

If a rigorous theory of teaching is to be achieved, some assumptions *must* be made about the nature of the student (the conditions under which he attends to the instruction and the kinds of conceptual abilities he brings to bear upon it) and the structure of the subject matter. In one way or another, provision *must* be made for comprehending the student's problem-solving processes and the mechanisms that underlie these processes. This in turn seems to call for a sizable network of concepts like the structured skill, the error factor, and the data-processing hierarchy. In the absence of such concepts it is just not possible to explicate the logical, psychological, and epistemological relationships that exist between one part of a complex subject matter and another.

As usual, there is a great deal of unfinished business. Although the outlined framework covers many important features of the teaching process, it is basically inelegant and in need of greater systematization. To strengthen and elucidate the "learning" aspect of the model, work is currently being done on the computer simulation of some of the student-machine interactions discussed. In these simulations the student is characterized as a hierarchically organized learning system which searches through a changing repertoire of problem-solving algorithms and creates new algorithms in cases where none can be found. Correspondence between the activities of the simulated student-machine interaction and the real student-machine interaction provides tentative evidence that the simulated learning model is correct.

Inquiries of this kind are illuminating because they reveal, as no other method can, the tremendous diversity of problem-solving methods that can underlie any one "terminal behavior." Even for the comparatively simple skill of Table 3, several distinct "repertoires" (of problem-solving methods) can be specified. These all have potentially different transfer of training properties and, within the experimental situation, they can be distinguished only by investigating the sequential characteristics of component responses (as in Table 3), or by differences in response latencies, or by some even more microscopic comparison. It is also of interest to note that learning, within a stabilized system of the (A, B) kind described in this chapter, can be explicated within a Piaget-like or Vygotsky-like framework, but not within the tenets of statistical learning theory or comparable disciplines.

References

1. Coulson, J. E., editor. *Programmed Learning and Computer-Based Instruction.* New York: John Wiley & Sons, 1962.
2. Evans, J. L.; Homme, L. E.; and Glaser, R. "The Ruleg System for the Construction of Programmed Verbal Learning Sequences." *Journal of Educational Research* 55: 513-18; June-July 1962.
3. Flavell, D. *The Developmental Psychology of Jean Piaget.* New York: D. Van Nostrand Co., 1960.
4. Glaser, R. "Some Research Problems in Automated Instruction." *Programmed Learning and Computer-Based Instruction.* (Edited by J. E. Coulson.) New York: John Wiley & Sons, 1962.
5. Gorn, S. "The Treatment of Ambiguity and Paradox in Mechanical Languages." *Symposium Proceedings in Pure Mathematics of the American Mathematical Society*, 1962. Vol. 5, pp. 201-18.

6. Harlow, H. F. "The Formation of Learning Sets." *Psychological Review* 56: 51-65; January 1949.
7. Harlow, H. F. "Learning Set and Error Factor Theory." *Psychology, A Study of a Science*. (Edited by S. Koch.) New York: McGraw-Hill Book Co., 1959. Vol. 2, Study 1.
8. Hovland, C. I. "A 'Communication Analysis' of Concept Learning." *Psychological Review* 59: 461-72; November 1952.
9. Hunt, E. B. *Concept Learning: An Information Processing Problem*. New York: John Wiley & Sons, 1962.
10. Jonckheere, A. R. "A Test of the Significance for the Relation Between *m* Rankings and *k* Ranked Categories." *British Journal of Statistical Psychology*, 1954. Vol. 7.
11. Lewis, B. N. "Adaptive Teaching Machines." *Programmed Learning* 1: 3-4; 1963.
12. Lewis, B. N. "Communication in Problem-Solving Groups." *Conference on Design Methods*. (Edited by J. C. Jones and D. G. Thornley.) London: Pergamon Press, 1963.
13. Lewis, B. N. "The Adaptive Control of Small Groups." *Programming '63*. (Edited by B. Dodd.) Sheffield, England: Department of Education, Sheffield University, 1963.
14. Lewis, B. N. "The Rationale of Adaptive Teaching Machines." *Mechanisation in the Classroom*. (Edited by M. Goldsmith.) London: Souvenir Press, 1963.
15. Lewis, B. N., and Pask, G. "The Development of Communication Skills Under Adaptively Controlled Conditions." *Programmed Learning* 1: 69-88; July 1964.
16. Mager, R. F. *Preparing Objectives for Programmed Instruction*. San Francisco: Fearon Publishers, 1961.
17. Martin, R. M. *Intension and Decision*. Englewood Cliffs, N.J.: Prentice-Hall, 1963.
18. Mead, G. H. *Mind, Self and Society*. Chicago: University of Chicago Press, 1934.
19. Miller, G. A. "The Magical Number Seven, Plus or Minus Two; Some Limits on Our Capacity for Processing Information." *Psychological Review* 63: 81-97; March 1956.
20. Miller, G. A.; Galanter E.; and Pribram, K. H. *Plans and the Structure of Behavior*. New York: Henry Holt, 1960.
21. Minsky, M. "Steps Toward Artificial Intelligence." *I.R.E. Proceedings* 49: 8-30; 1961.
22. Morris, D. *The Biology of Art*. London: Methuen, 1962.
23. Newell, A. "Learning, Generality and Problem-Solving." *Information Processing 62*. (Edited by C. M. Popplewell.) Amsterdam: Nth Holland Publishing Co., 1963.

24. Newell, A.; Shaw, J. C.; and Simon, H. A. "The Processes of Creative Thinking." *Contemporary Approaches to Creative Thinking.* (Edited by H. E. Gruber, G. Terrell, and M. Wertheimer.) New York: Atherton Press, 1962.
25. Pask, G. "The Teaching Machine as a Control Mechanism." *Transactions of the Society of Instrument Technology* 12: 72-89; June 1960.
26. Pask, G. "Interaction Between a Group of Subjects and an Adaptive Automaton To Produce a Self-Organising System for Decision-Making." *Self-Organizing Systems—1962.* (Edited by M. C. Yovits, G. T. Jacobi, and G. D. Goldstein.) Washington, D.C.: Spartan Books, 1962.
27. Pask, G. "The Simulation of Learning and Decision-Making Behaviour." *Aspects of the Theory of Artificial Intelligence.* (Edited by C. A. Muses.) New York: Plenum Press, 1962.
28. Pask, G. "A Model for Concept Learning." *Proceedings of the Tenth International Scientific Congress on Electronics,* Rome, 1963.
29. Pask, G. "A Model of Learning Applicable Within Systems Stabilised by an Adaptive Teaching Machine." U.S.A.F. Contract AF 61(052)—402, ASTIA. *Technical Note No. 1,* 1963.
30. Pask, G. "The Use of Analogy and Parable in Cybernetics with Emphasis upon Analogies for Learning and Creativity." *Dialetica* 17: 167-202; 1963.
31. Pask, G. *"Self-Organising Systems Involved in Human Learning and Performance."* U.S.A.F. Report ASD-TDR-63-946. *Proceedings of the Third Bionics Symposium,* Dayton, Ohio, March 1964.
32. Pask, G. "A Discussion of Artificial Intelligence and Self-Organisation." *Advances in Computers.* (Edited by M. Rubinoff.) New York: Academic Press, 1964.
33. Pask, G. *"An Investigation of Learning Under Normal and Automatically Controlled Conditions.* Doctor's thesis. London: London University, 1964.
34. Pask, G., and Lewis, B. N. "An Adaptive Automaton for Teaching Small Groups." *Perceptual and Motor Skills* 14: 183-88; 1962.
35. Pask, G., and Lewis, B. N. "Research on the Design of Adaptive Teaching Systems with a Capability for Selecting and Altering Criteria for Adaptation." U.S.A.F. Contract AF 61(052)—402. *Annual Summary Report No. 3,* 1963.
36. Piaget, J. *Logic and Psychology.* New York: Basic Books, 1957.
37. Quine, W. V. O. *Mathematical Logic.* Second edition. Cambridge, Mass.: Harvard University Press, 1951.
38. Reid, R. L. "The Simple Fixed-Sequence Program." *Mechanisation in the Classroom.* (Edited by M. Goldsmith.) London: Souvenir Press, 1963.
39. Rothkopf, E. Z. "Verbal Learning Theory, Inspection Behavior, and Programmed Instruction." *Proceedings of the First Berlin Conference*

on *Teaching Machines and Programmed Instruction*. Berlin: Sekretariat Pädagogisches Zentrum, 1963.

40. Shibutani, T. *Society and Personality*. Englewood Cliffs, N.J.: Prentice-Hall, 1961.
41. Singer, M. G. *Generalisation in Ethics*. London: Eyre and Spottiswoode, 1963.
42. Smallwood, R. D. *A Decision Structure for Teaching Machines*. Massachusetts Institute of Technology Monograph. New York: John Wiley & Sons, 1962.
43. Spiel, O. *Discipline Without Punishment*. London: Faber and Faber, 1962.
44. Thomas, C. A., and others. *Programmed Learning in Perspective*. London: Adelphi Press, 1963.
45. Vygotsky, L. S. *Thought and Language*. Massachusetts Institute of Technology Monograph. New York: John Wiley & Sons, 1962.
46. Welch, L., and Long, L. "The Higher Structural Phases of Concept Formation in Children." *Journal of Psychology* 9: 59-95; 1940.
47. Whitehead, A. N., and Russell, B. *Principia Mathematica*. Revised edition. London: Cambridge University Press, 1927.
48. Woodworth, R. S. *Experimental Psychology*. London: Methuen & Co., 1950.
49. Yovits, M. C.; Jacobi, G. T.; and Goldstein, G. D. *Self-Organizing Systems—1962*. Washington, D.C.: Spartan Books, 1962.

A. A. LUMSDAINE
University of California, Los Angeles

Assessing the Effectiveness of Instructional Programs*

This chapter is necessarily addressed to several audiences. Chief among these are (a) the program user or potential user interested in determining the suitability of a given program for his educational purposes; (b) the program producer, interested in providing data to attest to the merits of the programs he hopes to market or otherwise distribute for use; and (c) the behavioral scientist or educational technologist who, in addition to other interests, may be able to provide technical assistance to the user or producer in obtaining or interpreting assessment data.

Since the background and interests of these three groups may differ considerably, some compromise is necessary if the chapter is to be useful to all three. The attempt is made here to discuss major issues in a sufficiently simple, nontechnical manner to be intelligible to the

* The preparation of this paper was materially aided by research projects supported by the Ford Foundation and by the Educational Media program of the U.S. Office of Education, including support by the latter for the work of the AERA-APA-DAVI Joint Committee on Programed Instruction (see also footnote 1). Reproduction in whole or in part is authorized for any purpose of the U.S. Government. The writer, who serves as chairman of the J.C.P.I., would like to acknowledge the contributions of his colleagues on the Committee (H. F. Silberman, E. R. Keislar, and Robert Glaser [AERA]; R. S. Crutchfield, J. G. Holland, and L. M. Stolurow [APA]; and J. V. Edling, E. B. Fry, W. C. Meierhenry, and P. R. Wendt [DAVI]). He also wishes to thank E. Z. Rothkopf, L. C. Silvern, B. B. Hamilton, and other

seriously interested nontechnical person concerned with program assessment, either as user or producer, while also trying to identify some of the more important technical problems involved.

The Problem of Assessing Program Quality

The problem with which this chapter is concerned was anticipated in the following remarks, written in the spring of 1960: "In the production of programs a major problem could arise from premature publication and sale of hastily conceived and untested programs. . . . It would therefore appear that a high-priority objective is that of working out acceptable quality-control standards for programs" (64, p. 566).

Concern with evaluative criteria for assessing the quality of programed materials was primarily responsible for the formation, in 1961, of the Joint Committee on Programed Instruction (J.C.P.I.), representing the American Educational Research Association (AERA), the American Psychological Association (APA), and the Department of Audiovisual Instruction (DAVI) of the National Education Association (NEA).[1]

Many other individuals and groups have also been concerned with this problem. In addition to the J.C.P.I. reports (1, 2, 3, 56, 61, 81; see also 72, pp. 59-71) and previous papers by the present author (e.g., 54, 55, 57, 59, 62), discussions of the problem of program assessment have been provided by Geis (30), Eigen (22, 23), Gotkin (37), Rothkopf (78, 79), Silverman (91), Stolurow (93), Caulfield (3), Schutz, Baker, and Gerlach (87), Holland (45), Glaser (33), Hively (44), Maier, Stol-

---

consultants and staff assistants for their assistance in the Committee's work, to which several portions of the present paper are closely related. The author is indebted to J. C. Flanagan for helpful comments on an earlier version of the paper and to Harriet Foster, Susan Markle, M. J. Rosen, and other colleagues and students at UCLA for their contributions to his notions on program assessment. It is not, of course, implied that any of these individuals shares all of the opinions stated in the present paper or bears responsibility for any deficiencies of content or exposition which it contains.

[1] Most of the work of the Committee has been supported, under the provisions of Title VII of the National Defense Education Act, through a contract from the Educational Media Branch of the U.S. Office of Education to the American Educational Research Association. For brevity this committee is referred to herein simply as the "AERA Joint Committee," as well as by the abbreviation "J.C.P.I." The Committee's activities through 1962 were summarized in an article by the chairman (54), and its published reports are cited in a number of places in this chapter.

urow, and Jacobs (67), and others. The paper by Lumsdaine (62) presents a more extended discussion of some of the methodological problems encountered in assessing and describing the effects of program use.

Background and Perspectives

In 1961, the AERA Joint Committee pointed out that the contribution of self-instructional programed learning materials, used in teaching machines or otherwise, can be best realized only if users have adequate information with which to evaluate programed materials. Some of the interim guidelines prepared by the Joint Committee in 1961 are relevant as perspective for the present discussion. The concluding statement is as follows: "The effectiveness of a self-instructional program can be assessed by finding out what students actually learn and remember from the program. The prospective purchaser should find out whether such data are available and for what kinds of students and under what conditions the data were obtained" (1, p. 208). This statement suggests the perspective reflected in the main concern of the subsequent work of the Committee—namely, the assessment of individual instructional programs in terms of their demonstrable performance characteristics. In its second published report (2), the J.C.P.I. further developed this perspective and amplified the foregoing recommendations. The points of view given in this report, quoted several times herein, also represent a basic perspective for the present paper.

Product Testing vs. Evaluation of a "Method": A crucial distinction needs to be made between the question of assessing the quality of specific programs and the question of evaluating programed instruction as a general method. This chapter is exclusively concerned with the former question, considered as a useful form of *product* assessment. However, the restriction of product-assessment studies to the immediate aim of determining the quality or suitability of a particular program (with no attempt, as a primary objective, to derive generalizations about the methods represented) does not preclude the possibility that leads about such generalizations may emerge as important by-products of these studies (46, p. 259). Evaluation of programed instruction as a general method is a much more difficult and elusive question to answer. This is so because of the difficulty of defining the "method" of programed instruction in general terms, or of delimiting it—as well as alternative "methods"—in a way that would provide a basis for a generalizable answer for a question stated in such nonspecific terms.

The need to distinguish between assessment of a particular program and of the "method" it purports to represent has been stated in the 1962-63 AERA Joint Committee report (2, p. 85):

. . . the value of a method of instruction cannot be tested in the abstract. For example, evaluation of a particular textbook is not an assessment of the usefulness of textbooks in general. A properly constructed experimental tryout or field test of a program may provide an assessment of that particular program, but does not afford proof or disproof of the value of a general "method" of programed instruction.

Experimentation conducted thus far supports the expectation that good programs, carefully developed, *can* significantly improve the quality and economy of instruction. Whether any particular program *will* do so is subject to question until established by adequate tests of that program.

Merely recognizing this point does not, of course, insure its comprehension by the program-buying public. One of the problems which can only be solved as data on performance characteristics for each specific program are made widely available is the "halo" which boils down to the following invalid syllogism (examples of which, in hardly less blatant form, have appeared widely in advertising copy):

Some programs have been shown to teach very effectively;
These materials which I offer you are programs;
Therefore, these materials provide a superior way to teach your students.

In a continued attempt to combat the tendency to accept such spurious arguments, the J.C.P.I. has again highlighted in its 1964 report the need to judge each program individually, by restating the point as its first recommendation to prospective users: "Prospective users should evaluate each program on its own merits according to its demonstrated effectiveness rather than relying on general statements or findings purporting to support the value of the 'method' of programmed instruction" (3). The attempt to assess the general worth of any "method" or "medium," including programed instruction, really involves an essentially meaningless question. As has been elaborated elsewhere in more detail (60, pp. 596-600), attempts to compare any medium or method with another in the abstract, so as to support a generalization about the value of the medium or method, are inherently foredoomed to failure for the simple reason that a good film, for example, will always beat a poor lecture, and vice versa. Meaningful experiments thus must either have the purpose of determining the effects produced by specific programs or must seek to test propositions about the effects of definable, describable properties of programs.

The difference between this latter purpose and that of assessing specific programs reflects the distinction between the scientific and the technological goals of research and development on instruction. The technological goal is concerned with the development and description of demonstrably good *products*; the scientific goal comprises the generating and testing of hypotheses which can lead to the development of *principles*, ultimately comprising a science of instruction (see 53, 58, 60, 63). It is to be emphasized that the important long-range contributions in programed instruction will result from scientifically oriented studies which seek to identify and validate rules or principles of programing that transcend the properties of specific programs. The important short-range efforts on which this chapter focuses are, by contrast, directed at ascertaining the quality of specific individual programs in terms of what their use can contribute to specified instructional outcomes. Scientifically oriented studies for testing hypotheses or proposed principles of programing can be considered here only incidentally, insofar as they affect the choice of methods used in the assessment of specific programs.

Importance of Program Assessment

The State of the Art in Program Production

The author is convinced that most existing programs afford only a rough approximation of the potentiality for control over learning which could, in principle, realize a goal of assured mastery for all qualified students. This position can be argued both on a priori grounds and in terms of such limited data as are currently available on the effectiveness of existing programs (e.g., 8, 19, 27, 33, 35, 76, 84). Even casual inspection of a sample of programs suggests a tendency merely to follow superficially the general format implied by one programing rationale or another, while meeting neither the theoretical assumptions nor empirical characteristics that are supposed to be exemplified. In addition to lack of adequate tryout and revision, many other apparent weaknesses are to be seen in examining the existing programs, including inadequate analysis of subject matter content and inept use of what seem to be the more promising techniques of programing. Accordingly, it should not be surprising if, despite the acclaim accorded to programed instruction as a basis for a potential "educational revolution," many current programs do not prove to be more effective than alternative kinds of instruction. The existence of a gap between the promise of programed instruction and its realization, up to 1962 at least, is a major thesis of the provocative report by Schramm (83), who defends the position that while "programmed instruction is, in the best sense of the word, a truly revolutionary device," its "potential is, so far, largely unrealized." (See also 80.)

Knowledge of What Programs Are Available as a Basis for Choice: An elementary step in assessing any program, particularly in terms of its content, is simply to know what other programs are available in the same or similar subject matter. The publication of the USOE-sponsored survey edited by Hanson at the Center for Programed Instruction (40) and the compilation by Hendershot at Delta College (42) have been helpful in this respect. But mere knowledge of the availability of programs, while at least showing the prospective purchaser that he may need a basis for choosing among available alternatives, does not provide him with standards of judgment for making the choice.

Why "Standards" for Assessment?

The question may well be asked: Why have "standards" or "criteria" for assessing the quality of programs? Why are such criteria desirable, feasible, or justified, as compared with the case for other instructional resources like textbooks, films, simulators, or other training devices? Attempts have long been made to develop criteria for evaluating films, training devices, and other instructional tools (20, 51, 67, 70, 94). The main differences between these previous attempts and the problem as considered here lies in the attempt to develop validating criteria based on controlled measurement of what the use of a program demonstrably contributes to the attainment of behaviorally specified instructional goals. As the AERA Joint Committee has pointed out:

The tendency to empirically guided development of programs is coupled with an orientation toward testing the specific effects produced by a program, and toward more sharply focused objectives defined in terms of specified behavioral outcomes. In addition, the program is intended to generate a more predictable pattern of student behavior than does the study of a textbook, which generally has a less specialized purpose in aiming to serve as a reference source as well as a sequence of instruction (2, p. 87).

The Usefulness of Criteria for Assessing Program Effectiveness: A basic purpose for developing criteria to assess the quality of specific programs is to increase the usable potential of programed instruction, both through improving the selection and use of existing programs and through stimulating the development of more effective programs in the future. Both the wise selection and the effective utilization of present programs in schools clearly requires a dependable way to assess the merit of any given program.

Effect of Standards on Program Production: Part of the case for introducing dependable and widely accepted criteria of assessment lies in the effect on the standards of quality in future programs, particularly those produced by commercial publishers. We may assume that a stimulus to better quality production in this field, as in others, involves the dynamics of a competitive marketplace. If the consumers (e.g., school systems) have a dependable method for differentiating better programs from poorer programs, a demand for the former is effectively generated, and publishers must produce better programs in order to compete in the market. However, such competition cannot be effective unless there is indeed a basis for determining the quality or effectiveness of programs in unambiguous terms. In the absence of available unbiased and dependable information about program quality, programs can be promoted and sold on the basis of unsupported claims or dubious "data" purporting to show their merits, and the competitive incentive to produce genuinely superior programs is thereby weakened. Stimulation of program quality by the open competition of the marketplace is next to impossible in the absence of dependable and acceptable criteria for assessing the merits of any particular program (59).

What Kind of "Standards" Are Relevant?
Some Basic Distinctions Among the Main Kinds of Criteria
Three main kinds of considerations need to be distinguished as relevant bases for assessing the suitability or acceptability of a particular

program for meeting a given educational purpose: These may be termed "appropriateness," "effectiveness," and "practicality."

"*Appropriateness*," as used herein, refers to the nature of the "subject matter" or "content" that is "covered" by a program. The concept of "content" actually turns out to be a rather fuzzy and unsatisfactory one, with some ambiguous and troublesome connotations. For the present purpose, program content can be characterized as representing what the program tries to teach or, perhaps, what it "contains" that apparently could be learned by an optimally qualified student who learned everything that it was possible to learn from what is presented in that particular program. In other words, appropriateness may refer to prospective outcomes to which a program's use might lead, that is, to what is to be learned or may be learned from a program. Thus, appropriateness means, roughly, the extent to which program "content" is consonant with the objectives of a particular educational purpose or course, or the degree of correspondence between the user's objectives and those of the programer.

"*Effectiveness*" refers to how well the program does, in fact, attain certain prospective outcomes, how well it teaches whatever it is calculated to teach (rather than *what* it may teach), or, in other words, the extent to which its content is learned or the extent to which stated objectives are attained by students who use the program in a particular way. A further distinction can also be made between effectiveness and efficiency, the latter referring, broadly, to the extent to which a given degree of attainment is achieved economically in terms of the use of student time and other resources.

"*Practicality*" can be used to refer to matters of cost, feasibility, acceptance by students and teachers, and other factors which determine whether an appropriate program of given potential effectiveness can or will in fact be used so that its potential is realized in practice. This category involves, aside from factors of convenience that may influence effectiveness, considerations that are largely translatable into terms of cost.

Finally, the terms "*suitability*" or "*acceptability*" might be used in a generic sense to indicate over-all bases for evaluation or decision concerning program adoption or use, based on consideration of all three of the above classes of factors (appropriateness, effectiveness, and practicality).

Interrelation Between Appropriateness and Effectiveness

Obviously, both appropriateness and effectiveness are important considerations in assessing a program. Almost as obviously, they do not necessarily go hand in hand. As pointed out by Galanter (29), a program might be effective in teaching inappropriate content, or it might present appropriate content but fail to do so effectively; also, it might teach inappropriate content either effectively or ineffectively. One reason for largely bypassing the question of appropriateness as a primary concern here is simply that the determination of appropriateness is such a complex problem and involves many unsettled questions of value in terms of what should be taught. At present, at least, it can be held that each user or reviewer can claim to be as good an authority as the next.

However, even though primary emphasis is placed on the effectiveness with which a program teaches, the question of what the program is supposed to teach, and hence what should be measured in determining its effectiveness, will necessarily enter into this discussion to some extent. Furthermore, it should be recognized explicitly that "assessment" of program effects, in the sense of their measurement and description, clearly does not in itself provide "evaluation" of a program; at best it only provides an important basis on which, along with other relevant information, an evaluation can be made of the suitability of a program for meeting a given set of instructional objectives.

"Internal" and "External" Sources of Information About Programs

A useful terminological distinction suggested by Silverman (91) and by Rothkopf (78), which was also adopted by the AERA-APA-DAVI Joint Committee (2), can be made in terms of the locus or source of information about a program. This is the distinction between internal and external sources of information as possible criteria for program evaluation. "Internal" characteristics refer to features which can be revealed through inspection of the program material, including both its "content" and such pedagogical features of construction as length of frames, use of branching, techniques of prompting, patterns of repetition and review, kinds of responses called for, and the like. These may be viewed merely in a descriptive sense, but often are assumed to be predictive of the effectiveness of the program. Clearly, if there were a fully developed science of instruction, the effectiveness of a program could be predicted by determination of the extent to which such descriptive characteristics of a program were optimally selected and arranged to promote effective learning.

"External" information about a program refers to features which cannot be observed merely by inspecting the program itself, such as the history of the way in which it was developed and, in particular, its observed performance as a teaching instrument. Other kinds of external information could include such information as the qualifications of the author, the kind of student-response data obtained in revising the program, opinions of reviewers, and test data obtained to measure the achievement produced by the program.

Predictive vs. Validating Criteria of Effectiveness

A further important distinction can be made between (a) those external criteria that are believed to be *predictive* of program effectiveness (such as external evidence about the competence of the programer or the history of a program's development, including tryout and revision) and (b) *validating* criteria, which consist of direct evidence of the effects actually produced by the program in demonstrably changing students' behavior.

Experienced programers will undoubtedly continue to look at programs and state, possibly with some real basis for confidence, that they are good programs or poor ones. But this is an unvalidated opinion, though it may be an informed and illuminating one. It is a prediction of effectiveness, not a verification. It should not be greatly surprising, therefore, to find that some programs that looked poor may turn out to do a good job of teaching, or that frames which seemed beautifully fashioned may, when put to the test, do a poor job of teaching. The distinctions among major classes of criteria for judging a program's effectiveness (or efficiency) may thus be reoriented as follows:

1. *Predictive criteria of effectiveness*: rational or theoretical bases, involving inferences from general experience or extrapolations from laboratory science, on which the effects of a program are believed to be at least partly predictable. These include (a) *internal criteria*, derivable from inspection of the program, and (b) *external predictive criteria*, based on ancillary information about a program's development, or on external information such as expert

review or information about students' or teachers' opinions of a program.

2. *Validating criteria of effectiveness:* external criteria that provide measures of the actual effects of the program in demonstrably changing students' behavior.

Possible "Validating" Criteria for Assessing Program Effectiveness

Validating criteria have been characterized as measures of the actual effects of the program in changing students' behavior. The validity of such measures may vary, however, along a dimension of ultimate validity from responses the student makes within the program to measures of ultimate or long-term retention, transfer, or application. Measurement of such effects may also vary with respect to inclusiveness of *all* relevant effects (including transfer and motivational and other "indirect" effects as well as direct competence per se on the subject matter covered) and also with respect to how clearly the behaviors observed represent changes demonstrably shown by rigorous experiment to result from the use of the program. For example, the following kinds of evidence differ from each other in one or more of these respects:[2]

1. Error rate on prompted frames or over-all error rate.
2. Error rate on frames that are internally unprompted, but are located within or just following prompted program sequences, so that "sequence prompting" effects are present.
3. Error rate, or pattern of errors and correct responses, on review sequences placed so that they are minimally effected by sequence prompts.
4. Gains from preprogram to immediate postprogram tests.
5. Gains from preprogram to immediate postprogram tests, but with control for external influences.
6. Demonstrated changes on indirect motivation and transfer.
7. Persistent or "permanent" effects as shown by delayed tests of transfer and application, including sustained motivation.

The major factors that bear on deciding the suitability of a program are summarized, in relation to sources of information concerning them, in Figure 1.

[2] For definitions of technical terms used in describing program features, see 24, 69.

	Internal Information (Available from program inspection)	External Information
Appropriateness:	Content inspection	Stated objectives
	Table of contents	Test content
	Reading of program	Competence of authors
	Analysis of terminal-behavior frames	Opinions of reviews or advisers
	Publisher's statements of objectives and tests provided by publishers	
Effectiveness:		
1. Predictive criteria	Features of program style or construction	Reviewer's opinions
	Inferred direct and side effects based on program inspection	Developmental history, including tryout and revision
		Error rates within the program
2. Validating criteria	— — — — — —	Measured effects of program use and related data (time, etc.)
Practicality:		
	Ease of using	Cost factors:
	Reusability	program price, adapt-ability, characteristics
	Machine (instrumenta-tion) requirements	of presentation, machine (if required)

FIGURE 1. *Main Types of Criteria for Assessing the Suitability of a Program.*

Critical Reviews of Programs

In recognizing various levels of assessment for program quality, it is necessary to look further at the possibilities of critical reviews of programs, which furnish one possible basis for evaluation. Such reviews began to appear in professional journals starting around 1961. Examples are reviews published in *Contemporary Psychology*, such as the reviews by Eigen (21), Galanter (29), Saltzman (82), and Silberman (89) on algebra programs, by Markle (68) on a program in English grammar, by Carroll (12) on a program for teaching Russian script, and by Denova (17) on a program for teaching digital computer programing. Other periodicals in which reviews of programs may be found include *Audiovisual Instruction, AV Communication Review,* and the *NSPI Journal* (National Society for Programmed Instruction). As with reviews of tests, some program reviews include data—in this case, data on achievement attained by using the program—as well as reviewer opinion about the program based on its internal features (12, 17, 27, 29).

The emphasis on objective standards for assessing programs, on which this chapter is focused, should not minimize the potential usefulness of critical review based on inspection of programs. However, aside from the need to assess the competence and bias of reviewers, users should be made aware that reviewer opinions may conflict, and furthermore that no reviewer may correctly predict what the program will actually teach. The usefulness of reviews will thus be increased as provision is made for the collating and bringing together of several reviews on each program so as to have available something like the collection of reviews of tests provided by the O. K. Buros' *Mental Measurements Yearbooks* (9, 10).

Program reviews, even when only representing reviewer opinion, can be helpful in view of the need to make recommendations and decisions about the acceptability of programs in the absence of objective data about what a program's use can accomplish; lacking such data, one has to depend primarily on opinions of reviewers based on program inspection. Though opinions clearly do not qualify as criteria in terms of which programs can be objectively assessed, they may be viewed as signposts that are useful if accepted as advice rather than fact; they offer something to rely on "until the data comes," particularly in assessing the appropriateness of program content. Whatever its value, it seems certain that as with other educational materials (e.g., textbooks, films), reviewer opinion will be used as one basis for evaluation of programed materials.

As objective and valid data on demonstrated program effectiveness becomes increasingly available, the main function of reviews may be to provide a critical analysis of the validity of results from objective assessment studies and to furnish advice on over-all suitability of programs, taking into account content appropriateness and practicality of use as well as demonstrated effectiveness indicated by experimental data. Reviews, even by programing "experts," necessarily represent predictions of program effectiveness rather than objective evidence of it, except when based on data from objective studies of program effects. Data offered by a reviewer in support of conclusions about a program's effectiveness should, moreover, be weighed in the light of technical considerations influencing the validity of such data, discussed later in this chapter. Data for two or three students gathered informally by the reviewer may be indicative, especially for extremely poor or extremely good programs, but do not take the place of more formal and extensive assessment studies.

Guidelines for Reviewers: The J.C.P.I. (3) has recommended that those who prepare critical reviews of programs should, in addition to expressing their opinions about the suitability of the program content and objectives: (a) obtain and report all available data about program effects; (b) evaluate and interpret such data in the context of technical considerations such as those set forth by the Joint Committee; and (c) distinguish clearly and explicitly between their own opinions about the probable effectiveness of the program and the objective evidence on its demonstrable outcomes.

Checklists and Other Statements of Proposed Evaluative Criteria

Many checklists and statements of criteria for assessing programs have been proposed by a number of sources.[3] These have tended to represent a potpourri of criteria related to appropriateness, practicality, and both internal and external predictive criteria of effectiveness, together with external validating criteria (i.e., measured program effects). In such statements and checklists, little explicit differentiation or recognition has been made of the status of the differences in kinds of criteria proposed in terms of the foregoing kind of distinctions. How-

---

[3] Among these guidance statements and checklists, in addition to the previously mentioned statements by Rothkopf (78) and by the AERA Joint Committee (1, 2), have been those offered by Belton (6), Jacobs and others (48), Tracey (96), the USAF's Air Training Command (99), the New York Board of Education (75), the Rocky Mountain School Study Committee (77), the Center for Programed Instruction (14), the University of Michigan Center for Programed Learning for Business (98), and the National Society for Programmed Instruction (73, 74). Guidance statements or checklists have also been provided by several of the commercial program producers, including TMI-Grolier (95), Coronet (16), and the General Programmed Teaching Corporation (31). Internal criteria are also implied in various guides to programing procedure—e.g., Klaus (49) and Wiley (100)—as well as in several textbooks (cf., 65, p. 480).

ever, the distinctions seem to be useful ones even though the three primary classes of factors may interact and in some ways overlap. As one example of this overlap, in the above-noted distinction between effectiveness and efficiency it is evident that the latter involves cost factors, indirectly at least; also, on closer examination, the meaning of "content," as commonly used, will be found to be related both to appropriateness and effectiveness.

In the course of preparing this chapter, the writer and some of his students examined and attempted to classify several hundred statements put forth in published documents as criteria for the assessment of the suitability of a program in terms of its appropriateness and/or its presumed effectiveness. Most of these statements came from "checklist" formulations put forth for the guidance of parents, teachers, curriculum specialists, etc. (6, 14, 31, 48, 73, 74, 75, 77, 95, 96, 98, 99). These statements can be grouped in several broad categories. A considerable number of them refer to internal characteristics of the programs, either to factors of construction and organization presumed to be predictive of effectiveness or statements in which the above-noted overlap between effectiveness and appropriateness makes an unambiguous classification in this respect difficult or impossible. A second group of statements refers more unequivocally to appropriateness factors, either in terms of what is to be taught or the kinds of students for whom the program is appropriate. Another group of statements concerns questions of feasibility in pattern of use, questions which may, depending on point of view, be considered to relate either to the appropriateness or to over-all effectiveness in school use in a variety of use patterns. A smaller group of statements refers to external characteristics, particularly the history of developmental testing, tryout, and revision which the program has undergone. A final category refers to external validating data and their interpretation. There is often some ambiguity between developmental and descriptive or validation data due to vagueness in the way the data are reported; sometimes it is not possible, for example, to know whether "tryout" data refer to information used as a basis for revising the program or presented to attest its effectiveness.

Some such checklists seem to imply the possibility of deriving a "score" for a program, in which acceptability for a program can be determined from the number of favorable answers to the questions posed. In the opinion of the writer, such an implication is a mischievous one, particularly since there is no assurance of the validity of many of the questions asked (particularly those about internal characteristics). Even where the questions are clearly relevant, there is no assurance as to how they should be weighted. It would be interesting to apply such questions in systematic fashion to the effects actually produced by a number of parallel programs with similar objectives; this might serve to determine whether, regardless of theoretical rationale, they appear to have any empirical predictive validity (cf., 79).

It is also interesting, with respect to questions which appear to be clearly relevant, to consider the order in which it is most appropriate to ask questions. Such ordering has been implied by several checklists, including that of ETS (48). One might devise a kind of decision flowchart, algorithm, or structured "20-questions" game, on the basis of which one could examine programs efficiently. Such a 20-questions arrangement, in the figurative sense, would differ from the "20 questions" proposed by Belton (6), which do not form an algorithm, but merely a checklist of points to be considered. Undoubtedly some kind of spiral or alternation between several major categories of consideration—appropriateness, feasibility (including cost), and probable or demonstrated effectiveness—would be reasonable in considering the adoption of a program. One might ask a few over-all screening questions: for example, whether content appears to be at least "in the right ballpark" and whether its cost is conceivably feasible, etc., before proceeding to more detailed examination of the program in terms of presumed or demonstrated effectiveness and more detailed aspects of content suitability. If neither of these questions could be answered in the affirmative, the program would be ruled out for further consideration.

Any criteria for determining the suitability of any course of action, including the adoption of an instructional program, involves matching available means to desired ends. It follows that any such criteria must include a specification of the ends sought by the user. Neither the specialist in instructional programing nor the publisher of programs has, as such, any special competence, much less authority, to tell the user what his aims should be. The user must decide these for himself. In doing so, however, he may perhaps wish to examine the objectives which the programer has formulated in writing the program or other statements of possible outcomes relevant to the general field to which the program pertains.

Primary Reliance on External Validating Criteria

The notion of "standards" of effectiveness has suggested to some the development of authoritarian or restrictive criteria which attempt to dictate the way programs are written or presented. This unintended and quite unfortunate connotation has tripped off various tirades against the attempt to develop criteria (e.g., 25). Any such attempt to standardize or freeze program styles would be very undesirable, as was stressed in 1960 by Lumsdaine and Glaser:

> In the development of quality-control standards for programs, it is important to avoid the imposition of inflexible requirements which might inhibit creativity and experimental use of new techniques.

> It seems clear that standards for the adequacy of a program ought to be conceived primarily in terms of its effectiveness in attaining defined educational objectives, rather than by specifying the format, sequencing, or other aspects of the means whereby these ends are achieved (64, p. 566).

This emphasis on avoiding any prescription of internal form or style and advocacy of external, validating criteria as the primary basis for assessing the effectiveness of programs has also been consistently advocated by Rothkopf (78) and the AERA Joint Committee (2, pp. 87-89; see also 91). It is the empirically oriented position that ultimately the "proof of the pudding is in the eating," that is, that the ultimate measure of a program's effectiveness is what it teaches.

Dangers of Restrictive "Standards" Based on Internal Criteria Which Would Prejudge Program Effectiveness: Schramm (83) has pointed out the existence of a tendency toward premature "freezing" of particular programing styles. This fixing on a stereotyped style can be seen in many current programs, despite the warning given five years ago in the statement just quoted. Undoubtedly, it reflects an overpreoccupation with internal criteria inferred from early programs and a tendency to imitate their superficial characteristics rather than experimenting with new styles and relying on empirical proof to determine how well the resulting programs work.

Rationale for Reliance on Validating Criteria: The decision to limit criteria of effectiveness in this chapter's discussion of program assessment to validating criteria or measured effects produced by programs is suggested and made possible by the conception of programs as potentially autonomous vehicles of instruction. Such forms of assessment have not characteristically been applied to textbooks or other instructional materials. It is the tendency for development of programs to be based on an explicit statement of objectives—and for programers to take the responsibility for achieving these goals without dependence on other forms of instruction—that makes possible a policy of accepting empirical data as the validation of the program's effectiveness. There is some similarity here to the rationale underlying empirical validation of psychological and educational tests, as has been pointed out by the Joint Committee (2). Although programs and tests differ in objectives, with programs aiming primarily to instruct rather than to test students, both generate student-response data and are capable of being developed as well as validated in terms of empirical procedures. In both cases an external criterion can be specified, at least in principle, to indicate the extent to which an intended outcome has been achieved as evidenced by kinds of behavior which have been developed (in the case of a program) or differentiated (in the case of a test).

The risk in relying on inspection for assessing program effectiveness is that widely accepted precepts and current patterns of programs have not, as yet, been the subject of satisfactory experimental validation. Although some considerable number of experiments comparing the relative effectiveness or efficiency of alternative forms of programs have been conducted, inspection of the available evidence makes it clear that a great deal more evidence than is now available is necessary before a well-developed science or validated theory of programing, on the basis of which program effectiveness can be reliably predicted, can be delineated (2, 78, 79).

One form of evidence bearing on theories or principles of programing comes from comparative studies in which controlled variation of specific program features has been introduced. For example, the importance of having the student overtly compose responses, as stressed by Skinner (92) and others, has been studied in a number of investigations (see 53, 65, 83, 85). In general, such studies have come rather far from offering clear-cut support for the principles of programing which suggested the alternative forms of programs that were experimentally contrasted. Although many of the experiments thus far performed suffer from serious conceptual as well as methodological defects (58, 60), the fact is that they nonetheless do not provide convincing support for particular styles of programing in most instances (cf., 65, 85). Though they are not capable of logically showing that proposed principles are necessarily faulty, they do not offer sufficient evidence for putting forth such principles as bases for assessing programs in terms of their internal characteristics. A perhaps more direct form of evidence is supported in a study reported by Rothkopf (79), in which individuals who had been trained in programing principles were asked to predict the relative effectiveness of seven different forms of a program, and their pooled and individual predictions were subsequently compared with the effects as actually determined by experimental measurement for these same program variants. The scope of this investigation was limited, and the programs studied were doubtless too short to exemplify the operation of all of the factors believed important in determining the effectiveness of programs. Nevertheless, the results of the comparison were far from reassuring. Not only were Rothkopf's "prophets" of effectiveness unable to predict correctly; their predictions showed a high *negative* correlation with measured effectiveness.

Such findings lend weight to the rational grounds suggested by Lumsdaine and Glaser for the importance of avoiding premature "freezing" of program styles (64, p. 566). The evidence accumulated since that time has helped to illuminate some facets of the art of programing, but still falls far short of approaching a sufficient basis for any confident assessment of program effectiveness in terms of internal characteristics. The need for test data to assess a program's effectiveness is summarized by the Joint Committee in the following excerpt from their 1962-63 report (2): "At the present time, the principal recommended use of internal data obtained from inspection of the programed materials is for determining whether program *content* is appropriate to the educator's objectives."

Of course one should not despair of the eventual possibility of accurately predicting program effects, and the firm validation of some predictive criteria by experimentation ultimately is to be expected. Even at present, it of course does not follow that all judgments would be as bad as those found by Rothkopf. In the long run, quite aside from the matter of efficiency in reducing the amount of trial and error needed to develop effective programs, validation of internal criteria even on a probabilistic basis is obviously desirable. This would permit making demonstrably valid estimates (even if only approximate ones) of possible effects prior to their being actually determined or verified by experimental measurement.

Tryout and Revision as a Basis for Gauging Effectiveness

The requirement of program tryout and revision is a central one in the programing rationale and has even been made a critical characteristic in Markle's definition (24). It seems obvious that one should be able to improve a program by testing its outcomes and progressively revising it until one has corrected the difficulties shown by the tryout test data. Is it possible, however, to use information about the developmental tryout and revision as a basis for assessing a program's effectiveness? Surely the mere fact that a program is reported to have been subjected to a tryout and revision procedure does not by itself assure that it has thereby become perfected. Lacking a validated, well-defined, and reproducible procedure that will demonstrably assure satisfactory results, validating data are still necessary for each program tryout and revision.

The Nature of Defensible Effectiveness-Assessment Standards

From the foregoing it is evident that the kind of "standards" advocated here are not standards for prescribing program content, construction, or style. Rather, it follows from the empirical orientation here adopted that the standards of concern are *standards of adequacy in the conduct (and reporting) of studies to determine program effects*. Standards for program "quality control" are thus standards for the quality control of program *data*. If one is to rely on empirical data to gauge program effectiveness, he needs to have assurance that the data afford a valid measure of the relevant effects actually produced by a program. The rest of this chapter is mainly concerned with the question of how such assurance can be provided.

Description of Effects vs. "Effectiveness Standards": Program effects mean the changes in educational outcomes or attainments that can be shown to result from a program's use. The "effectiveness" of a program sometimes refers to the extent to which the program's effects are satisfactory in the light of the goals set for its use. Although one commonly speaks of assessing program effectiveness, experimental tests per se can only reveal a program's effects; whether these are satisfactory for a given purpose involves standards of judgment that cannot be dealt with more fully here.

Some agencies have thought to prescribe standards of minimum acceptable effectiveness in terms of test scores—such as the Air Training Command's "90-90" standard: "All programmed instruction packages (PIP's) will be designed to fulfill the terminal objectives to a 90% level for 90% of the students and therefore produce a mean test raw score of 90% minimum" (99). In commenting on an earlier version of this paper, J. C. Flanagan has seriously questioned the wisdom of promulgating such "standards" at the present time; certainly they are indefensible, and even dangerous, without more-nearly absolute measures of attainment than the kinds of tests generally used to measure program effects.

The term "effectiveness" as used in this chapter implies only the question of determining what effects a program *is* capable of producing, rather than standards for deciding how effective it *ought* to be in order to be regarded as of acceptable effectiveness. A disposition to think of program-effectiveness data as descriptive rather than "evaluative" seems likely to avoid misunderstandings, especially if it is recognized that any description of program effects will inevitably be to some extent incomplete.

What Is a "Program"?

The placing of reliance for the determination of program effectiveness primarily on empirical evidence concerning what the program teaches carries with it logical implications for the definition of what should be called a "program." Often the use of the term *program* has been restricted by various writers to materials which have particular characteristics of format and sequencing that are believed to exemplify principles derived from behavioral science. This is coupled with an emphasis on criteria for assessment of program quality in terms of internal characteristics determinable on the basis of inspection. Among experienced programers (Lumsdaine and Glaser [64], Rothkopf [78], and the J.C.P.I. to the contrary notwithstanding), we hear such "in-group" characterizations as: "That's a program? Why, it's nothing but a series of copying frames!" Characterizations of this kind may well turn out to be cogent evaluations when eventually validated by appropriate data on the effects achieved by competing "real" programs. But at present, such statements seem to imply the existence of a basis for validation which does not as yet exist as much more than an article of faith. They have the status of hypothesis rather than of verified principle.

The attempt to restrict the use of the term "program" to materials exemplifying particular preconceptions about the value of alternative program forms or styles, of course, may be a useful heuristic in teaching students a particular technique of programing. However, no matter how well based in behavioral science such notions may seem to their proponents, they will not do at present, as has been emphasized, as a basis for demonstrating or establishing the actual merits or deficiencies of specific programs. Any proposed instructional vehicle ought to be allowed at least to enter a competition in which its merits can be demonstrated on the basis of impartial evidence of what it can do; it ought not to be barred from competition because "it's not really a program" in terms of failing to adhere to preconceived notions of what a "program" should look like. Restricting the field by definition can only be self-defeating, particularly at the present state of the art. Even if there is a good reason to believe that a "series of copying frames" is an inept style of programing, precluding such a sequence from the chance to demonstrate what it actually teaches can set up a restrictive situation which can inhibit creativity and lead to dogma rather than to either a science or technology of instruction.

Thus, rather than attempting to prejudge *what a program should be*, at the present time a very inclusive definition is necessary in terms of what a program can be. The following definition has been proposed elsewhere: "An instructional program is a vehicle which generates an essentially reproducible sequence of instructional events and accepts responsibility for efficiently accomplishing a specified change from a given range of initial competences or behavioral tendencies to a specified terminal range of competences or behavioral tendencies" (63, p. 385). This definition, with a minimum of restrictive connotations, can encompass most of the forms of programs that have been proposed under the "programed instruction" banner. The definition not only makes no particular theoretical presuppositions, but does not even require individually paced progress or overt responses by the learner as qualifications for inclusion as a program. The variety of program types and styles admitted includes individual learning programs differing in terms of such factors as use of larger or smaller steps and varying kinds or amounts of student response, as well as any combination of linear or alternative ("branching") pathways. It also includes within its compass "programs" designed for fixed-pace and group presentation, as well as individually paced programs. It thus admits to a competition for demonstrable effectiveness programs for group presentation by film, television, or other media, as long as the instructional sequence is substantially reproducible, and the program, of whatever nature, is assessible in terms of its demonstrable effects on students. A somewhat similar but slightly less inclusive definition, given by Susan Markle (24, p. 64), requires empirical development of material in order for it to qualify as a "program."

Application to Individual and Group-Instruction Programs: Focusing on external or validating criteria of program effects makes most of the following discussion equally applicable to all styles and forms of programs because it concentrates attention on the changes in behavior effected by the program, regardless of the nature of the program that effected the change. Some special problems of measurement, discussed in a later section, do arise for self-paced programs as a direct consequence of individual variations in instructional time which they permit. But the main aspects of assessment methodology apply just as much to assessment of instructional television, or filmed instructional programs for group presentation, as they do to assessing the effects of individually paced programed instruction. (See also 52.) This generality, of course, does not apply to many of the proposed internal criteria, which relate to particular features of individually paced programed instruction following current patterns and which are dealt with in some of the proposed criteria, or checklists, for program assessment.

Program Assessment as a General Problem in Education
The broad definition of programs given above suggests also the realization that the basic problem in program assessment is not just that of assessing "programed-instructional" materials per se. This is only a facet of the total problem of being able to measure and predict the effects of all forms of instruction, whatever their nature, since it

treats effectiveness in terms of "output" as related to "input" (initial competence), without regard for the processes or program characteristics whereby this gain from input to output is achieved. In terms of a hardware-system analogy, the concern is with how to assess the effectiveness of programs in producing a given output in relation to a given input, considering the program as a "black box." The internal workings need not be known for this purpose.

Major Aspects of Program-Effects Assessment

In this chapter "program-effectiveness assessment" is roughly synonymous with measuring the *effects* produced by a program under some observed procedure of use. By "effects" are meant changes which can be directly observed or inferred from recorded observations of changes in the behavior of students as a result of the use of the program. Such changes may include gains or changes in knowledge, skills (both verbal and psychomotor), attitudes, interests, or motivations as identified by specific kinds of behavior which such terms are intended to connote. Furthermore, "effects of a program" means changes which can be validly ascribed to the use of a program when other sources of influence have been ruled out by appropriate scientific procedures.

Purposes of Determining the Effects That a Given Program Can Produce

Two quite different purposes of testing the effects produced by a particular program need to be distinguished, because differences in procedures as well as in measurement techniques are sometimes appropriate to these different purposes. Perhaps the most important distinction to make here is between studies that assess a program's effects in order to provide (a) *a diagnostic basis for program revision* and improvement, i.e., a basis for empirical guidance of program development or (b) a *reportorial* basis for describing performance characteristics of a specified, completed program. Data for a completed product indicate to a teacher or other user the outcomes he can expect the product's use to achieve. (Data showing what effects were achieved by use of a program that is *not* available for general use seem to serve little current purpose, except to demonstrate that some difficult-to-achieve kinds of outcomes can in fact be produced by program use.) The kinds of data appropriate to these two purposes have considerable overlap, however, though the uses may differ considerably, and the two purposes should not be confused.

For "diagnostic" purposes, the effects of a program on a *number of specific points* related to its objectives needs to be separately measured. These might include certain points of factual information and a variety of specific skills which it is desired to create. Here one is little interested in the total score: the relevant interest is in subscores for content units and even in what is learned on each specific test question or point. To achieve adequate stability of results, this of course requires a larger sample than to detect differences of the same magnitude in an over-all score.

Diagnostic subscores are not only of utility in the revision of a program; for a completed, published program they can indicate what specific additional instruction may be needed in order to achieve defined goals. Such data, for example, give the teacher guidance on what points of the subject matter need special attention in classroom instruction, as distinguished from those which can be achieved from the program. The usefulness of over-all total scores information, on the other hand, is mainly limited to indicating whether it is worthwhile to use the program at all.

Error Rate

"Error rate" is an *external* criterion in the sense defined above, but cannot, as such, be considered a *validating* criterion. Errors on unprompted criterion frames within a program come closer, and data for subtests on program units (which might include or consist of such frames) come closer still. An end-of-program test, preferably administered after an appreciable interval so as to measure retention freed from the cueing influence of immediate context (extended sequence-prompting effects), probably comes as close as is often likely to be practical for current program-construction practices, though still further delayed retention, transfer, and relearning (savings) tests deserve attention as further steps toward ultimate validation. A fairly low error rate may be and, at least for prevailing forms of nonbranching programs, probably often is a necessary condition for an effective program; but it is far from being a sufficient condition for effectiveness. Too low an error rate may, in fact, militate against optimum efficiency in many instances. It is easy to attain a low error rate by consistent overprompting or by a nonbranching or fixed sequence so slow as to produce very few errors by the least able of a highly heterogeneous population of learners that could hardly be of optimal efficiency for those at the able extreme of the distribution. In considering "error rate" as a datum, one should at least distinguish error rates of several types of items: prompted items in a linear sequence, items used to decide branching (whether prompted or not, review or otherwise), and terminal-behavior frames calling for unprompted performance of the to-be-learned behavior.

Whatever the usefulness of error rates (especially when classified by type of frame) may be for purposes of program revision, the uncritical use of over-all error rates, especially for entire programs or for heterogeneous sets of variously prompted and unprompted items, is by now largely discounted as a validating measure of program effectiveness. For other discussions or comments on the use of "error rates" or error counts as measures of program effectiveness, see the papers by Geis (30) and Lumsdaine (62).

Response Data as a Basis for Revision

The point-by-point or step-by-step feedback to the programer (as well as to the student) has been widely hailed as a crucial and even defining feature of the programed learning approach. However, feedback to the programer does not necessarily require overt response in the program. Few would doubt that feedback from the constant responding as a student goes through a program is a valuable source of leads to the programer. But one of the things that the programed instruction field at first seemed slow to realize is that correct responses within the program do not necessarily mean that the terminal behavior (that is, posttest or retention performance) will be adequate. If one must depend on satisfactory posttest or retention performance as a necessary basis for assurance that the program is "working" properly, then it could be argued that there is no special virtue in having a record of overt responses within the program as a way of providing feedback to the programer. There are as yet few instances where the value of feedback to the programer as a basis for revision has been demonstrated in terms of improved test performance for programs thus revised as compared with concurrent parallel test scores for earlier versions of the same program. Examples are studies by Silberman and others (90) in the field of individual programed instruction and by Gropper and Lumsdaine (38) in the case of instructional television. The main value of frame-by-frame response data, obtained for a relatively small number of subjects, is to provide leads to the programer as to where (and perhaps how) to revise his program. Such data may be a helpful basis for suggesting certain revisions; they are not an adequate basis for validating the program's effectiveness.

Major Considerations Entering into Assessment of Program Effects

Some of the main considerations that apply in the conduct and reporting of studies of program effects can be considered under three main topics: (a) Consideration of *criterion measures* encompasses the characteristics of tests used as indices of what students can do or "are like" after the program, as compared with what they can do or "are like" before going through a program. This includes the definition of program objectives or potential outcomes and development of appropriate criterion tests reflecting attainment of these outcomes. (b) Under *utilization procedures and experimental design* must be considered procedures and arrangements for sampling and administering programs to defined samples of students under controlled and reproducible conditions, together with procedures using the above-identified criterion tests, particularly in terms of the control of extraprogram factors that may influence criterion attainment. The procedures used may be either those of a "laboratory" test or a "field" test; in either case controls must be introduced such that the data will reflect in a valid manner gains produced by the program, as distinct from other possible sources of responses on the test. (c) Although *reporting of program effects* cuts directly across the above two aspects, it is useful to consider reporting also as a separate category. Critical problems are how to obtain reporting in uniform terms, so that terminology has the same meaning to all users, how to insure soundness of reported data in terms of its reproducibility, and how to provide meaningful reporting intelligible to the prospective program user.

Criterion Measures

Behaviorally Stated Objectives

The problem of describing precisely what is to be taught and what it is, therefore, that is to be measured as an outcome of instruction clearly is neither new nor peculiar to programed instruction; it is a general problem of educational planning and evaluation. Contributions to the question of behavioral specification of instructional outcomes stem in considerable part from the work of Ralph Tyler (97) at the University of Chicago, later reflected in Bloom's well-known *Taxonomy* (7). Perhaps the most influential contribution growing out of the more recent concern with programed instruction has been Mager's book (66) on the specification of instructional objectives.

Various aspects of the issues and problems involved in defining educational objectives are more fully treated in a series of papers by Lindvall, Krathwohl, Gagné, Glaser and Reynolds, Tyler, and others in the recent volume edited by Lindvall (50). The concepts of "task analysis" (cf., 28, 71) have had an important influence in increasing the emphasis on need for precise description of the specific behaviors comprised by such objectives. (See also 18, 37, and 69.)

A number of other writers (e.g., 32, 50, 55) have also stressed the conviction that relatively more attention needs to be given to defining objectives in relation to "what to teach" as contrasted with efforts to improve knowledge of "how to teach." The wiser definition of educational objectives need not remain solely a rational or judgmental matter, but may be aided by empirical data. In particular, it can be expected that improved knowledge of "what transfers to what" will give a better basis for identifying specific instructional objectives which demonstrably, rather than just as an article of faith, lead to the broader kinds of competencies and behaviors that can be agreed on in general terms as basic goals of education. The problems of such inquiry, basically a question of transfer of training, lie beyond the scope of the present paper.

Objectives and Outcomes: The orientation of focusing on criteria of demonstrated effectiveness suggests the appropriateness of providing program-assessment data in the form of stated "performance characteristics" which indicate what contribution the use of a particular program is actually capable of making toward the attainment of the specified instructional objectives. The specification of objectives may be done by the program producer and, separately, by the teacher, educational administrator, or other prospective program user. Some special questions arise from the fact that a given user's objectives may differ from those the program writer or publisher had in mind and also from the fact that in actual use a program may have effects that neither the producer nor the user necessarily had in mind in his original formulation of objectives (cf., 88). Part of the task for an ideally comprehensive program-assessment study is therefore to identify any likely relevant effects to which a program's use may lead—including but not necessarily limited to those proposed by the producer and user—and then to determine whether these possible effects are in fact produced by the use of the program.

Some Factors in the Design of Instruments for Measuring Instructional Outcomes

The following are illustrative of some major areas of concern that need to be considered in relation to criterion measures, or capability tests:

1. Definition of the universe of behaviors that constitutes the competence which the programer is trying to create or, in any case, with respect to which the evaluator is examining the accomplishments of the program. (The "*or*" implies that these could include definitions of *any* behavioral outcomes which might ensue from the program, even though they were not all necessarily intentions of the programer.) These definitions should be accompanied by examples. However, such a definition is not a test itself; it is an analytic definition of the behavior that specifies what test items are relevant (cf., 26, 34, 50).

2. The problem of item sampling and of how a specific test can be described, as completely as possible, as a sample of the universe of behaviors.

3. The formal or descriptive characteristics of the capability tests (e.g., the basic properties of reliability and validity, if this is applicable). Also, the test's origin: is it an *ad hoc* test, a standardized test, or a mixture? May it be best sometimes to use standardized tests, but with certain items excluded? How should the level of performance be specified? As a related topic, can the outcome or objective of a program be defined without reference to the content of the program, especially when transfer is part of the educational objective?

4. The question of what *kind* of a criterion of program effectiveness to use: specifically, the question of time to attain some specified

criterion level, as distinct from level achieved after going through the program, where performance time varies from subject to subject, so that time and achievement level are both dependent variables—as contrasted in the situation in which time is constant so that achievement level is the only dependent variable. This necessarily overlaps with the question of procedural design.

Sampling of Test Items: In assessing programs it is important to keep in mind the concept that an attainment test is, in general, only a sample of some total population of items that represent the criterion performance. But sometimes it is very difficult to define the relevant population of items in such a way that it does constitute the total teaching objective—and also so that, at least in principle, any number of independent samples can be drawn from this population so as to form equivalent tests. This is a problem which psychometricians seem not to have fully solved, perhaps because the kind of requirements they generally have do not require doing so.

What is needed is a definable population of potential items. It is not often feasible to enumerate all of them; however, two things might be used jointly as the bases for defining the population of items: first, one or more examples, and, second, some kind of "generating function." Given a generating rule that would define the population, and some illustrations that help show what it means, presumably a competent psychometrician can write any number of parallel test forms; one doesn't have to have all possible items constructed in advance and then sample from an already-written pool of test items. The importance of having a large pool of equivalent items from which successive samples can be drawn is made much more acute when tests are used repeatedly for the purpose of making successive determinations, in a branching program, as to whether a student is up to criterion or needs more instruction (see below).

Requirements for Program-Effectiveness Tests vs. Individual or Student Achievement Tests: The problem of measurement usually faced by the psychometrician is primarily one of assessing individual differences. Hammock (39) and Glaser (33) have discussed some differences in the theoretical requirements for "norm-referenced" attainment tests for use in measuring individual differences vs. "criterion-referenced" tests designed to measure the effects of programs. Whereas for the former purpose economic constraints often require "objective" types of questions to permit electromechanical scoring for large numbers of papers that must be processed, this restriction need not be imposed for the relatively small number of subjects needed to assess a program. (See also 41, 47 concerning other aspects of the use of tests in relation to programed instruction.)

Experimental Design

Utilization Conditions

In determining and reporting the effects produced by the use of a programed instruction package, conditions of utilization, in a classroom or in the use of a program for individual study, may obviously have considerable effect on its effectiveness. As emphasized in the J.C.P.I. 1962-63 report (2), it is recognized that programs will generally be used in conjunction with other instruction. However, unless the contribution of a program's use to the student's knowledge or competence can be separated out from the contribution of the sources of instruction, there is no defensible way to tell what the program itself contributed. This involves the experimental control of extraneous sources of influence, so that gains in knowledge, skills, or behavioral tendencies associated with the use of a program can be validly defended as results of the program itself, rather than other concurrent or prior sources of influence.

The need to control for related causal factors will also depend on the question that is being asked—on what is to be assessed. As noted above, it is often necessary to know the effects of the program per se when used under conditions which, however specified, involve a minimum of other related concurrent instruction. Even though the contemplated later use of the program may actually be in conjunction with other instruction, it can be contended that relatively unambiguous information about what it can accomplish by itself, without supplementation, is more useful than uninterpretable information about gains produced by some unknown mixture of program effects and other unspecified influences. On the other hand, it may often be the case that the real question for assessment—that is, the question that reflects

the decision to be made about a particular program's effectiveness—
is what the program will contribute when used collaterally with other
materials or procedures of instruction. This is not at all an impossible
question to answer experimentally, though it does generally involve
the need for specification as to what the "other" instruction is to be.
The usefulness of such information about joint effects of a program
and "other" instruction will obviously decrease as the "other" instruction departs from complete specifiability and reproducibility.

In this connection, the distinction between so-called "laboratory
tests" versus "field tests" may need to be reexamined and sharpened.
No doubt both of these kinds of program tests are needed. "Laboratory
tests" of programs, that is program tests which are conducted under
relatively describable, controllable, standardized conditions, are analogous to the "brake-horsepower" rating on an automobile, which is
a useful statistic even though one also wants data on hill-climbing and
other road tests. The latter may be thought of as analogous to the data
obtained from field tests of the program—less exact, but taking into
account factors not encountered in the laboratory (cf., 15, 35, 84).

Utilization Procedure vs. Experimental Design: The procedure for
utilization of a program (i.e., the way it is to be used) sets limits on
the experimental design that is appropriate for measuring the effects
the program produces within that pattern of utilization. However,
more than one experimental design may be employed to determine
the effects that are produced by a program when used in a particular
pattern of utilization. Conversely, the same general design may be
used with appropriate modifications for determining a program's use
under more than one condition of utilization. For example, either a
"before-after" or "after-only" design can be used to determine a program's effects under a given condition of use, and either basic design
can be used to compare a program's effects under two conditions of use.
(After-only is used here in the special sense employed by Hovland,
Lumsdaine, and Sheffield [46], where a nonexposed control group's
score, rather than preexposure scores for an experimental group, furnish the "before" measure.) But some of the important aspects of experimental design can be considered only in relation to the features
of certain patterns or procedures of program use such as those distinguished below.

Effects as Gains Due to Programs: Essentially, the question of measurement of program effects follows a "before-to-after" change paradigm. That is, the determination of the effects of any given program reduces to the problems of determining what the learners are like in terms of behavioral competencies and tendencies *following* the use of a program (or some segment thereof) as compared to what they would have been like had they not used the program, or what they would have been like had they used some specified alternative program. The same argument applies whether the program in question is a *total* program, as packaged for sale or distribution, or a program segment. The principal departure from this kind of model will be found in the case where program effectiveness or efficiency is measured in terms of time required by a person to reach a given criterion of accomplishment, rather than measured by achievement at the end of a fixed sequence of program materials.

Use of Statistical Significance Tests: A weakness of the statistical habits associated with before-after and gain experiments is that the statistical tests employed are addressed to hypothesis testing rather than to estimation (cf., 86). It is true that in determining the effects of a program, one wants to rule out the null hypothesis that observed gains can be dismissed as chance differences; i.e., one wants to show that effects produced were statistically reliable. However, what is obviously of more interest is a good estimate of the *size* of the gain; merely showing reliable evidence for *some* gain can be trivial. Unfortunately, as Lumsdaine and May have noted (65, p. 490), the practice of reporting the size of effects on an interpretable scale and with accompanying confidence intervals is as yet more the exception than the rule in experiments on the effects of programs.

Some Factors in Experimental Design as Related to Program Assessment

Some of the problems of experimental design are independent of measurement problems per se; others interact with the kind of criteria that are employed. Several recurrent questions are: (a) The experimental procedure—that is, how to specify what was done in using the program, the instructions under which it was used (including the test instructions), how long people worked at it, under what kind of supervision, with what kind of incentive factors, etc. (b) Questions of control (not necessarily implying a control group) for extraneous sources of influence. (c) The need for alternative or complementary evaluation procedures to answer two different questions, previously identified: (i) What do subjects learn when some form of control insures that they do, in some sense, go through the program? (ii) And if a program is merely made available to people, to what extent *will* they go through it (and learn from it)? In other words, to what extent is the program self-motivating? A related design problem is that of how to take account, in analysis and reporting, of dropouts which occur even under a relatively controlled situation. (d) Differences in the kinds of requirements that would apply for experimental design in the case of relatively *brief* programs as compared with quite lengthy programs.

In any study on assessing "effects" of a program as gain from "before" to "after," several methodological decisions must be made. If there is good reason not to be worried about the effect of concurrent extraneous events, it is possible to simply measure the same group before and after using the program. Thus less test data would probably be needed in the case of very short programs. But generally, with any lengthy program it is necessary to introduce a suitable control for what is happening in the meantime: what the students are reading on the outside, what help their parents are giving them, and so forth. This in turn generally means that to assess the effects of a long program, some form of control group is necessary; simply a before-and-after measure for one group will not suffice. Note that such a control group does not mean a group that was given "conventional instruction" as a base of comparison; rather it means a "nonexposure" control for extraneous influences so as to afford a measure of what the program group would have been like had they not received the program. But such a control suffices only for extraneous influences that act independently of the program's use; for other influences (e.g., outside help given on the program itself), other control strategies are needed.

The extent to which formal requirements of control actually are of practical importance in a particular assessment situation often can be tempered by the judgment of the experienced experimentalist. For example, the degree to which pre-to-post changes for a nonexposure control group must be subtracted from those found for the experimental group will depend on the likelihood that substantial changes will occur as a result of extraneous (nonprogram) influences. This likelihood will be much greater in some cases than in others.

One extreme might be the case of a semester-long program on a topic which figures largely in current discussion and public news. It is conceivable in such cases that *all* the gain observed from before-to-after a program might derive from outside sources and the program itself be wholly ineffective. Here the need for a control group not exposed to the program is more obvious than, to take an opposite extreme, in the case of a one-half hour program which can be given and tested without students leaving the experimental classroom, thus affording nearly complete control of extraneous informational sources. (For further discussion of alternative experimental designs for determining instructional effects, see 11, 60).

Reporting of Program Effects

Need for Technical Standards in Measuring Program Effects

A need to provide guidelines for the consistent and interpretable reporting of tests to assess the achievement of programs complements the need for standards to guide the conduct of such tests. The idea of technical recommendations for the assessment of programs in terms of what they demonstrably teach essentially implies some form of controlled experimental measurement which, as indicated by the 1962-63 Joint Committee report (2), can yield evidence to "document for the technical reader that the gains in achievement reported can rightly be attributed to the effects of the program's use rather than to extraneous causes." It is assumed that data on the effectiveness of programs will be obtained and reported by various agencies, including program producers, using agencies (including school systems), and projects conducted by universities and other research agencies. Three levels of reporting may be distinguished: (a) Summary reports, advertisements, general characterizations of program effects and uses; (b) teachers manuals, giving details of program effects demonstrated under described conditions of use, in sufficient detail that valid results may furnish a usable guide to selection and use of programs; (c) technical reports amplifying the teachers-manual information in the kind of detail needed for a technical expert or consultant to assess the validity and applicability of the data summarized in the teachers manual. (This could be a technical supplement to the teachers manual, or, since fewer copies will be needed, a separate technical report.)

Reporting Descriptive Information for Program Users

It seems very desirable to provide user's manuals (or teachers manuals) for programs, as a vehicle for presenting relevant external information about properties which are not apparent on inspection. Information presented in a manual might deal with (a) the program's purposes and intended use, (b) the source of program content, (c) the way the program was developed, including tryout and revision, and (d) the conduct and results of testing to determine empirically the effectiveness, or "performance characteristics," of the published program. The last of these kinds of information is, of course, the most relevant to the present discussion.

Reporting of Information About the Demonstrated Effectiveness of a Program

It is to be hoped that manuals for programs, at least for programs of considerable scope, will furnish evidence on the program's effectiveness based on measurement of student performance on pre- and postprogram criterion tests. The J.C.P.I. has recommended that these tests be exhibited either in the manual or in a supporting technical report, so as to exemplify what the producer expects students to learn as a result of program use. Suggested content of information for teachers manuals concerning reported program effects is presented in a supplement to the 1964 J.C.P.I. report (3, 72). Information on effects, presented in nontechnical terms helpful to the teacher or program purchaser, will generally need to be backed up by a more detailed technical supplement to permit technical assessment of the adequacy of the data presented. Outcomes resulting from the use of a program need to be described as concisely, objectively, and simply as possible, with the aim of communicating to teachers and supervisors how the program was used and what results this use produced.

The writer believes that the emphasis in the reporting of assessment data should be primarily descriptive rather than "evaluative" in the sense of passing judgment on the desirability of different kinds of objectives and outcomes. The aim of such data is to provide a clear picture of what each program *will do* under two or more conditions of use, rather than to pass judgment on what the program *should* do. This leaves it to schools to decide whether the kinds of outcomes that can be realized are the ones which they wish to attain. However, relevant normative data are obviously useful for comparison where available and appropriate.

Description of Effects for Published Programs

The writer believes that claims for the effectiveness of a published program should be supported by data from evidence of gains in student attainment produced by the *final, published version* of the program. A clear distinction should be made between this "effectiveness-test" data, for the final program, and any test data obtained in earlier tryouts of preliminary versions, used as a basis for revision of the program. The sole purpose of these earlier data is to point the way to program revision. By contrast, any changes made in the program after "effectiveness" data are obtained could throw doubt on the validity of these latter data for furnishing a demonstration of the program's effectiveness, since changing the program could lessen as well as increase its effectiveness. The prospective user should have data, if possible, based on the edition he is trying. If data based on an earlier edition are offered in support of a program, this fact should at least be clearly stated, since at the present state of the art there is no real guarantee that revision, particularly if based on editorial judgment, will necessarily have improved a program. In at least one case known to the writer, editorial revisions almost certainly reduced the quality of the program and thus impugned the validity of test data offered in support of it.

Standards in Reporting Findings of Educational Research

Assessment of purportedly factual statements in the literature about education is very difficult. For example, there is no way to assess the significance of statements such as "average students chose televised instruction 6 to 4 over face-to-face instruction" or "more questions are being asked than in classes taught by traditional methods." There are no standards of consistent reporting, no assurance of dependability, such as one would have in a summary abstract or a technical journal in physics, or even, to some extent, in *Psychological Abstracts*. This is not entirely just a difference in the rigor and precision obtainable by science, but is partly a question of the *recognition* of the existence of a technical literature, of technical bases for making statements, and of conventions about what is said on the basis of what kind of evidence —or, rather, what kind of evidence can reasonably be presumed to lie behind what kind of statement. One can expect loose statements in the press, but is often not so wary in reading a professional journal or book. The problem is that the line between journalism and technical reporting is much hazier in the field of education. Perhaps it may be possible to establish standards of consistent reporting or of evaluation of published statements which would reflect the kind of evidence which actually lies behind a given statement. A real inquiry into the possibilities would be a worthwhile effort. The importance of this problem will increase as more and more educational literature accumulates which tries to report scientific data about the effects of educational programs.

In relation to the problems of reporting program effectiveness, it should be noted that impressions of program effects often are not clearly differentiated from actual findings documented directly by quantitative evidence. Yet, the former, by virtue of the way they are stated, are likely to be given as much credence as documented findings. This seems particularly likely when conclusions based on mere impression are presented in the context of an actual research study in which certain data were found which do justify certain conclusions. The former thereby acquire an aura of validity ("gilt" by association?) which they do not, in fact, possess.

The J.C.P.I. (3) strongly recommends that summary reports describing a program's effects (in the form of press releases, advertising, or teachers manuals) be withheld until there is also available a technical report setting forth the procedures by which the data were obtained. Such technical information, in sufficient detail that the technically qualified adviser may be able to assess its soundness, should be available to back up claims made in summaries prepared for administrators or teachers. It is important that this basis be provided in order that data which are actually sound and valid indicators of the effects of a program will not be confused with those popularly presented data which, in fact, do not validly reflect the effects of a program.

Reproducibility

A general criterion of the value of criteria for reporting as well as conducting any assessment study is that the evaluation procedure and its results should be reproducible. This applies to the derivation, administration, and description of criterion measures as well as to the selection of the experimental population and all aspects of the design and procedure. The object of the reporting is to describe what the program accomplishes, in such a way that the process can be duplicated with substantially similar results. The reporting of evaluation tests should therefore describe the physical and social conditions of the program's use and the effectiveness-testing procedures in sufficient detail so that their essential features can be reproduced by another investigator if desired. Any discrepancies between recommended conditions of use and those that were employed in obtaining the effectiveness-test data should be noted.

Technical reports should indicate how many students started and completed the program, average completion time, the average level of performance on the specified pre- and postprogram tests of achievement, and the range or variability of these measures. Relevant further temporal data would include the amount of time learners of different ability spent on various portions of the program, how this time was distributed (especially for long programs), and how long after completion of the program the learners were given the criterion test. (See also 3, 78.)

The AERA Joint Committee General Recommendations on Reporting

The J.C.P.I. (3) makes the following three general recommendations about the reporting of evidence on a program's effectiveness:

First: *Evidence for the effectiveness of a program should be based on a carefully conducted study which shows what the program's use accomplished under specified conditions.*

Second: *The results of the evaluation study should be carefully documented in a technical report prepared in keeping with accepted standards of scientific reporting.*

Third: *All claims or statements about the effectiveness of a program should be supported by specific reference to the evidence contained in the technical report.*

The substance of the Committee's further recommendations for prospective purchasers or users of programs includes, in addition to the general caution of evaluating each program on its own merits, the following further recommendations: (a) That in determining the usefulness of any particular program, a prospective user should first try to formulate his own objectives in as much detail as possible and then evaluate the program, in relation to these objectives, in the light of the three criteria of suitability, practicality, and effectiveness in attaining outcomes relevant to his own objectives. (b) That the prospective user should ignore all claims for the effectiveness of a program which are not backed up by appropriate data that have been subjected to competent evaluation. It is further recommended that advice on the soundness of claims for program effectiveness preferably be obtained from a technical adviser who has competence in the fields of educational psychology, measurement, and experimental design. And (c) that users should seek all available data on the demonstrated characteristics of the program, both from information supplied by the producer and also from reports prepared by school systems, research projects, or other agencies that have conducted program-assessment studies of the particular program.

Additional recommendations for program publishers are proposed by the Committee to assist them in providing necessary information which will help the user make an intelligent choice of a program. These include the recommendations that (a) publishers state in detail the objectives of each program, preferably in terms of specific behavior or competence which its use is intended to achieve; (b) publishers cite the available evidence to document the statements they make about the effectiveness of the program, citing any pertinent evidence available both from their own studies and from other appropriate studies of the program; (c) publishers refrain from promoting a program on the basis of unsupported statements about its effectiveness or in terms of general statements about the value of the programed instruction "method"; (d) publishers provide a program manual, preferably one that can be updated or supplemented as new data on the program become available, and one that substantiates all claims made in this manual or elsewhere by citing documentary evidence from a technical report of a carefully conducted evaluation study. Publishers are also advised to differentiate explicitly between opinions about the effectiveness of the program and documented evidence on the outcomes it can be shown to produce.

Technical Consultation: It is recognized that the teacher or administrator will generally not wish to be burdened with the detailed technical information that is necessary to provide an adequate basis for determining the soundness of reported experimental findings. Consequently, data put forth purporting to indicate a program's accomplishments generally cannot be validly interpreted except with the consultation of a technical specialist who has examined the procedures and instruments whereby the data were obtained. The requirement for having such technical consultation available to appraise data on the effectiveness of instructional programs is a relatively new one in educational institutions. However, the utilization of other kinds of technical experts as consultants in educational decisions, for example, engineering and architectural consultants, is, of course, commonplace. As educational technology advances, it may be expected that a similar need may be more widely recognized for technical specialists to advise the educational administrator and curriculum supervisor on the validity of data about the effects of educational programs, just as he now calls on experts to advise him with respect to the characteristics of audiovisual equipment or the construction of instructional facilities.

Techniques for Describing Program Effects: Describing program effects in a useful way for teachers and administrators cannot be done by requiring them to pore over detailed tabulations of data. Simplified techniques of presentation are needed, yet must be reconciled with the fact that the data are basically rather complex. For example, in describing the performance of students on a program, a "three-dimensional" distribution is needed. Each person started at some level and got to a different level in a certain amount of time. There are, therefore, three descriptive dimensions: a starting point, a terminal point, and the time required to get there. There is also a need to present subscores as well as total scores, and for both there will often be considerable variation among learners in their starting points as well as variations in the terminal points or levels reached. In addition, individual differences in learning ability also lead to variations in how long it takes students to get to any specified level in using the program. Since each of these variables involves a frequency distribution, a quite complicated descriptive problem exists.

Various ways of attempting to cope with this problem can be seen.

In reporting gains in total score from pre- to posttests, evaluation studies by publishers (4, 5, 19) have simply tabulated the pre- and posttest scores individually for each subject for whom data are reported, with N's ranging from 3 up to 30 or more. Time spent on the program by each student is similarly reported. Glaser, Reynolds, and Fullick (35) present graphical distributions of scores on the pre- and posttests rather than tabulating individuals' scores. A recent paper by Hively (44) and graphic presentation techniques used by Hovland, Lumsdaine, and Sheffield (46) and Zuckerman and Jacobs (101) also suggest several graphical methods of presentation. None of these, however, has attempted to integrate the time and gain variables.

Some Methodological Problems in Improving Program-Assessment Practices

Various difficulties of a methodological sort are encountered in current program-assessment studies. Several key problems are identified below. (See additional discussion of some of these problems in an earlier paper [62].)

Learner Characteristics: Specification of prior knowledge and ability of learners can serve both to identify the preprogram baseline from which gains may be measured and also to indicate what prerequisites are needed in order to learn effectively from the program. The corresponding characteristics for the samples of students used in preliminary tryouts or, particularly, in the effectiveness testing of the program, need to be separately specified so as to indicate the degree to which these learners were typical or atypical of the learners for whom the program is intended. A special problem here that calls for some methodological research is that of determining "latent" initial knowledge, based on prior knowledge not recalled, but readily relearned, which is thus not revealed by a preinstructional achievement test.

Problems in Determining Initial Level or "Entering Behavior": There are two kinds of initial capabilities from which gain to terminal behavior capability takes place. The first is the degree of initial competence on the specific set of behaviors which are to be modified by instruction. The second comprises other, related initial capabilities which are not to be modified, but which are assumed to be prerequisites for the desired modification which the program is to accomplish. For example, in addition to "an initial and a terminal capability" in spelling or in ability to perform algebraic manipulations, an initial capability (not to be modified by the program as such) in reading ability and perhaps in competence in writing (or button pushing?), if the program calls for these kinds of responses, is also assumed. Some general intellectual competence, summarized under "IQ" or described by age level, school placement, etc., often without further analysis, is also assumed. The attempt to analyze fully and completely all the prerequisite capabilities would be a very demanding task. On the other hand, being as complete as is feasible is likely to pay off, since it may point to supplementary program requirements to augment additional prerequisite capabilities not initially thought of.

Adequate identification of initial capability is one of several problems encountered in assessment of program effects which suggest inherent deficiencies in programing rationale. The straight-through linear program not only does not lend itself well to measuring time to criterion (see below), it also invites a spuriously inflated gain if initial knowledge is present that is not revealed by a pretest. These two difficulties are interrelated; the latter one can be minimized if a brief review is given between two pretests before starting the main program. But a more fundamental solution is to change the nature of the program itself by branching sequences that skip over detailed coverage of the material on which an initial overview or brush-up has already shown satisfactory achievement.

Time vs. Criterion Achievement: A special problem is brought into focus by the assessment of self-instructional programs, where time spent in instruction is a dependent variable as well as gain in achievement level. In dealing only with fixed-pace programs such as films and television, one could readily compare, say, two versions of a film, each of which took one hour to show. In this case, the problem of evaluating time versus achievement was not as apparent. If one film produced higher achievement scores, and it could be demonstrated that this superiority was reliable, it could be said that it was the better film. The comparison of two self-instructional programs, one of which produces higher achievement scores than the other but also requires more time for students to finish is much more difficult. Of course, it is possible simply to report two separate sets of facts. This is perhaps about the best solution at present; it is not a very good long-range solution because it leads to no decisive basis for preferring one program over another when one program scores better in terms of achievement, but an alternate program scores better in terms of time. Gain in achievement level has sometimes been expressed as an "efficiency" ratio of gain divided by time (36). Objections to this procedure stem from such considerations as nonlinearity of the achievement-gain scales. These considerations, however, do not controvert the need to take time into account in some such fashion.

At present, a considerable advance in program description will be made if *any* objective records are presented that clearly identify the initial and terminal points and the gains that can be unambiguously attributed to the effect of using the program. As a complement to these "achievement-gain" data, it would be desirable to see the time-in-study data even if, for the present, no single achievement-time index seems defensible as a single figure of merit for a program's instructional efficiency. In describing the effects produced by the use of a program, any of the following may be useful (see 62):

1. Report gains in attainment of outcomes achieved by going through the program from beginning to end and separately report time spent on the program as a second, separate dependent variable.
2. Determine and report as the main dependent variable time required to achieve specified levels of attainment.
3. Hold time constant, reporting attainment achieved in some arbitrarily fixed period of time.
4. Let both time and attainment vary, using some devised single measure such as amount of attainment per unit time.

Time To Reach a Criterion: When agreed-upon minimum levels of proficiency to be attained can be set, the time that is required to get to these levels can be used as a criterion instead of comparisons between a gain from a given before-level to a given after-level (cf., 32, 92). In order to know more or less continuously whether a learner has reached the criterion or how closely he has approached it, one has to use frequent interspersed tests; certainly one cannot give the whole program and then measure at the end of it. But, in order not to spend all of the student's time in being tested, this requires some form of sequential-sampling test, in which one or two responses are used as the basis for a branching decision—that is, the decision of whether to stop testing and to proceed with further instruction, or ask more questions, as determined on the basis of the first question or two.

"Savings" Measures: There is a potential alternative to measuring time to criterion. This alternative is to use as a measure the time required to get the student up to (or back up to) some criterion by further instruction of a specifiable sort. If the student had initially achieved this criterion, such a "savings" measure is the time spent in *re*learning, as in the traditional use of "savings" measures of retention in the psychological laboratory.

Savings measures have the advantage of permitting translation of program effectiveness into time values that can be evaluated in terms of cost and yet which can be applied as an indication of retention at any time after a student has finished a program. Moreover, even if the student never attained criterion performance by the time he initially completed a program, a "savings" measure can still be used, indicating how much more instruction was required to get him initially up to a criterion level of performance. (Variants of the basic idea of using "savings" measures for assessing program effects seem to have been independently arrived at by R. Glaser and by E. Z. Rothkopf, in discussion with the present writer.)

Retention: In using retention as a criterion, the interest is not primarily, of course, in just how well a student does at the end of any given lesson or even in how well he does at the end of the semester. Furthermore, it may be of less interest to know whether he can get a perfect score on a recall test six months (or two years) after he has finished algebra than to know how fast he can relearn algebra when he needs it (and how fast he can relearn it with what kinds of refresher instruction). For many kinds of learning this is the criterion on which more and more premium will have to be placed as knowledge continues to expand. Thus, to assess the effectiveness of a program properly, the concern sooner or later must be not only with whether it gets a person up to some immediate criterion, but with how well it compares with some other program (that may have gone up faster or slower to perfect immediate performance) in terms of a "savings" score. The principal problem in the use of a "savings" measure, whether used to measure immediate or delayed retention, is that of specifying a standard or reproducible vehicle for providing the "refresher" or "finishing" instruction. Nevertheless, the "savings" approach is so attractive that considerable effort appears warranted to solve the methodological obstacles it presents.

Empiricism and Theory: Today and Tomorrow

Many challenging problems are posed for research needed to improve the methods of instructional program assessment. One of these, noted above, is the problem of how to predict, from intraprogram response data, what the long-term recall or relearning performance will be at a later date. Better solutions to this and other methodological problems need to be found, though optimum solutions are not likely to be obtained in the immediate future. For the present, however, useful work in assessing program effects can still be done with methods which fall far short of those that hopefully will be available five or ten years hence.

Many statements have been made about properties of programs regarded as related to their effectiveness, and a number of experiments have been conducted to test the predictive validity of such propositions. The fact that some reasonable propositions about the advantages of theoretically sound prompting techniques and sequencing of content are far from fully supported by available evidence does not necessarily mean that such propositions are without validity nor that they should necessarily be ignored as guides to programing. While this may be obvious, it seems well to make it explicit in view of the stress placed here on the need for reliance on empirical evidence to assess each program's effectiveness. This empirical emphasis does not deny the usefulness of theory as a basis of prediction or a guide to program construction. It merely takes the position that for the present, theoretical propositions and rules of programing derived from them are insufficient and therefore hazardous bases on which to rely for the assessment of a program's effectiveness. Obviously it would be more efficient as well as more elegant if results of empirical tests of effectiveness could be reliably predicted in advance by analysis of program construction features, i.e., on the basis of "internal criteria." It is certainly to be hoped that this will be the case in the future. At present, it is to be recognized that a mature science of instruction does not exist, and wishing won't make it so. How soon research will make it so remains to be seen.

In the meantime, as Candide had it, "We must cultivate our gardens." The weeds to be gotten out of the programed-instruction garden are generalizations about "the method" based on faith rather than evidence, unsupported claims about program effectiveness, and data advanced for such claims which, however extensive or neatly presented, actually fail to support the claims in terms of accepted standards of scientific evidence. We need to rid the programing field as rapidly as possible of these impediments to its orderly growth, and thus put on a sound basis of practice the philosophy of providing tested performance specifications for current programs. We may then profitably shift more of our research emphasis to the longer-range goals of cultivating the knowledges and understanding that will be needed to comprise a science of curriculum, which can afford a rational basis for deciding on what programs need to teach, and a science of instruction, which can more dependably guide our efforts to teach it efficiently.

References

1. American Educational Research Association, American Psychological Association, Department of Audiovisual Instruction, National Education Association: Joint Committee on Programed Instruction and Teaching Machines. "Joint Committee Prepares Interim Guidelines." *AV Communication Review* 9: 206-208; July-August 1961.
2. American Educational Research Association, American Psychological Association, Department of Audiovisual Instruction, National Education Association: Joint Committee on Programed Instruction and Teaching Machines. "Criteria for Assessing Programed Instructional Material." *Audiovisual Instruction* 8: 84-89; February 1963.
3. American Educational Research Association, American Psychological Association, Department of Audiovisual Instruction, National Education Association: Joint Committee on Programed Instruction and Teaching Machines. *Recommendations for Reporting of Information on the Performance Characteristics of Programmed Learning Materials: Third Interim Report.* Los Angeles: University of California, 1964. (Preliminary edition)

4. Basic Systems Program. *Chemistry 1, Atomic Structure and Bonding: Teacher's Manual.* New York: Appleton-Century-Crofts—Lyons & Carnahan, 1962.

5. Basic Systems Program. *Vectors, A Programmed Text for Introductory Physics: Teacher's Manual,* New York: Appleton-Century-Crofts—Lyons & Carnahan, 1962.

6. Belton, J. R. "Programmed Learning—20 Questions." *Bulletin of the National Association of Secondary School Principals* 46: 77-78; December 1962.

7. Bloom, B. S., editor. *Taxonomy of Educational Objectives. Handbook I: Cognitive Domain.* New York: Longmans, 1956.

8. Bolt, Beranek and Newman, Inc. *Test Results of Honor Roll Programs.* Brighton, Mass: the Author, 1963.

9. Buros, O. K., editor. *The Fourth Mental Measurements Yearbook.* Highland Park, N.J.: Gryphon Press, 1959.

10. Buros, O. K., editor. *The Fifth Mental Measurements Yearbook.* Highland Park, N.J.: Gryphon Press, 1959.

11. Campbell, D. T., and Stanley, J. C. "Experimental and Quasi-Experimental Designs for Research on Teaching." *Handbook of Research on Teaching.* (Edited by N. L. Gage.) Chicago: Rand McNally, 1963. pp. 171-246.

12. Carroll, J. B. "Sorcerer's Apprentice at Large?" *Contemporary Psychology* 9: 188-90; April 1964.

13. Caulfield, R. L. "Evaluation of Program Texts." *School and Society* 91: 116-17; March 7, 1963.

14. Center for Programed Instruction, Information Division. *A Parents' Guide to Teaching Machines and Programed Instruction.* New York: the Center, 1962.

15. Center for Programed Instruction. *The Use of Programed Instruction in U.S. Schools.* New York: the Center, 1963.

16. Coronet Learning Programs. *How Coronet Learning Programs Are Prepared and Tested.* Chicago: Coronet Instructional Films, n.d.

17. Denova, C. C. "Byways Through a FORTRAN Maze." *Contemporary Psychology* 8: 456-58; November 1963.

18. Deterline, W. A. "The Carpentry Revolution—A Fable." *Trends in Programmed Instruction.* (Edited by G. D. Ofiesh and W. C. Meierhenry.) Washington, D.C.: National Education Association and National Society for Programmed Instruction, 1964. p. xi.

19. Drooyan, I., and Wooton, W. *Teacher's Manual To Accompany "Programmed Beginning Algebra."* New York: John Wiley & Sons, 1964.

20. Edgerton, H. A. *The Acceptability and Effectiveness of the Casual Use of Auditory Training Aids.* ONR Technical Report No. NAVTRADEVCEN 373-1. Port Washington, N.Y.: U.S. Naval Training Device Center, March 1960.

21. Eigen, L. D. "Scrambled Bits." *Contemporary Psychology* 6: 25-27; January 1961.
22. Eigen, L. D. "Some Problems in Field Testing Programs for Teaching Machines." *Journal of Educational Sociology* 34: 372-76; April 1961.
\ 23. Eigen, L. D. "The Implications for Research Methodology of Some Behavioral Studies in Programed Instruction." *Psychology in the Schools* 1: 140-47; April 1964.
24. Ely, D. P., editor. "The Changing Role of the Audiovisual Process in Education: A Definition and a Glossary of Related Terms." *AV Communication Review* 11: 1-148; January-February 1963.
25. Esbensen, T. "The Programmer as Artist." *Auto-Instructional Devices* 2: 186-87; November 1962.
26. Flanagan, J. C. "The Use of Comprehensive Rationales in Test Development." *Educational and Psychological Measurement* 11: 151-55; Spring 1951.
27. Fletcher, L. "The Non-Programmed Program." *NSPI Journal* 3: 6-7; May 1964.
28. Gagné, R. M. "The Implications of Instructional Objectives for Learning." *Defining Educational Objectives.* (Edited by C. M. Lindvall.) Pittsburgh: University of Pittsburgh Press, 1964. pp. 37-46.
29. Galanter, E. "Common Statistics Uncommonly Taught." *Contemporary Psychology* 6: 104-106; March 1961.
30. Geis, G. L. "Some Considerations in the Evaluation of Programs." *AV Communication Review* 10: 64-69; January-February 1962.
31. General Programmed Teaching Corporation. "Judging Program Quality." *Guide to Programmed Teaching.* Albuquerque, N. Mex.: the Corporation, 1963. pp. 15-18.
32. Gilpin, J. "Design and Evaluation of Instructional Systems." *AV Communication Review* 10: 75-84; January-February 1962.
33. Glaser, R. "Instructional Technology and the Measurement of Learning Outcomes." *American Psychologist* 18: 519-21; August 1963.
34. Glaser, R., and Klaus, D. J. "Proficiency Measurement: Assessing Human Performance." *Psychological Principles in System Development.* (Edited by R. M. Gagné.) New York: Holt, 1962. pp. 419-74.
35. Glaser, R.; Reynolds, J. H.; and Fullick, Margaret. *Programmed Instruction in the Intact Classroom.* Pittsburgh: Learning Research and Development Center, University of Pittsburgh, December 1963.
36. Goldbeck, R. A., and Campbell, V. N. "The Effects of Response Mode and Response Difficulty on Programmed Learning." *Journal of Educational Psychology* 53: 110-18; June 1962.
37. Gotkin, L. G. *Some Guidelines for the Location, Selection, and Individual Testing of Programed Instruction for School Use.* Paper read at the National Conference on Selection and Use of Programed Instruction, Detroit, June 1963.

38. Gropper, G. L., and Lumsdaine, A. A. *The Use of Student Response To Improve Televised Instruction: An Overview*. Studies in Televised Instruction, Report No. 7. Pittsburgh: Metropolitan Pittsburgh Educational Television Stations WQED-WQEX and the American Institute for Research, June 1961.

39. Hammock, J. *Criterion Measures: Instruction vs. Selection Research*. Paper presented at the Annual Convention of the American Psychological Association, Chicago, September 1960.

40. Hanson, L. F., editor. *Programs, '63: A Guide to Programed Instructional Materials Available to Educators by September 1963*. Washington, D.C.: Government Printing Office, 1963.

41. Heath, R. W. "Some Uses of Tests in Programmed Instruction." *Nineteenth Yearbook of the National Council on Measurement in Education*. (Edited by M. Katz.) Ames, Iowa: National Council on Measurement in Education, 1962. pp. 46-48.

42. Hendershot, C. H. *Programmed Learning: A Bibliography of Programs and Presentation Devices*. Second edition. University Center, Mich.: Delta College, 1963.

43. Hively, W. *Defining Criterion Behavior for Programmed Instruction in Elementary Mathematics*. Cambridge, Mass.: Committee on Programmed Instruction, Harvard University, 1963.

44. Hively, W. *Some Guidelines for Evaluating Programs of Instruction in Mathematics*. Paper prepared for the Committee on Programmed Instruction of the National Council of Teachers of Mathematics, 1964.

45. Holland, J. G. "Evaluating Teaching Machines and Programs." *Teachers College Record* 63: 56-65; October 1961.

46. Hovland, C. I.; Lumsdaine, A. A.; and Sheffield, F. D. *Experiments on Mass Communication*. Princeton, N.J.: Princeton University Press, 1949.

47. Jacobs, P. I. "Some Relationships Between Testing and Auto-Instructional Programming." *AV Communication Review* 10: 317-27; November-December 1962.

48. Jacobs, P. I.; Maier, M. H.; and Stolurow, L. M. *A Guide To Evaluating Self-Instructional Programs*. Princeton, N.J.: Educational Testing Service, April 1964. (Revised draft)

49. Klaus, D. J. "The Art of Auto-Instructional Programming." *AV Communication Review* 9: 130-42; March-April 1961.

50. Lindvall, C. M., editor. *Defining Educational Objectives*. Pittsburgh: University of Pittsburgh Press, 1964.

51. Los Angeles County Board of Education. "An Approach to the Evaluation of Instructional Materials." *Our American Heritage*. Los Angeles: Our American Heritage Cooperative Project, May 1963.

52. Lumsdaine, A. A. "Partial and More Complete Automation of Teaching in Group and Individual Learning Situations." *Automatic Teach-*

ing: The State of the Art. (Edited by E. Galanter.) New York: John Wiley & Sons, 1959. pp. 147-66.

53. Lumsdaine, A. A. "Some Conclusions Concerning Student Response and a Science of Instruction." *Student Response in Programmed Instruction.* (Edited by A. A. Lumsdaine.) Washington, D.C.: National Academy of Sciences—National Research Council, 1961. pp. 471-527.

54. Lumsdaine, A. A. "Criteria for Evaluating Self-Instructional Programs." *School Life* 45: 15-17 ff.; November-December 1962.

55. Lumsdaine, A. A. "Improving the Quality of Instruction Through Programmed Learning." *Proceedings of the Twenty-Sixth Conference of the Educational Records Bureau and the American Council on Education.* New York: Educational Records Bureau, 1962.

56. Lumsdaine, A. A. "Report of the Committee on Auto-Instructional Programs and Devices." *1962 Annual Report of the American Educational Research Association.* Atlantic City, N.J.: American Educational Research Association, 1962.

57. Lumsdaine, A. A. "Some Critical Issues in the Improvement of Instruction Through Programed Learning." *AV Communication Review* 10: 61-64; January-February 1962.

58. Lumsdaine, A. A. "Some Theoretical and Practical Problems in Programmed Instruction." *Programmed Learning and Computer-Based Instruction.* (Edited by J. E. Coulson.) New York: John Wiley & Sons, 1962. pp. 134-51.

59. Lumsdaine, A. A. "Assessment and Improvement of Instructional Programs." *Educator* 6: 4-6; December 1963.

60. Lumsdaine, A. A. "Instruments and Media of Instruction." *Handbook of Research on Teaching.* (Edited by N. L. Gage.) Chicago: Rand-McNally, 1963.

61. Lumsdaine, A. A. "Report of the Committee on Auto-Instructional Programs and Devices." *1963 Annual Report of the American Educational Research Association.* Chicago: American Educational Research Association, Spring 1963.

62. Lumsdaine, A. A. "Some Problems in Assessing Instructional Programs." *Prospectives in Programing.* (Edited by R. T. Filep.) New York: Macmillan Co., 1963. pp. 228-62.

63. Lumsdaine, A. A. "Educational Technology, Programed Learning, and Instructional Science." *Theories of Learning and Instruction: Sixty-Third Yearbook, National Society for the Study of Education.* Chicago: University of Chicago Press, 1964. pp. 371-401.

64. Lumsdaine, A. A., and Glaser R., editors. *Teaching Machines and Programmed Learning.* Washington, D.C.: National Education Association, 1960.

65. Lumsdaine, A. A., and May, M. A. "Mass Communication and Educational Media." *Annual Review of Psychology.* (Edited by P. R.

Farnsworth, Olga McNemar, and Q. McNemar.) Palo Alto, Calif.: Annual Reviews, 1965. pp. 475-534.

66. Mager, R. F. *Preparing Objectives for Programed Instruction.* San Francisco: Fearon Publishers, 1962.

67. Maier, M. H.; Stolurow, L. M.; and Jacobs, P. I. *The Schoolman's Guide to Programed Instruction.* Princeton, N.J.: Educational Testing Service, February 1963. (Mimeo.)

68. Markle, Susan M. "Confusion Worse Confounded." *Contemporary Psychology* 6: 133-36; April 1961.

69. Markle, Susan M. *Good Frames and Bad: A Grammar of Frame Writing.* New York: John Wiley & Sons, 1964.

70. Miller, R. B. *Handbook on Training and Training Equipment Design.* WADC Technical Report No. 53-136. Wright-Patterson Air Force Base, Ohio: Wright Air Development Center, June 1953.

71. Miller, R. B. "Task Description and Analysis." *Psychological Principles in System Development.* (Edited by R. M. Gagné.) New York: Holt, Rinehart and Winston, 1962. pp. 187-230.

72. National Education Association, Department of Audiovisual Instruction. *Selection and Use of Programed Materials: A Handbook for Teachers.* Washington, D.C.: National Education Association, 1964.

73. National Society for Programmed Instruction. "Checklist for Selecting Programs." *NSPI Newsletter* 1: 6-7; October 1962.

74. National Society for Programmed Instruction. "Checklist for Selecting Programs." *NSPI Journal* 2: 4; July 1963.

75. New York City Board of Education, Division of Curriculum Development, Bureau of Audio-Visual Instruction. *Recommended Procedures for the Appraisal of Programed Audio-Visual Materials.* Brooklyn, N.Y.: Programed Audio-Visual Materials Evaluation Project, 1962.

76. Paulson, C. F. *The Effectiveness of the Self-Instructional Program "Longitude and Latitude."* Technical Report No. 1. Monmouth: Oregon State System of Higher Education, 1963.

77. Rocky Mountain School Study Council, Curriculum and Instruction Committee, Programmed Study Group. *Guidelines for the Selection of Programmed Materials,* 1962.

78. Rothkopf, E. Z. "Criteria for the Acceptance of Self-Instructional Programs." *Improving the Efficiency and Quality of Learning.* (Edited by A. E. Traxler.) Washington, D.C.: Educational Records Bureau and American Council on Education, 1961. pp. 30-38.

79. Rothkopf, E. Z. "Some Observations on Predicting Instructional Effectiveness by Simple Inspection." *Journal of Programmed Instruction* 2: 19-20; Summer 1963.

80. Rothkopf, E. Z. "The Epidemiology of Ignorance." *Contemporary Psychology* 9: 234-36; May 1964.

81. Ryans, D. G. "Report of the Committee on Auto-Instructional Programs and Devices." *1961 Annual Report of the American Educational Research Association.* Chicago: American Educational Research Association, 1961. pp. 23-24.

82. Saltzman, I. J. "Road Under Construction." *Contemporary Psychology* 6: 106-109; March 1961.

83. Schramm, W. *Programed Instruction.* New York: Fund for the Advancement of Education, 1962.

84. Schramm, W., editor. *Four Case Studies of Programed Instruction.* New York: Fund for the Advancement of Education, 1964.

85. Schramm, W. *The Research on Programed Instruction: An Annotated Bibliography.* Washington, D.C.: U.S. Department of Health, Education, and Welfare, Office of Education, 1964.

86. Schutz, R. E.; Baker, R. L.; and Gerlach, V. S. "Teaching Capitalization with a Programed Text." *AV Communication Review* 10: 359-63; November-December 1962.

87. Schutz, R. E.; Baker, R. L.; and Gerlach, V. S. *Measurement Procedures in Programmed Instruction.* Tempe: Classroom Learning Laboratory, Arizona State University, 1964.

88. Shettel, H. H. "Objectives, 'Ours' and 'Theirs.'" *NSPI Journal* 3: 12-14; May 1964.

89. Silberman, H. F. "Adventure or Fundamentals." *Contemporary Psychology* 6: 411-13; November 1961.

90. Silberman, H. F., and others. *Use of Exploratory Research and Individual Tutoring Techniques for the Development of Programming Methods and Theory.* Santa Monica, Calif.: System Development Corp., June 1964.

91. Silverman, R. E. "The Evaluation of Programmed Instruction: A Problem in Decision Making." *Psychology in the Schools* 1: 74-78; January 1964.

92. Skinner, B. F. "Teaching Machines." *Science* 128: 969-77; October 1958. [Reprinted in *Teaching Machines and Programmed Learning.* (Edited by A. A. Lumsdaine and R. Glaser.) Washington, D.C.: National Education Association, 1960.]

93. Stolurow, L. M. "Problems, Procedures, Pitfalls, and Promise of Programing Practices." *Bulletin of the National Association of Secondary School Principals* 48: 256-70; April 1964.

94. Stolurow, L. M., and Lumsdaine, A. A. *Training Characteristics for Illumination of Animated Classroom Trainers.* Technical Memo TARL-TM-56-1. Chanute Air Force Base, Ill.: Air Force Personnel and Training Research Center, Air Research and Development Command, Training Aids Research Laboratory, 1956.

95. Teaching Materials Corporation. *How Teachers Can Evaluate Teaching Machines and Learning Programs.* New York: the Corporation, 1962.

96. Tracey, W. R. "Editor's Checklist: Content and Construction Review." *NSPI Journal* 2 13-14; December 1963.

97. Tyler, R. W. *Basic Principles of Curriculum and Instruction: Syllabus for Education 305.* Chicago: University of Chicago Press, 1950.

98. University of Michigan, Center for Programed Learning for Business. "Criteria for the Evaluation of 'Off-the-Shelf' Programs." *Programmed Learning Bulletin* 1: 1-2; April 1963.

99. U.S. Air Force, Headquarters Air Training Command, Randolph Air Force Base, Texas. "Evaluation of Programmed Instruction Packages." Letter dated October 12, 1962.

100. Wiley, John & Sons. *A Guide for Wiley Authors in the Preparation of Linear Auto-Instructional Programs.* New York: the Author, 1961.

101. Zuckerman, J. V., and Jacobs, M. *Specific Effects of the Film "Flight Capabilities of the F86A" as Related to Points Covered in the Film.* HRRL Memo Report No. 10. Washington, D.C.: U.S. Air Force Human Resources Laboratories, 1951.

BERT Y. KERSH

Teaching Research Division
Oregon State System of Higher Education

Programing Classroom Instruction

It is almost inevitable that programed self-instruction will have an impact on conventional classroom instruction. It already has to some extent. Practicing teachers who attempt to learn the techniques of programed instruction in summer workshops and professional courses are finding that the rigor of specifying objectives in behavioral terms, reducing the instructional experience to small steps, and trying out the materials on students before actually using them makes them more sensitive to the shortcomings of their own classroom techniques. College instructors in psychological foundation courses are finding that the topic of programed instruction is ideally suited as a vehicle for teaching learning theory and psychological measurement. But these are all indirect benefits. Programing is still generally considered to be limited to self-instruction. This chapter will describe a direct application to group-paced classroom instruction.

It is frequently said that the classroom teacher will never be replaced by programs of self-instruction. Rather, he will be freed to guide the learning of his students in ways that only a human being can. Implicit in this statement is the assumption that some learning processes cannot be "automated" or learned independently. Learning processes which many say cannot be automated include such "complex processes" as reasoning, problem solving, and "learning how to learn." The behavioral components of these processes are elusive, so it is reasonable to believe they are best learned by interacting with another person who has mastered them or by wrestling with difficult problems under supervision. The thesis of this chapter is not that such complex learnings are adaptable to self-instructional programing techniques, but rather that the principles and techniques which underlie self-instructional programing can be employed equally as well in the development of suitable classroom instructional materials and procedures. The result may be very similar in appearance to classroom procedures which are presently employed by teachers, but the resemblance may end there. There will be no greater similarity between conventional classroom techniques and programed classroom techniques than exists between conventional self-study materials and programed self-instructional materials.

In this chapter, five plans for conventional classroom instruction will be described briefly, and their strengths and weaknesses will be discussed in terms of the technology of programed instruction. Next several requirements will be listed for a programing procedure that could transcend the limitations of existing plans, including programed self-instruction. Finally, one example of a programing procedure will be outlined which satisfies the essential requirements.

Of primary interest in this chapter is a procedure for designing instructional programs, not a set of rubrics for analyzing a program after it has been designed. None of the existing plans to be described is entirely sufficient in this respect, but each has other aspects which may be of considerable interest to anyone wishing to develop a new design procedure.

Instructional Design Today

Wallen and Travers (34) have pointed out that the systematic design of instruction involves two steps: (a) the specification of learning principles based on scientific research—principles which have relevance to school learning and (b) the design of teaching methods on the basis of the learning principles previously specified. Their comprehensive analysis and investigation of teaching methods led them to conclude that few plans or methods of teaching are presently based on principles of behavioral science. Most have been derived from teaching traditions, social learnings in the teacher's background, philosophical traditions, the teacher's own needs, and from conditions existing in the school and community. The Winnetka Plan developed by Washburne (36), the teaching model developed by Woodruff (40), and perhaps that developed by Olson (24) are listed as representing attempts to develop a teaching method on the basis of learning principles. In addition to the three plans Wallen and Travers recommend, the Unit Plan frequently referred to in textbooks on elementary and secondary methods (5, 13, 23, 27, 28, 31) and curriculum studies like the mathematics curriculum developed by the University of Illinois Committee on School Mathematics (2) could be included as examples. These plans and procedures will be described briefly below, but first to be considered are the learning principles upon which they are based.

Accepted Principles of Learning

The five instructional plans have one thing in common. They are based on principles of learning and behavior rather than on tradition, social need, or "teaching experience."

Almost any textbook dealing with educational psychology or teaching methods selected from the library shelf will contain a list of statements about human learning (e.g., 17, pp. 162-64; 10, pp. 287-88; 23, pp. 18-37; 28, pp. 32-50; and 27, pp. 69-103). Different wording is used, but all lists contain essentially the same basic concepts. Perhaps the most comprehensive and concise list has been prepared by Hilgard (16). It reads as follows:

1. In deciding who should learn what, the capacities of the learner are very important. Brighter people can learn things less bright ones cannot learn; in general, older children can learn more readily than younger ones; the decline of ability with age, in the adult years, depends upon what it is that is being learned.
2. A motivated learner acquires what he learns more readily than one who is not motivated. The relevant motives include both general and specific ones, for example, desire to learn, need for achievement (general), desire for a certain reward or to avoid a threatened punishment (specific).
3. Motivation that is too intense (especially pain, fear, anxiety) may be accompanied by distracting emotional states, so that excessive motivation may be less effective than moderate motivation for learning some kinds of tasks, especially those involving difficult discriminations.
4. Learning under the control of reward is usually preferable to learning under the control of punishment. Correspondingly, learning motivated

by success is preferable to learning motivated by failure. Even though the theoretical issue is still unresolved, the practical outcome must take into account the social by-products, which tend to be more favorable under reward than under punishment.

5. Learning under intrinsic motivation is preferable to learning under extrinsic motivation.
6. Tolerance for failure is best taught through providing a backlog of success that compensates for experienced failure.
7. Individuals need practice in setting realistic goals for themselves, goals neither so low as to elicit little effort nor so high as to foreordain to failure. Realistic goal-setting leads to more satisfactory improvement than unrealistic goal-setting.
8. The personal history of the individual, for example, his reaction to authority, may hamper or enhance his ability to learn from a given teacher.
9. Active participation by a learner is preferable to passive reception when learning, for example, from a lecture or a motion picture.
10. Meaningful materials and meaningful tasks are learned more readily than nonsense materials and more readily than tasks not understood by the learner.
11. There is no substitute for repetitive practice in the overlearning of skills (for instance, the performance of a concert pianist), or in the memorization of unrelated facts that have to be automatized.
12. Information about the nature of a good performance, knowledge of his own mistakes, and knowledge of successful results aid learning.
13. Transfer to new tasks will be better if, in learning, the learner can discover relationships for himself, and if he has experience during learning of applying the principles within a variety of tasks.
14. Spaced or distributed recalls are advantageous in fixing material that is to be long retained (16, pp. 486-87).

Each of the instructional design procedures described below are based on principles similar to those listed above. In some cases, these principles are not stated directly as in the Winnetka Plan, which was developed prior to 1926, but even with the Winnetka Plan the principles are implicit.

The Unit Plan

The Unit Plan anticipates that today's public school teacher will be provided with broadly stated objectives in a curriculum guide distributed by his State Department of Education. The teacher may begin then by planning a unit of work around a prescribed topic. The unit, variously described as the "resource unit," "unit of instruction," "unit of work," and "experience unit" may place emphasis on the resources (motivating devices, materials, references) or upon the learning experiences that the teacher develops in his classroom. Nordberg, Bradfield, and Odell (23) list the following characteristics of a good unit and unit teaching:

1. A unit is planned cooperatively by the teacher and students. When students have a role in selecting and planning areas for study, there is greater acceptance of and interest in the problem.
2. A unit is based upon a broad problem or area of investigation. All information and procedures are related and purposeful in that they are needed in arriving at conclusions pertinent to the problem.
3. Unit teaching lends itself to the problem solving approach. Being able to collect data, evaluate, and arrive at conclusions is recognized as a desirable skill to be learned by students.
4. There are abundant opportunities for providing for individual differences. The various abilities of the students can be utilized through group or individual contributions toward the achievement of the objectives of the unit.
5. Student initiative is encouraged. Everyone is not doing the same task in the same manner. Original thinking, therefore, is stimulated.
6. A wide variety of teaching techniques can be employed in unit teaching. Committee work, library research, field trips, and others are necessary in the pursuance of the unit.
7. Flexibility is inherent in a unit. A preplanned unit allows for the stimulation of further action in different, but related, areas than those originally considered (23, pp. 87-88).

At the elementary level the teacher attempts to integrate learning from all the content areas and to teach as many required skills as possible. For example, a fourth-grade teacher, planning a unit of work around the topic "living in Norway," may have several objectives in mind including skill in using the index, giving oral reports, and reading to find specific information, in addition to learning about life in Norway. The unit of work is expected to last more than a single lesson, generally extending over several weeks.

The teacher is free to develop any outline he wishes in working out a unit. In any event, units must include a statement of objectives, some means for pretesting the students, specification of problems and concepts to be studied, teaching techniques to be employed, resource materials, and some means for evaluating student progress.

The Daily Lesson Plan: From the Unit Plan, the teacher develops lesson plans. The daily lesson plan is organized much like the unit, except that it deals with specific skills, concepts, and understandings. Outlines vary, but they generally include a statement of objectives, the topic or problem to be considered, teaching-learning techniques employed, and a listing of resource materials. In planning his lesson for the day, the teacher is encouraged to give careful consideration to his students, with particular respect to their interests and abilities. The lesson plan is flexible, and the teacher may deviate from the plan during instruction. Even in preparing the lesson, the teacher has a choice of a variety of "methods," such as motion pictures, student projects, and textbook assignments.

It is clear that the Unit Plan attempts to provide for individual differences in student motivation and interest through cooperative planning, flexibility in instruction, and variation in activities and materials. Differences among individuals in learning rate and competency are provided for through the coordination of a wide variety of activities in the unit. Complex processes of problem solving, study habits, and cooperative work skills are developed by directing learner activity toward problems and encouraging the students to use their own initiative in resolving them.

In addition to learning the components of the learning process, teachers are taught that students should discover generalizations for themselves, should use punishment and competition sparingly, if at all, and should relate learning activities to specific and clearly defined purposes (28). Teachers are also taught that activities should be planned in a graduated sequence, starting with concrete experiences and progressing toward abstractions (27).

Most outstanding in contrast with programing procedures is that it is permissible to state teaching objectives as "purposes" (not behaviors) and that learning principles and procedures are recommended, but not systematically employed. Also notable is the fact that in the Unit Plan instructional procedures are rarely, if ever, pretried before being put to use and are frequently changed to suit what the teacher observes to be the student's interests and abilities. These differences are major and are enough to lead some educators to the conclusion that conventional classroom instruction and programed instruction have nothing in common. Others might prefer to say that procedures employed are similar, and differences are only a matter of degree. The programer develops his objectives with much greater precision and places much greater emphasis on entry and terminal behavior. Although the classroom teacher is much less systematic, he does develop his procedures through experience.

Plan for Developing UICSM Instructional Materials

The materials and procedures developed by the University of Illinois Committee on School Mathematics (UICSM) are illustrative of the newer curricula in science and mathematics. According to Beberman (2), their objective is to teach high school mathematics with understanding. They believe that understanding comes when (a) precise language is used and (b) when the learner can discover generalizations by himself. Both exposition and exercises are designed so that the learner will discover principles and rules. Consistent with Hendrix's position (15), the UICSM program delays the verbalization of important discoveries and claims this delaying technique as one of the distinguishing characteristics of the program. Delaying verbalization means the learner does not "say" a principle until he has demonstrated that he knows it.

Beberman defends the use of the discovery method on the grounds that ninth graders are attracted to the "what-would-happen-if" question regardless of its "practicality" from the adult point of view. He stresses the importance of success in discovering answers to such questions. If the learner is not successful, the questions become artificial and uninteresting. The fact that he can discover for himself is all he needs to justify mathematics. In Beberman's words: "Thus, the discovery method develops interest in mathematics, and power in mathematical thinking. Because of the student's independence of rote rules and routines, it also develops versatility in applying mathematics" (2, pp. 38-39).

Although objectives are not stated in behavioral terms, rather precise criteria are employed. For example, at the completion of a lesson in which the learner "discovers" a general law of mathematics, an "open sentence" may be provided and the learner asked to determine whether or not the sentence will always produce a "true statement." If the learner knows the general law involved, he can answer correctly; otherwise, it is presumed that he does not know the law. Such precision in determining terminal behavior comes about because the verbalization of generalizations by the learner is discouraged until the learner has demonstrated that he has learned the generalizations.

In addition, the UICSM materials have been thoroughly tested by trained teachers in conventional classrooms. Classroom teachers are trained in specific techniques of instruction including the use of a precise terminology. For example, when an arbitrary rule of mathematics is to be learned, such as the order of operations, the teacher is permitted to tell it to the learner directly. However, when a generalization is involved which can be induced from examples, the learner must discover the generalization. The teacher tells the learner when he is right or wrong, gives encouragement, and manages the classroom behavior of the students, but otherwise is limited to manipulating materials. In effect, the teacher acts as a logic-control center which determines for the learner when to branch, wash back, or skip ahead in the instructional sequence. The instructional "program" is flexible in that the teacher may deviate from the lesson plan, but only within prescribed limits. Actually, the lesson is broken down into small steps, and the materials are carefully sequenced. The UICSM instructor can often anticipate almost anything that might happen in the classroom before the lesson begins.

The UICSM instructional program is highly individualized at times and on other occasions relies heavily on competition. One technique, for instance, is to provide the learners with examples of a general law and to require them to work with the materials until they discover an "easier way" (employing the general law) to solve the problems. As the individual learners discover the law, they raise their hands and whisper the solution to the instructor. Often a great deal of excitement is generated in the classroom. At other times, the class interacts with the instructor and works out solutions to problems cooperatively. Conventions are agreed upon through class discussions, names are given to general laws, and loopholes in logical processes of thinking are identified.

The UICSM instructional program is an example of one of the most systematically developed instructional procedures employed in conventional classrooms today. Instructional procedure is fairly consistent and predictable, teaching objectives are relatively precise, and the materials and procedures are carefully developed by a procedure of trial and correction. Because the underlying principles of the instructional procedure are prescribed, the task of designing instructional methods for attaining new and different teaching objectives is rather clear-cut. The UICSM design procedure still falls short of the rigor and precision with which self-instructional programs are developed, however. Teaching objectives are not always measurable, and it is the understanding of this present writer that the instructional materials are developed on the basis of information from teachers regarding the effectiveness of the materials more often than on the student's performance records directly.

Woodruff's Teaching Model

The first tangible products of an extensive effort directed by Woodruff to reorganize a teacher education program are just beginning to appear (25, 41). At present there is available little more than an outline of a basic structure of an evolving teacher education program and a set of "workable ideas" concerning what the teacher does when he teaches a class. Woodruff's notions are based on "a deliberate and critical selection of the things a teacher should know, and the things he should be able to do, in order to teach students in school" (41, p. v). The selection was based on both philosophy and psychology. He recognizes the fact that many of the principles and practices of teaching today are based on philosophical points of view, not the psychology of human learning. Behavioral scientists have only recently accepted the fact that enough is known about human learning to develop a technology for teaching.

Woodruff's Concept of Teaching: According to Woodruff, teaching has three major elements: (a) specifying what is to be learned, (b) determining the action by which the student learns it, and (c) helping the students become receptive to the learning experience. Every teaching act is aimed at an objective, and objectives must be stated in very precise terms. Broad concepts or complex skills should be broken down into their respective components, and teaching should be directed at each component separately, one at a time. Finally, all components are brought together to form the single more complex concept or skill. In designing instruction, Woodruff prefers to keep attention on the objective and on the things the learner must do to reach the objective rather than on what the teacher must do. He does not identify with any particular methodology such as "child-centered teaching" or "an activity curriculum." Finally, it is specified that the learning experience for any given objective must be the same for any learner. Differences in the learner's capacities to learn will affect only the rate of learning.

Attaining Education Objectives: Learning takes place at different levels: Level A is the lowest level and involves experience with actual external referents. At the next higher level, Level B, learning is conceptual and is based largely on inductive thinking. Level C is also inductive, but involves application and practice of whatever was induced at Level B. The highest level, Level D, is based on deductive thinking and is where the learner analyzes, evaluates, and engages in problem solving and creative activities.

The activities of the teacher may either enhance or interfere with learning at the various levels. If the teacher limits the experiences for the learner to any one level, or skips over a lower level in an effort to provide experiences at a higher level, learning may be limited or thwarted. In planning lessons, the teacher is advised to present one concept or skill at a time and to treat the lessons as a sequence of learnings leading to some broader objective. The Unit Plan is recommended as a basis for organizing instruction.

The Winnetka Plan

The Winnetka Plan is of historical interest primarily because it represents one of the first comprehensive efforts to individualize classroom instruction. Washburne (35, pp. 247-84) gave credit to Frederic Burk for providing the basis for the Winnetka Plan. Burk's plan in brief was described by Washburne as follows:

1. Write text material simply, concretely, and very clearly, as if it were to be used as correspondence lessons for children. Those "Self-Instruction Bulletins," prepared by Burk's faculty, were the beginning of the modern "work books" and a potent influence in the great improvement of textbooks ever since.
2. Differentiate assignments, providing extra practice for the slow learners who need extra practice.
3. Provide for self-correction of their work by the pupils.

4. Stimulate maximum effort by each child through short periods of intensive work.
5. Let each child's work be individual—each child working on a unit for which he is ready and passing on to the next unit when one unit is complete, regardless of the progress of other children.
6. When a child is ready for the next grade's work in any subject at any time of the year, let him proceed to the next grade's work in that subject, without necessarily changing rooms.
7. Never have a child repeat a grade. If he has not finished a grade's work in June, let him go on in September from where he left off.
8. Have no homework.
9. Supplement individual work with creative and socialized activities— such as art, music, shop, dramatics, and especially "Socratic Discussions" in which children exchange *thinking* on topics, the factual part of which they already know (35, pp. 250-51).

The Winnetka Plan divided the curriculum into two parts, "the common essentials" and "the group and creative activities" (36, p. 15). The common essentials included knowledges and skills which all students must learn—that which are referred to commonly today as "the basic skills" of reading, writing, and arithmetic. "Group and creative activities" included those learnings in which students are expected to have varying competencies and interests, including physical activity, appreciation for art, public speaking, discussion skill, and handicraft skills.

It was assumed that progress in the common essentials was strictly an individual matter and that each child should be allowed to progress at his own rate. The stages in learning the basic skills were carefully delineated, and the student was required to master one phase of work before progressing to the next. The instructional phases were considered to be units of achievement, not units of time. The standards for achievement were the same for all children.

The design for individual instruction consisted of (a) dividing the curriculum into units of achievement, (b) using diagnostic testing procedures to determine when the learner had mastered the material included in each unit and for helping him attain mastery if he failed, and (c) employing "self-instructive, self-corrective practice materials" to full advantage. The units of achievement were identified in terms of specific "goals." "Instead of saying, for example, that a child must learn column addition during third grade, the Winnetka schools say that the child must be able, before leaving third-grade arithmetic, to add columns three digits wide and four digits high at the rate of three in three minutes with one hundred percent accuracy. An effort has been made to define each goal and each of the common essentials with equal definiteness" (36, p. 17). The goals were printed on large cards supplied for each child, and each child's progress was recorded on the cards. In format, the card was not unlike many used in cumulative record files today, except that each card traced the child's progress from goal to goal for each subject at six-week intervals.

Self-Instructional Materials: The self-instructional materials used in the Winnetka schools were developed by classroom teachers. They were tried, revised, and tried again two or three times. A complete set of "mimeographed books" was developed in arithmetic, language, and "history-geography." Reading skills were developed through a program of required reading. For studying spelling, the children were paired off so that one child could dictate words to another.

The self-instructional materials reportedly were written directly to the child as in a correspondence lesson. The child was led step by step gradually to the objective. He mastered each step before progressing to the next. The teacher was available to provide help and encouragement as needed. Occasionally, the teacher worked with small groups or presented a topic to the entire class when there appeared to be general confusion on a specific point. The teacher was considered to be as necessary in the self-instructional program as in any other system of classroom instruction. The practice materials were self-corrective. Each child corrected his own work by comparing his answers with answers in the back of the practice book. However, the daily work was not graded and did not count in the promotion of the child from one unit to the next. The children were oriented to the fact that the six-week tests were the deciding factor in promotions.

The term *grade* in the Winnetka Plan referred to the work units which made up the program of basic instruction ("common essentials"). Thus a single pupil could be working in two or more grades at the same time in different subjects. However, there were restrictions imposed on the child in the Winnetka Plan which prevented him from working at widely divergent levels in different subject areas at the same time. For example, if a pupil's most advanced subject was more than a grade beyond his most retarded one, he was required to drop the most advanced subject temporarily and to spend more time on the one in which he was progressing more slowly. Consequently, it was rare for an individual to be doing work at different levels in more than two grades simultaneously.

Classroom groupings in the basic program of instruction were flexible. A child could be placed in almost any group where he fitted in. In practically every classroom children could be found working at two and sometimes three different levels of work in one or more subjects at almost any time.

Group and Creative Activities: About half of each morning and half of each afternoon were devoted to group and creative activities such as physical education, self-government, discussions, dramatics, and related activities. The rest of each day, of course, was devoted to individual work.

Evaluation of the Winnetka Plan: Washburne claims that Burk's plan was the only feasible one that has ever been recommended and carried out in practice for individualizing classroom instruction. He wrote, "Schools that have tried Burk's plan intelligently have found that it worked, that it saved time, that it reduced retardation, that it made school life happier and more efficient for teacher and pupils, that it actually made possible the recognition of a wide range of individual differences in readiness among children in a given class" (35, p. 251). His conclusions were based on facts reported in the twenty-fourth yearbook of the National Society for the Study of Education (38) and on his own research (36). The reason why such individualized plans had not spread more widely by 1940, Washburne reported, could be attributed to the fact that adequate texts and tests for individual work had not been prepared, to the swing away from subject matter emphasis to the emphasis on the child-centered learning, and to the development of "compromise plans" of ability grouping and group projects in which each child participates according to his own ability.

It is interesting to note that after nearly 40 years, there is a trend back to the subject matter emphasis and planning for individualized instruction which apparently prevailed when the Winnetka Plan was developed. Perhaps now that more adequate self-instructional materials are being made available, Winnetka-type plans will become more widespread.

Olson's Teaching Model

Olson (24) provides a set of concepts and principles which indicates fairly clearly what the teacher should not do, but which suggests little in the way of direct action by the teacher. From a series of longitudinal studies of children, Olson has concluded that the developmental processes of children are highly individualized and are the result of complex forces of nature and the individual's experience. Single measures of an individual's growth tend to cluster in such a manner when transformed to the same scale of measurement that the development of the child as a whole can be indicated by a single measure of central tendency. The single index of a child's development is the average or "central age" called the "organismic age." The components of the organismic age of a child include almost any measurable aspect of the individual's development, including school achievement. Through numerous examples of individual children's growth records, Olson demonstrates that it is always wise to consider the child from the "holistic" view. The major generalizations growing out of his work are the following:

1. Growth has some unity when viewed as a whole.
2. Children differ in rate and level of growth.
3. Growth through time is an individual matter.
4. Children differ in the pattern of growth of the various components that are measured.
5. Familial resemblance appears in all measurements.
6. It is difficult to change growth patterns in a substantial fashion by conscious environmental manipulation.
7. Children tend to attain the mature status of the species and the family at different ages (24, pp. 221-22).

From these generalizations, Olson develops a "philosophy of growth" which, when applied to the growing child, says, "Each child is to be assisted in growing according to his natural design, without deprivation or forcing, in an environment and by a process which also supply a social direction to his achievement" (24, p. 449). Although he does not offer a detailed plan, Olson does provide the teacher with a body of research evidence and a set of guidelines which have implications for classroom instruction.

Instructional Design Requirements

The sections which follow will develop the basis for a programing procedure that attempts to build on the strengths of the five instructional plans identified at the beginning of this chapter and to transcend their weaknesses.

Teaching Complex Instructional Objectives

The most outstanding characteristic of the plans and procedures outlined above is the "broad brush" treatment given the specification of instructional objectives. Interestingly enough, the plan which places most stress on detailing the instructional objectives is also the oldest —the Winnetka Plan. Unless objectives are stated in behavioral terms, the known principles of behavioral science cannot be applied with precision. It is not uncommon for self-instructional programs to begin with a prediction regarding the learner's peformance when he has completed the program. By contrast, conventional lessons prepared according to the Unit Plan rarely begin with more than a very general statement of the kind of learning the teacher hopes will result. For example, the following is a list of objectives included in a lesson plan prepared by a junior high school teacher for the first two lessons in a unit on combustion.

1. To develop problem-solving skills.
2. To understand the scientific method.
3. To develop skills in using scientific apparatus, and in measurement.
4. To develop understanding of theory of combustion.
5. To learn to interpret and evaluate data (27, p. 166).

If the lesson were outlined for a self-instructional program, the instructor would probably not be so generous in the statement of objectives. Instead, the objectives might read somewhat as follows: When you (the learner) have completed this program, you will be able to—

1. Tell one way that a scientist might attempt to answer the question, "What is necessary for combustion?"
2. Demonstrate how water can be made to boil in a dish made of paper, without burning the paper.
3. State several hypotheses (guesses) as to why the paper will not burn in the demonstration.
4. Conduct experiments to determine which hypothesis is correct.

5. Tell how a scientist might explain the results of the experiments which you have conducted.
6. Tell how the findings of your experiments might be put to practical use.

The point of the comparison in teaching objectives is not to criticize conventional practice. Rather it is to determine whether or not self-instructional programing should be limited in application to specific instructional objectives. As stated previously, it is presumed by many educators that there is a point beyond which self-instructional materials are inadequate and more conventional classroom instructional techniques are required. Specifically, it was suggested that more conventional techniques of instruction are required when such complex processes as problem solving and reasoning are involved.

The first list of objectives referred to above includes some that would be considered very complex, such as skill in problem solving and the ability to interpret and evaluate data. When restated in behavioral terms, these become very much more specific, but no less complex. A student must have some problem-solving ability to be able to state several hypotheses about the boiling-water-in-a-paper-dish demonstration; and he must know how to interpret data himself in order to tell how a scientist would interpret data. Actually, even the more specifically stated behavioral objectives fail to specify the complex behavioral processes involved in forming hypotheses and interpreting data. Are self-instructional programing techniques sufficient to teach such complex intellectual skills as these?

The Adequacy of Self-Instructional Programs: Research indicates that it is extremely difficult to teach complex intellectual skills effectively by any method (see 3, 20, 22, 32, 37). Buswell (7) found that even such simple skills as estimating answers to arithmetic problems and distinguishing relevant from irrelevant data have not been mastered by many learners, even at the college level. Resnick (26) suggests that previous attempts to teach complex intellectual skills may have been ineffective because the behavioral components of such skills have never been clearly identified and because techniques for shaping up discriminations and for establishing stimulus control are not yet perfected.

It is conceivable that complex intellectual skills which can be clearly identified and discriminated by the learner (such as "withholding judgment" and "testing hypotheses") might be effectively shaped by self-instructional techniques because the learner could easily evaluate his own performance according to printed instructions. Also the reinforcing effect of "checking further" and "testing ideas" is often immediate. But, what about those complex intellectual skills for which the behaviors involved have not been specified, or which are difficult to distinguish from other behaviors, or for which the reinforcing effects are delayed?

Consider, for example, the complex behavior sometimes called "forming hypotheses." Hanson (14) has written an extremely penetrating account of this process of thinking. In formulating hypotheses, a person typically works from evidence regarding a particular phenomenon in an attempt to explain the phenomenon. Hanson refers to this process as "working from *explicanda* to *explicans*" (14, p. 85). A simple example of working from *explicanda* to *explicans* is illustrated by the task of discovering an "easy way" to sum a series of odd numbers beginning with one. Working with several series as concrete examples (e.g., $1 + 3 + 5 + 7 = 16$), a learner may ascertain that the sum is given by squaring the number of integers in the series. A more complex example is Hanson's account of Johannes Kepler's efforts to explain the collection of observations of Mars's orbit compiled by Tycho Brahe. In Hanson's words:

Kepler did not *begin* with the hypothesis that Mars' orbit was elliptical and then deduce statements confirmed by Brahe's observations. These latter observations were given, and they set the problem—they were Johannes Kepler's starting point. He struggled back from these, first to one hypothesis, then to another, then to another, and ultimately to the hypothesis of the elliptical orbit. Few detailed accounts have been given by philosophers of science of Kepler's achievements, although his discovery of Mars' orbit is physical thinking at its best. The philosopher of physics should not neglect what Peirce calls the finest retroduction ever made (14, pp. 72-73).

Another description of what is interpreted as being the same type of complex behavior is given by Duncker (8, p. 29): "In the course of a solution-process, the 'emphasis-relief' of the situation, its 'figure-ground' relief, for example, is restructured. . . . Parts and elements of the situation which, psychologically speaking, were either hardly in existence or remained in the background—unthematic—suddenly emerge, become the main point, the theme, the 'figure.' Of course, the reverse also happens."

Duncker refers to such changes as "restructurations." He considers the formulation of a "model of search" as a special case of such restructuration. Such descriptions may be meaningful to those who may have developed some degree of competency in forming hypotheses, but for the novice they probably communicate very little. The point is, it is difficult to describe such complex behavior as hypothesis formation in general terms.

Although it is difficult to describe hypothesis formation, it has been the experience of this present writer that it is not difficult to determine when a learner is attempting to formulate a hypothesis in a given problematic situation. In a recently completed research project (20), trained observers demonstrated remarkable agreement in their efforts to identify the occurrence of such behavior from verbal reports and written notes that the learners made as they attempted to ascertain a principle from a set of examples of the principle. In other words, although it may be difficult to verbalize in general terms the behavioral components of "hypothesis formation," examples of such behavior can be pointed out from among examples of behavior which are not representative. By analogy, it may be difficult to describe the concept of a "chair" (or "chairness"), yet not difficult to identify examples.

Since it is relatively easy to learn to recognize examples of "forming hypotheses" in the behavior of others, it should be possible for an individual to learn to recognize such behavior in himself as well. Persons who are in the process of learning to formulate hypotheses would have to undergo discrimination training at first, and this poses a problem to programers of self-instructional materials. The programing problems are probably not insurmountable, however. Conceivably, self-instructional techniques could be developed whereby a student could first be taught to discriminate examples of hypothesis-forming behavior from examples of other classes of behavior, then to recognize from his own behavior when he is forming hypotheses more or less adequately. By successively approximating the desired behavior and refining the distinctions between heuristic behavior and behavior which does not readily lead to solutions, perhaps the learner could attain the instructional objective. The most difficult problem would be that as the learner progressed, the distinctions undoubtedly would become increasingly more difficult, and the delays in reinforcement of "effective" behavior would increase. These problems are challenging to many who are researching instructional problems.

Employing the Unique Capabilities of a Teacher: Although programed self-instructional materials may prove adequate to teach most instructional objectives, they may not be the most effective way to teach all objectives—particularly those which involve complex behaviors. Perhaps the unique capability of a human instructor should be capitalized on to identify, elicit, and reinforce complex behavior in others. In addition to helping the learner make difficult distinctions, the human instructor could interact with a learner while the learner is engrossed in a problem-solving activity. It has been demonstrated in experiments that while a learner is engaged in a problem-solving task, a teacher can offer "encouragement" by making comments such as "you're doing fine" or "keep going" without interrupting the learner (e.g., 7, 18). Reasonably, the teacher would offer such encouragement only while the learner is employing some approximation of the criterion behavior. When the learner is not behaving in a way which is considered desirable (e.g., when the learner is unnecessarily rigid in that he employs a limited "search model" without deviation or begins "thinking in circles"), the human instructor could "cue" the learner by making such suggestions as "think broadly" or "can you think of another possible way?" Such procedures for cueing a learner so as to effectively "shape" his heuristic behavior without breaking the continuity of the learner's complex behavior have been studied by researchers interested in "discovery" and "inquiry" as a learning process (e.g., 1, 4, 12, 20, 21, 32, 39). Fortunately, many experienced teachers are capable of doing this effectively and would need only a little more training to be able to cue a learner precisely as an instructional designer or experimenter might dictate. Increasingly more effective techniques for training teachers in such interaction skills are under development (see 9, 19, 33).

It may be argued by some that the difficulties of employing self-instructional techniques to teach such complex intellectual skills are overshadowed by the teacher-training and financial problems involved in providing individualized instruction to learners on a wide scale. There can be little doubt that for some time to come education will be faced with the limitations of classroom instruction and inexperienced instructors operating with outdated instructional tools. One way to resolve this dilemma would be to develop a method of programing which would prescribe learning sequences for classroom (grouped) instruction just as carefully as they are for self-instruction. By using the materials as prescribed, even poorly trained teachers could be effective. Such programs of classroom instruction could incorporate the unique capabilities of the human instructor for interacting with learners individually or in small groups while appropriate instructional media effectively "teach" others in the group. This suggestion is developed more fully in sections which follow.

Two Kinds of Instructional Objectives: It was argued above that although it is certainly possible to teach some very complex instructional objectives by self-instructional techniques, the instructional requirements for some complex behaviors are such that they could be learned more readily with direct teacher guidance. Hereafter, instructional objectives will be classified in two categories: (a) as being amenable to "automatic" or self-instruction and (b) as being most readily attained through "human" instruction.

Instructional objectives which are most readily attained through human instruction may be distinguished from those which are amenable to automatic or self-instruction by identifying their instructional requirements. For example, assistance from another person may be required in the attainment of an instructional objective for any one or more of the following reasons:

1. The required behavior cannot be identified by machine processes presently available or by the learner himself without previous instruction.

2. The required behavior cannot be reliably elicited except through direct or indirect intercommunication with another person who is capable of identifying the required behavior once it has been elicited.

3. The learner cannot determine that he is making progress toward the instructional objective by independently comparing his own behavior against a behavioral standard or model.

Usually instructional objectives which involve the attainment of factual knowledge, concepts, principles, or even psychomotor skills will be amenable to automatic or self-instruction. Objectives which are most readily attained through human instruction will usually involve patterns of behavior occurring at unpredictable intervals and reflecting "mediational" processes. Examples of the second class of objectives will probably include what Duncker (8) calls formulating or restructuring problems during the problem-solving process and what was identified above as hypothesis formation or "retroductive reasoning" (see 14, p. 85). Of course, involved in such complex behaviors as reformulating problems and forming hypotheses are many other behaviors (or behavioral tendencies) which have been variously described as "shifting," "searching for patterns," and "being flexible."

In the past the present writer, for convenience, has referred to those objectives which could be described as being amenable to automatic or self-instruction as "simple" objectives and to those which call for human instruction as "complex." However, it has become evident that such terms as "simple" and "complex" objectives may be misleading. For example, behavioral scientists tend to equate "complex instructional objectives" with "complex behaviors," when apparently many complex behaviors may be taught effectively by self-instructional techniques (30).

"Compounded" Objectives: Public school teachers today do not often limit themselves to teaching one thing at a time. If they wish to teach some computational skill in arithmetic, for instance, they also concern themselves with such "by-products" of learning as the attitudes of their students toward arithmetic; if they wish to teach theory of combustion, they are also concerned with "understanding scientific method" and "skill in problem solving." Even if teachers were satisfied to deal with a single objective at a time, psychologists would remind them that they must not only consider the objective from the standpoint of immediate learning, but also they should give consideration to the maintenance and subsequent use (transfer) of the new learning. It is one thing to predict that the learner will be able to say something or do something that he is presently unable to do after completing the instruction, and something else to say that the learner will want to continue using it and will use it to good advantage in a great variety of appropriate situations. As was illustrated in the previous example of the ninth-grade lesson on combustion, a single unit of instruction may include some objectives which can be taught through

automatic or self-instructional techniques and other objectives which may call for human instruction. When this is the case, the instruction will be said to involve multiple or compounded objectives.

Each of the conventional plans and procedures reviewed above recognizes that both group and individualized teaching methods may be used effectively in the classroom. The Winnetka Plan actually organized the curriculum into individual and grouped instruction, but the two types of instruction were separated. Classes organized for self-study were held at one time and group-paced classes at another. Furthermore, Winnetka procedures for designing grouped instruction were not so clearly established as those for individualized instruction. This lack of clarity in procedure is exactly what is of primary concern in this present chapter, especially as it pertains to a procedure for designing and programing new instructional procedures. Woodruff's principles provide the basis for an effective design procedure because they are explicit even to the point of presuming that all children learn by the same process, differing only in rate of learning. This last assumption is very convenient from the programing standpoint. However, Woodruff's directions for actually building a lesson are not much more explicit than those provided by other authors under the Unit Plan. Each of the other plans reviewed above has similar shortcomings.

A new procedure is needed which will incorporate the techniques employed in developing automated self-instructional programs in the design and development of classroom instructional systems.

Automated Classrooms

The human being is far superior to any man-made device in searching for and identifying patterns and in making decisions. Consequently, most military and industrial systems involve both men and machines. From the engineering standpoint, man is frequently employed only as a practical expedient, not because the task he performs cannot be automated. When this is the case, the man-machine system sometimes suffers because man is an unreliable creature when "misused." Most often, however, the engineer employs a human because he has unique capabilities which cannot easily be duplicated. Man has the advantage of being lightweight, flexible, mobile, and completely independent. The fact that man is still accustomed to pilot complex air and spacecraft which are controlled to a great extent from ground stations illustrates this point.

For almost the same reasons, instructional systems designed to teach compounded instructional objectives will have to be man-machine systems. Ideally, these instructional man-machine systems should have the capability for individualizing instruction or employing group-paced techniques, as is possible, for example, in the System Development Corporation CLASS facility (6). Briefly, CLASS is an automated classroom using a Philco S-2000 computer as the central control mechanism. CLASS permits instruction through a variety of different media, including motion pictures and television. There is a visual display on the wall and at each student's desk. Each student receives an individualized sequence of instructional materials through a manually operated film viewer containing 2,000 frames of instructional materials. A response device, linked to the computer, tells the student which frame to turn to, enables the student to respond to questions, and presents knowledge of results. The computer keeps track of the performance of all students and makes these records available to the teacher. The teacher could have displayed the current progress of any student or group of students at any time during the instructional process period. Figure 1 shows more of the details in CLASS.

Another automated classroom of the type required for programed classroom instruction is represented by the Teaching Research Automated Classroom (TRAC) facility at Oregon College of Education. TRAC combines three instructional systems to equip the teacher with the capability for providing individualized feedback to students through light signals, for collating student responses to a single stimulus question or problem, for remotely controlling a motion picture projector, slide projector, overhead transparency projector (all on a single rear-projection screen), and for operating a tape recorder and voice amplifier. The room is also equipped with open and closed circuit TV receivers. Figure 2 pictures the TRAC system from the instructor's position. The Edling Teacher Console, one of the three systems comprising TRAC, is the desk unit with overhead screen for the various projectors housed in the desk. The second system is the Teletest Communication System which consists of the response units at each student position and the small teacher's console on the desk. The third system is the EDEX, the larger console to the right of the instructor in Figure 2. Such systems are available commercially and do not require additional control equipment or special power outlets. Of course, individualized instruction is limited in TRAC because it lacks

FIGURE 1.   *The CLASS facility is an automated classroom developed for research purposes by System Development Corporation. The instructor, Harry
F. Silberman, is seated in front of the class operating controls to the computer
which provides him with detailed information regarding student progress.
Students are responding to self-instructional materials by pushing buttons
on the consoles in front of them. Their responses serve as inputs to the computer system which, in turn, instructs the students to go ahead, branch, or
take some other action on an individual basis.*

a computer-based data processing system. Such individualized instruction could be provided through available self-instructional programed materials and devices, however. Another limitation of TRAC
is that the burden on the teacher of recordkeeping, storing, and retrieval still remains.

The primary advantage of such classrooms is that instruction can
be automated whenever it is appropriate, and the human instructor
can concentrate on those instructional processes which require his
unique competencies. When the teacher is free from any direct concern for displaying materials and providing instructions, he can
attend to whether or not individual students are employing "search"
behavior, shifting in their approach to problems and making effective
use of technical notation. He can deal directly with these complex
behaviors on an individual or a group basis, even while the students

FIGURE 2.   *The Teaching Research Automated Classroom (TRAC) is located on the Oregon College of Education campus in one of the Teaching Research Laboratories of the Oregon State System of Higher Education. The various projectors housed in the desk unit and a classroom communications system are controlled automatically by the EDEX system to the right of the instructor, Jack H. Bond.*

are in the process of learning something else by automated instruction.

In the automated classroom the disadvantages of group instruction are minimized. Problems associated with individual differences in learning rate or interest can be handled either by assigning individualized self-instructional materials or by grouping. Since permanent records of the individual's performance can be made and class summaries are more immediately available to the teacher, the teacher may employ more precise criteria for grouping and for scheduling the learner's experience. For example, since the teacher has the capability for determining exact proportions of the group who are responding correctly at each step of the way, he may employ such criteria as would read, "branch to review sequence if 95 percent of class fails to respond correctly after five frames," or "continue to next lesson when all class members respond correctly to three practice exercises in succession." This capability will be described in greater detail in another section of this chapter.

Methodology

Whereas conventional instruction places greatest emphasis on the use of materials, the modern instructional system should place emphasis on their development. The design of instruction in the classroom should become more technical and less artistic. At best, present-day classroom instruction is an attempt to attain ill-defined objectives through imprecise methods. It amounts to leading others in the pursuit of shadows along an unmarked pathway.

The attainment of compounded instructional objectives requires the capabilities of an automated classroom. Otherwise, the teacher would be taxed beyond his ability in the attempt to control the experiences of the learners. To reduce the burden on the teacher and to allow him to concentrate on those activities which require human guidance, a systematically developed set of instructional materials and validated procedure also must be available.

The complexity of designing and programing classroom instruction exceeds that of self-instructional programing. In self-instructional programing, the development of materials may usually follow directly from the statement of objectives. By following any one of several existing procedures, such as "ruleg" and "mathetics," and by incorporating more specific techniques pertaining to individual frame writing and sequencing, such as "vanishing" and "cueing," the programer typically may start composing frames immediately. These programing procedures and techniques are reviewed elsewhere (29). At best, such procedures are checklists which permit the programer to make a careful accounting of the various kinds of items included in his program. The techniques recommended by Gilbert, Barlow, Homme, and Glaser (29, pp. 96-99), for example, employ a matrix method or a coding technique for classifying items while the program is under construction and later when it is being refined.

While existing procedures may be adequate for programing objectives one at a time, in the experience of the present writer they have not been adaptable to programing multiple or compounded objectives. In dealing with compounded objectives, the programer must concern himself with two or more processes which will be operating at once in about the same fashion as a composer of music in developing a symphonic score. The essential characteristics of such a methodology would appear to be the following:

1. It should provide a notation and charting technique with which the programer can prepare in advance a detailed outline of the learning experience in terms of practice and reinforcement schedules, branching criteria, and related characteristics, without attending to the specifics of frame writing.

2. It should outline a procedure for preparing a basic program aimed at objectives which are amenable to automated instruction and then for "weaving in" programs involving human instruction, or vice versa. It should be possible to maintain one part of the over-all program intact (e.g., the basic program) while changing another part (e.g., that pertaining to the human instructor). In this way, different processes of learning could be employed simultaneously in a single program, or a single program could be systematically altered for purposes of research and development.

3. The methodology should enable the programer to deal separately with problems of program design, frame writing, and materials development so that these operations can be accomplished by different individuals concurrently.

In other words, it should be possible for an expert in human learning and a subject matter specialist to prepare an advanced outline of the learning process independently of the programer and materials development specialist. The special competencies required of a program writer should be distinguished from those required of the materials development specialist. In preparing standardized tests, the item writer is not required to develop the format for the test, to prepare the finished line drawings or diagrams that may be involved, or necessarily to try out the test materials in preparation for their revision.

An Example: the TRAC Procedure

One example of a methodology which meets the requirements specified above was developed in connection with a research project supported by a grant from the U.S. Office of Education (20). The plan is referred to simply as the TRAC procedure, because it was developed in connection with the TRAC facility. As is the case in most technological developments, the TRAC procedure consists of a new combination of existing procedures. The first step in the procedure follows the example of Gagné (11), and subsequent steps are applications of already familiar flow-charting methods employed in computer programing.

The following steps outline the procedure as it was used in the development of an instructional unit having six objectives, some of which were amenable to automatic instruction and others to human instruction.[1] The instructional procedure was designed for use in the TRAC facility, but it might also be adapted for use in other automated instructional facilities. The instruction program differs from conventional self-instructional programs in that it is group-paced, and a teacher is required to control the learning experience. The instructional materials include tape-recorded instructions, projections of problems and examples, and prepared worksheets for the learners. The instructional program employed the principles of instruction, terminology, and notation employed in the UICSM curriculum. It was designed for use at the fifth-grade level.

Step 1. Specification of Objectives in Terms of Both Content and Process

In the preparation of the instructional materials for the research project referred to above, consideration was given not only to the content objective (knowledge of the distributive law) but also to the attainment of some rather complex behaviors which might be called "interest," "transfer," and "discovery processes." The latter were written as specific instructional objectives. Specifically, the instructional program was planned and developed so that the learner, when through, would be able to do the following:

1. Specify that numerals put into the frames will always make this "open sentence" true:

$$(\triangle \times \square) + (\bigcirc \times \square) = (\triangle + \bigcirc) \times \square$$

[1] Credit for the development of the original unit of materials belongs to Vern D. Hiebert, assistant professor of mathematics, Oregon College of Education. Mrs. Cordelia A. Moritz, formerly assistant professor of mathematics at OCE, was the programer, and Jack H. Bond, research specialist, Teaching Research Division, Oregon State System of Higher Education, was the materials development specialist.

2. Specify that numerals put into the frames will *not* always make this open sentence true:

$$(\triangle + \square) \times (\bigcirc + \square) = (\triangle \times \bigcirc) + \square$$

3. Without instructions from the teacher (T), use the distributive law or related information after the formal learning period.

4. Without instructions from T, in a task employing a different principle and new examples, employ the same discovery processes taught in the original learning.

5. After initial learning, correctly identify examples of the distributive law from among examples of other numerical operations.

6. After initial learning, correctly employ the distributive law in the regrouping of numerals in mathematical sentences to form simpler sentences.

Note that the first two objectives involve knowledge or subject matter objectives. The third objective specifies behavior which is indicative of interest in the task; the fourth indicates transfer of "discovery processes." The last two objectives indicate the learner's ability to remember and apply what he learned. Which of these objectives should be taught automatically and which with human instruction is determined in subsequent steps described below.

Step. 2. Preparation of a Hierarchy of Subordinate Facts and Processes

This technique is modeled after Gagné (11). The procedure differs in that both complex behavioral processes and knowledge are dealt with as "ultimate" objectives. According to Gagné, the tasks to be learned in the acquisition of knowledge may be identified by working backward from the final task. The question is asked, "What would an individual have to know in order to perform this task successfully?" The answer to this question reveals subordinate knowledge which the individual must have in order to obtain the ultimate objective. The subordinate knowledge is presumably simpler and probably more general. This subordinate knowledge is again subjected to the question, "What does one have to know in order to achieve this?" And still more subordinate knowledge is revealed in the answer. By continuing this questioning procedure and working backward from the ultimate objective, a hierarchy of subordinate knowledge is established. In the end, the final content objective is seen to rest on a framework of subordinate knowledge which becomes increasingly more simple and more general.

So much for the acquisition of knowledge. What about the acquisition of such complex behaviors as those specified in the objectives listed above which involve motivational effects, discovery processes, and transfer? Gagné recommends that this be done by manipulating the programed "instructions" which determine the sequence of experiences, the criteria for determining the learner's route at choice points, and so forth. He has reported some attempts to study the effects of instructions designed to insure high recall ability of subordinate knowledge and to guide the learner's thinking (11).

The essential change which is made in Gagné's method is to identify clearly the complex behaviors (e.g., motivational effects, discovery processes, and transfer effects) which one wishes to teach and to deal with them independently of (but concurrently with) the knowledge which is to be acquired. The subordinate knowledge which must be acquired is identified by asking what the learner must *know* (after Gagné), and the subordinate learning processes are identified by asking what the learner must *do*. Consider, for example, the six instructional objectives listed under Step 1, above. The breakdown of the six objectives into subordinate facts and learning processes is shown in Figure 3. Some of the subordinate facts and processes for the six ultimate objectives are combined as they are under Objectives 1, 2, and 4. The other objectives in this case must be outlined separately as they are for Objectives 3, 5, and 6 in Figure 3.

For now, the reader's attention is directed to the breakdown for Objective 3. It requires that the learner generate enough interest in the distributive law to use it after the formal learning period without instructions to do so. What must the learner do to develop this interest? The answer is written in the four smaller boxes labeled 18, 19, 20, and 21. These subordinate process statements specify that the learner should employ subordinate knowledge in discovering higher-level tasks repeatedly, with the knowledge of results, on a schedule in which the teacher's instructions are gradually withdrawn and with approval provided intermittently, regardless of the learner's success or failure.

Objective 4, the "transfer of discovery process" objective in Figure 3, is combined with the "knowledge" objectives (Objectives 1 and 2).

Clearly it is a higher level of learning than the knowledge objectives and probably should be classed as a "learning set," but it rests on a framework of specific knowledge as indicated. The "discovery processes" employed by the learners are not precisely stated in Figure 3 primarily because, as with the example of "forming hypotheses" discussed previously, the behaviors involved cannot be adequately described in general terms. Instead, the instructors learned to identify examples of the complex behavior in the context of standardized instructional and test situations. For example, "frames" (e.g., $\square$, $\triangle$, $\bigcirc$) are used in the UICSM notation instead of more conventional algebraic symbols (e.g., x, y, z) in writing abstract mathematical expressions. All learners were taught how to use frames. However, "using frames" also referred to a specific and somewhat complex behavior which was classified as a "discovery process." When learning by discovery, a student may be given a set of mathematical statements such as the following:

$$3 + 3 = 2 \times 3$$
$$5 + 5 = 2 \times 5$$
$$8 + 8 = 2 \times 8$$

Then the student might be asked to determine whether or not each is an example of the same general law. If while trying to determine the correct answer the learner is observed to use frames in an effort to reduce the three examples to a single abstract expression (e.g., $\triangle + \triangle = 2 \times \triangle$), he is said to be "using frames" as a discovery process.

Step 3. Preparation of Flow Charts for Each Subordinate Fact and Process

Next, the instructional program was designed using flow charts. The flow charts were prepared for each of the subordinate facts and processes. A special notation was developed to indicate specific teaching operations so that the detailed instructions and materials could be completed by another person without consultation with the person preparing the flow charts. Some of the special notation is indicated in Figure 4. As is indicated, whenever the instructional program was to provide instructions to the learner (as if from a teacher), a square box was employed. Whenever there were problems or examples to be worked by the learners, they were indicated in a diamond-shaped box. Since the progress of the learners beyond a set of problems was

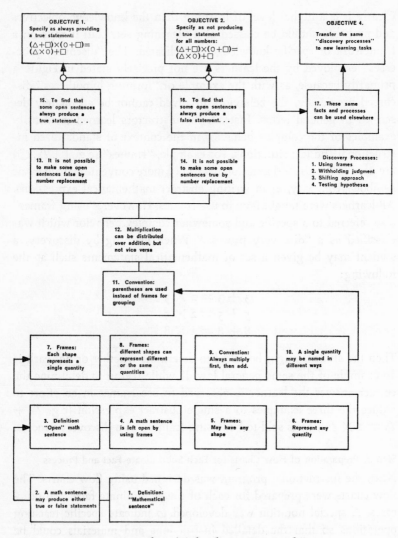

FIGURE 3. *Hierarchy of Subordinate Facts and Processes.*

usually determined by their performance with the problems, additional notation is included. For example, such notation as "3(1.0+)" was used to indicate that the examples were to be continued until the class as a whole achieved three problems in succession correctly. A less stringent criterion would be indicated by the notation, "3(.75+)."

Using the special notation, it was possible to outline for the pro-

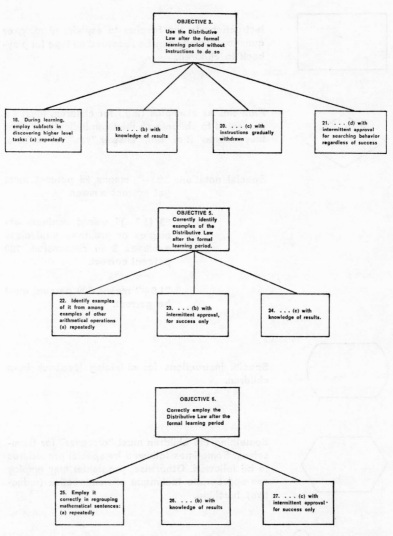

(FIGURE 3 *continued. Hierarchy of Subordinate Facts and Processes.*)

gramer the essential characteristics of the instructional program in sufficient detail for him to carry on independently. In practice, the subordinate facts were charted first. Each was handled separately, without particular regard for the programing requirements as spelled out by the process statements. The person doing the flow charting operated with the knowledge that he could alter the flow chart quite

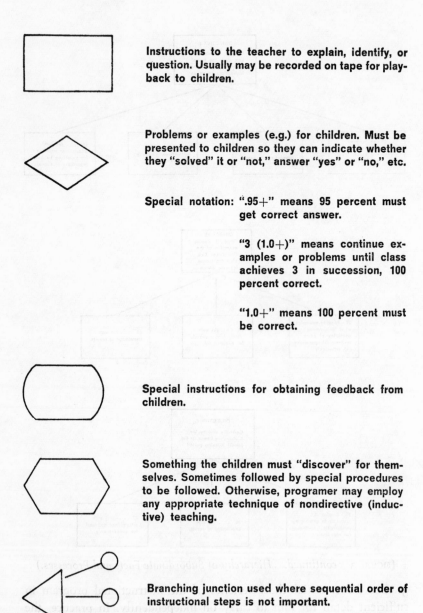

Instructions to the teacher to explain, identify, or question. Usually may be recorded on tape for play-back to children.

Problems or examples (e.g.) for children. Must be presented to children so they can indicate whether they "solved" it or "not," answer "yes" or "no," etc.

Special notation: ".95+" means 95 percent must get correct answer.

"3 (1.0+)" means continue ex-amples or problems until class achieves 3 in succession, 100 percent correct.

"1.0+" means 100 percent must be correct.

Special instructions for obtaining feedback from children.

Something the children must "discover" for them-selves. Sometimes followed by special procedures to be followed. Otherwise, programer may employ any appropriate technique of nondirective (induc-tive) teaching.

Branching junction used where sequential order of instructional steps is not important.

FIGURE 4.   *Examples of Flow-Chart Notation.*

simply according to the subordinate process requirements after he
had prepared the outlines for each of the subordinate facts. For example, subfact 10 in the list of subordinate objectives (see Figure 3)
specifies that the learners know that a single quantity may be named
in many different ways (e.g., the quantity 10 may be referred to as
"5 + 5," "6 + 4," or simply "10"). Without regard for any of the

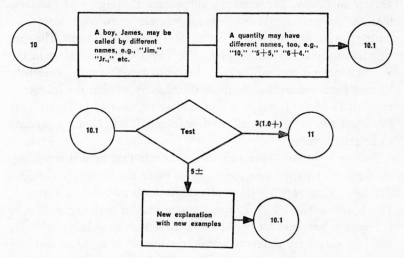

FIGURE 5.   *Plan A for Subfact 10, "A Single Quantity May Be Written
Different Ways."*

process statements, and following an established rule-example technique, the flow chart could be drawn first as shown in Figure 5. The
flow chart should be read from left to right starting with circle 10
(subfact 10).

The first box indicates to the programer that the instruction should
start with an example concerning a boy with several names. The next
box indicates that, by analogy, the rule is to be established that a
quantity such as 10 may be referred to in a number of different ways
including "5 + 5," and "6 + 4." At circle 10.1 (simply a location
point or connecting link), the flow chart moves to a diamond-shaped
frame which indicates that the program should follow with a test. The
notation "3(1.0+)" specifies that the learners should continue with
the test until they achieve three examples in succession correctly. The
notation "5±" specifies that should the learners fail to achieve the

criterion after five examples, the program should return them to a new explanation of subfact 10 and then test them again. Circle 11 indicates that when the learners pass the test they are to go to subfact 11.

After the subfacts were charted, the program "designer" turned his attention to the subordinate process statements. Instead of being flow charted, they were reduced to specific instructions for the pro-gramer to follow. For example, subprocess 18 (Figure 3) indicates that the learner should employ subordinate knowledge repeatedly during the learning process in discovering higher-level tasks. The spe-cific instructions tell the programer to identify every subfact in the instructional process which may be "discovered" using previously learned facts and to rewrite them if necessary so that the learner is required to do so. It happens that subfact 10, charted in Figure 5, is one which can be "discovered" and, written as it is in Figure 5, it needs to be rewritten.

Having identified subfact 10 among others that needed rewriting, the flow-chart writer then proceeded to make the necessary changes. The new "discovery" version of subfact 10 is outlined in Figure 6. This second version, Plan B, appears to be similar in design to Plan A in Figure 5, but there are two changes. First, instead of being told that numbers may have different names, the learner is asked to discover some other names for numbers. How this is to be done is indicated in the hexagon. Specifically, the learner is "cued" with subordinate knowledge learned previously ("mathematical sentences," "open sen-tences," and "frames"). For example, the learner knows from previous instruction that "$10 = \Box + \Box$" is an open sentence which can pro-duce either a true or a false mathematical statement when the boxes are replaced with numerals. He knows that any numeral can be used to replace the box so long as it is the same for both boxes. So when asked, "Are there names for 10?" and then shown open sentences such as those in the hexagon, the learner may more easily ascertain the cor-rect answer.

Second, in accordance with subprocess 21 (Figure 3), the flow chart indicates that the teacher should circulate among the learners, giving approval intermittently for their efforts to ascertain that 10 may have other names. It is at this point that the teacher is performing a task which cannot be automated. The teacher must discriminate between student behaviors which are indicative of "problem solving" or

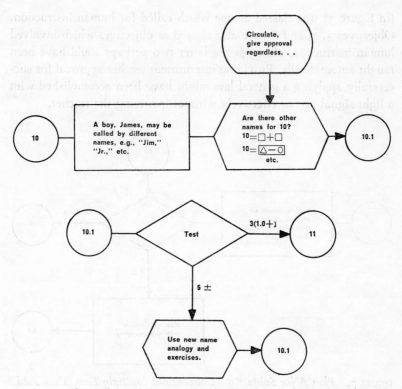

FIGURE 6. *Plan B for Subfact 10, "A Single Quantity May Be Written in Different Ways."*

"searching" and those which indicate that a learner is otherwise occupied. The teachers first must be shown examples of these complex behaviors and supervised during the first hours of instruction. Thereafter, it is not difficult for a skilled teacher to identify such complex behaviors without assistance.

It is the instructional designer ultimately who must determine whether an instructional objective calls for human instruction or can be automated. His decision is based partly on scientific principles or a theory of instruction and partly on the capabilities of the instructional system involved. For example, with the TRAC system, knowledge of results can be provided by a light signal directly to each learner, but these light signals are certainly not adequate for cueing a learner as he is attempting to discover a higher level task. Human instruction is called for in this case. For this reason Objective 4 (in Figure 3) was classed as one which called for human instruction. Objectives 3, 5, and 6 were also classed as objectives which involved human instruction, although the latter two perhaps could have been taught automatically. Providing intermittent teacher approval for successfully applying a general law might have been accomplished with a light signal just as effectively without involving the teacher.

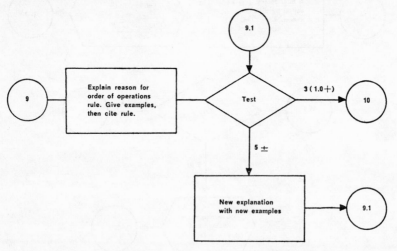

FIGURE 7. *Plan A for Subfact 9, "Convention: Multiply First, Then Add."*

Figures 7 and 8 illustrate two different plans for still another subordinate objective which can be learned through discovery or by other methods. Subfact 9 is the conventional order of operations (multiply first, then add). Typically, in the UICSM materials, students are not required to "discover" a convention; however, in the design of the present instructional materials, it was decided that the learners should have the experience of "discovering" that there is need for such a convention before being told the convention.

Plan A for subfact 9 (which is not the discovery plan) is outlined in Figure 7. The first box in the flow chart indicates that a teacher (or tape) first should explain to the student the reason for the order of operations rule, then give examples, and, finally, cite the rule. Next, the diamond indicates that a test should be given which continues until all learners answer three problems in a row correctly. Having reached the criterion, the flow chart indicates that the program should

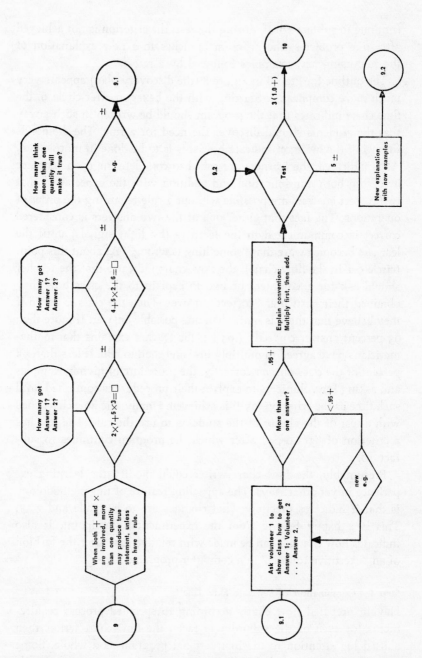

FIGURE 8. *Plan B for Subfact 9, "Convention: Multiply First, Then Add."*

continue to subfact 10. If, during the test, the criterion is not achieved after five problems, the program branches to a new explanation of the rule using new examples followed by a retest.

The outline for Plan B in Figure 8 (the discovery plan) appears very much more complicated. Starting with the hexagon after circle 9, the flow chart indicates that the program should be written in such a way that the students should discover the need for a rule. The diamonds following the hexagon indicate how this is to be done in more detail. As is indicated, the learners are asked to complete the open sentence involving both multiplication and addition with the expectation that two correct answers are possible without a rule regarding the order of operations. The fact that either one of the two answers is considered correct is communicated to the learners (by light signals) until the learners become aware that "something is wrong." At about this point (circle 9.1 in the flow chart), the flow chart indicates that the teacher should ask for a volunteer or two to explain to the class how they obtained their particular "correct" answer. Then the class is asked if they believe that there is more than one possible answer. If more than 95 percent answer correctly (.95+), the teacher explains that mathematicians have agreed to multiply first and then to add. If less than 95 percent of the class answer correctly, the procedure of giving examples and asking for volunteers to explain their procedure is continued until such time as the criterion .95+ is achieved. Finally, the flow chart ends with a test of the ability of the students to use the rule. The test has a criterion of "3(1.0+)" after which the program continues to subfact 10.

Presumably, the flow-chart writer could modify the learning experience in yet other ways. The appealing feature of this methodology is that it indicates precisely what changes are to be made and why. This is a happy feature from the experimental standpoint. It also indicates how changes can be made with relative ease after the fashion of an "executive routine" in a computer program.

Step 4. Combination of Separate Flow Charts

Having prepared flow charts according to specified process requirements for each of the subordinate facts, the flow-chart writer then shifted his attention to the instructional program as a whole. Some process statements can be applied only from the perspective of a single continuous program of instruction. For example, subprocess 20 specifies that instructions from the teacher (program) be withdrawn gradually. More detailed instructions to the programer specify that the instructional procedure for each of the "discovery" frames (hexagons) in the flow chart be examined to determine that more help (cues) is given to the learner in the beginning stages of the program than at the end. For example, in the actual program for subfact 10 (Figure 6), the learner is helped with frames and symbols in his efforts to answer the question, "Are there other names for 10?" If the same question were asked toward the end of the program, these cues would not be provided. Instead the learners would be expected to employ frames spontaneously. Since the discovery frames are clearly identified in the flow chart and the programing instructions are specific, this task is much easier for the programer than it otherwise might be.

Another place where the "over-all look" is required is in connection with the programer's attempt to insure that subordinate knowledge is immediately accessible to memory. To insure that information learned at the beginning of the instructional experience is remembered, the combined flow chart for the entire instructional program is scanned to insure that appropriate practice schedules or "review experiences" are built into the program. It is also necessary to anticipate future objectives in earlier ones. Such scanning is readily accomplished with the flow charts when it would be almost impossible working from a detailed instructional program.

Step 5. Development of Specific Instructions and Materials
Using the flow charts, a materials production specialist and programing specialist operated independently in the final preparation of the instructional materials. The programing specialist wrote the preliminary drafts of instructions to be tape recorded, problems to be projected on the overhead screen, and related materials. He also conducted the preliminary tryout of the materials. While preliminary drafts of instructional materials were being tested on one or two subjects individually by the programer, other materials were being converted to tapes and transparencies for overhead projection by the media specialist. The second assistant also tried the materials on small groups of children using the special classroom communication and display equipment for which the materials were prepared. Thus, a staff of three

specialists worked fairly independently in the production of a single instructional program. Each person was a specialist in his own right and worked at a different level in the development of the materials.

The Effectiveness of the TRAC Procedure

The particular program of classroom instruction described above was tried out with individuals and then with several small groups of fourth and fifth graders in the process of its development. A total of 15 children completed the instructional program before it was used in the experiment (20). Their IQ's ranged from 104 to 134 (California Test of Mental Maturity), and all were performing at or above grade level as measured by standardized achievement tests. Subsequently, over 100 pupils completed the program in the TRAC facility.

Solutions to Problems of "Individual Differences": Even though the instruction was paced to the slowest learner, individual differences in learning rate posed no great difficulty. At one point in the program, special handling of the learners was required when faster learners discovered the basic pattern several hours before slower learners. This problem was handled by removing the rapid learners from the group and providing them with work in other subject matter areas until the slower learners caught up. Thereafter the learners continued as a group to the completion of the program without difficulty.

Because the groups employed in the experiment were considerably larger than those employed in the development of the program of instruction (groups of 15-20 as contrasted with groups of 5), some problems arose in the experiment which were not anticipated during the developmental phase. Individuals in the larger groups, for instance, were much less likely to interact among themselves than those in the smaller groups, and because they were more heterogeneous with respect to ability and interest, problems of a disciplinary sort arose more frequently in the larger groups. Most problems were handled effectively by the classroom instructors who were skilled elementary school teachers. One group phenomenon was observed, which appeared to be unique to the instructional technique and which was partially resolved by a slight modification in the instructional system. The solution is worthy of special note because it has implications for the development of future man-machine systems of this sort.

Because the learners received individualized feedback through the electronic communications system (red and green light signals), there tended to be a much closer interaction between the individual learner and the materials with which he was working, even though the instruction was group paced. Consequently, the group appeared to "fractionate" during those phases of the instructional process which were largely automated. By this is meant that individuals who were more rapid learners tended to be less patient with the pace of instruction which of necessity was regulated to the slowest learner. Similarly, the slower learners, recognizing from the behavior of others in the classroom that they were slowing down the group, appeared frustrated and threatened. On occasion, the slow learners would simply give up and enter into distracting social behavior with their seatmates.

The solution to this problem was to redesign the instructional system so that individual learners in the classroom could see the meter which registered the proportion of learners in the class who responded correctly to each question. Then the teacher instructed the learners on his use of the meter and let them know at the beginning of each exercise that the exercise would continue until everyone succeeded in responding correctly to three problems in a row, or whatever the learning criteria happened to be. After the use of the meter was made known, the group appeared to become more cohesive. Faster learners reacted with greater tolerance toward the slower members in the group, and even offered comments of encouragement to them from time to time. Possibly because of the change in the reactions of the faster learners, the slower learners appeared more relaxed and challenged by the instructional process. It became more evident to individuals in the class that they were not always the ones who were last to respond when the needle of the meter continued to respond after they had registered their response. In effect, the meter acted as a kind of "governor" for the group.

Spontaneous Reactions of Learners: Another observation which indicates the effectiveness of the TRAC procedure has to do with the excitement with which the children sometimes reacted to the instructional materials. Excitement did occur more with the smaller groups employed in the preliminary development of the materials, and it tended to occur less frequently as instruction progressed beyond the first five or ten hours. Nevertheless, the children were observed to question each other and to argue and challenge "Mr. Console," which was the name given the tape-recording unit. In this respect, they displayed precisely the type of behavior children sometimes exhibit under the direction of skilled teachers in the UICSM program. In this case, however, the children were reacting to a highly structured set of materials being manipulated by a teacher who, in the beginning, was skilled only in conventional techniques of classroom instruction.

Orienting the Instructors: It is also worthy of special note that both instructors used in the experiment were relatively unfamiliar with the distributive law and with the UICSM notation initially. Furthermore, only one instructor had a working knowledge of electronic equipment. The teacher who was inexperienced with the equipment joined the project staff only a few months prior to the beginning of the experiment. He learned to operate the TRAC facility and successfully taught with the programed discovery materials after only a few days of orientation. Since he had no prior knowledge of the distributive law or of the UICSM notation, in effect, he was "teaching by rote." Still, the learners in his initial group were not significantly different in their measured performance than those who learned under the direction of the instructor who had been with the project from the beginning and who by then was thoroughly familiar with the instructional content and procedure. On the basis of this observation, it is reasonable to believe that almost any experienced teacher could teach the distributive law of arithmetic by the discovery method, using the programed materials developed for the present experiment.

Implications for Research and Development

Implications for research have been indicated in previous paragraphs and perhaps need not be made more explicit. Educational researchers will recognize the advantages inherent in a procedure which adds precision to the procedures for preparing instructional materials. From the flow-chart diagrams, it is quite possible to identify those portions of the instructional program which were designed for specific subordinate objectives or to represent particular methods of instruction. Furthermore, because the behavior of the teacher is standardized, comparisons can be made between variations in research treatments without having to contend with that source of error variance attributable to teacher effectiveness. Because the instructional experiences are standardized, design features of classroom experiments can be replicated systematically. In general, all benefits accruing from the use of self-instructional programed materials in research would also apply to classroom instructional materials developed in the way indicated above.

Developmental Implications: It was argued above that in order to attain certain "complex" educational objectives, the unique capabilities of a human observer are called for. This does not mean that each learner must be given individual instruction. Instead, by making appropriate use of the "hardware" associated with educational technology, a single teacher may operate effectively in an automated classroom with groups of learners. While learners are interacting with instructional materials presented and controlled automatically, the teacher can interact with individuals in a manner designed to change more complex behavioral patterns. Such procedures have been demonstrated to be workable and to be readily learned by classroom teachers. Differences among individual learners in learning rate create difficulties, particularly with a UICSM type "discovery" program in which some learners may experience a "sudden reorganization" and attain a particular objective before others in the group. At these points in a discovery program, more rapid learners must be separated from the others and provided the opportunity to study individually in different subject matter areas or to otherwise occupy themselves until the others ascertain the generalization involved. As an alternative procedure, the "early discoverers" can be regrouped separately and allowed to proceed at their own rate.

Ideally, the classroom teacher should employ an effective means by which learners can be rescheduled rapidly and efficiently into programs of self-study or more homogeneous groups based on learning rate. In other words, rather than beginning instruction on an individual basis with the learners working with self-instructional materials, then progressing into grouped instruction to work with a teacher, a classroom instructional procedure such as the TRAC procedure would begin with grouped instruction and proceed to increasingly more complex instructional patterns involving combinations of group-paced and individually paced programs of instruction.

The administrative and instructional patterns associated with either the Winnetka Plan or the more recently developed Continuous Progress Plan (25) would not be entirely appropriate for TRAC type instruction because they are based on the assumption that most instructional objectives are best attained when learners are independently paced. A plan of operation for the group-paced instructional programs outlined above should be equally flexible and adaptable to individual requirements, but for an entirely different reason. The rationale underlying the group-paced program is that some objectives cannot be attained easily without direct teacher guidance, and others can. Furthermore, because many instructional objectives are compounded, instruction can best be provided through man-machine systems to groups of learners.

To effectively employ either individualized or group-paced programs of instruction requires tools and techniques not presently available to many schools. Complex problems of scheduling are created in either type program which probably cannot be resolved effectively without the aid of computer-based data processing equipment. However, if the instructional materials and procedures are developed first, perhaps schoolmen will make it their business to acquire the necessary equipment to use them.

References

1. Ausubel, D. P. "Learning by Discovery: Rationale and Mystique." *Bulletin of the National Association of Secondary School Principals* 45: 18-58; December 1961.
2. Beberman, M. *An Emerging Program of Secondary School Mathematics.* Cambridge, Mass.: Harvard University Press, 1958.
3. Bloom, B. S., and Broder, Lois L. *Problem-Solving Processes of College Students.* Supplementary Education Monograph No. 73. Chicago: University of Chicago Press, 1950.
4. Bruner, J. S. "The Act of Discovery." *Harvard Educational Review* 31: 21-32; Winter 1961.
5. Burton, W. H. *The Guidance of Learning Activities.* Second edition. New York: Appleton-Century-Crofts, 1952.
6. Bushnell, D. D. "The Role of the Computer in Future Instructional Systems." *AV Communication Review* 11: 1-70; March-April 1963.
7. Buswell, G. T. "Patterns of Thinking in Solving Problems." *University of California Publications in Education,* 1956. Vol. 12, No. 2.

8. Duncker, K. "On Problem Solving." *Psychological Monographs* 58: 1-113; Whole No. 270, 1945.
9. Flanders, N. A. "Intent, Action, and Feedback: A Preparation for Teachers." *Journal of Teacher Education* 14: 251-60; September 1963.
10. Frandsen, A. N. *How Children Learn.* New York: McGraw-Hill Book Co., 1957.
11. Gagné, R. M. "The Acquisition of Knowledge." *Psychological Review* 69: 355-65; July 1962.
12. Gagné, R. M., and Brown, L. T. "Some Factors in the Programing of Conceptual Learning." *Journal of Experimental Psychology* 62: 313-21; 1961.
13. Hanna, Lavone A.; Potter, Gladys L.; and Hagaman, Neva. *Unit Teaching in the Elementary School.* New York: Holt, Rinehart & Winston, 1963.
14. Hanson, N. R. *Patterns of Discovery: An Inquiry into the Conceptual Foundations of Science.* London: Cambridge University Press, 1958.
15. Hendrix, Gertrude. "Learning by Discovery." *Mathematics Teacher* 54: 290-99; May 1961.
16. Hilgard, E. R. *Theories of Learning.* New York: Appleton-Century-Crofts, 1956.
17. Johnson, E. A., and Michael, R. E. *Principles of Teaching.* Boston: Allyn and Bacon, 1958.
18. Kersh, B. Y. "The Adequacy of 'Meaning' as an Explanation for the Superiority of Learning by Independent Discovery." *Journal of Educational Psychology* 49: 282-92; October 1958.
19. Kersh, B. Y. *Classroom Simulation: A New Dimension in Teacher Education.* Title VII Project No. 886, National Defense Education Act of 1958. Monmouth: Teaching Research Division, Oregon State System of Higher Education, 1963.
20. Kersh, B. Y. *Directed Discovery vs. Programed Instruction: A Test of a Theoretical Position Involving Educational Technology.* Title VII Research Project No. 907, National Defense Education Act of 1958. Monmouth: Teaching Research Division, Oregon State System of Higher Education, 1964.
21. Kersh, B. Y., and Wittrock, M. C. "Learning by Discovery: An Interpretation of Recent Research." *Journal of Teacher Education* 13: 461-68; December 1962.
22. Maltzman, I. "On the Training of Originality." *Psychological Review* 67: 229-42; July 1960.
23. Nordberg, H. O.; Bradfield, J. M.; and Odell, W. C. *Secondary School Teaching.* New York: Macmillan Co., 1962.
24. Olson, W. C. *Child Development.* Boston: D. C. Heath & Co., 1959.
25. Read, E. A., and Crnkovic, J. K. *The Continuous Progress Plan.* Provo, Utah: Brigham Young University, 1963.

26. Resnick, L. B. "Programmed Instruction and the Teaching of Complex Intellectual Skills: Problems and Prospects." *Harvard Educational Review* 33: 439-71; Fall 1963.

27. Rivlin, H. N. *Teaching Adolescents in the Secondary Schools.* New York: Appleton-Century-Crofts, 1961.

28. Stendler, Celia B. *Teaching in the Elementary School.* New York: Harcourt, Brace, 1958.

29. Stolurow, L. M. *Teaching by Machine.* Cooperative Research Monograph No. 6 (OE-34010). Washington, D.C.: Government Printing Office, 1961.

30. Stolurow, L. M., and Beberman, M. *Comparative Studies of Principles for Programming Mathematics in Automated Instruction.* Semi-Annual Report, June 6, 1962—December 6, 1962. Title VII Project No. 806, National Defense Education Act of 1958. Urbana: University of Illinois, 1962.

31. Strickland, R. G. *How To Build a Unit of Work.* U.S. Office of Education Bulletin No. 5. Washington, D.C.: Government Printing Office, 1946.

32. Suchman, J. R. *The Elementary School Training Program in Scientific Inquiry.* Title VII Project No. 216, National Defense Education Act of 1958. Urbana: University of Illinois, 1962.

33. Taba, Hilda. *Thinking in Elementary School Children.* Cooperative Research Project No. 1574. San Francisco: San Francisco State College, 1964.

34. Wallen, N. E., and Travers, R. M. W. "Analysis and Investigation of Teaching Methods." *Handbook of Research on Teaching.* (Edited by N. L. Gage.) Chicago: Rand McNally & Co., 1963. pp. 448-505.

35. Washburne, C. *A Living Philosophy of Education.* New York: John Day Co., 1940.

36. Washburne, C.; Vogel, Mabel; and Gray, W. S. "A Survey of Winnetka Public Schools." *Journal of Educational Research Supplementary Educational Monograph.* Bloomington, Ill.: Public School Publishing Co., 1926.

37. Wertheimer, M. *Productive Thinking.* Second edition. New York: Harper & Brothers, 1959.

38. Whipple, G. M., editor. *Adapting the Schools to Individual Differences.* Twenty-Third Yearbook, National Society for the Study of Education. Chicago: University of Chicago Press, 1924.

39. Wittrock, M. C. *Transfer Through Verbal Cueing in Concept Identification.* Cooperative Research Project No. 1684. Los Angeles: University of California, 1964.

40. Woodruff, A. W. *Fundamental Concepts of Teaching.* Minneapolis: Burgess Publishing Co., 1959.

41. Woodruff, A. W. *Basic Concepts of Teaching.* San Francisco: Chandler Publishing Co., 1961.

Technology and
Subject Matter

JAMES L. EVANS
Teaching Machines, Inc.

Programing in Mathematics and Logic

The primacy of mathematics in the field of teaching machines and programed learning is easily documented. Historically, Skinner chose mathematical behavior as a theme in his earliest paper (122) dealing explicitly with the necessity of inserting implementation into the learning process. The first machine he describes is an experimental model designed to teach arithmetic. The necessity for such a device follows Skinner's analysis that adequate establishment of mathematical behavior acquired in the first four school years requires some 25,000 to 50,000 "contingencies of reinforcement." Skinner states, "In this frame of reference the daily assignment in arithmetic seems pitifully meagre" (p. 151). He concludes, "If the teacher is to take advantage of recent advances in the study of learning, she must have the help of mechanical devices" (p. 154). So, even a decade ago, mathematics was the favored topic as formative ideas in the programed learning field were being developed.

Continued emphasis is found in many studies of the availability of programs (e.g., 22, 23, 46, 77) and their experimental use (e.g., 112). Without exception, the number of mathematics programs[1] exceeds,

---

[1] The affinity of mathematics and logic is such that, in the interest of concision, the phrase "mathematics programs" will generally include mathematics *and logic* programs in this review. Programs on classical and symbolic logic are not so numerous as those on arithmetic, algebra, geometry, set theory, and advanced mathematical topics. However, a substantial number of logic programs has been constructed and used in programing investigations.

often by a factor of two or more, the number of programs in the next most popular subject areas (generally, science or language). An examination of Schramm's annotated bibliography reveals that between 35 and 40 percent of the reported studies used mathematics programs. This range of percentages holds surprisingly well as an index of the proportion of available programs (cf., 22, 23, 46, 77) which are devoted to mathematical topics.

A concise answer as to why mathematics is the most popular subject matter for programing is found in Fry:

> In many ways, it is the ideal subject for programing. Mathematic items are all logically related, all carefully defined. The student's response can be specified precisely. It is fairly easy to determine why particular errors are made in mathematics and to anticipate them. Mathematics can be used with both constructed-response and multiple-choice programs with almost equal facility. And, of course, it is badly needed in this age of transition from traditional mathematics to the modern, logic-oriented view (22, p. 113).

Mathematics has had, and continues to have, an intimate and important relationship with the development of the field of programed learning. Programs in mathematics have served faithfully as vehicles for the investigation of fundamental problems in programed learning. A review of such studies will be the first order of business. However, the inverse operation is the use of programed learning as a vehicle to answer fundamental questions about the analysis of mathematical behavior. Studies of the latter variety, regrettably few in comparison with the first breed, are already resulting in exciting new concepts and techniques. These investigations give much promise of continued fruitful cross-fertilization between mathematics and programed learning. These studies will be the second order of business. Finally, the chapter will conclude with a bit of prophecy as to where the interaction of programing and mathematics may lead in the future.

The Nature of Research in Programed Learning

Even a casual examination of the research paradigms used in the reported experimental studies dealing with programs in mathematics and logic would reveal one consistent fact: almost without exception, studies reported involve hypothesis-testing using statistically based experimental designs. Such experimental procedures underlie the vast majority of all reports appearing in current psychological and educational research journals. Since psychologists and educators schooled in experimental design have been the chief contributors to programed learning, this is not surprising. What is surprising is that the reported research procedures are entirely different from the type of research long advocated and pursued by Skinner and his students (41, 114, 119, 120, 122, 123). Their research activities are characterized by the absence of explicitly stated hypotheses, by the use of small numbers of test subjects, and by attempts to establish laboratory (in contradistinction to statistical) control or elimination of variables.

And herein lies an anomaly. The impetus to the flurry of research on teaching machines and programed learning was unquestionably provided by Skinner and his associates. Although these researchers tend to eschew experimental design procedures, practically all reported research in programed learning has been in the experimental design paradigm. Speculation as to why this state of affairs exists would be out of place in this chapter. But it is of sufficient importance to make note of in the interests of presenting two facets of present-day psychological research for their relevance in the interpretation of the studies being reported here.

Research on the "Classic" Programing Variables

A popular activity in the early days of programing research was listing variables to be studied. At one time, the number of such lists outstripped the number of programing research investigations under way. Hopefully, this situation seems to be correcting itself. Certain variables, however, emerged as being disproportionately popular. Early favorites were investigated in the "X vs. Y" studies, where X and Y were teachers, teaching machines, and programed textbooks in various combinations. Several studies have been conducted (and will be reported later) in which the experimental group received programed instruction, while the control group received no instruction whatsoever. Fortunately for programed instruction, the experimental groups generally score significantly better on posttests. Vying for popularity with the "X vs. Y" studies, and sharing with them much of the same research methodology, were the "axiom-doubting" studies. If Skinner advocated composed responses and eschewed multiple-choice responses, researchers (this writer also pleads guilty) ineluctably constructed response-composition and multiple-choice versions of programs and started searching for two groups of test students. If Skinner recommended that students actively write out their responses, experiments were quickly designed in which one group was instructed to "think" responses.

The net worth of these "X vs. Y" and "axiom-doubting" studies, which can be placed under the rubric of the investigation of "classic" variables, will require the perspective of time for adequate evaluation. However, such hypothesis-testing studies in general, and comparative studies of teachers and programs in particular, have been roundly criticized. Evans, Glaser, and Homme (39) pointed out that such comparative studies were perhaps premature until more was known about the construction of effective programs and recommended that research be directed toward isolating the variables relevant to the production of such programs. Stolurow (134) makes the point this way: "No single program can represent 'the new method,' and no teacher can represent 'the average teacher.' Comparisons between a program and a teacher may be meaningless, because we cannot know where we are on either scale. The comparative study has to go" (p. 2). Gotkin (59) states that the comparison of programed and conventional instruction is neither practical nor useful, due to uncontrolled variables such as teacher competence, quality of program, and evaluative instruments. In a similar vein, Ellis (34) enumerates four types of experiments designed to evaluate program effectiveness: (a) comparison of the program with an existing instructional procedure and a teacher; (b) comparison of a given instructional procedure plus teacher plus program with instructional procedure plus teacher *without* a program; (c) a comparison of one type of program with another type of program, both of which treat the same subject matter; and (d) studies of pretest and posttest gain. Since the first three experiments involve relevant but nonidentifiable variables, Ellis rejects them as being essentially nonanalytic (cf., 145) and concludes, "The gain study appears to be the most useful for evaluating the teaching effectiveness of a program."

Roe (106) enumerates four reasons why he feels little of either statistical or social significance has emerged from programed learning research to date: (a) weak criteria measures; (b) limited number of variables which can be measured at one time; (c) failure either to satisfactorily separate or combine learning time and test scores—the two major performance measures; and (d) the lack of an adequate rationale for specifying the efficiency of the teaching-learning process. Holland (69 and Chapter 3 of this volume) deprecates hypothesis-testing studies in teaching machine research, particularly those involving only 100 or 200 items. And Gilbert (52) admonishes the researcher to "resist the temptation to design formal experiments. You don't want to know *whether* one method teaches better than another, you want to know *what* method teaches best" (p. 478).

In any event, these investigations of "classic" variables with mathematics and logic programs as vehicles were undertaken, and they constitute the preponderance of available research in the area of programed learning. This chapter now turns to consideration and review of those vehicles and the studies that have influenced programed learning.

Programs vs. Teachers

"Will machines replace teachers? On the contrary, they are capital equipment to be used by teachers to save time and labor. In assigning certain mechanizable functions to machines, the teacher emerges in his proper role as an indispensable human being" (124, p. 976). From this comment by Skinner in "Teaching Machines," it would not appear that Skinner is suggesting comparative investigations of the effectiveness of machines and teachers. Unfortunately, the concept of a machine (or program) replacing a teacher was an intriguing one, despite the *1984* overtones, and many early researchers yielded to the temptation of designing an experiment pitting machines and programs against teachers. The methodological difficulties inherent in such research designs have already been pointed out. Also, when many of these comparative experiments were started, few, if any, tested programs of sufficient length to result in a stabilization of the learners' behavior were available. Whether the efforts expended in these "program vs. teacher" investigations could have been more productively channeled into different research areas of programed instruction is a moot point.

In the studies now to be reported, programed instruction, either in a programed textbook or a machine format, was typically compared with conventional classroom procedures involving teachers, textbooks, and other conventional instructional procedures. With respect to the application of inferential statistics to performance measures from such studies, three logical possibilities exist: the programed instruction group can do significantly poorer than, not statistically different from, or significantly better than, the group receiving conventional instruction.[2] A review of these performance studies (using programs in mathematics and logic) indicates research showing programed instruction groups doing significantly worse than conventional instruction groups is in the minority. A more frequent finding is that of significant differences in favor of programed instruction. Finally, of the reports available to this reviewer, the finding of no significant difference between experimental and control groups has been most frequent. These differential results will be dealt with in the order presented above, and the results of tests of significance on learning time will be indicated when they are available.

A study comparing groups taught agricultural finance and credit by lecture-discussion and groups taught by a programed notebook (87) showed a highly significant difference favoring the lecture-discussion method. Similar results were found on a retest two months later. Legg indicates that the lecture-discussion group used an average of 12 hours while the programed-instruction group completed the task in an average of 5 hours. No statistical tests of significance on time are reported, nor is any attempt to adjust performance scores on the basis of time scores indicated. Legg does point out that a gain was made by students in each of the methods of teaching and concludes, "Appropriate, well-prepared programed instruction material, used by good teachers, is an aid to individual learning." Glaser, Reynolds, and Fullick (57) found that average-IQ students who had programed instruction in algebra did significantly poorer than matched controls (traditional instruction) or brighter students receiving either programed or traditional instruction. However, Glaser, Reynolds, and Fullick note that the average students completed significantly *fewer* programed units (approximately 18 units of a 30-unit program) in the time allotted them. This study and the study by Legg emphasize the difficulty the self-pacing feature of programed instruction poses in reaching a clear-cut interpretation of comparative results. If time is held constant, some students will not complete the program, and their mean posttest performance does not

---

[2] Unless otherwise noted, the word *significant* will refer to a probability value less than .05 ($p < .05$); *highly significant* will refer to a probability value less than .01 ($p < .01$).

necessarily reflect what the entire program might teach. On the other hand, suppose each student is allowed to finish the program at his own pace. It is common knowledge among workers in programed instruction that the slowest student may take as much as four times as long as the fastest student to complete a program. This fact makes it difficult to match the time spent by the control group with the widely varying times of the experimental group. A possibility which has apparently escaped investigation is to establish the median time required to complete the program and to use an equal amount of time on conventional instruction. But as long as programed instruction in individually self-paced and conventional instruction is by groups, definitive answers to such comparative studies will probably continue to elude investigators.

The reports of Legg (87) and of Glaser, Reynolds, and Fullick (57) are the only two this reviewer has been able to obtain which present statistically significant negative results for the groups who learned through programs. It is interesting to conjecture briefly why this might be so. Nonprogramed educational processes have been around for a long time and have had the benefit of uncountable man-hours devoted to improving them. Programing technology, on the other hand, is admittedly in its infancy. Yet, if the reported literature is believed, when the fledgling programer is pitted against conventional instruction, the odds to date are that he will win, or at least break even. Some possible hypotheses may be that conventional instruction is very bad, that even amateur programed instruction is very good, or that negative results of programed instruction effects are not routinely submitted for publication.

In contrast with the research above, a group of experiments will now be reported in which the investigators found significant differences favoring the groups receiving programed instruction. Roe and others (109) compared four modes of programed presentation (constructed response and multiple-choice response on a teaching machine and composed response and covert response on a programed textbook) with a group instructed through conventional lecture. Results indicate that all program groups performed significantly better than the groups who received the conventional lecture. However, the mean time of the students in the lecture group was less than the mean time required by the machine and programed textbook groups. Fine (44) reviews a study comparing bright students taught algebra by programed instruction and by "traditional" methods. He reports that 38 percent of the group that took programed instruction in algebra was above the 90th percentile (presumably on a standardized test) at the end of the course, compared with 21 percent of the group using traditional methods. This difference is reported as being statistically significant.

Keislar (83) has done a provocative study on an attempt to teach mathematics in terms of algebraic structures with teaching machines. In a number of the posttests following this investigation, the first-grade experimental group did significantly better than the first-grade controls, and in some instances this experimental group did not differ significantly in performance from a fourth-grade control group. Unfortunately (as Keislar is well aware), the study has several experimental flaws which serve to attenuate the results. Although a portion of the experimental group had individual multiple-choice teaching machines, another portion of the group was taught with a group teaching machine, due to a shortage of machines. This resulted in a loss of the self-pacing feature for a portion of the experimental group. Another difficulty is that a number of items on the postexperimental criterion measures involved symbols (e.g., ">" for "greater than," "<" for "less than," and " · " for "multiplication") to which the experimental group had been exposed, but which were unfamiliar to the control group. Of interest in this investigation is the performance of the first-grade experimental and control groups on one of the measures mentioned above, a 50-item addition and subtraction test. The experimental subjects received all their instruction in arithmetic from the machine program, and their mean postexperimental score was extremely close to, and nonsignificantly different from, the control group which received conventional instruction. Although the structure of the experiment precludes any formal statistically based conclusions from being drawn, Keislar's study certainly deserves attention as a bold and successful attempt in teaching rather sophisticated mathematical concepts to young children. Blyth (13), in reporting his experiences in teaching probability through programed instruction, indicates that the average grade on a yearly examination was raised by approximately 30 points over the corresponding examination of the previous year. No statistical analyses are presented, but it is likely that such a difference represents both practical and statistical differences.

Attention will now be directed to investigations of programed instruction vs. conventional instruction in which no significant differences were found. In an early study comparing conventional textbook presentation and a programed textbook presentation of a topic in statistics, Evans, Glaser, and Homme (39) report results of two experiments using college students. In both cases, the group receiving programed instruction had higher, but nonsignificant, mean performance posttest scores. Evans, Glaser, and Homme found, in both experiments, the conventional textbook group displayed significantly more variability in performance measures. This suggests that programed instruction may exert more control over individual variability. In this study it was also found that the programed textbook group took significantly more time to complete the material than did the textbook groups.

Smith (130) reports the results of a comparison of four programed instruction procedures with four conventional classroom procedures in the teaching of fractions concepts at the fifth-grade level. Items in the criterion test, in which terms in the questions were defined in the program material, were designated as *definitive* test questions. A set of test questions assumed to measure transfer or generalization was designated as *inferential* test questions. Using regression techniques on pre- and posttests, Smith computed residual learning scores. An analysis of variance of these scores based on definitive questions yielded significant differences between the eight treatment groups. During the *t*-test comparing the four programed treatments and any one or more of the teacher-taught treatments, six significant *t* values were found. Three of the values favored the programed instruction group, and three of the values favored the teacher taught group. An examination of the patterns of these significances reveals that apparently one programed instruction condition produced a sufficiently low score to be exceeded significantly by three of the four teacher taught conditions. On the other hand, one of the teacher taught conditions was sufficiently low to be significantly poorer than three of the four programed instruction conditions. Smith notes that the program used in the study was unrevised on the basis of student tryout. The question arises as to whether or not attempts at perfecting the program would not have resulted in markedly different experimental results.

A report by Brown (15) is concerned with the results of the use of programed materials prepared by the University of Illinois Committee on School Mathematics (UICSM) programed instruction project. This experiment was not strictly speaking a "teacher vs. program" experiment since the experimental group was taught by teacher, UICSM conventional text, and programed materials, while the control group was taught only by teacher and the conventional text. Comparison of eight specific achievement tests (including one test administered both as pre- and a posttest) revealed the program-supplemented experimental group scored slightly, but significantly better, on seven of the eight tests. As Brown points out, the experimental group had significantly higher scores on both a general ability and a math aptitude test administered at the outset of the school year. Brown also furnishes a figure which demonstrates that the experimental groups are maintaining a much more homogeneous performance level, while the mean scores of the control groups appear to be growing cumulatively more heterogeneous. Brown concludes his summary with the conservative statement, "No student was penalized in his level of mathematics achievement because of having used programed material" (p. 14).

In a study by Beane (11), a control group was used for comparison purposes with all-branching, all-linear, half-branching-half-linear, and half-linear-half-branching programed instruction groups. The instructor who normally taught the two experimental classes taught the control class. The control group had a higher mean score on posttest achievement than any of the four experimental groups, but the differences failed to reach statistical significance. Beane reports significant differences between control groups and the four experimental groups on time spent on the program. He attributes the greater amount of time spent by the control group to homework assignments given only to that group.

The Associated Public School Systems (6) reports on an experimental and a control group using a commercially available elementary algebra program. Although no tests of significance were reported, both groups were given the full-year Lankton First-Year Algebra Test (20) at the end of the first semester. The experimental group had percentiles ranging from 4 through 99, with a median of 44. The control group recorded percentiles from 21 through 80, with a median of 57. In a study of constructed answer responding to a program in elementary algebra, Austwick (7) found no significant difference between mean learning time, mean posttest score, and mean retention test score (taken after two weeks) between experimental and control groups. The control group was taught by the mathematics teacher who normally taught the course.

A branching program on topics in elementary statistics was utilized by Smith (131). He reports the results of programed instruction vs. a classroom-homework-textbook-teacher-instructed control group. Analysis of results reveals no statistically significant differences attributable to the differences in the two methods of instruction. Smith reports that the time consumed in completing the course was less for the experimental group, p between .05 and .10.

As mentioned before, a special case in experimental design is the control group which gets no instruction whatsoever. In one such study, Keislar (82) did find a significant difference favoring fifth and sixth graders learning arithmetic on a teaching machine over a matched control group which received no instruction. A somewhat similar experiment (88) administered a 180-frame program in informal geometry to 15 second graders. A test of significance on difference scores with matched control groups was highly significant ($p < .001$) in favor of the experimental group.

An intriguing potential of programed learning is that of teaching a subject matter to students several grade levels below where it is ordinarily taught. The efforts of Keislar (83) in teaching algebraic structures to first graders has already been mentioned. Eigen and Komoski (32) call for a reexamination of the contention that certain materials are best taught at a given level. A possible response to that plea might be seen in a study by Kalin (81), in which a programed text was compared with conventional methods in an experiment in teaching equations and inequalities to intellectually superior fifth and sixth graders. Kalin failed to find significant differences in test scores between the programed test group and the control group taught by conventional methods. A 20 percent saving in time for experimental groups was reported. On a 34-item criterion test, groups from the fifth and sixth grades had mean scores ranging from 26.2 to 30.8, in comparison with 35.0 for a ninth-grade algebra class.

In summary, and in spite of the methodological difficulties, programed learning appears at least to be able to hold its own with conventional instruction. This public relations job has been done. Hopefully, researchers will now devote their energies to the real problem: perfection of programed instruction. The locomotive can now tie or beat the stagecoach; it is time to build better locomotives.

Programed Textbooks vs. Teaching Machines

In setting forth his requirements for a "minimal teaching machine," Skinner (124) described two essentially different machines. For the lower grades, he recommended a device in which the student cannot proceed to the second step until he has composed a response by moving printed figures or letters. These are then compared by the machine with a coded response. For more advanced students, Skinner implies that responding can be adequately controlled by simply asking the student to compare his response with the correct response revealed by the machine. To gain access to the correct response, the student had to manipulate the machine so that his last answer was still visible, but had moved into a position where it was unavailable for change. In the second type of machine, the burden of discrimination of correctness or incorrectness of the answer is upon the student.

Perhaps due to a lack of research funds available in those early days, it soon occurred to interested researchers that all of the functions of Skinner's "write-in" machines, save that of preventing cheating, could be served by a modified book format (cf., 72). The term *programed textbook* quickly caught on, and two basic formats quickly appeared: (a) the horizontal format, in which the page containing the stimulus portion of an item masked the answer on the next page until the student turned for confirmation, and (b) the vertical format, in which the student read down the page as in a regular book, but covered the correct response with some slider device or mask until he was ready to check the answer to the preceding frame. Several versions of the programed textbook are reviewed by Stolurow (135, pp. 37, 43). The feasibility of investigating program variables using programed textbooks was soon established (e.g., 39). Evans, Glaser, and Homme cautioned, "Whether or not the machines have intrinsic properties which cannot be matched by non-machine techniques awaits controlled experimental comparisons of machine and non-machine presentation of sequences" (39, p. 446).

The results of such comparative studies were not long in coming. Eigen and Komoski (32), using a 707-frame sequence on *Sets, Relations and Functions*, found no significant differences on postprogram tests between the machine and the programed text groups, with the machine groups taking significantly more time. Similar results were found by Roe and others (109) who also found no significant difference in performance and significant differences favoring (using less time) the programed textbook condition. In a 90-frame program dealing with a binary system, Silverman and Alter (117) again found no significant effect due to methods when comparing machine and programed textbook, although no time data were reported. Silverman and Alter also report comparison of an elaborate electromechanical device, a crude spool-type machine, and a programed text using a vertical format with a sliding cardboard frame. No significant differences between programed text and the machines were found, and no time data were presented.

An investigation of machine, horizontal-text, and vertical-text modes of presentation (33) again failed to reveal any statistically significant differences between machine and program format presentation. Subjects using the programed text again completed the program in less time, although in this case the time difference was not significant. Finally, in a review of research of teaching machines vs. programed text presentation, Goldstein and Gotkin (58), whose report includes the results of an additional three programs in which the subject matter was not mathematics, conclude: "None of the studies report significant differences in mastery of subject material between machine and programed-text presentation of the same programed sequence. In four of the five studies in which time to complete the program was a variable, statistically significant differences were noted between the presentation modes. These studies report a saving in time varying from 10% to approximately 40% in favor of the programed text" (p. 34). Chapter 5 by Stolurow and Davis also considers programed textbook versus teaching machine studies.

Format Studies

As has been pointed out, the two basic formats for programed textbooks developed following the observations by Homme and Glaser (72). Several experiments have been done to see whether the format per se was a relevant variable. Results to date do not indicate that such a variable is relevant. For example, Eigen and others (33) compared horizontal, vertical, and machine instruction of the same program on a 65-frame program. No significant differences were found on posttest mastery measures between machine, horizontal-text, or vertical-text presentation. Delayed posttests of four weeks failed to reveal statistically significant differences among the groups. Similar results are reported by Smith (130) on work done by Alexander, Barlow, and Gilpin. In this experiment, horizontal and vertical format variations were studied as well as conditions in which students were not required to write their answers and a condition in which the answers were supplied by using capital letters in place of the words ordinarily left blank. Smith reports that the experiment gave no support to the notion that the horizontal format is superior to vertical format. The finding is consistent with the hypothesis of Evans (35) that in situations in which the probability of responding correctly is high, the mode or method of receiving feedback diminishes in importance.

Studies on the Nature of Feedback in Programs

". . . the machine, like the private tutor, reinforces the student for every correct response, using this immediate feedback not only to shape his behavior most efficiently but to maintain it in strength in a manner which the layman would describe as 'holding the student's interest' " (154, p. 164). In the early days of research in programed learning, programers rather uncritically accepted the reasonable assertion that the confirming or feedback stimulus available to them after responding was the reinforcer in programed learning. In the areas of mathematics and logic, little experimentation has been accomplished to date which has been addressed specifically to the problem of the necessity of a confirmation stimulus. However, a number of studies on different types of feedback procedures have been reported. (See the chapter by Holland for a related discussion of this topic.) For example, Alter, Eigen, and King (4) investigated a confirmation vs. a confirmation-plus-trinket situation in a program dealing with quantitative concepts and numerals in order from one to nine. They failed to find differences on either pre- or posttest score, number of errors on the program, or time taken to complete the program. Smith (129) found that machine confirmation with a buzzer was much more effective than confirmation through a light. Legg (87) used a nonconfirmation-type answer sheet and an answer sheet which provided the student with erasure feedback which gave immediate knowledge of the correct answers. Students taking the posttest with the erasure feedback-type answer sheet made a significant gain over those who used the nonconfirmation type answer sheet. McDonald and Allen (93) investigated the effectiveness of five programing techniques in teaching an "original two-person board game." In all five experimental conditions, the students were exposed to the same basic information at each frame. Variations in the experimental conditions were achieved by providing or not providing additional examples, questioning or not questioning the student on his comprehension of the information, providing or not providing correction of answers, and providing or not providing explanation of the correctness of answers and the correctness of alternatives. No significant differences were found either for mean scores on two criterion measures or on program error scores when such scores were available. Such studies provide interesting food for thought, but present very little systematic evidence which sheds light on the nature of reinforcement in the programing or teaching machine situation.

As Lumsdaine (92) points out, "In any case, the immediate feedback providing confirmation or correction in instructional programs cannot be equated theoretically to any simple conception of reinforcement in the sense of reward" (p. 143). Evans (35), who failed to find significant differences due to immediate confirmation as opposed to confirmation delayed for periods from 30 seconds up to five minutes, said: "The relevance of variables such as response mode and immediacy of confirmation is inversely related to the probability of correct responding. That is, in situations in which correct responses have low probability, factors such as overt responding and immediate feedback are more critical than in situations in which probabilities of correct responding are high" (p. 76).

Sequencing Studies

Skinner (124) states, ". . . technical terms, facts, laws, principles, and cases . . . must then be arranged in a plausible developmental order" (p. 974).

On an a priori basis, it seems highly unlikely that any topic of complexity can be taught through programing or through any other method in any sequence other than an orderly one. However, it is possible that with very short programs, scrambling of the order of items may make little difference. In particular, this would be true of a short program in which the "logical" order results in low net gains on performance measures. Such logic appears to be supported by studies on "scrambled" vs. "ordered" sequences reported to date. (See the studies by Roe, Case, and Roe (107), Levin and Baker (89), and Roe (106) reported in the chapter by Holland.) On the basis of this evidence and common sense, it seems highly unlikely that any successful, well-revised program of more than 100 frames in length, in highly structured topics such as mathematics or logic, could be successfully scrambled in its entirety and still do the job it was designed to do. It is interesting to conjecture, however, on the possibilities of scrambling within selected "blocks" of items to ascertain at what point randomization of items begins to result in a deficit in performance.

Individual Differences

A presumed function of an adequately designed learning program is to reduce or eliminate postprogram performance differences due to individual differences at the beginning of the program. As Skinner (124) emphasized, "A program designed for the slow student in the school system will probably not seriously delay the fast student, who will be free to progress at his own speed. . . . If this does not prove to be the case, programs can be constructed at two or more levels, and students can be shifted from one to the other as performances dictate" (p. 976). An earlier quoted, but as yet unrealized, goal of programed instruction is postprogram performance in which the mean postest score is 100 percent with a standard deviation of 0. How well has this ambitious attempt to reduce or eliminate individual differences in achievement on program performances been realized in practice?

Grade Level: In experimental situations in which the same program is administered to various grade levels, it is obviously easy to check the relevance of grade level per se on performance. Using a program on sets, relations, and functions, Eigen and Komoski (32) failed to find any significant differences on posttest performance for ninth, tenth, and eleventh graders and also no significant effect of grade level on completion time of the program. However, upon a transfer test, there were significant differences attributable to grade level. Evans (37), using a logic program, failed to find performance differences attributed to college class. On the other hand, Campbell (21) clearly differentiated test-score differences between fourth-, sixth-, eighth-, tenth-, and twelfth-grade students on a program involving variations on a branching procedure. Yet, on a very short program designed to teach an "original two-person board game," McDonald and Allen (93) did find significant differences between high school juniors and seniors on final posttest score and on error scores on the programs themselves.

In summarizing the relevance of grade level to program performance, it is probably safe to assert that for programs of some length and with grade level not too widely separated, relatively homogeneous performance can be expected. However, with very short programs, or with widely separated grade levels, heterogeneous results attributable to grade level can be expected. Although the evidence is far from conclusive to date, the sometimes surprising ability of a program to be used effectively at many grade levels has real implications for education. Eigen and Komoski (32) conclude that the traditional concepts that certain materials are best taught at a given grade level need serious reexamination.

Intelligence: What is the effect of general intelligence on program performance? Presumably, a well-constructed program should take moderately heterogeneous intelligence levels and bring them all to near perfection in postprogram performance. Alter (3), in a study which considered IQ level and retention, concludes that "if we are interested in improving retention, we should operate primarily on improving the learner's initial achievement" (p. 8). She also states, "These data give us no reason to believe that the lower IQ students will forget any more or less rapidly than the higher IQ students once they have been brought up to the same achievement level" (p. 8).

In a study of the relationship between intelligence and step size, Shay (113), using a program on Roman numerals, also divided subjects into three groups on the basis of IQ. Using pretest scores as a covariable, Shay found significant differences attributable to ability levels on the total posttest, new items introduced on the posttest, old items introduced on the posttest, and time to complete the program. Only in the case of percentage error on the program was a significant difference found attributable to the interaction of intelligence and size-of-item step. Shay concludes, "Failure to reject most of the null hypotheses asserted in this study supports Skinner's position that it is not necessary to provide more than one program on the basis of different initial ability" (p. 100).

In a study in which students had two repetitions of a 107-frame algebra program, Rigney (103) found that the high-IQ students made considerably fewer errors than the average and low-IQ students on both Trial 1 and Trial 2 of the program. Rigney notes, "With two trials, the dullest group's mean approached that of the bright group for one trial" (p. 164). Recognizing that repetition would be boring to the student, he also comments that it is at least a possibility for decreasing intrasubject differences for certain learning objectives. Although error scores on a program per se are tending to become a somewhat suspect dependent variable, the findings of Rigney suggest the possibility that some variation on a repetition sequence could be useful in making the postprogram performance of students with varied intelligence more homogeneous.

Beane (11), using a program in plane geometry, investigated several treatments involving both linear (951 frames) and branching (852 frames) sequences of some length. Using the Henmon-Nelson Tests of Mental Ability to divide students into high- and low-ability subgroups in each experimental group, Beane found high-ability students did significantly better than low-ability students in both achievement and retention. However, there were no significant differences on program error rate between high- and low-ability groups. Although the low-ability groups had a relatively low error rate on the program (8 percent), their ability to grasp logical sequences was not equal to that of high-ability classmates. Such a finding is another count against the use of program error rate as the chief dependent variable in program experimentation. Lambert, Miller, and Wiley (86) also used the Henmon-Nelson Tests of Mental Ability to divide students into high-, average-, and low-intelligence groups. Analysis of posttest scores following administration of a program of some length (Eigen's *Sets, Relations, and Functions*, 843 frames) showed intelligence to be a significant factor in posttest performance.

Somewhat puzzling findings relating IQ's (Pintner), reading level, and presentation mode utilizing a short (65-frame) program on numbers and numerals are reported by Eigen (30). On immediate posttest, gain, and four-week retention scores, significant correlations between IQ and performance scores of machine and horizontal textbook groups were found. Students using the vertical programed textbook format, however, in no instance showed significant correlations between IQ and performance. In light of repeated findings of no significant performance differences due to format (machine, vertical programed text, horizontal programed text), this particular finding would seem to require replication with a longer program.

In a study involving a fixed-sequence (linear) group versus a branching group, Coulson and others (25) failed to find significant correlations in either group between posttest criterion scores and scores on the Henmon-Nelson Tests of Mental Ability. More effective remedial materials in this experiment, in comparison with an earlier experiment, "raised the performance of lower aptitude students to that of the higher aptitude students, although the lower aptitude students required more training time to reach this level" (25, p. 392).

At its present state of technology, it seems clear that linear programing has not fulfilled its promise of markedly reducing or eliminating individual differences due to ability (IQ). On the other hand, the study by Coulson and others (25) shows some promise of reducing the effects of ability levels by using more effective branching material and improving remedial steps. In one study using variations of a very short (27-item) program, McDonald and Allen (93) found a moderate but significant relationship between criterion scores and aptitude scores (as measured by the Differential Aptitude Tests [20]). In general, then, the studies reported to date give no evidence that linear programs are eliminating performance differences due to aptitude. Does this constitute damning evidence against linear programing? Several considerations seem to contraindicate. As pointed out, the technology of linear programing is "admittedly in its infancy." It would be premature to assert that linear programing is ineffective in dealing with individual differences. In none of the reported cases were the programs pulling the "low end of the aptitude range" up to near perfect performance. In some cases, even the high-aptitude students were achieving far from perfect posttest scores. When programs are available which produce near-perfect postprogram performance in both low- and high-aptitude groups, correlations between aptitude scores and performance scores will obviously disappear. Is this begging the question for linear programing? Perhaps. However, until the effects of the enormous present effort to perfect programing technology are seen with more "modern" programs, it is dangerous to assert that experiments using programs of 1960 and 1961 vintage are giving definitive answers.

A relevant distinction is raised by Stolurow (134). In a series of studies involving the relationship between sequencing variations and measures of general ability, Stolurow states, "One of the earlier findings in this series was that sequences which led to the most rapid learning did not produce scores that were correlated with standardized test scores of general intellectual ability" (p. 4). In summarizing results of the use of "mixed" and "consecutive" sequence programs, Stolurow also points out, ". . . the scores on the consecutive sequence program correlated significantly with scores from specific ability tests (reading comprehension and arithmetic fundamentals)" (p. 5). Although Stolurow's results are more suggestive than definitive, it may be that certain relevant specific ability measures would prove more useful in program use than the more generalized measures. Again postulating an effective program, it seems reasonable that it is more important to know if the student has the prerequisite "entering" skills (e.g., a certain level of reading comprehension) than it is to have some generalized measure of his IQ. Broadly stated, a high-IQ child who cannot read will fail a program assuming reading knowledge, while a less bright reader may do very well on the same program. It may be that the program of the future will contain both a pretest on program content (on which he should score very low) as well as a test of assumed "entering abilities" (on which he should score very high). Granted the necessary entering skills and an adequate program, near-perfect posttest results might be expected. To date, little has been reported on the use of some test to assure the experimenter that students have the specific skills and knowledge necessary to complete the program successfully. Routine use of such a test might very well remove a major source of variability which is now obfuscating reported experimental results.

Several studies can be cited in partial support of the contention that specific relevant abilities may merit more attention than generalized measures of ability. For example, Gagné and Paradise (50) found negligible correlations between vocabulary (presumably closely correlated with general intelligence) and either learning rate or ability to achieve increasingly complex learning sets. On the other hand, tests of specific relevant abilities (e.g., tests of ability to add, subtract, multiply, recognize symbols, follow directions) had sizable significant correlations with performance, transfer, and speed-of-learning measures. For students who learned on consecutive sequence programs, Stolurow (135) reports no significant correlations between performances and either a full-scale IQ measure or a total language measure. On the other hand, specific (relevant) abilities such as reading comprehension and arithmetic fundamentals did correlate significantly with posttest performance.

It would seem reasonable that previous mathematical experience or grades in mathematics courses would correlate substantially with the method of instruction and with posttest performance in programed instruction in mathematics. Evans (37), Smith (131), and Roe and others (109) failed to find such relationships. However, Gagné and Dick (49), Campbell (21), and Silberman and others (115) did find significant correlations between previous mathematical achievement and program performance.

In summary, the effect of programed instruction on individual differences is by no means clear. Programs used in studies to date have simply not been effective in producing high posttest performance across the board. Whether such an ideal can be obtained is an empirical question. However, until criterion performance at a high level can be produced reliably through programs, the effects of individual differences will continue to plague investigators. The control achieved in the behavioral laboratory has not yet been reflected in the programed learning situation. It is regrettable that the sometimes prodigious efforts following the construction of a program have not been channeled into the perfection of the program prior to testing. For example, in one extensive study (128) involving eight treatments and some fifteen "mental abilities," Smith writes, "The program used in the study was unrevised and represented an initial attempt at programing by the experimenter" (pp. 147-48). Of 480 correlations between "mental abilities" and various performance measures, 22 were significant at the .05 level (note: $.05 \times 480 = 24$), and 4 were significant at the .01 level (note: $.01 \times 480 = 4.8$). To grind the axe once again, the experimental analysis investigations which gave birth to programed learning bear little relationship to the experimental design used in experiments currently being conducted in an attempt to increment knowledge about programed learning.

Student Attitude

"The student remains active. If he stops, the program stops . . . but there is no compulsion for he is not inclined to stop. Immediate and frequent reinforcement sustains a lively interest" (125, pp. 182.10-182.11). Motivation in a behavioral laboratory is no problem. Powerful reinforcers such as food, water, electrical brain stimulation, and avoidance of or escape from electric shock can be used to maintain a chosen behavior. If the "immediate and frequent" reinforcement of being right is a comparable reinforcer in the human organism, problems of sustaining motivation of "interest" in programed learning should disappear. Under such circumstances, one would expect strong positive attitudes from students toward programed instruction. Also, in light of the efforts of psychometricians to scale and measure attitude, one would expect that investigators of programed learning, presumably conversant with such techniques, would routinely gather data on this critical dependent variable. Such has not generally been the case, although some information is available.

Attitude studies toward programs in mathematics and logic to date present one consistent finding: the preponderance of students report a favorable attitude toward programed learning. In the face of such consistency, one has at least three choices: (a) to believe, (b) to suspect, as in comparative studies of programed learning and conventional instruction, negative findings for programed learning are not being reported, or (c) to question the methodology of attitude studies. Choices (a) and (b) are beyond the scope of this review; methodological considerations are not.

Most postprogram attitude questionnaires consist of a "multiple-choice" and a "free response" section. The "multiple-choice" section typically contains three- or five-choice elections (e.g., "I agree," "I have no opinion," "I disagree") to statements such as "I would rather learn from a program than from a textbook." The "free response" sections typically contain statements such as "The thing I liked *least* about this method of learning was —————." "Multiple-choice" responses do permit some quantification of attitudes, and "free responses" do permit categorization. The application of sophisticated scaling techniques to such questionnaires (cf., 29) is notable by its absence, as is any reported effort to construct a standardized postprogram attitude questionnaire.

Before turning to studies in which inferential statistics were applied to attitude measures, documentation of findings of a typical favorable disposition by Ss toward programed learning is desirable. Gagné and Dick (49) found that 92 percent of the students "enjoyed using the program to some extent." In another study utilizing a branching program in statistics, Smith (131) reports that 78 percent of his students marked "yes" to the question, "Did you enjoy taking this course by programed instruction?" Beane (11), in a study involving both linear and branching programs, found students highly favorable toward programed learning, both halfway through the experiment and at its termination. In two separate studies (35, 49), only approximately 30 percent were opposed to the notion of using programs in the classroom, with the remaining 70 percent ranging from "indifferent" to "highly enthusiastic." Similarly, Smith (131) found only 25 percent of his Ss answering "no" to the question, "Do you prefer programed instruction to conventional classroom discussion?" with 59 percent answering "yes." Eigen and Komoski (32) administered attitude questionnaires anonymously and also found indication of favorable attitudes toward programed instruction. When asked to compare learning algebra from a program with learning from a textbook (49), 42 percent of seventh graders felt the program was easier, while 28 percent felt it was more difficult. These results are in line with a similar question asked of college students who had learned symbolic logic with a program (37), where 56 percent recorded they would have learned better with a program, while 20 percent recorded they would have learned better from a textbook. Plumlee (99) reports "student response for the most part appears to be favorable to programed instruction" and offers some tangible evidence that programed learning is having a real effect. In the year previous to the availability of a programed course, only 64 percent of students who signed up for a course in descriptive statistics took the final examination. The following year, when a programed textbook in descriptive statistics was used, "eighty-seven percent of the students signing up took the final examination." The practical implications of this finding in areas where dropouts are costly are obvious.

Some attitudinal comparisons between variations in programed instruction are also available: Eigen and Komoski (32), Beane (11), Roe and others (109), and Smith (130). In the only study encountered to date to measure "retention" of attitude, Beane (11) compared attitude toward programed instruction (including both branching and linear conditions) and regular classroom instruction. Measures were taken halfway through the experiment, at its completion, and seven weeks following completion. Students declined from a strong favorable position toward programed learning to an essentially neutral position seven weeks later. Such a trend toward a somewhat neutral attitude toward programed instruction has also been observed by Eigen (31) who stated, "In my experience, the attitudes of students toward programed instruction (after they have gotten over the Hawthorne effect of their first exposure) are much the same as the attitudes of students toward any other educational situation" (p. 142).

Ability to sustain motivation over long periods in first graders with machine presentation of a program to teach algebraic structures is reported by Keislar (83). Keislar writes: "Informal observations of the pupils indicated that the experimental subjects were generally quite eager to appear each day for the auto-instructional lessons. Although records made by the research assistants contain a few isolated instances of boredom, there was little evidence of the "pall effect" sometimes found with programed instructional materials" (p. 64).

Despite a generally favorable predisposition toward programed instruction, students, given the opportunity, will complain about particular features of programed learning. Students often complain they miss the interpersonal contact with their teachers, their classmates, or both (e.g., 49, 99, 115).

There is evidence that programs do not contain enough review and that additional exercises and quizzes are helpful (e.g., 32, 99). A common observation among programers is that students "do not discriminate that they are learning" because of the gradual increment of knowledge in a program. It is likely that outside quizzes and exercises can facilitate this discrimination. A somewhat unexpected complaint (49) was that the proximity of the correct answer was "tempting"; 92 percent of the students admitted some temptation to peek ahead at the confirmation.

The data available on student attitude toward programed learning are still regrettably sparse. However, it seems a safe generalization that there is a positive reaction on the part of students ranging from first graders to college students. While this is encouraging, the variance in student attitude indicates that present motivational techniques give only a poor approximation of the control that might be achieved. It seems quite clear that immediate confirmation per se, at least as it has been employed to date, has been only a marginally successful reinforcement and maintenance device in human instruction. This leaves open the field of investigation of reinforcing properties of programed learning; possibly no other area of programed learning presents such opportunities for breakthroughs.

Size-of-Step Studies

"In acquiring complex behavior the student must pass through a carefully designed sequence of steps, often of considerable length. Each step must be so small that it can always be taken, yet in taking it the student moves somewhat closer to fully competent behavior" (124, p. 970). This "progression to mastery through small steps" has characterized programing and the programing process as a result of Skinner's guidance in his prescription of requirements for a "minimal teaching machine." As several writers (e.g., 56, 91) have pointed out, terms such as *step* and *step size* are not without their semantic and operational difficulties. Lumsdaine (91) notes that size of step could mean (a) the length of the program frame, as indexed by the number of words or sentences, (b) the difficulty of giving a correct answer at any point in the program, as reflected by the proportion of students making errors on that particular frame, (c) the complexity or length of the response, or (d) the number of responses to questions required of the student before he received correction, feedback, or reinforcement. Filby (43) reviewed size-of-step studies and suggests as additional indicators of step size (a) the number of items or examples used for concepts and (b) response latency. Early programs, particularly those generated at Harvard, did tend to be characterized by short two- or three-sentence frames. This is perhaps due to the persuasiveness of Skinner's prescription of small steps, combined with the physical constraint imposed by the wedge-shaped write-in disk machine developed and described by Skinner (124).

As Glaser (56) notes, however, there is nothing inherent in the concept of teaching machines or programed learning which dictates a special rationale for such short two- or three-sentence frames. Pennington and Slack (96) compare the characteristics of step sizes of the linear, branching, and mathetical approaches (cf., 51). They state, with respect to the amount of information given in each step, the linear approach is characterized as "small," the branching approach as "large," and the mathetical approach as "as large as possible." In his description of techniques for the preparation of mathetical lessons, Gilbert (53) suggests: "Always let your biases be in the direction of assuming too much about the student's repertory. This rule is determined by the simple fact that if you overestimate the student's repertory, you will discover the error instantly when the lessons are first tried out. If you err in the other direction, it will be very difficult to discover it" (pp. 31-32).

Difficulties in defining step and step size and the disagreements on what constitutes the optimal step size have not prevented a number of research studies on this variable from being conducted. Shay (113) investigated the relationship of intelligence to step size using a program on Roman numerals. In adjusting and evaluating step size in the construction of the program, Shay used both a criterion of an average probability of correct response and the probability of responding correctly to any given item. Shay's large-step program contained 103 frames, the medium-step program 150 frames, and the small-step program 199 frames. Ninety subjects were divided into above-average, average, and below-average ability groups, using IQ scores of 110 and 92 as cutoff points. Using a covariance analysis with pretest scores as the control, Shay found no significant posttest differences attributable either to the effect of programs or to the interaction of programs and intelligence. For all ability groups, there was a monotonic relationship between times spent on the program and step size, with the large step (fewer frames) taking the least time and the small steps (more frames) taking the most time. Differences in time spent on programs were highly significant. Shay concludes that if there is a relationship between intelligence and step size, it is not a strong one, and that his data do not suggest the necessity of alternate programs on the basis of intelligence alone.

Evans, Glaser, and Homme (39) found that better performance resulted from a smaller-step sequence than a shorter, large-step sequence. Small-step sequences produced significantly fewer response errors during learning despite increased opportunities for error due to the greater number of frames. Keislar (82) notes that when steps become too large, errors increase, and learning is not as maximal as it could be. He suggests the use of more examples and the reduction in the amount of reading per frame to reduce errors and improve learning. Silberman and others (115) report on a "hard" and an "easy" geometry program used in a study of the relationship of test anxiety and program difficulty. Since the "easy" program consisted of the same frames as the "hard" program and was supplemented by additional frames explaining the more difficult portions, this study can also be construed as being a size-of-step investigation. Silberman and others found, as did Shay (113), no significant differences related to program length. They commented that their "easy" and "hard" programs were not sufficiently dissimilar to produce the anticipated effect.

A general comment about size-of-step studies is in order. In the studies reported so far, in no case were the programs producing that desideratum of programed learning, namely, the near 100 percent posttest results by all students. This result is understandable, since these were all experimental programs constructed when little was known about the technology of program construction. As programs which reliably produce extremely high-criterion performance become available, more definitive investigations into the aspects of the size-of-step variable should be made possible.

Mode-of-Response Studies

Skinner's firmness on the necessity of an overt, composed (in contradistinction to multiple choice) response in the programed learning situation led to a rash of perhaps the most popular set of axiom-doubting studies. Since psychologists and educators are very good at making up multiple-choice items, and, since it is very easy to tell the student to "think" his answer rather than to write it down, overt-covert and response-composition vs. multiple-choice responding studies blossomed with great frequency. Gilbert (52) judged the multiple-choice selection vs. answer-construction experiment to be "the most popular experiment current in education." In a Cassandra-like prophecy, Gilbert says:

Briefly, the experiments comparing multiple-choice selection with answer construction will demonstrate considerable individual differences on whatever criteria are used. Some investigators will, with statistical equivocation, conclude in favor of the construction method; some in favor of multiple-choice; some will fail to conclude anything; and some will qualify their findings with reports of statistical interactions (p. 476).

Gilbert's prediction notwithstanding, many early investigators wanted
to see for themselves. With respect to experiments conducted using
programs in mathematics and logic, several consistent findings involving response mode have appeared. Generally the findings are (a) covert,
overt, and multiple-choice response comparisons do not result in any
significant postprogram performance differences, either immediate or
delayed, and (b) when covert (no active response required) responding
is employed, students complete the program in significantly less time.
The research supporting such findings is drawn from the following
studies: Roe, Lyman, and Moon (108), a 192-frame program on elementary probability; Lambert, Miller, and Wiley (86), an 843-frame
program on *Sets, Relations, and Functions*; Stolurow and Walker
(136), an introductory unit on descriptive statistics; Evans (35), a
72-frame and a 125-frame program in symbolic logic; and Gilpin,
Barlow, and Alexander (55). (See also the chapter by Holland.)

In summary, present data are inconclusive in establishing any clear-
cut performance advantage associated with a particular response mode.
Covert response conditions typically result in significantly less learning time and hence are more efficient. However, as Skinner (124)
points out, the overt response which the student makes provides the
programer with invaluable feedback in the construction of a program,
a point which may well be the most important feature of programed
learning.

Studies Involving Branching Programs

"A first step is to define the field. A second is to collect technical terms,
facts, laws, principles, and cases. These must then be arranged in a
plausible developmental order—linear if possible, branching if necessary."

Indulging in a whimsical desire, the author of this chapter presented the above quotation to approximately 10 of his colleagues, all
of whom had been actively engaged in programed learning for periods
of time ranging from two to seven years. Of those questioned, none
was able to identify the author on the first trial (under response-composition conditions). The source, of course, was Skinner in his 1958
article "Teaching Machines" in *Science* (124, p. 974). It is probably
due to the predilection of the popular (and, unfortunately, often of the
professional) writers who deal in contrast and dichotomies that one

so often hears of the "Skinner vs. Crowder controversy," with Skinner uncompromisingly defending linear programing and Crowder unflinchingly defending branching (intrinsic) programing. It is most likely that these two principals are less concerned about such matters than the members of the teaching machine community in general. Barlow (10) has done an excellent job of summarizing the "needlessly exaggerated" differences between Crowder and Skinner. In any event, some inevitable studies comparing linear and branching programs have been completed, as well as investigations of the effects of various branching sequences. For reasons beyond the ken of this reviewer, the number of studies involving branching is extremely small in comparison with the studies of linear programs. Studies to be cited are Beane (11), Silberman and others (117), Coulson and others (25), Roe (104, 105), Campbell (21), and Smith (129). (See also the chapter by Holland.)

In summary, no clear theme emerges from the "linear vs. branching" studies. The present technologies of construction of both linear and branching programs leave much to be desired. Such technologies should evolve, and the skill of programers in making relevant behavioral analyses should increase. It seems likely that linear and branching techniques simply serve different functions. When these functions have been identified, both techniques will be employed as needed. The "linear vs. branching" dichotomy will then disappear as the pseudoproblem which it is.

The Use of Programed Instruction To Investigate Mathematical Processes

The flurry of activity during the first decade of teaching machines and programed learning has obscured the central issue: the impact of the experimental analysis of behavior on education. The behavioral science which laid the foundation for programed instruction has been abandoned to experimental design methodology. If the problem were simply methodological, it might be resolved. At least it could be reduced to "You study programing your way; I'll study it mine." However, the experimental-analysis-of-behavior approach to education forces a focusing on fundamental issues: the nature of knowledge, the process of education, and the control of human behavior itself. Skinner, as the founder and chief proponent of the experimental analysis school, has firm but controversial opinions on the nature of knowledge and the manner in which it should be imparted to human beings. This last point can be made more forcefully. Consider two quotations:

. . . if man's intellectual excellence is the most his own among his perfections, it is also the case that the most personal of all that he knows is that which he has discovered for himself.

We can define terms like "information," "knowledge," and "verbal ability" by reference to the behavior from which we infer their presence. *We may then teach the behavior directly.*

It is a rare reader who can consider these two statements with equanimity. With the option of marking "strongly agree" on one and "violently disagree" on the other, the quotations become a two-item attitude scale toward the fundamental nature of education. (For those marking "strongly agree" to the second item, the quotation also doubles as a graduation exam for students of the experimental-analysis-of-behavior school.) The first quote is from Jerome Bruner (17, p. 82), surely one of the influential writers on education of this decade. The second quote is from Skinner (125, p. 182.07). Two students of the problems of education; two psychologists at Harvard with Ph.D.'s in psychology from Harvard; two creative experimenters; two respected scientists; two compelling writers; too far apart.

This brief introduction has been ominous. It hints darkly of dichotomy and diatribe, of confusion and chaos. Worse, it has yet to mention either programing or mathematics. The purpose of this chapter is to relate programed instruction to the study of mathematical processes; to attempt to put the "new" mathematics in perspective; to identify relevant new techniques and devices; and, having peered into the innards of both programing and mathematics, to augur the future. How then will aspects of the experimental analysis of behavior aid in accomplishing these objectives? There are four ways. First, to the degree that mathematics is important, potential contributions from the science of behavior to the understanding of mathematical processes are important. Psychology, as a science of the behavior of organisms, is derivative from behaviorism, which is a *philosophy of science.* Unfortunately, behaviorism is an 11-letter word to many students of education. As a result, studies which are too behavioristic tend to be avoided or ignored. This chapter will attempt a clear delineation of the orientation and techniques of the behavioral scientist. If such an exposition leads to reexaminations and reconsiderations of the potential of behavioral techniques for studying mathematical processes, a major purpose of this review will have been accomplished. Second, experimental behavioral analysis is historically important. No one would quarrel with the fact that Skinner's application of operant conditioning techniques to human education provided the impetus for present-day programed instruction. Third, studies by the experimental analysis school have made significant contributions to the analysis of mathematical behavior. The methodology and approach in such studies contrast sharply with those used by most investigators of mathematical behavior. The striking contrast allows one to see clearly both tactical and strategical differences in two diverse approaches to learning about mathematical processes. Fourth, mathematical behavior, whatever else it may be, is behavior. Experimental analysis provides an exhaustive, sequential model to examine any behavior. In applying the model to mathematical behavior, one should be able to focus on the critical aspects, topics, and issues, regardless of one's particular philosophy.

The last point must be amplified, since it forms the theme for the remainder of this review. It is the slender thread with which a whole cloth can be woven from such diverse filaments as Piaget, chaining, Begle, Suppes, Skinner, discovery, Premack, O. K. Moore, SMSG, mathetics, "new" math, induction, Ferster, reversibility, Eigen, validated instruction, UICSM, autotelic, Bruner, Page, nonverbal awareness, heuristics, Ausubel, Cuisenaire rods, discrimination training, Gagné, preoperational stage, Holland, structure, set theory, Beberman, and hierarchies of subordinate learning sets.

The model is this. Suppose an operant conditioner, one schooled in the experimental analysis of behavior, is given an organism and charged with teaching it something. He would first *select* the behavior he wishes to teach. He would then *analyze* the chosen behavior. Next, he would *produce* the behavior with the facilities at hand. Finally, he might make provisions to *maintain* and *extend* the selected behavior. It is under the topics of the *selection, analysis, production,* and *maintenance* and *extension* of mathematical behavior that this section will attempt to bind the concepts, conflicts, personalities, and problems which the intersection of mathematics and programed instruction has produced.

The Selection of Mathematical Behavior

Skinner (126) writes, "In studying such [operant] behavior we must make certain preliminary decisions. We begin by choosing an organism—one which we hope will be representative but which is first merely convenient. We must also choose a bit of behavior" (p. 101). In most studies of mathematical behavior, the most convenient organism has proved to be the human being. But in choosing the "bit of behavior" to be taught, Skinner allows considerable freedom. In the hands of a skilled operant conditioner, animals exhibit "complexities and subtleties of behavior probably never before reached by members of their species" (126). The relevance of these observations for the purposes of this chapter are stated clearly by Gilbert (53): "a technology of control will not supply wisdom about *what* to teach and *whom* to teach; nevertheless these principles of control do apply" (p. 7).

The question of what to teach is properly a curriculum problem. Sweeping curriculum reforms, stimulated in part by the ineluctable presence of Sputnik in 1957, have altered at least the façade of American education. The efforts of the Biological Sciences Curriculum Study (BSCS) and the Physical Science Study Committee (PSSC) are well known, but the activities among the mathematics groups have been far more extensive. The School Mathematics Study Group under Edward Begle, the University of Illinois Committee on School Mathematics under Max Beberman, the University of Illinois Arithmetic Project under David Page, and the Minnesota School Mathematics Center under Paul Rosenbloom are only four of the best known committees whose prodigious efforts have had profound effects on mathematics curricula.

But this strays from the model. If the first step is to *select* behavior to be taught, why should an effective technology of instruction be concerned with content changes recommended by top-flight experts in the field of mathematics? If set theory, inequalities, and a more careful distinction between number and numeral help update the old-fashioned curriculum, why not simply include them? Again the model pinpoints the difficulty.

Curriculum committees do more work than they are paid for. The work of curriculum committees is never confined to the selection of new behaviors to be taught; such committees inevitably get caught up in the analyses, production, and maintenance and extension phases of training. It is the failure to discriminate and separate these phases which can constrain the thinking and subsequent recommendation of such committee members. This can be illustrated with a quotation from Barbel Inhelder of the Geneva group, taken from Bruner (18):

Another matter relates particularly to the ordering of a mathematics curriculum. Often the sequence of psychological development follows more closely the axiomatic order of a subject matter than it does the historical order of development of concepts within the field. One observes, for instance, that certain topological notions such as connection, separation, being interior to, and so forth, precede the formation of Euclidian and projective notions in geometry, though the former ideas are newer in their formalism in the history of mathematics than the latter. If any special justification were needed for teaching the structure of a subject in its proper logical or axiomatic order rather than its order of historical development, this should provide it (pp. 43-44).

Inhelder's argument is scholarly, bold, and seductive. As is characteristic of the Geneva school, it also has the sanction of being based on the extensive observations of the development of mathematical and logical processes in children. But note that Inhelder's recommendations on sequences contain elements of *analysis* as well as elements of *selection*. As a result, she has reached the plausible conclusion that in presenting mathematics, logical order is superior to historical order. Unfortunately, by confounding the analysis phase with the selection phase, Inhelder has missed a very real logical possibility: neither axiomatic or historical sequencing may be optimum. As Gilbert (52) puts it, "You don't want to know *whether* one method teaches better than another, you want to know *what* method teaches best" (p. 478). More pointedly, the principle of chaining, developed by Skinner (120) and utilized extensively by Gilbert (53, 54) in constructing the teaching system he terms *mathetics*, raises serious doubt that a "logical" sequence is necessarily the most effective learning sequence.

Psychologists do not create mathematics. Mathematicians do. And, if mathematicians do not get caught in *how* mathematics should be taught, they generally have little difficulty in agreeing *what* should be taught. The frustrated parent who can no longer help his child with his arithmetic notwithstanding, the *content* now being selected for some mathematics textbooks (and programs) is excellent, even if most of it is 100 years late. In summary, the programer skilled in experimental analysis is not particularly concerned about *what* should be taught. In this, he will defer to the good judgment of his colleagues in other fields. He will properly question *how* a chosen content is to be taught, as will be seen in the remaining sections.

In spite of disparate and sometimes violent disagreement on *how* curriculum subjects should be taught, there is beginning to be an interesting concurrence of opinion among students of the educational process on *when* subject matter can be taught to children. The point is well expressed by Bruner (18): "We begin with the hypothesis that any subject can be taught effectively in some intellectually honest form to any child at any stage of development. It is a bold hypothesis and an essential one in thinking about the nature of a curriculum. No evidence exists to contradict it; considerable evidence is being amassed that supports it" (p. 33).

In outlining the possibility of special purpose teaching machines, Skinner (126) states "there is much . . . that could be done to increase the behavioral repertoires of children, even those who are younger than school age" (p. 101). And Inhelder, quoted by Bruner (18), suggests, "These examples lead us to think that it is possible to draw up methods of teaching the basic ideas in science and mathematics to children considerably younger than the traditional age" (p. 44). Page, again in a quote from Bruner (18), states, "As far as I am concerned young children learn almost anything faster than adults do if it can be given to them in terms they understand. . . . It is appropriate that we warn ourselves to be careful of assigning an absolute level of difficulty to any particular topic" (p. 40). Studies involving the use of programed instruction to teach advanced mathematical topics to students well below the age level at which such topics are ordinarily taught have been cited earlier in this review. Such investigations included the teaching of algebraic structures to first graders (83), geometry to second graders (88), and equations and inequalities to bright fifth and sixth graders (81). As previously mentioned, absences of significant differences in posttest performances of ninth, tenth, and eleventh graders who had learned from a program in modern mathematics led Eigen and Komoski (32) to conclude that the traditional concept that certain materials are best taught at a given grade level needs serious reexamination. Dramatic support for this last statement has been provided by Suppes (138). In a pilot-study class taught by Shirley Hill, bright fifth graders were given specially prepared materials in mathematical logic. No quantified results are presented, but the children appeared to achieve a level of accomplishment in deductive reasoning skills which compared favorably with achievement levels of college undergraduates taking mathematical logic. Understandably, the pace of the fifth graders was much slower. Suppes (138) concludes: "Evidence is mounting that logic is not too abstract for the elementary school child of age 10, 11, or 12, but on the contrary, that this age may represent the most propitious time for the introduction of abstract concepts" (p. 397).

Another contribution by Suppes and his associates, using material which more closely approximates programed textbooks, has been the teaching of the concept of sets to first graders (140, 141). Students were taught set concepts including union, difference of sets, set variable, and the empty set and zero. The basic teaching vehicle was a workbook which presented problems and required the child to make multiple-choice responses. Suppes and Hill (140) report: "Results from the first two years' experimentation show that notions of set and set operations are more easily comprehended than those of number. A special point of some interest is the striking evidence during this experiment for the early introduction of zero as the number of things in the empty set" (p. 52). The same report also cites evidence that experimental classes taught set concepts were superior in knowledge of number operations and concepts to comparable classes using more conventional approaches to arithmetic.

The bold and imaginative statements and experiments on *when* a selected topic can be taught allows this section to end on an optimistic note. It has been noted that the programer, like any good workman, is willing to accept any assignment. He will not quarrel about *what* is to be taught. As will be examined in detail in the section on the production of behavior, he may become fussy (like any good workman) if he is told *how* to teach. But he will happily join the growing throng who proclaim that much more can be taught, much better, at lower age levels than one would have dared to dream of 10 years ago. *What* can be taught *when* is a matter of empirical determination—which is exactly as it should be.

The Analysis[3] of Mathematical Behavior

In attempting to quantify the success of a rocket launching, it is possible to assign a score of "1" if the satellite is put successfully into orbit and to assign a score of "0" if it fails. Such binary scoring, in the event of failure, would contribute little toward improving the science of rocketry. A more reasonable procedure is to use high-speed cameras to document the progress of the rocket at various stages. If a failure occurs, the rocket scientist can determine the stage at which it occurred and those systems which were presumably in operation at the time of the failure. Corrections can then be made to increase the probability of success of the next launching. Without pressing the metaphor too far, programed learning is a process for taking high-speed pictures of the learning process. If a student goes wrong at any point, the program constructor can examine the sequence of frames leading up to the point of failure. He can scan the pattern of responses, summarize them, and in general get much information of value to aid him in diagnosing the difficulty which the student encountered. The opportunity to make this study of the human learning process results from the fact that in programed instruction, the student is responding to a series of steps and is leaving a written record of his response at each step. The step-by-step recording of answers provides the research worker with an unprecedented opportunity to learn about how students learn. After a student has been taught by a lecture or by a conventional textbook, he can be tested to ascertain how well he has learned. While there will be some diagnostic value gained from the study of the posttest following conventional instruction, no comparable records exist which permit the detailed reconstruction of the student's learning experience which programed learning provides. The chief vir-

---

[3] Analysis is a broad term. As Skinner uses the term (118), "experimental analysis" generally involves long-term studies of single organisms. Rate of responding is typically the dependent variable, and any of a variety of independent variables, such as schedules of reinforcement or drugs, may be studied. In a real sense, anyone who makes naturalistic or experimental observations of behaving organisms and abstracts some feature of that behavior to record and classify can be said to be *analyzing* that behavior. Furthermore, to the degree that words and symbols already represent abstractions, their manipulations and arrangements can likewise be considered analysis. In the model used here, analysis of behavior follows selection and precedes production. In this section, then, analysis will be defined as any abstraction of aspects of a selected behavior plus any arrangement of such abstractions made previous to attempting production of that behavior.

tue programed learning has to offer in the analysis of mathematical behavior is the opportunity of the experimenter to get detailed records on a reproducible sequence of learning events. Variables can then be manipulated, and consequent effects on a variety of dependent variables can then be examined. These advantages stem from the control which the program exerts over the behavior of the student.

A major contribution to the analysis of mathematical behavior has been made by Hively (67). Hively comes directly to grips with problems such as describing the behavior of a student who "understands counting" in a reasonably thorough and rigorous way. This necessarily leads to questions of test construction, which Hively treats at length. Since even for the most elementary mathematical behavior, the number of possible test items is generally infinite, some other tack must be taken. Hively points out that the behavior of Ss may be defined in terms of *classes* of responses and *classes* of stimuli which control them. Rather than making lists of criterion items, which is usually impossible, he suggests that it should be possible to write the rules which generate populations of equivalent items. These rules will then define, rather than exemplify, the criterion behavior. For example, suppose the problem is that of testing the student's "understanding" of counting in the decimal system. To exemplify all possible test items is patently impossible. However, criterion behavior can be defined with a rule which will generate acceptable test items. A typical "test-item form" for this behavior would be—

Write the numerals from m to n in the decimal system.

Restriction: m and n may be any numbers such that $|m - n| < 20$.

The problem then becomes the empirical one of finding the sample of items of this form which will provide the best prediction on a random sample of the infinite set of other items of this form. Hively draws attention to the fact that in this context, the classical notions of test validity and reliability lose their usefulness. In other words, if success on the empirically determined sample permits predictions of success on any sample drawn from items generated by the test-items form, it is a valid and reliable measure of the predefined behavior. Since such a measure of criterion behavior is now absolute in nature, Hively also questions the value of the conventional process of establishing norms. Hively's report contains many other provocative and ingenious notions on assessing criterion behavior in mathematics which space does not permit discussing. His presentation is strongly recommended to anyone interested in measurement, in mathematics, in programing, or in any combination of these three.

Workers in programed learning have developed, or adapted, a variety of analytical techniques for analyzing behavior. Csanyi, in a report by Homme (70), presents four such techniques, as well as a discussion of the importance of analysis previous to the programing of any topic. Two of the techniques, flow charts (cf., 37, 38) and decision tables, will be familiar to computer programers. The matrix technique (cf., 40), an early attempt at systematic behavioral analysis, is also presented. Finally, a format developed by Csanyi which he terms the critical discrimination (CD) chart is described. The CD chart is derivative from the flow chart. However, it appears to be superior to the flow chart as a presentation device, or panel, in cases where the S is given the chart as part of his program package (38). The paper by Evans (38) also presents the "set-permutational" technique, an extension of the matrix technique to more than two dimensions.

Gagné and his associates (47, 50, 51) have contributed both a provocative analytical technique and a formidable body of supportive data to the field of programed mathematics instruction. Gagné's basic concept is that any behavior (for example, solving linear equations) can be analyzed into a *hierarchy of learning sets*.

This analysis was based upon a theory to the effect that attainment of any given learning set is dependent upon recallability of certain subordinate learning sets. . . . Subordinate learning sets are conceived as having the function of mediating positive transfer to higher level learning sets throughout the hierarchy, and ultimately to the final task. Subordinate learning sets for a given class of tasks may be defined as the answer to the question: "What would the individual have to be able to know how to do, in order to be able to perform this (new) task, being given only instructions?" Beginning with the final task, the question is applied successively to each learning set so defined, and thus identifies a progression of learning sets which grow increasingly simple and increasingly general (50, pp. 16-17).

Based on his analysis, Gagné is then able to lay out in graphical form the basic structure under consideration. Basic sets or concepts necessary for higher-order sets are placed lower in the structure; specific relations between subordinate and superordinate sets are shown by interconnecting lines. By designing items to measure the attainment of each set in the hierarchy, Gagné is then able to do an analysis of the "pass-fail" pattern of achievement between adjacent lower and higher level related learning sets. Four logical patterns exist: passing both the higher learning set and the supporting lower set (+ +); failing both the higher set and the lower supporting set (— —); passing the higher and failing the lower (+ —); failing the higher and passing the lower (— +). Gagné's theory predicts higher positive transfer from a recalled learning set and attainment of the adjacent higher relevant learning set. Obviously, either passing both the higher and lower set or failing both would be in accord with the theory (+ + and — — patterns). Passing a higher set after having failed a related subordinate set is directly opposed to the theory (+ — pattern). Failing a higher set after passing a lower set (— + pattern) is not in opposition to the theory, but is taken by Gagné as being partially due to inadequacies in the instructional program. A measure of the proportion of positive transfer may be obtained by summing the (+ +), (— —), and (+ —) pattern and dividing this sum into the sum of the two patterns in accord with the theory (+ + ; — —). Ratios approaching 1.00 provide strong confirmation of the theory. In studies involving analyses of programs in nonmetric geometry (51) and equation solving (50), Gagné obtained strikingly high positive transfer indices in both studies. With the current emphasis on structure in mathematics, Gagne's techniques of structural analysis and empirical checking of the transfer components of mathematical learning set hierarchies merit serious consideration. Diagrammatic analysis of either existing or proposed programs are quite likely to have salutary effects on furthering the improvement of programing technology.

No account of current efforts to analyze behavior would be complete without mentioning the system of *mathetics*, developed by Gilbert (53, 54). Gilbert (53) defines mathetics[4] as "the systematic application of reinforcement theory to the analysis and reconstruction of those complex behavior repertoires usually known as 'subject-matter mastery,' 'knowledge,' and 'skill' " (p. 8). The two published volumes of *Mathetics* are, regretfully, either unknown to or disregarded by the programed learning community as a whole. There are several reasons

---

[4] Subtitle: The [sic] Technology of Education.

for this disregard. First, the claims made for mathetics strike some as presumptuous (e.g., "Mathetics is not just another point-of-view about teaching and learning; it is an authoritative scientific technology" [53, p. 9]). Second, Gilbert has a penchant for giving new names to old ideas and old names to new ideas. Third, the system is rigorously behavioristic, and behavioral terminology is offensive to many. Fourth, Gilbert fails to exemplify adequately many key concepts and operations in his system. As a result, the reader, however strong his motivations to learn the system, finds himself at the end unable to construct a mathetics lesson (the word "program" is taboo) of his own.

Nonetheless, in the opinion of this author, *Mathetics: The Technology of Education* must rank in the top three contributions to the field of programed learning. It is boldly original: it departs both from any known educational theory and from Skinnerian principles of programing. It is both analytic and synthetic[5]: it provides guidelines and notational systems for breaking a selected skill into its components and putting them back together in the form of a teaching sequence. And, if a clincher is needed, it is a scientific system with the historical sanction of being misunderstood and ignored by almost everyone who should be interested in it. Gilbert's techniques for analyzing behavior are too involved to be dealt with in detail here. An important aspect of mathetics, however, is that behavior can be analyzed exhaustively into generalizations, discriminations, and chains. Gilbert (53) provides a clever and flexible notation system incorporating symbols for these three basic behavior concepts.

In the somewhat broad definition of analysis, it was stated above that anyone who made naturalistic or experimental observations of behavior and abstracted from such behavior was doing "analysis." Such a conception allows one to fit the work of Piaget and others of the Geneva school into the present model. Piaget's writing (e.g., 79, 97, 98) on the development of concepts of mathematics and logic in children has had profound influence on many students of mathematical processes, both here and abroad. The work of Piaget is characterized by ingenious experiments and apparatus to determine how children at various age levels deal with assorted problems involving con-

---

[5] Note to matheticists: not "analytic" and "synthetic" as Gilbert uses the terms.

cepts of mathematics, logic, and science. Typical concepts would be that of conservation of number following rearrangement, transitivity of preferences (cf., 127), and conservation of volume under transformation. As a result of a formidable amount of experimentation, Piaget and his colleagues distinguished between at least three "stages" of logical development. Each stage can be characterized by logical concepts that a child is able or unable to demonstrate. The stage of "preoperational" thought, (roughly, 2-7 years) is characterized by the absence of the "reversibility" operations. "For example, when the child . . . pours liquid or beads from one glass bottle into another of a different shape, he still believes that the actual quantity in the recipient bottle is increased or diminished in the process. . . . When the most elementary forms of conservation are absent, it is a consequence of the absence of operational reversibility" (98, pp. 11-12). The stage of "concrete operations" (roughly, 7-11 years) is characterized by the presence of the concept of reversibility and also of "internalization," or the absence of the necessity of overt trial-and-error. The child eventually reaches the stage of "formal operations" (roughly, 14-15 years). When apparatus or problems are presented to children who have attained this stage, they "endeavor after a few trials to formulate all the possible hypotheses concerning the operative factors, and then arrange their experiments as a function of these factors" (98, p. 19). The work of Piaget and the Geneva school is characterized by careful experimentation and observation and almost complete absence of training and instruction. It qualifies clearly as *analysis* of behavior (under the present definition), but stops short of controlled *production* of behavior, which titles the next section.

In summary, there are many ways one can examine the behavior one has selected before one begins to control its production. It is regrettable that so much work in examining mathematical processes halts at the analysis stage.

The Production of Mathematical Behavior

A mathematician is an organism who takes scrupulous care in moving artificial objects following arbitrary rules. In so doing, he makes patterns. If the patterns are ugly and useful, he is called an *applied* mathematician. If the patterns are pretty and useless, he is called a *pure* mathematician. Applied mathematicians make more money while they are living, but pure mathematicians become more famous after they are dead. The objects and rules with which mathematicians play are called *concepts*. Psychologists have been interested in the formation of concepts for many years. At first, they concentrated their efforts on developing materials and techniques to *prevent* concept formation in order to study the process. Most of these efforts were highly successful (e.g., 19, 62, 78, 133), although some humans formed concepts anyway. Lately, some psychologists have become interested in developing materials and techniques to *facilitate* concept formation. Surprisingly enough, they have been somewhat successful also.

What is a concept? As Keller and Schoenfeld (84) point out, "Strictly speaking, one does not *have* a concept . . . rather, one demonstrates conceptual behavior, by acting in a certain way" (p. 154). A child (or a rat) demonstrates the concept of triangularity by responding in some appropriate manner to all triangles and by not responding in the same manner to nontriangles. Much of the art in conceptual programing lies in the selection and sequencing of exemplars which fall within and without the conceptual class being taught. "Generalization *within* classes and discrimination *between* classes—this is the essence of concepts" (84, p. 155). Generalization is typically produced by reinforcing correct responses to a wide variety of exemplars of the chosen conceptual class; discrimination is typically produced by extinguishing responses to nonexemplars, particularly those which contain all but the particular critical aspect of the concept in question. (See also Chapter 10 by Mechner.)

Teaching a concept to humans or animals by reinforcing appropriate responses to members of a chosen class and extinguishing inappropriate responses is neither new nor startling. Using these techniques over 30 years ago, Fields (42) demonstrated the ability of the white rat to generalize on the basis of the mathematical concept of triangularity. However, in the field of programed learning, there exists an anomaly of more than passing interest. In his classic article of 1958, Skinner makes a plausible case for the application of established laboratory results and techniques to human learning. It is no doubt a tribute to Skinner's persuasiveness that he was recommending "a right response at every step" when there existed no laboratory analogues, with or without human subjects, of *errorless* conceptual learning at that time.[6] The concept of errorless learning is the key to understanding the role of programed instruction in the production of mathematical behavior.

In 1960 Evans (37) noted:

Classical techniques for the investigation of verbal learning are characterized by the precautions taken to prevent learning from occurring. Nonsense-syllable lists are standardized for low-association value; concept-formation problems contain irrelevant stimulus dimensions; problem solving tasks are selected for their novelty. As a consequence, a characteristic of the initial stages of such learning is the number of response errors. For any increase in the probability of correct responding to occur, differential feedback as to the adequacy of such responses is obviously necessary.

In a learning program, however, the attempt is made to arrange a series of stimuli so that successive responses have a high probability of being correct from the beginning. As the learning progresses, the supporting stimuli or prompts are "faded" or withdrawn, but only at such a rate that correct responses continue to be emitted. At the termination of an "ideal" program, criterion responses should be under the control of the minimum set of stimuli which set the occasion for such responses (pp. 75-76).

Skinner's concept that human beings can acquire knowledge and skills without errors during that acquisition is surely one of the boldest propositions ever set forth before a trial-and-error world. Much of the controversy over programed instruction stems from this proposition and some of the attempts to implement it. Criticisms have ranged from the "life-is-not-a-bowl-of-cherries-and-errors-are-good-for-you" attitude (cf., 102) to the identification of the very real existence of errorless "small-step" programs which simultaneously insulted the students' intelligence as they systematically murdered their motivation for the programed topic (46). Philosophical aspects of errorless learning and techniques for combating the "pall effect" are beyond the scope of this review. However, if the task of this chapter is to relate the important concepts of programed instruction to the important concepts of modern mathematics teaching, one critical issue must be faced and resolved: the relationship between errorless learning and discovery learning.

---

[6] Relevant studies involving errorless *discrimination* learning will be reported later in this section. The reader will recognize that "errorless" learning is a conceptual convenience similar to the physicist's "perfect" vacuum or the chemist's "perfect" gas.

Discovery learning is trial-and-error learning. In mathematics, the teacher will present a series of exemplars or patterns. Students will attempt to discover, but not necessarily be able to verbalize (65), the concept or rule which permits the correct identification or generation of additional exemplars or patterns. In theory, the probability of success of a student in a true "discovery" situation is initially low or zero. As will be pointed out later, true "discovery" situations rarely exist in practice, so initial probability of success is above zero, but certainly not extremely high as in "errorless" programed learning.

Some feeling for the preeminent position of discovery learning in mathematics education in the United States can be gained from the following quotes. First, from the Report of the Secondary-School Curriculum Committee of the National Council of Teachers of Mathematics (112): "At all levels of instruction more emphasis should be placed upon pupil discovery and reasoning" (p. 397). Next, from the Commission on Mathematics of the College Entrance Examination Board (24): "Most if not all of the Commission members would prefer to see a developmental approach, which would encourage the student to discover as much of the mathematical subject matter for himself as his ability and the time available (for this is a time-consuming method) will permit" (p. 17). Discovery learning has also strongly influenced the activities of the mathematics curriculum study groups. For example, Wills (148) writes, "Another goal for our programers is to encourage students to discover the desired concept by providing them with sequences of developmental exercises" (p. 806). Also, the list of enthusiastic proponents of discovery learning is long and distinguished (e.g., 5, 16, 18, 27, 28, 63, 64, 65, 94, 137).

In the face of such unanimity of opinion by such an august group on the virtues of learning by discovery, it takes a first-class devil's advocate to stand up and ask, "Where is your evidence for the value of discovery learning?" In a scholarly, rational, and incisive manner, David Ausubel (8) has both asked and answered that question. He concludes:

Actual examination of the research literature allegedly supportive of learning by discovery reveals that valid evidence of this nature is virtually nonexistent. . . . The different curriculum reform projects using discovery techniques have not attempted the well-nigh impossible task of isolating the effects of the discovery variable from the effects of other significant variables and, in most instances, have not even attempted to collect adequate control data with which to evaluate the efficacy of a given project as a whole (p. 56).

Ausubel's searching study of the rationale and mystique of discovery learning merits the serious attention and consideration of any student of mathematical processes, regardless of his academic background.

Where then is one left with learning by discovery? And how may one draw it into meaningful relationship with the "errorless" learning of programed instruction? Fortunately, with much of the smoke-be-hind-the-altar on discovery having been cleared away by Ausubel,[7] one is in a position to take a fresh look at the production of mathe-matical behavior. There are two basic ways to establish concept for-mation in the human being without errors: (a) give him a carefully programed and tested series of exemplars which will allow him to in-duce the concept or (b) tell him the concept. The ability of the human organism to learn a concept in one expository trial has great survival value. As Ausubel (8) puts it, "This miracle of culture is made possible only because it is so much less time-consuming to communicate and explain an idea meaningfully to others than to have them rediscover it by themselves" (p. 27). Skinner (126) seems to have anticipated the objection of the discovery enthusiasts to expository instruction when he states, "The teacher-turned-programer . . . may find it difficult to allow an item to stand which 'gives the point away' " (p. 172). And, with respect to the first point above, Ausubel (8) notes, "In the UICSM program, therefore, students are given a prearranged sequence of suitable exemplars, and from these they 'spontaneously self-dis-cover' the appropriate generalization. . . . This type of discovery is

---

[7] It would be misleading to give the impression that Ausubel considers discovery learning without value. He clearly states: "In the early, unsophisticated stages of learning any abstract subject matter, particularly prior to adolescence, the discovery method is invaluable. It is also indispensable for teaching scientific method and effective problem-solving skills. Furthermore, various cognitive and motivational factors undoubtedly enhance the learning, retention, and transferability of mean-ingful material learned by discovery" (p. 22). However, he also points out: "The crucial points at issue, however, are not whether learning by discovery enhances learning, retention, and transferability, but (a) whether it does so *sufficiently*, for learners who are capable of learning principles meaningfully *without* it, to warrant the vastly increased expenditure of time it requires; and (b) whether, in view of this time consideration, the discovery method is a feasible technique for trans-mitting the substantive content of an intellectual or scientific discipline to cogni-tively mature students who have already mastered its rudiments and basic vocabu-lary" (p. 25).

perfectly compatible with the automated teaching movement (despite the howls of anguish which teaching machines elicit from discovery enthusiasts)" (p. 43).

In the reported research which formed the initial portion of this chapter, no studies of programed learning were reported in which either performance on frames or on criterion tests approximated errorless learning. In view of Ausubel's comment on the "programed" nature of the material produced by workers in discovery learning, it can be observed that proponents of "errorless" and "discovery" learning, although conceptually far apart, are empirically close together. A number of reviews of "learning by discovery" are available (9, 85). With one exception (48), the studies did not involve programed instruction, and, though interesting in their own right, are beyond the scope of this review.

Gagné and Brown (48) used an 89-item introductory program[8] to teach basic concepts and symbols to be used later in a task involving the sum of number series. After completing the introductory program, the students were assigned to three treatment groups. All groups were assigned the task of finding a general formula for the sum of four new number series. In the Rule and Example (R & E) program, S copied the correct formula in each case, identified terms in the formula, and found numerical values for the sum using the formula. In the Discovery (D) program, S was asked for the sum formula and was then given a series of hints as they were needed. In the Guided Discovery (GD) program, the items guided the student to observe certain relationships between the rows of term values, the series itself, and the row of sums, and called for a variety of verbal and symbolic responses. All Ss returned the next day and repeated the nonintroductory phase of their program. They were then asked to find the general sum formula for four *new* series. Solution time and number of hints were measured, and weighted time score based on these two measures also served as a dependent variable. On the transfer tasks, significant differences were found with the GD program producing the best performance, the R & E program the worst performance, and an intermediate performance for the D program. The authors conclude that the Guided Discovery pro-

---

[8] This is one of the few reports in the literature employing programed instruction to control learning variables previous to the introduction of the experimental variables.

gram requires the S to actively produce certain critical concepts, that the Discovery program requires the same active production in a less systematic manner, and that the Rule and Example program may lack this feature of active production or "reinstatement" of key concepts. On this basis they conclude that for problem-solving performance, "what is learned" is more important than "how it is learned."

Della-Piana and Eldridge (26) replicated the results of the Gagné and Brown (48) study and got essentially the same experimental results. However, Della-Piana and Eldridge also did a frame-by-frame analysis comparing the Rule and Example program with the Guided Discovery program. They point out differences in what is practiced and how it is practiced in each program. They conclude that at least part of the advantage of the GD program results from it being less highly prompted and more varied in the use of equivalent words and symbols. They recognize the impossibility of equating such treatments "without somehow destroying what is meant by discovery" (p. 9). One is again reminded of Gilbert's admonition: "You don't want to know whether one method teaches better than another, you want to know what method teaches best" (52, p. 478).

One final "guided discovery" study in which the guide was an IBM 650 computer is worthy of mention (60). A half-semester's work in college-level statistics was completed by six students. The decision logic in the core of the statistics program, among other things, permits the student to make up to three errors (and receive an error cue following the first two errors) before the correct solution and an alternate problem is presented. The student can also request cues from the machine before attempting the solution to a problem. On the same midterm posttest, the computer group averaged over 94 percent compared with the 58 percent of eight students receiving the same material by lecture and homework. Equally impressive was an approximately 1:9 advantage in instructional time in favor of the computer group.

Despite the paucity of studies of variations on discovery which involve programed learning, the results to date seem to be consistent with Ausubel's (9) conclusion: "Providing guidance to the learner in the form of verbal explanation of the underlying principles almost invariably facilitates learning and retention and sometimes transfer as well. *Self*-discovery methods and the furnishing of completely explicit rules, on the other hand, are relatively less effective" (p. 171).

At this point it is appropriate to introduce two concept formation investigations which are not studies in programed learning. That is, the learning tasks were not arranged to produce and maintain high probabilities of correct responding from the beginning. However, as can be shown, each of these investigations are highly relevant to the production of mathematical behavior, although for quite different reasons. The first investigation involves a series of studies of mathematical concept formation in young children (139). In the first study, Ss learned the binary equivalents of the Arabic numerals 4 and 5 (100 and 101) with different symbols substituted for the two binary digits (0 and 1). All children were told whether they were correct or incorrect after each trial. Half of the Ss were instructed to correct their responses following an error. This latter group performed significantly better than the half who did not correct their errors. Suppes and Ginsberg (139) found that without modification, a simple paired-associate mathematical model produced eight out of eight excellent fits between predicted and observed statistics. Only one *observed* value was used to estimate the single parameter of this model. Due to the small number (6) of different stimuli in this first experiment, the authors point out that the children may have acquired associations between specific stimuli and appropriate responses; hence the initial good fit by the paired-associate model. In subsequent experiments, no stimulus display was ever repeated to insure that the tasks were indeed concept formation exercises. In a second experiment, the authors used combinations of the concepts of *equipollence* (number of objects in two sets equal), *identity* of sets (sets with same objects, order disregarded), and *ordered* sets (same objects, same order) in an attempt to find the most efficient sequence to produce the concepts. In spite of *logical* reasons to expect facilitation (e.g., identical sets are always equipollent; therefore, identity might be expected to facilitate equipollence), no appreciable facilitating effects were found in presenting any of the three concepts before presentation of the second of these concepts. A later experiment demonstrated that no incidental learning of equipollence occurred when Ss could get the correct answer on the basis of spurious color cues—which is consistent with the programer's dictum to make sure that Ss do not get "the right answer for the wrong reason." However, learning of equipollence was enhanced in a group which started out with spurious color cues that were slowly "fused" so that discrimination based on color was not possible. Their "fusing" apparently forced closer attention to the stimuli; hence the enhanced learning. A final empirical result is of particular interest to programers interested in multiple-choice responding. In learning equipollence, it is possible to present S with two sets and have his response indicate presence or absence of equipollence of the two sets. Or, he can be given a stimulus set and be required to pick one of two or one of three multiple-choice alternatives. These three treatments were employed, and the ability of Ss to transfer the equipollence concept on the second day was checked. Ss who learn presence-absence of equipollence transferred to the new task (three-choice multiple-choice) more effectively than did either of the multiple-choice groups to the presence-absence condition. Of the two- and three-multiple-choice groups, the three-choice group transferred more effectively than the two-choice group.

Again, these results, although interesting in their own right, were obtained from a nonprogramed sequence. That is, Ss presumably began all tasks at chance levels and, through differential feedback, built up to whatever point of competence the training situation permitted. It is interesting to conjecture whether an attempt to program the concepts would markedly alter the results obtained by Suppes and Ginsberg. After examination of both programed and nonprogramed learning studies, Evans (37) concluded that the relevance of variables such as response mode and immediacy of confirmation are inversely related to the probability of correct responding. Put more simply, perhaps the same laws do not hold in programed versus nonprogramed situations.

An intriguing series of studies on "hypothesis formation" or "learning without awareness" have been reported by Verplanck (146). Again, as in the study by Suppes and Ginsberg, the concept-formation tasks used were not "programed" in the sense of attempting to achieve high probabilities of correct responding from the beginning. However, Verplanck's techniques and findings should be of considerable interest to anyone concerned with the relationship between concept-formation behavior and correlated verbal statements *about* that behavior. Verplanck's experimental procedure was straightforward. Ss were provided with a number of children's "trading cards." Each card was different from the other cards, and the cards varied in many dimensions with respect to pictures and designs. Ss were instructed to guess whether each card in turn belonged on the left or on the right. They were fur-

ther instructed on each trial to state the rule followed in attempting
to place the card correctly.[9] Verplanck treats the rule-statement and
the motor response of placing the cards right or left as separate operants. This permits verbal reinforcement ("right" and "wrong") of
either a predetermined rule-statement ("e.g., single objects to the right;
more than one object to the left") or of the actual placement of the card.
In the experiment of most immediate interest, one group was differentially reinforced for correct placement; the other group was differentially reinforced for emitting the correct rule-statement. The results
were striking. The group reinforced for placement stated the correct
rule, or a version of it, on 48.4 percent of the trials; they placed the
cards correctly on 71.8 percent—a discrepancy of 23.4 percent in the
direction of the operant (placement) which was reinforced. The group
reinforced for the correct rule statement was correct on 94.2 percent
of the trials; they placed their cards correctly on 76.8 percent of the
trials—a discrepancy of 17.4 percent in the direction of the operant
(rule-statement) which was reinforced. (There were no significant differences in the two groups during acquisition to a criterion of 10 successive correct responses.) In Verplanck's words, "The rule-statement,
and the behavior for which it is presumably a discriminative stimulus,
have been dissociated by manipulating their contingencies of reinforcement" (pp. 137-38).

Whatever one's orientation about the role of verbalization in discovery and concept formation may be, such a dramatic separation of
what the S does from what the S says he does merits serious consideration. For the classroom, where one has much less systematic control
over the consistency and timing of verbal reinforcements for student
behavior, Verplanck's results, if taken seriously, are actually discon-
certing.

Verplanck's conclusion following an extended series of investigations on the effect of verbal reinforcement on "hypotheses" and
"awareness" is highly pertinent:

In all these experiments, the behavior of individual subjects was orderly
to a high degree; subject's "thinking" came under experimenter's control in

---

[5] Verplanck terms the operant vocal response of stating the rule a *monent* to
avoid some of the surplus meaning of the word "hypothesis." The procedure of
requesting overt rule-statements at each trial, of course, is at odds with the procedures recommended by some members of the "discovery" school (cf., 65).

very much the way the behavior of a rat does when a response is being shaped. On the other hand, questioning a subject at the end of these experiments on what he was doing, or what he thought was going on, or how he solved the problem, yields a good deal of verbal behavior that usually corresponds poorly with what the subject had in fact been doing, or how frequently he had been reinforced. It reflects very seldom the environmental variables whose control led this subject to behave as other subjects do under the same procedure. . . . Rationalizing, not reasoning, seems to be the appropriate term (p. 145).

Verplanck's investigations have shed much light on the effect of verbal reinforcement on concept formation and related verbal behavior. To the degree that his procedures parallel "discovery" learning in mathematics, they should be both provocative and useful. However, as Verplanck clearly indicates, the availability of a particular "notate" (a Verplanckian term almost identical with "concept") is directly related to the sequence in which cards are presented. In Verplanck's words:

. . . (e.g., "border" vs. "no border" is ordinarily a very difficult notate. However, it may be produced on trial number 1 by presenting the subject with a pair of cards about which there is nothing to say but "border," that is, two blank cards, one with a border.) The availability of a particular notate . . . proves to be a simple function of the sequence of environmental events, and of the subject's previous experimental history. It is readily manipulable by the experimenter (p. 147).

Again the central theme of this section emerges: the possibility of errorless learning through programing the sequence of exemplars in a concept formation task. Verplanck does not mention the other technique available to produce errorless concept formation in humans, i.e., telling them the concept. To restate a point made earlier, it is the ability of the human organism to tell others where to look or to what to attend that permits the rapid communication on which our culture is built. Gilbert (53) chooses to use the word *theory* in talking about the behavior of attending and develops this key concept in mathetics as follows: "The word *theory* is derived from a Greek word meaning "to look at," and its etymology is a guide to a useful way of understanding it. . . . Theory can be thought of as a repertory of selective looking behavior, as a set of words that we use to stimulate ourselves to look at the key and relevant features of an otherwise confusing jumble of details" (p. 39). The critical importance of this "selective looking behavior" in discrimination training was first clearly described and demonstrated by Wyckoff (149) and termed by him the *observing response*. As is characteristic of science, the "pure" research of a decade ago turns up in the technology of today.

Two current studies by Terrace (142, 143) of discrimination learning in lower organisms are provocative with respect to their implications for errorless human learning. Terrace (143) demonstrated that a red-green discrimination and a vertical line-horizontal-line discrimination could be produced in pigeons virtually without error under certain conditions. (In a sense, the pigeon was "labeling" lines as being vertical or horizontal by responding or not responding to exemplars. Those who have ever experienced confusion in responding appropriately when labeling lines as "horizontal" or "vertical" might ask if errorless performance on a similar task by a pigeon qualifies as rudimentary mathematical behavior.)

Of considerable theoretical interest to those interested in errorless human learning were these findings: (a) In the first study, birds which had learned without errors never showed "emotional" responses (e.g., wing flapping, stamping on the chamber floor) to the "incorrect" stimulus, as did birds which had learned with errors. (b) Birds which had learned without errors did not produce the occasional bursts of responses to the "incorrect" stimulus, as did birds which had learned with errors. (c) Birds trained without errors in both the original red-green discrimination and in the vertical-horizontal transfer made no errors in subsequent red-green testing. Birds trained without errors in the red-green discrimination but with error in the transfer task made errors in subsequent red-green testing. It would be going beyond these data to predict that errorless human learning (wherever someone produces it) will result in better retention and in better mental health for students, but these data also do not contraindicate this.

It should be noted that Terrace's work is in discrimination learning, not concept formation. Also, as Terrace points out, errorless discrimination learning has been demonstrated on at least two previous occasions: Skinner (119) on a brightness discrimination and Schlosberg and Solomon (110) on two narrowly separated grays using gradual changes from original black-and-white cards. However, it can safely be predicted that the techniques developed for producing errorless discrimination learning can be modified without major difficulty to the production of errorless concept formation. Some generalization usually accompanies the establishment of any discriminative stimulus. As Terrace (143) notes, generalization gradients have been constructed for many continua, e.g., wave length of light (61), visual intensity (12, 14), auditory frequency (75, 80), and auditory intensity (76). At the infrahuman level, these "natural" gradients should supply at least part of the generalization component of concept formation, with some adaptation of Terrace's procedure to sharpen the discrimination component without error. At the human level, similar procedures coupled with the availability of producing "instant" observing responses through language mediation should be similarly successful in the production of errorless learning.

The obvious question at this point is, "Why do you want errorless conceptual learning?" The obvious answer is, "We don't know." It is known, however, that even with the prodigious efforts of the last decade to produce error-free programed instruction, such learning, except in trivial cases, is yet to be attained. On the other hand, there is a rather long human history of "errorful" learning. There also exists the most serious educational crisis of all time. And all agree that something has to change.

With the exception of the few studies in this chapter utilizing computers in programed instruction, the equipment used by Terrace (142, 143) to study errorless discrimination learning in pigeons was more sophisticated than the devices (if any) used to study mathematics learning in humans. This is due in part to Skinner's insistence that "the student must *compose* his response rather than select it from a set of alternatives, as in a multiple-choice self-rater . . . although it is much easier to build a machine to score multiple-choice answers than to evaluate a composed response" (124, p. 970). As was indicated earlier in this chapter, with the quality of programing to date, experimental evidence has not borne Skinner out on the necessity of the composed response. Indeed, with the repeated success of multiple-choice responses in at least holding their own with constructed responses, many experimenters began taking second looks at multiple-choice responding. (Several papers are available which treat in detail both the behavioral advantages of multiple-choice programs as well as techniques for the construction of more effective multiple-choice frames [36, 71, 145].) For Skinner was correct in one assertion: it is easier to build machines which score multiple-choice answers. At the same time, such machines can provide immediate, differential feedback to the S as to the correctness of his answer. Such features appear to be particularly important with younger children who have difficulty discriminating the correctness of their responses themselves.

Several relevant studies using multiple-choice teaching machines to teach mathematical or quasimathematical skills are of interest here. An early paper by Holland (68) presents no data, but does describe a three-choice "preverbal" machine and sample program frames prepared by Skinner to teach young children to respond in terms of the abstract property of form. A brief but lucid description of techniques of "freeing" the concept of form from the control of irrelevant dimensions such as size, color, or position is given. Hively (66) describes a series of exploratory and control experiments using a two-choice machine to teach matching-to-sample to preschool and first-grade children. In his attempts to maximize criterion matching-to-sample performance, Hively checked variables such as removing the alternative answer, orienting the stimulus to be matched over the choice stimulus, and "fading in" the incorrect choice stimulus. Training in progressively difficult discrimination tasks was found to be much more efficient than training in the final discriminations alone. Hively also notes that of the conditions tried, programs too long as well as too short resulted in increased errors. Discontinuities in size of consecutive discriminations (step size) were also associated with increased errors. Evans (36) used an all multiple-choice program to teach counting and numeral-making behavior to preschool children. During the program, no numerals were actually constructed by writing: Ss responded either by circling correct answers or by pushing appropriate buttons on a four-choice machine. (The machine featured automatic answer evaluation and advance and so was functionally similar to the devices described by Holland [68] and Hively [66].) Pre- and posttest results on a numeral-writing task showed marked gains in ability to write numerals, although no actual numeral-making behavior was practiced during the program. Discrimination training was also successful in correcting all four "figure-reversal" errors made by one child who already knew her numbers. Evans concludes that after learning to discriminate between "good" and "bad" examples of numerals, the child is enabled to monitor the adequacy of his own corresponding productions.

A study by Holland (69) in collaboration with Eugene Long is concerned with inductive reasoning behavior in young children (ages 6-9). This investigation is perhaps the clearest example of the differences in philosophy and approach of those schooled in the experimental analysis of behavior. As Holland expresses it, "This approach to learning research is novel in that it is directed toward development of techniques that will establish a given behavior. It can be contrasted with research directed toward discovering some supposed 'learning function' or to discover whether one arbitrary condition is better than another arbitrary condition" (p. 57). A five-choice multiple-choice machine was employed. In common with the machines previously described, this device featured automatic answer evaluation and advance following correct responses. However, presumably to increase the probability of the observing response to the stimulus, the illuminated stimulus panel had to be pressed before the five-choice windows were illuminated. If an error was made, the student had to try again until he responded correctly. He was then "branched" back to the previous frame. The stimulus window displayed a series of bottle-shaped objects of constant shape, but varied in color, orientation, and pattern. The task of the child was to induce and select the response choice which correctly extended the series. The program progressed from "easy" frames in which only a single dimension such as color was relevant to terminal frames in which orientation, color, and pattern might be relevant or irrelevant in varying combinations. For example, for one terminal item Holland presents, the child must discriminate (a) the single alternation of figures between right-side-up and up-side-down and (b) a color pattern which repeats after every third figure. Further, the series presented has not been extended far enough for the choice which correctly extends the series to have yet appeared. That is, the child has to induce and select a figure which has never appeared in the stimulus window. The original 187-item version of the inductive reasoning program was administered to a single S and revised the basis of his recorded errors. Revision never involved removal of difficult slides; rather, it involved rearrangement and addition of slides at trouble spots, as well as an increase in the number of difficult items at the end. The performance records of six children provides striking evidence for the effectiveness of the revision and of the program as a whole. Only two Ss were in the vicinity of a 10 percent error rate, and most of those errors were bunched in the last 10 frames. One S made only two errors in the entire

234-frame sequence. Holland (69) concludes: "Through careful analytical research of procedures, one can often attain behavioral control.
The real product of such work is a technique and procedure for establishing such control rather than the usual confirmation of an hypothesis" (p. 57). Holland's statement that "one understands inductive reasoning when he knows how to create the ability" (p. 57) is a significant
expression of an attitude on how an important mathematical process
may be viewed and can be studied.

An early section of this review examined the results of comparative
studies using programed textbooks and teaching machines. It will be
recalled that teaching machines barely broke even (though they often
broke down) with programed textbooks in terms of performance measures. With respect to time, they did even worse: 10 to 40 percent saving
in time favoring programed texts. And yet, in the studies just reviewed,
teaching machines were associated with the production of quite cred-
itable results. Can it be that the poor old teaching machine, which
started all this fuss in the first place, is only down, not out? It may be
that the appropriate devices are only now being designed (125) or are
yet to be designed (36, 108). The day may yet come when one will
explain to his friend, "Now don't let the term 'programed learning'
fool you. It's not the program that teaches; it's the machine."

The Maintenance and Extension of Mathematical Behavior

As the end of this chapter approaches, research papers to review have
run out. Not many people have reported much work in programing
the maintenance and extension of mathematical behavior. Where is the
work on motivation, on problem solving, on creativity in mathematics?
Where is the analysis of mathematical thinking? Where is the study on
programing the ability to generalize and to transfer concepts to new
areas of mathematics? Well, these things are out there somewhere.
There are not many. They are hard to find. They are usually not even
labeled "Programed Instruction." But they are important, and it would
be remiss not to conclude by mentioning them.[10] What about motivation? How does one go about the practical business of getting the stu-

---

[10] The author will be forever grateful to Wilbur Schramm for his public suggestion
and encouragement that the author "blue sky" the final portion of this chapter.

dent to the task and keeping him at it? Gilbert (53) has the simplest solution; he postulates motivation: "The principles and procedures I describe will assume a motivated student, one that possesses a genuine educational objective" (p. 12). Skinner (124) trusts the machine and the program to do the job: "Lastly, of course, the machine, like the private tutor, reinforces the student for every correct response, using this immediate feedback not only to shape his behavior most efficiently but to maintain it in strength in a manner which the layman would describe as 'holding the student's interest' " (p. 971). Bruner (17) seems to take this, but then counterpunches with: "When learning leads only to pellets of this or that in the short run rather than to mastery in the long run, this behavior can be readily "shaped" by extrinsic rewards. But when behavior becomes more extended and competence-oriented, it comes under the control of more complex cognitive structures and operates more from the inside out" (p. 90). Moore (94) adds: "Motivation is sustained throughout by seeing to it that the child is not robbed of the opportunity of making a series of interrelated discoveries which lead to the acquisition of some basic intellectual skills." By this time the reader may be a bit overwhelmed at the task of attempting to grasp and reconcile such statements from such eminent students of human motivation.

Relating the problem back to programed instruction, Glaser (56) suggests a possible rapprochement between some of these positions:

The notion I am trying to convey here is similar to O. K. Moore's term "autotelic," which he coined to describe the quality of an instructional sequence which becomes an end in itself so that performing the sequence is "intrinsically" reinforcing. If a frame offers a stimulus which has a high probability of eliciting the desired response, the foundation for an autotelic frame has been laid. Finishing such a frame (i.e., giving the correct response) is an end in itself. In this sense a frame that is "peaked" in difficulty (neither too easy nor too difficult) can provide the stimulus for an intrinsically re-inforcing frame (p. 84).

Just how far this or any other attempt at reconciliation between the inventor of teaching machines, the chief proponent of discovery learning, the constructor of mathetics, and the creator of the autotelic concept would get is problematical.

Fortunately, there is a new and useful way of looking at reinforcement and motivation which is independent of all the previous approaches. It has the advantage of conceptual simplicity, practicability, the sanction of the behavioral laboratory, and demonstrated success in application. The reference here is to a concept developed by Premack (101) and termed the "Premack Principle" by Homme (70, 73) in reporting field application of its effectiveness. Premack's concept deals with response probabilities or frequencies and their sequencing. It may be stated: if behavior B is of higher probability than behavior A, then behavior A can be made more probable by making behavior B contingent upon it. An obvious example is that eating can be used to reinforce bar-pressing, since eating is more likely or probable than bar-pressing. Homme and his colleagues have demonstrated the potency of this principle in controlling and motivating nursery school children (73) and low-achieving adolescents (70). It is interesting to note that among other behaviors controlled with the Premack principle were counting behavior in nursery school children and programed instruction in mathematics in low-achieving adolescents. The Premack principle, if it continues to prove workable, would provide Gilbert with a stronger system by removing the assumptions of motivation. It would provide Skinner with other reinforcers, if the material itself proves not to be sufficiently reinforcing (cf., 121, p. 156). And it appears to be perfectly compatible with discovery and autotelic learning, if they are indeed the high-probability behavior their proponents say they are when the environment is properly constructed. No mention of autotelic learning would be complete without acknowledging the efforts of Allen (1, 2) and his colleagues in developing autotelic games to teach mathematics logic and arithmetic. These games have the happy property of producing, maintaining, and extending the student's symbolic, arithmetic, and deductive logic skills to highly sophisticated levels.

Turning attention to problem solving in mathematics, there is an existing program to point to (74). The technique is straightforward. It takes a standard problem-type ("Andy disliked the catcher. Ed's sister was engaged to the second baseman. . . .") and a standard technique (use of a grid with fielding positions on one axis, and players' names on the other axis). The program then proceeds in small-step fashion, with confirmation, to lead the student to the solution as he learns to make the deductions and inferences necessary to complete the solution. The most amazing thing about the program is why it has not been done more often with other problem-solving techniques.

The peculiar disinterest in techniques of problem solving and discovery is well stated by Polya (100): "*Heuristic,* or heuretic, or 'ars inveniendi' was the name of a certain branch of study, not very clearly circumscribed, belonging to logic, or to philosophy, or to psychology, often outlined, seldom presented in detail, and as good as forgotten today. The aim of heuristic is to study the methods of rules of discovery and invention" (p. 112).

It is one of the paradoxes of civilization that the study of the "methods and rules of discovery and invention" by which that civilization advances is rarely formally taught, has a pitifully meager literature, and is a new vocabulary item for many whose livelihood depends on its application. For the purposes of this chapter, only two possibly useful references can be cited (95, 118). In the first study, a heuristic program was written for a computer and proceeded to generate valid logic proofs from the first volume of *Principia Mathematica* (147). In the second case a heuristic program simple enough to be simulated by hand appears to be able to discover the combination in about 52 of the 136 positions presented in a chapter on mating attacks in a chess book by Fine (45). Slight modification of the heuristic program will add 10 more mating combinations. For the chess study, Simon and Simon (118) conclude: "The conclusion we reach from our investigation is that the discovery of 'deep' mating combinations by expert chess players requires neither prodigious memory, ultra-rapid processing capacities, nor flashes of insight. Combinations as difficult as any that have been recorded in chess history will be discovered by the selective heuristics we have outlined" (p. 429).

The only problem for which no suitable heuristic seems to exist is this: why don't we develop the best heuristics possible in all areas of science and mathematics and then proceed to teach them by the best available methods? Perhaps part of the answer is supplied by Skinner (125). Perhaps in it one can see why man, whose geocentric position was stolen by Copernicus, whose separation from the beasts was stolen by Darwin, and whose total rationality was partly stolen by Freud, is reluctant to surrender the remainder of that rationality:

Logicians, mathematicians, and scientists have often tried to record and understand their own thinking processes, but we are still far from a satisfactory formulation of all relevant behaviors. Much remains to be learned about how a skillful thinker examines a situation, alters it, samples his own responses with respect to it, carries out specific verbal manipulations appropriate to it, and so on. It is quite possible that we cannot teach thinking adequately until all this has been analyzed. Once we have specified the behavior, however, we have no reason to suppose that it will be any less adaptable to programed instruction than simple verbal repertoires (p. 182.21).

The problems of selecting, analyzing, producing, maintaining, and extending mathematical behavior will not be resolved by this chapter, or by a committee meeting. They will not be solved by a mathematician, or by an educator, or by a psychologist. The problems will be resolved as students of behavior and of mathematics continue to play together that grand old game of axiom-doubting, remembering that one must ante his own most precious axioms to begin. Programed learning in mathematics promises to be a good version of the game. The rules require only that one try new things. In so doing, one loses some of his ante, but he gets to know the other players better. And those who are lucky enough to discover something new are always willing to split the pot.

References

1. Allen, L. E. "Toward Autotelic Learning of Mathematical Logic." *Mathematics Teacher* 56: 8-21; January 1963.
2. Allen, L. E., and others. "The All Project (Accelerated Learning of Logic)." *American Mathematical Monthly* 68: 497-500; May 1961.
3. Alter, M. *Retention in Programed Instruction.* New York: Center for Programed Instruction, 1962.
4. Alter, M.; Eigen, L. D.; and King, S. *The Effectiveness of Confirmation Plus Trinket Reinforcers in Young Children.* New York: Center for Programed Instruction, 1962.
5. Anderson, A. R., and Moore O. K. *Autotelic Folk-Models.* Paper presented at the Current Sociological Theory section meeting of the American Sociological Association, New York, August 1959.
6. Associated Public School Systems (Affiliate of the Institute of Administrative Research, Teachers College, Columbia University). "Teaching Machines." *Know How* 13: 17; May-June 1962.
7. Austwick, K. "Automated Teaching." *Research* 15: 477-82; November 1962.
8. Ausubel, D. P. "Learning by Discovery: Rationale and Mystique." *Bulletin of the National Association of Secondary School Principals* 45: 18-58; December 1961.
9. Ausubel, D. P. *The Psychology of Meaningful Verbal Learning.* New York: Grune and Stratton, 1963. 255 pp.

10. Barlow, J. A. "Programed Instruction in Perspective: Yesterday, To-day, and Tomorrow." *Prospectives in Programing.* (Edited by R. Filep.) New York: Macmillan Co., 1963.

11. Beane, D. G. *A Comparison of Linear and Branching Techniques of Programed Instruction in Plane Geometry.* Urbana: University of Illinois, July 1962.

12. Blough, D. B. "Generalization and Preference on a Stimulus-Intensity Continuum." *Journal of the Experimental Analysis of Behavior* 2: 307-17; October 1959.

13. Blyth, J. W. "Teaching Machines and Logic." *American Mathematical Monthly* 67: 285-86; March 1960.

14. Brown, J. S. "The Generalization of Approach Responses as a Function of Stimulus Intensity and Strength of Motivation." *Journal of Comparative Psychology* 33: 209-26; April 1942.

15. Brown, O. R., Jr. *A Comparison of Test Scores of Students Using Programed Instructional Materials with Those of Students Not Using Programed Instructional Materials.* Urbana: University of Illinois, July 1962.

16. Bruner, J. S. "The Act of Discovery." *Harvard Educational Review* 31: 21-32; Winter 1961.

17. Bruner, J. S. *On Knowing: Essays for the Left Hand.* Cambridge: Belknap Press of Harvard University Press, 1962.

18. Bruner, J. S. *The Process of Education.* Garden City, N.Y.: Doubleday Anchor Books, 1963. [Also Cambridge, Mass.: Harvard University Press, 1960.]

19. Bruner, J. S.; Goodnow, J. J.; and Austin, G. A. *A Study of Thinking.* New York: John Wiley & Sons, 1956. 330 pp.

20. Buros, O. K. *The Fifth Mental Measurements Yearbook.* Highland Park, N.J.: Gryphon Press, 1959. 1,292 pp.

21. Campbell, V. N. *Studies of Bypassing as a Way of Adapting Self-Instruction Programs to Individual Differences.* Pittsburgh: American Institute for Research, May 1962.

22. Center for Programed Instruction. *Programs, '62: A Guide to Programed Instructional Materials Available to Educators by September 1962.* Washington, D.C.: U.S. Office of Education, 1962. 383 pp.

23. Center for Programed Instruction. *Programs, '63: A Guide to Programed Instructional Materials Available to Educators by September 1963.* Washington, D.C.: U.S. Office of Education, 1963. 814 pp.

24. Commission on Mathematics of the College Entrance Examination Board. *Program for College Preparatory Mathematics.* New York: the Commission, 1959. 63 pp.

25. Coulson, J. E., and others. "Effects of Branching in a Computer Controlled Autoinstructional Device." *Journal of Applied Psychology* 46: 389-92; December 1962.

26. Della-Piana, G., and Eldridge, G. *Discovery Learning in Programed Instruction*. Paper presented at the Convention of the National Society for Programed Instruction, San Antonio, Texas, April 1964.

27. Easley, J. A., Jr. "Is the Teaching of Scientific Method a Significant Educational Objective?" *Philosophy and Education*. (Edited by I. Scheffler.) Boston: Allyn and Bacon, 1958.

28. Easley, J. A., Jr. "The Physical Science Study Committee and Educational Theory." *Harvard Educational Review* 29: 4-11; Winter 1959.

29. Edwards, A. L. *Techniques of Attitude Scale Construction*. New York: Appleton-Century-Crofts, 1957. 256 pp.

30. Eigen, L. D. "A Comparison of Three Modes of Presenting a Programmed Instruction Sequence." *Journal of Educational Research* 55: 453-60; June-July 1962.

31. Eigen, L. D. "Since You Asked." *New York State Mathematics Teachers Journal* 12: 140-44; October 1962.

32. Eigen, L. D., and Komoski, P. K. "Research Summary No. 1 of the Collegiate School Automated Teaching Project." *Programed Instruction* 1: 7; May 1961.

33. Eigen, L. D., and others. "A Comparison of Modes of Presenting a Programed Instruction Sequence." *Programed Instruction* 1: 2-5; February 1962.

34. Ellis, H. C. *Research Designs in Studies of Programmed Learning*. Portion of an address presented at a conference on "Methods Appropriate to Studies of Classroom Learning," Washington University, St. Louis, Missouri, May 1962.

35. Evans, J. L. *An Investigation of 'Teaching Machine' Variables Using Learning Programs in Symbolic Logic*. Doctor's thesis. Pittsburgh: University of Pittsburgh, 1960. [Cf., Evans, J. L.; Glaser, R.; and Homme, L. E. *Journal of Educational Research* 55: 433-52; June-July 1962.]

36. Evans, J. L. *Multiple Choice Discrimination Programing*. Paper presented at the American Psychological Association Convention, New York, September 1961.

37. Evans, J. L. *Programers, Experts, and the Analysis of Knowledge*. Paper delivered to the American Association for the Advancement of Science, Denver, Colorado, December 1961.

38. Evans, J. L. "A Potpourri of Programing Technology." *Trends in Programmed Instruction*. (Edited by G. D. Ofiesh and W. C. Meierhenry.) Washington, D.C.: National Education Association and National Society for Programmed Instruction, 1964.

39. Evans, J. L.; Glaser, R.; and Homme, L. E. *A Preliminary Investigation of Variation in the Properties of Verbal Learning Sequences of the "Teaching Machine" Type*. Paper presented at the Annual Con-

vention of the Eastern Psychological Association, Atlantic City, N.J., April 1959. [Reprinted in *Teaching Machines and Programmed Learning*. (Edited by A. A. Lumsdaine and R. Glaser.) Washington, D.C.: National Education Association, 1960.]

40. Evans, J. L.; Homme, L. E.; and Glaser, R. "The Ruleg System for the Construction of Programmed Verbal Learning Sequences." *Journal of Educational Research* 55: 9; June-July 1962.

41. Ferster, C. B., and Skinner, B. F. *Schedules of Reinforcement*. New York: Appleton-Century-Crofts, 1957. 741 pp.

42. Fields, P. E. "Studies in Concept Formation: I. The Development of the Concept of Triangularity by the White Rat." *Comparative Psychological Monographs* 9: 1-70; December 1932.

43. Filby, Y. *Teaching Machines: A Review of Theory and Research*. Nordisk Psykologi Monograph No. 13. Copenhagen: Forlag, 1961.

44. Fine, B. *Teaching Machines*. New York: Sterling Publishing Co., 1962. 176 pp.

45. Fine, R. *Middle Game in Chess*. New York: David McKay, 1952.

46. Fry, E. B. *Teaching Machines and Programmed Instruction*. New York: McGraw-Hill Book Co., 1963. 176 pp.

47. Gagné, R. M. "The Acquisition of Knowledge." *Psychological Review* 69: 355-65; July 1962.

48. Gagné, R. M., and Brown, L. T. "Some Factors in the Programing of Conceptual Learning." *Journal of Experimental Psychology* 62: 313-21; October 1961.

49. Gagné, R. M., and Dick, W. "Learning Measures in a Self-Instructional Program in Solving Equations." *Psychological Reports* 10: 131-46; February 1962.

50. Gagné, R. M., and Paradise, N. E. "Abilities and Learning Sets in Knowledge Acquisition." *Psychological Monographs* 75: 1-23; Whole No. 518, 1961.

51. Gagné, R. M., and staff (University of Maryland Mathematics Project). "Some Factors in Learning Non-Metric Geometry." *Society for Research in Child Development Monographs*, 1965. (In press)

52. Gilbert, T. F. *On the Relevance of Laboratory Investigation of Learning to Self-Instructorial Programming*. Paper presented at the American Psychological Association Convention, Cincinnati, Ohio, September 1959. [Reprinted in *Teaching Machines and Programmed Learning*. (Edited by A. A. Lumsdaine and R. Glaser.) Washington, D.C.: National Education Association, 1960.]

53. Gilbert, T. F. "Mathetics: The Technology of Education." *Journal of Mathetics* 1: 7-73; January 1962.

54. Gilbert, T. F. "Mathetics: The Design of Teaching Exercises." *Journal of Mathetics* 2: 7-56; April 1962.

55. Gilpin, J.; Barlow, J.; and Alexander, H. *Type of Format, Mode of Response, and Efficiency of Learning with a Self-Instruction Program.* Richmond, Ind.: Earlham College, 1960. (Unpublished)

56. Glaser, R. "Some Research Problems in Automated Instruction." *Programmed Learning and Computer-Based Instruction.* (Edited by J. E. Coulson.) New York: John Wiley & Sons, 1962. pp. 67-85.

57. Glaser, R.; Reynolds, J. H.; and Fullick, M. G. *Programmed Instruction in the Intact Classroom.* Pittsburgh: Learning Research and Development Center, University of Pittsburgh, 1963.

58. Goldstein, Leo. S., and Gotkin, L. G. "A Review of Research: Teaching Machines vs. Programed Textbooks as Presentation Modes." *Journal of Programed Instruction* 1: 29-36; No. 1, 1962.

59. Gotkin, L. G. "Experimentation with Programed Instruction: Some Suggestions for Educators." *Programed Instruction* 1: 3-7; December 1961.

60. Grubb, R. E., and Selfridge, L. E. *The Computer Tutoring of Statistics: A Preliminary Report.* Yorktown Heights, N.Y.: Thomas J. Watson Research Center, International Business Machines Corp., July 1962.

61. Guttman, N., and Kalish, H. I. "Discriminability and Stimulus Generalization." *Journal of Experimental Psychology* 51: 79-88; January 1956.

62. Heidbreder, E. "The Attainment of Concepts. 6. Exploratory Experiments on Conceptualizations at Perceptual Levels." *Journal of Psychology* 26: 193-216; July 1948.

63. Hendrix, G. "A New Clue to Transfer of Training." *Elementary School Journal* 48: 197-208; December 1947.

64. Hendrix, G. "Prerequisite to Meaning." *Mathematics Teacher* 43: 334-39; November 1950.

65. Hendrix, G. "Learning by Discovery." *Mathematics Teacher* 54: 290-99; May 1961.

66. Hively, W. "Programming Stimuli in Matching to Sample." *Journal of the Experimental Analysis of Behavior* 5: 279-98; July 1962.

67. Hively, W. *Defining Criterion Behavior for Programmed Instruction in Elementary Mathematics.* Cambridge, Mass.: Elementary Mathematics Project, Committee on Programmed Instruction, Harvard University, June 1963.

68. Holland, J. G. "Teaching Machines: An Application of Principles from the Laboratory." *Journal of the Experimental Analysis of Behavior* 3: 275-87; October 1960.

69. Holland, J. L. "New Directions in Teaching Machine Research." *Programmed Learning and Computer-Based Instruction.* (Edited by J. E. Coulson.) New York: John Wiley & Sons, 1962. pp. 46-57.

70. Homme, L. E. *A Demonstration of the Use of Self-Instructional and Other Teaching Techniques for Remedial Instruction of Low Achiev-*

ing Adolescents in Reading and Mathematics. Contract No. OE-4-16-033. Washington, D.C.: U.S. Office of Education, 1964.

71. Homme, L. E. "Programming and the Stimulus Control of Behavior." *Programmed Instruction and Teaching Machines.* Report of the International Conference on Teaching Machines, Berlin, 1963. Berlin: Pädagogische Arbeitsstelle, Sekretariat Pädagogisches Zentrum, 1964.

72. Homme, L. E., and Glaser, R. "Relationships Between the Programed Textbook and Teaching Machines." *Automatic Teaching: The State of the Art.* (Edited by E. Galanter.) New York: John Wiley & Sons, 1959. pp. 103-107.

73. Homme, L. E., and others. "Use of the Premack Principle in Controlling the Behavior of the Nursery School Children." *Journal of the Experimental Analysis of Behavior* 6: 544; October 1963.

74. Horvath, R. W. *An Excursion into Programmed Problem-Solving.* Endicott, N.Y.: International Business Machines Corp. 1962.

75. Hovland, C. I. "The Generalization of Conditioned Responses. I. The Sensory Generalization of Conditioned Responses with Varying Frequencies of Tone." *Journal of General Psychology* 17: 125-48; July 1937.

76. Hovland, C. I. "The Generalization of Conditioned Responses. II. The Sensory Generalization of Conditioned Responses with Varying Intensities of Tones." *Journal of Genetic Psychology* 51: 279-91; December 1937.

77. Hughes, J. L. *Programed Instruction for Schools and Industry.* Chicago: Science Research Associates, 1962.

78. Hull, C. L. "Quantitative Aspects of the Evolution of Concepts: An Experimental Study." *Psychology Monographs* 28: 1-86; No. 23, 1920.

79. Inhelder, B., and Piaget, J. *The Growth of Logical Thinking from Childhood to Adolescence.* New York: Basic Books, 1958. 356 pp.

80. Jenkins, H. M., and Harrison, R. H. "The Effect of Discrimination Training on Auditory Generalization." *Journal of Experimental Psychology* 59: 246-53; April 1960.

81. Kalin, R. "Development and Evaluation of a Programed Text in an Advanced Mathematical Topic for Intellectually Superior Fifth and Sixth Grade Pupils." *Programed Instruction* 1: 4; December 1961.

82. Keislar, E. R. "The Development of Understanding in Arithmetic by a Teaching Machine." *Journal of Educational Psychology* 50: 247-53; December 1959.

83. Keislar, E. R. *Abilities of First Grade Pupils to Learn Mathematics in Terms of Algebraic Structures by Teaching Machines.* Cooperative Research Program Project SAE 8998, No. 1090. Washington, D.C.: U.S. Office of Education, December 1961.

84. Keller, F. S., and Schoenfeld, W. N. *Principles of Psychology*. New York: Appleton-Century-Crofts, 1950. 431 pp.

85. Kersh, B. Y., and Wittrock, M. C. "Learning by Discovery: An Interpretation of Recent Research." *Journal of Teacher Education* 13: 461-88; October 1962.

86. Lambert, P.; Miller, D. M.; and Wiley, D. E. "Experimental Folklore and Experimentation: The Study of Programmed Learning in the Wauwatosa Public Schools." *Journal of Educational Research* 55: 485-94; June-July 1962.

87. Legg, O. "Programmed-Instruction and Lecture-Discussion Methods Compared for Effectiveness in Teaching Agricultural Finance to Vocational Agriculture Students." *Auto-Instructional Devices* 2: 135; June 1962.

88. Levin, G. R. *Informal Geometry for the Second Grade, Part 1. An Instructional Program. Part 2. Measuring Achievement*. Providence, R.I.: Brown University, July 1961.

89. Levin, G. R., and Baker, B. L. "Item Scrambling in a Self-Instructional Program." *Programed Instruction* 1: 4; April 1962.

90. Levine, S. L., and Silvern, L. C. "The Evolution and Revolution of the Teaching Machine: Part 1 and Part 2." *Journal of the American Society of Training Directors* 14: 4-16; December 1960 and 15: 14-25; January 1961.

91. Lumsdaine, A. A. "Some Issues Concerning Devices and Programs for Automated Learning." *Teaching Machines and Programmed Learning*. (Edited by A. A. Lumsdaine and R. Glaser.) Washington, D.C.: National Education Association, 1960. pp. 517-39.

92. Lumsdaine, A. A. "Some Theoretical and Practical Problems in Programmed Instruction." *Programmed Learning and Computer-Based Instruction*. (Edited by J. E. Coulson.) New York: John Wiley & Sons, 1962. pp. 134-51.

93. McDonald, F. J., and Allen, D. W. "An Investigation of Presentation, Response, and Correction Factors in Programmed Instruction." *Journal of Educational Research* 55: 502-507; June-July 1962.

94. Moore, O. K. *The Motivation and Training of Students for Intellectual Pursuits: A New Approach*. Address given at the Tenth Thomas Alva Edison Foundation Institution, New York University, November 1959.

95. Newell, A.; Shaw, J. C.; and Simon, H. A. "Elements of a Theory of Human Problem Solving." *Psychological Review* 65: 151-66; May 1958.

96. Pennington, D. F., and Slack, C. W. "The Mathetical Design of Effective Lessons." *Applied Programed Instruction*. (Edited by S. Margulies and L. D. Eigen.) New York: John Wiley & Sons, 1962.

97. Piaget, J. "How Children Form Mathematical Concepts." *Scientific American* 189: 74-79; November 1953.
98. Piaget, J. *Logic and Psychology.* New York: Basic Books, 1957.
99. Plumlee, L. B. *Report on Use of a Programmed Text in Teaching Statistics.* Albuquerque, N. Mex.: Sandia Corp., February 1962.
100. Polya, G. *How To Solve It.* Garden City, N.Y.: Doubleday Anchor Books, 1957.
101. Premack, D. "Toward Empirical Behavior Laws: I. Positive Reinforcement." *Psychological Review* 66: 219-33; July 1959.
102. Pressey, S. L. "Certain Major Psycho-Educational Issues Appearing in the Conference on Teaching Machines." *Automatic Teaching: The State of the Art.* (Edited by E. Galanter.) New York: John Wiley & Sons, 1959. 198 pp.
103. Rigney, J. W. "Potential Uses of Computers as Teaching Machines." *Programmed Learning and Computer-Based Instruction.* (Edited by J. E. Coulson.) New York: John Wiley & Sons, 1962. pp. 155-70.
104. Roe, A. "A Comparison of Branching Methods for Programmed Learning." *Journal of Educational Research* 55: 407-16; June-July 1962.
105. Roe, A. *Branching Programs in Automated Instruction: A Simplified Format.* Report No. 61-72. Los Angeles: Department of Engineering, University of California, August 1962.
106. Roe, A. "Research in Programmed Learning." *Programmed Learning and Computer-Based Instruction.* (Edited by J. E. Coulson.) New York: John Wiley & Sons, 1962. pp. 113-19.
107. Roe, V. K.; Case, H. W.; and Roe, A. *Scrambled vs. Ordered Sequence in Auto-Instructional Programs.* Los Angeles: Department of Engineering, University of California, 1961. [Same data also in Roe, K. V.; Case, H. W.; and Roe, A. "Scrambled vs. Ordered Sequence in Auto-Instructional Programs." *Journal of Educational Psychology* 53: 101-104; April 1962.]
108. Roe, A.; Lyman, J.; and Moon, H. "The Dynamics of an Automated Teaching System." *Automated Teaching Bulletin* 1: 16-25; Spring 1961.
109. Roe, A., and others. *Automated Teaching Methods Using Linear Programs.* Los Angeles: Department of Engineering, UCLA, 1960. [Some data also in Roe, A. "Automated Teaching Methods Using Linear Programs." *Journal of Applied Psychology* 40: 198-201; June 1962.]
110. Schlosberg, H., and Solomon, R. L. "Latency of Response in a Choice Discrimination." *Journal of Experimental Psychology* 33: 22-39; July 1943.
111. Schramm, W. *The Research on Programmed Instruction: An Annotated Bibliography.* Stanford, Calif.: Institute for Communication Research, Stanford University, 1962.

112. Secondary-School Curriculum Committee of the National Council of Teachers of Mathematics. "The Secondary Mathematics Curriculum." *Mathematics Teacher* 52: 389-417; February 1959.

113. Shay, C. B. "Relationship of Intelligence to Step Size on a Teaching Machine Program." *Journal of Educational Psychology* 52: 98-103; April 1961.

114. Sidman, M. *Tactics of Scientific Research: Evaluating Experimental Data in Psychology.* New York: Basic Books, 1960. 428 pp.

115. Silberman, H. F., and others. *Development and Evaluation of Self-Instructional Materials for Underachieving and Overachieving Students.* Santa Monica, Calif.: System Development Corp., July 1962.

116. Silberman, H. F., and others. "Fixed-Sequence versus Branching Auto-Instruction Methods." *Journal of Educational Psychology*, 1965. (In press)

117. Silverman, R. E., and Alter, M. "Response Mode, Pacing, and Motivational Effects in Teaching Machines." *Programed Instruction* 1: 7; October 1961.

118. Simon, H. A., and Simon, P. A. *Trial and Error Search in Solving Difficult Problems: Evidence from the Game of Chess.* Graduate School of Industrial Administration Reprint No. 108. Pittsburgh: Carnegie Institute of Technology, 1962.

119. Skinner, B. F. *The Behavior of Organisms.* New York: Appleton-Century-Crofts, 1938. 457 pp.

120. Skinner, B. F. *Science and Human Behavior.* New York: Macmillan Co., 1953. 461 pp.

121. Skinner, B. F. "The Science of Learning and the Art of Teaching." *Harvard Educational Review* 24: 86-97; Spring 1954. [Reprinted in Skinner B. F. *Cumulative Record.* (Enlarged edition.) New York: Appleton-Century-Crofts, 1961. 426 pp.]

122. Skinner, B. F. "A Case History in Scientific Method." *American Psychologist* 11: 221-33; April 1956. [Reprinted in Skinner, B. F. *Cumulative Record.* (Enlarged edition.) New York: Appleton-Century-Crofts, 1961. 426 pp.]

123. Skinner. B. F. *Verbal Behavior.* New York: Appleton-Century-Crofts, 1957. 478 pp.

124. Skinner, B. F. "Teaching Machines." *Science* 128: 969-77; October 1958. [Reprinted in Skinner, B. F. *Cumulative Record.* (Enlarged edition.) New York: Appleton-Century-Crofts, 1961. pp. 158-82.]

125. Skinner, B. F. *Cumulative Record.* (Enlarged edition.) New York: Appleton-Century-Crofts, 1961.

126. Skinner, B. F. "Teaching Machines." *Scientific American* 205: 90-102; No. 3, 1961.

127. Smedslund, J. "Transitivity of Preference Patterns as Seen by Pre-School Children." *Scandinavian Journal of Psychology* 1: 49-54; January 1960.

128. Smith, L. M. "Programed Learning in Elementary School: An Experimental Study of Relationships Between Mental Abilities and Performance." *Comparative Studies of Principles for Programing Mathematics in Automated Instruction.* Title VII Project No. 711151.01. Washington, D.C.: Educational Media Branch, U.S. Office of Education, August 1962.

129. Smith, M. D. *An Exploration of Non-Wordal Programming in Mathematics and Science.* Richmond, Ind.: Earlham College, 1961.

130. Smith, M. D. *New Instruction Media: Self Instruction—Guided Instruction and the Role of the Teacher.* Richmond, Ind.: Earlham College, 1962.

131. Smith, N. H. "The Teaching of Elementary Statistics by the Conventional Classroom Method of Programmed Instruction." *Journal of Educational Research,* 55: 417-20; June-July 1962.

132. Smoke, K. L. "An Objective Study of Concept Formation." *Psychological Monographs* 42: 1-46; Whole No. 4, 1932.

133. Stolurow, L. M. *Teaching by Machine.* Washington, D.C.: Government Printing Office, 1961.

134. Stolurow, L. M. "A Response to 'Inside Opinion.'" *Programmed Instruction* 1: 2; June 1962.

135. Stolurow, L. M. *Social Impact of Programed Instruction—Aptitudes and Abilities Revisited.* Paper presented at the American Psychological Association Annual Convention, Symposium on Programmed Instruction, St. Louis, Missouri, September 1962.

136. Stolurow, L. M., and Walker, C. C. "A Comparison of Overt and Covert Response in Programmed Learning." *Journal of Educational Research* 55: 421-29; June-July 1962.

137. Suchman, J. R. "Inquiry Training in the Elementary School." *Science Teacher* 27: 42-47; November 1960.

138. Suppes, P. "Mathematical Logic for the Schools." *Arithmetic Teacher* 9: 396-99; November 1962.

139. Suppes, P., and Ginsberg, R. "Experimental Studies of Mathematical Concept Formation in Young Children." *Science Education* 46: 230-40; April 1962.

140. Suppes, P., and Hill, S. A. "The Concept of Set." *Grade Teacher* 79: 51-52; April 1962.

141. Suppes, P., and McKnight, B. A. "Sets and Numbers in Grade One 1959-60." *Arithmetic Teacher* 8: 287-90; October 1961.

142. Terrace, H. S. "Discrimination Learning with and Without Errors." *Journal of the Experimental Analysis of Behavior* 6: 1-27; January 1963.

143. Terrace, H. S. "Errorless Transfer of Discrimination Across Two Continua." *Journal of the Experimental Analysis of Behavior* 6: 223-32; April 1963.

144. Tosto, D. *Some Behavioral Considerations of Multiple-Choice Frames.* Paper presented at the Convention of the National Society for Programed Instruction, San Antonio, Texas, April 1964.

145. Underwood, B. J. *Psychological Research.* New York: Appleton-Century-Crofts, 1957.

146. Verplanck, W. S. "Unaware of Where's Awareness: Some Verbal Operants-Notates, Monents, and Notants." *Behavior and Awareness: A Symposium of Research and Interpretation.* (Edited by C. Ericksen.) Durham, N.C.: Duke University Press, 1962.

147. Whitehead, A. N., and Russell, B. *Principia Mathematica.* New York: Cambridge University Press, 1925.

148. Wills, H. "The UICSM Programmed Instruction Project." *American Mathematical Monthly* 69: 804-806; October 1962.

149. Wyckoff, L. B. "The Role of Observing Responses in Discrimination Learning." *Psychological Review* 59: 431-42; November 1952.

FRANCIS MECHNER
Basic Systems, Incorporated

Science Education and Behavioral Technology

When the behavioral technologist approaches the problem of science teaching, he must begin by asking the question, "What does one teach when one teaches 'science' and to whom does one teach it?" In his technical jargon, he would ask, "What are the terminal behavior specifications and the target population?" The answer to this question is becoming increasingly dependent on whom one asks. Should one ask scientists? School principals? State boards of education? Research directors in industry? Foremen in factories? Science teachers at the grass-roots level? Perhaps the students themselves? Publishers of scientific literature? Clearly, each of these authorities will provide a different answer. This dilemma is not a trivial one. The problem of science education cannot be considered independently of the frame of reference.

Each frame of reference imposes a different set of terminal behavior specifications and is concerned with a different target population. Our educational system attempts to accommodate these varying requirements with trade schools, specialized vocational schools, technical institutes, and curricula based on "major subjects" in high schools, colleges, and professional schools. These specialized curricula always end with some form of practical training, called "on-the-job" training, "doctoral thesis," or "internship," depending on the field.

This chapter is addressed to two groups: the educators, educational administrators, and educational planners who will significantly control what is produced and the behavioral technologists and subject matter experts who will actually produce the science education systems of the future.

The main emphasis of the chapter will be the objectives of science education and the application of behavioral technology to the implementation of these objectives. It is hoped that the present chapter, by presenting in perspective what has been accomplished to date and the tasks that lie ahead, will help science educators and educational planners to chart the course of science education in the future.

The Application of Behavioral Technology to Education

Readers for whom this is familiar terrain may skip this section and proceed directly to the next section on terminal behavior for science education. For readers who are not familiar with the principles of behavioral technology, the description below will provide a summary of the basic methodology and mode of thought.

Behavioral technology involves the detailed application of learning theory to practical problems of training and education. Much as an aeronautical engineer feels that he can design an airplane by applying a few basic physical principles plus a little art and intuition, so, too, a behavioral technologist feels that he can design a complex repertoire of knowledge or behavior by applying a few basic principles of learning theory plus a little art and intuition. The behavioral technologist approaches his task with a basically deterministic and operational attitude. This attitude may be characterized as follows:

1. The objective is that an individual "understand x," "know x," "be able to do x."
2. First, an acceptable way of determining whether an individual "understands x," "knows x," "can do x" must be found.
3. The conditions which will be accepted as evidence that the individual "understands x," "knows x," "can do x" must be operationally specified.
4. The specification of these conditions always involves the specification of behavior. The specifications are met when the individual does or says certain things under certain conditions.

5. The conditions which have been specified are brought about by operating on the individual's behavior in accordance with known principles of behavior theory (or learning theory).
6. When the individual exhibits the specified behavior under the specified conditions, it can then be said that he "understands x," "knows x," "can do x."

The behavioral technologist equates "knowledge" and "understanding" with behavior. He argues that there need not be any concern as to whether knowledge is basically behavior or not. The significant consideration is that the only tangible evidence of "knowledge" is behavioral evidence. The only way to determine whether an individual "knows" something is to see what he does or says under certain conditions. "Well, then," it may be argued, "suppose I teach one of my students mechanically to wire up some dry cells and resistors to an ammeter, and then to vary the resistance so as to show a change in current. I then teach him in equally robot-like fashion to substitute the correct values in the equation $E=IR$ and to solve for I. He has then exhibited a lot of behavior, and yet I would not be willing to say that he 'understands' Ohm's Law." True enough. But the fault here lies not in the fact that the student merely exhibited behavior. The fault lies, rather, in the way in which the behavior that was supposed to constitute evidence of "knowledge of Ohm's Law" was specified. If the behavior specifications had included solving a set of well-chosen problems in which Ohm's Law had to be applied and the manipulations of the dry cell-resistor circuit with accompanying verbal explanations of the principle being demonstrated, then the behavioral evidence of an "understanding of Ohm's Law" would have been much more convincing.

To sum up, then, the behavioral technologist approaches a problem by going through the following basic steps:

1. He specifies the behavior which the student is to acquire. (Behavior may be considered as evidence of knowledge.)
2. He specifies the relevant characteristics of the student, including the student's present level of knowledge.
3. He performs a behavioral analysis of the material to be taught. This involves "atomizing" the knowledge to be imparted according to learning theory principles. The knowledge is broken down into concepts, discriminations, generalizations, and chains.

4. He constructs a teaching system or program by which the behavior may be built into the student's repertoire.
5. He tests the teaching system on sample students and revises it according to the results, until the desired result is obtained reliably in student after student.

The operational specification of the educational objectives, which is the first step in the application of behavioral technology to an educational problem, offers the following benefits which are particularly significant in science education:

1. It provides a way of determining and measuring the extent to which the objectives of the course have in fact been met, after a student has completed the course.
2. It provides a set of guidelines for anyone wishing to teach the course, whether by means of a behaviorally designed instructional system or by conventional means.
3. It provides a terse, and yet exhaustive, summary of the content of the course for anyone who wishes to know what the course teaches. This feature is of particular significance in connection with evaluation.
4. It provides a discussion framework and a set of working documents on which science educators and designers of the course can reach agreement prior to making a major investment of time and effort in developing the course itself.
5. It serve as a final examination, in the event that such an examination should be desired.

A behaviorally designed course may be thought of as an instructional system for attaining the course objectives as efficiently as the resources of modern behavioral technology allow, without commitment to any particular set of media, techniques, or modes of administration.

Terminal Behavior for Science Education

Gross Categorization of Terminal Behavior

Educators are accustomed to thinking about terminal behavior from two complementary points of view: the functional point of view, which considers the ultimate occupation or profession of the student, and the substantive point of view, which considers the subject matter which the student is to master. This dual approach will be taken here, in preparation for the more detailed treatment used in the following sections. Table 1 on page 447 is a matrix which combines the functional with the substantive categorization. It distinguishes five occupational categories corresponding to different types of involvement in science and crosses these with five terminal behavior classes.

Occupational or Functional Categories: It must be understood that the occupational categories are not mutually exclusive; they merely designate the type of involvement with science for which the student is being prepared. The categories may be described as—

1. The consumer of science. The consumer of science is the car owner, the TV set owner, the individual who is called upon to vote on such matters as fluoridation of drinking water and atomic testing, the individual who must decide when he should go to see a doctor and whether or not his house needs a lightning rod.

2. The skilled worker. He may be an automobile mechanic, a carpenter, a plumber, a draftsman, a TV or radio repairman, an electrician, or a printer.

3. The technician. The technician is essentially the assistant to the scientist and the technologist. He carries out routine functions in laboratories, such as setting up equipment and carrying out procedures. He may install and program computers, make measurements in a physics laboratory, carry out chemical syntheses, administer new drugs to experimental animals, perform blood tests, and carry out statistical calculations.

4. The technologist. The technologist is the engineer who applies scientific knowledge to the solution of practical problems. Electrical engineers, mechanical engineers, nuclear engineers, chemical engineers, doctors, and dentists are all technologists. They all turn the findings of science to the service of society.

5. The scientist. He is the producer of science. While there is considerable division of labor among scientists, the scientist's functions include the identification of problems that deserve attention, the formulation of these problems in a manner that makes them susceptible to the scientific approach, and the solution of these problems.

The above are the five broadest occupational categories from the science education standpoint. The teacher and administrator of science are not classified separately because they cut across all of those categories. In a sense, each of the five groups has its own teachers and administrators. It is impossible to consider the training of a teacher or an administrator without specifying whom he is to teach or administer.

Substantive or Behavioral Categories: Below are the five major classes of terminal behavior in which each of the five occupational groups must be trained to various degrees. The five categories are called "terminal behavior classes" in Table 1. It should be noted that they are certainly not "terminal behavior specifications"; they are merely gross classes. The various forms the terminal behavior specifications for these classes might take are described in a following section, Terminal Behavior Specifications in the Five Substantive Categories.

1. Formal descriptive and analytic systems. The most significant descriptive and analytic system used by scientists is mathematics, which includes logic and statistics as well as arithmetic and various more specialized techniques like information theory and differential equations.
2. Current body of knowledge. This includes all the generalizations and principles that have become accepted and that are said to constitute the "body of scientific knowledge."
3. Experimental and theoretical bases of scientific knowledge. The distinction between this category and the preceding one is the distinction between the statement "F=ma" and the reasons why scientists believe that F=ma. In science, the reasons why a principle or theory is accepted are always given in terms of the experimental procedures by which the principle or theory is demonstrated or in terms of the theoretical framework within which the principle or theory may be deduced.
4. Scientific method and research skills. This is a broad category, which includes the ability to formulate problems so that they may be attacked scientifically, skill in experimental design, techniques of measurement, techniques for generating hypotheses, skill in selecting fruitful hypotheses, criteria for deciding which experiments

TABLE 1

Categories of Terminal Behavior for Science Education by Occupation and Area of Training

	Formal descriptive and analytic systems	Current body of scientific knowledge	Empirical and theoretical bases of scientific knowledge	Scientific method and research skills						Scientific personality traits		
				deductive	inferential	generating hypotheses	selecting hypotheses	testing hypotheses	formulating problems for attack by sci.	patience	perseverance	scientific curiosity
Consumer of science	elementary	elementary		elementary	elementary							
Skilled worker	elementary	elementary		elementary	elementary					✓	✓	
Technician	intermediate	intermediate	elementary	intermediate	intermediate	elementary				✓	✓	
Technologist	advanced	advanced	intermediate	advanced	advanced	intermediate		✓	✓	✓	✓	✓
Scientist	advanced	advanced	advanced	advanced	advanced	advanced	✓	✓	✓	✓	✓	✓

to perform, skill in designing "crucial test cases," and all the various data evaluation techniques, including the proper application of logic and statistics.

5. Generalized traits useful in scientific activity. It takes more than just skill and knowledge to make a scientist. Certain personality traits and thought habits are necessary also. Science teachers often cite such traits as "scientific curiosity," "perseverance," "patience," and "a logical mind" (the disposition to think logically) as desirable traits for scientists to possess. While these terms may sound rather vague, it is nevertheless possible to identify and specify a set of behavior patterns to which these terms somewhat loosely refer.

Table 1 is intended to illustrate how the educational requirements of various gross occupational categories may be stated in terms of these five terminal behavior classes. It must be emphasized that the table is intended merely as an illustration; the positions of the check-marks are not to be interpreted as proposals or recommendations regarding the occupational requirements of different occupations. They are intended only to illustrate a method of analysis and categorization in an area in which methods of analysis and categorization are still largely lacking. They are also intended to illustrate the types of decisions that must be made before behavioral technology can have a full impact.

Terminal Behavior Specifications in the Five Substantive Categories

Formal Descriptive and Analytic Systems: Mathematics is the language of science in two senses: It is the means for summarizing and codifying knowledge and the means for deducing the implications of the summaries and codifications. Different branches of mathematics are used by members of different occupational categories. The consumer of science certainly needs to be skilled in arithmetic and could probably benefit from an understanding of statistics, probability theory, and algebra. A working research scientist, on the other hand, usually puts to use as much mathematics as he knows; the more he knows, the more he uses.

The terminal behavior specifications for programs on formal descriptive and analytic systems can take many different forms, depending upon the functional and substantive categories involved. They could form the subject of an entire chapter and will therefore not be treated in great detail here. Some of the broadest skill categories are suggested by the questions and exercises below:

1. Applied Mathematics.
    a. Convert 1.5 miles into inches.
    b. Three pencils cost 15 cents. How much does one pencil cost?
    c. Problems in probability theory.
    d. Problems in operations research.
    e. Problems in calculus and differential equations.
    f. Applying algebra to practical problems.

2. Pure Mathematics.
    a. Devising proofs of theorems.
    b. Stating previously learned proofs of theorems.
    c. Developing derivations.
    d. Discovering relationships.

3. Descriptive Mathematics.
    a. Which function would you use to describe the data below?
    b. Fit a parabola to the points of this graph, using the method of least squares.
    c. Use the appropriate transformation of axes in the graph below to simplify the functional relationship.
    d. What transformation would you want to apply to these data so as to summarize them best?
    e. Derive the equations that follow from assumptions *A*, *B*, and *C*, so that you may test the theory against the data given below.
    f. What simplifying assumptions would you want to make in theory X before testing this theory against the data obtained in the experiment described below?

4. Deciding Which Branch of Mathematics To Use in Particular Applications.
    a. In solving the following problem, would you use algebra or calculus?
    b. Is the following a statistics or a probability theory problem?
    c. What branch of mathematics would help you solve the problem below?

Current Body of Scientific Knowledge: Almost all of the "science" programs developed thus far fall into this category. The distinction is being made here between "scientific knowledge proper" and "the empirical basis for scientific knowledge." The distinction is more traditional than real; working scientists often do not make the distinction, although it usually has been made in science education.

Examples of terminal behavior specifications for teaching scientific knowledge are as follows:

1. In which case is a covalent bond more likely: when the two atoms in the molecule are similar in electronegativity or when they are different in electronegativity? Explain.
2. A gun shoots a bullet up into the air at an angle of 30 degrees to the ground. The bullet leaves the muzzle at 100 miles per hour. How far away will the bullet land?
3. Draw the circuit diagram for a circuit which you could use to make a temperature measurement using a thermistor and a Wheatstone bridge and describe in words the procedure which you would use to make the measurement.
4. Define electrical power in terms of energy and use this definition in conjunction with Ohm's Law to derive the power equation.
5. Name three important genera in each animal phylum and show their approximate placement in the evolutionary tree.
6. Name four important substances in female endocrinology and describe their role in the control of the ovulatory cycle.
7. Sketch the curves that show the graphic relationship between visual sensitivity and frequency of light, for high and low illuminations. Label the axes and show the approximate scales on the axes.
8. Write the chemical reactions you would use to synthesize trinitrotoluene from chemicals that are easily available, using ordinary laboratory equipment.

Experimental and Theoretical Bases of Scientific Knowledge: The reforms which science education is currently undergoing are of two separate kinds: (a) modernization of curricula and (b) introduction of scientific knowledge to the student by stressing the empirical and theoretical bases for the acceptance of the "knowledge." The present section is concerned with the latter.

The major contributions have come during the past few years from curriculum study groups. Such groups as the Physical Sciences Study Committee and the Biological Sciences Curriculum Study of the American Institute for Biological Science have devised tests and measuring instruments that represent perhaps the most significant forward steps in defining the goals of science teaching. One important reason for the quality of these contributions is the fact that terminal behavior objectives are being developed by scientists who are conscious of the interplay between knowledge and experimental findings and who appreciate, more than professional educators can, the fact that all scientific knowledge is tentative. From the behavioral technologist's standpoint, the advent of actual scientists upon the science education scene is an essential development. If the premise that science is what scientists do and know is to be accepted, then the corollary conclusion that scientists are the best qualified experts on science is necessary. It is from them that the terminal behavior specifications must be obtained.

That this point of view is gaining rapidly is evidenced by the increasing number of curriculum study groups in which scientists are active members and the increasing experimentation with curriculum alterations and laboratory approaches to science teaching, in primary schools, secondary schools, and colleges. National and international organizations that have responsibility for science education and manpower development, including NSF, Ford, Carnegie, UNESCO, and the Organization for Economic Cooperation and Development, are appropriating increasing funds for experimentation with science instruction that stresses the skills which approximate those of the scientist. Examples of terminal behavior specifications for this type of science teaching are as follows:

1. What are the main pieces of supporting data for the theory of the evolution of species?
2. Describe the experiment you would perform to persuade somebody that water is made up of hydrogen and oxygen in the ratio of 2 to 1. Give the accompanying reason.
3. Describe one experiment that would lead to acceptance of the wave theory of light and one experiment that would lead to acceptance of the particle theory of light. Give an explanation of each feature of your experimental design, and for each experiment explain why the result would lead you to one theory or the other.

This last item is taken from the terminal behavior specifications being developed for a behaviorally designed physics course in São Paulo,
Brazil. The project is being supported by UNESCO as a demonstration
of the modern approach to physics teaching and the applications of behavioral technology. It should be noted that question "3" above does
not require the student to conceive the experiments or even to design
them. He will have been taught and shown these experiments during
the programed course. But in order to answer the question satisfactorily, he must be able to reason his way through all the phases of the
experiments and also through the logic that leads to one theory of
light propagation or the other. The student must understand the experimental bases for the theoretical formulations. The theories are not
handed to him in a dogmatic, authoritarian fashion. Rather he is taught
why these theories are accepted, why there are two alternative theories,
and that his confidence in either of them should be only as strong as
his experimental evidence. Another example of a program which takes
this approach is supplied in a subsequent section of this chapter which
describes teaching an empirical law by experimental induction (see
pp. 484 ff.).

Scientific Method and Research Techniques: This is an area in which
relatively little progress has yet been made, but in which some work
is now beginning to appear. As has been said, many science educators
point out that science is what scientists do; it is an approach to the
solution of problems; it is a method by which problems may be attacked; it is a philosophic attitude. The subject matter of science, they
point out, is the knowledge that has already been obtained as a result
of the application of the scientific method. It is the method, however,
not the knowledge so far obtained, which is the important and distinguishing aspect of science. This point of view, widely accepted among
scientists, suggests that scientific method is an area that demands more
emphasis than it is usually given. However, the area of scientific method and research skills must be subdivided into more manageable pieces
before it can be treated successfully. The following are some possible
subdivisions:

1. Deductive Reasoning Skills. The skills implied by this category in-
    clude both informal deduction and the sophisticated application of
    mathematics or logic. Terminal behavior specifications for these
    skills might take the following forms:

a. The dog was given one injection of drug X per day. After two months, the dog died. What can you conclude? Explain.

b. Given data X, Y, and Z, what can you conclude about W? Why can you not conclude A?

2. Inferential Reasoning Skills. The scientist's formal tool for making inferences is, of course, statistics. It would therefore seem that this aspect of science education belongs more properly under *Formal Descriptive and Analytic Systems*, discussed previously. However, a scientist's skill in the use of statistics must extend beyond the ability to apply statistics to his data. Scientists must also possess "statistical intuition," which is the ability to make good guesses about the likely outcomes of rigorous statistical analyses and thereby save enormous time and effort. The following are examples of terminal behavior specifications for statistical intuition. (Each of these questions is to be answered within 10 seconds, without formal statistical calculation.)

a. Out of 50 tubes you tested, 3 were defective. What would you guess is the probability that 10 percent of all tubes in the batch are defective?

b. The distribution shown below is slightly bimodal. The number of cases is 56. What do you think is the probability that the bimodality would persist if the number of cases were increased to 1 million?

c. Each of the curves shown in the graph below represents the number of errors for successive learning trials in teaching six rats to learn a maze. You will note that rat number 5 learned the maze faster than any of the other rats. At which probability level do you think that the difference between this rat and the other rats is statistically significant?

d. You have made four determinations under each of two conditions, A and B. How many more determinations do you think you will need so that the difference between the two means will be statistically significant at the .01 level of confidence?

Condition A	Condition B
3	4
6	9
2	11
4	6

e. You have obtained a time-course function for blood pressure following injection for six animals that had received a drug and for six animals that had received saline. The time-course functions are shown below. What do you think is the probability that the drug affects blood pressure? How many more animals do you think you would need in each group to bring your confidence up to the .01 level? To the .001 level?

A scientist makes many judgments of this type every day, without applying formal statistics. Clearly, his skill at making these judgments accurately determines the effectiveness and efficiency of his research activities.

3. Skill in generating hypotheses. Good scientists are often distinguished from poor ones in their ability to generate useful or interesting hypotheses. Some scientists claim that they spend a great deal of their time thinking up "crazy" ideas and then refuting them. Refuting a hypothesis involves scanning the available data of previous experimental findings and seeing whether the hypothesis is in accord with these data. One time in a thousand, one of these "crazy" ideas turns out to be not so crazy after all. This hypothesis-generating activity in which scientists claim to engage is often largely covert. When they test their hypotheses, they do most of it mentally. Only when they are unable to refute the hypothesis in a reasonable time do they begin to talk to people about it or to suggest physical experiments. It appears likely that claims of the "it came to me in a flash" variety are often true. What these scientists usually neglect to mention are the other 999 ideas that had come to them in similar flashes, but were promptly dismissed as absurd. This type of activity may be described as a type of scanning, like free association, except that it always involves statements about the world. Each statement is checked against experience until it is refuted. If it is not refuted, it becomes a scientific contribution. This process is, in a sense, mechanical. The skill involved certainly can be specified in operational terms and measured. This skill is one of the elements of what is frequently termed "imagination" or "creativity." The terminal behavior test for this skill would require the student to generate and test, at a certain minimal rate, hypotheses about a universe with which he has had

some previous experience. The behavioral technologist, in developing the terminal behavior specifications, would have to (a) make the behavior overt rather than covert, (b) circumscribe the universe for the hypotheses, and (c) circumscribe the range of data against which the successive hypotheses are tested by the student. Here, the use of a computer suggests itself. It should be possible to develop a program for the computer that would make the computer behave like a small, artificial, circumscribed universe. This universe would be described by a set of specific input-output relationships, some of them determined and others probabilistic. The student of "creativity" would start out by learning his "subject matter," i.e., how this computer behaves under various specific conditions. At the end of this subject matter training, there would still be a great deal about the computer universe that would be unknown to him. Here he must begin to generate hypotheses and test them. A program could be designed to develop this skill. The program would teach the student in the standard step-by-step fashion how to generate hypotheses on the basis of some available data and then to test the hypotheses in a brute force manner against other available data until the hypothesis is refuted or until the data are exhausted. At the end of the program, the student would be generating and testing hypotheses at the desired rate.

4. Skill in selecting "fruitful" hypotheses. A higher-order skill in this category is how to discriminate between alternative hypotheses before starting to test any of them. Great scientists seem to have a peculiar ability to pick out "fruitful" hypotheses. The behavioral technologist, in developing a specification of "ability to choose fruitful hypotheses" would have to interview scientists and try to get them to verbalize what criteria they employ. It is likely that there exist criteria that cut across different disciplines. Structured interview techniques, in which the scientists are given sets of hypotheses among which to choose, might be used to supplement the interview data. In the final terminal behavior specification, the student's task would be to answer questions of the form, "Which of the following hypotheses is the most promising on the basis of present knowledge?" The development of this type of skill is certainly a much more formidable problem than that of generating hypotheses indiscriminately.

5. Skill in testing hypotheses and in deciding which experiments to perform. Skinner and other scientists who have attempted to describe their own thought processes have pointed out that the research process does not generally follow the lines advocated by the logicians or the philosophers of science. Very often, scientists engage in a type of experimental activity which may be characterized as "I wonder what will happen if I change this variable" or "Let's see what happens if. . . ." This type of exploratory activity appears to be a very important component of scientific research and can be performed with varying degrees of skill. It may be thought of as a physical extension of the type of activity described in the preceding category. Skinner (16), in his paper "A Case History in Scientific Method," impresses the reader with his remarkable "luck," as it would seem. Good scientists know, however, that only good scientists are lucky, just as only good poker players seem always to be lucky. What must be examined is how scientists decide which variables to play with, in what direction and over what range to vary them. Again, a structured interview technique or even a behavioral analysis by naturalistic observation may help in the identification of the criteria that good scientists use, consciously or unconsciously. Once some of these criteria have been identified, the next step is to program them into the computer-mediated artificial universe and to pose to the students such problems as, "Given what you know now, which variable would you manipulate at this point, and in which way?" This is perhaps the most important skill for an experimentalist to develop.

Another important skill which the experimentalist must have is the ability to find "crucial test cases" for tentative hypotheses. An experimentalist looks at a set of data and says, "I seem to notice the same phenomenon here, here, and also here. I wonder if this is a universal phenomenon." Now he must formulate some stringent test cases. Frequently, this involves taking extreme values of some variables in the experimental situation and seeing whether the phenomenon still holds up. Sometimes it involves introducing a new variable; at other times it may involve eliminating a variable. In any case, there are rules which may be applied in the design of crucial tests that challenge the generality of a finding. The process is similar to the process used by a mathematician in determining whether a new theorem he has just thought up is true. He may start out by letting x equal zero, and then letting it equal infinity. If the theorem still holds up, he may put other strains on it, such as choosing a value of x such that the function is maximized or minimized, etc. A mathematician usually goes through all this empirical testing before he undertakes any formal proofs. The terminal behavior test for this type of skill would include such items as, "On the basis of the data you have been given so far, it would seem that x is always true. What experiment would you do to determine whether this finding is general?"

6. Skill in formulating problems so that they can be solved by the scientific method. When a problem is stated in the form of a general empirical question—e.g., What is the effect of salary on productivity?—the statement always requires further elaboration. To make the problem susceptible to experimental attack, the independent variable, the dependent variable, and the over-all experimental setting must be operationally defined. This type of refinement of an experimental question is a necessary skill for a scientist. An experienced scientist can usually offer several alternative refinements of any general statement of an experimental question within his own field. Some examples of terminal behavior specifications for this skill are the following:

    a. What effect does alcohol have on thought processes? The student's answer will have to include a specification of the behavior to be used as the dependent variable, the manner in which the independent variable will be controlled and administered, and the species of organism used.

    b. Which is harder, wood or chalk? Here, the student must specify how he will define and measure hardness and how he will decide what type of wood and what type of chalk to use.

The skill of reformulating problems is related to experimental design, but stops short of the details of equipment and design and meticulous control of variables, which would fall more properly under the category of experimental technique.

Generalized Traits Useful in Scientific Activity: Scientific knowledge and technical skill are only part of the scientist's behavioral repertoire. There is almost universal agreement among scientists and science teachers alike that certain personality traits and temperamental characteristics are just as important to the scientist, if not more so. The terminology used to describe these traits is, of course, still very loose. Rigor becomes necessary only when there is a desire to measure, predict, and control. Some of the terms that are most commonly associated with the scientific personality are "logical mind," "scientific curiosity," "perseverance," and "patience." Everyone feels that he knows more or less what these things are, but few individuals could offer operational definitions that would receive widespread acceptance. In spite of this, teachers of science frequently claim that it is these traits that they try to teach, rather than mere facts and subject matter knowledge. Advocating the teaching of these desirable traits is somewhat like advocating righteousness. Because most educators know so little about the measurement or establishment of these traits, such advocacy is relatively safe; teachers of "logical thought," "scientific curiosity," etc., are always doing a good thing. Because these traits are so difficult to specify or measure, the teacher runs little risk of being held accountable for not succeeding.

All this is no reason to deny the importance of teaching these traits or even to reduce the amount of emphasis placed upon them. The task is, clearly, to develop adequate terminal behavior specifications for these traits. The question to be posed is, "How can it be determined by testing whether and to what degree an individual has 'a logical mind,' 'perseverance,' or 'patience'?" Once these traits can be specified and measured in an operational manner, the methods of behavioral science can be applied to generate them. If the methods of behavioral science have been successful in teaching scientific subject matter or mathematics, it is because objectives have been adequately specified. If the methods of behavioral technology do not at present seem applicable to the teaching of scientific personality traits, this may not be a failing of behavioral technology, but rather a failure to specify in operational and measurable terms what these traits are. Few educators are aware of the large amount of excellent work and thought that already has been devoted to the problem of specifying in operational terms what is meant by "perseverance," "patience," and "scientific curiosity."

1.   Patience. Scientists are subject to the contingencies imposed by the physical universe. A real-life contingency in which "patience" or

"waiting ability" is required is fishing. A fisherman is considered patient if he keeps fishing in spite of long intervals between catches. It is not difficult to think of a variety of situations that test patience, and any combination of these may be used as the terminal behavior specifications for the teaching of patience as a personality trait. The question of how patience may be taught will be discussed later in this chapter.

2. Perseverance. A related trait is "perseverance." In his *Behavior of Organisms*, Skinner (14) introduced the concept of "schedules of reinforcement for free operants." He showed that behavior can be maintained at high strength even if reinforcement is the exception rather than the rule. Some responses are reinforced, but most responses are allowed to go unreinforced. Ferster and Skinner (2), in a major research report on the subject of schedules of reinforcement, showed, among other things, that extreme tolerance of nonreinforcement may be built up in an organism by gradually increasing the number of responses that are allowed to go unreinforced. By means of a carefully designed program of schedules, an animal may be brought to a state where it will continue to respond for weeks and months without a single reinforcement, just as scientists do. A pigeon trained in this manner may peck at a key thousands and tens of thousands of times before finally quitting. This may well be called extreme perseverance. Skinner implies in his *Science and Human Behavior* (15) that human beings develop perseverance and tolerance for nonreinforcement in much the same way: They are exposed to longer and longer stretches of nonreinforcement. Later in training, very little of the behavior is reinforced, yet the strength of the behavior remains high. There are many different names for the resulting behavioral state, including "frustration tolerance," "resistance to extinction," and "high ratios." The layman usually settles for "perseverance." Perseverance tests seem easy to construct; all sorts of games and puzzles provide straightforward tests of perseverance. The problem of teaching perseverance as a generalized trait will be considered in a later section.

3. Scientific curiosity. The trait of "curiosity" has received attention from many psychologists. Some of the work in this area has been done by Harlow and his co-workers. Psychologists generally define curiosity as the capacity to be reinforced by novel stimuli. Monkeys

will work long and hard for an opportunity to peek out of a window and watch a toy train or to play with a lock. The "novelty" of stimuli appears to be closely related to their predictability for the observer. Exploration behavior is based upon the reinforcing effect of bringing novel stimuli under predictive control. When an animal explores a novel environment, stimuli which are initially unpredictable become predictable. Developmental psychologists point out that when children are very young, they too have a natural capacity to be reinforced by the ability to predict and control. Children are forever exploring and playing. When they explore, they learn to predict. Apparently, they like to be able to predict. When they play, they are learning to control aspects of their environment. The improved ability to control probably reinforces play. Further evidence that children are strongly reinforced by the ability to control their environment is that many young boys take great delight in "making things happen," such as producing sounds, causing people to pay attention to them, building startling contraptions (building involves modifying and thus controlling the environment), and transporting themselves about at high speeds. It would certainly seem, then, that children are strongly reinforced by the ability to predict and control.

Prediction and control are, of course, the main objectives of scientific activity. Scientists are particularly susceptible to the reinforcement inherent in the ability to predict and control. Such people are said to have "scientific curiosity." It would seem that scientific curiosity could be developed by developing the capacity to be reinforced by the ability to predict and control. The developmental psychologists claim that children have a natural capacity to be reinforced by this ability. They point out, further, that the socialization process is often the enemy of these capacities. Children are intermittently punished for playing, especially when the kind of control they are imposing on the world begins to conflict with the kind of control their elders wish to impose on the world. "Stop that noise," or "Don't touch that" are familiar household expressions. O.K. Moore (12), in his experiments with teaching young children how to read and write, utilizes the child's natural exploratory activity. The child's main reinforcement is his increasing ability to control the environment in which Moore allows him to "play." In short, it appears that the problem of creating "scientific curiosity" is less a problem of building a trait than a problem of not destroying a trait that all children start out with. It may be that permissiveness and encouragement of exploratory activity and play, on the part of parents and school teachers, would achieve a great deal more than many forms of imposed training.

Science Programing

So far, the terminal populations and the terminal behavior specifications, or objectives, of science teaching have been discussed. This section will be devoted to the problems of establishing the specified terminal behavior in the student.

The Teaching of Concepts and Chains

It can safely be said that most of the behavior discussed in the previous section falls into the gross categories of concept formation and chaining, in the sense in which psychologists such as Hull (4), Skinner (14), Piaget (13), and Keller and Schoenfeld (5) understand the terms. In this section, therefore, the nature of concepts and chains and how these are taught will be discussed.

What Is a Concept? To a psychologist, conceptual behavior involves generalizing within classes and discriminating between classes (4, 5). An individual discriminates between things when he makes different responses to different things. He generalizes among things when he makes the same response to different things. When he makes the response "triangle" to any three-sided figure and the response "quadrilateral" to any four-sided figure, he is discriminating between triangles and quadrilaterals, and he is generalizing among triangles and among quadrilaterals. In general, when he makes the same response to some members of a set and different responses to other members of the set, then he is both discriminating and generalizing among members of the set, and a psychologist would say that he has a "concept." When he makes the response "triangle" to different kinds of three-sided figures, but not to other kinds of figures, he is said to "have the concept" of "triangle." The situation may be schematized as in Figure 1.

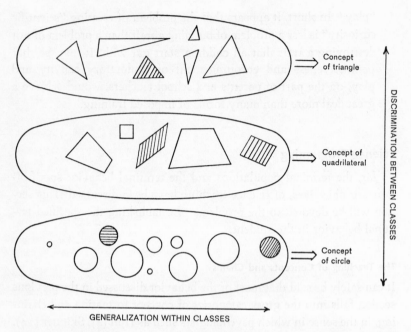

FIGURE 1.   *Each of the three ovals surrounds a set of geometric figures which have something in common: The figures in the top oval are all triangles; the figures in the center oval are all quadrilaterals; and the figures in the bottom oval are all circles. The student has learned the three concepts when he has learned to generalize among the figures in each oval by calling them all "triangle," "quadrilateral," and "circle," respectively, and to discriminate between figures in different ovals by calling them different names.*

When a child makes the response "horse" to small and large horses, to live horses and to horses in pictures, and to horses of different colors and breeds, then he is generalizing within the class of horses. But we cannot say that he has the concept of horse unless he *does not* make the response "horse" to other things, like dogs, cats, cows, and automobiles. In other words, he must not only generalize within the class of horses, but he must also discriminate between the class of horses and other classes.

How Are Concepts Taught?   The basic procedure for forming concepts may be summarized by saying that it involves teaching the student to generalize within classes and to discriminate between classes. The student must learn to make the same response to all members falling within a class and to make different responses to members of different classes.

A psychologist teaching a child who does not yet know the concepts "red" and "blue" might proceed as follows: He might choose objects around the room, some red, some blue, and some other colors. First, he might show the child a set of three objects, two of them red and one not red. Each time he would ask, "Which one is not red?" thereby asking the child to discriminate the different, nonred one. He would repeat this with blue objects. Once these discriminations are established, he might start showing the child pairs of colored objects, asking each time, "Which one is red?" or "Which one is blue?" Then, he would increase the number of nonred and nonblue objects in each set until only one out of four or five objects is red or blue. In choosing the objects, he would be careful to include large ones and small ones, distant and near ones, coarse and smooth ones, dark and light ones, whole objects and parts of many-colored objects. This would prevent attributes other than redness and blueness from becoming associated with the responses "red" and "blue" through inadvertent selection. With the properties of the objects varied, the child would learn to generalize among objects having in common no characteristics other than their color. Once the child says "red" only to red objects, and never to nonred objects, and says "blue" only to blue objects, he may be said to have acquired the concepts of redness and blueness. The method outlined above, of course, can be modified to include the simultaneous teaching of any number of color names.

As a further illustration, this method of analysis will be applied to three medical concepts which are related to each other: the electrocardiographic patterns of ischemia, injury, and infarction. Note that no attempt is made here to analyze or teach the concepts of ischemia, injury, or infarction. The concepts being analyzed are only the electrocardiographic patterns of ischemia, injury, and infarction as these are seen on Lead 1 of the electrocardiogram. It is assumed that the doctor for whom the instruction is intended already has the concepts of ischemia, injury, and infarction: He knows that the heart muscle tissue is said to be ischemic when it has a deficit of oxygenated blood, that it is said to be injured when this deficit has produced some damage which is still reversible, and is said to be infarcted when it is dead. These concepts are prerequisite and are not being taught in the illustration which follows (see Figure 2). Each of the three ovals surrounds a set of tracings that are examples of one of the three types of patterns. When an individual can discriminate between tracings shown to him at random on the basis of whether they show the pattern of ischemia, injury, or infarction, and can generalize among patterns of ischemia, patterns of injury, and patterns of infarction, then it can be said that he has those three concepts. Such a test is provided by Frame 12 of the sequence which follows (see p. 474).

This method of concept analysis may be extended to many concepts in science. Here are some additional examples: (a) Each tracing could be replaced with a disease syndrome, and the concepts, for example, could be hyperthyroidism and hypothyroidism. (b) Each tracing could be replaced with a description of a clinical case, complete with history, just the way a physician would see it. The concept would be the appropriate diagnosis. (c) Each tracing could be replaced with a set of chemical data and observations; the concepts could be "alcohol," "aldehyde," "ketone," and "organic acid."

What Is a Chain?   In spite of the large number of concepts in science that yield to this form of analysis, there is nevertheless another important category of knowledge which is not merely a matter of concept formation. Examples of forms of knowledge that cannot be analyzed merely as concepts might be—

1. Figuring out the appropriate power rating of a resistor to put in a circuit.
2. Going through a sequential decision process in troubleshooting.
3. Dissecting a frog.
4. Doing a qualitative chemical analysis.
5. Explaining a procedure in a technical report.

These examples all have something in common. Each one of them involves a sequence of actions, not just a single discrimination or generalization. They all involve sequences of discriminations and generalizations. In short, they involve sequences of concepts. In the terminology of behavior theory, a form of behavior which involves a sequence of actions in which each action depends upon the outcome of the last action is called a chain. Some other examples of chains are—

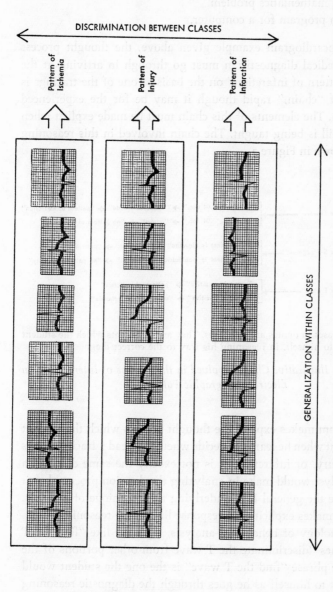

DISCRIMINATION BETWEEN CLASSES

Pattern of Ischemia

Pattern of Injury

Pattern of Infarction

GENERALIZATION WITHIN CLASSES

FIGURE 2. *Each of the three boxes surrounds a set of tracings that have something in common. The tracings in the top box all show the pattern of ischemia; the tracings in the center box all show the pattern of injury; and the tracings in the bottom box all show the pattern of infarction. The student has learned the three concepts when he has learned to discriminate between tracings in different boxes. To have a concept is to generalize within classes and to discriminate between classes.*

1. Reciting a poem.
2. Tying a shoelace.
3. Solving a mathematics problem.
4. Writing a program for a computer.

In the electrocardiogram example given above, the thought process which the medical diagnostician must go through in arriving at the response "pattern of infarction" on the basis of one of the tracings is really a brief "chain," rapid though it may be for the experienced diagnostician. The elements of this chain must be made explicit when diagnostic skill is being taught. The chain involved in this reasoning process is shown in Figure 3.

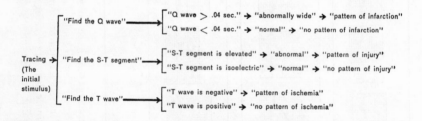

Note: All phrases in quotes are responses. They are statements which the student makes silently, to himself, in reasoning his way to the correct diagnosis.

FIGURE 3.   *An Illustrative Chain Involved in the Process of Interpreting an Electrocardiographic Pattern.*

This diagram makes explicit the thought process which the student must be taught when he learns to decide whether a Lead 1 tracing shows ischemia, injury, or infarction. It is not exactly the same diagram a behavior analyst would make in analyzing the decision process, but it does illustrate the general idea underlying this technique of analysis. The diagram makes explicit each response link in the reasoning chain. In the terminology of behavioral analysis, a phrase like "find the T wave" becomes "discriminate the T wave from other portions of the tracing." The phrase "find the T wave" is the one the student would learn to think to himself as he goes through the diagnostic reasoning process.

Note that the first decision point, after the arrow leading away from the word "tracing," represents a so-called "and" junction. This means that all three paths leading away from that point must be followed in succession. The next decision point (after "find the Q wave," "find the S-T segment," etc.) is an "or" junction, in that the diagnostician makes a discrimination here according to what he sees and continues along only one of the alternative paths. Figure 3 does not attempt to make the distinction between "and" and "or" junctions, although these are important in analyzing reasoning processes and behavioral chains. The reason for presenting this analysis is only to illustrate a technique for making explicit the detailed sequence of responses and decisions that the student must learn to make.

In constructing the analysis of the reasoning process or decision process, as in Figure 3, the behavior analyst makes some decisions which will have an ultimate effect on the size of the steps in the first-draft version of the instructional program. For example, had the behavior analyst had a lower opinion of his target population, or had he been writing for college students instead of doctors, he might have inserted an intermediate response after "Find the Q wave." The intermediate response might have been, "Determine whether the Q wave is wider or narrower than one subdivision of the graph." This intermediate step would have an impact on the construction of Frame 3 in the program below and would probably have increased the total length of the program by one or two frames.

In analyzing concepts, also, the behavior analyst makes decisions which take into account the sophistication and learning ability of his target population. For example, in constructing Figure 2, the behavior analyst made a judgment concerning the level of this target population when he decided to present six examples each of patterns of ischemia, injury, and infarction. Had he been preparing the analysis for nurses, for example, he might have included 8 or 10 examples of each, or he might have taught the physiological aspects of the three concepts first. Usually, the estimates made by the behavior analyst at this stage in the development of an instructional program have to be corrected later on when the actual frames of the program are being tested on the target population. If the program proves too easy or repetitious, examples are sometimes eliminated. The main point being made here is that the behavior analyst, prior to writing any frames of the instructional program, makes some initial guesses concerning the ability of the target population. These guesses function as first approximations, to be corrected and adjusted during the testing phase.

Once these behavioral analyses have been completed, the behavior analyst must decide in which order to teach the behavioral elements that have been identified. In the case of a concept, he must decide in which order to teach the discriminations and generalizations and also how many of them to teach at one time. In the case of a chain, he must decide at which end of the chain to begin, in what order to teach the various links, and how many links to teach at one time. When the behavioral analysis consists of both chains and concepts, he must arrange these in an optimal teaching sequence.

Behavior theory is able to provide answers to many questions of this type. The answers are sometimes easy and obvious, on the basis of directly relevant experimental evidence. For example, learning theory suggests strongly that the last links in a chain should be taught before the early links, that discriminations are best taught by random alternation of examples, and that related concepts should be taught concurrently. At other times, the answers are less obvious and must be arrived at by judging the relative importance of different features of the teaching problem or by extrapolating the results of experiments that are only indirectly relevant. In still other cases, behavior theory cannot provide any answers at all, even when all available experimental data are stretched to their limit. For example, learning theory provides few guidelines for deciding how many concepts to teach concurrently when there are too many (say, 26) for it to be possible to take them all at one time. In many cases of practical importance, however, behavior theory provides significant guidelines. A behavior analyst who knows the behavior literature well—and has experience in analyzing complex behavior—is usually able to make educated guesses and is rarely driven to the position of having to "flip a coin."

The Relationship of the Frames of a Program to the Behavioral Analysis: The following example shows how the behavioral analysis presented in Figures 2 and 3 for diagnosing the Lead 1 tracing is translated into a sequence of teaching frames. The frame-by-frame account is not an exhaustive explanation of every aspect of the construction of the sequence. In Frame 4, for instance, the answers to items (a) and (b) ("elevated" and "isoelectric," respectively) are provided as samples. This has a very definite purpose, as do the positioning and layout techniques employed in Frames 5-9. To go into these aspects of the behavioral analysis any further at this point, however, would go too far afield.

Questions	Answers

1 *The diagram below, taken from the Lead 1 tracing of a normal subject, shows the standard deflections of the electrocardiogram.*

Label the five deflections,
using the conventional letters P, Q, R, S, and T:
   Circle the QRS complex.
   The T wave is ☐ positive ☐ negative

positive

EXPLANATION OF THE RELATIONSHIP OF FRAME 1 TO THE BEHAVIORAL ANALYSIS

The QRS complex is discriminated from other portions of the tracing.

The T wave is discriminated from other portions of the tracing.

The positivity of the T wave is discriminated from the possible negativity of the T wave.

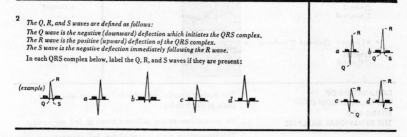

2 *The Q, R, and S waves are defined as follows:*
The Q wave is the negative (downward) deflection which initiates the QRS complex.
The R wave is the positive (upward) deflection of the QRS complex.
The S wave is the negative deflection immediately following the R wave.

In each QRS complex below, label the Q, R, and S waves if they are present:

(example)   a   b   c   d

EXPLANATION OF THE RELATIONSHIP OF FRAME 2 TO THE BEHAVIORAL ANALYSIS

The student generalizes among different types of Q waves, R waves, and S waves.

The student discriminates between Q waves, R waves, and S waves.

Thus, the concepts of the Q wave, the R wave, and the S wave are formed.

3 *A Q wave wider than one standard division, i.e., longer than*
0.04 seconds in duration, is considered abnormal.

Under each diagram, indicate whether the Q wave is normal or abnormal:

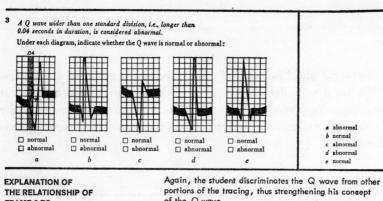

□ normal	□ normal	□ normal	□ normal	□ normal
□ abnormal	□ abnormal	□ abnormal	□ abnormal	□ abnormal
a	*b*	*c*	*d*	*e*

a	abnormal
b	normal
c	abnormal
d	abnormal
e	normal

EXPLANATION OF
THE RELATIONSHIP OF
FRAME 3 TO
THE BEHAVIORAL ANALYSIS

Again, the student discriminates the Q wave from other
portions of the tracing, thus strengthening his concept
of the Q wave.

The student discriminates between Q waves wider than
.04 sec. and Q waves narrower than .04 sec.

Two links of the chain are formed:

    "Q wave wider than .04 sec." ⟶ "abnormal"
    "Q wave narrower than .04 sec."⟶ "normal"

---

4 *The S-T segment begins at the end of the QRS complex and ends at the beginning*
of the T wave. An elevated S-T segment is abnormal.

For each diagram below, indicate whether the S-T segment is normal or abnormal:

a S-T segment elevated   *a*
  □ normal
  □ abnormal

b S-T segment isoelectric   *b*
  □ normal
  □ abnormal

c S-T segment □ elevated □ isoelectric   *c*
  □ normal
  □ abnormal

d S-T segment □ elevated □ isoelectric   *d*
  □ normal
  □ abnormal

e S-T segment □ elevated □ isoelectric   *e*
  □ normal
  □ abnormal

a	abnormal
b	normal
c	elevated abnormal
d	elevated abnormal
e	isoelectric normal

EXPLANATION OF
THE RELATIONSHIP OF
FRAME 4 TO
THE BEHAVIORAL ANALYSIS

The student discriminates the S-T segment from other
parts of the tracing.

He generalizes among different kinds of S-T segments.

This strengthens the concept of the S-T segment.

The student discriminates between elevated and
isoelectric S-T segments.

He generalizes among different kinds of elevated
S-T segments.

This strengthens the concept of the elevated S-T
segment.

Two links in the chain shown in Fig. 2 are formed:

    "S-T segment is elevated" ⟶ "abnormal"
    "S-T segment is isoelectric" ⟶ "normal"

5

Referring to the diagrams in the panel below, check the correct box:

a. An elevated S-T segment suggests ... □ ischemia □ injury □ infarction.
b. A negative T wave suggests .... □ ischemia □ injury □ infarction.
c. An abnormally wide Q wave suggests □ ischemia □ injury □ infarction.

a injury
b ischemia
c infarction

These diagrams show the ECG changes which, in various combinations, may be observed in myocardial infarction.

| Normal Pattern | Pattern of Ischemia | Pattern of Injury | Pattern of Infarction |

EXPLANATION OF THE RELATIONSHIP OF FRAME 5 TO THE BEHAVIORAL ANALYSIS

a. The student discriminates between an elevated S-T segment and the normal S-T segment.

The chain link:

"elevated S-T segment" ⟶ "injury"

is strengthened, this time with omission of the auxiliary mediating link:

"elevated S-T segment" ⟶ "abnormal"

b. The student discriminates between a negative and a normal T wave.
The chain link:

"negative T wave" ⟶ "ischemia"

is strengthened.

c. The student discriminates between an abnormally wide Q wave and a normal Q wave.

The chain link:

"abnormally wide Q wave" ⟶ "infarction"

is strengthened, this time with omission of the auxiliary mediating link:

"abnormally wide Q wave" ⟶ "abnormal"

6

Again referring to the above diagrams, check the correct box:

a. The difference between the pattern of infarction and the normal pattern is the
□ negative T wave   □ elevated S-T segment   □ abnormally wide Q wave

b. The difference between the pattern of injury and the normal pattern is the
□ negative T wave   □ elevated S-T segment   □ abnormally wide Q wave

c. The difference between the pattern of ischemia and the normal pattern is the
□ negative T wave   □ elevated S-T segment   □ abnormally wide Q wave

a abnormally wide Q wave
b elevated S-T segment
c negative T wave

EXPLANATION OF THE RELATIONSHIP OF FRAME 6 TO THE BEHAVIORAL ANALYSIS

The chain links:

"tracing showing an infarction pattern" ⟶ "abnormally" wide Q wave"

"tracing showing an injury pattern" ⟶ "elevated S-T segment"

and

"tracing showing an ischemia pattern" ⟶ "negative T wave"

are formed.

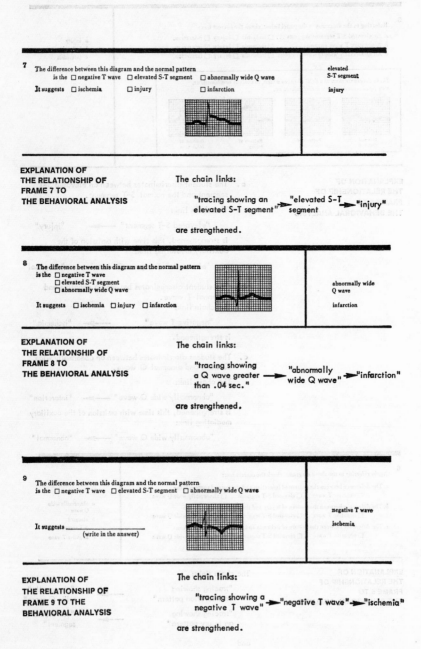

7 The difference between this diagram and the normal pattern
is the ☐ negative T wave   ☐ elevated S-T segment   ☐ abnormally wide Q wave

It suggests   ☐ ischemia   ☐ injury   ☐ infarction

elevated
S-T segment

injury

**EXPLANATION OF
THE RELATIONSHIP OF
FRAME 7 TO
THE BEHAVIORAL ANALYSIS**

The chain links:

"tracing showing an   "elevated S-T   "injury"
elevated S-T segment"   segment

are strengthened.

8 The difference between this diagram and the normal pattern
is the ☐ negative T wave
☐ elevated S-T segment
☐ abnormally wide Q wave

It suggests   ☐ ischemia   ☐ injury   ☐ infarction

abnormally wide
Q wave

infarction

**EXPLANATION OF
THE RELATIONSHIP OF
FRAME 8 TO
THE BEHAVIORAL ANALYSIS**

The chain links:

"tracing showing
a Q wave greater   "abnormally   "infarction"
than .04 sec."   wide Q wave"

are strengthened.

9 The difference between this diagram and the normal pattern
is the ☐ negative T wave   ☐ elevated S-T segment   ☐ abnormally wide Q wave

negative T wave

ischemia

It suggests _____
        (write in the answer)

**EXPLANATION OF
THE RELATIONSHIP OF
FRAME 9 TO THE
BEHAVIORAL ANALYSIS**

The chain links:

"tracing showing a
negative T wave"   "negative T wave"   "ischemia"

are strengthened.

10 Check the myocardial state suggested by each diagram:

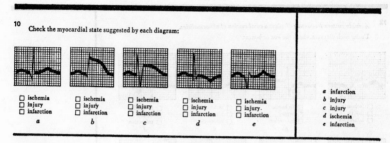

☐ ischemia   ☐ ischemia   ☐ ischemia   ☐ ischemia   ☐ ischemia
☐ injury   ☐ injury   ☐ injury   ☐ injury   ☐ injury.
☐ infarction   ☐ infarction   ☐ infarction   ☐ infarction   ☐ infarction
    a   *b*   *c*   *d*   *e*

a infarction
b injury
c injury
d ischemia
e infarction

**EXPLANATION OF
THE RELATIONSHIP OF
FRAME 10 TO
THE BEHAVIORAL ANALYSIS**

The student discriminates negative T waves from normal T waves, and generalizes among different kinds of negative T waves.

The complete chain:

"tracing showing a negative T wave"   ⟶   "ischemia"

is strengthened.

The student discriminates elevated S-T segments from normal S-T segments, and generalizes among different kinds of elevated S-T segments, thereby further strengthening the concept.

The complete chain:

"tracing showing an elevated S-T segment"   ⟶   "injury"

is strengthened.

The student discriminates between abnormally wide Q waves and normal Q waves, and generalizes among different kinds of abnormally wide Q waves, thereby further strengthening the concept of abnormally wide Q waves.

The complete chain:

"tracing showing an abnormally wide Q wave"   ⟶   "infarction"

is strengthened.

11 Check the myocardial state suggested by each diagram:

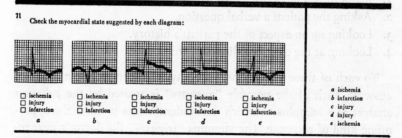

☐ ischemia   ☐ ischemia   ☐ ischemia   ☐ ischemia   ☐ ischemia
☐ injury   ☐ injury   ☐ injury   ☐ injury   ☐ injury
☐ infarction   ☐ infarction   ☐ infarction   ☐ infarction   ☐ infarction
    a   *b*   *c*   *d*   *e*

a ischemia
b infarction
c injury
d injury
e ischemia

**EXPLANATION OF
THE RELATIONSHIP OF FRAME 11
TO THE BEHAVIORAL ANALYSIS**

Same as Frame 10, to provide further strengthening of the three concepts and chains.

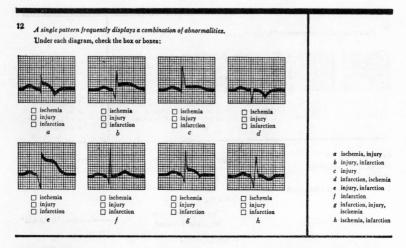

12 *A single pattern frequently displays a combination of abnormalities.*
Under each diagram, check the box or boxes:

☐ ischemia   ☐ ischemia   ☐ ischemia   ☐ ischemia
☐ injury   ☐ injury   ☐ injury   ☐ injury
☐ infarction ☐ infarction ☐ infarction ☐ infarction
   a   *b*   *c*   *d*

☐ ischemia   ☐ ischemia   ☐ ischemia   ☐ ischemia
☐ injury   ☐ injury   ☐ injury   ☐ injury
☐ infarction ☐ infarction ☐ infarction ☐ infarction
   e   *f*   *g*   *h*

a ischemia, injury
b injury, infarction
c injury
d infarction, ischemia
e injury, infarction
f infarction
g infarction, injury, ischemia
h ischemia, infarction

**EXPLANATION OF
THE RELATIONSHIP OF
FRAME 12 TO
THE BEHAVIORAL ANALYSIS**

Same as Frames 10 and 11, with the difference that this time each tracing is examined by the student three times, once for ischemia, once for injury, and once for infarction, because more than one of the three abnormalities may be present. This establishes the "and" nature of the first junction in the chain shown in Fig. 3.

Applications of Behavioral Analysis to Other Problems in Science Teaching: Experience suggests that all diagnostic problems in medicine, troubleshooting procedures in engineering, and problem-solving procedures in a variety of contexts are susceptible to this form of analysis. It is always possible to break the process down into a series of decisions. In dealing with medical diagnosis, at each decision point the physician "asks a question." Asking a question can mean any of the following:

1. Requesting a laboratory test.
2. Asking the patient a verbal question.
3. Looking up an aspect of the patient's history.
4. Looking at the electrocardiogram, etc.

To each of these "questions," the physician can receive a range of answers. Each of the possible "answers" is treated by the behavior analyst as a stimulus to which the student learns to make the appropriate kind of response. The stimulus "triggers" the doctor's next response, which may be another question, or an observation, or a diagnosis. Thus the entire diagnostic process is analyzed as a decision process consisting of stimuli and responses to these stimuli. The foregoing analysis for the diagnosis of the Lead 1 tracing was an example of the analysis of a decision process in terms of "concepts" and "chains." To reformulate what appears to be a simple, old-fashioned decision process into esoteric behavioristic terminology like "concepts" and "chains" is not merely an idle exercise in academic psychology. The application of concept formation theory and chaining theory to this type of decision process *brings the decision process within the domain of instructional technology.* Once the reformulation in terms of concepts and chains is accomplished, learning theory can be applied to the development of the instructional program. Learning theory does not tell how to teach decision processes as such, but it does tell how to go about teaching concepts and chains. Since a decision process turns out to be nothing other than a network of concepts and chains, such a decision process can be taught. Below is the general schema for translating any decision process into a network of concepts and chains. This schema also applies to troubleshooting, computer programing, and any other kind of problem solving (see Figure 4).

Each of the ovals represents a class of conditions among which gen-

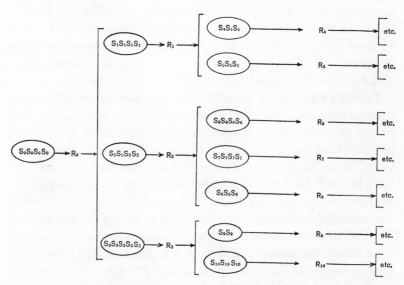

FIGURE 4. *A General Scheme for Translating a Decision Process into a Network of Concepts and Chains.*

eralization is to occur, in the sense that the same response is appropriate to all members of the set. Thus, the entire Figure 2 (patterns of ischemia, injury, and infarction) could be included in one of the brackets, say the center bracket which contains three ovals. Each of the S's would correspond to one of the tracings shown in Figure 2, and the responses R_6, R_7, and R_8 in Figure 4 would correspond to the diagnoses "pattern of ischemia," "pattern of injury," or "pattern of infarction."

The techniques of behavioral analysis illustrated above are fundamental to any mode of teaching or interpersonal communication. They are applicable to the construction of lectures, to individual tutoring, to the writing of textbooks, to film-making, and to ordinary conversation. Even great works of art, in music, poetry, and literature, can be shown to be consistent with certain principles of concept formation and chaining (8, 11).

Programed instruction, in the sense of a sequence of printed frames which require the student to write in a response, for which he receives immediate feedback, is only one particular technique for presenting the outcome of a behavioral analysis of knowledge. Small steps, active response, and immediate feedback, in and of themselves, are not very useful concepts. They enhance instruction only when the "small steps" are relevant to the behavioral structure of the knowledge being taught and when the "active response" is actually a building block of the behavioral repertoire which is being established. Small steps and active response are useful when the nature of the steps and of the responses is in accord with a sound behavioral analysis of the material.

Teaching a student to generalize within a class and to discriminate between that class and other classes is generally a straightforward process and poses technical problems only insofar as the properties to be generalized and discriminated are very subtle. When the concept is very difficult, such as, for instance, the concepts "early Mozart" and "late Mozart" for a tone-deaf individual, it may be necessary to administer some preliminary discrimination and generalization training. The tone-deaf individual might first have to learn pitch and interval discrimination and acquire various harmonic and melodic concepts. Even though the concept is a difficult one and may take a very long time to teach, the basic concept formation process still applies. The chief problem in teaching advanced or complex concepts is not so much the procedure as the definition of the classes. The definition of classes becomes particularly problematical where there is disagreement among the "experts" or where the semantics are imprecise. The reason why it would be difficult to teach the concept of "good rhythm in prose writing" is that it is difficult to develop a sufficient number of good rhythm examples and bad rhythm examples on which different experts would agree. Once the classes have been adequately defined, however, and a sufficient number of examples are available, the remainder of the teaching process poses few problems. With this formulation of concept formation, it becomes possible to consider the problems of teaching some of the concepts discussed previously in the section on Terminal Behavior Specifications (see pp. 448 ff.). The approach described in the foregoing analysis of concept formation implies a method of teaching which is related to what is sometimes called the "case method." Difficult and critical training tasks are frequently taught by this method. Other names given to the "case" method are "simulator training" and "field training." Much sales training and military training is done by this method.

The "case" method is also used in academic settings, especially on the graduate training level. "Original research projects" and "term projects" are illustrations of reasonably unsystematic applications of the case method in the academic sphere. The "case" method has also appeared in some textbooks. The most brilliant book of this type in the science field is Conant's *Harvard Case Histories in Experimental Science* (1). The two volumes of this book lead the reader through a series of eight case studies taken from the history of science. In each one, the reader is given a detailed account of the historic development of the concept, the false hypotheses and their fates, the experimental efforts of all the investigators who tackled the problem over years and sometimes centuries, and the eventual stabilization of views on the issue. In reading through these specific cases, the reader develops a concept of how scientists work. His concept increases in richness and generality with each successive case. Another example of this approach is Herrnstein and Boring's *A Source Book in the History of Psychology* (3). Case history methods apply an important principle of behavior theory—the principle that general concepts are built up in the behavior repertoire through a series of specific instances. To apply this principle is a good beginning, but a beginning is all that it is. Behavior theory would further suggest, for example, that at every point in the learning process the student must emit relevant responses and that the cases or specific instances should be arranged in order of systematically increasing complexity and generality.

Examples of Frequently Neglected Scientific Concepts: The application of concept formation procedures to the teaching of complex scientific skills can be illustrated in connection with the problem of teaching a science student to apply mathematics to the solution of problems he will encounter. The first step certainly is to teach him mathematics. He must learn arithmetic, elementary algebra, set theory, probability theory, calculus, statistics, etc. But an equally important step is to teach him the occasions on which to use each branch of mathematics. This vital step is usually omitted from the curriculum, with the result that few are able to use mathematics in practical situations, even though they may have a fairly good mastery of the techniques proper.

This second step, which branch of mathematics to use and when, is an example of concept formation. The programer can begin his behavioral analysis by developing an extensive table of the following sort:

Differential Equations	Arithmetic	Algebra	Probability Theory	Statistics	etc.
1. Heat transmission.	1. Division	1. Coin problems	1. Card problems	1. Sampling problems	
2. Movement where friction, viscosity, acceleration, and mass must be considered.	2. Multiplication	2. Compound interest problems	2. Balls in urns problems	2. Distribution problems	
	3. Subtraction	3. Projectile trajectory problems etc.	3. Genetics problems etc.	3. Reliability problems	
	4. Addition			4. Confidence limits problems etc.	
3. Electrical circuits involving capacitance, inductance.	5. Decimals etc.				
4. Analysis of the rates of chemical reactions.					

The columns of the table would contain specific problems to which the branch of mathematics named on top is applicable. Once this table is available, the programer can proceed with the construction of the program, following essentially the formula described in the earlier example where the psychologist was teaching the concepts "red" and "blue."

A second example of concept formation in the development of complex scientific skills may be found in the teaching of inferential reasoning skills and "statistical intuition." Each one of the five terminal behavior examples given previously refers to a major domain of concepts. Consider the first question: "Out of 50 tubes you tested, three were defective. What would you guess is the probability that 10 percent of all tubes in the batch are defective? Give your answer in 10 seconds." The domain of the examples might be defined as follows by the psychologist in developing his classes: "Out of x tubes tested, y were defective. What is the probability that z percent of all tubes in the batch are defective?" The response required of the student is the probability statement. He could be required to state into which of the following 10 classes the probability falls: .001-.002; .002-.004; .004-.008; .008-.016; .016-.032; etc. It may well be that thousands of combinations of x, y, and z would be needed in an instructional program to teach the student to estimate the probability accurately if he is given the values of x, y, and z. This teaching process must be repeated for a variety of statements like the one above. It might be noted that this procedure is not very different from "giving the student extensive experience." It is different only in that the experience is planned and controlled, with immediate feedback provided after each response.

Thus, application of behavioral science to the teaching of abstract concepts demands the presentation to the student of a series of specific cases arranged in a systematic order of gradually increasing complexity and abstraction. Each case should require the student to make an active response which builds toward the type of behavior specified as the behavioral objective. This is a key point in teaching complex conceptual skills.

Behavioral Analysis Applied to the Teaching of Experimental Science

As was stated earlier, interest in the application of behavioral technology to the teaching of experimental science has grown considerably during recent years. This trend must be distinguished from numerous attempts to develop science programs, in the sense of programs which teach "the facts," or the current state of theoretical knowledge, with little reference to the empirical bases of the knowledge.

One good example of research and development effort in the area of experimental science teaching is the UNESCO-sponsored science teaching project in São Paulo, Brazil, discussed earlier (9). While the project is concerned primarily with the teaching of experimental physics, its findings have implications for the teaching of science in general. One portion of the course has as its objective to teach students to describe, in experimental terms, the properties that light shares with particles and the properties that light shares with waves. The teaching materials for this course consist of programed textbooks in which the students write their answers, a set of kit materials which the students use to perform experiments in conjunction with the text, a set of optional film loops which shows experiments, and a set of optional concept films. This project generated some significant advances in the application of behavioral technology to science teaching. Some examples follow:

The Systematic Extension of Concept Formation Principles to Science Teaching: Applied to science teaching, the definition of the concept which states that a concept involves "generalization within a class and discrimination between that class and other classes" becomes "generalization within a class of observations or experiments, and discrimination between that class and other classes of observations and experiments." One immediate corollary of this definition is that concept formation in science teaching requires that the student make observations and perform experiments. This conclusion is in accord with the views of many modern science teachers and curriculum reform groups. In the case of the UNESCO project, the application of this definition to the subject matter of the physics of light resulted in a syllabus similar to that suggested by the Physical Science Study Committee (17).

A second corollary of this definition is that one single experiment or observation is not enough for the formation of a concept, for two reasons: (a) it is not possible to generalize from one instance, and (b) in order to form a discrimination, the student needs at least one instance and one noninstance of the concept in question.

Techniques for Applying Behavioral Analysis to the Design of Laboratory Work: Objections which are often leveled at the "cookbook" approach to laboratory teaching are circumvented by isolating six distinct aspects of laboratory instruction, each of which requires a separate teaching approach. The six aspects are—

1. Guiding the student through the steps of a procedure without any intent of *teaching* the procedure, as when the student is instructed to assemble a piece of equipment.
2. Teaching the student a procedure which he must learn to follow by heart, without prompts.
3. Teaching the student the reasons underlying the procedure.
4. Using the outcome of the experiment to provide one of the observations which is to be generalized with, and discriminated from, other observations in the formation of a concept.
5. Teaching incidental subconcepts within a single experiment.
6. Teaching the student to conceive, design, and carry out his own experiments.

This separation of categories of possible alternative objectives allows the techniques of behavioral analysis to be applied fruitfully to laboratory teaching.

The Problem of Generality and Transfer of Training

Another way of formulating this colossal problem is as follows: How do you know when you have built a sufficient variety of specific cases into the program, and what is "variety" anyway? How do you determine whether two specific examples are, in fact, "different"? How do you know that all your specific cases are not just a lot of variations of one basic case? In psychological terms, this is the problem of generalization gradients. For some stimulus dimensions, there is no ambiguity about the intervals along the scale. When it comes to specifying "degree of difference" between two examples involving scientific inference, say, one in physics and one in biology, anyone would be hard pressed to quantify the degree of difference. In such a case, the decision must be left to "programing art" or impressionistic judgment. It is up to the programer's ingenuity to find as wide a range of examples as possible. The wider the range he is able to cover in his program, the more general the resulting concept will be, and the greater the eventual transfer of training.

To illustrate the problem more concretely, the task of teaching "patience" and "perseverance" will serve as an example. Suppose the student is asked to sit down at the edge of a stream with his fishing rod. A hungry fish is released into the stream whenever it is desirable to reinforce the student. The time interval between fish is gradually increased according to a carefully worked-out schedule. The student becomes more and more patient. But does he? The truth is that he becomes a more and more patient *fisherman*. But he does not, because of that experience alone, become a more and more patient person. In order to develop generalized patience, exposure to a wide variety of patience-building situations would be required. The wider the range and diversity of situations in which such training is given, the greater the likelihood that the training will generalize to the types of situations in which a scientist functions. Psychologists have, as yet, very little experience with this type of personality training, but a carefully worked out program of this sort would no doubt produce definite changes in the individual's capacity to tolerate delays.

In the area of perseverance training, there is again the problem of the generality of the perseverance which is established. If a pinball machine at which the student is working is manipulated in such a way that his payoffs gradually decreased in frequency, the teacher would soon have an inveterate gambler on his hands. Skinner describes this procedure in his *Science and Human Behavior* (15). This student would have enormous perseverance at the pinball machine. This perseverance might even transfer to a one-armed bandit or a gambling table. But would it carry over to threading a needle? Or to getting a paper published? Probably not. In order to develop generalized perseverance, it would be necessary to administer perseverance training in a wide variety of situations.

One serious practical problem in developing effective programs of this sort is to invent a set of training situations that is sufficiently varied to be managed in a school and to be administered economically. Clearly, it is not feasible to lead the student from the fishing pond to the gambling casino every day. This problem will pose a major challenge to the programer and the behavioral engineer. Actually, it is the type of problem which the programer faces all the time, whether he realizes it or not. The problem of transfer of training is not unique to the teaching of patience and perseverance. The problem exists whether the subject matter is salesmanship or English grammar. A good instructional program varies the range of examples and applications as much as is possible and practical within the economic and administrative constraints that are prescribed on the basis of over-all considerations. A program to teach salesmen how to converse with their clients includes a wide variety of client's voices: deep voices and shrill ones, mellow voices and harsh ones, fast speech and slow speech. The trick is to vary the trainee's experience in the training situation as much as is feasible within the limitations imposed by the medium. The program stops short of taking the student into live client situations, rigged into a programed series of interviews, because this would be too expensive. The amount of transfer actually achieved by the program may be far from complete and may even be inadequate, but it may still provide ample justification for the investment of training time that is required. A similar argument will have to be accepted in the case of personality training for scientists. It is surely possible to develop a wide assortment of patience exercises that can be conveniently administered in the classroom with an inexpensive set of materials. While such training may not encompass the complete range of situations the student may ever encounter, it may produce enough transfer to make it worth his time.

These principles apply to all of the concept formation tasks described earlier, including—

1. Deductive reasoning skill.
2. Scientific inference skill.
3. Skill in generating hypotheses.
4. Discriminating fruitful from nonfruitful hypotheses.
5. Skill in testing hypotheses.
6. Formulating problems so that they can be solved by the scientific method.

All of these skills must be developed inductively through a long series of specific cases of gradually increasing complexity. It will not be surprising if it turns out that thousands of hours of training may be involved in developing some of these skills to any high degree.

To sum up, it can be said that behavioral technology has not yet addressed itself to the problems of science teaching in any significant way. Programs that have been written have barely begun to scratch the surface of science teaching, and that has been teaching only in the area of subject matter. Even there, the most important steps have not yet been taken.

Case Studies in Science Programing

The purpose of this section is to show some examples of science programs that have met with at least moderate success. The examples chosen do not address the most interesting ones of the science teaching problems discussed above. They do illustrate, however, some of the techniques that have proven useful. For each example presented, the underlying behavioral analysis is discussed.

Case I: Teaching an Empirical Law by Experimental Induction: The point was made previously that science educators are becoming increasingly conscious of the need to teach science students the empirical or experimental basis of laws and principles, in addition to the principles themselves. The sample presented below teaches Ohm's Law by experimental induction with the aid of a laboratory kit. The kit includes electric batteries, wire, light bulbs, and a switch. At the point in the program where the sample starts, the student has already learned from the program how an incandescent light bulb works, about electron flow, conductors, insulators, resistance, voltage, switches, and symbolic circuit representation. In reading through the frames, note the progression from manipulations of the physical equipment, to specific observations, and then to generalizations.

QUESTIONS   ANSWERS

211

DRAW the circuit diagram of the circuit you have just built.

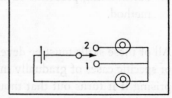

212

Throw the switch to position 1, then to position 2. What happens to the light bulbs in each case? _____

In position 1, one bulb glows brightly. In position 2, both bulbs glow dimly.

(or equivalent response)

213

Suppose each light bulb has a resistance of 10 ohms. How much resistance would two light bulbs in series have?

_____

20 ohms (10 ohms + 10 ohms
= 20 ohms)

214

How can you tell by looking at a bulb how much current is in it? _____

The brighter a bulb is, the more current there is in it.

215

Is a bulb brighter when the electrons go through both bulbs in series, or when they go through just one bulb? _____

A bulb is brighter when the electrons go through just one bulb.

216

What can you conclude about the relationship between the number of light bulbs in series and the amount of current in the circuit? _____

The more light bulbs, the less current.
or
The fewer light bulbs, the more current.

217

What can you conclude about the relationship between the amount of resistance in the circuit and the amount of current? _____

The more resistance in the circuit, the less current.
or
The less resistance in the circuit, the more current.

218

The ohm is the unit of _____.

The ampere is the unit of _____.

resistance

current

219

The more _____ s (unit) in a circuit, the fewer _____ s (unit) will flow.

ohms
amperes

In the next 24 frames, the student learns that voltages add when dry cells are placed in series, and that voltage is measured in volts. Then the student interchanges the light bulbs and dry cells in his circuit.

244

DRAW the diagram of the circuit you have just built.

245

In which circuit is there more voltage?

☐ in the circuit with two dry cells in series and one light bulb

☐ in the circuit with two light bulbs in series and one dry cell

in the circuit with two dry cells in series and one light bulb

246

Try the switch in both positions.

What do you observe? _____

When the circuit has two dry cells in series, the bulb is brighter than when the circuit has only one dry cell.

(or equivalent response)

247

You observed that the bulb glowed more brightly when there were two dry cells in series. What does this tell you about the effect of voltage on current? _____

The more voltage, the more current.

(or equivalent response)

248

When you increased the voltage, the current:

☐ increased
☐ remained the same
☐ decreased

increased

249

When you increased the resistance, the current:

☐ increased
☐ remained the same
☐ decreased

decreased

250

In your experiments you observed that:

1. the higher the _____, the higher the current.
2. the higher the _____, the lower the current.

voltage

resistance

251

WRITE this observation in the form of an equation:

$$current = \frac{(?)}{(?)}$$

$$current = \frac{voltage}{resistance}$$

252

Now WRITE the equation again, from memory, using the proper units in place of current, resistance, and voltage.

$$amperes = \frac{volts}{ohms}$$

In Frame 217, the student is ready to state the general relationship between resistance in a circuit and the amount of current flowing through that circuit. The student arrived at this statement by generalizing from his own empirical observations. Similarly, in Frame 247, he arrives at the relationship between voltage and current. In Frames

248-52 he combines these two statements into a single statement and translates it into mathematical form. This sample is another illustration of the technique of advancing from the concrete to the abstract in the teaching of concepts.

Case 2: Terms and Concepts in Medicine for General Practitioners: As has been explained, the formation of a concept involves the formation of generalization within a class and discrimination between that class and other classes. The first four frames of the example below form the concepts of "allergy" and "immunity" by teaching some similarities and some differences between the two. The first frame in the sequence (Frame 1) is designed to insure that one of the very important terms, "antigen-antibody reaction," is present in the doctor's repertoire before the concept formation process is initiated.

The second concept taught in the program is that of "specificity." Note how the term "specificity" is brought under the control of three stimuli: (a) the word "complementary," (b) the diagram which shows the geometric representation of specificity, and (c) the words "will react only with." Only after the term "specificity" has been brought

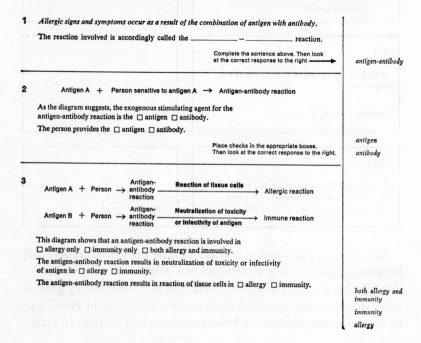

1 *Allergic signs and symptoms occur as a result of the combination of antigen with antibody.*

The reaction involved is accordingly called the _____ – _____ reaction.

Complete the sentence above. Then look
at the correct response to the right ⟶   *antigen-antibody*

2   Antigen A + Person sensitive to antigen A → Antigen-antibody reaction

As the diagram suggests, the exogenous stimulating agent for the
antigen-antibody reaction is the ☐ antigen ☐ antibody.

The person provides the ☐ antigen ☐ antibody.

Place checks in the appropriate boxes.   *antigen*
Then look at the correct response to the right.   *antibody*

3   Antigen-   **Reaction of tissue cells**
         Antigen A + Person → antibody ————————————→ Allergic reaction
                              reaction

                              Antigen-   **Neutralization of toxicity**
         Antigen B + Person → antibody ————————————→ Immune reaction
                              reaction   **or infectivity of antigen**

This diagram shows that an antigen-antibody reaction is involved in
☐ allergy only ☐ immunity only ☐ both allergy and immunity.

The antigen-antibody reaction results in neutralization of toxicity or infectivity
of antigen in ☐ allergy ☐ immunity.

The antigen-antibody reaction results in reaction of tissue cells in ☐ allergy ☐ immunity.

both allergy and
immunity

immunity

allergy

4 Compare allergy and immunity by checking one or both boxes for each statement below:

Allergy	Immunity		Allergy	Immunity
☐	☐	Person has antibodies.	☑	☑
☐	☐	Antigen-antibody reaction occurs.	☑	☑
☐	☐	Antigen-antibody reaction occurs on contact with antigen.	☑	☑
☐	☐	Antigen-antibody reaction results in tissue reaction.	☑	☐
☐	☐	Antigen-antibody reaction results in neutralization of toxicity or infectivity of antigen.	☐	☑

5 *The geometric forms below depict the relation between antigens and antibodies. (In reality, these substances are complex chemical entities, not geometric forms.)*

○ + ▰ → Antigen-antibody reaction
○ + ◣ → No antigen-antibody reaction
○ + ◤ → No antigen-antibody reaction

When we say that an antibody will react only with an antigen specific for it, we mean that their configurations must be ☐ complementary ☐ identical.

Draw the shape of the antibody that is specific for the antigen depicted below:

○ + ⬦ → Antigen-antibody reaction

complementary

◤

6 The term SPECIFICITY refers to the fact that the ☐ antigen ☐ antibody elicited by a particular ☐ antigen ☐ antibody will react only with that ☐ antigen ☐ antibody.

antibody
antigen
antigen

7 Check the combination(s) of antigen and antibody that would **not** produce an antigen-antibody reaction:

☐ ○ + ▰
☐ ○ + ◣
☐ ○ + ◤

For an antigen-antibody reaction to occur the antibody must be _____ for the antigen.

☐
☑
☐

specific

8 *The diagram below depicts the process of sensitization.*

Susceptible person without antibodies specific for antigen A + Antigen A → Person with antibodies specific for antigen A

When a person acquires specific ☐ antigens ☐ antibodies as the result of contact with ☐ antigen ☐ antibody, he is said to be _____ ed.

antibodies
antigen
sensitized

9 *Some persons are more likely than others to develop allergies. When such a person is exposed to an antigen for the first time, he may develop antibodies to it. These will make him allergic to that antigen.*

This process is called _____.

The antibodies produced as a result of exposure to the antigen are_____ for that antigen.

sensitization
specific

° *Chas. Pfizer & Co., Inc., 1963.*

under the control of these three stimuli is the doctor required to use the term "specificity" as an active response.

In Frames 8 and 9, the new term "sensitization" is introduced. The term is developed conceptually over the next six or seven frames, but note how it is juxtaposed with the previously taught term "specificity" in Frame 9. The purpose of this juxtaposition is to prevent the development of an unintended generalization between the new concept being taught and the one which has just been developed. By an immediate juxtaposition, the discrimination between the two classes is made sharper. This is not only good concept-formation technique, but it is also one of the important devices for enhancing retention.

An interesting sidelight on this 400-frame, six-hour program is that 153,000 individual physicians have requested a total of over 170,000 copies of the program from the Pfizer Laboratories over a one-year period (10).

Case 3: The Formation of a Highly Abstract Concept: The Behavioral Contingency: The sample program on the succeeding pages is the introduction to a program which teaches the use of a symbolic notation system for describing and analyzing behavioral contingencies (7). The introduction teaches the rather difficult concept of "behavioral contingency." Prior to teaching this concept, the program teaches two prerequisite concepts: "response-event" and "stimulus-event." The concept formation process illustrated in this program is particularly instructive because of the elaborateness of the generalization training. In the myocardial infarction case presented above, the behavior analyst has a relatively easy job of choosing examples of "normal" and "enlarged" Q waves and examples and nonexamples of the various types of other abnormalities. In the following case, the behavior analyst must make some very difficult decisions in selecting the members of the classes within which generalization must be brought about. Equally difficult is the choice of classes from which the concept class must become discriminated. In the myocardial infarction program, each of the three concept classes (ischemia, injury, and infarction) had to be discriminated from each of the two other classes and from nothing else. In teaching a concept like behavioral contingency, on the other hand, the behavior analyst must anticipate the likely areas of confusion for the learner and must introduce these classes during the discrimination training process as "almost-but-not-quite" classes that the student must learn to discriminate from the real thing. The techniques used are discussed in more detail at the end of the sample.

1

Your being born <u>was not</u> a "response-event" for you.
That is, it <u>was not</u> an action you initiated.

Your throwing your rattle out of your crib, however,
<u>was</u> an action initiated by you. It <u>was</u> a "response-
event" for you.

CHECK each sentence below that describes a response-
event for the person or animal named in the sentence
(note that there is no limit to the number of sentences
you can check):

☐ a. Clara dyed her hair red.   a

☐ b. Herman died of old age.

☐ c. The dog has fleas.

☐ d. The cat meowed.   d

2

When you hit someone, it (☐ is ☐ is not) your action.   is
It (☐ is ☐ is not) your response-event.   is

When the other person hits you back, it (☐ is ☐ is not)   is not
your response-event.

CHECK each sentence below that describes a response-
event for the person or animal named in the sentence:

☐ a. Philip ran fast.   a

☐ b. Gregory was run over.

☐ c. Alice cheated on the exam.   c

☐ d. Mary was reprimanded for cheating.

☐ e. The canary lost all its feathers.

☐ f. The parrot said "Polly wants a cracker."   f

3

The sentence, "The officer gave Mr. Smith a summons,"
<u>describes</u> the officer's giving the ticket, but merely
<u>implies</u> Mr. Smith's speeding or going through the red
<u>light</u>.

Does the sentence describe a response-event for
Mr. Smith? ☐ yes   ☐ no   no

CHECK the statements below that describe, not merely
imply, response-events for <u>you</u>:

☐ a. You solved a hard math example.   a

☐ b. Your teacher gave you a good grade
in math.

☐ c. You are a doctor.

☐ d. You are studying to be a doctor.   d

4

Psychology is often called the science of behavior.
That is, it is the study of how living creatures behave,
how they act, what response-events they initiate
under what circumstances.

The sentence "The telephone rang" does not refer to
a response-event, because only people or animals can
initiate response-events.

CHECK the response-events below:

☐ a. The hurricane struck here yesterday.
       (for the hurricane)

☐ b. Tom struck Harry.
       (for Tom)

☐ c. Tom struck Harry.
       (for Harry)

☐ d. The clock struck ten.
       (for the clock)

b

5

COMPLETE the definition of the term "response-event"
below. Your definition should include the word
"action."

A response-event is _____.

any action initiated
by a person or animal
(or by a living crea-
ture).

(or equivalent re-
sponse)

6

When you get into the bathtub, your environment
changes: you get wet.

When you are just sitting in the bathtub, your
environment does not change: you are already wet.

When you are standing on the corner and the traffic
light is red, your environment (☐ changes ☐ does not
change).

does not change

When you are standing on the corner and the traffic
light turns from red to green, your environment
(☐ changes ☐ does not change).

changes

When you are standing on the corner and someone
right behind you calls your name, your environment
(☐ changes ☐ does not change).

changes

7

The sentence "Tommy finished his spinach" <u>describes</u> the response-event "finishing the spinach," but it merely <u>implies</u> the environmental changes "The spinach disappeared from the plate" and "Tommy's stomach got fuller."

CHECK the sentences below which describe, not merely imply, <u>changes</u> in your environment:

   □ a. You have a scar on your forehead.

   □ b. You are walking along and a ladder comes into view.

   □ c. Your alarm clock goes off in your ear.

   □ d. You set the alarm for 8:00.

b

c

8

We call a change in someone's environment a "stimulus-event" for that person.

Consider this sentence: Fred is stretched out on a sandy beach.

Does it describe a change in Fred's environment?
□ yes □ no

Does it describe a stimulus-event for Fred? □ yes □ no

Consider this sentence: Fred is stretched out on the beach and a wave washes over him.

Does it describe a change in Fred's environment?
□ yes □ no

Does it describe a stimulus-event for Fred? □ yes □ no

no

no

yes

yes

9

CHECK the stimulus-events below:

   □ a. The rat is sitting in a cage with a light bulb in front of him.

   □ b. The light goes on.

   □ c. He presses the bar in front of him.

   □ d. The pellet dispenser drops him a pellet of food.

   □ e. He eats the pellet.

b

d

10

The action of John's hitting Al on the nose is a
(☐ response-event ☐ stimulus-event) for John and a
(☐ response-event ☐ stimulus-event) for Al.

| response-event |
| stimulus-event |

In front of each sentence below, WRITE:

"R" if it describes (not just implies) a response-
event for you

"S" if it describes (not just implies) a stimulus-
event for you

"O" if it describes neither a response-event
nor a stimulus-event for you

_____ You pick up the telephone receiver. → R

_____ A dial tone sounds. → S

_____ Your mother-in-law, who is listening in on
the extension phone, hears the dial tone, too. → O

_____ You dial your friend's number. → R

_____ You get a busy signal. → S

11

To summarize: For a given individual, a stimulus-
event can be initiated by:

☐ that individual → that individual

☐ another individual → another individual

☐ the inanimate world → the inanimate world

A response-event can be initiated by:

☐ that individual → that individual

☐ another individual

☐ the inanimate world

12

If you walk in the rain, then you'll get wet.
   ‾‾‾‾‾‾‾‾‾‾‾‾‾   ‾‾‾‾‾‾‾‾‾‾‾
        R   S

In the sentence above, the response-event
has been underlined and labeled _____. → R

The stimulus-event has been underlined and
labeled _____. → S

13

In the sentences below, UNDERLINE each response-event and LABEL it with an "R." Also UNDERLINE each stimulus-event and LABEL it with an "S," as in the example.

Example: Unless <u>you cash your check</u> within thirty
R

days, <u>it will become void.</u>
S

a. Your hand will turn pale if you hold it above

your head for a long time.

b. Arnold goes to the doctor once a year and never

gets a serious disease.

---

a. <u>Your hand will turn</u>
<u>pale</u> if <u>you hold it</u>
S   R
above your head
for a long time.

b. <u>Arnold goes to the</u>
<u>doctor</u> once a year
R
and never <u>gets a</u>
<u>serious disease.</u>
S

14

Unless <u>you cash your check</u> within thirty days, <u>it</u>
R
<u>will become void.</u>
S

Unless R within thirty days, S.

In the model above, we have rewritten the sentence, substituting "R" for the whole response-event and "S" for the whole stimulus-event.

REWRITE the sentences below according to the model:

a. <u>Your hand will turn pale</u> if <u>you hold it above</u>
S   R
<u>your head</u> for a long time.

_____

b. <u>Arnold goes to the doctor</u> once a year and never
R
<u>gets a serious disease.</u>
S

_____

---

a. S if R for a long time.

b. R once a year and
never S.

15

Consider this sentence:

If you flick the light switch, then the light will go on.

It states that the light will go on:

☐ whether or not you flick the switch
☐ since you will flick the switch
☐ only on the condition that you flick
the switch

---

only on the condition
that you flick the
switch

16

Sometimes a change in the environment follows behavior without being conditional upon (or contingent upon) the behavior.

For example, in both sentences below, an S-event (environmental change) follows an R-event (behavior). CHECK the one that states a relation of conditionality or contingency between the R-event and the S-event that follows it:

☐ John pushed button "6" and then the elevator stopped at the sixth floor.

☐ If John pushes button "6" then the elevator will stop at the sixth floor.

> If John pushes button "6" then the elevator will stop at the sixth floor.

17

First, UNDERLINE and LABEL all response-events and stimulus-events in the sentences below.

Second, REWRITE the sentences, substituting "R" for the whole response-event and "S" for the whole stimulus-event.

Third, CHECK the sentence if it states (not merely implies) that the S-event is contingent upon the R-event.

☐ a. A recorded announcement of the time played on

the phone once when Alice dialed ME 7-1212.

REWRITTEN: _____

☐ b. A recorded announcement of the time plays on

the phone whenever Alice dials ME 7-1212.

REWRITTEN: _____

> ☐ a. A recorded an-
> nouncement of the
> time <u>played on the
> phone once</u> when
> S
> Alice <u>dialed ME-
> 7-1212.</u>
> R
>
> S once when R.
>
> ☑ b. A recorded an-
> nouncement of the
> time <u>plays on the
> phone</u> whenever
> S
> Alice <u>dials ME 7-
> 1212.</u>
> R
>
> S whenever R.

18

Below are four types of statements. As psychologists, we are interested only in situations in which an environmental change is contingent upon behavior.

CHECK the one sentence that represents this type of situation:

☐ If R then R.   (or: R if R.)
☐ If R then S.   (or: S if R.)
☐ If S then R.   (or: R if S.)
☐ If S then S.   (or: S if S.)

> If R then S.   (or: S if R.)

19

As psychologists, we are interested in situations in which _____-events are contingent upon _____-events.

Why do we call such situations "behavioral contingencies"? (Include the words <u>behavior</u> and <u>contingent</u> in your answer.) _____

> stimulus (or S)
> response (or R)
>
> because an environmental change (or stimulus-event) is contingent upon behavior
>
> (or equivalent response)

20

First, REWRITE each sentence below, substituting "R" for any response-event and "S" for any stimulus-event.

Then, CHECK a sentence only if it describes a behavioral contingency; that is, if it describes a situation in which an <u>S</u> is contingent upon an <u>R</u>.

☐ a. The radio will go on if you turn the knob to the right.

     REWRITTEN: _____

☐ b. The trees will get smashed if the hurricane comes this way.

     REWRITTEN: _____

☐ c. If you behave yourself all year long, then there'll be nice presents under the tree for you on Christmas morning.

     REWRITTEN: _____

☐ d. If it snows this weekend, then I'll go skiing.

     REWRITTEN: _____

> ☑ a. <u>The radio will go on</u>
>   S
>   if <u>you turn the knob to the right.</u>
>   R
>   S if R.
>
> ☐ b. <u>The trees will get smashed</u> if <u>the hurri-</u>
>   S   S
>   <u>cane comes this way.</u>
>   S if S.
>
> ☑ c. If <u>you behave yourself all year long,</u>
>   R
>   then <u>there'll be nice presents under the tree</u>
>   S
>   <u>for you on Christmas morning.</u>
>   If R, then S.
>
> ☐ d. If <u>it snows this weekend,</u>
>   S
>   then <u>I'll go skiing.</u>
>   R
>   If S, then R.

21

UNDERLINE and LABEL the R-event and the S-event in the following sentence:

     If the swelling in Mrs. Jones's leg gets worse,

     then she'll go to a doctor.

In this sentence, the _____-event is conditional upon the _____-event.

Therefore, the sentence (☐ describes   ☐ does not describe) a behavioral contingency.

> If <u>the swelling in Mrs. Jones's leg gets worse,</u>
>   S
> then <u>she'll go to a</u>
>   R
> <u>doctor.</u>
>
> R
> S
>
> does not describe

22

When deciding whether a sentence does or does not
describe a behavioral contingency, it is important
to look for the R and S in relation to the SAME
person.

Consider, for example, the sentence, "If John
hits Tom, then Tom will hit John."

REWRITE the sentence, substituting "R" for John's
response-event and "S" for John's stimulus-event:

_____

REWRITE the same sentence, substituting "R" for
Tom's response-event and "S" for Tom's stimulus-
event: _____

For whom does the sentence "If John hits Tom,
then Tom will hit John" describe a behavioral
contingency?

    ☐ for Tom

    ☐ for John

If R, then S.
If S, then R.
for John

23

Behavioral contingencies are often described in
the form(s):

    ☐ a. A stimulus-event occurs when a response-
          event occurs.

    ☐ b. If a stimulus-event occurs, then a
          response-event occurs.

    ☐ c. If a response-event occurs, then a stimulus-
          event occurs.

    ☐ d. If one response-event occurs, then another
          response-event occurs.

    ☐ e. If one stimulus-event occurs, then another
          stimulus-event occurs.

    ☐ f. A response-event occurs when a stimulus-
          event occurs.

a
c

24

REWRITE the sentence below, substituting "R" for
the response-event and "S" for the stimulus-event:

Unless you put that cat down, you'll get a spanking.

REWRITTEN: _____

Do the same for this sentence:

If you do not put that cat down, you'll get a
spanking.

REWRITTEN: _____

Unless R, S.
If not R, S.

25

Unless <u>you put that cat down</u>, <u>you'll get a spanking</u>.
            R   S

Unless R, S.

If <u>you do not put that cat down</u>, <u>you'll get a</u>
              R   S
<u>spanking</u>.

If not R, S.

The two sentences above are equivalent, because in both cases, the occurrence of the stimulus-event is contingent upon:

☐ the occurrence of the response-event, "put that cat down."

☐ the non-occurrence of the response-event, "put that cat down."

the non-occurrence
of the response-event,
"put that cat down"

26

REWRITE this sentence, substituting "R" for the response-event and "S" for the stimulus-event.

You'll get hurt if you do not cross streets carefully.

REWRITTEN: _____

S if not R.

In the sentence above, whether or not the _____ occurs depends upon whether or not the _____ occurs.

S
R

Thus, we say that the sentence (☐ describes ☐ does not describe) a behavioral contingency.

describes

27

CHECK the behavioral contingencies below:

☐ a. If you put off that visit to the dentist, your cavity will grow bigger.

☐ b. More people take their vacations in summer than in winter.

☐ c. You get the weather report when you dial WE 6-1212.

☐ d. If it rains tomorrow, I will go for a walk.

☐ e. If we go to the beach, then we'll take a picnic lunch.

☐ f. Your wish will come true if you wish on the first star you see at night.

☐ g. If someone is born in New York, then he is a native New Yorker.

☐ h. If I were you, I'd tell him a thing or two!

a

c

f

The discrimination training for the concept "response-event" begins with matching-to-sample Frames 1 and 2. Frame 3 withdraws the sample and at the same time teaches the discrimination between stated and implied response-events. Frame 4 enlarges the class of noninstances, and by Frame 5, the student is ready to give the definition. Frames 6-9 follow a similar procedure for the concept "stimulus-event." The decision, "Is x a stimulus-event or not?" is made a two-step chain: "Is x an environmental change? If so, then it is a stimulus-event. If not, then it is not a stimulus-event." This chain makes use of the concept "environmental change," which the student already has, so that he can learn the concept "stimulus-event" with fewer examples than would otherwise be needed. In Frame 10, the two concepts, "response-event" and "stimulus-event" are juxtaposed to initiate the discrimination training for those two classes. The frame also picks up a loose end from Frame 2: In Frame 2, "a response-event by another person" was a nonmember of the class in question. In Frame 10, a new class is available, so that "a response-event by another person" can be "a stimulus-event for you." Frame 11 requires the student to summarize the two concepts from a novel point of view. Frames 12, 13, 14, and 17 teach a method of abbreviating response-events and stimulus-events so that their relationship to one another is more easily recognized. This abbreviation is one link in the chain, "Identify the response-event and stimulus-event; rewrite the sentence, substituting R for the response-event and S for the stimulus-event; is the S contingent upon the R? If so, then the sentence describes a behavioral contingency. If not, it doesn't describe one." Frame 15 introduces the concept of contingency. This concept is further sharpened in Frames 16 and 17. Frame 18 introduces the concept of behavioral contingency as one type of contingency, the definition of which is called for in Frame 19. Frame 20 teaches the student to generalize between "S if S" and "If S then R" statements as nonmembers of the class "behavioral contingency" and at the same time to generalize between "S if R" and "If R then S" statements as members of the class of behavioral contingencies. Frame 21 asks for the student to decide without a supporting definition whether a statement describes a behavioral contingency. Frame 22 teaches that a given statement can describe a behavioral contingency for one organism and not for another. Frame 23 requires the identification of behavioral contingencies stated in abstract form. Frames 24-26 extend the concept of behavioral contingency to instances in which the stimulus-event is contingent upon the nonoccurrence of the response-event. Frame 27 brings together all the generalizations and discriminations that had previously been taught.

The behavior analyst needs a thorough knowledge not only of the subject matter to be taught but also of the student population. The discrimination training between explicit and implicit statements of events and contingencies was included in the program not because it is prerequisite to the concepts of response-event, stimulus-event, and behavioral contingency, but rather because the student population tends to read into a given statement events and contingencies that are not really described. Similarly, the chains dealing with how to identify a response-event, a stimulus-event, and a behavioral contingency were included not because the definitions are necessary for the concept, but rather because the student population on the whole cannot make the discriminations in one step until they have had more practice than could be included in a short program. A student can drop the intermediate links of the chain as they become unnecessary, but they are at least always available if needed.

Behavioral Technology and Science Education Today

Defects in Existing Programs

Thoughtful and competent science teachers have expressed disappointment with existing programed instruction courses in science. Common verdicts are that programed instruction may be "fine for rote material," "a convenient way of administering drill work," "a useful way of teaching 'facts' as opposed to 'concepts,' " "good for the slow student who needs remedial spoon feeding." These comments represent generous attempts to stress the positive, to find a grain of value, in a basically sterile method of teaching. Less generous verdicts state that programed instruction "stultifies inquisitive or creative thought" and "presents scientific knowledge as dogma instead of as tentative theory."

These views are based on the evaluation of existing programs. During the past five years, several hundred science programs have been published and used in hundreds of classrooms and other settings. Almost all of these programs have suffered from the following defects (6, 10):

1. They require the student to write out unimportant words which are omitted in text passages which read like a somewhat repetitious textbook. The inexpert programer who writes such material often justifies the technique in terms of "forcing the student to read carefully" or "introducing repetition to improve retention." Neither of these justifications has any basis in learning theory.

2. They attempt to teach interverbally, or "by rote," concepts which should be taught by examples (instances and noninstances) or by empirical reference. This includes the error of teaching words *about* a concept instead of the concept itself. This type of error reflects a lack of understanding of the nature of concepts and is often committed by the same programers who state that programed instruction is not well suited to teaching concepts.

3. They fail to teach the differences and similarities between related entities and fail to teach the student to organize, categorize, or classify his knowledge. The result of this error is that the student fails to develop any overview. He may complain that he "doesn't know where he is going" and may, in fact, forget the material soon after he has completed the program.

4. They limit the responses the student makes to one- or two-word answers or to selecting one of three or four given alternative choices, instead of occasionally requiring the student to provide an explanation, to give a definition, to draw a complete, labeled diagram, to draw a graph, or to describe an observation. This error has the effect that the knowledge being established by the program does not transfer beyond the program to the real world. The student learns to respond to highly structured questions to which there are brief and clear-cut answers, but does not learn to answer more open-ended questions, which may require longer or more complex answers. The student who takes such a program may complain that he "is not learning anything." This sensation is due to the fact that when the student "tests himself" by asking himself an open-ended question, he finds himself unable to respond.

5. They are not designed in the appropriate medium or response modality. Examples of this error include attempts to teach oral communication skills, such as selling or interviewing, by paper-and-pencil programs instead of audiolingual programs, to teach an aspect of engineering or experimental science without providing

access to the relevant laboratory equipment, or to teach the operation of a machine by paper and pencil instead of at the machine to be operated.

These are the most serious drawbacks of the large majority of existing programed instruction courses. The criticisms which educators frequently level against programed instruction are justified criticisms of most existing programs.

Some Causes of the Poor State of the Art

Before a remedy can be discussed, it is necessary to examine some of the reasons why the technology of programed instruction has not advanced more rapidly. Here are some of the more obvious contributing factors:

1. When one describes programed instruction to someone who is not familiar with it, it is easiest to say that it consists of a teaching technique which uses "small steps, active responses by the student, and immediate confirmation." This is the way programed instruction has been presented to the layman, to the country's teachers, and to industrial managers. It is much more difficult to promote and sell programed instruction by referring to "the operational specification of behavioral objectives" and to "techniques of behavioral analysis." The result, however, is that the "small-step, active response, immediate feedback" definition has been taken seriously by many people who never became aware of the fact that "activeness" of the student's response is far less important than the *nature* of the response and that the "size" of the step is far less significant than the dimension of knowledge along which the "step" is being taken. These people are therefore not convinced that behavioral science and learning theory have anything significant to contribute or that behavioral analysis is anything more than a slogan used by behavioral scientists in attempting to stake an unjustified claim in a significant new field.

2. The vigorous publicity which programed instruction has received during the past few years has attracted into the field many individuals with no background in behavioral science or behavioral technology. Under pressure to become "experts," these individuals

produced programs as best they could and wrote articles and papers which in one way or another denied the applicability of learning theory. This antilearning theory point of view is appealing to the vast majority of those who are active in the field of programed instruction and who could not qualify as experts if a knowledge of learning theory were accepted as an important qualification.

3. It is far less expensive to produce programed instruction courses which consist of text passages with many blanks than it is to produce programed courses based on operational specification of behavioral objectives, behavioral analysis, and behaviorally designed frame sequences which have been subjected to several cycles of testing and revision until the specifications are met. It costs between $2,000 and $6,000 to produce one student hour of top-quality, behaviorally designed instructional material. This economic factor, in conjunction with the factors described in paragraphs 1 and 2, above, has exerted strong pressures against the systematic application of behavioral technology in the development of programed instruction courses. This pressure has been felt particularly by textbook publishers. The publishers, in attempting to anticipate a promising new way of writing textbooks, tried to secure programs by the same methods they have used to procure textbook manuscripts: by making a contract with a university teacher and paying him an advance against royalties. Because a single individual working by himself cannot produce a programed course of high quality, especially if he does not have the backup of good behavior analysts, and because the cost of producing a behaviorally designed programed course is about 20 times as high as the cost of producing a textbook covering comparable material, this method of obtaining and publishing programs has resulted in many programs of very inferior quality, even though many of these bear the names of distinguished subject matter experts (9, 10).

4. In numerous, poorly controlled experiments conducted during the past four years, inadequately designed programs have appeared to work better than "conventional instruction." This literature is for the most part invalid. Most of the experiments reported suffer from a combination of the following defects:

a. The "conventional instruction" was directed toward a different set of objectives than the programed instruction. The final evaluation test on which the comparison is based favors the objectives toward which the program was written.

b. The "conventional instruction" suffered from a combination of faults which are not necessary components of nonprogramed instruction. This touches upon the problem of defining "conventional instruction" to begin with.

Results of such studies, uncritically interpreted, have encouraged the proponents of a nonbehavioral approach to programed instruction.

Summary

This entire chapter makes the following main points:

1. The most important problems in science education, which are also the most difficult problems—how to develop skills in scientific method, research skills, and personality traits—are being avoided by the workers in the field. They are being avoided for several reasons:

   a. The technology which could implement an attack upon these problems is not yet widely understood.

   b. The correct application of this technology is expensive.

   c. The market for science teaching systems that utilize behavioral technology is not yet ripe.

2. Programed instruction, which is one application of behavioral technology, has been applied, during the past few years, to some of the more straightforward problems of science education, especially science subject matter. Most of these attempts have been unsuccessful because of failure to apply behavioral technology correctly.

Issues That Remain To Be Solved

It is beyond the scope of this chapter to set objectives or to propose solutions. The setting of national goals for science education and the implementation of such goals is an extremely difficult and complex task. It is possible, however, to state some fundamental issues that will have to be taken into account by those who will eventually face this task:

1. Research and development in the application of behavioral technology to science education cannot be supported by private invest-

ment. The return on such investment is, by any criteria in current use, too delayed, too uncertain, and too small to justify making the investment. This implies that research and development must be supported by public or foundation funds.

2. The unavoidable high cost of developing science teaching systems based on the application of behavioral technology argues against duplication of effort. And yet, attempts to avoid duplication will exert pressure against diversity, innovation, and creativity. Such pressure would slow down progress and invention. But it contains an even greater danger: It would promote centralization of educational control. The funding agency and the recipient of the funds who is first in any given field would acquire a very strong voice in the setting of educational objectives in that field, at the expense of other educators who might favor other approaches and objectives. Such centralization of educational control can be stultifying and dangerous. This issue and some others are discussed at greater length by Mechner and Cook (10).

However, the challenge must be faced. A powerful new technology for addressing the problems of science education is available. The application of this technology could have a vast social impact during the next few decades. The initial steps must involve the development of experts in the new technology and intensive research and development. In such situations, the most promising form of research and development is the attempt to implement. The only way to chart unknown terrain is to explore it.

References

1. Conant, J. B., editor. *Harvard Case Histories in Experimental Science.* Cambridge, Mass.: Harvard University Press, 1948.
2. Ferster, C. B., and Skinner, B. F. *Schedules of Reinforcement.* New York: Appleton-Century-Crofts, 1957.
3. Herrnstein, R. J., and Boring, E. G. *A Source Book in the History of Psychology.* Cambridge, Mass.: Harvard University Press. (In press)
4. Hull, C. L. "Quantitative Aspects of the Evolution of Concepts; An Experimental Study." *Psychological Monographs* 28: 1-25; Whole No. 123, 1920.
5. Keller, F. S., and Schoenfeld, W. N. *Principles of Psychology.* New York: Appleton-Century-Crofts, 1950.

6. Margulies, S. *Some General Rules of Frame Construction.* New York: Basic Systems, 1963.

7. Mechner, F. "A Notation System for the Description of Behavioral Procedures." *Journal of the Experimental Analysis of Behavior* 2: 133-50; April 1959.

8. Mechner, F. *Programming for Automated Instruction, III.* New York: Basic Systems, 1961.

9. Mechner, F. *Behavioral Technology and Medical Education.* Paper presented at Rochester Conference on Programmed Instruction in Medical Education, June 26, 1964.

10. Mechner, F., and Cook, D. A. *Behavioral Technology and Manpower Development.* Background paper prepared for the Directorate of Scientific Affairs, Organization for Economic Cooperation and Development, 1963.

11. Mechner, F.; Cook, D. A.; and Margulies, S. *Introduction to Programmed Instruction.* New York: Basic Systems, 1964.

12. Moore, O. K., and Anderson, A. R. *Early Reading and Writing.* 15 min., 16mm, sound, color. Basic Education, Hamden, Connecticut, 1960.

13. Piaget, J. *The Child's Conception of the World.* New York: Harcourt, 1929.

14. Skinner, B. F. *The Behavior of Organisms: An Experimental Analysis.* New York: Appleton-Century-Crofts, 1938.

15. Skinner, B. F. *Science and Human Behavior.* New York: Macmillan Co., 1953.

16. Skinner, B. F. "A Case History in Scientific Method." *American Psychologist* 11: 221-33; May 1956.

17. Zacharias, J. "The Age of Science." *The Nation's Children.* (Edited by Eli Ginzberg.) New York: Columbia University Press, 1960. Vol. 2, Development and Education, pp. 93-115.

HARRY F. SILBERMAN
System Development Corporation

Reading and Related Verbal Learning

This chapter includes studies which are relevant to the application of programing principles to reading instruction. The main emphasis is on beginning reading. The organization of this paper differs from the usual division of reading research into such topics as methods, materials, comprehension, and remediation. Instead, the following topics have been used: sequencing factors, stimulus-response factors, reinforcement factors, mediation effects, individual differences, and program evaluations. This structure corresponds with the paradigm of programed instruction in which desired overt and covert responses are defined, stimuli are designed to evoke them, reinforcers are applied as needed, items are arranged in a systematic sequence with provision for individual differences in learning rate, and procedures are modified on the basis of learner performance.

Sequencing Factors

The task of sequencing reading material in a progression of increasing difficulty seems to be a problem of finding an optimal solution to ordering the material on more than one dimension. Word frequency is only one of these dimensions; letter frequency, syntactic structure, meaningfulness, redundancy, pronunciability, word and sentence length, familiarity, stimulus similarity, and grapheme-phoneme correspondence are also dimensions which are related to learning difficulty. Careful manipulation of all these variables may prove to be of considerable value in improving the effectiveness of reading instruction.

Gradual Progression

In the psychological literature, there is some evidence that learning a difficult discrimination is easier if it is preceded by training on a similar but easier discrimination. Hively (35) taught preschool and first-grade children to discriminate stimuli differing in shape, size, and color. Training methods featuring progressively more difficult discrimination tasks were compared with training in the final most difficult discrimination alone. A control experiment confirmed the finding of five exploratory experiments that approaching the criterion task through a sequence of progressively difficult discriminations was more efficient than training on the criterion task alone.

Grapheme-Phoneme Correspondence

One dimension on which reading material may be ordered is phonemic regularity. Bloomfield, in Bloomfield and Barnhart (3), made a strong plea that reading instruction should take advantage of the fact that English writing is alphabetic and urged, "Our teaching ought to distinguish, then, between *regular* spellings, which involve only the alphabetic principle, and *irregular* spellings, which depart from this principle, and it ought to classify the irregular spellings according to the various types of deviation from the alphabetic principle" (p. 29). He wanted to modify existing primers and readers so that words are graded on phonemic regularity, with regularly spelled words appearing before irregularly spelled words. In *Let's Read* (3), Bloomfield presented words in rhyming groups like hat, cat, and rat. He began by teaching the short sounds of all the vowels in consonant-vowel-consonant (CVC) trigrams. These words are practiced until they are overlearned. They are practiced in groups arranged according to final letters (bat, hat, cat, rat); initial letters (cat, cap, can, cab); in groups with contrasting vowels (hat, hit, hot, hut); and in irregular orders (bat, hop, pin, cut). There are some hazards in organizing words into groups with rhyming endings, e.g., bump, dump, hump, jump. As the child reads these words, he need only respond to the initial consonant to obtain his reinforcement. Consequently, when the same child is confronted with a new block of words—e.g., damp, lamp, ramp, he says dump, lump, and rump—since he has not learned to respond to anything but the initial consonants.

The practice of grouping together words with a common grapheme-to-phoneme correspondence has also been questioned by Levin and Watson (44) on the grounds that discrimination among elements in a more variable list, using words in which the medial vowel is associated with two phonemes, is more easily established and is more likely to facilitate transfer to a new list. Levin and Watson (44) tested and confirmed the hypothesis that some degree of variability is more useful than Bloomfield's categorical training. Using 40 third-grade children, 20 boys and 20 girls, two treatment conditions were compared. One group learned a constant list (words with medial vowels associated with only one phoneme) followed by a variable list of words; the other group learned a variable list followed by a variable list. Both groups were then given a transfer list to learn. The group which learned a variable list of four words followed by a second variable list of four words learned more efficiently than the group which learned a constant followed by a variable list. It is evident from the choice of words used in the variable lists that the variable lists were not representative of the entire range of variability that is possible, but rather indicates that a small degree of variability is better than a constant list. The question of how much variability is desirable remains to be answered.

In a follow-up study (45), instead of the medial vowel being associated with two phonemes, the variation was applied to the initial elements in the words. The results showed that the task of learning the constant list is easier than that of learning the variable list. Once acquired, however, the initial learning of a variable list facilitates the subsequent learning of a different variable list. This may be a "learning how to learn" phenomenon rather than the effect of the variable list per se.

An alternative to solving problems associated with grouping words according to spelling-sound consistency is the modification of the alphabet itself. Downing (9) and others have been studying the use of an augmented Roman alphabet (A.R.) for teaching beginning reading and find it quite successful on initial trials. An interim report (9) described a comparison of 14 seven-year-old children classified as reading failures with 20 children of equivalent IQ and home environment.

The children in experimental and control groups were treated alike, except that during four half-hour periods per week and during their free reading periods the experimental group used books printed in A.R., while the control group used books in the conventional alphabet. After 16 hours of training time with the A.R. material (32 half-hour lessons), the gains in test results showed a significant advantage for the experimental groups. After a further four hours' teaching, the A.R. group had made the transition to normal print. The small number of children tested is probably of less concern than that only one teacher was responsible for the experimental A.R. group. Generalizations concerning the effectiveness of the augmented Roman alphabet will await further evaluation with a larger number of teachers.

Gibson and her associates (27) have recently proposed that the proper unit of the reading process is neither the single letter nor the whole word, but a higher-order invariant derived from grapheme-phoneme correspondences. These are constants which are presumably discovered by exposure to both the graphic and phonemic stimuli at the same time and in different contexts, so that the invariant combinations can be recognized in many different words. From this hypothesis it was predicted that meaningless and unfamiliar pseudo-words would be perceived more accurately with tachistoscopic presentation when they followed the grapheme-phoneme correspondence rules found in the structure of written and spoken English than ones which did not. Experimental results showed that pronounceable pseudowords (e.g., dink, vuns) were recognized and written more accurately than unpronounceable pseudowords (e.g., nkid, nsuv) which were matched for summed letter frequency.

Gibson, Osser, and Pick (26) raised the question of how the spelling-to-sound correspondence rules are learned. Two different possibilities are considered: either the child begins by memorizing whole words and later learns to formulate some of the correspondence rules, or the correspondence rules might develop as soon as he learns to speak even though the sequence is short and the grammar very simple. If the first alternative is correct, first-grade children would read words, but not pseudowords which have never been encountered even though they fit the correspondence rules (i.e., have a predictable, invariant pronunciation). But if the second alternative is correct, even the first graders would read pronounceable pseudowords more efficiently than unpronounceable ones. A comparison was made of the ability of children, at the completion of grade 1 and grade 3, to recognize three-letter familiar words, pronounceable trigrams, and unpronounceable trigrams. By either hypothesis, the familiar words should be easy to recognize; the question was whether there would be a difference between the two types of trigrams at the two grade levels. Pronounceable items and unpronounceable items had the same trigram frequency, but no indication that letters were controlled for position in a word was reported. The results showed that words were read correctly with greatest frequency, and the pronounceable trigrams were read more accurately than unpronounceable ones by the same children. Tentatively, it was concluded that a child in the early stages of reading skill typically reads in short units, but has already generalized certain consistent predictions of grapheme-phoneme correspondence, so that units which fit these simple "rules" are more easily read. Thus, the results were interpreted in favor of the second alternative that correspondence rules develop right from the beginning of speech acquisition.

In brief, there is sufficient evidence that grapheme-phoneme correspondence is a significant factor in word recognition to warrant its inclusion as a dimension for ordering reading material.

Analytic vs. Synthetic Sequences

A sequencing question which has received considerable attention is whether reading instruction should be "synthetic" (directed toward building wholes out of parts) rather than "analytic" (directed toward finding parts in previously learned wholes). Carroll (4), in a review of research on the teaching of reading, discusses five arguments which have been used to support the analytic approach that beginning reading should start with training in "whole word" recognition, delaying phonic analysis until a second stage. According to Carroll, advocates of analytic approaches argue that children who are just beginning to read will find synthetic approaches difficult, uninteresting, and meaningless; that mature readers perceive whole words and phrases; and, moreover, that published comparisons of synthetic and analytic methods find in favor of analytic methods. In opposition to this view, advocates of synthetic approaches reply that phonic training can be conducted so that it is easy, interesting, and meaningful and that perception of the whole word is a function of detailed perception of its parts. With respect to the evidence favoring whole-word approaches, Carroll writes:

For emphasis and clarity, let us comment once again that the issue is not between "phonics" and "no phonics," but between "good programming" and "poor programming." It is our contention that the reason for the generally poor showing of "phonics" training in many of the earlier educational experiments was that it was poorly programmed. With the aid of vocabulary control and other factors, the instruction which began with the teaching of sight vocabulary and continued with "incidental phonics" was in those experiments better "programmed," over-all, than the instruction which had a large amount of phonics training, but the possibility of better programming of phonic instruction was not precluded by these results.

Programing by Carroll is used here in the loose sense of any teaching procedure that introduces new elements gradually (one or a few at a time), requires mastery of these elements before further elements are introduced, and has prepared for the new elements by the prior introduction of simpler prerequisite elements. For whole-word approaches, programing the introduction of new words may be sufficient, but for synthetic or phonic approaches, the element to be programed probably should be the letter or groups of letters. When the rate of introduction of letters and letter meanings, as well as words, is controlled in reading material, comparisons of phonic and whole-word approaches tend to favor the phonic approaches, contrary to earlier comparisons using phonic material with no letter control (1, 8, 11, 49).

Woolman (96) developed a synthetic approach to reading instruction called the Progressive Choice Reading Method (P.C.). In the P.C. materials, the learner starts with only one letter-sound relationship, then two, three, etc. Advancement to new letters is contingent on his ability to discriminate meaningful combinations of the previous letter elements. For example, he must know that OMO and MO are meaningless and that MOM is meaningful. As the pool of known letters gets larger, the number of words and letter shape combinations rapidly expands. In addition to the progressive growth in the size of the learning units, the P.C. materials incorporate maximal stimulus discriminability among successive letter sounds and shapes and use phonetically consistent stories. A programed teachers manual accompanies the P.C. reading materials. The P.C. method has been evaluated by Bloomer (2) and Davy (7). Bloomer summarized a comparison of four P.C. and six control classes in a 17-week beginning reading program in which experimental materials controlling word length and the frequency of letter occurrence and sounds were used. When readiness was held constant by covariance control, the P.C. method was superior to the controls on word recognition and sentence reading. The experimental groups read their basal readers (preprimer, primer, and reader) in less than half the time required by the control group. This finding is particularly interesting because the progressive-choice subjects were taught by relatively inexperienced teachers compared with the control groups. Control teachers followed basal reader material they had used the previous year.

Davy (7) used the P.C. materials on 26 retarded children. Subjects who participated in the program for one year progressed from a nonreading level and achieved ability to recognize and write most of the letters in the alphabet and to use these letters in a few simple words. This study unfortunately has all of the disadvantages of the one-group pretest-posttest design. Nevertheless, the results of both of these studies suggest that programed phonics may be very effective for beginning reading instruction. It would be interesting to have data on the relative contribution to learning provided by the various principles used in the design of these materials (e.g., letter and word-length control, discriminability, etc.).

Harris (33) described a reading method that incorporated both synthetic and analytic approaches. The synthetic and analytic approaches were carried out as separate but parallel activities. In one period the child received a whole-word-meaning approach featuring experience-chart work, and in another separate period he received a phonic approach emphasizing discrimination training.

The effectiveness of the dual synthetic-analytic approach has been evaluated by Sparks and Fay (81), Greenman (31), and Kelly (41). Greenman compared the dual approach with the analytic or meaning-first approach and found significant differences favoring the dual approach for each of three consecutive years. All too often in experimental-control comparison-type research, the novel method taught by a highly skilled, deeply committed, enthusiastic teacher produces results which do not hold up when the number of teachers in the sample and the teaching interval are extended. But the data collected at the end of the investigation involving 29 teachers and over 660 pupils were substantially the same as the data collected at the beginning involving 5 teachers and 88 pupils, which suggests that the Hawthorne effect is probably not a factor in this study. In another study, Kelly (41) found the dual approach superior to a standard basal reading series. Sparks and Fay (81), and Fay (18), reported that the dual approach was superior to an analytic approach for children at the completion of the first grade in reading comprehension and reading vocabulary. By the end of the second-grade year, however, there were no differences between the groups, and no significant differences were later found between the groups at the completion of grades five and six.

Although all global comparison studies such as these may be easily criticized on methodological grounds, the general findings at least provide assurance that no great harm and possibly considerable gain will come from introducing words which illustrate grapheme-phoneme correspondences before irregularly spelled words in a synthetic fashion.

Frequency

Another dimension for ordering beginning reading material is frequency. Word lists, such as the Thorndike and Lorge list, have been compiled and are used as a guide in the development of basic readers and consequently help to determine the sequence of reading instruction in most schools (21, 71, 88, 91). The use of word lists is based on the assumption that children should learn those words which they will encounter most frequently and should progress from the most common words to the less frequent words.

There is evidence that frequency counts of words in printed material are correlated with other measures of word response strength such as latency and probability. Erlebacher and Harris (14) confirmed the hypothesis that mean production of words beginning with specified bigrams is associated with the number of words in the Thorndike and Lorge list which begin with those bigrams (pool size). Word production increases as a function of pool size; hence the difficulty of the word-production task can be ordered in advance from knowledge of the pool size.

Meaningfulness and Frequency

Data on the relationship between frequency of use of a word and reading difficulty are also provided by research on meaningfulness. Using
the number of associates which an item elicits as a definition of meaningfulness, in general the greater the word frequency, the greater the
meaningfulness. In paired-associate tasks when stimulus and response
meaningfulness are varied independently, both are directly related to
rate of learning, but the effect is greater for response meaningfulness
than for stimulus meaningfulness (92). One might conclude from this
that the greater the frequency of the word in printed English, the
more rapidly is a child likely to learn to read it. However, from studies
of the effect of meaningfulness on the rate at which verbal units are
learned, Underwood and Schulz (92) found that the one predictor of
learning which held up throughout their experiments was the pronunciability of the verbal units. They concluded that the factor most responsible for the degree of associative connection between letters may
be emitted frequency in a vocal sense—the subject actually speaking—
and not frequency of printed letter sequences. This suggests that the
frequency of specifiable sounds and sound sequences in verbal behavior ought to be used as a guide in letter and word control, rather
than frequency counts based on printed text.

Syntactical Structure

Frequency counts also do not reflect linguistic structure of the sentences
used by children in the act of connected speech. Furthermore, these
counts were compiled many years ago and do not take into account
the wide vocabulary children have today as a result of the mass media
and greater opportunity for verbal stimulation. Epstein (13) demonstrated that syntactical structure facilitates verbal learning apart from
the contributions of meaningfulness, familiarity, and sequential probability.

In a study of the relationship of the language of elementary school
children to the language of reading textbooks, Strickland (89) found
that patterns of sentence structure appeared to be introduced in the
readers in a random, haphazard manner. There appeared to be no
scheme for the development of control over sentence structure which
paralleled the generally accepted scheme for the development of control over vocabulary. She also found that the oral language children

use is far more advanced than the language of the books in which they were taught to read. The implication here is that when children have mastered certain language patterns in their speaking, these patterns should perhaps begin to appear in the materials designed for teaching them to read.

Miller and Ervin (57), and Ervin and Miller (15), cited evidence that even in the earliest two-word sentences there are systematic regularities of order and suggested that these regularities reflect the child's memorization of sequential probabilities in adult speech. If the child uses constructions that have analogues in adult speech, adults reinforce the child's pattern and enable him to approximate adult patterns more closely. If the constructions do not reflect patterns in the model language, they drop out.

Redundancy

Carterette and Jones (5) are measuring the amount of letter redundancy in children's written and spoken language and of that written for and spoken to children. They are studying the influence of different amounts of redundancy on learning in the second, fourth, and sixth grades. Perhaps control of sequential constraints of letter sequences (redundancy) will facilitate learning rate to a greater extent than will control of either meaningfulness or pronunciability.

Miller and Selfridge (56) constructed words varying in degree of approximation to English from zero order to seventh order. They found that as order of approximation to English increased from zero to five, so did percent of words correctly recalled. However, fifth-order approximations were recalled almost as well as English text. They concluded that the rapid rate of learning meaningful material was not due to meaningfulness per se, but rather to the greater redundancy of meaningful material. The probability or frequency with which given letters follow or precede other letters in English has been tabulated (55, 92), and data have been obtained (55) which show that subjects can rank letters and digrams in terms of the frequency with which they follow single letters in words. It was suggested that such digram and single-letter frequencies are "stored" by subjects as a frequency-response hierarchy. Although these studies used only adult subjects, the analysis of letter redundancy in children's speech may prove to be a valuable guide in sequencing reading instruction.

Perhaps the success often reported by primary teachers in the use of the experience chart in beginning reading instruction stems from its preservation of the amount of redundancy found in children's expression and vocabulary. On the other hand, since it is known that the responses have already been well established, the contributing factor may be the meaningfulness of the task, inasmuch as the children dictate the material on the chart, and all that remains is for them to associate these responses to the appropriate stimuli. Since these responses generally describe a recently completed exciting activity, they must elicit a high number of associations which enhance the chances for efficient learning.

Stimulus Similarity

Another variable which has been the subject of considerable study in verbal learning research and may be important in designing reading programs is stimulus similarity. In a program in which the stimulus words are quite similar and where difficult discriminations must be made, errors of generalization are more likely, and learning difficulty will increase. Thus, words like ran, rat, pan, and pin will be harder to learn in a sequence than words like boy, children, look, and father. The more difficult element-sharing list would be expected to discourage the beginning reader from attempting to discriminate among the words on the basis of letter differences and depend more on context cues or other stimuli for his response. Newman and Taylor (62), in studying context effects in paired-associate learning as a function of element sharing (number of consonants shared by CVC trigrams) among stimulus terms, found an increased tendency for the response to be to a context element (background color) as the similarity of the stimulus terms increased. The learner responded to background color cues more often when the words in the list had more letters in common—were more similar.

Paradoxically, while stimulus similarity should be minimized for efficient learning, the population of reading stimuli to which the instruction must transfer does involve many fine discriminations. Using Osgood's transfer surface as a guide (64), it would be expected that the instructional stimuli should similarly require fine discriminations for maximum positive transfer. The simple answer to this problem is to begin with maximally dissimilar stimuli and successively approximate the finer discriminations in terminal frames. Such a procedure unfortunately is more readily described than achieved. When stimuli are maximally dissimilar (e.g., boy, children), there are more stimulus dimensions which distinguish the words, thus increasing the probability that the child's behavior will come under the control of irrelevant dimensions such as word length or word shape. For example, in trying out a sequence on compound words in the laboratory at System Development Corporation, it was found that pupils were responding to word length, position of multiple-choice options, responses of other children, and other irrelevant cues rather than to the component words within the compound words being presented to them. Children are extremely adept at "beating the game" and show a remarkable capacity for giving the correct responses to the wrong stimuli. In some cases cueing techniques, rather than facilitating learning, may impede it. Presumably, with appropriate stimulus variation, such problems will not occur. However, in the author's research, it has been repeatedly observed that if the stimuli differ on many dimensions, the alert child will always manage to fixate on one dimension, while other dimensions are being varied. Then, when the dimension on which he is fixated is varied, interference effects are observed quite similar to those obtained by Kendler and Kendler (42) in studies of reversal and nonreversal shifts. One solution is to restrict the boundaries of dissimilarity so that all the irrelevant dimensions may be varied before the child has a chance to come under their control. For example, letterform confusion such as b, d; p, q; o, c, e; u, n; and m, w can be reduced by starting with a more limited set of letters within which correct stimulus control can be established by suitable variations and contrasts. The Language for Learning program (17), also known as the Richards-Gibson material, contains sequences that start with seven letters (a, h, i, m, n, s, and t) from which such sentences as the following can be formed: "This is a man. This is a hat. This hat is his hat. It is his hat." Such letter groups can be introduced in order of increasing similarity, and, within each of these groups, combinations of letters may also be ordered on a progression of increasing difficulty. As the child overlearns the initial group of letters and their combinations, new letters may be more easily discriminated from members of the original group.

In short, interference effects resulting from loss of stimulus control can be expected with either too much or too little stimulus similarity.

Programing a sequence of reading material on the dimension of stimulus similarity is complicated by the fact that similarity of visual stimuli may be defined in terms of semantic properties as well as structural characteristics. The overwhelming effect of associations established in different individuals by the culture may relegate attempts at controlling stimulus similarity to a trivial category. Providing a child with a carefully graded sequence of minimally contrasting words, with the hope that he will induce the difference between short a and short i sounds corresponding to those letters, may be less efficient than prompting the discrimination by means of some mnemonic like "a is for apple and i is for Indian" or by using picture cues, as do most practice materials for reading instruction.

It remains for future researchers to develop a reading program with a synthetic sequence established on dimensions of grapheme-phoneme correspondence, word frequency, meaningfulness, syntactic structure, language redundancy, and stimulus similarity, all of which have been shown to influence learning efficiency.

Stimulus-Response Factors

After the general sequence of a program has been determined, it is necessary to decide what specific responses are desired and to determine what stimuli will evoke them. The use of a simple matrix has been helpful in suggesting stimulus-response requirements in programing (29). A useful framework for describing language behavior can also be constructed from a stimulus-response matrix (Table 1). A set of stimulus or display categories—e.g., phoneme, grapheme—may be specified along the rows, and a set of response modes—e.g., multiple

TABLE 1

Stimulus-Response Combinations in Verbal Behavior

				Stimulus Mode		
				pictorial	grapheme	phoneme
Response Mode	Overt	multiple choice	grapheme	1	2	3
			phoneme	4	5	6
		constructed response	grapheme	7	8	9
			phoneme	10	11	12
	Covert			13	14	15

choice, constructed response—may be listed along the columns. The cells of the matrix then represent language skills such as listening, speaking, reading, writing, and spelling. For example, Table 2, prepared by Hively and Popp (36), shows four stimulus-response categories involved in teaching phonic relationships.

TABLE 2

Situations in Which Phonic Relationships May Be Taught

Stimulus	*Response*	*Examples*
1. Phoneme*	Child selects corresponding grapheme from among a set of alternatives.	1. Given written words, e.g., *sad, lad,* point out one that has been pronounced.
2. Phoneme	Child composes corresponding grapheme.	2. Given a spoken word, e.g., *lad,* write or compose it from letters of the alphabet.
3. Grapheme	Child selects corresponding phoneme from among a set of alternatives.	3. Given alternative spoken words, select one which matches a written sample: "Is this word pronounced 'sad' or 'lad'?"
4. Grapheme	Child composes corresponding phoneme.	4. Given a written word, e.g., *lad,* pronounce it.

* The terms "phoneme" or "grapheme" refer to either one or a sequence of phonemes or graphemes.

The programing task for some cells will depend on the prior acquisition of behavior specified in other cells. For example, cell 11 in Table 1 presumes completion of cells 2 and 6. That is, auditory discrimination and visual training precedes acquisition of textual skills (vocal response to graphemes). Any of these cells would be analyzed much further if they were to be programed. For instance, cell 11 might be divided into a series of separate matrices—e.g., consonant-vowel combinations, trigram combinations, grammatical frame combinations—which comprise a definitive sample of the behaviors represented by that cell. The analysis of stimulus and response elements is a useful device for determining what goes into a program, but does not necessarily mean that the various skills—e.g., reading, writing, spelling—must be compartmentalized in the program itself.

The behavior represented by some cells in the matrix is more readily acquired than that for others. For example, McNeil (52) used two forms of a word recognition program on 188 kindergarten children during 15 15-minute sessions to compare oral and nonoral response modes. An examination which called for silent reading was given at the end of the last lesson. The oral response mode was superior to the nonoral mode, especially for lower IQ children. Wechkin (94), using 32 delinquent adolescents, compared a procedure of teaching two lists of six paired associates by presenting the word visually and requiring subjects to choose between two auditory alternatives (cell 5), with the reverse procedure in which visual response alternatives were coupled with an auditory stimulus (cell 3). The latter procedure resulted in more rapid acquisition and superior retention. Wepman (95) suggested that children be screened and classified as auditory or visual learners at school entrance. Thus the choice of cell for initial instruction would depend upon the behavioral repertoire of the child on entering the program.

Once the behavioral objectives have been defined and the entry behavior has been assessed, the programing strategy becomes more apparent. For example, if the student is to learn to compose phonemes corresponding to displayed graphemes and does not have the appropriate pronunciation of the phonemes in his initial repertoire, then the program will probably begin by shaping the correct pronunciation by a process of response differentiation (40). If the pronunciation responses have already been learned, then the program will concentrate on bringing those responses under control of the appropriate grapheme stimuli by a process of discrimination training. Beginning reading programs generally assume that the child has the phonemes in his speaking repertoire, and the problem becomes one of bringing them under control of the appropriate stimuli. This is often accomplished by evoking the desired response in the presence of the appropriate grapheme by using some form of stimulus cue or prompt; when the prompt is withdrawn, the child can emit the desired response to the grapheme without being prompted. A wide variety of positive and negative instances are practiced until the desired response is well under the control of the appropriate grapheme.

A common practice is to use pictures to evoke appropriate phonemic responses (cell 10 in Table 1). McNeil and Keislar (53) noted that while pictures are desirable as response alternatives, they are not desirable as cue stimuli; they do distract, regardless of the intended purpose. An irrelevant but attractive picture is likely to be chosen by the child just because he likes it. Fowler (20) also had difficulty with picture prompts. He found that individual letter or word flash cards nearly always proved better than any form of picture-word association techniques whether the picture-word combinations were presented on fabricated word cards or in preprimer texts. A similar disenchantment with picture prompts was expressed by Ellson and others (12) with programed teaching of a sight vocabulary to retarded children. They reported that too few words can be pictured unambiguously and felt that the use of pictures in teaching some words might increase the difficulty of teaching nonpicturable words. Hall (32) felt that pictures encourage a child to guess "not on the basis of the letters he sees printed, but from what he sees in the picture or drawing, so that, if asked to read off *ship*, he is likely to come out with *boat* or the likes." Of course the ambiguity of pictures can be eliminated by first using oral prompts to evoke the appropriate verbal response in the presence of the picture (e.g., "This is the picture of a *ship;* say *ship*"—cells 10 and 12 in Table 1). The difficult problem is to transfer control of the verbal response to the letters. Evans (16) used a method of progressively vanishing portions of a picture cue to effect transfer of control to the letter stimuli (Figure 1). Popp and Porter (65) and Taber and

FIGURE 1. *"Fading" Sequence for the Letter* H.

Glaser (90) also reported using this fading procedure with beginning reading tasks.

A variant of the fading procedure has also been used to teach difficult discrimination tasks. Initially only dissimilar elements of the graphemes to be discriminated are displayed. After the child can discriminate between these distinctive elements, the remaining elements are faded *in* gradually, while the response is still under control of the distinctive element. Hively and Popp (36) used this method in teaching the l and s initial consonant sounds. They isolated the phonemes and graphemes upon which the discrimination was based—first teaching subjects to discriminate between the letters s and l in response to the phonemes /s/ and /l/ and then gradually fading in the remaining auditory and visual elements of the words being taught. These procedures did not work too well, but for those few children who did learn the isolated letter sounds, fading in the remaining visual elements while holding the initial consonant phoneme constant was a successful procedure.

The temporal location of the prompting stimulus has also been studied. Prompting refers to the procedure in which the prompt is presented before the response is made, while confirmation refers to the procedure wherein the information follows the response. Stolurow and Lippers (87) compared prompting and confirmation procedures in teaching vocabulary to retarded children at two degrees of overlearning. With the shorter practice period, prompting was superior to confirmation; but with overlearning, confirmation proved superior to prompting with respect to retention.

Although the analysis of stimulus and response factors in reading have resulted in much work with visual and auditory media, the full range of these channels has not been explored, e.g., novel visual and sound effects; nor has there been sufficient exploration of other sensory and motor channels, e.g., kinesthetic, tactual, olfactory, temperature.

Mediation Effects

When the learner has acquired units of grapheme-phoneme correspondence and is able to blend or compound these units by responding successively to the elements in a word, he will be able to give appropriate vocal responses to new words. Before he can be called a reader, however, the child must be able to comprehend the meaning of words in context. It is for this reason that reading teachers present new words in meaningful context before drawing attention to them for separate study. Children are taught to cross-check the "sense" of a new word which they have sounded out against the context in which it appears. The authors of most reading texts thus urge a "pattern or variety of word attack skills." Judd (38) concluded from a series of studies that in the later stages of reading, during the middle grades, oral reading should give way to silent reading and phonic analysis should give place to word analysis and that meanings should be emphasized and not the mechanical pronunciation of words.

Of course, unless "meaning" or mediating responses are already in their repertoires, the children will not "understand" what they are reading. Reading new words foreign to the child's experience, however, may facilitate the acquisition of new concepts by sensitizing the child to references to those new words. Diack (8) implies this possibility when he writes: "Great care was taken to ensure us in reading books that only words the child knew the meaning of were used, and used in sentences so simple that the child could not fail to understand them. Yet the constant argument was that children were being taught to get meaning from the printed words. Having made certain there was nothing the child could not understand, you proceeded to teach him to understand it."

The relationship between meanings and oral pronunciation responses to printed material is often a matter of dispute. Skinner (78) rejects the traditional formulation of verbal behavior in terms of meaning. He denies mysterious processes which cause verbal behavior and views such processes simply as behavior, whether verbal or nonverbal, covert or overt. Printed material may provide the occasion either for textual behavior (vocal responses to printed text) or nontextual (meaning) behavior or both since they are affected by the same stimuli. Textual behavior may influence nontextual behavior; nontextual behavior may influence textual behavior or they may be mutually independent. Normally, however, according to Skinner, "the reader's reactions are first a consequence of textual behavior and then a collateral activity in which textual responses are short-circuited (p. 159).

The notion that meaning is a stimulus-producing response which serves to mediate other behavior, and as such is amenable to conditioning in the same manner as any other response, receives support from a variety of sources (30, 43, 63, 82). Feigenbaum and Simon (19) provided an illustration of verbal mediation in a computer program (EPAM) which learned to read words. EPAM first learned to pair objects with spoken words. Next it learned to pair spoken words with printed words. Finally it demonstrated reading ability, responding to printed words by pointing to the objects they named. Thus the association between the printed word and its "meaning" was mediated via the spoken response. Using a similar computer program, Rogers[1] obtained reading errors which closely approximated those observed in first-grade children who had been given the same reading task by Silberman (77).

In an operant analysis of reading, Resnick (70) points out that the controlling stimuli in reading include characteristics of language and its logical organization as well as the letter groups. Reading with understanding involves extended "chains" of behavior in which the individual's own responses serve as stimuli for his next response. The description of reading as a covert chain of "thinking" behavior suggests that the elements of the chain may be taught overtly and slowly, later to be interiorized and speeded up.

Several reading programs use such a chaining approach. Following the early stages of beginning reading, Keislar, McNeil, and Mace (39) used a process of verbal chaining in a programed reading task for kindergarten children. They selected meaningful word sequences, on the basis of a child's being able to respond appropriately to the sequences, and programed them with a forward chaining procedure. By this procedure, a newly taught response to a particular stimulus is added to an existing chain of behavior. For example, a child who has previously been taught to say "the boy" when he sees *the boy* written, next learns to say "runs" when he sees *runs* written. The response "runs" is then added to the chain "the boy" so that the child comes to say "the boy runs" in the presence of the written stimulus *the boy runs.*

Evans (16) reported a backward chaining procedure to teach three-year-old children to read. Using meaningful words, he brought their vocal responses under control of phoneticized pronunciations of the same words. This was accomplished by playing "sounding games" with the children. Proceeding by a series of approximations, the first soundings are drawn out very little, but later in the game the words are drawn out markedly, e.g., "cuh-ah-tuh." The child soon starts sounding out words of his own for the adult to translate. The next step was to bring the children's phoneticized pronunciations under control of the printed words. With further practice, the phoneticizing

---

[1] M. Rogers, personal communication, 1963.

response drops out of the chain, and the children read the words normally. Three students were tested at the end of their programed reading sessions. All three were reading novel phonetic words and sentences. Out of a possible 223 phonetic words, the three children read correctly 218, 193, and 161 words, respectively.

The work cited above gives encouraging evidence that it is possible to program textual behavior of young children. However, even though textual responses are essential in the reading process, mediating responses must also be analyzed and programed if reading instruction is to become a technology. Further work is needed in this area.

Reinforcement Factors

The search for effective reinforcers is a persisting activity in the research on programed reading. Of particular interest is the notion that self-selection of reading material by children is both motivating and reinforcing. Perhaps freedom from the teacher has as much to do with this effect as the design of the physical materials and environment to which the teacher delegates the responsibility for instruction by her nonintervention. Teacher threats, frowns, ridicule, and other aversive stimuli may serve as reinforcers when their removal is contingent on appropriate reading responses by the child. Unfortunately, while such negative reinforcement may produce efficient learning, it also may produce fear responses and avoidance or escape behavior that will interfere with subsequent reading objectives. When a child enters a program with well-established avoidance responses, their intensity can be reduced by introducing the reading stimuli so gradually that these responses do not occur. Snyder (79) described a "desensitization" procedure using a graded series of activities along visual, auditory, motor, and environmental continua for the introduction of reading stimuli. The gradual presentation of the negative reading stimuli and the simultaneous presentation of positive reinforcement tended to increase the amounts of negative stimuli needed to elicit avoidance behavior in a group of low-reading-level boys.

The use of interesting reading material as a reinforcer is generally preferred to negative reinforcement. In most classrooms, materials are selected which capitalize on the children's interests and purposes. Teachers discuss stories, comment on illustrations, and help children establish a purpose in reading for meaning. Skinner (78) pointed out, however, that "automatic consequences are used to motivate the beginning reader when a textbook is designed to be 'interesting.' Such reinforcement is not, however, contingent upon accuracy of response in the manner needed to shape skillful behavior" (p. 66). If reading is viewed as "texting" (giving appropriate vocal responses to printed words), this is a reasonable position since an interesting text cannot differentially reinforce correct phonemic responses. If reading is viewed as obtaining meaning from printed material, however, then exciting, humorous, or informative material will reinforce meaning-getting behavior, whatever its form, be it simply interpreting pictures or guessing from context clues. The practice of using relatively meaningless and uninteresting material such as consonant-vowel combinations in order to obtain smooth learning curves (84) may be introducing an artifact that limits the generalizability of such research. Although the effects of changing reinforcement schedules are readily observed on a smooth curve, more variegated material might have obviated the need for such careful scheduling of extrinsic reinforcers.

The problem is to determine what constitutes interesting material. The prior conditioning history of each child specifies what will be interesting for that child. One technique which appears in many instructional methods is self-selection of material (86). Ostensibly the child's history of conditioning will predispose him to choose material or activities which have been reinforced in the past. Thus exploratory or manipulative behavior which has previously led to desirable consequences will be pursued. The Montessori principle of nonintervention in the child's exploratory behavior takes advantage of this. There is no necessary contradiction between providing free choices of activity to the child and the programing of his behavior. In both cases, there is an attempt to begin with the existing behavioral repertoire of the learner. And in both cases, the structure of the environment determines the learning outcomes. Whether one uses "Froebelian Gifts," "Montessori Materials" (86), "Talking Typewriters" (59), or other self-instructional devices, the decisive influence of the environmental characteristics in determining the course of learning is inescapable. Complete nonintervention by the teacher merely transfers control of the learning objectives to other sources such as the social and physical environment of the classroom. There is little empirical support for the practice of allowing the child to choose his own curriculum. The advantage of a self-instructional physical environment lies in the contingent, consistent, efficient, persistent, and uncompromising manner in which it provides differential reinforcement. Silberman (76) reported evidence of the ineffectiveness of noncontingent reinforcement in changing reading behavior in the classroom.

In using interest to motivate the beginning reader, it is important to distinguish the interests of the teacher or programer from that of the child. Adults often view activities as boring which do not appeal to them, but may nevertheless be quite effective for the child. Rothkopf (74) asked 12 educators to predict the effectiveness of seven self-instructional arrangements and obtained a rank correlation between these predictions and observed effectiveness of − .75. In some cases, an excessive concern with making instruction gamelike and interesting reflects a history of pupil reinforcement of the teacher's entertainment behavior. Such behavior is not necessarily related to student learning. The possibility of constructing interesting material with a highly constrained vocabulary has been admirably demonstrated in the Dr. Suess books.

Although social approval and knowledge of correctness of response are adequate reinforcers for many children, there are those who require more tangible reinforcers in the early stages of reading until the skill itself acquires secondary reinforcing properties (93). Staats, and others (84) explored the effect of extrinsic reinforcers on six four-year-old children on a reading program consisting of 26 words arranged so the word stimuli were gradually combined into sentences and then into short stories. A Gerbrands Universal Feeder was filled with a variety of edibles, trinkets, and tokens which were dispensed as reinforcers by the experimenter using a foot pedal. On the third day of the experiment, each child was told the machine was broken. The children made no more progress and dramatically reverted to actions of the stereotyped kindergartner with short attention span. The experimenter continued to use verbal reinforcement, but after a few sessions the subjects were ready to leave. Then the feeder was resumed and the subjects once again began to make progress. Extrinsic reinforcers reduced escape behavior and maintained sustained attention. In a follow-up study, the same group (85) ran four four-year-old children for 30 training sessions. The procedures and apparatus produced learning curves that were sensitive to different reinforcement contingencies presented in various multiple-schedule designs and indicated that long-term studies of reading acquisition may be conducted with this type of reinforcing system.

Response rate also seems to act as a reinforcer. Keislar, McNeil, and Mace (39) found that motivational problems were solved by keeping the children responding rapidly to a reading program. This was accomplished by using a minimum of taped instructions and using instead a bell and horn arrangement to signal responses. Evans (16) also reports sustained activity at a reading program under conditions of high response rates (10 to 15 responses per minute) using six three-year-old subjects, teaching letter sounds and words with pictures and mnemonic prompts.

Premack (66) postulated that of any two responses, the one that occurs, more often when both are available can reinforce the one that occurs less often, but not vice versa. He found that for children who preferred playing to eating, playing could be used to reinforce eating. McIntire (51) used high- and low-frequency words (Thorndike-Lorge list) as reinforcers following responses to each of 10 paired associates. The group with the high-frequency words as reinforcers learned faster than the group with the low-frequency words. The notion that any kind of response can produce a stimulus which is a conditioned reinforcer for any other kind of less frequent response has extensive practical implications.

Control of the physical environment has also proven to be an effective reinforcer. Moore (59) has shown that children can be taught successfully to read at the age of three years using an automated responsive environment. He pointed out that the children's activity within the responsive environment is *autotelic*. "An activity is autotelic if it is engaged in for its own sake and not because of extrinsic rewards or punishments. Every effort was made to protect the experimental environment from extraneous influences." Moore indicated that instructors sometimes err by showing signs of approval or disapproval and speculated that in a fully automated responsive environment with a computer as an instructor, there would be no inadvertent expressions of approval or disapproval. One might argue that a responsive environment is the best example of an extrinsic reinforcer and that giving a smile or a trinket for a correct response is merely a special case—to be sure, a very limited and restricted case—of a responsive environment. The individual human tutor gains his status primarily by virtue of his unique capacity to confront the learner with such a responsive environment. What better example of differential reinforcement than when a typewriter and tape are unresponsive to a child's erroneous responses, but immediately responsive to his correct actions. Perhaps a better measure of an *autotelic* activity would be the continued behavior of a child in the absence of a responsive environment. The effectiveness of Moore's responsive environment might well be attributed to the efficiency with which it dispenses reinforcement.

A question persists of how to maintain the reinforcement properties of stimuli over long periods such as might be encountered in an ongoing school situation. Perhaps gradual increase in reinforcement ratios (97); back-up token systems, e.g., exchanging marbles for toys (83); or multiple schedules (47, 48) are steps in this direction.

Individual Differences

Readiness

One of the more visceral words in the reading literature is *readiness*. When should a child begin reading instruction? Some writers claim that readiness was invented to excuse poor reading instruction by shifting the blame to the child (50). Others feel that "it is impossible to draw satisfactory conclusions about individual differences in reading readiness until the relation between readiness factors and success in learning to read has been ascertained in the context of demonstrable optimal methods of teaching" (4). Studies show no differences between performances of children for whom reading instruction was delayed on the basis of readiness tests and children for whom such instruction was not delayed. Indeed, the delayed groups may eventually surpass the early starters after a year (22).

There may be some question in these early studies as to the extent to which the instruction for the early starters took into account the limited repertoire of behavior of those children. There is a growing literature on perceptual learning (25) to support the notion that very young children can learn the distinguishing features which differentiate printed letters provided they receive appropriate early experiences. Commercial reading-readiness material contains visual-discrimination exercises using geometric or animal forms and pictures rather than printed words, letters, or letterlike forms. Gibson and others (28) studied the development of visual discrimination of letterlike forms in children from four through eight. The implications of the study are that greater potential transfer value would be obtained from readiness tasks which are crucial to letter discrimination. Studies in discrimination pretaining generally show positive transfer to subsequent tasks using the same visual stimuli, but altered responses. Muehl (60) found that pretraining practice in matching words which later appeared in a learning task was superior to pretraining on different words or on geometric forms. Levin, Watson, and Feldman (46), testing a lead from Spalding and Spalding (80), found that pretraining on tracing initial graphemes of words resulted in a higher number of correct associates and better recognition than tracing the terminal or the medial graphemes or looking at pictures. Stimulus pretraining usually facilitates learning as a result of acquired distinctiveness of cues or increased attention to relevant cues. Sometimes, however, pretraining results in interference effects, which is not surprising, since the stimuli remain the same, but the response changes. Muehl (61) found that the acquisition of letter names by kindergartners interfered with subsequent performance in learning to associate picture names with nonsense words containing these same letters as the critical stimuli.

Early research by Davidson (6) indicated that children are not normally capable of discriminating b from d until seven and a half years of age. Jeffrey (37) gave three- and four-year-old children pretraining in pushing a button on the left or the right depending on which direction the arms of certain stick figures pointed; these children learned the names of the stick figures, which differed only in the direction an arm pointed, more readily than a control group lacking the pretraining. Hendrickson and Muehl (34) found that pretraining on a similar motor response to b and d facilitated learning names for these letters. It appears that a child incapable of discriminating between b and d at a given time can be taught it very quickly if conditions are properly arranged.

The important point is not that training be continued in the face of failure, but rather that it continue at a different level and thus achieve the desired results without concomitant frustration and escape behavior. That the age at which a given skill might first be taught and learned depends on the effectiveness of the learning conditions has been demonstrated in the pretraining literature and in reading laboratories such as the one at Yale (58). In a longitudinal study of children who read early, Durkin (10) found that the lower the child's IQ, the greater seems to be the advantage of starting his reading early, giving him more time for learning.

Branching

With more complex equipment, elaborate branching networks may be programed which adapt the instructional sequence to individual differences on the basis of the pattern of errors made by a student, the student's own self-evaluation, and on how long it takes the student to respond to items. Within a classroom setting, the use of such complex branching contingencies is not feasible without elaborate equipment. Even without elaborate equipment, a measure of individualization of instruction is provided by programs since children may progress at their own rate. Various school districts are now trying different organizational structures to permit the operation of instructional programs which demand an individualized rate of progress. Theoretically, branching would be unnecessary if all learning requirements in the student could be anticipated before he started the program and rectified by suitable modifications to the program or by inserting prerequisite programs. Unfortunately, many learning deficiencies can be assessed only *after* the student has completed portions of the program and is tested on his ability to integrate the program content with his previous knowledge. If he cannot assimilate the new behavior into his existing repertoire, he may be branched to a remedial program segment. The general problem of adapting programed instruction to individual differences is virtually ignored in the research on programed reading. This is surprising in light of the publicity which programed instruction has received as a method of individualizing instruction.

Program Evaluations

As a result of the popularity of programed instruction, a wide variety of materials is being published and advertised as programed material. Some of these materials are little more than lessons in sequence, tachistoscope exercises, or booklets which have some way of providing

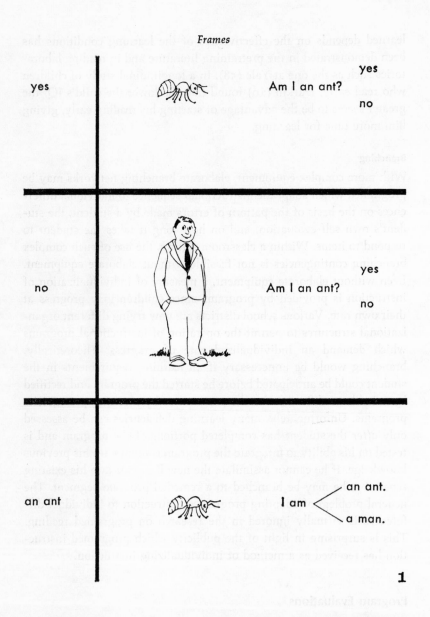

FIGURE 2. *Frames and Accompanying Dialogue After Buchanan's*
"Programmed Reading," page 1, book 1, Copyright McGraw-Hill
Book Company, Inc.

(Used by permission)

Dialogue

1. Have you covered the answer column with your slider?
2. Now, read what the ant is saying.
3. Is it a question?
4. What is the answer to the question?
5. What will you do, then? (circle *yes*)
6. Circle *yes*; then pull your slider down to the black line and check your answer.

1. Read the question.
2. Circle the right answer.
3. Check your answer.

1. What is this a picture of?
2. Read the sentence.
3. What letter is missing?
4. Fill it in.
5. Check your answer.
6. Look at the word in the answer column. What letter is underlined?
7. Is that the letter you filled in the blank?
8. The letter you filled in will always be underlined in the answer.
9. Turn your page.

(FIGURE 2 *continued. Frames and Accompanying Dialogue After Buchanan's "Programmed Reading."*)

the student with knowledge of results. Perhaps such efforts are more to be applauded than decried, for they represent at least an effort to adopt some of the principles of programed instruction.

A program for beginning reading has been prepared by Cynthia Dee Buchanan of Sullivan Associates and published by the McGraw-Hill Book Company. The program is arranged in order of phonetic regularity. A sample of its items and accompanying dialogue is given in Figure 2. Individual letters are presented only in context of words and have a one-to-one correspondence with sounds. The program proceeds from gross discriminations to minute discriminations in increasingly complex situations. Each sentence is accompanied by a picture for meaning and motivation. The program is student paced and provides immediate knowledge of results. This program is preceded by a prereading program that teaches the letter names and how to print them; that letters stand for sounds; what sounds to associate with the letters a, f, m, n, t, th, and i; that groups of letters form words which are read from left to right; the words "yes" and "no" by sight; how to discriminate the words "ant," "man," and "mat" from each other; and how to read the sentence, "I am an ant." At the end of the first series of readers, the child "can read and write all the consonants and all the short vowels in all combinations that occur in a basic vocabulary of over 500 words plus their inflected forms." The program has been tested with normal groups of five- and six-year-old children and with remedial reading groups. At the Crittenden School in Mountain View, California, a remedial class of 15 first- through fourth-grade children used the program for 25 minutes a day, five days a week, for three weeks, after which they showed a mean gain on the Gates Reading Test of four months. Another program on beginning reading is being tested at Teaching Machines, Incorporated. It begins with a phonics approach and uses the teacher to pronounce the letters and evaluate the children's reproductions.

In sharp contrast to the programed book described above is the work on responsive physical environments. O. K. Moore (58) has prepared filmed reports of two- and three-year-old children printing, typing, and reading first- and second-grade stories and even taking dictation after working in an automated responsive environment. In addition to a typewriter and speaker, his system includes a rear-projection screen and a card display with an attention arrow permitting messages of varying length to be exhibited. At the beginning of the training, the child explores the booth which provides him with only one accessible component—the keyboard. When he eventually strikes a key, the character is typed on paper, and the pronunciation of the character is presented over the speaker. When he gets tired of this procedure, a letter will be displayed on the card for him to copy. The only key which will work is the one which matches the character. The stimulus material becomes increasingly more complex (e.g., letters, words, sentences, paragraphs, and stories). Thus far, 102 children (ages 2 1/2 to 6) have been taught in the laboratory. Some children exhibit intelligence test score increases of 20 to 30 points; and there is indication that the younger the child is when he begins training, the greater the amount of learning. Children typically spend a maximum of 30 minutes in the booth per day. Both gifted and retarded children have benefited from this type of laboratory experience. The key feature of the laboratory is its responsiveness to the child's behavior.

In addition to the material being developed by commercial publishers and the experimental programs being developed as research vehicles to explore problems of beginning reading instruction, many program evaluations are concerned with reading problems at advanced educational levels (see Chapter 12 by Markle). For example, programs have been evaluated on such topics as capitalization (75), reading comprehension (67, 68, 73), sentence structure (72), word analysis (54), grammar (69), and visual tracking (23, 24).

Summary

1. Reading material should be sequenced on a number of different dimensions such as pronunciability, syntactic structure, and stimulus similarity. Each dimension should be assigned a priority weighting corresponding to its relative contribution to ease of learning. Although multidimensional sorting of language material is a formidable task, the possible gain is great. The digital computer is admirably suited to such a task and will undoubtedly be used in the near future to arrange the sequence of reading material.

2. Analysis of stimulus and response factors before constructing a reading program helps to avoid gross instructional errors. For example, reading programs have been constructed which require, as

prerequisite behavior, that the learner already have the skill which the program was intended to establish. Some reading programs teach the learner to verbalize rules *about* reading rather than to perform the reading skill itself. The analysis of terminal behavior and the assessment of the initial repertoire of the child determines the programing procedures required. Generally, beginning reading programs assume the child already has in his speaking vocabulary the words which are to be read. Response learning is not the main problem. Rather the task is one of bringing his existing responses under control of the appropriate written stimuli. A variety of cueing and prompting techniques has been used to evoke the desired responses, and fading procedures have been developed to bring these responses under stimulus control.

3. Recent criticisms of reading instruction focus on the lack of transfer obtained with "look-say" methods. The inability of certain children to read novel words is accepted as evidence that phonics are being neglected. An unnecessary dichotomy is often made between phonic and meaning approaches, since the acquisition of mediating responses and grapheme-phoneme correspondences are not mutually exclusive. Both textual responses and mediating responses must be programed for effective reading instruction. The task of estabishing stimulus control over such behavior has been successfully accomplished by using chaining procedures.

4. Reinforcers which are effective in programed reading are the following: interesting material, social approval, knowledge of results, edibles, novelty, trinkets, tokens, high response rates, high frequency responses, and equipment that is responsive to the child's exploratory behavior. The successful control of the child's behavior by responsive physical environments is attributable to the consistency with which they reinforce desired behavior. The technology of programed reading is limited by the lack of a device which will evaluate and confirm the child's vocal responses to written material. The question of how to sustain the reinforcing properties of existing techniques, over long periods of time, although unanswered, is receiving increased attention.

5. The restriction of maturation on children's readiness to begin reading instruction is being reappraised. Reports of successful reading programs with preschool children indicate that many children can

and should begin reading much earlier than first grade. The processes characterizing the young child's efforts in learning to read are not dissimilar to those found in older children, except that learning gradients have to be reduced, play techniques emphasized, and more explicit provision made for shaping attention or observing responses. Individual differences among children require that they move at their own rate and that the program be capable of branching them to appropriate remedial or enrichment material. The inflexibility of the self-contained classroom makes individualization of instruction difficult to achieve, and efforts to eliminate the lock-step system may be expected as effective programs become more available.

6. Programed instruction in beginning reading is just now being translated into commercially available products. The trend in development appears to move in a downward direction. The primary grades where the effect of programed instruction promises to be the greatest seems to be the last to benefit from the systematic attention of the programer.

Research in the reading area generally seems to be either too global or too molecular. The global studies use large samples and long training periods, but do not have the experimental control necessary to isolate specific learning variables. The molecular studies are very precise and isolate specific variables, but have small sample sizes, brief training intervals, and use contrived tasks which are seldom generalizable to practical instructional problems. The research on programed reading promises a rapprochement between these poles. Increased emphasis on the design of instructional material and the arrangement of the physical environment in such a way that incorrect responses are prevented and correct responses are immediately reinforced is an encouraging development. Greater control of the physical environment is an important factor in improving instructional efficiency. The work on sequencing, reinforcement, and stimulus-response factors is moving ahead rapidly, and results of such research are being applied in the design of physical environments and materials. However, greater effort in the analysis of mediating responses and the provision for individual differences within programed reading environments is a prerequisite to a viable technology of reading instruction.

References

1. Bear, D. E. "Phonics for First Grade: A Comparison of Two Methods." *Elementary School Journal* 59: 394-402; April 1958-59.

2. Bloomer, R. H. "Reading Methodology: Some Alternative Organizational Principles." *Reading Teacher* 14: 167-71; January 1961.

3. Bloomfield, L., and Barnhart, C. *Let's Read: A Linguistic Approach.* Detroit: Wayne State University Press, 1961.

4. Carroll, J. B. *Research on Reading and Its Teaching.* Cambridge, Mass.: Harvard University Press, 1963.

5. Carterette, E. C., and Jones, M. J. "Contextual Constraints in the Language of the Child." *Project English Newsletter.* Issue No. 2, OE-30006-2. Washington, D.C.: U.S. Department of Health, Education, and Welfare, Office of Education, September 1962.

6. Davidson, H. P. "A Study of the Confusing Letters, D, B, P, and Q." *Journal of Genetic Psychology* 47: 458-68; December 1935.

7. Davy, R. A. "Adaptation of Progressive-Choice Method for Teaching Reading to Retarded Children." *American Journal of Mental Deficiency* 67: 274-80; September 1962.

8. Diack, H. *Reading and the Psychology of Perception.* New York: Philosophical Library, 1960.

9. Downing, J. A. "The Augmented Roman Alphabet for Learning To Read." *Reading Teacher* 16: 325-26; March 1963.

10. Durkin, Dolores. "An Earlier Start in Reading?" *Reading Teacher* 16: 479-81; May 1963.

11. Durrell, D. D., and others. "Success in First Grade Reading." *Journal of Education* 140: 2-48; February 1958.

12. Ellson, D. G., and others. *Programmed Teaching of Elementary Reading—A Progress Report.* Bloomington: Indiana University, September 1962.

13. Epstein, W. "The Influence of Syntactical Structure on Learning." *American Journal of Psychology* 74: 80-85; March 1961.

14. Erlebacher, Adrienne, and Harris, C. "Parameters of Word Fluency Tasks." *Journal of Educational Psychology* 53: 198-202; August 1962.

15. Ervin, S. M., and Miller, W. R. "Language Development." *Child Psychology.* Sixty-Second Yearbook, National Society for the Study of Education. Chicago: University of Chicago Press, 1963.

16. Evans, J. L. *A Behavioral Approach to the Teaching of Phonetic Reading.* Paper presented at the International Reading Association Convention, Miami, Florida, May 1963.

17. Everett, R. M., Jr. *Comparison Between Conventional Basic Reading Programs and the Language for Learning Program.* New York: Washington Square Press, 1960.

18. Fay, L. C. "A Look at Two Approaches to the Teaching of Reading." *Changing Concepts of Reading Instruction.* Proceedings of the Inter-

national Reading Association Conference, Chicago, Illinois, 1961. pp. 161-63.
19. Feigenbaum, E. A., and Simon, H. A. "Performance of a Reading Task by an Elementary Perceiving and Memorizing Program." *Behavioral Science* 8: 72-76; January 1963.
20. Fowler, W. "Teaching a Two-Year-Old To Read: An Experiment in Early Childhood Learning." *Genetic Psychology Monographs* 66: 181-283; November 1962.
21. Gates, A. I. *A Reading Vocabulary for the Primary Grades.* New York: Bureau of Publications, Teachers College, Columbia University, 1935.
22. Gates, A. I., and Russell, D. H. "The Effects of Delaying Beginning Reading a Half Year in the Case of Underprivileged Pupils with I.Q.'s 75-95." *Journal of Educational Research* 32: 321-28; January 1939.
23. Geake, R. R., and Smith, D. E. P. *Manual for Visual Tracking.* Ann Arbor, Mich.: Ann Arbor Publishers, 1962.
24. Geake, R. R., and Smith, D. E. P. *Visual Tracking: A Self-Instructional Workbook for Perceptual Skills in Reading.* Ann Arbor, Mich.: Ann Arbor Publishers, 1962.
25. Gibson, Eleanor J. "Perceptual Learning." *Annual Review of Psychology.* (Edited by Paul Farnsworth.) Palo Alto, Calif.: Annual Reviews, 1963. pp. 29-56.
26. Gibson, Eleanor J.; Osser, H.; and Pick, A. *A Study of the Development of Grapheme-Phoneme Correspondences.* New York: Cornell University, 1963.
27. Gibson, Eleanor J., and others. "The Role of Grapheme-Phoneme Correspondence in the Perception of Words." *American Journal of Psychology* 75: 554-70; December 1962.
28. Gibson, Eleanor J., and others. "A Developmental Study of the Discrimination of Letter-Like Forms." *Journal of Comparative and Physiological Psychology* 55: 897-906; December 1963.
29. Glaser, R. "Some Research Problems in Automated Instruction: Instructional Programming and Subject-Matter Structure." *Programmed Learning and Computer-Based Instruction.* (Edited by John E. Coulson.) New York: John Wiley & Sons, 1962. pp. 76-85.
30. Goss, A. E. "Verbal Mediating Responses and Concept Formation." *Psychological Review* 68: 248-74; July 1961.
31. Greenman, Margaret H. "A Six-Year Experimental Study of Two Methods of Teaching Reading in the Elementary School." In Harris, T. L. "Some Issues in Beginning Reading Instruction." *Journal of Educational Research* 56: 5-19; September 1962.
32. Hall, R. A., Jr. *Sound and Spelling in English.* Philadelphia: Chilton Books, 1961.
33. Harris, T. L. "Some Issues in Beginning Reading Instruction." *Journal of Educational Research* 56: 5-19; September 1962.

34. Hendrickson, L. N., and Muehl, S. "The Effect of Attention and Motor Response Pretraining on Learning To Discriminate B & D in Kindergarten Children." *Journal of Educational Psychology* 53: 236-41; October 1962.

35. Hively, W. "Programming Stimuli in Matching to Sample." *Journal of the Experimental Analysis of Behavior* 5: 279-98; July 1962.

36. Hively, W., and Popp, H. *Attempts To Program Materials To Teach Certain Elements of a Phonic Repertoire.* Cambridge, Mass.: Harvard University, 1963.

37. Jeffrey, W. E. "Variables in Early Discrimination Learning: I. Motor Responses in the Training of a Left-Right Discrimination." *Child Development* 29: 269-75; June 1958.

38. Judd, C. H. "Reading: Its Nature and Development." *Supplementary Educational Monographs,* 1918. Vol. 2.

39. Keislar, E.; McNeil, J.; and Mace, L. *Verbal Chaining in an Auto-Instructional Reading Program for Kindergarten Children.* Paper presented at a symposium on Programmed Instruction, California Educational Research Association, Los Angeles, March 9, 1963.

40. Keller, F. S., and Schoenfeld, W. N. *Principles of Psychology.* New York: Appleton-Century-Crofts, 1950.

41. Kelly, Barbara C. "The Economy Method Versus the Scott-Foresman Method in Teaching Second-Grade Reading in the Murphysboro Public Schools." *Journal of Educational Research* 51: 465-69; February 1958.

42. Kendler, H. H., and Kendler, T. S. "Vertical and Horizontal Processes in Problem Solving." *Psychological Review* 69: 1-16; January 1962.

43. Kjeldergaard, P. M. "The Psychology of Language." *Review of Educational Research* 31: 119-29; April 1961.

44. Levin, H., and Watson, J. *The Learning of Variable Grapheme-to-Phoneme Correspondences.* New York: Cornell University, 1961.

45. Levin, H., and Watson, J. *The Learning of Variable Grapheme-to-Phoneme Correspondences: Variations in the Initial Consonant Position.* New York: Cornell University, 1961.

46. Levin, H.; Watson, J.; and Feldman, M. *Writing as Pretraining for Association Learning.* New York: Cornell University, August 1961.

47. Long, E. R. "Multiple Scheduling in Children." *Journal of the Experimental Analysis of Behavior* 2: 268; July 1959.

48. Long, E. R. "Multiple-Schedule Control in Children." *Journal of the Experimental Analysis of Behavior* 4: 443-55; October 1962.

49. MacKinnon, A. R. *How DO Children Learn To Read? An Experimental Investigation of Children's Early Growth in Awareness of the Meanings of Printed Symbols.* Vancouver, British Columbia: Copp Clark Publishing Co., 1959.

50. McCracken, G. "Reading Readiness in Theory and Practice." *Tomor-*

row's Illiterates. (Edited by C. Walcutt.) Boston: Little, Brown and Co., 1961.

51. McIntire, R. W. "Reinforcement and Verbal Learning." *Psychological Reports* 12: 103-106; February 1962.

52. McNeil, J. D. "Programed Instruction as a Research Tool in Reading: An Annotated Case." *Journal of Programed Instruction* 1: 37-42; January 1962.

53. McNeil, J. D., and Kieslar, E. R. *Value of the Oral Response in Beginning Reading: An Experimental Study Using Programed Instruction.* Grant No. 1413. Washington, D.C.: U.S. Office of Education, Department of Health, Education, and Welfare, 1962.

54. Markle, S. M. *Words: A Programed Course in Vocabulary Development; Teacher's Manual.* Chicago: Science Research Associates, 1962.

55. Mayzner, M. S., and Tresselt, M. E. "The Ranking of Letter Pairs and Single Letters To Match Digram and Single-Letter Frequency Counts." *Journal of Verbal Learning and Verbal Behavior* 1: 203-207; October 1962.

56. Miller, G. A., and Selfridge, J. A. "Verbal Context and the Recall of Meaningful Material." *American Journal of Psychology* 63: 176-85; April 1950.

57. Miller, W., and Ervin, S. *The Development of Grammar in Child Language.* Berkeley: University of California, 1963.

58. Moore, O. K. "Orthographic Symbols and the Preschool Child—A New Approach." *Proceedings of the Third Minnesota Conference on Gifted Children.* Minneapolis: University of Minnesota Press, 1961.

59. Moore, O. K. *The Automated Responsive Environment.* New Haven: Yale University, 1962.

60. Muehl, S. "The Effects of Visual Discrimination Pretraining on Learning To Read a Vocabulary List in Kindergarten Children." *Journal of Educational Psychology* 51: 217-21; August 1960.

61. Muehl, S. "The Effects of Letter-Name Knowledge on Learning To Read a Word List in Kindergarten Children." *Journal of Educational Psychology* 4: 181-86; August 1962.

62. Newman, S. E., and Taylor, L. R. "Context Effects in Paired-Associate Learning as a Function of Element-Sharing Among Stimulus Terms." *Journal of Verbal Learning and Verbal Behavior* 1: 243-49; January 1963.

63. Osgood, C. E. "The Similarity Paradox in Human Learning." *Psychological Review* 56: 132-43; May 1949.

64. Osgood, C. E. "The Nature and Measurement of Meaning." *Psychological Bulletin* 49: 197-237; May 1952.

65. Popp, Helen, and Porter, D. "Programming Verbal Skills for Primary Grades." *AV Communication Review* 8: 165-75; July-August 1960.

66. Premack, D. "Toward Empirical Behavior Laws: I. Positive Reinforcement." *Psychological Review* 66: 219-33; July 1959.

67. Raygor, A. L., and Summers, E. G. *A Comparison of Two Methods of Teaching Reading Comprehension to High School and College Students*. Paper presented at National Reading Conference, Miami, Florida, December 7, 1962.

68. Raygor, A. L., and Wark, D. M. *An Evaluation of Programmed Learning in Teaching Reading Comprehension*. Paper presented at the National Reading Conference, Miami, Florida, December 7, 1962.

69. Reed, J. E., and Hayman, J. L., Jr. "Experiment Involving Use of English 2600: An Automated Instruction Text." *Journal of Educational Research* 55: 476-84; June 1962.

70. Resnick, L. B. *Programmed Instruction and the Teaching of Complex Intellectual Skills: Problems and Prospects*. New York: City University of New York, 1962.

71. Rinsland, H. D. *A Basic Vocabulary of Elementary and Secondary School Children*. New York: Macmillan Co., 1945.

72. Rogovin, S. *Modern English Sentence Structure: A Programed Textbook*. New York: Random House, 1963.

73. Roossinck, Pearl A. *A Learning Program in Paragraph Comprehension*. Master's thesis. Ann Arbor: University of Michigan, June 1962. (Typewritten)

74. Rothkopf, E. Z. *Some Observations on Predicting Instructional Effectiveness by Simple Inspection*. Murray Hill, N.J.: Bell Telephone Laboratories, 1963.

75. Schutz, R. E.; Baker, R. L.; and Gerlach, V. S. "Teaching Capitalization with a Programmed Text." *AV Communication Review* 10: 359-63; November-December 1962.

76. Silberman, H. F. "Effects of Praise and Reproof on Reading Growth in a Nonlaboratory Classroom Setting." *Journal of Educational Psychology* 48: 199-206; April 1957.

77. Silberman, H. F. *Exploratory Research on a Beginning Reading Program*. TM 895/100/00. Santa Monica, Calif.: System Development Corporation, 1964.

78. Skinner, B. F. *Verbal Behavior*. New York: Appleton-Century-Crofts, 1957.

79. Snyder, Marjorie S. *An Experiment in the Effectiveness of Desensitization in the Teaching of Remedial Reading*. Doctor's thesis. Nashville, Tenn.: George Peabody College for Teachers, 1962. (Typewritten)

80. Spalding, R. B., and Spalding, W. R. *The Writing Road to Reading*. New York: Whiteside and Morrow, 1957.

81. Sparks, P. E., and Fay, L. C. "An Evaluation of Two Methods of Teaching Reading." *Elementary School Journal* 57: 386-90; April 1957.

82. Staats, A. W. "Verbal Habit-Families, Concepts and the Operant Conditioning of Word Classes." *Psychological Review* 68: 190-204; May 1961.

83. Staats, A. W., and others. *A Reinforced System and Experimental Procedure for the Laboratory Study of Reading Acquisition.* Contract Nonr-2794 (02), Technical Report No. 22. Tempe: Arizona State University, September 1962.

84. Staats, A. W., and others. "The Conditioning of Textual Responses Using 'Extrinsic' Reinforcers." *Journal of the Experimental Analysis of Behavior* 5: 33-40; January 1962.

85. Staats, A. W., and others. *Reinforcement Variables in the Control of Unit Textual Responses.* Contract Nonr-2794 (02), Technical Report No. 23. Tempe: Arizona State University, March 1963.

86. Standing, E. M. *Maria Montessori.* New York: New American Library, 1962.

87. Stolurow, L. M., and Lippert H. *Prompting, Confirmation and Vanishing in the Teaching of a Sight Vocabulary.* Technical Report, Cooperative Research Project, Contract No. SAE 8370. Washington, D.C.: U.S. Department of Health, Education, and Welfare, Office of Education, 1961.

88. Stone, C. R. *Stone's Graded Vocabulary for Primary Reading.* St. Louis, Mo.: Webster Publishing Co., 1941.

89. Strickland, Ruth G. "The Language of Elementary School Children: Its Relationship to the Language of Reading Textbooks and the Quality of Reading of Selected Children." *Bulletin of the School of Education, Indiana University* 38: 1-131; July 1962.

90. Taber, J. I., and Glaser, R. "An Exploratory Evaluation of a Discriminative Transfer Learning Program Using Literal Prompts." *Journal of Educational Research* 55: 508-12; June-July 1962.

91. Thorndike, E. L., and Lorge, I. *Teacher's Word Book of 30.000 Words.* New York: Bureau of Publications, Teachers College, Columbia University, 1944.

92. Underwood, B. J., and Schulz, R. W. *Meaningfulness and Verbal Learning.* Philadelphia: J. B. Lippincott Co., 1960.

93. Walters, R. H., and Kosowski, I. "Symbolic Learning and Reading Retardation." *Journal of Consulting Psychology* 27: 75-82; February 1963.

94. Wechkin, S. "Word Learning in an Automated Teaching Situation as a Function of Display Condition." *Journal of Educational Psychology* 53: 165-69; August 1962.

95. Wepman, J. M. "Auditory Discrimination, Speech, and Reading." *Elementary School Journal* 60: 325-33; March 1960.

96. Woolman, M. *The Programming of Reading Skills (The Progressive Choice Reading Method).* Washington, D.C.: Institute of Educational Research, 1962.

97. Zimmerman, D. W. "Durable Secondary Reinforcement: Method and Theory." *Psychological Review* 64: 373-83; November 1957.

SUSAN MEYER MARKLE*
University of California, Los Angeles

Programed Instruction in English

Should English Be Programed? Three Negative Indications

Overheard in a Brooklyn classroom:

"Why've we gotta study this stuff anyway? We was born in this here country."

"It would be nice if you spoke a language besides your own."

The exasperated reply of this unidentified teacher, reported by a source long since forgotten, epitomizes one aspect of the struggle of English teachers around the country. It is their task to train youngsters in a particular dialect of English, called "Standard English," which often conflicts with the dialects, normally lumped under the expressive rubric, "Vulgar English," learned in the home and on the streets. The grammatical structures that are allowable, the phonemes that are comprehended, and even the meaning of many words vary from community to community, taken in both the geographic and the socioeconomic sense. "His [the student's] teachers must ponder the extent to which they can simply build upon his previously acquired capabilities and the extent to which they can attempt to alter a system of habits which are not only highly practiced, but which also probably serve a supportive role in the child's adjustment to his non-school environment" (4, p.

* The author wishes to thank Professor Richard M. Bossone, University of California, Riverside, for a critical reading of the first draft of the paper and for many helpful suggestions.

342). In a programer's terminology, the "entering behaviors" or "initial repertoires" of students in English vary in ways not yet fully known, although work is in progress on linguistic atlases which will provide such information. More is known about the problems of teaching English to speakers of Tagalog (36) or of teaching a foreign language to native English speakers (see Chapter 13 by Lane) than is known about the problems of teaching a dialect we might call "academic English" to native speakers of "Brooklynese" or "Georgia drawl." The programer will not find a clear specification of the characteristics of the target population to aid him in determining the starting point of instruction. He has one strike against him.

A psychology instructor must teach his students to talk intelligently about conditioning, the id, the autonomic nervous system, and so forth. A mathematics instructor must teach his students to talk intelligently about matrices, probability, exponents, and so forth. A musicology instructor must teach his students to talk intelligently about sonatas, Palestrina, tone rows, and so forth. An English instructor must teach his students to talk intelligently. The behavior which constitutes "knowing English" is difficult to specify. It is possible to talk nonsense grammatically, as Chomsky's (6) classic sentence, "Colorless green ideas sleep furiously," purports to show. It is also possible to make eminent sense in "poor" English, as readers of student papers know. The objectives of English instruction, as defined by the National Council of Teachers of English (33), lie in four skills: speaking, listening, reading, and writing. One assumes that an implied "correctly" or "effectively" modifies this statement. Children enter school with a large capacity for speaking and a similar (if smaller) capacity for listening; for most, the problems of making appropriate noises when confronted with a text and constructing appropriate symbols on paper are fairly well solved in the first few years of school. And yet English instruction continues yearly on into the college years. "Freshman English," Kitzhaber remarked, "is one of those things like spinach and tetanus shots that young people put up with because their elders say they must" (20, p. 1). Presumably, throughout these years, something is being taught. Just what the "terminal behaviors" are is unclear. The programer will not find a clear statement of objectives set out for him in behavioral terms to aid in determining the end point of instruction. The English language programer is not in the happy state de-

scribed by Lane (see pp. 584-85), in which a whole discipline is devoted
to the specification of terminal behaviors.

If the highest-level objectives of English instruction are not so easily
specifiable, there is a lower level on which one would hope to find
greater specificity. In the course of learning to talk, listen, read, and
write, most students are exposed to a body of material to talk about,
especially grammar and literature. Grammar, long a singular noun,
has recently attained plurality. Competing for a place in the curriculum
are no less than three grammars. Literature, which contributes to the
literate or well-read product of long years in school, is equally a house
divided. For every school system that excises an old classic as no longer
relevant to the needs of modern youth, there is a comparable school
system which reinstates that classic as necessary to the production of
a cultured human being. An argument continues on the virtues of extensive reading (wide-ranging but somewhat superficial acquaintance
with many books) as against intensive reading (the critical and detailed analysis of a few texts). Courses in literature seem to have one
objective in common: that the student interact with books. Which
books and what sort of interaction differ. The closer the objectives of
English instruction approach specificity, it would appear, the hotter
the conflicts between the advocates of one approach and another. The
programer who selects any of these sets of specifiable objectives—for
instance, one of the grammars—will find himself in conflict with and
criticized by advocates of other approaches. He has two strikes against
him.

On what basis do judges of freshman writing decide that one piece of
writing is better than another? . . . We used 53 outstanding judges, known
to be deeply concerned with student writing, in six different fields: college
English teachers, social scientists, natural scientists, writers and editors, law-
yers and law professors, and business executives. Each one read multilithed
copies of 300 short essays on two topics . . . written by first-year men and
women students [at three colleges]. . . . The judges sorted them [the papers]
into nine piles in order of merit, observing only the rules that all nine piles
should be used, and not less than 4% of the papers should appear in the
smallest piles. No judge knew how any other judge ranked the papers. . . .
The judges were *not* asked to rate the papers on particular qualities. . . . 34%
of these essays received all nine possible grades; 37% received eight; 23%
received seven; 5% received six; 1% received five; and none received less
than five different grades from the 53 readers (10).

This startling demonstration of total disagreement, of course, does not represent a normal grading situation in which members of an English department are grading student themes on specified criteria of "good writing." In his paper, Diederich emphasized that any implication of a standard which might be used to judge the papers had deliberately been removed from the set of directions given his 53 readers. In an earlier paper, however, Diederich gave the teacher who must judge the writings of students no reason for complacency, when he reported that "the College Entrance Examination Board subsidized a long series of experiments from 1951 through 1956 with a two-hour essay examination for writing ability . . . until the cumulative weight of evidence forced us to the conclusion that scores on such a sample of free writing cannot be made either sufficiently *reliable* or sufficiently *valid* to be used as one basis for admission to college" (9, p. 1). Given evidence that even highly trained readers produce grades on the same paper that can be expected to correlate around .70, and that grades on two papers from the same student can be expected to correlate around .60, he concluded that "the essay examination is about as trustworthy as an African witch-doctor."

There is no reason to expect that the criteria for effective speaking are more generally agreed upon. There is little question on the criteria for reading, when reading is taken to mean that the student's oral performance shows a recognizable formal relationship to the text. As the objectives move from reading for facts to reading for understanding to critical reading, however, the criteria become progressively hazier. The same disintegration of consensus may be observable in listening skills, if tests of "critical listening" exist. The programer has three strikes against him.

A programer surveying the English scene could hardly be blamed for moving to the simpler problems of another discipline. According to the dicta of his craft, construction of a program of instruction requires a clearly specifiable goal, the attainment of which can be measured with some accuracy, and a clear starting point or set of assumptions upon which to build new behavior. None of these factors seems to exist to any degree in the higher level objectives of English instruction.

The reflection of this fact is seen in a nose-count of existing programs available (5, 18). At the lowest level, where no controversy

exists and the criterion behavior is clear and unassailable, the proliferation of programs almost matches that shown in the field of mathematics. Programs on set theory and programs on spelling are almost
equally numerous. Where controversy exists, such as in grammar, but
where a reasonable specificity exists in measurable objectives, a few
programs have reached the market. While rumors continue to appear
that one or another individual has a "composition program," nothing
satisfying that classification has appeared. Whether English is un-
programable or not, it is, to a large extent, unprogramed.

Should English Be Programed? Four Positive Indications

"English is taught more extensively to more pupils than is any other
subject" (34, p. 18). Between the first year when he studies reading
(see Chapter 11 by Silberman) and the final year in which he passes
Freshman English in college, almost every student in every school is
exposed to required instruction in English every year. The importance
of the subject is as great as the size of the population. "Competence in
using English is essential in every subject. Unless English is taught
well, every subject suffers. . . . The task of educating students to use
language is the special responsibility of the English teacher, but his
success or failure ultimately affects instruction in all other subjects"
(34, p. 17). One criterion for choosing to program an area of instruction, that of an adequate audience for a program, is assured. The significance of the subject is equally apparent.

Not only is there the usual well-known shortage of teachers in the
field of English, but, in the words of their own professional organization, "most of the English majors who were graduated in June, 1960,
and are now teaching in high schools are simply not equipped either
to deal with problems of teaching the language and composition or to
keep up with current developments in the application of linguistics to
the teaching of English" (34, p. 75). The problem is further compounded by an inadequate supply of college instructors trained in these
same fields who could contribute to the reduction of this cultural lag.
At the elementary level, where "two of the three R's" are English, the
preparation of teachers is even weaker: "Except for work in freshman
composition, the average college requires that only ten per cent of the
total program be spent on English or the teaching of English. . . . The

preparation of elementary teachers for teaching students to write and speak seems very limited indeed" (34, p. 48). A teacher cannot teach what he does not know himself. Among all the aids that bring the world to the classroom, programed instruction in its classical sense—written materials requiring writing and reading—seems best suited to the problem of closing the gap between the frontiers of knowledge about language and the "superstitions" now being taught about language. As this author has noted before (29), not only can students be permitted up-to-date instruction via self-instructional materials, but their teachers also may utilize such materials (or perhaps more difficult versions of such programs) to update their own knowledge. An important criterion for choosing to program an area, namely, the lack of qualified instructors available in sufficient numbers, is satisfied—at least at the moment.

The NCTE (34) estimated that 150,000 students ("somewhat more than 20 per cent" of those tested) failed the qualifying entering examinations in college English. The cost of testing was high; the cost of the resulting remedial teaching, astounding. Many students who would have failed, of course, did not take the examinations. They did not enter college. The area of composition fully qualifies as an area in which there is a "depressed level of learning" (25) suggesting the application of programed techniques. Nor is the area of interpretive reading much less depressed. On a test of "interpretation of the writer's broader ideas and the implications of these ideas" conducted by Project Talent, the results reported by Flanagan were not encouraging:

According to this test the average 12th-grade student in the nation's high school was able to answer correctly 78 percent of the questions based on paragraphs selected from *Modern Screen* or *Silver Screen*. On selections chosen from the *Saturday Evening Post, Look,* and the *Reader's Digest,* the average 12th-grade student answered correctly about half of the questions testing his ability to understand and interpret the paragraphs. This dropped to about 40 percent for *Pageant* and *McCall's* and to about 33 percent for *Time* and *Fortune.* For the remaining two periodicals, the *Atlantic Monthly* and the *Saturday Review,* the percentage of questions answered correctly by the average 12th-grade student was 28 (13, p. 82).

The need for improved teaching techniques is apparent.

A mobile population moving from one school district to another and the American habit of advancing each student to the next grade regardless of attainment create problems for all instructors. It would be rare, however, for an instructor in geometry or physics to meet on the opening day a class in which knowledge of his particular subject matter varied from third-grade competence to college-level competence. English teachers face such problems yearly. It may be possible to find a literary work that all students in a class have not read; it is impossible to find a step forward in compositional skills which any large proportion of students are at one time prepared to take or in need of taking. Instruction in grammar and usage begins somewhere in the early grades when elementary teachers suggest to young students better ways to construct sentences. Formal instruction in grammar is usually placed at the junior-high level, but is continued year after year. It is often rehashed again in the college composition course. At all levels, then, instruction to the "grade" as a group must be beneath the level of the talented and well-trained, yet above the level of the least talented or least trained. There can be little doubt that individualized instruction is a necessity, not a luxury, in English class. English teachers are well aware of this. "As any experienced teacher knows, the range of ability in any one grade in any one school may vary enormously; consequently, the concept of grade-level requirements has been abandoned by most progressive systems. For it has been substituted the concept of 'points of emphasis' for various grades and for students of differing abilities and needs" (22, p. 45). The difficulties of pacing to group learning rates an instructional sequence which begins at a specific point and covers specified points in some specified order are well known. The English instructor must go further than that: he must begin at many points and go at many paces while covering a multitude of points. Even with competently trained instructors, the depressing results shown in the above-described surveys of the effectiveness of English instruction are predictable. The task is impossible.

Should English Be Programed?

All indications for the application of programing are there: a broad audience, a need for valid instruction where the supply of available competent instructors is insufficient, present instructional techniques that are producing less than perfect results, and the need for individualized instruction. There is no doubt that programers will rise to such a challenge. Given the negative side of the coin, however—the difficulties in specifying the entering behavior and the terminal behavior, the complexities of constructing adequate measures of success of any programed effort, and the controversies within the field—progress will doubtless be slow. English teachers will be required to do a great deal of serious thinking about their objectives; no less, programers will be required to do a great deal of serious thinking about their technology. The interaction may be mutually advantageous.

Issues in Programing of English: An Overview

To many people, a program is an odd sort of book containing an interminable series of short sentences with holes in them. A variant, of course, is the book with an interminable series of paragraphs followed by multiple-choice questions. Neither of these restricted media appears to hold much promise in guiding the development of composition skills, speaking skills, or listening skills. In the words of one insightful professor:

Although programmed instruction may offer hope of greater efficiency in teaching some things such as spelling and mechanics, there is considerable doubt that composition in a real sense can be taught any better by this method. Programmed instruction is especially suitable for giving a student command of the data of an organized body of knowledge such as psychology or arithmetic or physics, and an *understanding* of this body of knowledge. But composition is not a body of knowledge; instead it is a highly complex skill—perhaps the most complex of all human skills. It seems likely that the behavior patterns involved in writing well are too complex to be isolated one by one and systematically programmed for machine instruction. This is only hypothesis, however, not fact (20, p. 92).

When the English instructor surveys the split-level books and the small-apertured machines, it is little wonder that his conclusion is in accord with Professor Kitzhaber. They do indeed seem to have little to offer in the shaping of lengthy, complicated, and "artful" (read "not entirely predictable") sequences of verbal behavior.

In the interests of focusing attention on those characteristics of programed instruction which are intended in this chapter, a definition is needed. "An instructional program is a vehicle which generates an essentially reproducible sequence of instructional events and accepts responsibility for efficiently accomplishing a specified change from a

given range of initial competences or behavioral tendencies to a specified terminal range of competences or behavioral tendencies" (24, p.
385). From this definition one cannot derive the specifications of the
medium of presentation or of the theory of learning upon which the
program is based. The essential characteristics are two: reproducibility
and consistent effectiveness.[1]

In the sense that a master teacher produces consistent effects year
after year, his techniques satisfy half of the definition given above.
If he could be reproduced, or if another teacher using the "same" techniques achieved identical results, the whole definition would be satisfied. On the other hand, almost all teaching aids of the type usually
classed as audiovisual devices satisfy the first part of the definition
only minimally: "the definition implies a programed sequence of learner *behavior*, not merely a reproducible set of stimulus materials" (24,
p. 385). If the total definition is taken literally, many of the programs
(those that look like programs) now available do not really fit the definition at all (see Chapter 14 by Hanson and Komoski).

Accepting the responsibility for assuring an outcome of an instructional sequence is a problem in any discipline. The technology of programing is at best half-formed; its precepts change from one year to
the next (see Chapter 4 by Klaus), and those which do not change are
open to the widest possible interpretation. The difficulties of translating a subject into an efficient sequence of instructional events are not
peculiar to English. There are, however, special problems in English,
among them specification of the kinds and ranges of competencies desired, measurement of both initial and terminal behavior, articulation
or ordering of sequences, and sheer bulk of the materials which will
probably be required to perform the task. English, as a subject for
programers, will require advances in programing technology at the
same time that programers are demanding better specifications of the
behaviors to be taught from the English teachers.

Those examples of programs which have led many English teachers
to say that programed instruction cannot accomplish certain desirable

---

[1] Considerably more heat than light has been generated by arguments between
proponents of "anything that resembles an existing program is a program" and
proponents of "a program is any instructional sequence that works, no matter
what it looks like." The issue will not be resolved, obviously, by the author's advocacy of the latter.

goals do not adequately sample the range of possibilities implied by Lumsdaine's definition. Programed instruction is not limited to one medium, such as the book or its surrogate—the filmed page which a machine presents—nor is it limited to any particular school of programing technology. The small-step linear program is familiar to most teachers at this point and is assumed to be the full measure of programed instruction. English teachers rightfully question the capabilities of the limited technology to which they have been exposed. Perhaps in the future, they will come to contribute to the growth of the new technology in directions that approach their own needs rather than, as at present, relegating it to a minor role. Among improvements suggested by one instructor, for instance, was "greater experimentation with and understanding of the 'multiple-right-answer' technique . . . to destroy the one-question–one-answer syndrome" (3, p. 76). Obviously, inputs or stimulus materials larger than those generally used to date will be required to extend a student's reading skills and larger outputs or responses to extend his compositional skills. Some trends observable in available and prospective programs in English suggest that English as a subject is already affecting programing as a technology.

Trends in Grammar and Language Study

Grammar, as every English teacher knows, is a battleground. Arguments and counterarguments fill journals and occupy seekers after degrees as to what grammar to teach if you must teach it, how it should be taught, at what level it should be taught, why grammar is being taught, and whether grammar should be taught at all.

[The National Council of Teachers of English] drew up a momentous programmatic statement which was published in the Council's *English Journal* in December of 1928. This report pointed to the chasm between genuine language knowledge and the current language superstitions taught in the schools and sought a specific means of bringing about the gradual substitution of a scientific attitude for the eighteenth-century assumptions then being taught. . . . During the quarter century since that survey, spectacular advances have been made in the field of descriptive linguistics, particularly with respect to the analysis of English structure. These advances, linguists have pointed out, constitute a breakthrough comparable to those in physics and mathematics. The progress makes obsolete much of what was doctrinal in the discipline before 1930 (34, p. 62).

In the 1928 recommendations, the means for attaining the revolution in language teaching was to be a complete revision of what was taught *to* teachers in their college years. The effects of this strong recommendation on actual practices in teacher education were described earlier in this chapter. This "greatest cultural lag in any academic discipline" (34) still exists. It has been further compounded by the appearance of a powerful new approach to grammar emanating from work by Chomsky (6) and his disciples (see also 40).

The traditional grammar has been defended on two interesting counts: first, it seems to some to have positive effects on compositional skills, and second, it is a stable body of knowledge in contrast to the disputes and controversies evidenced among the proponents of the "scientific grammars." The defense of grammar in terms of its effects on composition is testable empirically, but even startling empirical results would hardly seem to justify the teaching of a false description of the language.[2] As stated by Kitzhaber, "Parents would rightly be shocked to learn that their children were studying psychology or physics under teachers and out of textbooks that were untouched by an awareness of developments in those fields since 1900" (20, pp. 81-82). While parents might find the psychology of the "soul" (or "mind") less threatening to their traditional values than modern behaviorism, the emphasis on modern physics would certainly be supported by PTA's, no matter how effective eighteenth-century physics might be in the construction of adequate bridges and internal combustion engines. As an excuse for retaining the old grammar, the avoidance of controversy has been roundly attacked by W. N. Francis:

The present ferment in what was for long a passive if not petrified subject is to me a healthy sign. I believe that just as every generation must rewrite history and literary criticism, and apparently every decade must reformulate physics and medicine, so every generation or so must revise if not completely rewrite grammar. If this seems like an attack upon eternal verities, it is so intended. All I ask of anyone who deplores it is that he point out any other field, from archeology to zoology, where eternal verities have survived the intellectual revolution of the last century. Grammar is a way of looking at and formulating the facts of language; it changes as modes of observation and formulation change (14, p. 50).

---

[2] If, of course, the composition instructor insists upon the grammatical structures taught by prescriptive grammarians, but no longer upheld by scientific grammarians, grades in composition of necessity will be correlated with mastery of usage patterns dictated by traditional grammar.

Although the analogy may stretch the truth a bit,[3] the three major approaches to grammar suggest a somewhat similar difference in approach within certain fields of psychology. Prescriptive grammar most closely parallels more directive types of clinical psychology; descriptive or structural grammar, the data-collecting normative orientation of differential psychology; and transformational or generative grammar, the hypothetico-deductive strain of psychology. The prescriptive clinical grammarian is concerned with a change in behavior toward an agreed-upon standard; the descriptive data-collecting grammarian is concerned with tabulating and classifying the "facts" of language behavior; and the transformational theoretical grammarian is concerned with demonstrating the consistency and completeness of a limited set of postulates.

The clinician accepts certain standards of behavior as "normal," "adjusted," and so forth, and seeks to remold his patient in the direction of these standards. Likewise, the prescriptive grammarian accepts certain standards of language behavior as "correct," "elegant," and so forth, and seeks to remold his student in the direction of these standards. It is as equally unlikely that in our upward-mobility-oriented school culture, the full development of a child's slum dialect will be encouraged by his grammar teacher as that in our predominantly monogamous culture, a patient's polygamous tendencies will be encouraged by his clinician. The issue lies not in such extremes, but in difficulties with the standards, both in the consistency of the explanatory system on which they are based and in their reality. The vituperative discussions generated by the informed and the less-informed on the subject of the reality of the standards of "good" English[4] remind one of nothing so much as the emotional declarations elicited by Kinsey's work.

The three grammatical systems may be compared on their approach to one of the real training problems confronting the English teacher: the nature of a "complete" sentence. Fries (15) presented the arguments of the structuralist against the definitions of a sentence common

---

[3] For a more technical discussion of the issues involved, see Saporta, S., editor. *Psycholinguistics.* New York: Holt, Rinehart & Winston, 1961.

[4] For one of the most amusing and definitive discussions of the pros and cons in this emotionally loaded area, the author recommends Sledd, J., and Ebbit, W. R., editors. *Dictionaries and That Dictionary.* Chicago: Scott, Foresman & Co., 1962. See also, Bloomfield, M. W., and Newmark, L. *A Linguistic Introduction to the History of English.* New York: Alfred Knopf, 1963.

in prescriptive grammars. The definitions stressing meaning (a sentence expresses a complete thought) have produced no teachable criteria for completeness because no one has defined a complete thought (except that which is expressed by a complete sentence). Definition in terms of word content (something named and something stated about the thing named) does not include all members of the population of sentences acceptable to even the most traditional of grammarians. To Fries and others, what is important in a sentence is not its "meaningful" content but its grammatical structure. The concept of a sentence as a minimal independent utterance already exists; instances may be identified in speech by the full stop or shift of speaker and in writing by the capital letter and period. The task of the observer is to identify the criterial attributes. Taking 50 hours of recorded conversations as data, Fries searched these data for the structural components of the minimal utterance—the smallest bits of conversation that a person who was not interrupted would allow to stand alone. From such an empirical base, utterances including more than minimal units could be classified as well, and the structure of all observed types of minimal utterances and more complex utterances built upon them described. Many of the observed instances of "complete" utterances would not satisfy the watchful ear of the guardian of pure English, even spoken English. The data represent informal conversations, only one of the conditions relevant to the description of English speakers' verbal behavior.

The observational methodology of structural linguistics has produced great quantities of data collected on many of the world's natural languages. To the English teacher, the generalizations derived from empirical observation of actual language performance under a variety of conditions could offer a firm basis from which to teach children to do as their elders do. But a problem new to English teachers accompanies the more scientific approach. Not only is the methodology expected to advance, as noted above by Francis, but as the language continues to evolve and new forms become acceptable within the working lifetime of the teacher, the "facts" will continue to change. The role of guardian of linguistic purity will be a difficult one indeed.

In contradistinction to the inductive approach of the structuralists is the axiomatically given "kernel" sentence of the generative grammarian. A limited number of "simple" sentence structures are identified and rules for forming them are basic postulates of the system. All other English sentences may then be derived from these givens by applying a set of transformations to the kernel sentences. For example, the question transformation involves a subject-auxiliary reversal: "The man was . . ." becomes "Was the man. . . ." Any rule that generates a sentence which would be rejected by a "native speaker" is invalid. An acceptable sentence which cannot be derived by applying the extant rules obviously calls for a new rule.

The transformational approach has shown one advantage not available to the structural approach, namely, it can identify the causes of ambiguity in many cases. To the taxonomist, "Flying airplanes can be dangerous," is one sentence. To the grammarian who can operate in reverse the rules which generated that sequence, the same sentence is two sentences, derived, as he can show, from two separate sets of rules. Miller (31, 32) has shown a relationship between the number and kind of transformations required to produce a sentence and perceptual responses to these sentences. However, the elegance of the theory, its power in certain cases, and its relevance to reaction times in deciphering sentences do not necessarily indicate that the approach is most suitable for classroom training. To this author's knowledge, there is no existing transformation rule that will take the speaker from the kernel sentence "He loves me" to the sentence "He don't love me no more." The deductive approach, of course, does not preclude such a rule, but the generators of generative grammar are speakers of Standard English. Likewise, no known rule in the system will generate a sentence fragment of the type used in "good" writing by acceptable authors. Although the English teacher may wish his students to use complete sentences most of the time, he knows that occasional sentence fragments are acceptable. At the moment, generative grammar as a description of American practices is incomplete. And, since the "facts" derived from the deductive system are the responses "Yes, it is grammatical" or "No, it is not," given by unspecified native speakers, sentences which are judged as grammatical in English—or, more likely, disagreements about those which are not—will vary with the population of speakers chosen as judges.

In summary, the three grammars provide the teacher with radically different tools. In the extreme, prescriptive grammar provides a set of rules to be learned and followed. The excuse "everybody else does it (including the teacher)" is no excuse. Descriptive grammar provides a set of empirically derived regularities about who says what to whom under what conditions. Because correctness is not an absolute, but is contingent upon complex and shifting conditions, the problems of teaching correct English are greatly magnified. Transformational grammar provides an elegant if as yet incomplete systematic approach to the study of sentence structure. What problems this newcomer will present as a teaching tool remain to be found. The choice among these tools is a difficult one.

Part of the difficulty seems to lie, not in intellectual archaism on the part of English teachers, but in a confusion in objectives. The traditional grammars of the eighteenth century, on which "modern traditional" grammars are still based, were written, not as scientific descriptions of the language, but as prescriptions for "correct usage." As Kitzhaber observed, "Since the people for whom these books were being written hungered for certainty, the books were dogmatic, prescriptive, making little pretense of describing the language as it was but instead laying down a plan for the language as these self-appointed authorities thought it should be" (20, p. 76). Changing one's language as a tool for upward mobility is still with us, as advertisements for language improvement courses show. In contrast, the scientific approach to the study of language "as she is spoke" is seen as a threat to the role of the English teacher as the guardian of good English and the shaper of correct usage. In Fries's words, "A linguist records and studies all the actual forms and uses of the language that occur, but that recording and that study, of Vulgar English as well as of Standard English, *should certainly not be taken as evidence that he therefore recommends or believes that the forms of Vulgar English can or should be substituted for the forms of Standard English*" (15, p. 5). Despite such statements by well-known linguists, scientific objectivity in describing "substandard" forms is taken not as objectivity, but as recommendation by default. The traditional grammar supports the efforts of the English teacher to change verbal habits; the descriptive grammar is taken to conflict with these objectives. A clarification of objectives—of "why grammar?"—is called for.

Programed instruction, with its heavy emphasis on the detailed statement of objectives and its equally heavy emphasis on measuring the attainment of these objectives, will undoubtedly have a healthy influence on controversies in this field. A behavioral analysis of the conflicting objectives of grammar instruction as described above indicates at least two widely varying goals which quite possibly are most efficiently attainable by equally widely varying types of programs. The conflict is often openly expressed in the titles of grammar texts. *Grammar*, an analysis of the language, is not identical with *usage*, the habits of certain classes of speakers.

There is no reason to believe that the problems of replacing one dialect (a substandard one) with another (the Standard one) are not amenable to the approach described in Lane's chapter (see especially pp. 598-99), given a contrastive analysis of the original dialect and the target dialect. The target dialect, of course, is closer to the student's original language than a foreign language would be, but it nevertheless involves new patterns of response which must be brought under the control of discriminative stimuli. When applying for a job or giving a speech to a mixed audience, certain patterns of speaking are expected to be automatic, so that embarrassing "errors" simply do not occur, and the behavior flows along smoothly. And, as in foreign language teaching, the most appropriate goal of such teaching would be the creation of two dialects, not the suppression of the original dialect which the student may need in order to be a "regular guy" in his own community. The NCTE suggested such an approach in 1952: "Since correctness is a relative matter derived from the needs of communication, the teaching of correct English requires the development in pupils of a sensitivity to the requirements of language in all kinds of situations and the gradual development of skill to use English appropriately in each situation" (33, p. 278). The audience, as a discriminative stimulus controlling large verbal repertoires, is given an important place in Skinner's analysis of verbal behavior (41). The audience variable, in different terminology, is no stranger to informed English teachers, as the preceding quotation demonstrates.

A program of instruction which aims at automatic responding under the control of such a discriminative stimulus as the audience (in the broadest sense) has certain requirements, such as extensive practice, which are not necessarily the same as the requirements for a program aimed at the "understanding" of a body of knowledge. The study of grammar as a systematic body of knowledge would seem to fall within the competence of a program paralleling more closely the techniques used in the programing of comprehension of mathematics and the sciences rather than those used in the programing of foreign languages. Talking *about* the language, as has been said many times by many people, is not the same behavior as fluent use of the language. The value of grammar—or more broadly, the study of his native language—as a humanistic discipline is *not* unquestioned *if* such study should prove to have no practical consequences in making the student a better speaker or writer. The expectations of English teachers may come in open conflict with the precise statement of objectives and exhibition of the criterion test expected of a programer. A physics programer would rightly object if the criterion applied to his program which effectively taught toward a verbal test were taken to be the ability to build a rocket. Such transfer might indeed occur as an unexpected bonus, but if rocket building is what is wanted, a program directed at the skill itself might be far more efficient. The analogous problem of transfer from grammar as a discipline to language fluency as a skill demands clarification and experimentation. The excuse for teaching grammar has lain in its supposed contribution to correct usage and better composition. Meckel, summarizing research in the teaching of composition, pointed out that no convincing evidence exists that instruction in grammar either has any significant effect on composition or that it has not. After quoting a study in which large numbers of children were tested for knowledge of grammar and found wanting, he added: "These data suggest one reason why studies of the transfer value of grammar have shown so little evidence of transfer. The pupils in the various studies have apparently acquired little knowledge that could be transferred" (30, p. 981). The first requirement, then, for successful research on transfer will be an effective teaching tool.

A program in grammar, using the word *program* in the sense intended by the definition given earlier, would contribute to the solution of this research problem. A program in each of the variants of grammar would offer some interesting research possibilities on the comparative effect on composition attributable to these variants. The problems of designing such a study would be immense, but a reproducible instructional sequence which enabled each student to reach the objectives of the program, namely demonstrable "knowledge about" the language, is at least a *sine qua non*. And, because the program is observable to all, proponents of each school (and opponents of grammar in general) could be forced to agree that "knowledge about" language had been taught without prejudicial introduction of specific training in usage; therefore, any transfer effects were indeed transfer effects. If no transfer were observed from any one or ones of the grammar programs, this could not be taken as a criticism of the program's effectiveness in attaining the objectives it was designed to attain. (See Chapter 7 by Lumsdaine for further discussion of this issue.) Nor, as was concluded at a conference sponsored by Project English, would such a finding necessarily invalidate the study of grammar as a legitimate discipline in the curriculum (44). Programed instruction may contribute to the solution of "why grammar," but "whether grammar" is not a scientific issue. If transfer is achieved, the old justification for teaching it will remain. If transfer does not occur, then the decision to teach it must be justified in other ways.

In the near future, English teachers will be able to select a grammar program conforming to their preferred major "school" of grammar. Seniority goes to Blumenthal's *English 2600*, one of the most widely used programs, representing the traditional grammar with a strong dose of usage drill included (see 26). Its upper-level sequel, *English 3200*, falls in the same category.[5] The Macmillan Company has published M. W. Sullivan's *Programmed English*, an entrant in the field of structural grammar. "It acquaints the student with what are traditionally termed 'the parts of speech.' (This term is never used in the program.) He also learns to describe and manipulate the indicative verb system, to identify the most important patterns in the simple sentence, to distinguish between form and function in a number of critical instances, and to correct a series of the most common errors found in the writings of high school and college students" (45, p. 2). By the programer's admission, therefore, the program is not purely knowledge-about—it includes usage drill. Nor is it exclusively structural.

Both teachers and students insisted on having recourse to meaning wherever it proved useful. *Semantically* a noun is a word that refers to a person, place, thing or idea. Most of the students had already profited from a semantic approach to grammar in their previous course work; they were loath to abandon a type of description which was already meaningful to

---

[5] Less widely known programs, not described here but listed in *Programs*, '63, tend to fall into this category, as far as can be determined by inspection of the frames printed there.

them. As a consequence, the final course is a synthesis of structural, formal, and semantic approaches to the description of English (45, pp. 7-8).

Another major contender will appear soon: *Modern English Sentence Structure,* programed by Syrell Rogovin (39). This last program most nearly approaches "pure" grammar, in the sense that it includes no drill attempting to eliminate common usage errors. It represents transformational grammar and therefore discusses the basic rules for generating sentences and transforming "kernel" sentences into more complex patterns. At no time in the program is the student confronted with a "substandard" English sentence, nor, if he follows the rules of sentence construction, can he generate one.

A further addition to the continuum of "schools of grammar" is expected when Harcourt, Brace & World releases a program by Paul Roberts. If Roberts' latest book, *English Sentences* (38), is a predictor of the program's content, it will represent an attempt at fusing generative (or transformational) and descriptive (or structural) grammars.[6] A "pure" structural program, the existence of which has not come to this writer's attention, would complete the continuum, giving teachers a selection from pure traditional (Blumenthal), combined structural-traditional (Sullivan), pure structural (?), combined structural-generative (Roberts) to pure generative (Rogovin). Since the programs were not written with the research suggested above in mind, the contribution of "grammar per se" is not yet testable. At least two—Sullivan and Blumenthal—include usage, and one—Rogovin—does not, so the variables are confounded. If usage drill produces the effect it is intended to produce, the die is loaded against the transformational grammar program at the outset.

Rogovin[7] reported difficulties similar to those encountered by Sullivan, as described above. The entering behavior of students included responses which conflicted with the behavior the program was trying to establish, especially in the precise use of terms as demanded by this rigorous deductive system. Such problems are not the exclusive property of English instruction, since intellectual revolutions seem to be the present rule in most disciplines, and their course is generally from

[6] On publication of the program, *English Syntax,* in September 1964, this prediction proved false. Roberts' program, like Rogovin's, is pure transformational grammar.

[7] Personal communication.

the graduate school downward, leaving the elementary school as the last stronghold of the "old" approach. This author has confronted similar problems in teaching morphemic analysis and is less hesitant than the two grammarians in labeling the previously acquired responses "misinformation."[8] Competing responses, especially when they legitimately may be classed as wrong, affect the design of a program, necessitating in many cases special sequences directed at the elimination of the previous response before the new and "more adequate" response can be trained. Programers undoubtedly will concur heartily with the request of the NCTE, quoted earlier, that instruction in modern views of language be part of the background of every elementary teacher. Had such been the case, Sullivan could have avoided including a set of definitions unacceptable to "pure" structuralists.

Among the strong recommendations offered by Lumsdaine (Chapter 7) on evaluating programs, the necessity for pretesting students is one of particular value to English teachers. In no other field is student variability as much in evidence, ranging from no information to misinformation to adequate knowledge. The majority of presently available programs in English make no provision for diagnosing the needs of individual students and tracking them through the program according to these needs. Being permitted to skip already known material will undoubtedly reduce the boredom in taking a lengthy program. As Glaser (16) noted, pretesting may also influence learning in a positive fashion by making the objectives of the program more apparent to the student. As indicated in Gotkin and Goldstein (17), a school system can make up for the oversights of the programer by constructing its own pretests or utilizing the programer's posttests as pretests. Grammar programs in which usage is a significant part, as is true of all but Rogovin's program, lend themselves most easily to such a system, since one error or kind of error is not necessarily correlated with another. Students who use "him and me" as a subject are not necessarily the same group as those who dangle participles. As noted by Lumsdaine, time to complete the program is not of much value as a measure

---

[8] An example of such competing responses is the "standard" eighth-grade definition of a prefix as "a couple of letters that go in front of a word to change its meaning slightly." Such a definition excludes lengthy prefixes and prefixes affixed to morphemes that are not words. It also reduces an important part of a word to a subordinate position. If a student gives such a definition on the pretest, he is likely to give it again on the posttest, despite the intervening training.

of the program's efficiency if half the students know half the material before beginning. English as a subject matter will force programing as a technology to change some of its early rules and procedures, perhaps to the benefit of other disciplines as well. The needs of English teachers for efficient individualized instruction may also force programers in the field to approximate the recommended standards more closely.

Two of the grammar programs offer interesting deviations from standard programing practice. Sullivan's *Programmed English* makes use of "oral" (presumably subvocal) responses, a device which makes it difficult for the teacher or experimenter to determine where and how frequently errors occur, but which saves the student a great deal of time. As described by J. M. Reid,[9] Roberts' program will utilize the teacher as the confirmation mechanism and on-the-spot writer of remedial branches.

The program is to be placed in the hands of each pupil in the class but no answers are supplied in the pupil's edition. The teacher controls the pace and gives each pupil a chance to write his answer. Then she calls on various individuals to give their answers, and then usually asks if other pupils have a different answer. If there are differences, they discuss them and come to an agreement. The correct answers, of course, are furnished in the Teacher's Edition. . . . It gives the teacher a chance to correct wrong thinking and wrong answers right on the spot.

(Reid, a kindly gentleman of the old school, also notes that "the old hobgoblin of replacing the teacher is gone forever.") The procedure is somewhat parallel to that described by Kersh in Chapter 8. Flexible approaches to programing are not only necessary in English, they are appearing.

None of the grammar programs presently available distinguish themselves when measured by the recommendations of the Joint Committee on Programed Instruction (see Chapter 7 by Lumsdaine.) While all have teachers manuals, none report pretest-posttest gains on the final published edition of the program. Rogovin notes that the field tests of the program led to extensive revision.[10] Sullivan describes many revisions of his program (45), but the manual is not clear on whether revisions were made after the program returned from its final

[9] Personal communication.
[10] Personal communication.

trial.[11] The complex and precise data on conditions of use and variability of the student population are also missing. It remains for the purchaser to determine the effectiveness of the program with his own student population. The full promise of programing, as intended in Lumsdaine's definition and as described by him in Chapter 7, has not yet been achieved. Lest there be nothing to transfer, to take Meckel's advice seriously, studies of the effectiveness of these programs in altering student composition skills must await data demonstrating that the more limited objectives of the programs are indeed achieved. It is necessary to know to whom these programs teach their respective grammatical positions before testing their effects on composition.

Many science educators have noted that the overwhelming amount of factual material that could be taught and the constant shift in points of view are forcing science teachers into a position of teaching students how to "think like scientists" and out of the position of creating walking encyclopedias. As Mechner points out in Chapter 10, the objectives in science education are changing as a result of the participation of scientists in curriculum revision. Because of the revolution in language study, instructors in grammar presumably must adopt the same position; linguists will find their activities as well as their findings incorporated into the curriculum. This is foreshadowed in the NCTE statement: "The teaching of correctness in school and college courses must shift in emphasis from the laying down of negative rules to the development of positive insights. Instead of teaching rules for the avoidance of error, pupils must be taught to observe and understand the way in which their language operates today for all the various needs of communication" (33, p. 278). The objectives of such a proposed program would seem to be the creation of English speakers who "think like linguists," who recognize that the usage which is most frequent in any particular situation is permissible and advisable, and who have been instructed in methods of determining such usage.

In his summary of research in the teaching of English, Meckel comes to the following conclusion:

We need a five-dimensional model to describe American usage, a model that includes social, situational, methodological, temporal, and regional fac-

---

[11] The author here is not criticizing from an Olympian position. The teachers manual for her own program contains an explicit statement that revisions were made after the final student completed the final frame (39).

tors. For example, in marked contrast to the superficial characterization of an item of usage as grammatically correct or incorrect, a description of usage based upon linguistic atlas research would point out that either standard or nonstandard forms of language (social) may be used, on formal or informal occasions (situational), in either speech or writing (methodological), by either young speakers or older speakers (temporal), in either isolated rural areas or urban centers of culture, in any given dialect area (regional) (30, p. 977).

The instructional goal implied in this description falls neatly into the category of discrimination, or, as Gagné terms it in Chapter 2, "multiple discrimination." For some students, not only the discriminations but also the responses will have to be learned. Almost all students acquire the forms peculiar to written English in school; for some, formal usage in spoken English and even standard usage requires instruction. Because language is fluid, because today's argot is tomorrow's colloquialism, such a program would require a further objective: not only instruction in existing discriminations but also instruction in how to discriminate. Such an objective implies a far different set of instructional events and a different population of test items from that required by the more prescriptive approaches. At the least, the "tell-'em-test-'em" methods so common in present programing styles would have to give way to something more closely approximating "guided discovery," difficult as that term is to pin down tightly (see Chapter 8 by Kersh). In grammar, no such approach has been attempted. The prescriptive nature of the traditional grammar has apparently settled in prescriptive methods of instruction, even when the content has changed.

Had this section of this chapter been labeled as linguists would like to have it, the label should have been "language study." Here again, the potential contribution of programed instruction to English instruction has hardly been tapped. At experimental centers, rumors of programs in semantics can be heard. A program on the history of English does not exist. Standards of usage and stylistic devices have been touched upon in some programs mentioned below, but generally from the viewpoint of prescription rather than description. A large area of language study was called for by Francis: "the [English] program should contain substantial material on words—not with the aim of artificially increasing vocabulary, but with the idea of developing an understanding of the nature of meaning, the derivational and morphological relationships of words, and the reasons for vocabulary and semantic change. A thorough introduction to dictionaries belongs here" (14, p. 49). While no behavioral scientist would be quite certain whether "an understanding of the nature of meaning" were part of a program without further specification of the behaviors involved in such an "understanding" and further specification of the discriminations and generalizations involved in what was to be understood, this author's program is a small start in the direction of "derivational and morphological relationships of words," with an occasional bow to "semantic change." The program's objectives state that "a student who has mastered such a skill can inspect an unfamiliar word, divide it into plausible units, search his own vocabulary for words containing these units, arrive at an approximate definition of each unit, construct therefrom an approximate definition of the new word, and test this definition for its reasonableness in the context in which the word occurs" (27, p. 5). The skill is developed through presentation of large families of words derived from Latin and Greek morphemes, which the student analyzes for "family meaning" and general rules of word construction. Semantic change, the shift in meaning over the centuries, enters as a qualification on the wholesale use of word analysis as the sole clue to modern meanings. As with grammatical analysis, morphemic analysis is commonly a "tool" subject; its intent for most school systems is vocabulary improvement rather than understanding of the subject matter itself. One school system has reported dissatisfaction with the program because of the limited vocabulary acquired (8). As with grammar programs, the contribution of the technique of morphemic analysis to the more general goal of vocabulary development depends upon a program which does indeed teach the subject matter. Once a program has been located which unfailingly produces competent students, failure to transfer to the broader goal merely presents the school systems with the same curricular decision over again—is the knowledge per se worth the time?

The program, which spent four years as a research tool, was shaped by the realities of the classroom. The variability of eighth-grade students in ability and previous knowledge demanded a flexible program and suggested the introduction of diagnostic testing, multiple-tracking for fast and slow students, and the use of branching techniques within an over-all linear approach. As with the innovations mentioned above, the nature of the subject matter and the wide differences in students peculiar to English classes interacted with the prejudices of the programer to create new, if as yet not perfected, solutions to the problems of designing efficient materials. As in the studies reported by Hanson and Komoski in Chapter 14, the effectiveness of the program is sensitive to the "teacher variable." A "super-program" involving a great deal of teacher activity, developed by a teacher who knew the subject and the printed program, has produced high achievement and high motivation in classes of highly intelligent fourth and fifth graders (17). Under another pattern of use, the same printed program produced highly negative attitudes and low achievement in seventh, eighth, and ninth graders (8). A great deal remains to be learned, by English teachers and programers, about the "programing" in the broadest sense of instructional events involving programs in the narrowest sense (see Chapter 7 by Lumsdaine).

The study of language, as part of the English trio of language, literature, and composition, is a "body of knowledge" of the sort that even so critical an observer of programed instruction as Professor Kitzhaber will allow is amenable to programed instruction. That there are more spelling programs than grammar programs and more grammar programs than "language arts" programs is not necessarily related to "programability." It could be equally attributed to coolness on the part of the subject matter experts in one of the most humanistic disciplines to the notion of scientifically designed teaching materials, coupled with a perhaps not unwarranted distaste for those examplars of the methodology that have come to their attention. More undoubtedly will be done, and done better, if the experts in the subject can be persuaded to contribute to the development of curricular materials with the same ardor shown by the PSSC group and others in the sciences and mathematics.

Trends in Literature and Reading

While English teachers question whether grammar should be taught at all, there is no such question about literature. The "why" of literature, however, has been an area of conflict. Is the teacher of literature to teach literary "types" (e.g., the short story, the epic poem, etc.), great themes (e.g., the struggle against evil), the historical development of a national or world literature, or great books? Are individuals differing in ability and interest to be forced to read the same books, or should each student proceed at his own pace in his own direction? Loban suggested that a synthesis of all these approaches was most satisfying: "A sound program of literature for any semester or year of the secondary school could very well feature a multiple approach: several thematic units, some established classics, at least one modern great book or document, some study of types of literature, and a considerable amount of individual reading with teacher guidance" (23, p. 78).

A persistent current underlying most discussions of how to teach literature is an openly expressed objective: that the student will "love to read" and keep reading after leaving school. "The important consideration [in the selection of books for students] is the value of a selection to an individual student—the extent to which it contributes to his insights into his own behavior and that of others, and the extent to which it promotes in him a value system consonant with the ideals of a democratic society" (33, p. 195). Such an objective is indeed hard to measure. In many discussions of what literature students should be exposed to, there is a thinly veiled concern that any attempt to teach "knowledge about" literature may interfere with attainment of the more highly valued objective. The desire to transmit a cultural heritage and to teach literary types or the historical development of literature is seen as conflicting with the needs of individual students to "grow" at their own rates. Thorough knowledge of particular works conflicts in an overcrowded curriculum with broad but superficial acquaintance with a wide range of books. While few worry whether a student likes grammar and therefore he can be taught precisely what the teacher feels he ought to know, literature teachers are extremely sensitive to any variable which, it might be said, suppresses the rate of "reading responses." The result is a tendency to allow the student to read what he pleases, as long as the book is acceptable and as long as the book can be related to some "topic" of discussion in class.

The effects of such completely individualized curricula, which Meckel (30) dates as commencing in 1917, has led to a restlessness with the product and a movement for reform well characterized by Squire:

During the past year, William Riley Parker, Distinguished Service Professor of English at Indiana University, has publicly observed that 'Without the least exaggeration, I can say that, as a teacher of graduate students in

English, there is not one single assumption I can make about either knowledge or skill already acquired. I cannot assume knowledge of the simplest technical term or the simplest Bible story or myth or fairy tale or piece of children's literature. . . . Is there no basic knowledge about English which college majors must learn during their undergraduate years if they are to succeed in graduate school? Is there no basic knowledge about English which students should learn in our high schools? Is there nothing which all should share in the elementary school? We talk much about presenting our common heritage in literature, but the commonness of the heritage seems singularly uncertain if Parker's observation can be supported by others. Somewhere between the Scylla of restrictive uniformity in literary programs and the Charybdis of a permissive anarchy, the Nation's English programs must find their way (43, p. 35).

The word *articulation* occurs with high frequency in recent discussions of the English curriculum (34, 43). It is of vital interest to programers contemplating a plunge into literature. A planned sequence of instruction leads to a specification of entering behavior which does not begin at zero—the implication of Parker's blast directed at his randomly educated students. While many programing concerns will undoubtedly produce a program in poetry reading (a few already exist), the day will arrive when someone will have to produce the second program, based on the assumption that the first poem is available in the student's memory for comparison with the new learning. The concept of "modular" programing—of small units which can be fitted into the teacher's over-all plan at her option—is nowhere more questionable than in the teaching of literature. The student will surely revolt if his third encounter with Shakespeare is a third "introduction" to Shakespeare. While techniques of branching have been successfully used to take account of individual differences in previous knowledge (see Chapter 4 by Klaus and 28), there is an obvious economic limit to such techniques. Taking account of a myriad of varying depths of exposure to books randomly selected is simply not feasible. And yet the assumption of no previous knowledge is not only obviously invalid but is also severely restrictive of a program's content.

Articulation will arise from two separate sources which may not be in complete agreement with each other. One developmental sequence is already in preparation and about to burst on the market from a venturesome publisher. Harcourt, Brace and World has prepared a series of programs to accompany its series of readers.[12] Other pub-

---

[12] Personal communication from J. M. Reid.

lishers may follow suit. Squire's comments, quoted above, were directed to a committee of Project English, a group sponsored by the Office of Education and dedicated to the improvement of English instruction (19). Among the Project's activities are curriculum study centers. From these centers recommendations for some standardization of the English curriculum are expected. Whatever the final source of articulation, there can be no doubt that programs in literature will be more literate if the programer can assume that his students have read a book before.

Perhaps of all fields, literature as a subject will contribute most strongly to the development of programing technology in the broadest sense. Although Finn (12) has castigated the literary tradition for its negativism toward technology in education, Meckel asked, "How can concepts of characterization, plot, and style be effectively taught through the use of supplemental aids such as recordings and films?" (30, p. 1,000), and the Project English conference suggested studying "the use of audiovisual aids, field trips, and other devices to motivate the student uninterested in English" (44, p. 115). As part of the proposed curriculum, a Commission of the NCTE recommended the use of records, films, TV shows, and so forth as adjuncts to the study of literature (33). In this author's opinion, the kind of objectives established for instruction in literature will require a new look at the media employed in present-day programs. The book with the holes in its sentences will have to be integrated with films in which, given appropriate background for comprehending the drama, the response is a lump in the throat (and the film is worked on until it achieves its objective), with tapes in which the response is discrimination between appropriate and inappropriate renderings of a poem (and such tapes are programed—or sequenced—so that each student with the requisite entering skills achieves the discrimination). There has been talk of such integration. The final objective of such a program might be the establishment of the printed word as a sufficient stimulus for "hearing the sound of a poem" or "visualizing the stage business in a play." The printed word may be the terminal stimulus, but it is not necessarily the most efficient (or even effective) transitional stimulus or training technique. English instructors have given programers a green light for the full use of every audiovisual device and instructional aid, although the objective of the instruction is to be literate behavior without such props.

Among the goals of reading instruction at the high school and college level is the production of critical or evaluative readers. The "students should learn to ask who is talking and why and on what authority. It is imperative that they note whether ideas follow in logical sequence or whether they contradict one another; whether inferences are sound and generalizations are backed up by evidence. It is important also that they recognize the emotional power of words and the techniques of the propagandist. . . . Evaluation of literary materials often involves still another kind of critical judgment—the application of standards of literary appreciation to works under consideration" (33, p. 404). This is a large order. It is easily labeled within the categories of behavior listed by Gagné in Chapter 2; obviously it is a discrimination task following the acquisition of principles and class concepts. The behavior is clear; it is the definition of the stimulus conditions under which the behavior occurs which brings the programer up short. What, for instance, is the population of "unsound inferences"? By judicious sampling of this population, the programer might expect to lead the student to recognize any instance of the class. If the student is taught to discriminate examples drawn from politics, for instance, will the critical behavior transfer to recognition of unsound inferences in a field such as popular magazine advice on the rearing of children based on so-called "scientific research"? Professional journals in almost any discipline provide instances of one subject matter expert criticizing the unsound inferences of another, many of which inferences are beyond the ken of the uninitiated. As was mentioned earlier (p. 547), the problems of teaching a "contentless skill" are inherent in many of the objectives which English instructors have identified for themselves. Critical reading is, as is composition, one of those "contentless skills," the limits of which are difficult to define. No student can be expected to read critically material he cannot even comprehend. Presumably, however, the skill which he has been taught will be applied to new subjects as he learns to comprehend them. If it does not, he cannot be said to have fully attained the skill. The programer is limited to instances of "unsound inferences" that, at any particular point in the student's career, fall within the student's understanding; yet the skill to be taught may be said to subsume the total population of unsound inferences, some of which even the programer cannot comprehend.

In a real sense, a program which has successfully achieved its objectives in an area such as this is not legitimately measurable in terms of transfer to new situations. A student has attained the objectives or he has not. A student who recognizes an unsound inference, who has attained that terminal behavior, should be capable of recognizing *any* unsound inference, provided he can comprehend the text. A student who can recognize the emotional appeal of advertising techniques should be equally capable of recognizing the emotional content of a patriotic speech, even though he chooses to agree with the latter.[13] To teach such a skill successfully, then, the programer must have specified the characteristics of the "universe" of unsound inferences or emotional loadings and provided for his student sufficient practice to cause the student to behave appropriately when confronted with a new member of this class. This requires a wise programer indeed.

Of those experimental programs that have attempted to reach such an objective in any one of the skills mentioned in the above quote, many exhibit a common failing. The programs teach a vocabulary rather than a skill, a set of labels attached to a few limited examples rather than a set of discriminations between widely ranging examples (e.g., of good and bad inference). That textbooks and teachers have done the same in the past is no excuse. To achieve any of the objectives set out in the quotation, what is required is a set of examples which sample the range of the class and which are graded for difficulty. Klaus (21) has demonstrated with a few students that art judgment could be so taught, provided the initial examples of good and bad art are obvious and the judgments were gradually made more and more difficult. In the case of the critical and evaluative skills in literature, not the technology of designing frames but the technology of task analysis is crucial.

Trends in Composition

The temptation is great to state that there are no trends in the programing of composition and dismiss this section at once. There are

---

[13] Such an instance occurred while the author was testing an experimental program in identification of propaganda techniques. One student who had successfully "unloaded" the well-known biases of a national news magazine under programed guidance offered the unsolicited statement that her social studies text was equally biased. The consequences of an effective critical reading program may not be acceptable to some members of the tax-paying public!

no composition programs, if composition is taken in the usual academic sense of a broad skill in writing lengthy manuscripts. If the subject is approached from another point of view, that of the English teacher confronted with a freshman composition, quite the opposite can be concluded. Of those "errors" generally granted a dose of red ink, many are the subjects of programs. Hendershot (18) listed 17 spelling programs, some not yet available, aimed at all educational levels. Punctuation runs a close second to spelling. The usage sections of the grammar programs might also be included, since incorrect usage elicits red ink. Of eight categories listed by Professor Kitzhaber in his report on freshman English at Dartmouth (20, p. 43), three causes for disapproval are at least somewhat programed: grammar, punctuation and mechanics, and misspelling. For the other categories in which errors fall—words, sentences, paragraphs, material, and focus—no significant amount of programed material exists.

"There is a good reason why spelling should lend itself to programing. The goal of instruction in spelling can be clearly and unequivocally specified: the student is to be taught to spell a given word in only one way. The goal is correctness according to a rigid standard. The student's success or lack of it can be easily determined: the word is rightly spelled or it is not. No element of personal judgment enters in" (20, p. 88). Programers apparently have agreed with Kitzhaber, if the nose count of programs indicates what they think they can do well.

An alternative explanation suggests itself: while the teacher confronted with a student's composition is allowed to express his preferences in red ink privately, a program is a public document and hence assailable. Given the controversies about what is and what is not good writing (see pp. 548-49 of this chapter), a programer without tenure might reasonably be shy about teaching students to do it *his* preferred way. A daring program, already drawing darts from the staid, is Scott Parry's *Improving Your Written Communications* (35). A chatty frontal attack on overstuffed language in business communications, the program recommends practices which some will find questionable, such as "earthy colloquialisms." By implication, the sentence, "We'll let our slide rule boys tackle this toughie" is preferable to "We plan to have our engineering staff take up this problem." The program is not likely to be used by English teachers instructing high school students

Klaus[14] has suggested a model for the teaching of composition in a discussion of a program on "creative writing." The student's first activity is judging sentences along the dimensions of creativity. When at the end of a graded sequence of examples, his judgments become sufficiently acute, he is confronted with "bad" sentences to be edited. Capable now of judging good and bad, the student knows when he has "groped to," a process which may require several revisions of the given sentence before he accepts his version. As a final examination, the student confronts a bit of the world about which he must say something "creative." He gropes. He may reject three or four formulations before he quits, satisfied that he has reached his goal. The situation is precisely that which has led many people to say that programed instruction cannot teach composition or creativity because programing is "only good for" questions to which there is one right answer. In Klaus's procedure, not only are there multiple right answers, but the right answer that the student will arrive at is unpredictable. The question is a "probe," a term defined by Skinner as a question the answer to which is unknown to the asker (41, p. 255). It can only be confirmed by the instructor after it has occurred, based on the instructor's discriminations, and these discriminations can be taught to the student, making him independent of the instructor.

The goals of a composition program are considerably different from the goals of a program aimed at automatic production of "acceptable" English, as discussed on page 561. As noted above by Ciardi, the written word may be edited. The polish expected in sentence structure and diction when the communication is in writing is considerably above that expected in extemporaneous speech. Neither speed nor automaticity is necessary; persistence ("Ideally, there can be no real end to that groping. To reread is to revise" [7, p. 10]) and fine discriminations or judgment are. Although English teachers will groan at the analogy, the process of learning to write resembles more closely than many school subjects the process of shaping according to which a pigeon is led to perform complex sequences of behavior through successive approximations to the final desired performance. Pigeons, as many a programer has forgotten, make "mistakes" in the sense that their behavior

---

[14] Personal communication, 1963. See also Klaus (21).

does not operate the reinforcement mechanism. But they continue to behave, to respond, until the payoff is delivered. As the behavior approaches efficiency, the rules are changed to more difficult requirements. If composition were efficiently programed, the reading to which the student was being exposed would always be ahead of the writing that was required of him, so that the discriminations between "right" and "wrong" or "good" and "bad" were being taught before the student had a chance to practice the latter member of each pair. The payoff mechanism should operate, and operate reliably, at the point at which the student decides to stop editing what he has written. Later is too late. The common saying that the teacher is the only efficient teaching machine for teaching composition because the discriminations involved are too difficult to be contained in a program and the behavior too variable to be predicted or controlled is false. The teacher is a very inefficient teaching machine. Only the student can deliver the immediate reinforcement that his own progress demands.

The discriminations the student learns to make in such a procedure are no better than the discriminations the programer makes, but is this not equally true of any other form of instruction? A program of this type could teach students to prefer pompous, overblown prose (as some college instructors accuse high school teachers of doing), "earthy colloquialisms," outmoded usage, or any other style, and to dutifully edit their sentences until they achieve what they have been taught to recognize as acceptable. If programed instruction can contribute significantly to the attainment of the composition teacher's objectives, as this author insists it can, its success or failure will hang upon the clear statement of linguistically sound objectives to be achieved. The program can be no better than the subject matter expert who defines its goals.

References

1. Bloomfield, M. W., and Newmark, L. *A Linguistic Introduction to the History of English.* New York: Alfred A. Knopf, 1963.
2. Blumenthal, J. *English 2600.* New York: Harcourt, Brace and World, 1960.
3. Briggs, F. A., and Branson, R. K. "Programs in the Language Arts: Available and Desirable." *Trends in Programmed Instruction.* (Edited by G. D. Ofiesh and W. C. Meierhenry.) Washington, D.C.: National

Education Association and National Society for Programmed Instruction, 1964. pp. 75-77.

4. Carroll, J. B. "Language Development in Children." *Psycholinguistics: A Book of Readings.* (Edited by S. Saporta.) New York: Holt, Rinehart & Winston, 1963. pp. 331-45.

5. Center for Programed Instruction. *Programs, '63: A Guide to Programed Instructional Materials.* U.S. Department of Health, Education, and Welfare, Office of Education. Washington, D.C.: Government Printing Office, 1963.

6. Chomsky, N. *Syntactic Structures.* The Hague, Netherlands: Mouton & Co., 1957.

7. Ciardi, J. "On Writing and Bad Writing." *Saturday Review,* December 15, 1962. pp. 10-12.

8. Cincinnati Public Schools, Department of Instruction. *Words: An Evaluation of a Programed Course in Vocabulary Development in the Cincinnati Public Schools.* Cincinnati: Division of Evaluation Services, Department of Instruction, 1963.

9. Diederich, P. B. *The Problem of Grading Essays.* Adapted from a paper presented to the College Testing Conference, Mount Union College, Alliance, Ohio, February 15, 1957. (Mimeo.)

10. Diederich, P. B.; French, J. W.; and Carlton, S. T. *Factors in Judgments of Writing Ability.* Research Bulletin Series RB-61-15. Princeton, N.J.: Educational Testing Service, 1961. (Mimeo.)

11. Evans, J. L. *Multiple-Choice Discrimination Programming.* Paper read at American Psychological Association Convention, New York, September 1961.

12. Finn, J. D. "The Tradition in the Iron Mask." *Audiovisual Instruction* 6: 238-43; June 1961.

13. Flanagan, J. C. "Implications of Project Talent for Research in the Teaching of English." *Needed Research in the Teaching of English.* Cooperative Research Monograph No. 11, OE-30010. Washington, D.C.: Office of Education, U.S. Department of Health, Education, and Welfare, 1963. pp. 80-97.

14. Francis, W. N. "The Study of Language in English Teaching." *Needed Research in the Teaching of English.* Cooperative Research Monograph No. 11, OE-30010. Washington, D.C.: Office of Education, U.S. Department of Health, Education, and Welfare, 1963. pp. 45-51.

15. Fries, C. C. *The Structure of English* New York: Harcourt, Brace and Co., 1952.

16. Glaser, R. "Instructional Technology and the Measurement of Learning Outcomes: Some Questions." *American Psychologist* 18: 519-21; August 1963.

17. Gotkin, L. G., and Goldstein, L. S. "Programed Instruction in the Schools: Innovation and Innovator." *Innovation in Education.* (Edited

by M. B. Miles.) New York: Bureau of Publications, Teachers College, Columbia University, 1964. pp. 231, 248.

18. Hendershot, C. H. *Programmed Learning: A Bibliography of Programs and Presentation Devices.* University Center, Mich.: Delta College, 1963.

19. Hook, J. N. "The Importance of the Conference to Project English." *Needed Research in the Teaching of English.* Cooperative Research Monograph No. 11, OE-30010. Washington, D.C.: Office of Education, U.S. Department of Health, Education, and Welfare, 1963. pp. 5-9.

20. Kitzhaber, A. R. *Themes, Theories, and Therapy: The Teaching of Writing in College.* New York: McGraw-Hill Book Co., 1963.

21. Klaus, D. J. "Programming the Impossible." *Trends in Programmed Instruction.* (Edited by G. D. Ofiesh and W. C. Meierhenry.) Washington, D.C.: National Education Association and National Society for Programmed Instruction, 1964. pp. 19-23.

22. Lewis, J. S., and Sisk, J. C. *Teaching English 7-12.* New York: American Book Co., 1963.

23. Loban, W. "Teaching Literature: A Multiple Approach." *English Journal* 45: 75-78; February 1956.

24. Lumsdaine, A. A. "Educational Technology, Programmed Learning, and Instructional Science." *The Psychology of Learning as Bearing on Educational Practice.* Sixty-Third Yearbook, National Society for the Study of Education. Chicago: University of Chicago Press, 1964. pp. 371-401.

25. Lysaught, J., and Williams, C. *A Guide to Programmed Instruction.* New York: John Wiley & Sons, 1962.

26. Markle, S. M. "Review of English 2600." *Contemporary Psychology* 6: 133-36; April 1961.

27. Markle, S. M. *Words: A Programed Course in Vocabulary Development, Teachers' Manual.* Chicago: Science Research Associates, 1962.

28. Markle, S. M. "The Lowest Common Denominator: A Persistent Problem in Programing." *Programed Instruction* 2: 4-5; February 1963.

29. Markle, S. M., and Bossone, R. M. "Programed Materials: A Teaching Aid." *Clearinghouse* 38: 148-50; November 1963.

30. Meckel, H. C. "Research on Teaching Composition and Literature." *Handbook of Research on Teaching.* (Edited by N. L. Gage.) Chicago: Rand McNally & Co., 1963. pp. 966-1,006.

31. Miller, G. A. "Some Psychological Studies of Grammar." *American Psychologist* 17: 748-61; November 1962.

32. Miller, G. A., and Isard, S. "Some Perceptual Consequences of Linguistic Rules." *Journal of Verbal Learning and Verbal Behavior* 2: 217-27; September 1963.

33. National Council of Teachers of English. *The English Language Arts.* New York: Appleton-Century-Crofts, 1952.

34. National Council of Teachers of English. *The National Interest and the Teaching of English.* Champaign, Ill.: National Council of Teachers of English, 1961.
35. Parry, S. *Improving Your Written Communications.* New York: Lord Products, 1963.
36. Philippine Center for Language Study. *Teacher's Guide for English in Grade I.* Manila, Philippines: Bureau of Public Schools and Philippine Center for Language Study, 1961.
37. Porter, D. "The Behavioral Repertoire of Writing." *College Composition and Communication* 13: 1-4; October 1962.
38. Roberts, P. *English Sentences.* New York: Harcourt, Brace and World, 1962.
39. Rogovin, S. *Modern English Sentence Structure.* New York: Random House, 1964.
40. Saporta, S., editor. *Psycholinguistics: A Book of Readings.* New York: Holt, Rinehart & Winston, 1963.
41. Skinner, B. F. *Verbal Behavior.* New York: Appleton-Century-Crofts, 1957.
42. Sledd, J., and Ebbitt, W. R. *Dictionaries and That Dictionary.* Chicago: Scott, Foresman & Co., 1962.
43. Squire, J. R. " 'Multilevel' Research in English: Imperatives for the Sixties." *Needed Research in the Teaching of English.* Cooperative Research Monograph No. 11, OE-30010. Washington, D.C.: Office of Education, U.S. Department of Health, Education, and Welfare, 1963. pp. 26-44.
44. Steinberg, E. R., editor. *Needed Research in the Teaching of English.* Cooperative Research Monograph No. 11, OE-30010. Washington, D.C.: Office of Education, U.S. Department of Health, Education, and Welfare, 1963.
45. Sullivan, M. W. *Programmed English, Teachers Manual.* New York: Macmillan Co., 1963.

HARLAN LANE
University of Michigan

Programed Learning of a
Second Language*

The cardinal requirement of programing, "specify the terminal behaviors," nowhere has had a more salutary effect on educational technology than in the area of second-language learning. Although language pedagogy turned to linguistic science for these specifications over two decades ago, the later arrival of programed instruction emphasized and placed a new perspective on the contribution of descriptive linguistics. The new emphasis is that linguistic specifications are a *sine qua non* for the conditioning enterprise; they codify group norms for verbal behavior in the relevant language community and, therefore, provide the programer with criteria for acceptable forms and sequences of responses. The new perspective is that a linguistic analysis of terminal behaviors is not a prescription for second-language learning; this is the task of the programer.

The good fortune of the language programer (and student) in finding an entire discipline devoted to the systematic specification of terminal behaviors is overreached by an even greater good fortune: the techniques of the laboratory analysis and control of behavior, upon which

* The preparation of this article and certain of the experiments reported herein were supported in part by a contract with the Language Development Section, U.S. Office of Education. I am indebted to F. R. Morton and A. B. Gaarder, who respectively inspired and financed my interest in second-language learning, and to D. M. Brethower, G. L. Geis, and S. Sapon, for helpful suggestions concerning this article.

programing is based, are more literally applicable to the conditioning of second-language behavior than to most of the other repertoires that programing has confronted. The objectives of most programs are restricted to changing the written, verbal behavior of a student in response to textual stimuli. The prerequisite motor responses and discriminations among orthographic stimuli already have been conditioned and are taken for granted. The behaviors involved in reading and understanding English and in writing at least a "reasonable" answer are also assumed. As Gilbert has put it: "Our student is not a master of the subject because he cannot make the mastery responses on the right occasions, not because he is unable to make those responses at all. . . . The responses of mastery are there. . ." (24, p. 11). This type of verbal conditioning, involving a restructuring of the student's highly articulate first-language repertoires, has a limited resemblance to laboratory research on the control of behavior. Transitional behavior affected by shifting contingencies of reinforcement, patterns of discriminative stimuli, or both, is little studied and poorly understood in comparison with the shaping, maintenance, and extinction of behavior in initially naïve organisms.

The programing task of restructuring an extant verbal repertoire may be contrasted to that of conditioning second-language fluency. In the latter case, there is nothing extrapolative in the application of laboratory techniques and nothing metaphorical in the use of concepts gained from a functional analysis of behavior in the laboratory. New discriminations (auditory, textual) must be conditioned, new forms of response (vocal, written) must be differentiated, concurrent responses of differing topography each must be brought under the control of appropriate discriminative stimuli, novel chains of topographically novel responses must be established, and so forth. These behaviors must be conditioned largely *de novo*, although it is never possible, as this chapter will point out, to overlook sources of interference and enhancement from the first-language repertoires.

Two other developments augur well for the success of second-language programing. The interest of the communication sciences in verbal, especially vocal, behavior has led to a greater sophistication and instrumental capability in describing and analyzing the vocal response than is available for any other behavior (18). These disciplines have also contributed significant techniques and data toward an understanding of the listener's behavior as well as of the speaker's (53). Another source of methods and findings for the control of verbal behavior is less well developed, but bound to have equal or greater impact on language pedagogy; this source is the rapidly growing discipline of psycholinguistics (88).

If second-language programing is aided by these four "sources of strength," it is also obstructed by four countervailing antecedents in language pedagogy: an unsuitable model of learning, undue emphasis on language aptitude, subjective evaluation of student performance, and incompetent classroom research.

The language teacher has operated frankly with a sunburn model of learning (36), and his techniques are as inefficient as this characterization of learning is inappropriate. The teacher, prime source of knowledge and light (and, occasionally, heat), "exposes" students to the language and its principles. He is aided in this endeavor by the language laboratory, now commonplace in secondary education (64), which also exposes the students to the material in limited doses; 20 minutes is generally considered the maximum safe exposure in one treatment. When classroom practice permits active participation by the student at all, it is usually in the form of repetitive drills which are presumed to "fix" or "stamp in" the material through repetition alone. The "brighter" students "soak up" the material and become "enlightened." Dull students, who fail to learn, are simply not "sensitive" or "receptive."

The remarkable plasticity of behavior is ignored by this model. Instead of acknowledging that the inadequacies of the students are the product of inadequate technique, and then spending all effort to improve technique, teachers often assign the key role in language learning to ability or endowment, and thus place the process beyond their control—and responsibility. The construct "language aptitude" is the *deus ex machina* that spares the language-learning story its tragic ending. In constructing so-called aptitude tests, psychologists have not helped to refocus attention on the critical variables, the manipulable variables, in language learning. Indeed, since it is invariably true that the student who takes the test is assigned an aptitude score, the presence of the score lends credence to the reality of aptitudes. This gambit has as much practical effect as lifting oneself by one's own bootstraps and leaves the language teacher in about the stance implied. The naïve assumption that aptitude tests measure innate capacity is no longer acceptable. As one noted student of individual differences points out, "It should be obvious that all psychological tests measure the individual's current behavior, which inevitably reflects the influence of prior learning" (1, p. 425). The task of the language teacher or programer is to destroy the test-retest reliability of language aptitude tests.

Evaluations of pedagogical techniques in second-language learning are most often grossly multidimensional, idiosyncratic, and subjective. As Sapon has put it, "The objectives of foreign language study still include such goals as understanding the foreign culture, appreciating the great works of literature in the language, increasing English vocabulary, learning about grammar—Latin even taught us how to think!"[1] The merit of multiple and complex objectives such as these is that the inadequacy of language pedagogy in attaining them cannot be assessed; thus, "achievement" in these areas may be offered as mitigating the limited effect of the teacher in conditioning the language behaviors themselves. Even when the objectives are somewhat more circumscribed, as "a spoken command of the language," the criteria for an acceptable response include such notions as phonetic accuracy, response latency, intonational accuracy, appropriateness of vocabulary, richness of vocabulary, use of idioms, propriety of style, etc. Only rarely has the criterion behavior been adequately specified, and even under those circumstances, the assessment device usually involves a panel of judges and is heir to the traditional problems of interjudge and intrajudge reliability and validity.

Prior research on second-language learning[2] has been, with few exceptions, seriously inadequate. Carroll seems to damn it all, in an extensive survey of research in this area, by concluding with the faint praise: "It is clearly within the realm of possibility that the results of such research could make language teaching more effectve and efficient" (13, p. 1094).

The inadequacies of the research are multiple. "Whereas psychologists perform experiments with insufficient relevance to foreign language teaching, members of the foreign language teaching profession perform studies with insufficient experimental rigor" (13, p. 1,066).

---

[1] Personal communication from S. M. Sapon, 1963.
[2] See Carroll (13), Nostrand (71), and Pimsleur (72).

Even when relevance and rigor have prevailed, studies in this area have suffered the many evils of comparison-group designs (see 35). Furthermore, the comparison is usually among the effects of complex experimental treatments, many-faceted and extending over many months, evaluated all too often either anecdotally or by tests of doubtful validity and reliability. These properties of the experimental method are in part the result of competing pedagogical and research objectives in the classroom setting. As a consequence, the findings of even the most carefully executed studies have little generality. No wonder that Carroll finds no research basis for educational policy on foreign language teaching: "However sympathetic we may be to [current] recommendations, they are often based on assumptions about which the most charitable thing to say is that they have not been proven" (10, p. 137).

The character of current second-language programing reflects these several antecedents. Many programs draw extensively from the findings of linguistics, both in specifying the terminal behaviors and in determining sequencing based on a contrastive analysis of the student's first and second languages. A few have systematically applied laboratory techniques for the control of behavior. A lesser number reveal the impress of findings in the communication sciences, especially in acoustic phonetics; psycholinguistics has had little impact as yet. Finally, many programing efforts have inherited the tradition of educational research in language pedagogy. The program is admixed with arbitrary amounts of classroom and language-laboratory instruction and drill, and the effects of the complex enterprise are compared in cursory fashion with those of more traditional methods. The failure to provide a detailed account of the terminal repertoires actually attained by students who have completed the second-language program is almost universal.

The present discussion of the basic research underpinnings and applied findings in second-language programing proceeds in terms of a functional analysis of verbal behavior (92). The discussion is *behavioral*, because the objective of second-language programing is to condition certain terminal behaviors (largely spoken and written); the discussion draws heavily on a *functional analysis*, because it is this analysis which describes the relations between the antecedents and consequences of behavior and the behavior itself; these controlling relations must be known if effective and efficient second-language learning is to be arranged.

A functional analysis of the terminal behaviors for a second-language program will usefully distinguish between *formal* repertoires, in which there is a point-to-point correspondence between stimulus and response, and *thematic* repertoires, in which responses are controlled by common sets of variables but without formal correspondences (93). The student (or child) who has learned only to imitate, read, and copy in a new language has acquired purely formal repertoires; the topography of his behavior in each case shows a point-to-point correspondence to the form of the stimulus conditions. However, he is as yet unable to respond appropriately to the nature of the stimulus conditions, and this lack of thematic repertoires leaves him unprepared to join the verbal community. In sum, he knows *how* to say things, but he does not know *what* to say. Talking birds, mimics, typists, and stenographers may earn their keep by purely formal repertoires, but most adult verbal behavior reflects both formal and thematic sources of strength. Thus, the terminal behavior of the student will be determined phonetically (or orthographically) by the audience and thematically by the environmental conditions.

The distinction between the two repertoires may be sharpened by noting that a minimal unit of behavior may be identified for a purely formal repertoire, and formal repertoires may therefore be extended readily to new stimuli. The minimal unit may be the phoneme or the grapheme, or it may be even more fragmentary. Once these stimulus-response units are made available through the conditioning of a formal repertoire, the student can respond adequately to novel stimuli by responding piecemeal—that is, with a series of unit responses never before arranged in that order. For example, minimal command of the formal repertoire involved in reading English text permits a passable attempt at, say, "marmoset," but nothing in the thematic repertoires that the student may have acquired previously enables him to say "marmoset" in the presence of marmosets, to make statements about marmosets, and so forth. The ability of formal repertoires to be extended to new stimuli is predicated on the availability of minimal units which require, in turn, the point-to-point correspondence of stimulus and response that characterizes these repertoires.

Formal Repertoires

The formal repertoires involved in second-language learning may be subdivided according to whether the stimulus and the response are each written or spoken. The distinction is important not only because the two classes of stimuli have different modalities and the two classes of responses have different topographies but also because the four possible functional relations have different dynamic properties. When both stimulus and response are spoken, the behavior is termed *echoic;* the name implies the point-to-point acoustic correspondence which characterizes this repertoire. In *transcription,* both stimulus and response are written. In *textual* behavior, a spoken response is controlled by a written stimulus. In *dictation,* the stimulus is spoken; the response, written. In each of the first two formal classes, the stimulus and the response have similar form, acoustic or visual, but in all four classes it is possible to predict the response given the stimulus or to infer the nature of the stimulus if the response is known; this is another way of stating the point-to-point correspondence between stimulus and response that defines a formal repertoire.

Each of the four formal repertoires obviously requires that the student make different responses to physically different stimuli; it is perhaps less obvious that he must make the same response to different stimuli more often; different fonts of type typically evoke the same textual behavior, differing rates of speaking the same transcriptions, and so forth. When the properties of responding change following a change in the stimulus, we speak of stimulus discrimination; to the degree that responding remains invariant under this change, we speak of stimulus generalization. The first requirement of a formal repertoire, then, concerns stimulus control: there must be generalization within arbitrarily defined classes of stimuli and discriminations between these classes. The second requirement concerns the properties of responding: response topography must show small, systematic variation within arbitrarily defined classes and large and abrupt changes from one class to the next. The third requirement of a formal repertoire concerns the coordination of changes in the stimulus with changes in the response. To take an example from a textual repertoire in English, in order to read the pair of words "pin pan," these requirements must be met: (a) The orthographic symbol "i" must be visually discriminated from "a," etc., but generalized with "*i*," "I," and that letter in various type fonts; similar requirements apply to "a" and to the other letters. (b) Response topography must include distinct response classes such as [pʰ], [ɪ], and [æ], but there is also a range of permissible and necessary variation within each class; thus, the reading of "pin" may range from [pʰɪn] to [pʰɪːn] or to [pɪn]. (c) [pʰ] must occur in the presence of initial "p," [ɪ] in the presence of "i," and so forth. Even if the letters "i" and "a" are *discriminated* and the responses [ɪ] and [æ] are *differentiated*, without the *coordination* required, the textual behavior would be incorrect (e.g., [pʰæn - pʰɪn]).

Before considering each of the four formal repertoires, the sections that follow describe some recent experiments on discrimination, differentiation, and coordination. Laboratory research on these behavioral processes provides methods and findings that may be used to arrange their acquisition in second-language programing.

Discrimination Learning and Transfer: The acquisition and maintenance of stimulus discriminations have been studied extensively with human and infrahuman organisms in the psychological laboratory. These experiments involve most often stimuli that are synthesized in the laboratory and varied along a single dimension, such as pure tone frequency. Controlled experiments on discrimination learning with synthetic stimuli varying in several dimensions, or with stimuli from "natural language" (spoken or written), are rare. A description of four representative experiments will illustrate methods and findings that are relevant to the programing of second-language discriminations involved in the formal repertoires.

In a series of experiments on discrimination learning with speech stimuli in a second language, Lane (41) has observed extremely rapid acquisition of differential stimulus control, suggesting the transfer of the subject's first-language discriminations. When a Spanish phoneme was presented as S^D (a stimulus correlated with reinforcement for responding), and a variety of English approximations were presented as S^Δ's (correlated with nonreinforcement), the subjects stopped responding to S^Δ's after the first few presentations. Indeed, most of the errors in learning were due to "overdiscriminating," that is, failing to respond to the allophonic variants of S^D throughout the sequence of stimuli. In one study, a self-instruction program was prepared to teach discriminations among the vowels and consonants of Spanish. The program was subdivided into 14 frames, each of which included allophones of a particular Spanish phoneme (S^D) and those of other English and Spanish phonemes (S^Δ's). The 14 frames as well as the 60 stimuli within each frame were sequenced according to a tentative schedule of difficulty for the English-speaking student. When the subject responded (button-press) to an S^D or failed to respond to an S^Δ during the 4-second interstimulus interval, a point was added to a counter in front of him. Failure to respond to S^D, or a response to an S^Δ, cost him a point. Figure 1 shows that most of the frames in this program were mastered to a criterion of eight or less errors in a single trial. These data and others reported suggest that discrimination learning among the sounds of a second language, at least one within the same

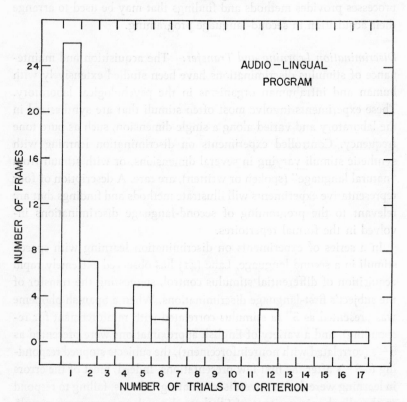

FIGURE 1. *Discrimination learning of Spanish phonemes with an audiolingual program. The average number of frames in which three subjects reached criterion within 1 through 17 trials (from 41).*

family as the subject's native language, may be expected to proceed quite rapidly when conditions are optimized because the subject transfers first-language discriminations to the new task. Additional support for this conclusion was obtained when the program described above was administered without reinforcement both before (pretest) and after (posttest) programed learning. For each of the 14 frames, Figure 2

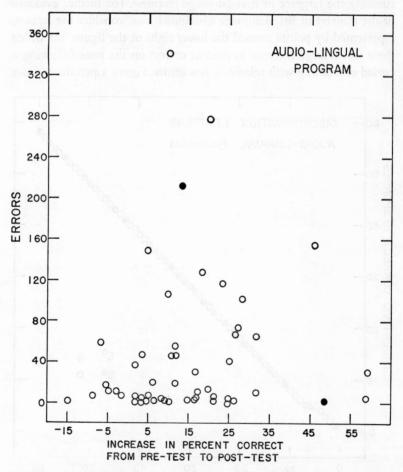

FIGURE 2. *Discrimination learning with an audiolingual program. For each of 14 frames, the number of errors made during discrimination training is plotted against the percent increase in correct responses from a pretest to a posttest, in which the program was administered without reinforcement (from 41).*

shows the number of errors made during programed learning plotted against the percent increase in correct responses from the pretest to the posttest. There are some frames in which the increase in percent correct on the tests is small and so is the number of errors during programed learning. These frames, represented by points at the lower left of Figure 2, evidenced a high baseline of discrimination, which is presumably the largesse of first-language learning. For further evidence of the transfer of first-language discriminations, consider the frames, represented by points toward the lower right of the figure, for which there was a *large* increase in percent correct on the tests following a period of learning with relatively few errors. Figure 3 permits a closer

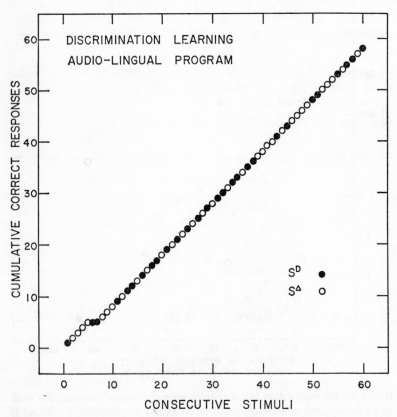

FIGURE 3. *Abrupt discrimination learning during one frame of an audio-lingual program in Spanish. Cumulative correct responses to consecutive stimuli by one S (from 41).*

look at the time-course of discrimination learning during one of these frames (the one showing a 47 percent increase in accuracy). This graph of cumulative correct responses to successive stimuli shows that the subject responded to the first S^D (as instructed), then failed to respond to the next two presentations of S^D, and responded correctly thereafter. The abrupt increase to near-perfect performance after but a few errors represents the transfer rather than the acquisition of a discrimination; it has been called "concept attainment" in other quarters. The transfer of first-language discriminations reflected by the function in Figure 3 may be contrasted with the more rare case of genuine acquisition of a speech discrimination, shown by the cumulative curve in Figure 4, obtained from the same subject. This graph corresponds to the filled circle toward the top of Figure 2: the numerous errors during discrimination learning are evident, but they were not in vain, for the subject's posttest revealed a 15 percent increase in accuracy. In this frame, which involved the trilled Spanish /r̃/ in intervocalic position as S^D and the general American /r̃/ in that position as S^Δ, the more gradual development of differential stimulus control that is normally associated with discrimination learning is evident.

Suppes and others (97) have performed several studies of discrimination among Russian phonemes and have examined the fit of mathematical models to the observed time-course of discrimination learning. In one study, a basic list of Russian syllables was constructed with 32 initial consonant phonemes and 5 vowels. The 144 syllables were grouped into contrasting pairs, differing only in the initial consonant. Twenty-six consonant-vowel (CV) contrasts were selected, and each was presented in four permutations: $C_1V_1:C_2V_2$; $C_2V_2:C_1V_1$; C_1V_1: C_1V_1; and $C_2V_2:C_2V_2$. The list of 104 contrast pairs was recorded in random order by a linguist and presented for one-half hour daily, on five days, to individual subjects for judgments of same or different. Incorrect responses were followed by a flash of light. A contrastive analysis of English and Russian and some pilot studies suggested that certain contrast pairs would prove easier to discriminate than others; these were presented to one group of 20 subjects, while those considered difficult were presented to another group of 20.

The first group showed a drop in errors over the five days from 11 to 2 percent; the second, from 22 to 10 percent. The low initial error rates (high baselines of discrimination) probably reflect transfer of

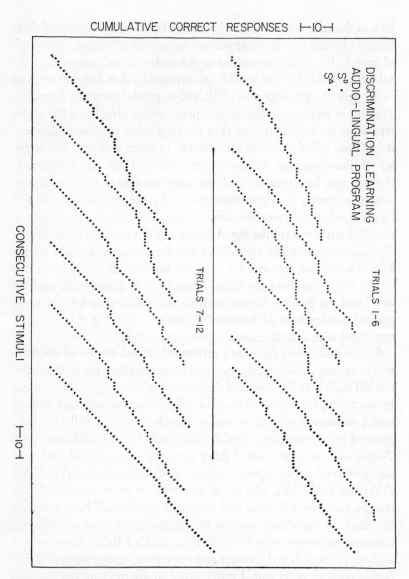

FIGURE 4.   *Gradual discrimination learning during one frame of an audio-lingual program in Spanish. Cumulative correct responses to consecutive stimuli by one S during 12 trials (from 41).*

first-language discriminations discussed above. Based on the error distributions obtained in this experiment, the authors present a rank ordering of the Russian consonants and vowels with respect to difficulty in discrimination learning for English-speaking subjects; the order accords well with that predicted from a contrastive analysis of the two languages.

In a subsequent study, Suppes, Crothers, and Weir (96) examined discrimination learning among Russian vowel phonemes and the effect of sequencing stimulus presentations according to expected difficulty. The subject was presented with a recorded series of sets of five stimuli during six daily 15-minute sessions distributed over a period of 11 days. Each stimulus was a Russian word containing one vowel preceded and/or followed by a consonant. The subject was instructed to select the alternate stimulus in each set which contained the same vowel as the first stimulus in the set; he was then told the correct answer. One group of subjects (N = 44) received a fixed series of items in random order (R); a second (N = 54) received progressively longer and more difficult items in each daily session (P).

Figure 5 shows the proportion of errors on each experimental day for the subjects in each group. On day 1, the programed subgroups naturally show fewer errors since they were presented with only the easier discriminations in the fixed series presented to group R. On days 5 and 6, when both groups were presented the same discrimination series, the programed group committed a reliably greater number of errors. In interpreting this finding it must be remembered that the programed group had less training on certain of the difficult discriminations because of the sequencing of stimuli presented to them. The procedure of vowel-phoneme matching from a set of alternatives permits the preparation of a confusion matrix which can serve as a guide to sequencing and repetition in programing the acquisition of the relevant discriminatons (cf., 87 and discussion below).

These three studies and others (41, 43, 73) illustrate the extensive transfer of first-language discriminations in second-language learning, whether the task be identification, detection of a difference, or recognition, respectively (see 21). The second experiment by Suppes, Crothers, and Weir (96) and that by Swets and others—to be described —show, however, that rapid and relatively error-free discrimination learning cannot be assured solely on the basis of an a priori sequencing of item difficulty. Among other requirements, there must be an iterative process of program revision, including the revision, addition, and de-

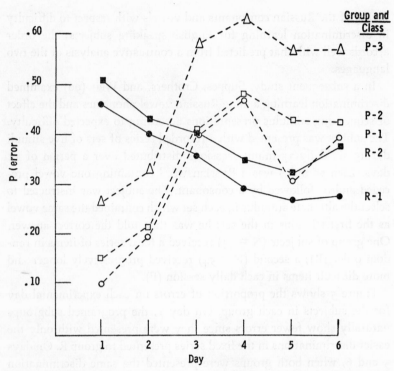

FIGURE 5. *Proportion of errors on each day of discrimination training with Russian vowel phonemes. One group of 44 subjects ("R") received a fixed set of items in random order; a second group of 54 subjects ("P") received progressively longer and more difficult items (from 96).*

letion of frames and sequences, based on an analysis of student errors.

Swets and co-workers (101) applied computer-based programed instruction to examine the usefulness of overt response, immediate reinforcement, adaptive sequencing, and self-pacing in learning to identify multidimensional sounds. They found that these procedures "produced results that are comparable to those obtained previously with conventional training methods. Certain of the central features of automated instruction were found to hinder learning in the task studied" (p. 928). A description of one of their series of four experiments will illustrate method and results. While seated in front of a typewriter connected to a computer, the subject was presented with one of a set of 32 stimuli over a pair of earphones. Each sound assumed one of two possible values along five dimensions: frequency, amplitude,

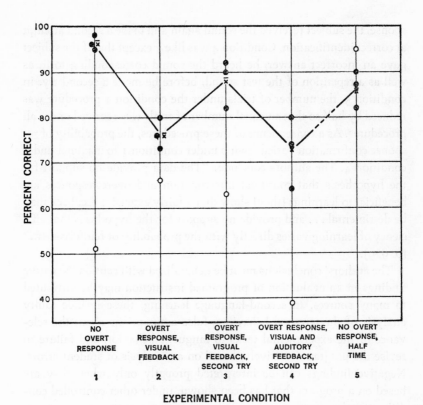

FIGURE 6. *Learning to identify multidimensional nonverbal sounds with a computer-based program. The effects of two types of response, two types of feedback, conditional and unconditional selection of successive items, and three levels of reinforcement probability, on percentage of correct identification (from 101).*

interruption rate, duty cycle, and duration. Figure 6 shows the percent correct attained on an identification test after a one-hour training session with one of five procedures. In condition 1, at the subject's command, the computer typed a five-digit number that specified the stimulus and then played the sound; the subject did not emit an overt identification response, but proceeded to give the next command. In condition 2, the subject initiated the presentation of the stimulus, then typed the five-digit number he believed to identify the sound; the computer typed OK or WRONG and, if wrong, typed the correct answer. Condition 3 was like condition 2 except that after an erroneous response, the subject received the sound again and made a second attempt at correct identification. Condition 4 was like 3 except that if the subject gave an incorrect answer, he heard the sound corresponding to it, as well as a repetition of the test sound, before he made a second try. In condition 5, the number of trials under the condition 1 procedure was reduced by half so that an equal number of trials was received under all procedures. As a consequence of these procedures, the probability of response confirmation varied from 0 under condition 1 to maximal under condition 4. The authors conclude: "The data provide no support for the hypothesis that continual interrogation and overt responses are beneficial to learning; [they] show that a fairly extensive feedback may be detrimental . . . and provide no support for the hypothesis that efficiency of learning varies directly with the probability of reinforcement" (p. 929).

The authors' conclusions must be generalized with caution. Negative findings in an evaluation of programed instruction may be attributed to many sources. In second-language learning, these include faulty analysis of the terminal behaviors, false assumptions about the relevance of the experimental tasks to language behavior, and failure to revise the program iteratively, based on an analysis of student errors. Negative findings can be interpreted properly only when they are based on a program that has been shown, under other controlled conditions, to be effective.

The use of auditory stimuli which are synthesized electronically, as in the preceding experiment, rather than speech stimuli uttered by an informant, often provides findings that are more systematic, sensitive, and stable—but at a loss in immediate relevance to the applied problem of second-language learning. Recent advances in speech synthesis (15, 18, 46) make it increasingly possible to perform comparably well-controlled experiments in programed learning with speech stimuli; regrettably, these devices have not found application in this area as yet.

Stimulus Generalization: Stimulus generalization, that is, the degree of invariance in responding under changes in stimulus conditions, has received extensive study in the laboratory with both nonspeech and speech stimuli.[3]

___

[3] For example, see the review by Mednick and Freedman (57) and studies reported in Mostofsky (67).

An experiment by Cross and Lane (17), employing stimuli varying along a single dimension (intensity of a 500-cps tone), is of particular interest because two incompatible responses were conditioned to two disparate stimuli, and then the probability of emission of each response to intermediate stimulus intensities was determined. This paradigm for discrimination learning and generalization testing bears some resemblance to the language-learning situation in which responses from the student's first- and second-language repertoires compete for emission. Figure 7 shows that response probability is maximal and latency minimal when the stimulus associated with reinforcement (S^D_1 or S^D_2) is presented. When the probabilities of emission of the responses are equal, at a median stimulus loudness, the latency of responding is greatest. Curiously enough, the same findings were obtained when two compatible responses were employed (low-pitch vowel and high-pitch vowel); when response probabilities were equal, latency was maximal, and there was no evidence of response "blending," i.e., intermediate pitch, under these conditions.

This experimental paradigm has recently been extended to multidimensional synthetic stimuli with essentially the same results (16). It turns out that if a discriminative response is conditioned to a stimulus with the properties (a_i, b_i), the degree of generalization to another stimulus, differing along both dimensions, (a_j, b_j), is equal to the degree of generalization due to the change in a ($a_j - a_i$), plus the degree of generalization due to the change in b ($b_j - b_i$). It would be interesting to explore generalization in the two-dimensional stimulus array defined by the first- and second-formant frequencies of synthetic vowels. Departures from this simple additive rule of generalization might occur in the region of points which define vowels in the subject's native language.

Over the past two decades, investigators at the Haskins Laboratories have greatly enhanced our understanding of the perception of speech by measuring the generalization of responses to synthetic speech stimuli. Illustrative of a segment of this research is a study by Liberman and others (50) of the perception of the voiced stops /d/ and /t/. Spectrographic patterns were prepared and converted to sound by means of a device called Pattern Playback. The patterns were identical except for the relative onset times of their first and second formants: the first formant was cut back in 10-msec steps from

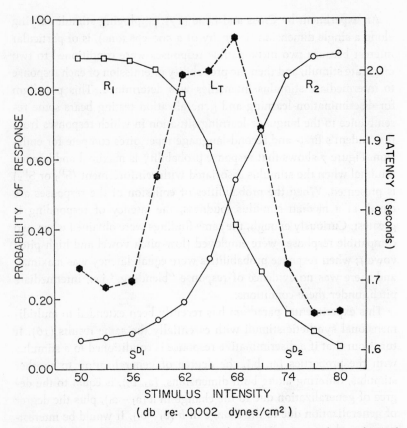

FIGURE 7. *Generalization gradients for pure tone intensity. The conditional probabilities were estimated from the total number of /ka/ responses (R_1) and /ti/ responses (R_2) emitted in 10 presentations of each stimulus intensity to each of 20 subjects. The total latency (hexagons) at each intensity is the unweighted mean of the average latency of responding by each of 20 subjects (from 17).*

o to 60 msec. They were presented in random order to subjects with instructions to label each stimulus as either /do/ or /to/. Cross and Lane (17) replicated this study with six subjects and also measured response latency; their findings are shown in Figure 8. Since the /do/ and /to/ response-gradients are complementary, only the former is presented. The reader may wish to compare these data with those in Figure 7; both experiments measure stimulus generalization after two incompatible responses have been conditioned to two discriminative stimuli. In

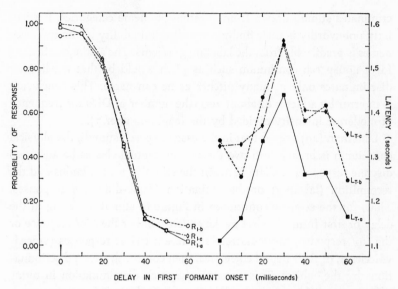

FIGURE 8. *Generalization gradients for synthetic speech stimuli, ranging from /do/ to /to/. The conditional probability and average latency of an identification response in 10 presentations of each stimulus to each of six subjects. The functions labeled (a), (b), and (c) were obtained under instructions to label the stimuli as /do/ - /to/, /to/ - /do/, and /ka/ - /ti/, respectively (from 17).*

studies of generalization among first-language speech stimuli, prior discrimination training has been arranged, of course, by the verbal community and is not controlled by the experimenter.

The average generalization gradient in Figure 8 is more shallow than that for individual subjects. A very steep phoneme labeling gradient (in the extreme case, a step function) means that the subject responds alike (generalizes) to all stimuli within a phoneme class and discriminates completely between stimuli drawn from the separate classes. In other words, discrimination training has effectively partitioned the stimulus *continuum* into two discrete classes of stimuli: /do/-stimuli and /to/-stimuli; that is, into two phoneme categories. Support for this conclusion comes from further experiments by Liberman and his co-workers (50, 51) with a number of phonemic contrasts. They find that a subject has great difficulty in distinguishing (in a psychophysical task) between those stimuli which he labels alike, i.e., those drawn from the same phoneme category, while he readily discriminates stimuli drawn from different phoneme categories. Particularly noteworthy is their finding that discriminability of the two phonemes is predictable from the labeling gradients. The analogous finding for a nonspeech continuum such as pitch would be that the listener discriminates only as many pitches as he can name. This conclusion is in error by a factor of about 200 (the number of DL's for frequency at moderate intensity divided by the magic number 7).

Liberman (49) argues that in the case of speech stimuli, the physical continuum is broken into two discrete perceptual classes because two discrete responses mediate between the stimulus presentations and the recognition (labeling) or discrimination (same-different) responses. Thus, for the acoustic continuum in Figure 8, stimuli differing in the delay of first-formant onset evoke covertly either the /do/ response or the /to/ response; these discretely different covert responses (voiced-voiceless), or their neural correlates, then control the overt discriminations by the subject. This account of speech discrimination in terms of response differentiation, called the motor theory of speech perception (55), has important implications for selecting a procedure by which these two components of formal repertoires shall be conditioned and coordinated (see below).

The experiments in stimulus generalization described above sampled the formal repertoire called dictation since nonvocal responses were under the control of an array of auditory stimuli. With only two responses employed in each of the studies, an extensive, differentiated repertoire of responses was not required. A number of experiments on generalization among speech stimuli that differ along several dimensions have capitalized on the extensive repertoire of vocal and written responses that is the largesse of first-language learning. With this technique, a confusion matrix may be obtained: the discrete stimuli are the column headings, the discrete responses are the row headings, and the frequency of occurrence of R_i over the n presentations of S_i gives the entry in the ith cell.

A study by Sapon and Carroll (87), who determined confusion matrices for selected words from English, French, Spanish, Portuguese, Italian, and Russian, illustrates this type of experiment. The procedure was similar to one later employed by Suppes, Crothers, and Weir (96), described above. Japanese, American, and Latin-American listeners with virtually no second-language training were employed. The pattern of errors in phoneme matching was found to be nonrandom; significant differences among the three language groups of listeners were obtained. To cite one example, stop consonants were always matched with other stop consonants by Latin-American listeners, while American and Japanese subjects often chose fricatives. In the light of these findings, the authors properly warn against interpreting confusion data obtained with one language group as generally characteristic of human sensory processes or stimulus generalization.

As indicated earlier, these confusion matrices provide a valuable guide to the second-language programer and an empirical check on the order of discrimination difficulty based on contrastive analysis. Reiff (78) has suggested that this analysis ideally would contrast each student's idiolect with that of the target language. Short of this extreme, he mentions that the Linguistic Atlas of the United States may serve as a guide when the student's residence is known. For example, "a native of Eastern Pennsylvania will need a heavier preponderance of the discrimination [ó] [ɔw] – or [éw] – than between [ó] and [ów]" (p. 91). It does not seem implausible that programs to condition second-language echoic behavior which are developed in different regions of the United States may differ in their emphasis on certain discriminations.

Response Differentiation: The differentiation of spoken or written responding, which is the second requirement of a formal repertoire, is predicated on the inherent variability of all behavior. In the laboratory, the technique of shaping or response-differentiation amounts to this: "We select one (or more) of the 'natural' variations of a well-conditioned response and give it *exclusive* reinforcement; the remaining variations are subjected to *extinction*. If we pick out, in advance, a variation that has been of fairly frequent occurrence, and if we apply this selective reinforcement rigorously, we can soon produce an increase in the frequency of the response that possesses the property or properties that we have chosen" (34, p. 186).

Differential reinforcement of vocal responding has rarely been studied in the laboratory; this is particularly regrettable in view of its importance in the acquisition of second-language fluency and the relative ease with which the topography of this behavior may be measured (see 45). A study of shaping vocal duration, reported by Lane (40), illustrates the method and findings in this application. The subject is seated in an audiometric room in front of a microphone, light, and coin dispenser. He is told to say /u/ when the light flashes, and he is told that the only pay he will receive will be dispensed in front of him, contingent on appropriate behavior. Each of the first 20 responses receives reinforcement (1 cent), and its duration is noted. A subclass of this operant is then chosen for selective reinforcement. In the experiment whose findings are shown in Figure 9, the mean (M) and average deviation (AD) of the set of 20 responses was computed, and in the second phase of the experiment, all responses whose duration exceeded $M_1 + AD_1$ were reinforced. The phase was continued until 10 succes-

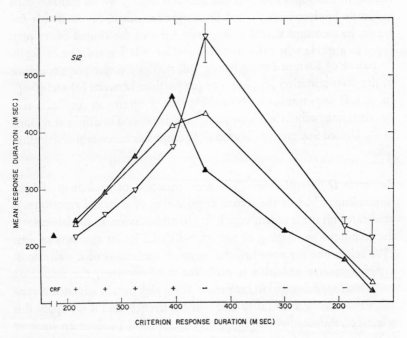

FIGURE 9. *Differential reinforcement of vocal duration with one subject (S12), shaping longer and then shorter durations. The relation between criterion response duration for differential reinforcement and the mean duration of unreinforced responses (inverted triangles), nonterminal reinforced responses (open triangles), and the 10 terminal reinforced responses (filled triangles) in each phase. (The pluses indicate the reinforcement criterion for each successive phase during the shaping of longer durations; the minuses indicate the criteria during the shaping of shorter durations.) (From 40)*

sive reinforcements were received. Then, $M_2 + AD_2$ was computed for these 10 responses, and this value was set as criterion for phase 3. In this fashion, the vocal duration of the subject was shaped (filled triangles) from approximately one-fifth second to nearly one-half second. After the fifth phase, the experimenter reversed the direction of shaping, now reinforcing all responses with duration less than $M_5 - AD_5$. The experiment was terminated when the subject's vocal duration was reduced to one-tenth second. This subject, like most of the others whose behavior was similarly manipulated, was unable to report the property of his behavior that produced the money ("unable" in the sense that extensive prompting by a carefully worded questionnaire, presented after the experiment, failed to yield an accurate report, if any at all).

Other experiments in this series varied the "size of step" that the subject had to take from one phase to the next; that is, the difference between the mean duration of ongoing responding and the new criterion $(C - M)$ was varied. A significant generalization arose from the data for over 30 subjects and a wide variety of step sizes. It was not possible to predict, from the size of step alone, either the success of the shaping process, that is, whether the subject would reach criterion, or the amount of shaping necessary before criterion was reached. However, it was possible to predict the length and outcome of the shaping process when the step size $(C - M)$ was expressed in terms of the variability (σ) of ongoing behavior. The statistic $\frac{C - M}{\sigma}$, called the shaping index, was correlated 0.4 with the number of responses that were emitted before criterion was reached, and it was found to be large whenever the shaping process failed.

When the shaping index is large—either because the step size is large, the variability small, or both—the a priori probability of a reinforced response is low, and the success of the shaping process is endangered. When the shaping index is small, the probability of a reinforced response is high and the success of shaping is secured; however, this may require many small steps to lead from the student's initial repertoire to the desired terminal repertoire. Therefore, the security of the shaping process and its efficiency are maximized when the probability of a reinforced response is set at some value, as yet unexplored, between zero and one, through a suitable choice of step size. It may not be too great an extrapolation of the initial findings of this research to suggest that the widely discussed issue of step size in programing various subject matters should be viewed in this light: the optimal size of a step is best defined in terms of the behavior of the individual student just before taking that step, so that the probability of a correct response has some constant, intermediate value (cf., 23).

The technique illustrated by these experiments in shaping response topography should provide a basis for measuring the interference produced by the first-language repertoire during shaping of second-language fluency. Just as the predictions of difficulty in discrimination learning provided by a contrastive analysis may be verified by studies of stimulus generalization, so too these predictions for difficulty in response differentiation may be verified by measurement of response topography during experiments in shaping.

An article by R. J. Sweet (98) describes the application of contrastive analysis to the prediction of difficulty in response shaping, with particular relevance to sources of interference between English and French repertoires. "The control of pronunciation, then, involves the sequencing of phonemic elements and their combinations so as to minimize the possibility of confusing phonemes and their combinations in the new language with others already acquired in the native tongue. Sequencing of these elements depends upon the existence of varying degrees of difficulty in their pronunciation" (p. 56). The author reports that pupils in his classroom research most often mispronounce those French words which are nearly approximated in English; e.g., *papier* and paper, *brosse* and brush, *personne* and person.

Several writers, among them Sweet (100) and Hayes and others (29), have suggested that the shaping of new response topographies may be accelerated by employing those in the first-language repertoire. For example, the student may be led to a correct pronunciation of the German *ich* via the following steps: (a) "fish," (b) "fish" said through spread lips, (c) "fish" said through spread lips while opening the teeth slowly (after 29). The danger of such techniques is, of course, that they evoke the very responses in the first language which are sources of interference and must be weakened. Here the language programer faces a choice, unguided as yet by research findings, which recurs in programing other repertoires as well (see *textual behavior* below). By calling into play first-language discriminations and patterns of responding, an *approximation* to the desired terminal behavior is more quickly attained, but it may then be more difficult to move precisely onto target.

Coordinating Discrimination and Differentiation: In any formal repertoire, there is a point-to-point correspondence between stimulus and response, whether these be spoken or written. The second-language programer, after engineering discrimination and differentiation separately, must undertake to coordinate them. The mastery of international Morse code illustrates the paradigm; there are 36 basic stimulus patterns, each connected with a differentiated response pattern. "When one learns to *receive* code, his problem is mainly *discriminative*, since the written or spoken responses have already been well differentiated; in *sending* code, however, the problem is one of differentiation, since the discriminative work was done when the student learned to read his ABC's" (34, p. 193). As stated at the outset of this chapter, conditioning a formal repertoire, such as receiving or sending code, establishes a minimal functional unit of behavior and permits the appropriate extension of this repertoire to new cases. The "minimal textual repertoire" involved in sending Morse code, for example, is extended whenever the telegrapher sends words from English text which he has never seen before.

A consideration of the development of echoic behavior will illustrate the problems of coordinating discrimination and differentiation in any of the four formal repertoires. The attention of this chapter will be restricted to strategies for conditioning a minimal echoic repertoire which is later extended to new stimuli as the occasion demands. This minimal repertoire is vital to second-language learning for once it is conditioned, the programer can evoke new responses as an assemblage of small echoic units never before arranged in this order; this behavior may then be reinforced.

When programing echoic behavior in a second language, certain auxiliary behaviors by the student, which are normally taken for granted in other kinds of programing, are not available. In the more common "subject matter" programs, confirmation is contingent upon not only a correct response but also upon a correct discrimination by the student; namely, that his written response "is the same as" the printed answer. This requirement of a discrimination is rarely mentioned and remains unobtrusive until the student erroneously considers equivalent such response-confirmation pairs as "cannot" and "does not" (32). Under these circumstances, an incorrect response is strengthened to the degree that the confirmation stimulus acts as a reinforcer.

The requirement of a discrimination for self-reinforcement obtrudes from the start, however, in programing second-language acquisition, for these discriminations are not part of the initial repertoire of the student. For example, Pimsleur writes: "The popular notion is that the student who is able to compare his pronunciation with that of a native speaker will acquire native-like speech. Many teachers have already realized that this hope is far too optimistic. It is evident that students are rather poor judges of their own pronunciation. They are prone to think their pronunciation is "good enough" when actually it is not acceptable. They are unable to note which features are relevant and which are not" (73, p. 199). In conditioning echoic behavior, the programer's task is further confounded by the fact that the confirmation stimulus and the subject's response are both fleeting and presented via different modalities; an aural stimulus in the first instance, sidetone and bone conduction in the second. Furthermore, psychophysical differences in the perception of external vs. "autophonic" (self-generated) sounds probably impede the development of accurate echoic behavior (see 37).

How then shall the student's echoic behavior be reinforced selectively? Assuming that each student shall not have access to a private tutor or to an automatic speech recognizer, there seems to be little choice but to condition the prerequisite discriminations in the first place and arrange for their maintenance during later conditions of *self-shaping* echoic behavior. There is inadequate laboratory evidence, however, to confirm that the relevant discriminations, once conditioned, are effective in self-shaping echoic behavior, although the pedagogical success of programs predicated on this assumption suggests its validity (see 65 and the section on echoic behavior below).

A series of 11 pilot studies and three major experiments by Pimsleur, Mace, and Keislar (75) are among the few that examine the effects of discrimination training on response differentiation. The central problem of their research was "to determine the value of preliminary discrimination training in increasing the effectiveness of language laboratory practices on the pronunciation of French sounds." They found the following: "(1) Training in discriminating the French nasal vowel phonemes /ð/, /ʒ/, /ɛ̃/ rendered subsequent language laboratory practice more effective in producing good pronunciation of these phonemes. (2) Training in discriminating between the diphthongized and the undiphthongized final /o/ did not render language laboratory practice measurably more effective in producing good pronunciation of this French phoneme" (p. 25). Note that the first discrimination is among phonemes in the target language, while the second is between a French phoneme and a troublesome English approximate. Pimsleur (73) attributes the different outcomes to the greater degree of response differentiation that existed in the former case for native speakers of English.

A close relation between speech discrimination and differentiation is again implied by the outcome of a programing experiment in speech correction. With a carefully designed and executed program that should serve as a model for others, Holland and Matthews (31) taught /s/ discriminations to children who misarticulated /s/. The discriminative response was button-press; correct responses simply led to the next item; incorrect responses caused the tape recorder to rewind and repeat the last item. Phase 1 of their program involved discrimination of /s/ in isolation from other isolated speech sounds. The latter were sequenced according to difficulty and faded in toward equal intensity with the S^D. In Phase 2, the subject was required to discriminate the sound in words. Sequencing of difficulty and fading were again employed. For example, words with initial /s/, terminal /s/, and medial /s/ were presented in that order. In Phase 3, the child was asked to identify the position of /s/ within a word. Phase 4 involved discrimination of correctly articulated from misarticulated /s/ sounds within words; omission, substitution, and distortion comprised the misarticulations. The group of children who worked through this program showed significantly improved /s/ discrimination, sibilant discrimination, and, of particular interest here, improved /s/ *articulation* on a series of tests.

There are several considerations, however, that strongly question the value of discrimination training before response differentiation. The first of these is the outcome of an experiment by Lane and Schneider (44) that measured the accuracy of self-shaping echoic responding to Thai tonemes under several procedures. These authors report that discrimination training, in which the target toneme was contrasted with segments of the same form but different durations and pitch slopes, did not lead to a marked improvement in echoic accuracy. The further introduction of delayed auditory feedback of the subject's response, facilitating comparison of the model and his attempt at imitation, also failed to produce an appreciable improvement in the correspondence of stimulus and response pitch or duration. The juxtaposition of model and imitation did not lead to an improvement in echoic accuracy despite the fact that the subjects had previously shown perfect discrimination between tonemes that were more similar than the model and their attempts at imitating it. This high level of discrimination was reached rapidly during training and probably reflected transfer of first-language discriminations, as discussed earlier in this article in the section on discrimination. The findings reported in that section, taken together with these data on echoic behavior, indicate that inadequate response differentiation can persist despite a very fine-grained discriminative repertoire.

Research at the Haskins Laboratories on the generalization of responses to synthetic speech stimuli, discussed earlier, casts further doubt on the necessity of discrimination preceding differentiation in the conditioning of formal repertoires. Indeed, inference from these findings suggests that discrimination training ideally should follow response differentiation. In a review of research on speech perception, Liberman writes: "All of this strongly suggests . . . that speech is perceived by reference to articulation—that is, that the articulatory movements and their sensory effects mediate between the acoustic stimulus and the event we call perception" (49, p. 122). It follows from this motor theory of speech perception that two relatively similar external stimuli could be made more discriminable "if we could attach to those stimuli two very different mediating responses and hence gain the added distinctiveness of their very different proprioceptive returns" (p. 123).

A study by Liberman and others (51) on the discrimination of /p/ and /b/ in intervocalic position will illustrate the application of the motor theory of speech perception to a particular phonemic contrast. An experiment similar to the /do/-/to/ study described earlier was performed with the synthetic speech stimuli, /ræbɪd/-/ræpɪd/. These stimuli varied only in the duration of the silent interval between the two syllables in each word, which ranged from 20 to 130 msec. Labeling responses by native Americans "partition" the stimulus continuum into two perceptual classes: /ræbɪd/ stimuli and

/ræpɪd/ stimuli. This outcome is attributed to covert mediating responses which provide discrete cues (e.g., voiced-voiceless) for the labeling judgments. A modest extension of Liberman's hypothesis suggests that a foreign student who has not learned the differentiated response patterns /b/-/p/ in English should find this auditory *discrimination* much more difficult than a native American. Moreover, if the new responses /b/ and /p/ are differentiated out of the student's current vocal repertoire, this should enhance the discrimination of /b/ and /p/ when presented to him as auditory patterns, for now the student's responding may be controlled by intervening articulations that provide very different proprioceptive cues.

Further support for the suggestion that vocalization may facilitate the development of speech-sound discrimination comes from some observations reported by Holland and Matthews in their study of /s/ discrimination, discussed above. The authors actually compared several programs for conditioning this discriminative behavior; they note that the one described earlier produced the most spontaneous vocalizing by students who worked through the program as well as the greatest improvement on the /s/ discrimination tests. They suggest that "these vocalizations might force careful observation of auditory cues, or they might provide supplemental kinesthetic stimuli which could be useful in close discriminations" (31, p. 481).

It is unfortunate that the pedagogical implications of the motor theory of speech perception have not been put to empirical test. The outcome might have importance not only for second-language learning but also for an evaluation of the theory itself; Lane (39) has provided evidence that the theory lacks a firm empirical basis.

Echoic Behavior

Among the four formal repertoires delineated earlier, echoic behavior, involving a spoken response to a spoken stimulus, receives the major emphasis in modern language pedagogy. "Today we are pretty much in agreement that the grammar-and-translation method, patterned largely on the traditional study of Latin, is obsolete at the least" (58, p. 168). Instead, the major emphasis is on aural presentation of stimuli and oral response—the *audiolingual* method. The objectives of the method include thematic repertoires to be discussed later, but its *modus operandi* involves the purely formal components of an echoic repertoire. "The justification for this emphasis is found in the observation that a language is first of all a system of sounds for social communication; writing is a secondary derivative system for the recording of spoken language. . ." (13, p. 1,063).

The audiolingual method may be characterized by Brooks' well-known dicta: "1. The learner should hear only authentic foreign speech. 2. He should hear much more than he speaks. 3. He should speak only on the basis of what he has heard. 4. He should read only what he has spoken. 5. He should write only what he has read. 6. He should analyze, if he does so at all, only what he has heard, spoken, read, written, and learned" (7, p. 45).

Despite the widespread use of the audiolingual method and the related proliferation of language laboratories (30), considerable uncertainty remains about the value of this approach to second-language learning. Questions such as these, posed by K. A. Mueller (68), are largely unanswered by available research findings: Does withholding texts, and the absence of reading and writing, in the early stages of language learning by this method affect performance in pronunciation, oral comprehension, reading, writing, and syntax at various stages in the course? Does the use of the language laboratory contribute to performance on audiolingual skills and on others, too? What types of language laboratory facilities are most valuable (see 64) in producing second-language fluency?

Scherer and Wertheimer summarize the dispute over the audiolingual method:

Inherent in the assumptions underlying an audio-lingual approach to foreign language learning is that students trained only audio-lingually at the beginning will subsequently reach, and perhaps surpass, in reading and writing ability, students who have been trained in the more conventional manner, while exhibiting a far higher level of achievement in auditory comprehension and speaking; advocates of the traditional multiple approach, with its heavy emphasis on grammar and reading, are of a contrary opinion. Little evidence based on controlled experimentation exists (91, p. 298).

These authors have performed a rigorous and comprehensive experiment to contrast the effects of the audiolingual method, which employs primarily echoic behavior, to those of "traditional" methods, which rely more heavily on textual behavior. Noteworthy among their criteria were several novel tests of "habituated direct association" (roughly, "the ability to think in German"), which are described by Wertheimer and Scherer (105). To précis their findings: audiolingual students were superior in listening and speaking ability, comparable in reading and writing, and inferior in translating when compared to a control group taught by traditional methods. The former were also superior in responding to spoken German rapidly, appropriately, and in a fashion comparable with that of German bilinguals. (Other comparisons of traditional and audiolingual methods are cited by Carroll [13].)

The third tenet of the audiolingual method—the student should speak only on the basis of what he has heard—may be reflected in the decision of many language programers to condition discrimination before response differentiation. The decision cannot be based presently on laboratory research, for the findings, discussed in the earlier section on coordination, are equivocal. Sapon (85) incorporates the audiolingual principle in his program in elementary Spanish: "In evaluating any program, one must remember that an individual can say only what he can hear, and one of the great strengths of this program is its training in auditory discrimination" (pp. 8-9). Morton's (63) audiolingual program for Spanish also has this approach. His first "hypothesis" and procedure in the program is called phonematization:

Essentially, this would hold that the incipient language learner learns first to "hear" and discriminate between all "significant" classes of sounds in the new language before a conscious effort is made to reproduce them; or, indeed, before any real capability exists for reproducing them. It is an aural conditioning necessary to set up the "phonemic areas" which will work finally in his acoustico-neurological system like a series of narrow-band filters, passing appropriate sounds, rejecting others automatically. . . (p. 14).

When discrimination learning is accomplished, most second-language programs move on to echoic behavior, in the hope that the prerequisite response differentiation will literally take care of itself (through some mechanism of self-shaping). For example, in Morton's audiolingual Spanish program the procedure of phonematization is followed by one called sound reproduction: ". . . automatic reproduction of all speech sounds as individual acoustic segments is achieved *after* phonematization of these sounds. . . . By means of the 230 individual sound reproduction drills, the student was expected to learn to render correctly, both in isolation and in combination, all of the sounds and sound groups (syllables and utterances) phonematisized earlier" (pp. 16, 17).

Similarly, programs in elementary French by Valdman (103) and by T. Mueller (70) begin with discrimination training, followed by response differentiation through echoic behavior. In Mueller's program, each vowel and consonant defines a separate unit in discrimination training. Each unit "teaches the student to discriminate against the S$^\triangle$ sounds and, after that, against the various intonational features such as: pitch, stress, rhythm, and syllabification" (p. 1). Self-shaping of echoic behavior follows this discrimination training.

Lermontoff (48) advocates the early introduction of textual material in programing echoic behavior. He argues that "some subjects find it easier to discriminate two sounds after they have read words in which they occur." Consequently, this author's program in elementary French has the following features: "We first present a new word aurally; and next we have the subject listen to it again and repeat it; then we have him listen to it and repeat it while he is at the same time presented with its written form; and finally we have him read the word aloud and then let him hear the correct pronunciation on the tape" (p. 75).

A French program by Moraud (62) also integrates echoic and textual behavior. The conditioning procedure has six steps.

1. [The students] hear a sentence . . . and read the text presented . . . unless the text has been faded out completely. 2. They repeat the sentence into the microphone or give answer into microphone. 3. They write answer on answer sheet unless instructions call exclusively for an oral response. 4. They listen to correct oral response and read correct written response. 5. They make appropriate connections. 6. They move to the next frame (p. 24).

Rocklyn (79) and his collaborators have prepared programs in several languages to condition echoic behaviors concurrent with a limited thematic repertoire. Their effort is of particular interest because they have applied linguistic and behavioral analysis to the choice of terminal behaviors as well as to the design of a program. Usually, the second-language programer must accept the target language as given. However, programing should be viewed as one technique among many in educational technology and, whenever it is possible to do so, the entire learning task should come within the purview of the behavioral engineer. A report by Rocklyn and Moren (81) describes the programing technique of this group as applied to the acquisition of a limited tactical language in Russian. The language was designed to include 16 commands (e.g., "hands up"), 10 question frames ("how many"), 100 inserts ("tanks, guns"), and 100 answers (yes, no, numbers, etc.). The conditioning paradigm included a recorded Russian or English stimulus, a student response in either Russian or English, depending on the stage in the program, and a recorded correct utterance as confirmation.

Although the acquisition of echoic behavior overlaps with that of thematic repertoires in most second-language programs, in a few the two repertoires are strictly sequenced. For example, Morton writes concerning his Spanish program: ". . . automatic reproduction of all speech sounds . . . is achieved . . . *before* the consistent use of the sounds in meaningful utterances" (63, p. 16), and Valdman reports on his program in elementary French: "We begin with a sound discrimination and production sequence followed by grammatical transformations dealing with features comprised exclusively of sounds that the student has been taught to discriminate and differentiate."[4]

To summarize: Echoic behavior receives the greatest emphasis among the formal repertoires, partly because of the widespread acceptance of an audiolingual approach to language pedagogy in general. Most often, the development of echoic behavior skips from discrimination training to imitation, with the intervening steps—response differentiation and coordination—largely omitted. In so doing, the programer capitalizes initially on the student's differentiated first-language repertoire, leaving to the self-shaping process the resolution of phonetic differences between the two languages. Echoic behavior is taught before thematic repertoires in some second-language programs and concurrently with them in others.

Several specialized devices have been designed to implement programed acquisition of echoic behavior. Gilpin (25) has described a system composed of two tape recorders (master and student) and relay circuitry which is operated by the student with a control panel. Fifteen buttons permit control of the two recorders in a variety of ways that provide an extremely flexible arrangement of stimulus and response

---

[4] Personal communication from A. Valdman, 1963.

recording and presentation. Carroll (12) has designed and constructed an audiovisual device, shown in Figure 10. The device has three operational modes. In the "familiarization mode," the student is first presented with instructions, new material, and the like; then he is given some task to perform, such as answering a question; then he finds out

FIGURE 10. *An audiovisual device for self-instruction in language learning. A sample film loop is resting above the projection screen; a sample magnetic tape cartridge is alongside the screen. To the left of the screen are a loudspeaker and a box containing relay circuitry. In the foreground is the control panel operated by the student and a write-in paper tape (from 12).*

whether the response he made was correct or not. There is provision for vocal, written, and multiple-choice (button-press) responding. When the student meets a criterion performance in this mode, he proceeds to the "learning mode" which omits instructions and provides only questions and confirmation. After criterion is reached in this mode, the student goes on to the "test mode" where only questions are presented.

Lane and Buiten (42) have implemented a computer-based system to permit programing and selective reinforcement of echoic behavior restricted to the prosodic features of speech. This system extracts the intonation, tempo, and relative amplitude parameters of a recorded stimulus pattern and of the subject's echoic response, compares one or more parameters of the stimulus and response, and presents either an analog or discrete representation of the parameter mismatch to the subject. Depending on the magnitude of the error voltage and a programable criterion, the subject is automatically presented either with a repeat of the last pattern or with the next pattern in the program.

Porter has surveyed the use of audiovisual aids (76) and of other instructional devices (77) in foreign language teaching with emphasis on the implementation of programed instruction. Carroll (11) provides a list of teaching machines designed for second-language programs.

Transcription

When both the stimulus and response are written, all the properties of echoic behavior apply in the conditioning and maintenance of transcription. If the second-language orthography is not common to English, the development of a purely formal repertoire will require both discrimination training and response differentiation. Such problems as the minimal unit, extension to new stimuli, coordination, and automatic self-reinforcement, which arose in the discussion of echoic behavior, are pertinent to transcription—and their solutions are analogous. For example, because the stimulus and the response-product are commensurate in transcription, as they are in echoic behavior, a possible programing strategy is to condition orthographic discriminations and responses initially, and then trust that the student will discriminate the accuracy of his transcriptions, automatically shaping his own behavior to minimize the mismatch between his response and the model pattern. If the second-language orthography is largely the same as in English, the required stimulus discriminations and response differentiation have already been acquired. This is the case for most second-language programs. Noteworthy exceptions are the programs that condition transcription in Russian (83) and Hebrew (26).

Textual Behavior

Textual behavior is vocal responding under the control of a nonauditory, verbal stimulus. The emphasis here is on the formal properties of such behaviors as reading aloud from a second-language text in that language. Formal and thematic repertoires are combined when a student reads a second-language text while translating into his native language. Many of the problems in programing the acquisition of textual behavior in a second language are similar to those associated with echoic behavior and transcription discussed earlier. Discriminations within the second-language orthography must be conditioned, and vocal responses must, of course, be shaped out of the student's initial repertoire. If the target language employs fundamentally the same orthography as in English, these discriminations require only minimal attention from the programer. Furthermore, if textual behavior is programed following echoic behavior, then the requisite response differentiation is available without further conditioning. It remains only to set up correspondences between discriminative stimuli—usually printed text —and differentiated vocal responses.

This strategy in programing corresponds to the fourth tenet of the audiolingual method—the student should read only what he has spoken—and it has a counterpart in the classroom practice of teaching audiolingual skills before reading. As Scherer and Wertheimer (91), K. A. Mueller (68), and others have pointed out, there is little research evidence in support of this practice. Indeed, when audiolingual methods have been compared with sight methods in producing speed and retention in reading, all four possible outcomes have been reported: (1) "Oral-aural and reading proficiency constitute separate, independent skills which do not develop one from the other" (13, p. 1,067); (2) "aural learning facilitates visual relearning; this facilitation is greater than the facilitation of aural relearning by visual learning" (74, p. 107); (3) "subjects who learned visually and relearned aurally achieved superior performances in comparison with performances of subjects who learned aurally and relearned visually" (2, p. 38); (4) "students taught by the audio-lingual method . . . were almost on the same level with students taught by the traditional method in new-type reading and writing tests" (91, p. 302).

The greatest difficulty in programing textual behavior arises from a difference between this repertoire and transcription or echoic behavior. The latter repertoires have in common that the response product and the stimulus occur in the same modality, visual in the first case, auditory in the second. Hence, it is possible to discriminate an improper response by direct comparison with the stimulus. On the other hand, dictation and textual behavior have in common that the stimulus and the response product are dissimilar—they impinge on different modalities. Thus, penmanship can be learned by transcription but not by dictation alone, and pronunciation can be learned from echoic behavior but not solely from textual behavior. Although there is a point-to-point correspondence between stimulus and response in textual behavior, there is no formal similarity between the two which, coupled with speech discriminations, could maintain response differentiation. Skinner draws the contrast clearly:

In echoic behavior, the correspondence upon which reinforcement is based may serve as an automatic conditioned reinforcer. The speaker who is also an accomplished listener "knows when he has correctly echoed a response" and is reinforced thereby. Such reinforcement brings the form of the response closer and closer to the form of the stimulus, the limit being the most precise correspondence possible either with respect to the vocal capacity of the speaker or his capacity to judge similarity. . . . The automatic reinforcement of reading an "interesting" text, however, has merely the effect of increasing the probability of occurrence of such behavior; it does not differentially reinforce correct forms at the phonetic level (92, pp. 68-69).

Although the speaker who is reading text is not able to assess the accuracy of his pronunciation by direct comparison with a model, nonetheless he is able to listen to his own speech, and this probably has some editing effect on gross mispronunciation. It would be interesting to determine whether the maintenance of response differentiation in textual behavior would be impaired by removing the auditory feedback to the speaker, as through masking of sidetone. The difficulty of maintaining differentiation in textual behavior need not be a problem for the second-language programer who desires only to condition "reading a foreign text for understanding." The widespread practice of conditioning students to respond aloud to text in a second language with accurate pronunciation, or with the English approximations that the text evokes through generalization with English orthography, seems most inefficient when only translation of text is the goal. Most efficient would be a procedure which brought English vocal responses directly under intraverbal control by the text; no responses in the second language need intervene covertly. A formal repertoire, of course, is sacrificed by this procedure.

Although the acquisition of discriminative control in textual behavior is expedited when the student's first and second languages have largely the same orthography, the maintenance of the differentiative component of textual behavior is hampered by the same tokens. Sapon (84) advocates the elimination of orthography in the early stages of language learning for this reason. He cites as an example the difficulty of teaching an English student learning Spanish to forsake a lateral continuant in response to the textual stimulus *r* (the product of some years of conditioning) and to emit instead an alveolar vibrant. On the other hand, Lermontoff (48) was quoted earlier as favoring the introduction of textual stimuli during the conditioning of echoic behavior. The question, unresolved by research, is: Does a common orthography in the two languages facilitate the acquisition of textual behavior, by rapidly yielding an approximation to the desired response, more than it impedes this acquisition, by interfering with accurate pronunciation through the evocation of competing responses in the native language? Sweet (100) disowns the problem in his Latin program, where response differentiation is of little concern. Programs for languages whose orthography is not common to English, as is the case with the Cyrillic, Hebrew, and Arabic alphabets and Chinese, Japanese, and Korean characters, need not concern themselves with this problem, but face another: discriminations among the orthographic symbols must be conditioned (12, 26, 83).

Dictation
Dictation in a second language is a formal repertoire that requires the conditioning of speech discriminations as in echoic behavior and, less often, response differentiation as in some cases of transcriptive behavior. The unit of the minimal repertoire may be orthographic, stenographic, phonetic, etc. The lack of formal similarity between stimulus and response is the source of several of the problems encountered in the previous discussion of textual behavior.

Among the programs that condition dictation, those by Morton (63) and Harms (27) bear special mention. Morton conditions dictation as a part of discrimination training; the responses are arbitrary orthographic symbols called grammalogs; they are transitional behaviors, eventually replaced by differentiated vocal responding during the conditioning of echoic behavior. Harms has developed a program to take a student from no knowledge of phonetic notation to a level of competence whereby he is able to give the phonetic notation at 95 percent accuracy for words selected at random from the Kenyon-Knott dictionary. The program proceeds from dictation of simple sounds through diphthongs and affricates, voiced-voiceless oppositions, stop-nasal oppositions, vowels in CVC frames, consonants with common places of articulation, semivowels, voiced and voiceless consonants, stress, and randomly selected units. The procedure is as follows: The student hears the word on tape, consults a corresponding card for prompting, writes the phonetic notation for the entire word, checks his response against confirmation on the back of the card, and repeats the sequence. Harms presents evaluation data for native and foreign-born students who worked through the program.

Thematic Repertoires

Purely *formal* repertoires are of little functional value in their own right either for the speaker (or writer) or his audience.[5] By virtue of the point-to-point correspondence between stimulus and response that characterizes these repertoires, the behavior is highly predictable and, in that sense, conveys little information. It is only when formal and thematic sources of strength combine in determining a response that it can be said to be meaningful. Because it has the proper form the response is, first of all, "intelligible"; that is, it has a form appropriate to the discriminative training of the audience. Because the response is also under the control of environmental conditions, or operations on the speaker, or his own prior verbal behavior, or that of other people, or several of these acting concurrently, it "tells the audience about" these controlling variables—and is likely to be reinforced.

In formal repertoires there is a point-to-point correspondence between stimulus and response—within one dimensional system for echoic and transcriptive behaviors, across two such systems for textual behavior and for dictation. In thematic repertoires, the response shows no such correspondence to the controlling variables.[6] The term *thematic repertoires* will be used broadly here to encompass several functional

[5] Apologies to my secretary.

[6] Additional contrasts, cited earlier, are the minimal units and their extension to new stimuli that characterize the formal but not the thematic repertoires. This distinction may now be qualified by noting that thematic repertoires partake of both properties to a limited degree. Morphemes often approximate thematic units. Extension to new stimuli is feasible for sets such as the following: concur, recur, incur, etc. Larger thematic units may also be extended; the student who knows the meaning of *elephant* has some notion, however crude, of the meaning of *elephantiasis* and so forth.

classes of verbal behavior including *intraverbal* responses, which are under the control of prior verbal behavior, *tacts*, which are under the control of nonverbal environmental stimuli, and *mands*, which are under the control of characteristic reinforcing consequences (see 92).

Although it is useful to distinguish the controlling relations involved in intraverbals, tacts, and mands, it is important to note that most verbal responses are multiply-determined by several sets of variables acting in concert. For example, the response "fire" may be a tact under the control of a conflagration in one's apartment, or it may be a mand for a characteristic reinforcer ("somebody sound the alarm!"), but it is probably both. It should also be noted that the same "word" may appear in one or more functional classes (in addition to a mand or a tact, "fire" could be an intraverbal response to "Ready, aim, . . .").

Intraverbal Responses

Intraverbal relations *within* one language include response patterns variously called syntactic frames or sequences, grammatical structures, redundant strings, contextual constraints, etc. Skinner (92) treats these under the special heading "autoclitics" in a functional analysis of verbal behavior. Grammatical models, among them Markovian, immediate constituent, and transformational, describe this patterning by different analytical techniques. Although these models are of interest to the second-language programer, especially insofar as they describe the terminal repertoire that the program is designed to produce, a functional analysis of intraverbal chains is of preeminent importance since the programer's task is primarily manipulative.

Unfortunately, there is a great dearth of laboratory research on the analysis and control of intraverbal chaining. Classic studies by Miller and Selfridge (61) and Miller (59) describe the potent effects of patterning in recall; recent psycholinguistic studies by Berko (4), Brown and Berko (8), and Brown and Fraser (9) describe this patterning in the language of children; Miller (60) reports several experiments on the effects of patterning on speech perception; techniques for conditioning and maintaining intraverbal chains, however, have not been examined experimentally. Saporta (89) has undertaken an evaluation of three grammatical models in the teaching of foreign languages which should prove illuminating in this respect. Sapon's "reflections on models of linguistic structure and language programing" (86) reflect, as

well, the synthesis of analytical and functional approaches to patterning adopted by many language programers:

What has generally emerged from my own experience in programming
Spanish is the recognition that the straight "economical" line of language
description [in linguistics] is neither the shortest nor the most direct route
to student performance in the language being taught. What does seem to
offer much promise is a first approach to the language via a series of transformations and expansions of basic sentence material. This material can then
be sequenced to exploit usable existing habits and to avoid conflicting ones
. . . a kind of contrastive psycholinguistic grammar . . . and finally fixed
through the use of pattern and substitution drill (86, p. 6).

In view of the widespread use of drill to condition intraverbal patterns, it is unfortunate that this technique has not been put to careful
laboratory test. Under controlled conditions, it would not be surprising
to find sheer repetition minimally effective. This technique should be
contrasted with that of programing, in which gradual progression and
the development of abstraction through multiple examples replaces
repetition. Skinner has contended that no one learns by repeating: "He
may learn so little that he needs to repeat and will learn more upon
successive occasions, but the repetition itself is not involved" (93, p.
171). "Stamping in" or "fixing" through repetition alone has not been
found to be an effective technique for the control of behavior in the
laboratory.

Intraverbal relations *between* first and second languages comprise
translation for the beginning student.

Faced with a passage in the new language, the translator emits appropriate
intraverbal responses. If these fall into something like a familiar pattern,
he may then react in any or all of the ways appropriate to a listener. . . .
Eventually the translator improves upon this crude procedure by developing
more efficient intraverbal operants, mainly of larger patterns, and by acquiring normal listening or reading behavior under the control of the new
language without the aid of translation" (92, p. 77).

Several language programers agree that whereas the evocation of
formal repertoires in English interferes with the development of these
repertoires in the second language, the evocation of intraverbal relations between the languages hinders not only the maintenance of formal repertoires in the second language but also the development of
intraverbal chains in that language. Mueller writes: "Developing automatic control over the sound patterns of the language is retarded when

the student's attention is directed toward meaningful utterances" (69, p. 43). A similar statement by Morton (63) has been quoted earlier (see also 70). On the other hand, some programers have argued for and implemented the early introduction of thematic repertoires such as translation (intraverbals) and question-and-answer (mands), on the grounds that motivation is sustained or enhanced by this procedure. Presumably, the reinforcing consequences of acquiring an intraverbal repertoire such as translation derive initially from the fact that the student may react to his own speech in his native language as a listener.

It remains to be shown by controlled experiments whether the introduction of thematic repertoires does in fact impair the formal repertoires established earlier; if interference is demonstrated, it is necessary to know the sources and their relative importance. The greatest difficulty in this kind of research is accurate specification of the dependent variable—the accuracy of the formal repertoire. Subjective techniques of evaluation are undesirable, but acoustic specification of the stimulus and the response is at present unwieldy. It may not be premature, however, to undertake to assess the effects of introducing thematic repertoires on the *prosodic* features of formal repertoires, measured electronically.

Any of the four formal repertoires may serve as the vehicle for the acquisition of thematic repertoires such as intraverbals. Some programs employ a written stimulus and written response. These include a program in Hebrew by Hammond (26), one in German by Ferster and Sapon (19), and a computer-based program to condition Russian vocabulary by Licklider (52). Valdman (103), Moraud (62), Harris (28), and others condition intraverbal responses by means of dialogues supplemented by English translation. A Latin program by W. E. Sweet (99) employs a less common procedure: a written stimulus is connected intraverbally to a spoken response. Most of the available second-language programs, however, condition spoken second-language stimuli to spoken English responses. Morton describes the procedure employed in his Spanish program as follows: "Practice rather than theory guided us in assuming that once the structural clues of Spanish had been mastered . . . the student, working with the minimal meanings afforded him by these in each new utterance, could be expected to 'fill in the gaps' with the help of 'broad hints' in English (i.e., nonliteral translations)" (63, p. 23).

Although most language programers and teachers would agree that literal translation is not the solution to the problem of how to introduce an intraverbal repertoire most effectively, the available alternatives also seem unsatisfactory; these include nonliteral interlinear translations, alternate pages of English and second-language texts, tape-recorded second-language phrases with their English "equivalents" in the text, paired associate learning with flash cards or lists, and so forth. Morton's "broad hint" approach, cited above, shows greater promise; it is related to a variably blurred prompting technique, developed by Israel (33), to study vocabulary learning. The auditory analog of Israel's technique would be worth exploring: English prompts might be recorded on a tape track parallel to one containing foreign language narrative or questions. The prompts could be masked by a noise whose level was under the student's control, or the prompts could be faded over the course of the recorded program by the experimenter, or both.

The crucial difficulty with all these techniques, however, is the attempt to transfer a response from one functional class to another. Initially, the student says "apple," for example, as a simple and well-conditioned textual or echoic response to the English "apple." It is desired, however, that this response come under the control of (be evoked by) a formally *dissimilar* stimulus, e.g., the spoken or written "manzana." *That* association has no status in the student's native language. It is not surprising, therefore, that as long as the translation is available, the English stimuli arrogate control of the English responses. But, without the translation, there is no reason initially for the response "apple" to occur in the presence of "manzana."

One solution to the apparent paradox is to evoke the English responses by means of collateral stimuli that do not exercise extensive control over these responses, and then to fade these collateral sources of strength as the intraverbal linkages between the two languages become established. This formula seems to characterize the ingenious technique developed by Schaefer (90) to condition English intraverbal responses to German text.[7] Among the collateral sources of strength for a response to English text, there are, in addition to thematic prompts, intraverbal prompts provided by the syntactic structure and

---

[7] The technique has been used, perhaps independently, by Van Riper and Smith (104) in conditioning a textual repertoire: reading phonetic transcription.

by common phrases, as suggested earlier. These collateral sources of strength are nicely illustrated by the procedure for generating order approximations to English with successive subjects, employed by Miller and Selfridge (61). The redundancy of the text is one way of expressing the degree of control exerted over responding by collateral sources of strength. Consequently, when Schaefer replaces high-redundancy words in the English text with their German counterparts—as in "But why will you say that ich am mad?"—the correct intraverbal is emitted, and it is emitted in the presence of the German textual stimuli. It remains to fade these collateral sources of strength by replacing both more words and words of lower redundancy. For example, the above excerpt is soon followed by "Ich heard all things. . ." where "I" is less determined by context. In six pages the text works up to "Es war laut, aber es grew lauter, ich say, lauter every moment!"

The auditory analog of this procedure for conditioning intraverbal responses would be worth trying and might prove superior on at least two counts. First, Schaefer's procedure evokes English pronunciations of the German words, because of the common orthography employed and because German words are interspersed at varying intervals among the English words in the text. If echoic rather than textual behavior were employed, there would be less tendency for English pronunciation of the German words to occur and, because the stimulus and response-product in echoic behavior is formally similar, it would be possible to discriminate the improper pronunciations. This is not possible in textual behavior, as emphasized earlier. The second potential advantage of an auditory adaptation of Schaefer's technique is the greater number of collateral sources of strength that may be manipulated. In addition to the intraverbal and thematic cues available in text, there is a multiplicity of acoustic cues—including stress, intonation, and tempo—which may be used as prompts and vanished as necessary.

Tacts

The tact is a class of verbal operant characterized by a three-term relation: nonverbal discriminative stimulus, verbal response, generalized reinforcement. "The three-term contingency in this type of operant is exemplified when, in the presence of a doll, a child frequently achieves some sort of generalized reinforcement by saying *doll*; or when a teleost fish, or picture thereof, is the occasion upon which the student of zoology is reinforced when he says *teleost fish*" (92, p. 81). Tacting comprises a large part of the thematic repertoire in first-language learning and a minute part in second-language learning; in the latter case, intraverbal responses "carry the thematic load" (see 6). Instead of conditioning the response "manzana" with some generalized reinforcer in the presence of an apple or a picture of one, the response is conditioned as an intraverbal to textual or auditory stimuli, such as: "Say 'apple' in Spanish," or "Eva comio una manzana envenenada." Once again, the means by which a thematic repertoire is taught in second-language learning is to establish one sort of functional control and hope for transfer to another. Thus, when the student eventually confronts an apple and it is appropriate to say "manzana," it is not expected that he will be speechless in the face of this novel situation; it is expected that manzana-the-intraverbal will become manzana-the-tact. The transfer of functional control presumably occurs through mediated generalization; that is, at the first confrontation the tact "apple" is emitted covertly, and "manzana" is uttered aloud as an intraverbal to "apple." If this leads to some sort of reinforcement on a number of occasions, "manzana" will acquire the functional properties of a tact.

The mediating responses in the student's native language required by this approach to the conditioning of tacts (i.e., transfer from intraverbal control) probably impair the acquisition and maintenance of second-language fluency. Carroll concludes in a survey of research that "foreign words are best learned (and probably better retained) when presented in association with the objects, actions, qualities, and conditions which are their referents" (13, p. 1,077). Several programs employ pictorial material to this end (e.g., 56); much greater versatility is provided by educational television (3) and specialized audiovisual devices (12, 76).

The direct approach to conditioning second-language tacts, however, also faces several problems. First, it is difficult to maintain these tacts outside the classroom, where the student responds to his environment in his native language. Second, the nonverbal controlling stimulus may evoke English responses that will interfere with both the formal and thematic properties of the second-language tact.

The nature of thematic interference between first- and second-language tacts is well revealed in an experiment by Lenneberg (47) on learning color names in six different experimental "languages." The languages consisted of four color words, and the subject's task was to discover the "meaning" of the words by observing their use by the experimenter. The nonsense words of the first language were distributed over the Munsell color series exactly as the English words: brown, green, blue, and pink. The other five languages had words whose frequency distributions (generalization gradients) represented systematic distortions from the previously established English distributions. There were two types of distortions: of the slope of the gradients (increasing or decreasing the determinancy of the color names) and of the location on the physical continuum (making colors which in English have no specific names, a perfect example of a color category in the nonsense language). Lenneberg found that if the tact generalization gradients ("reference relationships") of English were undistorted in the second language, the color words in that language were learned most easily; if only the locations of the gradients on the stimulus continuum were distorted, a small impairment in learning was observed. Learning the color names was most retarded when the shapes of the English color gradients were distorted in the second language to yield gradually rising slopes, that is, less well-defined boundaries between stimulus classes.

Mands

A mand is a verbal operant in which a response of a given form is reinforced by a characteristic consequence. The major variables that control a mand are the level of deprivation or of aversive stimulation applied to the speaker and his reinforcement history for similar responses. Questions, commands, entreaties, and the like are characterized by this kind of functional control (see 92). Mands are difficult to condition in a self-instruction setting because an active listener, required to present appropriate reinforcement, is not available. It is unwieldly, if not impossible, to arrange characteristic reinforcing consequences, such as providing the time if the student should inquire, or complying with a command such as "stop," or granting an entreaty, and so forth. As was the case with tacts, the functional class of mands is largely neglected in second-language programing in the hope that the transfer of certain intraverbals will take place when deprivation or aversive stimulation occasions a mand. As is the case with tacts, this slight of mand presumably depends on mediated generalization, which may be a mixed blessing: facilitating the thematic accuracy of the response, but degrading its formal properties. Although several second-language programs, notably those of Lermontoff (48), Morton (63), and Rocklyn and Moren (81), indirectly condition mands by conditioning intraverbals of appropriate form (e.g., "ask for an apple in Spanish"), this may not be the only way of proceeding. An audio-lingual program could be so carefully sequenced that the occurrence of particular mands by the student was predictable and, therefore, the characteristic (verbal) reinforcers could be prerecorded on the master tape.

Transfer Within and Between Repertoires

The concept of transfer has played a large role in this disquisition on programed learning of a second language; it has turned up as an observation, an explanation, and an assumption at many points, so it may be well to summarize the sources of transfer available to, and often relied upon by, the second-language programer. In echoic behavior and dictation, transfer of first-language auditory discriminations will occur, enhancing the acquisition of discriminations between sound classes, but impeding the learning of equivalences (generalization) within these classes. The typical effect is overdiscrimination, and the emphasis in conditioning must be on the equivalences among discriminably different sounds. In textual behavior and transcription, transfer of first-language orthographic discriminations will occur when the second language employs an orthography that overlaps with English orthography.

In echoic and textual behaviors, transfer of the differentiated vocal repertoire of the student's first language will occur to the degree that the two languages share a similar sound system or orthography. This greatly expedites the acquisition of a rough approximation to the desired repertoire, but it impedes the development of accurate pronunciation to the degree that the first- and second-language vocal repertoires differ. The consequences of transfer are similar for the differentiated manual repertoire involved in dictation and transcription.

A textual response will transfer to an echoic repertoire if the relevant auditory discriminations have been conditioned, and the converse can occur if the necessary orthographic discriminations have been learned in the first or second language. Similarly, transfer may occur between dictation and transcription if the relevant discriminations have been acquired. In complementary fashion, the student with an echoic repertoire should acquire dictation more readily when taught how to write the orthography than one who does not possess that repertoire; a similar transfer of discriminations may be expected to occur between transcription and textual behavior. These transfer effects are most obvious when the second-language orthography differs from that of the student's native language.

Within the thematic repertoires, an intraverbal response may transfer to the status of a tact in the second language; this requires nonverbal stimuli that evoke tacts in the student's native language which are linked intraverbally to responses in the second language. Intraverbal responses similarly may transfer to the status of mands in the second language when deprivation or aversive stimulation makes a mand likely and first-language responses intervene.

Transfer also takes place between the formal and thematic repertoires. A spoken response, whose form was conditioned during the acquisition of a purely echoic or textual repertoire, can take on the functional properties of an intraverbal through the replacement of one kind of stimulus control (formal) for another (thematic). This intraverbal response may then become a tact or a mand, in the manner described above. Similarly, written responses, learned as a part of the formal repertoires of dictation or transcription, may transfer to the thematic repertoires under suitable conditioning procedures. Finally, it should be noted that the formal and thematic repertoires acquired in the language laboratory and in the language classroom do transfer, in some measure, to the second-language community.

References

1. Anastasi, A. *Psychological Testing*. Second edition. New York: Macmillan Co., 1961.
2. Asher, J. J. "Sensory Interrelationships in the Automated Teaching of Foreign Languages." *Perceptual and Motor Skills* 14: 38; January 1962.
3. Barcus, D. L.; Hayman, J. L.; and Johnson, J. T. *Development of Programmed Learning Materials for Use with Televised Spanish Instruc-*

tion. Stanford, Calif.: Institute for Communication Research, Stanford University, 1961. (Unpublished report)

4. Berko, J. "The Child's Learning of English Morphology." *Word* 14: 150-77; August-December 1958.

5. Blyth, J. W., editor. *The Hamilton College Experiment in Programmed Learning.* Clinton, N.Y.: Hamilton College, September 1961. (Unpublished report)

6. Brethower, D. M. "On Linguists and Psychologists in Second Language Learning, Or the Necessity of Strange Bedfellows." *Programming of Audio-Lingual Language Skills for Self-Instructional Presentation.* (Edited by F. R. Morton.) Series Preprints and Reprints. Ann Arbor: University of Michigan Language Laboratory, 1961. Vol. 6.

7. Brooks, N. *Language and Language Learning; Theory and Practice.* New York: Harcourt, Brace, 1960.

8. Brown, R., and Berko, J. "Word Association and the Acquisition of Grammar." *Child Development* 31: 1-14; March 1960.

9. Brown, R., and Fraser, C. "The Acquisition of Syntax." *Verbal Behavior and Learning: Problems and Processes.* (Edited by C. N. Cofer and Barbara S. Musgrave.) New York: McGraw-Hill Book Co., 1963.

10. Carroll, J. B. "Wanted: A Research Basis for Educational Policy on Foreign Language Teaching." *Harvard Educational Review* 30: 128-40; Spring 1960.

11. Carroll, J. B. "A Primer of Programmed Instruction in Foreign Language Teaching." *International Review of Applied Linguistics* 1: 115-41; No. 2, 1963.

12. Carroll, J. B. *Programmed Self-Instruction in Mandarin Chinese.* Wellesley, Mass.: Language Testing Fund, 1963.

13. Carroll, J. B. "Research on Teaching Foreign Languages." *Handbook of Research on Teaching.* (Edited by N. L. Gage.) New York: Rand McNally, 1963. pp. 1,060-1,100.

14. Center for Programed Instruction. *Programs, '62: A Guide to Programed Instructional Materials.* U.S. Department of Health, Education, and Welfare, Office of Education. Washington, D.C.: Government Printing Office, 1962.

15. Cooper, F. S.; Liberman, A. M.; and Borst, J. "The Interconversion of Audible and Visible Patterns as a Basis for Research in the Perception of Speech." *Proceedings of the National Academy of Science* 37: 318-25; May 1951.

16. Cross, D. V. "Metric Properties of Multidimensional Stimulus Control." *Proceedings of the Conference on Stimulus Generalization.* (Edited by D. Mostofsky.) Stanford, Calif.: Stanford University Press, 1964.

17. Cross, D. V., and Lane, H. L. "On the Discriminative Control of Concurrent Responses: The Relations Among Response Frequency, Latency

and Topography in Auditory Generalization." *Journal of the Experimental Analysis of Behavior* 5: 487-96; October 1962.

18. Fant, C. G. M. "Modern Instruments and Methods for Acoustic Studies of Speech." *Acta Polytechnica Scandinavica* 1: 1-81; Whole No. 246, 1958.

19. Ferster, C. B., and Sapon, S. M. "An Application of Recent Developments in Psychology to the Teaching of German." *Teaching Machines and Programmed Learning.* (Edited by A. A. Lumsdaine and R. Glaser.) Washington, D.C.: National Education Association, 1960. pp. 173-85.

20. Fiks, A. I., and Garvey, C. J. *Construction and Evaluation of a Short, Automated, Vietnamese Course.* Washington, D.C.: Human Resources Research Office, January 1963.

21. Galanter, E. "Contemporary Psychophysics." *New Directions in Psychology.* (Edited by T. M. Newcombe.) New York: Holt, Rinehart and Winston, 1962.

22. Garvey, C. J., and Clark, J. W. *Investigation of the Procedures for Limited Tactical Language Training in Mandarin Chinese.* Washington, D.C.: Human Resources Research Office, September 1962.

23. Geis, G. "Possible Reinforcements in a Program." *Programming of Audio-Lingual Language Skills for Self-Instructional Presentation.* (Edited by F. R. Morton.) Series Preprints and Reprints. Ann Arbor: University of Michigan Language Laboratory, 1961. Vol. 6.

24. Gilbert, T. F. "Mathetics: The Technology of Education." *Journal of Mathetics* 1: 7-73; January 1962.

25. Gilpin, J. "A Versatile Apparatus for Audio Self-Instruction (the 'Poly-Audio')." *Programming of Audio-Lingual Language Skills for Self-Instructional Presentation.* (Edited by F. R. Morton.) Series Preprints and Reprints. Ann Arbor: University of Michigan Language Laboratory, 1961. Vol. 6.

26. Hammond, P. C. *The Elementary Biblical Hebrew Program of Princeton Theological Seminary.* Princeton, N.J.: Princeton University Press, 1962.

27. Harms, L. S. *A Self-Instructional Program for Phonetic Transcription.* Baton Rouge: Louisiana State University, February 1962. (Unpublished report)

28. Harris, C. C. "An Experience in Self-Teaching." *Programming of Audio-Lingual Language Skills for Self-Instructional Presentation.* (Edited by F. R. Morton.) Series Preprints and Reprints. Ann Arbor: University of Michigan Language Laboratory, 1961. Vol. 6.

29. Hayes, A. S., working committee chairman. "A New Look at Learning." *Reports of the Working Committees.* 1962 Northeast Conference on the Teaching of Foreign Languages. (Edited by William Bottiglia.) Oxford, Ohio: American Classical League Service Bureau, Miami University, 1962. pp. 19-60.

30. Hayes, A. S. *Technical Guide for the Selection, Purchase, Use and Main-*

tenance of Language Laboratory Facilities. U.S. Office of Education Bulletin 1963, No. 37, OE-21024. Washington, D.C.: Government Printing Office, 1963.

31. Holland, A. L., and Matthews, J. "Application of Teaching Machine Concepts to Speech Pathology and Audiology." *Asha* 5: 474-82; January 1963.

32. Holland, J. G. "Teaching Psychology by a Teaching Machine Program." *American Psychologist* 14: 414; July 1959.

33. Israel, M. L. "Variably Blurred Prompting: I. Methodology and Application to the Analysis of Paired Associate Learning." *Journal of Psychology* 50: 43-52; July 1960.

34. Keller, F. S., and Schoenfeld, W. N. *Principles of Psychology*. New York: Appleton-Century-Crofts, 1950.

35. Lane, H. L. "Teaching Machines and Programmed Learning." *Harvard Educational Review* 31: 469-76; Fall 1961.

36. Lane, H. L. "Experimentation in the Language Classroom: Guidelines and Suggested Procedures for the Classroom Teacher." *Language Learning* 12: 115-21; No. 3, 1962.

37. Lane, H. L. "Psychophysical Parameters of Vowel Perception." *Psychological Monographs* 76: 1-25; Whole No. 563, 1962.

38. Lane, H. L. "Some Differences Between First and Second Language Learning." *Language Learning* 12: 1-14; No. 1, 1962.

39. Lane, H. L. *The Motor Theory of Speech Perception: A Critical Review*. Ann Arbor: University of Michigan, 1963. (Unpublished report 05613-1-P)

40. Lane, H. L. "Differential Reinforcement of Vocal Duration." *Journal of the Experimental Analysis of Behavior* 7: 107-115; January 1964.

41. Lane, H. L. "Acquisition and Transfer in Auditory Discrimination." *American Journal of Psychology* 77: 240-48; June 1964.

42. Lane, H. L., and Buiten, R. L. *Preliminary Manual for the Speech Auto-Instructional Device*. Ann Arbor: University of Michigan, 1964. (Unpublished report 05613-2-P)

43. Lane, H. L., and Moore, D. J. "Reconditioning a Consonant Discrimination in an Aphasic: An Experimental Case History." *Journal of Speech and Hearing Disorders* 27: 232-43; August 1962.

44. Lane, H. L., and Schneider, B. A. "Methods for Self-Shaping Echoic Behavior." *Modern Language Journal* 47: 154-60; April 1963.

45. Lane, H. L., and Shinkman, P. G. "Methods and Findings in an Analysis of a Vocal Operant." *Journal of the Experimental Analysis of Behavior* 6: 179-88; April 1963.

46. Lawrence, W. "The Synthesis of Speech from Signals Which Have a Low Information Rate." *Communication Theory*. (Edited by W. Jackson.) New York: Academic Press, 1953.

47. Lenneberg, E. H. "A Probabilistic Approach to Language Learning." *Behavioral Science* 2: 1-12; January 1957.

48. Lermontoff, A. "Some Aspects of Programming a Direct-Method French Course." *Programming of Audio-Lingual Language Skills for Self-Instructional Presentation.* (Edited by F. R. Morton.) Series Preprints and Reprints. Ann Arbor: University of Michigan Language Laboratory, 1961. Vol. 6.

49. Liberman, A. M. "Some Results of Research on Speech Perception." *Journal of the Acoustical Society of America* 29: 117-23; January 1957.

50. Liberman, A. M., and others. "The Discrimination of Relative Onset-Time of the Components of Certain Speech and Non-Speech Patterns." *Journal of Experimental Psychology* 61: 379-88; May 1961.

51. Liberman, A. M., and others. "An Effect of Learning on Speech Perception: The Discrimination of Durations of Silence with and Without Phonemic Significance." *Language and Speech* 4: 175-95; October 1961.

52. Licklider, J. C. R. "Preliminary Experiments in Computer-Aided Teaching." *Programmed Learning and Computer-Based Instruction.* (Edited by J. E. Coulson.) New York: John Wiley & Sons, 1962. pp. 217-39.

53. Licklider, J. C. R., and Miller, G. A. "The Perception of Speech." *Handbook of Experimental Psychology.* (Edited by S. S. Stevens.) New York: John Wiley & Sons, 1951. Chapter 26, pp. 1,040-74.

54. Liedke, O. K. "The Programmed Course in Elementary German." *The Hamilton College Experiment in Programmed Learning.* Clinton, N.Y.: Hamilton College, September 1961. Appendix II. (Unpublished report)

55. Lisker, L.; Cooper, F. S.; and Liberman, A. M. "The Uses of Experiment in Language Description." *Word* 18: 82-106; April-August 1962.

56. Marty, F. *Programming a Basic Foreign Language Course; Prospects for Self-Instruction.* Roanoke, Va.: Audio-Visual Publications, 1962.

57. Mednick, S. A., and Freedman, J. L. "Stimulus Generalization." *Psychological Bulletin* 57: 169-200; May 1960.

58. Mildenberger, K. W. "Problems, Perspectives, and Projections." *International Journal of American Linguistics* 28: 168-72; 1962.

59. Miller, G. A. "Free Recall of Redundant Strings of Letters." *Journal of Experimental Psychology* 56: 485-91; December 1958.

60. Miller, G. A. "Some Psychological Studies of Grammar." *American Psychologist* 17: 748-62; November 1962.

61. Miller, G. A., and Selfridge, J. A. "Verbal Context and the Recall of Meaningful Material." *American Journal of Psychology* 63: 176-85; April 1950.

62. Moraud, M. "Report on the Programming of French." *The Hamilton College Experiment in Programmed Learning.* (Edited by J. W. Blyth.) Clinton, N.Y.: Hamilton College, September 1961. Appendix I. (Unpublished report)

63. Morton, F. R. *The Language Laboratory as a Teaching Machine.* Series Preprints and Reprints. Ann Arbor: University of Michigan Language Laboratory, 1960. Vol. 1.

64. Morton, F. R., editor. *Proceedings of the First Conference on the Role of the Language Laboratory in the Secondary School.* Series Preprints and Reprints. Ann Arbor: University of Michigan Language Laboratory, 1961. Vol. 4.

65. Morton, F. R., editor. *Programming of Audio-Lingual Language Skills for Self-Instructional Presentation.* Series Preprints and Reprints. Ann Arbor: University of Michigan Language Laboratory, 1961. Vol. 6.

66. Morton, F. R.; Mayer, E.; and Brethower, D. M. *Report to the Language Development Section, U.S. Office of Education.* Ann Arbor: University of Michigan, 1963. (Unpublished)

67. Mostofsky, D., editor. *Stimulus Generalization Conference.* Boston: Boston University, 1963. (Unpublished report)

68. Mueller, K. A. "Experimentation and Research in the Development of Modern Foreign Language Materials and Teaching Methods." *Materials and Techniques for the Language Laboratory.* (Edited by E. W. Najam.) Publication No. 18, International Journal of American Linguistics Supplement, January 1962. Vol. 28, Part 2, No. 1.

69. Mueller, T. "Programming Morphemic Structures: The Concept of Minute Steps." *Programming of Audio-Lingual Language Skills for Self-Instructional Presentation.* (Edited by F. R. Morton.) Series Preprints and Reprints. Ann Arbor: University of Michigan Language Laboratory, 1961. Vol. 6.

70. Mueller, T. *Revising Phase 1 of the Programmed French Course; A Work Paper.* Gainesville: University of Florida, 1962. (Unpublished report)

71. Nostrand, H., editor. *Research on Language Teaching.* Seattle: University of Washington Press, 1962.

72. Pimsleur, P., editor. *Report of the Conference on Psychological Experiments Related to Second-Language Learning.* Washington, D.C.: Language Development Program, U.S. Office of Education, January 1960. (Unpublished report)

73. Pimsleur, P. "Discrimination Training in the Teaching of French Pronunciation." *Modern Language Journal* 47: 199-203; May 1963.

74. Pimsleur, P., and Bonkowski, R. J. "Transfer of Verbal Material Across Sense Modalities." *Journal of Educational Psychology* 52: 104-107; April 1961.

75. Pimsleur, P.; Mace, L.; and Keislar, E. *Preliminary Discrimination Training in the Teaching of French Pronunciation.* Contract SAE 8950. Washington, D.C.: U.S. Office of Education, 1961. (Unpublished report)

76. Porter, D. A. *A Report on the Use of Audio-Visual Aids in Foreign Language Teaching.* Cambridge, Mass.: Harvard University, 1958. (Unpublished report)

77. Porter, D. "A Report on Instructional Devices in Foreign Language Teaching." *Teaching Machines and Programmed Learning.* (Edited by A. A. Lumsdaine and R. Glaser.) Washington, D.C.: National Education Association, 1960. pp. 186-205.

78. Reiff, D. G. "Molecular Analysis of Spanish Phonology." *Programming in Audio-Lingual Language Skills for Self-Instructional Presentation.* (Edited by F. R. Morton.) Series Preprints and Reprints. Ann Arbor: University of Michigan Language Laboratory, 1961. Vol. 6.

79. Rocklyn, E. H. "Problems in Programming an Intensive Aural-Oral Language Course." *Programming of Audio-Lingual Language Skills for Self-Instructional Presentation.* (Edited by F. R. Morton.) Series Preprints and Reprints. Ann Arbor: University of Michigan Language Laboratory, 1961. Vol. 6.

80. Rocklyn, E. H., and Clark, J. W. *Construction, Programming, and Evaluation of a Limited Tactical Language Course.* Washington, D.C.: Human Resources Research Office, September 1962. (Unpublished report)

81. Rocklyn, E. H., and Moren, R. I. "A Feasibility Study of a Special Machine-Taught Oral-Aural Russian-Language Course." *Applied Programmed Instruction.* (Edited by S. Margulies and L. D. Eigen.) New York: John Wiley & Sons, 1962. pp. 73-77.

82. Rocklyn, E. H.; Moren, R. I.; and Zinovieff, A. *Development and Evaluation of Training Methods for the Rapid Acquisition of Language Skills.* Washington, D.C.: Human Resources Research Office, 1962. (Unpublished report)

83. Saltzman, I. J. "Programmed Self-Instruction and Second-Language Learning." *International Review of Applied Linguistics* 1: 104-114; 1963.

84. Sapon, S. M. "An Application of Psychological Theory to Pronunciation Problems in Second-Language Learning." *Modern Language Journal* 36: 111-14; March 1952.

85. Sapon, S. M. *Report on the Use of a Programmed Course in Spanish.* Columbus: Ohio State University, 1961. (Unpublished report)

86. Sapon, S. M. "Some Reflections on Models of Linguistic Structure and Language Programming." *Programming of Audio-Lingual Language Skills for Self-Instructional Presentation.* (Edited by F. R. Morton.) Series Preprints and Reprints. Ann Arbor: University of Michigan Language Laboratory, 1961. Vol. 6.

87. Sapon, S. M., and Carroll, J. B. "Discriminative Perception of Speech Sounds as a Function of Native Language." *General Linguistics* 3: 62-72; Spring 1958.

88. Saporta, S., editor. *Psycholinguistics.* New York: Holt, Rinehart & Winston, 1961.

89. Saporta, S. "Evaluation of Three Grammatical Models in the Teaching of Foreign Languages." *National Defense Language Development Research and Studies.* OE 12014-62. Washington, D.C.: Government Printing Office, 1963.

90. Schaefer, H. "E. A. Poe as a Reinforcer." *Psychological Reports* 8: 398; June 1961.

91. Scherer, G. A. C., and Wertheimer, M. "The German Teaching Experiment at the University of Colorado." *German Quarterly* 35: 298-308; May 1962.

92. Skinner, B. F. *Verbal Behavior.* New York: Appleton-Century-Crofts, 1957.

93. Skinner, B. F. "Special Problems in Programming Language Instruction for Teaching Machines." *Language Teaching Today.* (Edited by F. N. Oinas.) Publication No. 14, International Journal of American Linguistics Supplement, October 1960. Vol. 26, Part 2, No. 4.

94. Smith, M. D. *New Instruction Media.* Report to the New Media Branch, U.S. Office of Education. Richmond, Ind.: Earlham College, 1963. (Unpublished)

95. Stevens, S. S. "Mathematics, Measurement, and Psychophysics." *Handbook of Experimental Psychology.* (Edited by S. S. Stevens.) New York: John Wiley & Sons, 1951. pp. 1-49.

96. Suppes, P.; Crothers, E.; and Weir, Ruth. *Application of Mathematical Learning Theory and Linguistic Analysis to Vowel Phoneme Matching in Russian Words.* Stanford, Calif.: Stanford University Institute for Mathematical Studies in the Social Sciences, 1962. (Unpublished Report No. 51)

97. Suppes, P., and others. *Some Quantitative Studies of Russian Consonant Phoneme Discrimination.* Stanford, Calif.: Stanford University Institute for Mathematical Studies in the Social Sciences, September 1962. (Unpublished Report No. 49)

98. Sweet, R. J. "Programming Control To Elicit Maximum Effectiveness in Pronunciation." *Programming of Audio-Visual Language Skills for Self-Instructional Presentation.* (Edited by F. R. Morton.) Series Preprints and Reprints. Ann Arbor: University of Michigan Language Laboratory, 1961. Vol. 6.

99. Sweet, W. E. "The Choice of Syntactical and Morphological Discriminations in an Elementary Latin Program." *Programming of Audio-Lingual Language Skills for Self-Instructional Presentation.* (Edited by F. R. Morton.) Series Preprints and Reprints. Ann Arbor: University of Michigan Language Laboratory, 1961. Vol. 6.

100. Sweet, W. E. *Outline and Description of Proposed Latin Programs.* Ann Arbor: University of Michigan, September 1962. (Unpublished report)

101. Swets, J. A., and others. "Learning To Identify Nonverbal Sounds: An Application of a Computer as a Teaching Machine." *Journal of the Acoustical Society of America* 34: 928-35; July 1962.

102. Uttal, W. R. "On Conversational Interaction." *Programmed Learning and Computer-Based Instruction.* (Edited by J. E. Coulson.) New York: John Wiley & Sons, 1962, pp. 171-90.

Summary Table Second-Language Programs [8]
Available and in Preparation

Authors	Language	Formal Repertoires				Thematic Repertoires		
		Echoic	Textual	Transcription	Dictation	Intraverbal	Tacts	Mands
Carroll	Chinese	x	x	x	x	x	x	x
Chou & Peterson	Chinese	x				x	x	x
Garvey & Clark	Chinese	x				x		x
Burroughs	French	x			x			
Mueller	French	x			x	x	x	x
Hanzelli	French	x	x	x	x	x	x	x
Lermontoff	French	x	x			x		x
Marty	French	x	x	x	x	x	x	x
Moraud	French	x	x	x	x	x	x	x
Ricket & Dubois	French	x		x		x		x
Valdman	French	x			x	x		x
Eilert	German	x	x	x	x	x	?	?
Ferster & Sapon	German				x	x		
Liedke	German	x	x	x			x	x
Ventola & Wilson	German				x	x		
Bloom & Smith	Hebrew	x	x			x		
Hammond	Hebrew				x	x		
Sweet	Latin			x		x	x	x

[8] This summary of available language programs is based on a survey conducted by the author in August 1963. Additional information and listings may be found in the reference for the Center for Programed Instruction (14).

103. Valdman, A. *The Implementation and Evaluation of a Multiple-Credit Intensive Audio-Lingual Approach in Elementary French*. Fourth and Sixth Progress Reports. Contract SAE 9498. Washington, D.C.: U.S. Office of Education, 1962.

104. Van Riper, C. G., and Smith, D. E. *An Introduction to General American Phonetics*. Second edition. New York: Harper & Row, 1962.

105. Wertheimer, M., and Scherer, G. A. C. *The Audiolingual Teaching of German: A Psycholinguistic Experiment*. Paper read at the Psychonomic Society, St. Louis, 1962.

Summary Table Second-Language Programs
Available and in Preparation

Special Presentation Device	Approximate Hours to Completion	Location of Research	Comments and Source S-Study discussed here E-Evaluation data reported	
yes	undetermined	Harvard	(12)	S
yes	200	Univ. of Michigan		
tape recorder				
tape recorder	14-16	Encyclopaedia Britannica Films		
yes	250	Univ. of Michigan		
tape recorder	year course	Univ. of Washington		
yes	200	Center for Programed Instruction		S
yes	year course	Hollins College	(56)	S
tape recorder	year course	Hamilton College	(5)	S, E
no	18-23	General Program Teaching Corporation	(11)	
tape recorder	year course	Indiana	(104)	S, E
tape recorder	60-75	Encyclopaedia Britannica Films	(11)	
no	48	Harvard	(19)	S, E
tape recorder	year course	Hamilton College	(5)	S, E
no	17-30	TMI-Grolier	(11)	
no	15-25	TMI-Grolier	(11)	
no	48	Princeton	(26)	E
			Biblical material	
tape recorder	two-year course	Univ. of Michigan	(100)	S

Summary Table Second-Language Programs (Continued)
Available and in Preparation

| | | Behaviors Receiving Major Emphasis | | | | | | |
| | | Formal Repertoires | | | | Thematic Repertoires | | |
Authors	Language	Echoic	Textual	Transcription	Dictation	Intraverbal	Tacts	Mands
Thilson	Latin	x	x			x	x	x
Licklider	Russian		x			x		
Myers	Russian	x	x	x	x	x	x	x
Morton, Mayer, & Brethower	Russian	x			x	x	x	x
Rocklyn, Moren, & Zinovieff	Russian	x				x		x
Saltzman, Wilson, & Ventola	Russian	x	x	x	x	x		x
Barcus	Spanish			x				x
Gilbert	Spanish		x	x		x		
Harris	Spanish	x	x	x	x	x		x
Morton, Mayer, & Brethower	Spanish	x			x	x	x	x
Sapon	Spanish	x	x	x	x	x	x	x
Sullivan	Spanish	x	x	x	x	x	x	?
Universal Teaching Machines	Spanish	x	x	x				x
Wilson & Ventola	Spanish				x			
Morton, Mayer & Brethower	Thai	x				x	x	x
Fiks & Garvey	Vietnamese	x				x		x
Details not available for:								
Bailey	Latin							
Newmark	French							
Unknown	Spanish			x		x		
Unknown	French							
Unknown	Spanish							
Unknown	German			x		x		
Unknown	Hebrew							
Unknown	Russian			x				
Unknown	Russian							
Koppitz	German			x		x		
Allen	English							

Summary Table Second-Language Programs (Continued)
Available and in Preparation

Special Presentation Device	Approximate Hours to Completion	Location of Research	Comments and Source S-Study discussed here E-Evaluation data reported
no	undetermined	Center for Programed Instruction	
computer based	undetermined	Bolt, Beranek & Newman	(52) S
yes	1/2 year course	Earlham College	(94) S, E
yes	275	Univ. of Michigan	
tape recorder	140	George Washington Univ.	(82) S Limited tactical language
tape recorder	1/2 year course	Indiana	(83)
no	18-22	TMI-Grolier	(11)
no	20	Denver Public Schools	(11)
no		TOR Labs	(11)
tape recorder	260	Louisiana State Univ.	(28) S, E
yes	225	Univ. of Michigan	(66) S
tape recorder	50-85	Encyclopaedia Britannica Films	(11) S, E
tape recorder	40-45	Encyclopaedia Britannica Films	(11) S, E
tape recorder	24-35	Universal Electric	
no	17-30	TMI-Grolier	(11)
yes	200	Univ. of Michigan	
tape recorder		George Washington Univ.	(20) S Limited tactical language
		Hollins College	
		System Development Corporation	
no	year course	AVTA Corporation	
		American Teaching Systems	
		American Teaching Systems	
no		AVTA Corporation	
		AVTA Corporation	
		AVTA Corporation	
		International Teaching Systems	
computer based		IBM	(102)
		Thompson Ramo Woolridge	

Implementation

LINCOLN F. HANSON
Columbia University

P. KENNETH KOMOSKI
Teachers College
Columbia University

School Use of Programed Instruction*

Programed instruction represents many things to many educators. To provide a vicarious background against which local decisions may be made with greater confidence, this chapter attempts to outline some of the basic assumptions school systems have invoked, the operating principles and practices they have employed, and the criteria by which they have selected, adapted, and evaluated programed materials. How does a schoolman introduce an innovation such as programed instruction into a classroom, a school, a school system? How does one fit programed instruction to the extant curriculum and schedule? How does one evaluate the attempt? These are basic questions with which this chapter will deal. Neither the survey nor the case histories presented in this chapter are likely to provide definitive answers; on the other hand, a great deal may be gained by seeing some of the usage patterns which exist.

In 1962 (4) and again in 1963, the Center for Programed Instruction, at the request of the U.S. Office of Education, conducted a survey to determine patterns of use of programed instruction in schools

* The survey reported in this chapter was carried out while the authors were at the Center for Programed Instruction.

throughout the country.[1] In each year a questionnaire was sent to over 14,000 school systems listed by the Office of Education. The questionnaire was constructed to supply data concerning general familiarity with programed instruction and amount and manner of usage.

In each year, the largest single category of responses was obtained from school administrators who considered themselves "nonusers" of programed materials. Of 1,830 forms returned in 1962, 1,621 indicated nonuse of programed instructional materials. In 1963, 1,686 forms were returned; 1,073 of these indicated nonuse. It was indicated, however, that nonusers were at least familiar with the terms "programed instruction," "teaching machines," and "programed learning," and reported having seen programed instructional materials of some kind. Professional publications play the dominant role in providing initial information about programed instruction, and the Lumsdaine and Glaser (14) collection of articles was apparent in its dominance of the early literature which both users and nonusers have read. Of the number of forms returned in each year, 11.42 percent indicated some use of programed materials in 1962; 36.36 percent indicated use in 1963.

The gathering of sample programs was a major activity of both users and nonusers. In 1962, 34 percent of the schools using programs were employing consultants; and in 1963, this figure was reduced to approximately 20 percent. In 1962, some 14 percent described their systems as using programs for research; in 1963, approximately 5 percent indicated present use for this purpose, and approximately 29 percent reported contemplated usage for this purpose. Activity among nonusers leaned toward the setting up of planning groups, and a number of school systems had sent staff members to workshops and conferences.

Within those schools using programs in the spring of 1962, teachers and curriculum coordinators were responsible for initiating most of the program use, although there was considerable variety in this role. In 1963, the principal had replaced the curriculum coordinator in influence in this capacity. While most programs were obtained from commercial sources, approximately 17 percent were locally pro-

[1] Detailed statistics from these surveys are presented in a report by Lewis D. Eigen, Marilyn Clayton, and Lincoln F. Hanson, *Programed Instruction in the Schools*. Washington, D.C.: Government Printing Office. (In press)

gramed, a good indication of the active involvement of these early users. As indicated in detail in the following case histories, provision made for teacher activity in either creation or use of programs ranges from a substantial commitment of both time and money down to completely voluntary efforts by teachers themselves. It is also the teacher who is most often the director of any program project.

Patterns of Usage

During both the 1961-62 and 1962-63 school years, mathematics programs were the most available and the most used (61 percent in 1962, 64 percent in 1963). The cost of these programs (as well as those in other subjects) appeared to be between $10 and $15 per copy, and it is therefore not surprising that most were reused several times. Those that have been designed as "consumable" were being made reusable by means of locally developed answer sheets. The major use of these programs was reported at the junior and senior high school levels, but approximately half of the total number of programs used was also reported as receiving some use at or below the sixth grade. The students using programs were generally considered of average intelligence or above, and for the most part (68 percent in 1962, 62 percent in 1963) the programs were a scheduled part of regular classroom instruction. The teacher in such classes most often (approximately 60 percent in each year) was engaged in actively supplementing the program.

In 1961-62, 73 percent and in 1962-63, 79 percent of users employed programed material without any machine. Whatever other factors may also have been invoked in these decisions, the point of the Goldstein and Gotkin (10) review of research comparing machines and texts is well taken. In their survey, no significant mastery differences were found, and more often than not the text proved faster. Most programs were used without any supplementary materials, although the program itself may have constituted only a part of the total instruction within a given course.

Eighty percent of the schools using programs in 1962 were using them with only a few students or groups of students, but about 70 percent of these schools did indicate that they were in the process of incorporating materials into regular instruction. In 1963, 60 percent actually report such regular classroom use. Approximately 45 percent of the users in each year indicated that they were using programs as an integral part of the curriculum, although for only a portion of a course. Approximately 85 percent of the usage both years was in class; 20 percent in 1962 and 14 percent in 1963 were in study hall; and 22 percent in 1962 and 30 percent in 1963 were at home. (Due to overlapping categories these totals add to more than 100 percent.) Some schools restricted the use of programed materials to the classroom, while others let youngsters work on programs both in class and out. Homework in programs appeared to be increasing.

The Teacher's Role

In the two years surveyed, approximately 60 percent of the users reported that the teacher participated as an active supplement to the program, and 40 percent reported that the teacher was "available for questions." Approximately 11 percent of the users reported teachers were being employed as "proctors only" in 1962; in 1963 the number of teachers used for this function had dropped to approximately 4 percent. (Even though these categories seem to be mutually exclusive, the respondents did not in all cases interpret them as such, and as a result the total exceeds 100 percent.) Presumably, to a great extent, this last group was trying to minimize the "teacher variable" in order to evaluate the effectiveness of programed materials in and of themselves.

Evalation

Evaluations of program content were generous (almost half considered their program content "modern"), and while many respondents thought that it was too soon for over-all evaluation, in general the evaluations that were made clearly leaned toward the favorable side. Reactions of the schools and those closely associated with them, such as parents, to the use of these early products of programed instruction were also favorable. Parents, teachers, administrators, boards of education, and students all showed remarkably similar profiles of opinion. Very little of this opinion was unfavorable.

No unfavorable reports at all were found by another survey of 30 effectiveness studies done by Quackenbush at Pennsylvania State University.[2] Most of the benefits he found reported by users of programed

[2] Personal communication, 1963.

material were peripheral or auxiliary. The regularly reported lack of significant differences in content mastery was often offset by improved attitude and increased student activity.

A substantial (N=327) return from a more intensive 1963 survey of individual school principals in New York State reproduces almost all percentages of the nationwide survey quoted above. Virtually the only change in the proportions reported turns up in the over-all efficiency evaluations; the "adequate" range is maintained (56 percent), but those who feel the use of programs was extremely worthwhile was doubled (from 18 percent to 36 percent).

The most common early use of programed materials has been within large school systems. However, it is interesting to note that over 40 percent of both 1962 and 1963 users tried out programs with individual students or small groups of students rather than with whole classes. The pattern of both 1962 and 1963 usage shows that while most administrators initially plan to use programs for remedial or enrichment purposes, the actual usage pattern both years has very slightly favored regular instruction (68 percent and 62 percent, respectively) over enrichment (60 percent both years) and remedial instruction (55 percent and 51 percent). It should be pointed out that many of the respondents considered programed instruction to be helping in two or more areas, thus accounting for the overlapping categories. These figures show a growing readiness on the part of school administrators, after limited experimentation with a few students, to move more firmly into the use of programed materials as a regular part of their instructional curriculum. By no means may this decision to incorporate programs into the curriculum be regarded as a large-scale educational commitment. The trend, however, is firm, and an increase from 3 percent to 10 percent of the schools who have reported the use of programs as part of the curriculum represents an involvement of three times as many administrators, teachers, and students throughout the country.

History of School Use

Any serious discussion of the use of programed instruction in schools must take into account the fact that programed instruction was not a direct product of the elementary and secondary school world, the world which it is currently affecting most. Programed instruction hap-

pened because of the willingness of a number of experimental psychologists to extrapolate from research with lower organisms to the
human learning situation. As a result, programing was first employed
on a regular basis in 1957 at Harvard University as a part of B. F.
Skinner's "The Analysis of Behavior," a course designed to teach many
of the behavioral principles on which programed instruction is found-
ed. Other early applications of these principles in settings that were
even more remote from the schoolroom occurred in the training program of the Bell Telephone Company and at an Air Force Research
Center near Denver, Colorado. Developments in industry and the government are covered in other chapters in this volume (Chapter 15 by
Shoemaker and Holt, and Chapter 16 by Bryan and Nagay).

The first sustained use of programed instruction in a public school
occurred when Douglas Porter (16) conducted, under the sponsorship
of the U.S. Office of Education, a year-long experiment in teaching
programed spelling to 102 second and sixth graders at the Mystic
School in Winchester, Massachusetts. (A shorter program was also
used with 63 fourth graders.) This use of programed instruction, like
Skinner's initial use, presented the programed material to students
via individual teaching machines designed by the experimenter. The
results of this first use of programing in elementary education were
not startling from the standpoint of the amount learned; students
learned about as much from the program as comparable groups have
learned from usual classroom instruction. However, notable gains in
time were recorded. In the experimenter's words, "When efficiency of
the teaching techniques were taken into account . . . the machine treatment resulted in a time advantage of approximately 3:1 for the entire
group" (16).

Much the same findings resulted from the first use of programed
instruction in secondary school in 1959 when Eigen and Komoski (5)
conducted an experiment in teaching modern mathematics to 74 ninth
and tenth graders at the Collegiate School in New York City. An additional aspect of the work at Collegiate was a comparison between the
presentation of a program via teaching machines on the one hand
and via programed textbooks on the other. The results showed a significant time advantage for the programed texts. This concept of the
programed textbook had grown out of a second pioneering use of
programed instruction at the university level in 1958 when Evans,

Glaser, and Homme (6) of the University of Pittsburgh printed programs in a unique book format designed to simulate certain characteristics of a teaching machine. The Eigen-Komoski study pointed out no significant difference in learning between the two presentation modes (10). Programed texts were also used in the first trials of programed instruction in public secondary schools in the Baldwin-Whitehall schools in suburban Pittsburgh, Pennsylvania, and in Roanoke, Virginia. These trials occurred almost simultaneously during the academic year 1960-61. In 1960, the Roanoke city schools tried their first programs using teaching machines; however, in all subsequent use they have used the simpler programed textbooks (19). Both Baldwin-Whitehall and Roanoke have subsequently expanded their use of programed materials.

It seems appropriate to point out that the general agreement upon the relatively poor showing of teaching machines to date is attributed largely to poor designs hurriedly produced. More than three years after his first experience with machines, Porter (15) openly criticized commercially produced devices as still inappropriate for use in the classroom. Komoski (13), who had taken a similar position in March 1960, felt justified in reiterating it two years later. It will be important to note the difference between the basically crude machine that seems to make little contribution to increased learning and subject matter presentation and the rapidly developing computer-based teaching machines (see Chapter 5 by Stolurow and Davis and Chapter 6 by Lewis and Pask).

At about the same time that Baldwin-Whitehall and Roanoke were early proving grounds, two other school systems were taking a somewhat different approach to the introduction and use of programed instruction. In the schools of Denver, Colorado, and Newton, Massachusetts, decisions were made to free small groups of teachers to be trained on a part-time basis as programers and to have them create programed materials designed to meet the specific curriculum needs of each school system.

The spectrum of usage has increased each year, and the trend seems to be in the direction of finding increasingly flexible use of programed (and other) materials to free the individual student to proceed at his own rate. A large school system in Manhasset, New York, and its surrounding schools have proven most adept in achieving such flexibility for the individual student. At the other corner of the country, in Tucson, Arizona, an individual teacher operating on her own in a single classroom has developed another highly individualized pattern. Both of these procedures will be discussed in more detail.

The Case Studies
Urban Schools: Roanoke, Virginia

The first large-scale field testing of programed instruction in secondary schools was done in the Roanoke city schools as a result of an invitation by Allen Calvin, a psychologist at Hollins College, to Edward Rushton, Roanoke's superintendent. President John Everett of Hollins had requested Calvin to design an experiment which would assess the possibilities of programed learning materials. A single eighth-grade class used ninth-grade algebra materials in some of Skinner's early machines in February 1960. The results of this pilot test were favorable, and in the fall of 1960 some 900 ninth graders in all of the Roanoke high schools participated in the field test of three mathematics programs, Algebra I and II and geometry (19). The two main goals of this large-scale field test were to determine the effect of programed materials without machines and the retention of learning acquired during these three mathematics courses taught by programed instruction. Some of the students finished algebra as early as December 1960 and were "encouraged to take other mathematics material." Three-quarters of the students who used programs finished before the end of the year, and less than one-quarter continued with their programs into summer school. One girl continued with Algebra I until November of the following year. She then demanded Algebra II which she again continued over into summer session. Her score of over 500 in the College Board algebra test is cited as an indication of the importance of allowing an individual student to proceed at his own rate.

The results in terms of student achievement of this early large-scale test were scarcely overwhelming; Algebra I program groups tested significantly better than the conventional classes taught by the same teachers, the Algebra II conventional group tested better than the program groups, and there was no significant difference between the plane geometry program and conventional groups (19). None of the retention tests showed significant differences. Despite the lack of spectacular success, Roanoke decided that student and teacher reaction was positive enough to justify the inclusion of programed materials in the regular curriculum for the following year.

In the summer of 1961, a summer work conference developed teacher-made tests and teachers manuals for the programs that were to be incorporated into the regular curriculum. In addition to the mathematics materials already tested, programs in Spanish, French phonetics, and first-year Latin were made available. In the fall of 1961, teachers were given the option of using programed materials, and if they were interested they were given an opportunity, not available to all of the mathematics teachers the prior year, to become familiar with the materials before their use. Further, students who specified preference for traditional texts were not assigned to classes using programed materials. Programed texts have been subsequently purchased by school appropriation starting with these fall 1961 adoptions, and since that time more than one-third of the seventh- to twelfth-grade population has used programed instructional materials in mathematics.

In 1962-63, Roanoke involved 200 additional students with second-year German materials, and during the 1963-64 term, teachers expanded their use of programs into 18 different subjects. Current usage patterns are more diverse than before, ranging from some time every day to once or twice a week to the occasional reference of a student through an appropriate advanced or remedial supplementary unit. Some classes stay with a schedule and let students use extra class time for studying; others have fewer group meetings and/or allow individual students to move into advanced material as they complete the basic course.

Perhaps because of its early involvement in field testing of material developed by outside subject matter experts, Roanoke has developed no programs of its own. Most other pioneer school systems were forced to develop their own programs without the opportunity for field testing commercially supplied materials. Denver, the next case study, is such an example.

In retrospect (19), Roanoke feels that it has learned "the hard way" that teachers should be involved far earlier in the adoption of new materials. Superintendent Rushton estimates that it took four months of the first large-scale test year for the teachers to feel at all confident about what they were doing. His feeling is based on the confusion of the first fall semester and the noticeable change in the way teachers handled visitors after the first year. He strongly recommends that no school system introduce programs without the most thorough orientation possible for teachers. He further feels that teachers and, if possible, students should participate only at their own option.

Denver, Colorado

The public school system of Denver, Colorado, was among the first large city systems to investigate programed instruction. It was through the superintendent's personal interest that in 1959 Denver became the first school system in the country to free a teacher from classroom duties to receive training in programing. As might be expected, therefore, Denver is among the few school systems to have developed a substantial amount of programed materials for use within its own curriculum. To date, instruction in English usage, the mechanics of writing, Spanish, and the U.S. Constitution have been programed by Denver teachers, who have been employed by the school system to write programs during the summer and on their free time during the school year.

Other facets of Denver's experience with programed instruction have included (a) a research study designed to investigate the attributes of a particular programed textbook; (b) research into the effects of various schedules of "confirmation of response" during the use of a mathematics program by students of low, average, and above-average ability; and (c) a study designed to test the use of programed instruction in combination with educational television in the teaching of Spanish. This latter experiment, which was part of a larger project, was unique in that it was the first large-scale attempt (involving 75 schools) to use individually paced programed material as a complement to group-paced televised instruction. This experiment is of interest also because it utilized the audiovisual resources of television to present the "conversational" portions of the Spanish course, while leaving instruction in reading and writing to teacher-prepared programed textbooks. Thus, this experiment represents a conscious division of an instructional task between an audiovisual medium and the printed word, with both employed to teach specific and separate behavioral objectives. One only wishes that research in language learning were able to supply evidence on which to base such a "division." Nevertheless, after its first year of experimenting, Denver was able to offer some pragmatic proof that such a division of instructional labor in language teaching is both workable and effective (12).

The initial use of programed instruction in the schools of Denver in 1960 occurred before their teacher-made programs were available and was within the narrower context of an experiment designed to answer four specific questions about a particular programed textbook, in fact, the first such book to be published commercially, a program in English grammar (1). The questions asked were (a) Does this grammar program, as a learning instrument, work equally well with pupils who have low academic achievement as it does with those who have average and high achievement? (b) How does learning compare for students who have worked through the program and those with more traditional learning experiences? (c) How long does it take for students of varying abilities to work through the program? and (d) Which parts of the books are especially difficult?

These four questions were asked in direct reference to a particular (but hardly unique) problem faced by the Denver schools, the problem of how to improve students' ability to write coherently. While perennial in most schools, this problem was somewhat intensified in Denver during the late 1950's by an increasingly mobile school population and an influx of large groups of Spanish-speaking children into the city's schools. To meet its needs, therefore, Denver was looking for a self-instructional program that might be used for bringing a large, diverse group of students up to a baseline of acceptable achievement in certain aspects of English usage.

As a result of its first experiment, Denver discovered (18) that this programed course did produce substantial learning in all ability groups and, furthermore, that the range in working time (9.68 to 14.23 hours) indicated that the programed method made allowance for individual differences in reading speed and working habits. However, it was also discovered that the program "proved to be more effective with students who have high achievement" (p. 478). Bright students in the experimental group scored higher on both standardized measures than did their counterparts in the control group who did not use the program. On the other hand, the low achievers "who did not use [the program] scored higher (on both measures) than those who did" (p. 478). With average students there was no significant difference in achievement between the experimental and the control groups (18).

On the completion of this study, Denver has an important question to answer: namely, did the grammar program meet the particular instructional needs of the Denver English curriculum? An answer to this question is to be found by observing practice in Denver three academic years after the study was launched. The particular program involved in the study was not used; however, as has been indicated, programed instruction was. The version of the grammar program used in 1960 did not meet Denver's needs for low-ability students, and a second version of the program seemed no better equipped to meet these needs. The frames that had been identified by the Denver study as being especially difficult had not been (in the opinion of the Denver staff) sufficiently revised to indicate that the program could now meet the needs of low-ability students.

As a result, Denver has done what many other schools using programed instruction have attempted; namely, set out to design and create programs specifically aimed at its own particular needs. In this case, as has been indicated earlier, Denver has employed a group of its English teachers to create a series of programed text units, each dealing with a specific need of the students engaged in the "Lay Reader System" of teaching English composition. This system was developed by Paul Diederich of the Educational Testing Service and pioneered in the Denver schools. Under this system, the student first of all writes; then his work is graded by a "lay" or nonprofessional reader who has been trained by members of Denver's professional teaching staff to spot certain key errors. Each type of error a student makes is recorded on an error grid which eventually supplies his English instructor with a profile of that particular student. Then and only then does programed instruction enter the picture. Using the error grid as a diagnostic instrument, the student is assigned to a series of programed units designed especially to remedy the types of errors he has made in his written work. As the directors of this program put it: ". . . if it becomes evident that a pupil is having difficulty with dangling modifiers . . . the program will be designed specifically to help him overcome his trouble" (12). In an informal study, Wahler (20) has reported an experimental variation in Denver's handling of the problem of adjusting to individual student entering levels: Each student punctuates a graded series of sentences, and on the basis of his performance, he is referred to appropriate program units.

In reviewing Denver's experience during four years of a growing commitment to programed instruction, one is tempted to conclude that the value of the new technique is in the construction of materials by a school system that knows its needs and is willing to give gifted teachers both encouragement and the time in which to meet these needs. Indeed, it would seem that Denver has benefited more from designing and using homegrown materials than from the use of commercially available programs. This may be quite true, and if it is, it adds support to the many advocates of programed instruction who contend that its greatest value lies in the effect it can have on teachers who learn the discipline of programing (see also 17).

Newton, Massachusetts

The interest in programed instruction in the schools of Newton, Massachusetts, developed almost simultaneously with that of Denver and Roanoke. While this interest stemmed from much the same motivation as Denver's, Newton had no instructional problems comparable to Denver's highly mobile population or students for whom English was a second language. Newton had participated in pioneering other educational innovations and therefore welcomed its responsibility for investigating and evaluating the potential of programed instruction. This attitude is clearly illustrated by the statement made in 1961 by J. Bernard Everett (7), the director of instruction:

It seems to be increasingly evident, therefore, that the major responsibility for the future of programed learning rests primarily with public school educators like myself. We cannot afford to wait for the academic schools, the professors of education or our professional associates to tell us what to do. We must take the initiative, for if we don't it will be seized by others less qualified than we are to decide what should happen in the schools.

Three factors, then, led to Newton's receptivity to programed instruction:

1. Newton is, by tradition, receptive to new ideas; it is a well-to-do community with considerable parental and community interest in its schools.
2. Perhaps a critical item, Newton had a director of instruction who was highly interested in learning about the nature of programed instruction and its suitability for the Newton school system.

3. Excellent relationships existed between Newton and some of the book publishing companies, manifesting itself at this point in a willingness by the publishers to supply funds and materials with which Newton was encouraged to experiment.

Newton at this time was working with the ATA (Academically Talented in Arithmetic) program and was interested in finding ways in which teachers, in a self-contained classroom, could work with a wide variety of arithmetic talents. The results of this confluence of interests led Newton very shortly, after informational visits to Harvard and the Center for Programed Instruction, to start writing programs to meet their special local need. After a general informational meeting, the Newton teachers who were interested in program writing and/or use were provided additional guidance, discussion opportunities, and finally summer workshops. Three programs have emerged from this effort, *Prime Numbers and Factoring*, *Number Systems*, and *Sets*, all of which have been used for several years in the sixth and some fifth grades in the Newton school system. They are not used across the board, but are available to any interested teacher. Newton described its interest during this study as wishing to satisfy a specific local need in the ATA program and wishing to keep very good control of the reins of program usage.

Newton does not hesitate to say that it is still looking for answers with programed materials. In 1962 it invested very heavily in both time and money in a Spanish program for some 13 children. While the taped materials seemed to produce better spoken Spanish, the teachers felt that the loss of grammar rendered the students quite vulnerable to the demands of a more conventional examination or subsequent course. Furthermore, the fact that a second-year program was not immediately available left them somewhat high and dry. The Spanish program was not officially used again in 1963-64, but two or three students used the material on their own because of inability to get into regular classes. Present plans call for obtaining from 5 to 10 copies of similarly individualized language materials in German, Russian, and Latin for upper-class students who would otherwise not be able to schedule these subjects. Other evaluations of programs which have been used at the high school level in Newton have resulted in the familiar criticism that linear programs, even in modern mathematics, become boring the further one gets into them, a phenomenon which accumulates quite severely with a two- or three-year sequence. Two different English word analysis programs seemed profitable for about 50 percent of the students who took them, but reading level proved to be a screening device and forced some of the intended student population to drop out early.

On the whole, the Newton teachers most involved with programed materials are very pleased at the trend toward shorter programs, and it is perhaps no coincidence that all programs developed by the teachers themselves are of this unitary nature. There is clearly a demand by the teachers for short units in many subject matter areas, and the state of production both in the commercial world and from their own colleagues will not soon be able to fill their requests.

In introducing programed instruction, Newton went through a number of specific activities, the exact sequence of which, as they are careful to point out, is not necessarily the only suitable one. Newton had a consultant talk with their top administrators and then held a large meeting, open to all interested teachers, at which the same consultant spoke and answered questions. Newton then presented a three-day workshop for approximately 30 of its own teachers. Subsequently, it sent 19 teachers to a 40-hour workshop at Harvard (21).

One teacher was sent to New York City for training in program writing with expenses paid by a grant from a publisher. An illustrated lecture was prepared for teacher groups and was made available upon request to any school; it was requested perhaps five or six times the first year and more often each year since. Simultaneously the Newton Office of Instruction made it a point to assemble, circulate, and disseminate all the information on programed instruction and all the sample programs that it could obtain.

After three years of such preliminary activities the acting Director of Instruction, Donald Welch,[3] felt that the pressure and the time were right; almost half of the schools held staff meetings on the subject of programed instruction. Throughout all of this activity the Office of Instruction tried to maintain a helpful clearinghouse role; whenever a program came under consideration by any teacher, he had but to request information, and a sample was obtained along with such evaluative data as might be available.

[3] Newton data based on visits and personal communications, 1963.

Because of this long-term, low-pressure method of introduction, programed instruction has never been considered, as far as is known to the administration, by even one teacher as a "threat." Furthermore, the Office of Instruction is not aware of any critical comments other than the common performance problems of boredom, lack of suitable materials, etc. Over 30 teachers have now taken courses in programed instruction; between 75 and 100 actually have used programed materials in connection with their teaching. Welch estimates that of the 900 people involved in teaching and administration, some 200 may be said to have reasonable knowledge of programed instruction.

Questioned as to specific behaviors actually traceable to the use of programed instruction, an elementary mathematics teacher using the local program says, "I never could have taught this much this quickly." Another said she had learned a great deal herself, and the supervisor mentions the high interest and even excitement among his staff with these materials. A second change observed by the Office of Instruction occurs in the way in which teachers who have used programed materials, particularly those who have written them, seem to be working with the children. Specifically, these teachers seem to be more sensitized to the needs and reactions of their students.

Manhasset, Long Island, New York

In a suburb of New York City, an alert associate superintendent brought several teachers to visit one of the early programing centers, and it was one of those teachers, John MacGowan of Manhasset High School, who several months later initiated the use of the same English grammar program used in Denver almost as soon as it was off the press. From the start, Manhasset was concerned with comparing these new materials with existing techniques. Recognizing the importance of surveillance in the early stages of innovation, Manhasset also elected to use its programed materials exclusively in class. But, being bolder than most other schools, they decided very early to try the experiment with one-quarter of their eighth-grade grammar students, plus 25 seventh graders. This meant that Manhasset was using 75 pupils as its very first experimental population, with 150 eighth graders and 175 seventh graders taking conventional grammar instruction as controls.

After three months of preliminary study, during which the groups were selected for the experiment and during which no formal grammar instruction was given to the experimental groups, the experiment was started in January 1961. Three of the five 40-minute periods scheduled for an English and social studies block were spent with the program. On a typical day, each student picked up a copy of the programed text and a response sheet as he entered the room. He first wrote the number of the frame at which his day's work began and proceeded informally at his own pace, writing each response (and each correction) on the separate sheet. Since this was an experiment, the student was given only minimum assistance by the monitoring teachers (underlining and clarification of terms for the most part).

As soon as the student finished a unit of the subject matter, he went to the front desk and received a copy of the appropriate unit test, which he completed, returned to the teacher, and saw immediately graded. If he did not achieve at least 80 percent mastery on this test, he returned to the unit for more study and subsequently tried an alternate form of the unit test. If he missed 80 percent a second or third time, using the tests alternately, he was either kept at the unit until he mastered it or else was moved along mechanically with the few students who had not mastered the unit. Bright students moved very rapidly with this system, average students made satisfactory progress, and only the few for whom grammar is always a problem had to be moved along without making the 80 percent criterion "on their own."

Of the 75 students starting this experiment in January, the first, a girl, completed the whole programed text in early March in just over nine working hours, and she was started immediately on composition writing under individual teacher guidance.[4] This meant that composition writing (ostensibly the rationale for studying grammar) began in early March and occupied the rest of the student's year. Each student subsequently completing the program was similarly freed for semi-independent writing, and the whole group completed its grammar requirements on or before the end of the school year, despite the delayed start. This eliminated, for bright students especially, the need for dragging out grammar instruction at the slower class pace. The school, the students, and the parents felt the results to be highly satisfactory. However, the school did not feel that it had a sufficiently objective measure of achievement for either the experimental or control groups.

[4] Personal communication, 1963. (See also 17.)

Only recently has an adequately standardized grammar test been available and used to get such a measure. While the experimental teachers
felt at the time that the students, as a group, showed marked improvement in capitalization, punctuation, and subordination, it was only
with the administration of this standardized test two years after the
experiment was run that these students showed up not only as well as
the other tenth graders still in the school, but with a saving of 4,000
hours in grammar instruction.

In October 1961, the program was adopted for a larger testing with
50 percent of the eighth-grade students. A somewhat unwieldy 519-
item pretest, correlated with the units of the book, was given to all
100 experimental students. Any unit score of 100 percent released the
student from having to go through the appropriate unit of English
grammar. Before Thanksgiving, the first student, taking full advantage of the pretest exemptions, completed her grammar requirements
in 7 1/2 working hours. By early December there were five students
who were removed from the program room and given individual attention in their composition writing. This newly established "class,"
chosen on the basis of three months' performance rather than on mere
opinion or a single selection test, was filled in January, with obvious
gains in opportunity to write compositions for the rest of the year.
Such 60 percent to 80 percent gains in freed time, especially for bright
students, constitute quite an addition to the student's own curriculum,
particularly in a period when there "never seems to be enough time
to teach everything."

Another unusual occurrence helped shape Manhasset's subsequent
employment of programed material. Even before the first student had
finished use of the program, 28 of the 100 experimental students informed the teachers in charge that they were having difficulties with
the program. These students became the first group to be pulled out
of the program sessions and were given immediate supplemental help.
This group was given a separate classroom, along with a teacher who
was well aware of the special nature of the group. These students still
used the programed text and worked at it regularly, as judged appropriate by the teacher, but where the programed unit did not do the job,
this group received both supplemental class discussion and tutoring.
As soon as any student in this group seemed to be moving ahead satisfactorily, he was allowed to rejoin the large group, once again back
completely at his own pace.

Even with the slowest students who had to be helped to complete the course, Manhasset teachers feel that the program offered a very considerable advantage over regular class activities. Every response made by the student had been recorded, not only in the program but also in each unit test that he had taken, in addition to the pretests and posttests. Rarely has such a quantity of diagnostic assistance been available to a teacher as existed for the teachers of these students.

Manhasset, then, is an example of unusual administrative flexibility emerging from the handling of the problems of slower individuals. The perceptive teacher response to restive students having trouble with the program meant that individual treatment was available to the student well before such problem accumulation became dangerous.

The teachers were also aware of the increased number of compositions that their students had time to write. An indication of the effect of the increased composition writing done by Manhasset's eighth graders is furnished by the following event. Near the close of the school year, a suggestion was made that some of the good compositions of the spring be reproduced. So plentiful was the supply of acceptable compositions that a noteworthy literary magazine was assembled in just three days.[5]

Present usage of the English grammar program in Manhasset is even more flexible. In the present brighter student population (defined and selected so that no student has an IQ below 100), there is a self-identified subgroup, which any student may join at will, where he will get individual and class attention as necessary. Such a student may also rejoin the larger and less personal section as soon as he gets over the problem which he has himself diagnosed. As one teacher says, "We have refined and refined to make this imperfect thing (the program) go, and the encouraging thing is that it gets easier and easier to do. All teachers involved have been through each step of the process, and new wrinkles can be added to individualize the material as long as rooms and teachers are available. While the program was not what we thought we would be getting, we have begun to achieve a system in which the status of the individual student is remarkably free. He can move out of the main group into a smaller help unit almost at will, and rejoin it as soon as he gets moving again."[6] This teacher has reported that formerly he had "known" only his one class of 25 gram-

---

[5] Personal communication, 1963.
[6] John MacGowan, personal communication, 1962.

mar students and felt like a relative stranger in the eighth-grade wing of the school. In correcting the unit tests and going over them with the students to spot problems, he found that he now knew almost all 200 students in the eighth grade and in many cases knew more about them than he had known about most of the 25 he had formerly had in class.

If the first student through such a program saves 40 or more of the 50 hours heretofore allowed for grammar instruction and if the average savings is only 20 instructional hours, when the number of students is increased to 200 the savings are undeniably impressive. Couple this with the fact that the teachers report an increased knowledge of the progress and problems of each student, and the specter of mass education by impersonal instruction is less threatening.

Manhasset is currently a key unit in a larger neighboring educational community experiment which may be considered an expansion of the Manhasset effort. With professional experimental guidance from a local university, six neighboring Long Island school districts have joined Manhasset in a full-scale trial of the grammar program based largely upon Manhasset's earlier experiences. Manhasset, Port Washington, Roslyn, Garden City, Mineola, and East Williston all have used this program as their method of teaching English grammar, while Great Neck provided the control population with "conventional" grammar instruction.

As a final note to Manhasset's work, the first 12 students to finish in the current experiment with the grammar program had a minimum final mastery score of 90 percent, and one can see how both teachers and administrators feel most handsomely rewarded for their attention to and flexible use of programed instructional material.

An interesting comparison may be made regarding the use of this same program in English grammar in Manhasset and Denver. Obviously both school systems feel that work in composition is the central work to be done in the English curriculum at the junior high school level. Both systems also seem to agree that the teaching of formal grammar as such does little to make students better writers. As a result of one experiment, Denver chose to discard this "broadside" grammar program in favor of units specifically designed to remedy particular aspects of a student's work in composition. Manhasset, on the other hand, has taken the attitude that formal grammar is a kind of necessary evil in the curriculum and should be gotten out of the way as soon as possible. Manhasset considers programs an ideal way of doing this because they save the time of teachers and pupils alike and can make it possible to devote more class time to the teaching of writing skills. Obviously, both strategies have something to be said for them and serve to illustrate the variety of ways in which different schools with similar outlooks to the same problem can use an experimental approach to programed instruction. The flexible experimental approach is the key point here and is of greater importance than the particular solutions of the moment.

Baldwin-Whitehall Schools, Pittsburgh, Pennsylvania

During the 1962-63 and 1963-64 school years, the Learning Research and Development Center at the University of Pittsburgh conducted, in the Baldwin-Whitehall School System, a study of the use of programed instructional materials within existing classroom structures (9). At elementary and junior high school levels, intact classroom groups, that is, the class as a whole, received instruction with specially prepared and commercially available programed materials in arithmetic, time-telling, general science, and algebra. Using these materials, the effects of teacher-program coordination, review and acceleration, variations in IQ, and enrichment activities were studied, and appropriate criterion and statistical measures were used to evaluate student performance.

Use of a program in addition and subtraction at the first-grade level indicated that the program was not as efficient as should have been expected and that different types of teacher-program combinations (initial instruction from the teacher followed by the program, initial instruction from the program followed by teacher direction, and all instruction from the program) made little difference in student gains.

Students in the first grade were also taught to tell time to the one-minute interval by means of a program that combined structured teacher instruction and paced individual student responding. The distribution of work on the program was different for three groups of children (one 20-minute period a day for 14 days, two 20-minute periods a day for 7 days, or one 20-minute period every other day for 28 days). This variable appeared to have no effect on final performance. However, with this experimental program, many children were successful in learning to tell time after the intensive instruction provided by the program. Programs of this kind may be useful to teach difficult special skills which are usually taught more incidentally.

Use of a program in fourth-grade multiplication and division indicated that difference in IQ between classroom groups apparently had little effect upon final achievement and the amount of learning (gain scores) that took place. After completing the program, one group continued with regular fourth-grade work which included review and additional work in multiplication and division at the same time that another group (of equivalent IQ level) was given accelerated instruction in fractions. No differences between groups were found in end-of-year multiplication and division scores, indicating that the accelerated fractions instruction did not detract from the learning or retention of multiplication and division topics which would normally have been reviewed by the teacher during the time used for fractions instruction. At the same time, the fractions group attained high scores on a fractions test, normally a fifth-grade subject.

In fourth-grade programed spelling instruction, program groups were compared with groups who received conventional instruction. It was found that there was no significant difference between these groups on a nationally standardized spelling test. On a test measuring ability to spell the 354 words taught by the program, however, the program group achieved significantly higher scores. The data from both tests were interpreted to mean that students were able to learn more spelling words in the same period of time by being required to do so, but that this acceleration did not detract from their learning to spell words usually taught at this level.

In seventh-grade general science, it was found that the length of "enrichment" periods related to program content following programed instruction had a facilitating effect on achievement immediately following learning. There was no effect upon the amount of programed material retained over a longer period of time. Also in seventh-grade general science, some teachers used familiarization procedures prior to programed instruction by presenting an overview of the subject matter and requiring students to learn to spell the new terms they were to encounter during the program. No reliable differences were found when this group was compared with those students who did not receive prefamiliarization instruction.

A ninth-grade algebra program was found to be less effective for an average-IQ group than for an above-average group. This was attributed to the fact that the average group was not able to complete the entire program in the time allotted, and thus had less instructional material to draw upon when tested at the end of the term.

The broad conclusions that were gathered from detailed analysis of these studies are the following:

1. There is extensive variation in rate of learning within a class when students are given the opportunity to proceed at their own rate with programed learning materials.
2. Program pretest scores show that many students know the subject being taught, and some few students are not ready to learn it.
3. Different types of teacher-program combinations may make little difference in student achievement.
4. Young children can be taught a subject intensively with little loss in retention, at least over the short period of time (two weeks) measured in this study.
5. The extent of the correlation between general intelligence and achievement as a result of programed instruction depends upon the particular program involved. In general, intelligence appears to be related to the pace at which a student goes through a program.
6. Extension of the curriculum with programed materials, necessarily taking away from time spent in conventional grade-level instruction, produced additional learning without being detrimental to the learning of materials usually taught at that grade level. In general, students required to learn more can learn more.

Rural Schools in Utah

Having covered in some detail several urban and suburban experiences with programed materials, it is time to look at the other end of the continuum. What has been done by or for the small rural school which is so isolated and so different from its more populous neighbors?

The Western States Small Schools Project (WSSSP) is a coordinated, regional effort to provide the necessary assistance to develop local experimentation that will answer some of the unique problems of the small school. A recent report by Ford and Walker (8) suggests that the problems of such small schools may exist in all but four of the 50 states. The five cooperating states of the WSSSP have parceled out the study of some of their common problem areas, such as Small Group Technique, In-Service Programs, Flexible Scheduling, Shared Services, and TV; however, all of the states involved (Arizona, Colorado, Nevada, New Mexico, and Utah) are experimenting with programed materials. In order to be specific, the experiences of one state have been selected as an example of some needs which programed instruction seems to be helping to meet.

The background which prompted the state education department of Utah to use programed instruction was the perennial problem of small rural schools with small groups of students in each class, needing more varieties or levels of subject matter than any single, or even area, school system could possibly provide. Stated simply, their needs ran far ahead of their ability to provide curricula suitable for a broad range of students.

The small schools of Utah, for some time, had been using "supervised correspondence courses." The student desiring a course available by correspondence would request it; a local teacher would then take on part-time supervision of the student's work and attempt to answer his questions, as well as monitor and correct examinations. This system had been considered modestly successful and is still used, but many subjects are not thus available. Another need in this particular geographical area was in the field of language teaching. Language teachers are difficult to obtain and at least as difficult to retain. The limited amount of language instruction available in books and on record is apt to be expensive and rarely successful in the conditions under which they would have had to be used.

When it came to an initial selection of programed materials, the Utah experience was common to most of the other pioneers; they simply took anything available that even remotely seemed to match their many needs. (Only recently have they felt that they had any choice; still more recently have they felt that they had anywhere near enough know-how to make intelligent choices.) All of their program usage obviously involves only limited numbers of copies; perhaps the largest group observed by the authors consisted of a dozen students. Their evaluation of programed instruction, based as much upon their very great need as upon any program effectiveness criteria, is best indicated by the fact that in any current multiple-class situation they immediately look for programed materials in the subject area involved.

When questioned as to "the best method in introducing programed instruction into a system," the Utah project lists the following procedures which they have adopted. First, since most new supplementary materials, such as programed instruction, have to be adapted to the special needs of the small school, everyone on the staff is aware of the experimental nature of their use. Second, all administrators receive information about programed instruction and, as soon as possible, sample materials. Third, on the basis of interest shown by either teachers or students, the local administration then recommends purchase. Fourth, the material is tried with students; hopefully a teacher is able to get through it ahead of, or at least along with, the students.

After three years, the Utah project still regards itself in the experimental phase of program usage; this means that having started to use programs as expedient or stop-gap measures, the participants in this experiment only now feel that they are beginning to make creative use of programs and may at last be on the way to establishing a philosophy of use. Utah is also careful to point out that they do not consider that they have yet made a full evaluation of programed materials, but they also admit that they are not likely to discard them.[7]

No programs have been introduced in this project on the basis of authority only. Teachers, perhaps as a result, do not consider programed materials as a threat at all. The one trend which the Utah group would like to encourage in the interests of flexibility is that already started by publishers to produce shorter subject matter units. The teachers in this project have rarely, if at all, tried their hands at writing programs, although the advantage as a teacher-training device has not escaped official notice. At the moment the project has no plans for producing programs, although other schools and universities in Utah are involved in program production, and the Small Schools Project will continue to do some experimental testing of these. Rowan Stutz, director of the Utah Project, reports that they would like to relate programed materials better to the rest of their curriculum, but they are struggling to find a way to do so. For example, they would like very much to use a program as the core of a course and have materials available to supplement it, enrich it, or provide related background material for students for whom the program is too difficult. While the teachers who first used programed materials found them-

[7] Personal communication, 1963.

selves cast largely in the role of monitors, the project has now advanced to the stage where teachers consider a program as another tool to help them. The only change foreseen in the role of the teacher awaits the availability of a greater variety of programed materials. The teacher will then have a greater possibility of matching material to his own teaching objectives. In other words, it is anticipated that the control of learning materials will very clearly remain in the hands of the teacher.

In an informal statement summing up the present stage of the Utah project experience, Stutz reports several changes. The teachers find their students more independent and more responsible. Even an improvement in motivation can be demonstrated by the extra work that the students do. The presence of the teacher is perceptibly less necessary in the classes working with programed materials, and the youngsters choose their own next experience without waiting for, or relying upon, a teacher. Another most pleasing and readily observable behavior brought about by the introduction of programed materials has been noted by even casual visitors: teachers using programs are seldom seen talking in front of the class. Instead, the class is busy in varied activities or at various places in a program, and the teacher is free to circulate to discuss individual questions and problems.[8]

Other Small School Systems

In Middletown (New York) High School, a scheduled study hall is set up to allow students to work on programs or other individual material under the guidance of an assigned teacher. Students request material at the beginning of each semester, and the school is gradually accumulating a small library of independent study materials. Students have profited from such programs as calculus, the slide rule, and beginning chess.

The Catskill Area Project in New York State contains one high school in Fleischmanns which has a student population of 72 and is able to offer over 40 courses, largely with the aid of programed materials which cover subjects for which they would normally have neither schedule time nor teaching personnel.

[8] Personal communication, 1963.

A third rural pattern is furnished by the director and coordinator of the Ulster County Board of Cooperative Educational Services. They felt that programed instruction was important to their member school systems, yet was not feasible for any school or system to tackle by itself. The coordinator took on the cautious task of introducing a real understanding of programed materials to the teachers of the county. First an introductory general session was presented for teachers. A one-day working session was offered some weeks later, and enough interest emerged from this active group so that the school administrators, for whom the Board provides services, approved a year-long workshop the following year. After this gradual two-year introduction of its teachers, Ulster County presently has a dozen individual school or school system projects under way. Involvement ranges from the assembling of potentially suitable materials in local learning aids centers all the way to small groups of teachers who work together on individualizing the instruction in a shared subject matter and have actually created some programed materials to cover needs not satisfied elsewhere.[9]

Cooperative efforts are obviously appropriate in innovation, and Ulster County took full advantage of an existing but informally structured administrative mechanism. Such experiences in the Western States Small Schools Project offer ample evidence to educators that programed instruction and its experimental use are far from large-school or large-system monopolies. The advantages of banding together for mutual sharing of information are also clear. The next example is chosen to show that even a single isolated classroom can formulate a suitable base for profitable learning about, as well as with, programed materials.

Tucson, Arizona

Having looked at the use of programed instruction in urban, suburban, and rural settings, this chapter turns to a description of the way it has been introduced into the curriculum of a typical American high school to answer the needs of a specific group of learners. A classroom in Tucson, Arizona, represents a typical situation, that is to say, a school

[9] Coordinator George Fernandez, personal communication, 1963.

in which the administration was interested in (but not overly excited about) programed instruction and hence was willing to allow one teacher (who was indeed very excited about the potential of this technique) to experiment freely in teaching a group of slow learners at the ninth-grade level.

Confronted with the lower end of a normal distribution and despite the knowledge that for such a group of students the curriculum may be justifiably narrowed to manageable limits, the teacher still found great problems in meeting the needs of a group of slow learners whose slowness derived from a great variety of factors. She stated that "to ignore this reality by trying to teach such slow learners as a group invites the frustration of at least five-sixths of the class and encourages the discipline problems which tend to abound with these students under the best of circumstances" (11).

This teacher turned to programed instruction in an attempt to establish a tutorial system of teaching her English classes within what otherwise would be a typical classroom situation. The teacher describes her tutorial classroom in the following way:

The outsider observing the classroom for the first time might well conclude that he is observing a supervised study hall. . . . Instruction per se is carried on by means of the materials in the room, most of which are auto-instructional in nature. The teacher interviews each student in turn, reviewing work completed, clearing up difficulties and making new assignments. Assignment sheets are kept in duplicate. The student retains the original in his folder as a working paper and the teacher keeps a carbon in a master notebook. On the teacher's carbon of the assignment sheet are kept the student's standardized test results which serve as a guide in assigning various learning tasks. . . . Monitors in each of the three classes distribute and collect the folders at the beginning and end of each period (11).

In describing the tutorial sessions, the teacher pointed out that four 10- to 15-minute interviews can be fitted into each class period. This means that she can see each student in the class about once a week except for some particularly slow learners who need to be interviewed more often. But even these seem to be counterbalanced by an equal number of self-reliant students who take the initiative in assigning themselves tasks if the time between interviews happens to run longer than a week.

While the teacher states that 20 students seem to be optimum class size with slow learners, she feels that it is not only possible but probable that with more mature students classes of 30, 40, or even 50 might not be out of the question. Here, however, she introduces a big "if": "*if* the proper instructional materials become available." The programs being used with this group are a mixture of commercial and teacher-made programed texts. In addition, the teacher has also prepared a number of self-teaching tapes which are used in student-operated recorders. Programs are worked on in a classroom, and homework for the group consists of reading for pleasure.

This teacher clearly views her job as one of controlling the learning environment, and she views programed materials as a great aid in maintaining such control. She is very tolerant of the inadequacies of present programs, saying simply, "If the materials do a faulty job of teaching, then we will develop other better materials which do a better job. This is a commercial problem in the same way that the manufacturer of physician's pills and serums is a commercial problem. The teacher's problems are those of motivation, diagnosis, prescription, and supervision." Commenting further on the teacher's role in such a tutorial method, she says, "The demand for adequate preparation is immediate, merciless, and inexorable. In prescribing learning materials the teacher must know what those materials will do and won't do, how they are to be used, how to judge whether or not mastery of these materials has been achieved. . . ." The teacher goes on to say that her output of energy in class must be extremely high because she must make every moment she spends with each student count. She must spot-check work and compare it with past achievement. She must try to motivate the student for days of work ahead during which she will not see him. She must lead him to an accurate evaluation of his own progress and create a list of tasks which will be educationally effective, varied, and interesting. While all of this is going on, she must keep a weather eye on the rest of the class as well.

The compensations are great, the teacher reports:

At the end of the school day she has no papers to grade, she has no lesson plans to make—she has made and effected the lesson plans as she went along, she has no grades to post. Any grades which have been decided upon are already on the student's assignment sheet and the teacher's carbon. . . . Most important of all she does not carry home with her the nagging frustration that comes from watching her students leave the class day after day half taught because the work was not geared to their individual abilities (11).

Throughout the description of her work, the teacher emphasizes that such a tutorial method is not applicable just to slow learners and clearly recommends that such utilization of programed materials could be adopted broadly in any school situation.

Hamden Hall, Hamden, Connecticut

Perhaps the most extreme example (within an actual school setting) of handling individual differences among students through automated instruction is represented by the work of O. K. Moore at Hamden Hall Country Day School near New Haven, Connecticut. Moore calls his instructional situation an autotelic responsive environment. The major goal of his work to date is to allow each child (starting as young as two years' old) to acquire reading and writing skills comparable to the listening and speaking skills which most preschoolers possess. No child begins instruction in Moore's laboratory except with the assistance and encouragement of an already enrolled child; the initiative must come from either child rather than from the parent, teacher, or any other adult.

In the course of his early sessions, the child acclimates himself to the surroundings and has an opportunity to "play with" an electric typewriter (which has the attendant advantages of requiring only light pressure, yet producing uniform, attractive, and well-formed letters). When the child adapts to the environment, the computer behind the typewriter—or a patient and specially trained teacher—becomes actively responsive to the keys pressed by the child, naming each symbol in turn and eventually helping the child to "recognize" simple three-letter words already in the child's vocabulary, which he types first at random and later in response to visual and/or auditory suggestion.

After a variety of related activities, the child is able to take "dictation" from the computer, pressing keys and forming words and sentences with virtually no error. It is but a short step, then, to allow the child to compose sentences on his own; and the "newspaper" put out during the third year of the experimental work by a couple of six-year-old editors is most impressive evidence of the efficacy of responsive environment teaching. Moore regularly resists any notion that his material, or the moment-to-moment procedure, is sequenced in the usual "programed" sense. Sixty children exposed to this technique during its first two years entered first grade with fourth-grade or higher level of reading ability.[11]

Despite this impressive electronic teacher, much of the secret of Moore's success in getting these youngsters to read by the time they are three or four years' old seems to lie in the great sensitivity and patience of the human teachers he has trained as an interim "device" pending the availability of more units of his electronic responsive environment. These teachers are selected for their sensitivity, their lack of authoritarian approach, and their ability to move the child ahead as rapidly as the child seems to want to go. These three qualities are, strangely enough, quite characteristic of a modern computer. It is as sensitive to content and handling as its makers care to build it; it is, or may be, completely nonauthoritarian; and it has both great speed and infinite patience. Moore's work, provocative as it now stands, is but the first of many steps toward an instructional system which will eventually be sensitive to the student so that the program sequences itself in reaction to each student's response and is available at the student's convenience and pace. As a consequence, no student should ever get or need to get the same item or sequence that any other student gets or complete the program at any pace other than his own.

There are three major components to this system development. Computers have long been available with capacities and speeds suitable for handling (by multiplex) many students simultaneously. Input and output devices are improving and will surely be expedited as educational pressures mount. However, a highly sensitive and enormously flexible arrangement of the subject material (i.e., the program) is likely to remain the missing link in the system for some time to come. Moore's electronic typewriter and sensitive staff have already obtained much fame for the fascinating accomplishments in reading and writing of their first graders, who have been allowed to assist materially in determining their own "programs" of instruction. The implications of an environment which is so responsive to the young learner are most challenging. The specific arrangement of detailed programed items turns out to be nowhere near as important as the existence of quite clear terminal goals and the delegation of "apparent control" to the learner.

[11] Personal communication, 1963.

A Look to the Future

It is evident from the foregoing descriptions of the use of programed instruction that this new instructional technique is acting as a substantial agent of educational change and is kicking over the traces of the educational past. The question one is prompted to ask is twofold: First of all, which of these traces is most likely to be affected in the near future; secondly, what kind of school will the advent of programed instruction and the teaching machine bring about in the more distant future?

Judging from the evidence of the schools represented, certain facets of a school's existence are *necessarily* affected when programed instruction is introduced. The first of these is the immediate learning environment as experienced by the individual student. The second is the nature of the relationship between the student and his teacher with a concomitant effect on the general administration of the classroom. The third is the effect of these programed-instruction-geared classrooms on such things as a school's deployment of its teaching staff, the size and nature of the curriculum, the logistics of student movement (both physically and academically), and the over-all administration of the school.

It is of course possible to use programed instruction without affecting a school as broadly as this, for schools do exist in which programs are administered in such a way that students are not able to proceed at their own pace. There are unfortunately some schools in which responses to the *teaching* frames of a program are graded as if they were test items. In such cases one can hardly say that programed instruction is effecting any change of attitude or procedure on the part of educators. However, if teachers and administrators understand the basic principles of programed instruction and are willing to create an environment within which these principles are consistently applied, then certain changes become natural if not inevitable.

The change that programed instruction is bringing to education is of a radical nature. It is radical because it starts with the root of the educational enterprise; i.e., the *learning individual*. In doing this it forces educators to ask questions about the entering behavior of the learner and about the particular ways in which the behavior of that learner may be changed. The next step becomes the structuring of the most appropriate learning environment in which to bring about those changes. Because the structure of such a learning environment often runs counter to the arrangement of the existing classroom or school, it is frequently necessary to modify that structure to meet the requirements for optimal learning. Viewed in this way, using programed instruction does not simply mean using new kinds of textbooks or audio-visual devices. In this context, using programed instruction means taking a fresh look at the whole structure of the school. The work at Hamden Hall is perhaps the most dramatic example of this reexamination in that the entire K-12 curriculum must be redesigned, not simply because youngsters come to first grade having learned how to read, but because of the environment in which their learning has taken place. It is an environment that is as radically different from existing classroom environment as was the progressive classroom from its stiff, rigid precursor.

One can hasten to point out that all programed instructional materials are not as flexible and completely adaptable to individual student needs as the material being used at Hamden Hall. But as is seen in the descriptions of the use of a program in English grammar in Denver and Manhasset, even programs as they now exist can be used in such a way as to answer the needs of a great variety of students. There should be no question that programs of the future will be designed and presented for a still greater variety of students to use them in increasingly varied ways. If research into the design and use of programed materials is carried out on a large scale, there is little doubt that the school of the not-too-distant future will be able to boast a curriculum that may be offered in as many different ways as there are pupils in the school. In such a school, each learner will seek and achieve mastery of a subject matter or a skill by proceeding along a path largely of his own choosing, a path that is neither too easy nor too difficult for him to traverse. Ideally the teacher will help the learner to discover a system of learning that suits his own capabilities. In other words, the learner will be taught how to learn; he will be provided with new tools for learning. These tools will consist of far more than learning to read and being group-paced through a 12-year parade of textbooks. Both the techniques and the materials of learning will be very different in the schools of tomorrow, and there can be little question that today's programed instruction is helping to lay the foundation for such schools.

How To Get Started

Having taken a quick glance into the future, this picture of program usage can be concluded by pulling together information of immediate use to school systems which are ready to take the first (or next) step into program usage themselves.

Administrative Support

While programed instruction and other innovations have at times achieved some success with a minimum of administrative cooperation, there can be little doubt that no significant program implementation is possible without at least an informed administration. Henry Brickell, associate superintendent of schools in Manhasset, points out, however, that more than information is needed (3). While acquiescence is better than opposition and while a high degree of enthusiasm is far from necessary, the greatest likelihood for educational change is found where there is substantial and continuing assistance to teachers.

The Western States Small Schools Project goes even further than Newton's Bernard Everett in the matter of the public school responsibility. One of the assumptions upon which the whole regional project was based is that "state departments of education, by eliminating restrictive regulation, giving support, and by aggressive assistance and consultation, can influence the rate, direction, and quality of public education in America" (2). For "state departments of education" read any lower administrative echelon, and the point still stands. All but two of the school systems discussed in this chapter have shown the importance of informed support from above. The methods by which administrators become informed are so many that they scarcely warrant cataloguing here, but it is clear that the influence of administrators upon their colleagues and neighbors is an important factor which must be consciously acknowledged and actively sought.

Low Pressure from Administration

A second element common to successful innovation with programed instruction seems to be a highly permissive atmosphere. (Low administrative pressure seems to be more effective than authority.) Not reported here are the many large and small school systems where programed instruction was "brought in" and administratively "imposed." If any such school or system is still using programed instruction, it is inevitably to a smaller and less effective extent than any of the systems here reported. One large suburban system, for example, introduced a ninth-grade algebra program into several high schools one fall with a minimum of teacher preparation. The following year the program was dropped, so disastrous were the results. On the other hand, some of the teachers who had not been impressed or pleased with these materials as an across-the-board technique are now finding that they can send individual students to these materials for help in specific topics, for remedial work, for enrichment, or to fill in gaps stemming from weak background (transfer from another school system) or prolonged absence.

The permissive environment seems to be highly correlated with an active interest in and experimentation with a variety of new approaches to education. Experimentation in the schools cited in this chapter is rarely limited to programed instruction. Experiments in modern mathematics, team teaching, language laboratories, and in-service workshops are all typical of the activities found in schools who are trying out programed instruction.

Clearinghouse

A third form of active support which facilitates an experimental environment lies in the maintenance of some sort of local information clearinghouse, preferably with active dissemination of informational materials and periodicals, as well as actual samples of the instructional materials themselves. The availability of such materials is obviously important, and the evidence from various school systems is that such a dissemination facility not only fails to place a large financial burden upon schools, but it actually saves time and effort in the long run. Well-publicized and central locations allow a few periodical subscriptions to cover a large staff. A coordinated and active center invariably gets more sample materials faster from the publishers and suppliers.

Test Population

While the day of publisher-supported field testing may never come as a means for obtaining any significant proportion of a school's supplies, the publishers' need for developmental and experimental populations is still on the increase rather than on the wane. Colleges, universities, and schools of education similarly have many researchers in need of test subjects, and many are having to settle for token populations simply because they do not have the contacts necessary to arrange for the larger test population most schools could and would freely provide.

Means of Support

Finally, a modestly well-thought-out proposal concerning either some general or highly specialized problem is increasingly eligible for support from foundations, smaller philanthropies, local business, and as a legitimate use of tax funds. When the results of such experiments offer the chance to save both student and teacher time or when the scope and flexibility of a school's offerings can materially be expanded, there is considerable logic for such financial support. Longer-range goals, such as workshops for teachers, usually emerge out of the positive experiences of a few individual teachers with a small sampling of their own students.

Programing by Teachers

Longest-range gains begin to accrue when the teachers, often from efforts to write programs themselves, become more sensitive to the students. Because programed instruction has grown from the learning laboratories, it brings to teaching an approximation of laboratory rigor and a spirit of experimentation through which teachers often gain new perspectives on their role in the learning process.

Conclusion

Certain frequently reiterated points of programed instruction contribute to the assurance with which it may be used by school systems.

1. It is the student whose activity is under observation.
2. With most programed materials, an unusual opportunity exists for obtaining and maintaining extensive records of the responses of students.
3. The diagnostic potential of such records is considerable.
4. The teacher is relieved from most of the straightforward textual transmission and is at the same time freed to be more sensitive in attending to individual student needs.

5. A program or a unit which successfully achieves its goal, however small, can be readily retained and shared, while material that is not satisfactory may be dropped or locally revised until it approaches its goal.

6. Because of the student activity and records obtained, these materials tend to improve with successive trials. Over the years new and better programing techniques will make their contribution.

7. The continuing evaluation of experimental materials against the longest range educational goals will almost surely become a more conscious process.

It is no accident that such procedural advantages should accrue with the use of a technique which itself emerged from the procedures of behavioral science laboratories. What educators seem to be finding is that despite the present rudimentary state of programed instructional materials, the experimental point of view which accompanies so many of the innovations discussed in this chapter is the best insurance of a gradual and inevitable educational improvement.

References

1. Blumenthal, J. C. *English 2600.* New York: Harcourt, Brace and World, 1960.
2. Bohrson, R. G. *An Introduction to the Western States Small Schools Project.* Denver, Colo.: State Department of Education, 1963.
3. Brickell, H. *Organizing New York State for Educational Change.* Albany, N.Y.: State Education Department, 1961.
4. Center for Programed Instruction. *The Use of Programed Instruction in U.S. Schools.* Washington, D.C.: Government Printing Office, 1963.
5. Eigen, L. D., and Komoski, P. K. *Research Summary No. 1 of the Collegiate School Automated Teaching Project.* New York: Center for Programed Instruction, 1960.
6. Evans, J. L.; Glaser, R.; and Homme, L. E. "An Investigation of 'Teaching Machine' Variables Using Learning Programs in Symbolic Logic." *Journal of Educational Research* 55: 433-50; June-July 1962.
7. Everett, J. B. "Quotable Quotes." *Programed Instruction* 1: 1; No. 1, 1961.
8. Ford, E. A., and Walker, V. R. *Public Secondary Schools of the United States.* Washington, D.C.: U.S. Office of Education, 1961.
9. Glaser, R.; Reynolds, J. H.; and Fullick, Margaret G. *Programmed Instruction in the Intact Classroom.* Pittsburgh: Learning Research and Development Center, University of Pittsburgh, 1963.

10. Goldstein, L. S., and Gotkin, L. G. "A Review of Research: Teaching Machines vs. Programed Textbooks as Presentation Modes." *Journal of Programed Instruction* 1: 29-36; No. 1, 1962.

11. Gray, Genevieve, and others. *Tutorial Method in English Instruction for Ninth-Grade Slow Learners.* An Exploratory Project. Tucson, Ariz.: Palo Verde High School, First Semester Report, 1963.

12. Jones, L. B. *New Patterns of Instruction in English Composition.* Report to the Board of Education. Denver, Colorado, 1962.

13. Komoski, P. K. *An Immodest Proposal Concerning the Use of Programed Instruction in Emerging Nations.* New York: Center for Programed Instruction, 1962.

14. Lumsdaine, A. A., and Glaser, R., editors. *Teaching Machines and Programmed Learning.* Washington, D.C.: National Education Association, 1960.

15. Moore, O. K. "Autotelic Responsive Environments and Exceptional Children." *Special Children in Century 21.* Seattle, Wash.: Special Child Publications, 1964.

16. Porter, D. *An Application of Reinforcement Principles to Classroom Teaching.* Cambridge, Mass.: Graduate School of Education, Harvard University, May 1961.

17. Schramm, W., editor. *Four Case Studies of Programed Instruction.* New York: Fund for the Advancement of Education, 1964.

18. Reed, J. E., and Hayman, J. L., Jr. "An Experiment Involving Use of 'English 2600,' An Automated Instructional Text." *Journal of Educational Research* 55: 476-84; June-July 1962.

19. Rushton, E. *The Roanoke Story.* Chicago: Encyclopaedia Britannica Press, 1963.

20. Wahler, T. G. "A Selective Reference System." *NSPI Journal* 2: 14; November 1963.

21. Welch, D. "Newton's Experience in Programed Instruction." *Bulletin of Programed Instruction* 1: 1; No. 6, 1962.

H. A. SHOEMAKER
H. O. HOLT
American Telephone and Telegraph Company

The Use of Programed
Instruction in Industry

This chapter is concerned with the use of programed instruction in industry. It is based, in part, on the results of a survey of programed instruction activity in a sample of large industrial companies conducted in the spring of 1963. The survey information is supplemented to some extent by published articles, though the activities of most companies are not publicized. The authors give their views concerning the place of programed instruction in industry, and, in a majority of cases, survey data are available and are cited to support these views. In many of these, however, the data are limited in amount and precision.

Programed instruction definitely has found a place in industry, and its use is growing. When one considers that in 1960 there was practically no programed instruction in industry, the growth of its use seems phenomenal. At the time the current survey was made, some 40 companies, in the sample of 277, reported having an in-house capability for producing their own programs, many of them in a sophisticated way. For most of these, and some others, programed instruction is well past the novelty or "gimmick" stage and is looked upon as a potentially powerful training method that can fulfill specific needs better than present methods. If one looks at the situation in a somewhat different way, however, the over-all use of programed instruction is relatively modest. For example, many more of the survey sample of companies reported *not* using programed instruction than reported using it. And with a few notable exceptions, the number of training hours programed is small in relation to the total number of hours of instruction. Nevertheless, the signs of acceptance and growth are unmistakable, and it will be most surprising if the present rapid rate of growth does not continue.

The Survey

Survey Techniques

The survey involved two phases. First, a questionnaire was sent to a large number of companies. Subsequently, representatives of those companies which reported in-house programing activities were contacted by telephone and asked for more information. The initial questionnaire was sent to 370 companies. Of these, 300 constituted a random sample from the list of the 500 largest companies published by *Fortune* magazine. These 300 were supplemented by 70 companies selected on the basis of informal leads indicating that their activities in programed instruction might merit attention. The initial mailing and a follow-up letter brought a total return of 75 percent (277 replies).

The questionnaire was designed to obtain information of the following general types:

1. Is programed instruction used in the company?
2. How are programs obtained or developed?
3. If programs are developed in-company, what types of skills are involved in their development?
4. If programs are in use, what are the subjects they cover, how many persons have taken them, etc.?
5. What are the characteristics of the programs, i.e., linear, branching, etc.?
6. How are the programs designed to be used, i.e., formal training school, directly on the job, during working hours, etc.?

From questionnaire returns, companies were identified which have developed programs in-house. A number of them were contacted by telephone, and loosely structured interviews were conducted to obtain more detailed information of the following types:

1. What types of personnel are involved in program development, i.e., training and responsibilities?
2. What is the program development procedure?
3. What is the evaluation procedure?
4. Are any special programing techniques used?
5. What are difficulties encountered in program development?
6. How are the introduction, implementation, and maintenance of programs handled?
7. What are advantageous and disadvantageous features of programed instruction?

In addition to the telephone interviews of representatives of companies which had developed programs, telephone contacts were made with other companies as necessary to clarify questionnaire responses.

General Information on Usage

Respondents were asked, "Has your company used, or is it now using, programed instruction either on a regular or experimental basis?" Table 1 summarizes the replies. It should be noted that the summaries in Table 1 reflect experimental as well as operational use. "Experi-

TABLE 1

Survey Results on Use of Programed Instruction

	Percent of companies $N = 277$
Have used programed instruction	33.6
Plan to use in near future	9.8
No plans for use	56.6

mental use" is interpreted by many companies to include a very limited use of one or two commercially obtained programs. If such companies are excluded and only those companies which reported having programs in operational use are considered, they total 30 percent of the sample. If only those companies are included which report at least one program in operational use by 10 or more persons, 22 percent of the respondents qualify as "users."

Figure 1 shows the percentages of companies reporting various numbers of programs in operational use. The number of programs in use in these companies probably reflects the length of experience companies have had in programed instruction. Many companies still are in the exploratory stages, and this may account for the high per-

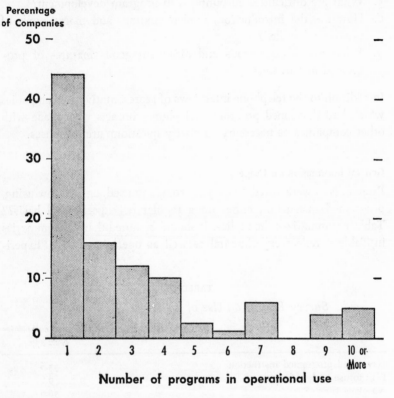

FIGURE 1: *Distribution of companies in terms of the number of programs in operational use. (N = 81 companies.)*

centage (45 percent) of those using only one program. There are some indications that companies who have used programed instruction extensively are those in which central staff training personnel have more or less direct responsibility for a large share of company vocational training which would lend itself to programed instruction. In some companies, however, the central training staff under the title "director of training" or "director of education" is concerned primarily with management development and has very little control over vocational or "craft" training. Vocational training in such companies often is not formalized. There is some evidence, in fact, for the allegation that training directors as a group are more concerned with management development than with vocational training.[1] This state of affairs is general enough so that it probably constitutes an obstacle to the greater use of programed instruction for vocational training in industry. Examples of this are furnished by manufacturing organizations which make a variety of products and have plants in various locations. Except for some phases of management development, the training responsibility and function is dispersed to plants, departments, and even small individual shops and separate operations. No records are maintained of the scope or cost of vocational training, although there is agreement that "there is a lot of it."

The programed instruction movement has not gone unnoticed in many of these companies, however. A few management people here and there have attended one-week programing workshop sessions. Some of these people are wise enough to realize that one week of contact does not qualify them to prepare programs; others, unfortunately, have returned full of enthusiasm and desire to write programs or to teach others to write them. But at least two essential ingredients are lacking which would make success probable. First, there is no centralized training organization around which a programing team could be built, and second, there are no professionally trained persons (usually psychologists) who could aid in the job analysis, behavioral objective setting, and evaluation phases of program building.

Figure 2 shows the distribution of programs in terms of number of persons who took them. This figure is read to indicate, for example, that 10 percent of the programs in use were used by one to nine people and that over 20 percent were used by 200 or more persons.

[1] As a check on this, a count was made on articles dealing with management development and vocational training in the *Journal of the American Society of Training Directors* for the years 1961-63. Of a total of 133 articles that could be classified in one or the other category, 40 percent were classified as vocational and 60 percent as management oriented.

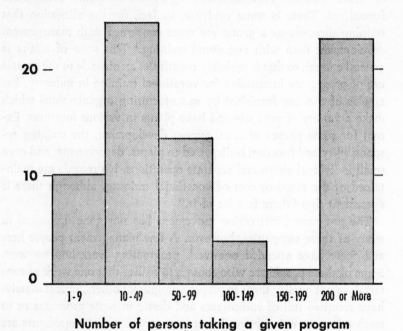

FIGURE 2: *Distribution of programs in terms of number of persons having taken them. (N = 316 programs; number of persons unspecified for 24 per cent of programs.)*

The Place of Programed Instruction in Industry

The place of programed instruction in industry can be examined from a number of points of view. Those considered to be of most importance are type of subject matter programed, roles of programed instruction in training, settings in which it is used, potential advantages and benefits of programed instruction, and limitations.

Type of Subject Matter Programed

The programs reported in the survey were classified by subject matter. An effort was made to assign each program to one (and sometimes two) classifications which most accurately characterized its subject matter.[2] Table 2 shows the distribution of programs among various

TABLE 2

Distribution of Programs Among Subject Matter Classifications

Subject matter classification (with examples of each)		Percent of programs* N = 316
Basic Concepts—General Knowledge (e.g., basic mathematics, human anatomy, logarithms)		27%
Specific Job Knowledge or Information (e.g., Know Your Motor Oil, Diabinese, New Employee Orientation)		17%
Job Procedures		52%**
General Procedural Rules or Skills—Not Company Specific (e.g., Computer Programing, Spelling Improvement, Effective Business Writing)	20%	
Specific Procedural Rules or Skills—Not Company Specific (e.g., Blood Typing, Key Punch Operating, Reading Vernier Micrometer, psychomotor tasks such as Touch System on 10-Key Adding Machine, Proof Machine Operator)	14%	
General Procedural Rules or Skills—Company Specific (e.g., Navy Test Equipment Usage, Back Office Purchase and Sales, Weapons System Safety Procedures)	14%	
Specific Procedural Rules or Skills—Company Specific (e.g., Decoding the Aviation Weather Report, How To Read RPIE Lists, Order Filling)	14%	
Other Information—Not Company Specific, Not Basic (e.g., Introduction to Mexico Documentation)		3%

* The percentages do not add to 100 because of overlapping categories.
** The sum of overlapping categories for job procedures.

[2] The classification procedure must be considered inexact because the classification was based primarily on the program titles given by survey respondents, and a large percentage of the programs cut across several subject matter classes. It was usually possible to identify one class which best characterized a given program, but it was sometimes necessary to assign a program to more than one class.

classes of subject matter. A distinction can be made between job-oriented programs, i.e., programs which deal with job knowledge and job procedures, on the one hand, and academically oriented programs, i.e., those dealing with general knowledge, on the other. Sixty-nine percent of the programs reported in the survey fall into the job-oriented categories.

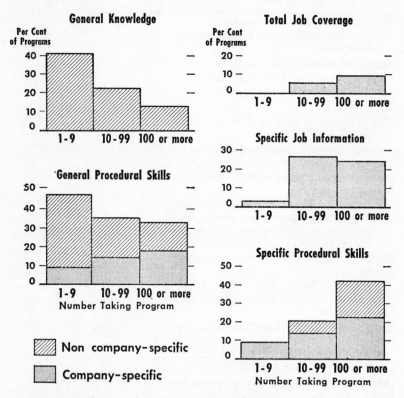

FIGURE 3: *Distribution of programs among subject matter classes as a function of numbers of persons taking programs. (Note: Percentages do not add to 100 because of overlapping categories.)*

Figure 3 shows a breakdown of programs by subject matter as it varies with extent-of-use. Programs were divided into three groups: those taken by one to nine persons ($N = 32$); those taken by 11 to 100 persons ($N = 120$); and those taken by more than 100 persons ($N = 89$). For 75 programs the number of persons involved was not specified. It is clear that the number of programs devoted to general knowledge decreases with increased extent-of-use and that there is an opposite trend for classes of subject matter which are more company- and job-oriented. The trends for general procedural skills represent a mixed picture, but conform to the main trend in that company-specific programs show an increase with increased usage. The proportion of programs dealing with specific procedural skills is markedly greater among the more extensively used programs. The shift toward a greater use of job- and company-oriented programs with an increased extent-of-use may simply reflect increased amounts of experience with programed instruction. That is, as companies gain more experience with programed instruction, they make more extensive use of it, and at the same time, they are more likely to use it in job-oriented applications. The shift may also be explained partly by the fact that the incidence of vocational training for which job-oriented programs are appropriate is greater than training or education which would use general knowledge programs.

The percentage of programs which provide training in psychomotor or manipulative skills is quite small considering that such skills are important in a great many industrial jobs. One cause for this may lie in the fact that techniques for programing manipulative skills are at an early stage in their development. A few companies have used audio-visual equipment for guiding assembly operations. Such devices are more properly classified as *job aids* rather than training devices, since in most cases workers remain dependent on them for guidance in performing job activities. However, some use has been made of these and other devices for training in manipulative skills such as the use of small tools, and these offer promising beginnings in this important area of training. In a few cases, programs have been built around equipment or training devices which simulate the equipment that persons are being trained to operate or maintain.

Roles of Programed Instruction in Training

The following represent the major functions or roles of programed instruction as they are revealed in the survey:

1. *Initial "total job" training* (programs which carry the entire or main burden of instruction for a job), e.g., programs for telephone information operators, secretarial training, and bank tellers.

2. *Segments of initial training*, e.g., basic electricity, use of the slide rule, and reading engineering drawings.
3. *Continuation or supplemental training*, e.g., programs on product knowledge for salesmen and new equipment characteristics for maintenance personnel.
4. *Remedial training*, e.g., an audiotape program to increase effective typing speed of stenographers. (The use of programed instruction for remedial training is relatively infrequent in industry.)
5. *Refresher training*, e.g., the use of a program as a refresher on mathematics or other technical subjects prior to taking a specialized engineering course.
6. *Review training*, e.g., the use of a program at the end of a middle-management training course for the review of concepts and factual information taught in the course. This use of programed instruction is closely similar to that of "adjunct" programing associated with Pressey (68, 69). Apparently, this use is infrequent in industry.
7. *Education or self-development*, e.g., the use of programs in basic subjects such as mathematics on a voluntary basis by employees. In a utility company, for example, employees have the opportunity to enroll in a basic electricity course on an out-of-hours basis for their own development.

Unfortunately, precise information concerning the relative frequency of uses listed above was not obtained in the survey. However, the available evidence points to segments of initial training and continuation training as the major functions of programed instruction, with an emphasis on continuation or supplemental training. Based on an examination of program titles, total-job programs were estimated to comprise only about 5 percent of the total programs. This percentage is strikingly small considering the presumably large number of jobs for which training would be appropriate, e.g., clerks and salesmen.

Information from the survey suggests several reasons for the low incidence of total-job programs. It may reflect the infancy of programing in industry. As the first step in exploring programed instruction, trainers are likely to use commercially available programs which are often not even job-oriented. They are unlikely to hazard the development of extensive job-oriented programs for two reasons. First, such programs must be custom built and must require a great deal of well-directed effort and cost to produce. In addition, programing technology may not be equal to the problems that arise, e.g., programing of manipulative skills, complex conceptual reasoning behavior, etc. Secondly, companies, at first, are unlikely to risk displacing a present training method for important jobs by a new and relatively unproved method. Even when they do develop some in-house capabilities for the custom development of programs, they are not likely to make an initially heavy investment in the development of total-job programs.

The low incidence of total-job programs also, in part, may be due to the fact that training for many such jobs never has been formalized, and thus they have not been considered for programed instruction. This may be particularly true for manufacturing operations where apprenticeship or man-to-man training has been the rule. As mentioned earlier, the responsibility for such training is apt to be local and outside the control of the central training staff. Finally, the low incidence of total job programs may reflect a tendency to aim programs toward skills and knowledge that are abstracted from particular jobs, e.g., general electronics for maintenance technicians, general sales techniques for salesmen, etc. This tendency, in part, may be a heritage from the academic forebears of programed instruction, whose early programs dealing with general subject matter served as the prototypes for programs built in and for industry. On the other hand, in total-job programs (as the term is used here), the subject matter is tailored to specific jobs, and greater dependence is thereby placed on a knowledge of specific job requirements in developing such programs. The data summarized in Figure 3 seem to indicate a trend toward increased use of job-specific programs as the field has developed, assuming that increased extent-of-use reflects increased emphasis. One implication of such a trend is that greater emphasis will need to be given to the need for careful analysis of job requirements to serve as the basis for programs.

Programed instruction either may be used alone or closely integrated with other training. Indications are that in industry most programs are used alone. (This is not to say that they are not followed or preceded by other courses as would be the case when they are used as segments of initial training.) There are cases, however, in which training courses contain a blend of instructional methods. Training courses for toll telephone operators and service representatives, for example, contain blends of self-instructional materials, conventional lecture-discussion sessions, and supervised practice.

Settings for Programed Instruction

Table 3 shows a summary of the survey results concerning the settings in which programed instruction is used. It is interesting to find so many programs used on a home-study or correspondence basis. A large portion of home-study uses involves programs dealing with general knowledge, e.g., mathematics. Forty-eight percent of the pro-

TABLE 3

Settings in Which Programed Instruction Is Used

Type of Setting	Percent of Companies (N=81)	Percent of Programs* (N=316)
Formal training school	43	29
During working hours—released time basis on the job	77	62
Home study—correspondence	42	34

*Percentages do not add to 100 because of overlapping categories.

grams used on a home-study basis were of the general knowledge type, compared with 18 percent of the programs teaching on-the-job skills. This suggests an extensive use of home-study programs for self-development purposes.

Since many programs require no instructor, home-study use appears to be an economical way to achieve training objectives with a minimum disruption of work operations. For programs used on a voluntary self-development basis, there seem to be no drawbacks to home study. On the other hand, assurance often is required that a given employee will complete a certain job-training course at a particular time. Such assurance can be secured with more confidence if the program is administered during working hours where greater control can be exercised over the training.

Lengths of Industrial Programs

Figure 4 shows the distribution of programs reported in terms of hours to completion. The programs included in this summary are limited to those taken by 10 or more persons. Although the majority of the

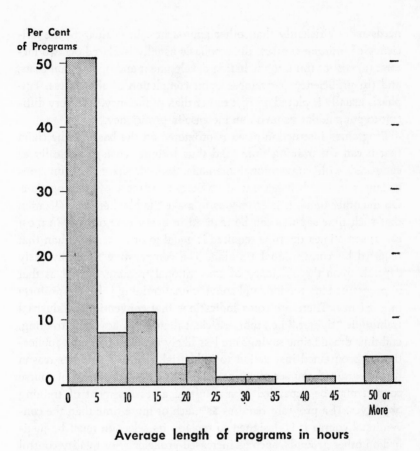

Per Cent of Programs

Average length of programs in hours

FIGURE 4: *Distribution of programs in terms of length. Average length reported for programs taken by 10 or more persons. (N = 208 programs; length unspecified in 17 percent of programs.)*

programs are short, a few programs are quite lengthy. The longest program reported was 192 hours. It is predicted that there will be a trend toward increasing length of programs as the field continues to develop. This should be the case particularly in an increase in the number of total-job programs.

Potential Benefits

The decision to use programed instruction for any given training can be justified if it can be demonstrated that this method meets training needs more efficiently than other approaches. In evaluating the efficiency of training courses, the emphasis usually is placed on two factors: (a) cost of training, including development and operational costs, and (b) proficiency of trainees upon completion of the course. Emphasis usually is placed on cost rather than proficiency. It is very difficult to put a dollar value on an increase in proficiency.

Programed instruction often is promoted on the basis of the claim that it can cut training time (and thus training costs) drastically as compared with conventional methods. Indeed, there are numerous instances in which it has saved 50 percent or more of training time. On the other hand, it is erroneous to make the blanket generalization that such time savings can be realized in every case or even in most cases; sometimes the time required is equal to or even more than that required by conventional training. The comparative time obviously depends upon the efficiency of conventional training as well as that of programed instruction, and conventional training is hardly uniform in efficiency. There are some indications that conventional industrial training is "tighter," i.e., more efficient than much academic training, and thus drastic time savings are less likely to result from the application of programed instruction to industrial courses.[3] Another reason that programed courses may not save time is that the scope of course content may be expanded as a result of a reassessment of training objectives. If a program requires as much or more time than the conventional course it is designed to replace, its selection must be justified on other grounds, such as increased proficiency or quality control of instruction. As indicated, the effects of increased proficiency in terms of dollars may be indirect and hard to measure. Nevertheless, increased training time should result in increased proficiency in a high proportion of cases, and especially in those situations where proficiency levels have been marginal due to mediocre instructor quality. For that matter, higher proficiency, more than savings of time, should be the catchphrase representing the dependable advantage of programed instruction. The program development process is so designed

---

[3] A reasonable explanation for such alleged greater efficiency of industrial training is the close relation between the training and the operations which use the training product. In some cases, the operational departments directly pay training costs. A man is unproductive while he is being trained, and organizational pressure exists to get him back on the job as soon as possible and to get assurance that the training time is well spent.

that programs are not released for operational use until their effectiveness has been demonstrated. Conventional courses rarely, if ever, are developed in this manner.

There are other benefits from the use of programed instruction in industry aside from possible savings in training time and increases in proficiency. These have an important, and sometimes a crucial, bearing on the efficiency of programed instruction. Those listed below were cited by one or more survey respondents.

Self-Pacing: Self-pacing usually is considered to be of general value because it enables different individuals to work toward and achieve a relatively uniform level of proficiency at rates which are commensurate with their individual rates of learning and performance. In industry, self-pacing allows rapid learners to return to the job sooner. Moreover, the company often is willing to allow slower students more time to complete a course of instruction if they are able to achieve the desired level of proficiency upon completion of training. In conventional training, such slow learners may not be able to complete the course satisfactorily.

An example of the above is contained in a study reported by Holt and Valentine (25). A self-instruction program was prepared to match the content of an existing lecture-discussion course in basic electricity. When proficiency in basic electricity was measured by means of two final examinations, both immediately after training and six months later, mean scores of a program-taught group were found to be significantly greater than mean scores of the lecture-discussion group. Mean time of the program-taught group was about the same as the classroom time of the other group, although there was considerable variation in individual completion times among the program-taught group. A further analysis of the Holt-Valentine data indicates that the low aptitude program-taught trainee benefited particularly from the extra time allowed by the self-pacing feature. Specifically, there is a considerably greater spread of scores toward the low end of the distribution for the low aptitude lecture-taught group than for the program-taught group. Since low-aptitude trainees also took more time for the program, it can be inferred that the reduced spread of scores toward the low end is attributable to the extra time allowed by the self-pacing feature.

Scheduling Flexibility: In conventional training, it usually is necessary to form classes to economize on instructor expenses. This creates problems of five types: (a) It may be difficult to schedule classes at times when all trainees are able to attend. (b) When the trainee input rate is quite low, considerable time may be required to form a class of economical size. This can result in expensive delays while trainees wait for a class to be formed. (c) Formation of classes for supplemental training of production workers requires that employees be taken away from the job in groups, thus disrupting production. (d) The formation of classes sometimes requires that employees be brought to a central location from distant locations for training. This can result in considerable travel and living-in expenses. (e) Employees often must be replaced on their jobs while they are away attending school.

Programed instruction ordinarily is administered on an individual basis, and usually it is unnecessary to form classes. It is true that some programs contain integrated lecture-discussion sessions, but this is relatively unusual. With respect to the problems enumerated above, the effects of individual learning are as follows: (a) Training sessions can be arranged to meet individual scheduling needs. (b) For training with a low input rate of trainees, employees simply are trained as the needs arise, thus eliminating delays. (c) Whereas group training can disrupt company operations, employees can be trained on a staggered basis with programed instruction. In the case of a chemical company, for example, it was possible to release a very limited number of employees at a time from production to take a program. Beyond that, production would have been disrupted. (d) When it is desired to train personnel who are widely dispersed, sometimes it is possible to mail programs to them instead of requiring them to travel to central locations. (e) Trainees may be allowed released time off the job to complete a program. A trainee, for example, may work every other morning on the program and spend the balance of his time on the job.

An example from a large manufacturing, sales, and maintenance organization will serve to illustrate most of the above points. The company installs large computers on customer's premises which it must maintain in working condition. The maintenance tasks are complex and require that the company offer a comprehensive maintenance training program. Until recently, training was given at a central school in the conventional manner. Trainees traveled to the school from the surrounding area, joined other trainees, were formed into a class, and were taught by an instructor. Self-instruction programs were prepared for this training; the programs were tested and found to take less time than conventional training and to do a better job of training. As a consequence, the administrative situation has changed considerably. Men no longer come into the central school for their training, but perform it during released time on the job. This results in several advantages in addition to time saving and higher proficiency: travel time and costs and per diem costs at the school are saved, the man does not have to be replaced but works part-time at his job, and the trainee lives at home while "going to school." The company is particularly proud of this last point. A study revealed that a man of this type with six years' service normally has spent one year and four months away from home going to the central school. The company feels that the new system does much for family morale.

Quality Control: There are several advantages of programed self-instruction which fall under the category of "quality control." Any time that a conventional lecture-discussion course is taught by more than one instructor, it is almost certain that there will be significant differences in content. It is difficult, too, for an instructor to maintain consistency in a course as he teaches successive classes. Thus, there can be no assurance that one is getting a high-quality product across several lecture-discussion classes. Moreover, instruction often is done by supervisors, and instructional duties therefore often interfere with other supervisory duties. Since supervisors usually are not selected on the basis of their instructional abilities or potential, there is no assurance that they can do an effective job of instruction. Consequently, when the burden of instruction falls on the supervisor, the quality is likely to be very uneven.

The situation is quite different with a properly developed self-instruction program. In the first place, the standard procedure for producing a high-quality product is to "cut and try" a program throughout its development. Specifically, this means that it is subjected to empirical trials on sample groups of the trainees for which it is intended. It is tested and revised as many times as necessary to make it meet training objectives. The final product, then, not only has been demonstrated to be effective, but remains constant. That is, all students who take a particular programed course take the same course (most programs in use are nonbranching). Thus the instructional product can be expected to be much more uniform than the lecture-discussion product, even though different groups of trainees work through the program in widely separated locations.

Standardization of Practices: Industries often have widely dispersed operations. For many reasons, many of the operations must be uniform from one operating branch to another. For example, the long-distance telephone operator in California must follow the same general practices as a long-distance telephone operator in Maine. Documents specifying the practices to be followed are prepared centrally and distributed to the various operating units. In conventional instruction, the burden of interpreting these materials often falls upon the local training personnel and, conscientious though they may be, idiosyncratic interpretations are bound to creep into the training, resulting in variations in practices. On the other hand, if self-instructional programs are developed centrally and in close cooperation with the agencies which write the practices and then are distributed to the operational subdivisions for training, there is greater assurance that all trainees will learn the practices in the same way.

Limitations of Programed Instruction

It would be rare, indeed, if programed instruction could meet all training needs. It does have limitations and disadvantages. Some of these may be overcome in time, while others are likely to be more lasting. Those considered to be most important are described below.

Difficulties in Procuring Suitable Programs: A large number of commercially produced programs are available, and the number is increasing rapidly. Some use can be made of these "off-the-shelf" programs in industrial training, especially for self-development and job-support purposes. However, a major share of industrial training is specialized, and thus no programs are available commercially to meet needs. In such cases, the company either must develop its own in-house capabilities for program development or engage a contractor to build a custom program to meet specialized needs. The development of an in-house capability to develop extensive programs usually requires a heavy commitment of resources. Such a commitment would not be economically feasible unless the company could foresee future continuing requirements for program development. If the company cannot foresee a requirement beyond a very limited number of programs, or cannot muster the necessary resources, the only course of action is to engage an outside contractor to develop the program.

The High Cost of Program Development: As mentioned before, the initial cost of program development is high compared with the initial cost of developing conventional instruction. In some cases, especially for short programs, the costs have run as high as $3,000 to $3,500 per instructional hour. Costs as low as $500 per instructional hour have been reported, although costs for a complete job, including an analysis of job requirements, seem to lie between $1,000 and $2,000 per instructional hour for longer programs. The question arises as to why the initial cost of program development is so high compared with conventional construction. There are several factors accounting for the increased cost: (a) The product of the initial program development is the complete course, whereas in ordinary instruction, the product usually consists of a course *outline.* Therefore, a larger volume of material is prepared in programed instruction than usually is the case with conventional instruction. Also, since programed instruction involves specialized skills, salary costs for personnel may be higher than those for persons who customarily build conventional courses. (b) In the course of development, programed materials undergo tryouts and revisions. This adds significantly to the preparation costs. (As the technology of program development advances, much of the trial and error which characterizes present program development should disappear.) (c) Job analyses sometimes are done as a first step in the development of a program, and these can be very costly. They are less often done in conventional instruction. (d) The program often undergoes an intensive evaluation which can be costly. This is not nearly as often done with conventional training.

An example can be given of a cost analysis for a particular program to furnish a general picture of the relative costs involved in various stages, as described above. The particular program in question was designed to teach the characteristics and alignment procedures for a complex mechanical device. In general terms, the subject matter would be classified as specific job information and company-specific procedural rules or skills. The program is 761 frames long and is linear in format. For evaluation, an experiment was conducted in which the program was compared with a conventional lecture course which included audiovisual materials, supervised study, and discussion periods. The instructor was judged to be highly skilled. Two matched groups of 10 experimental and nine control subjects were used. The average proficiency scores for the two groups, 88.9 percent for experimental and 90.7 percent for control, were not significantly different, but the programed group completed the instruction in 20 percent less time than the lecture group.

The development and operational training costs for the programed course are broken down as shown in the form reproduced in Table 4. One can obtain from the form a general notion of the cost factors in programed instruction; unfortunately, a cost analysis for the conventional course is not available. The form also is helpful in bringing to light a very important facet in the cost comparison of programed and conventional instruction, namely, that a comparison based on development costs alone is very misleading. This is because the distribution of costs is quite different in the two approaches. In programed instruction, the *development* categories, i.e., 1, 2, 3, and 12, account for the major share of the total cost. In most conventional courses, the major cost would fall into categories concerned with training operation, i.e., categories 4-11.

The high initial cost of programs per se is not a limitation of programed instruction. It becomes a limitation only when the cost of training, per trainee, over the long run is excessive in relation to the benefits that programed instruction can provide. If it is possible to amortize expenses over a long period of time, if travel and central school costs are saved, etc., considerable savings in training costs may be realized. Though programed instruction may result in cost savings in the long run, the high, immediate development costs may appear formidable and stand as an obstacle to its use. This is particularly likely in cases where some of the operating costs of a competing conventional course are concealed, as often is the case.

Another example of a cost analysis, though less detailed, concerns a program developed by the Martin Company dealing with "Weapons

TABLE 4

Form for Cost Analysis with Cost Breakdown for a Programed Course[a]

	Traditional Instruction	Programed Instruction
Number of people involved*	240 per yr.	240 per yr.
Length of time involved	20 hours	16.2 hours
Job for which training was provided	Equipment Adjustment	

Training Cost Factors	Cost Comparison	
	Traditional	Programed
1. Training analysis		
Research		$1,500
Job analysis		1,130
2. Curriculum development		1,065
3. Materials preparation—first complete writing for programed instruction	INFORMATION NOT AVAILABLE	3,750
Final revision of program		1,700
4. Instructor training and familiarization		
5. Instructor salary and benefits		700
6. Administrative** salary and benefits		2,000
7. Trainee salary and benefits		
8. Travel and per diem subsistence		291
9. Training materials production		4,630
10. Facilities		
11. Lost production in training or replacement		
12. Evaluation		3,214
13. Dropout during training or on the job		
14. Transition from end-of-training to proficiency		
15. Supervisor training time		
16. Quality of trainee output		
TOTAL		$19,980

[a] The cost analysis form was developed by the Programed Instruction Association, New York City, and is reproduced with permission.
*Refers to trainees for whom training is supplied.
**Includes all personnel, other than instructors or trainees, utilized for training.

Systems Familiarization" (95). The complete program, which was linear, consisted of 613 frames and 50 panel illustrations. It required three and one-half man-months to develop and so was developed at a rate of about 180 frames per month. The total program development cost was $5,600, including overhead, but excluding reproduction costs. The program can be completed by trainees in an average time of 10.3 hours. The development cost per instructional hour was $550 (a value considerably less than for other programs). When the expenses are amortized over 1,500 students, the program costs $3.75 per student, exclusive of reproduction costs, and $5.25 with reproduction expenses included. The program, on the average, requires 34 percent less time than the conventional text-lecture training, and there is an increase of proficiency for the program-type group of 9.3 percent over the conventionally taught group. Based upon savings in instructors' travel expenses and salaries and reduced training time, it is estimated that there was a savings in training costs of approximately $30 per student.

The cost of program development varies and is affected by a number of factors. A cost study carried out at the Martin Company emphasized the following factors among others:

1. *Program writers' skill and subject matter familiarity.* An experienced program writer can produce as much as 40 percent more finished, acceptable frames per unit of time than an inexperienced programer.
2. *Stability of subject matter.* The cost of programing subject matter of a changing nature may be as much as 50 percent more than the cost of programing material that remains static.
3. *Standards of quality.* The cost of meeting a criterion of 1 or 2 percent error rate is vastly greater than for a criterion of 5 percent error rate. (It is to be noted here that there is considerable question as to the desirability of an error rate as low as 2 percent, or even 5 percent.)
4. *Length.* Longer programs were cheaper to produce than short programs on the basis of cost per instructional hour.

An important factor in the cost of program development which was not stressed in the report cited above is the extent of job or task analysis often required as the initial phase of program development. In some cases, the objectives of existing training may be sufficiently detailed and their job relevance adequately established so that a separate job analysis is considered unnecessary. However, it appears that in a large share of cases, there can be little confidence that present training is sufficiently job relevant to make job analysis unnecessary. In much existing training, the objectives and content are not well documented because the burden is placed upon instructors to furnish detailed instructional content from their own experiences. On the other hand, the development of a programed course requires that the content and objectives of training be very carefully documented. Objectives, in turn, depend for their validity on an accurate knowledge of job requirements. If the development of a program is contemplated which will require a high initial cost and the expectation is that the program will be used for considerable future training, there is too much at stake to settle for less than a complete analysis of job requirements. As one writer has pointed out, "If our objectives are erroneous, we may do a beautiful job of teaching—the wrong thing."

Limited Application of Programs: One of the main factors affecting the per-trainee cost of the program is the size of the trainee population. If the number of trainees is small, the high cost of developing programs may not be justified. A program may also have a short life expectancy because of the obsolescence of the material. For example, in an electronics manufacturing company, it was decided not to use programed instruction for teaching an assembly operation (for which it would have been appropriate) simply because the total number of devices to be assembled was small. Similarly, programed instruction might not be an appropriate approach to instruction in new product information for salesmen in those cases where there is a rapid turnover of products. It is partly the obsolescence factor that inclines the program developers in companies to favor the more stable, basic subjects in their training programs. Programs in basic electricity, mechanical drawing, or the use of a slide rule can be expected to have long life expectancies.

Long Development Time: If a training program is needed in a hurry, programed instruction may not be a feasible approach, since development of programs is time consuming. A crude estimate is that 40 man-hours of development time are required to prepare finished materials for one hour of instruction. That does not include publication time. A program averaging approximately 50 hours in length would require approximately one year to develop, if done by a single person. If a job analysis is required before the program is written, the time can be expected to increase considerably.

The development time is an especially important consideration for training occasioned by the marketing of new products, especially those of a complex nature, such as new computing equipment. Salesmen need to be familiarized with the characteristics of new products, and training is necessary for personnel who will maintain equipment. In some cases, work is not begun on the development of training for new products until the product is about ready to be introduced into the market. The result is that the training courses sometimes have to be put together hastily and often are not ready when they are needed. Programed instruction often is out of the question for such training. If the company were so organized as to make possible a close cooperation between training personnel and development personnel at an early period in the development of new products, sufficient time might be available for the development of self-instructional programs. In some cases, development time can be reduced by using a team approach in program production. Some program writing agencies divide the subject matter into manageable segments and assign them simultaneously to several frame writers for production. Review by a single editor and a subject matter expert gives some assurance of homogeneity of the final program.

Finally, it should be kept in mind that long development time is not necessarily unique to programed instruction. It has been dawning upon many trainers that many of these aspects of a complete "programing" job, i.e., analysis of job requirements, tryout and revision of program, criterion test building, evaluation, etc., are no less necessary for other instructional treatments such as films and instructional outlines. In other words, one of the main reasons that preparation of self-instruction programs takes so long is that a *complete* job has been done. When an instructor's outline is done with the same thoroughness, the process can take about the same time as preparing a program. Thus, it seems that the long development time limitation on programed instruction is artificial and can be expected to diminish in importance.

Unstable Subject Matter: If there are frequent and unpredictable changes in job procedures or information which serves as a basis for the content of programs, programed instruction may not be an efficient approach to training. Some changes may affect only a few frames and require only minor changes, but other changes may pervade the entire program and therefore require costly revisions. This requirement however, cannot be considered a limitation restricted to programed instruction. It is no less important to change instructors' outlines and supporting materials in conventional training when source material changes.

Limitations in Subject Matter: It would be a serious mistake at this early stage in the history of programed instruction to attempt the specification of the type of subject matter to which it is amenable. Most existing programs are concerned with verbal concepts, verbal knowledge, and rules and procedures. Some effort has been made to program materials that would teach changes in values and attitudes, with apparent success. Some promising starts also have been made in programing manipulative skills.

Additional information from the survey which is relevant to a discussion of limitations of programed instruction was provided by respondents who indicated that their companies had not used programed instruction and were asked to check a list of possible reasons. A summary of the reasons is presented in Table 5. There is no assurance that the judgments made by respondents were based upon substantial

TABLE 5

Reasons Given for Not Using Programed Instruction
(N=157 Companies)

Reason	*Percent of Companies**
At present it may be too costly for what we would get out of it.	31
The company is not equipped for developing programed courses.	29
I believe that other training techniques are superior for our needs.	24
I don't know of any programs that are available which are applicable to company training.	20
The technique is not applicable to company training to a sufficient degree.	17
I am not now convinced of its general merit.	13
I don't know how programed instruction can be used for any company training.	6
The subject matter of training is not stable enough to justify its use.	6
My superiors in the company are opposed to its use.	1

* The percentages do not add to 100 because of overlapping categories.

knowledge of programed instruction rather than hearsay and supposition. Consequently, these data are valuable only for indicating the general attitude held toward programed instruction by those who are not yet using it. Taken together, the reasons most frequently checked suggest that there are companies which might like to use programs, but have not found any on the market which meet their specialized needs. At the same time they are not equipped to build programs and are as yet unwilling to commit their resources to facilities for program development. Other companies do not see possibilities for programed instruction in their training.

The Procurement and Development of Self-Instructional Programs

This section concerns the development of programed instruction for industrial use. First, survey results regarding the sources of programs are summarized. Next, the "systems" viewpoint toward training development within the larger context of organizational goals is briefly presented, and a general framework for training development is outlined. Examples are then given of procedures followed in program development, followed by a discussion of survey findings concerning the development procedures of companies.

Sources of Programs

There are three sources of self-instructional programs: (a) open market or "off the shelf," (b) custom development by a contractor, and (c) in-house development by the using company. Table 6 shows the survey findings regarding the frequency with which each source was used. From the standpoint of the number of programs, it would appear

TABLE 6

How Companies Obtain Programs

Source	Percent of Companies N = 86	Percent of Programs N = 316
In-company development	58.1	45.8
With help of outside consultant	12.8	18.8
Without help of outside consultant	45.3	26.9
Contract development	12.8	9.1
Purchased on market	29.1	45.1

that in-house development and the open market are about equally important sources of programs. However, a different picture emerges when extent-of-use of a program is taken into account. Figure 5 shows relative frequencies of program sources as they vary with extent-of-use. It is apparent from Figure 5 that the more extensively used pro-

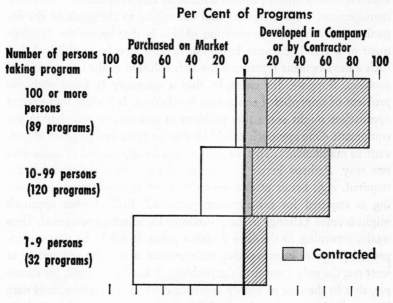

FIGURE 5: *Program sources as a function of number of persons taking programs. (Number of persons unspecified in 24 percent of the programs; not included above.)*

grams are those developed in-house and by a contractor. This is believed to be due to the fact that high volume training needs often involve company-specific subject matter, for which no programs are commercially available. The use of off-the-shelf programs on a low-volume basis probably reflects the exploratory efforts of trainers wishing to gain initial familiarization with programed instruction.

The Systems Viewpoint and Steps in Training Development

The danger of a discussion focused on programed instruction is that one can easily lose sight of the important steps that should take place *before* confronting the problem of how to obtain the particular instructional program that is needed. The point of view represented here is that of a *systems* approach to training. The reader is directed elsewhere for a detailed treatment of this approach (17, 53). Only a brief account of it can be given here.

According to the systems concept, training is viewed as one factor which is closely interdependent with other factors (personnel selection, management, work methods) that contribute to the goals of the organization. A specific implication of this is that before the development of a training course is begun, it must first be established that such a development represents the best solution to the organizational problem. Suppose, for example, that a company is faced with the problem of unpredicted equipment breakdown. It is clear that several approaches might solve this problem in addition to redesigning the equipment. One approach would be a more extensive program of preventive maintenance. This, in turn, might be approached in more than one way. Perhaps better procedures of preventive maintenance are required, e.g., better testing procedures, or perhaps improved training is required for maintenance personnel. Still another approach might involve a change in the procedures for selecting personnel. Then again, returning to the first decision point, it might be that an improved program in preventive maintenance is not the answer, or at least not the only answer to the problem. It has been found, for example, that in the case of highly sensitive equipment, malfunctions may be actually increased as the result of preventive maintenance. Perhaps the better solution is a forecasting of equipment breakdowns through an analysis of the history of past failures. This course of action may in turn create requirements for training, job aids, selection and/or changed operating procedures. The point of importance here is the interdependence among the various parts of the system: the design of operating procedures, job aids, personnel selection, and training.

The Training Development Subsystem: The systems approach has important implications for the strategy of training development. Of course, the first step is to determine that a training development need exists. Then attention can be given to steps in the training development proper. Figure 6 pictures the general steps involved in what is called "The Training Development Subsystem" which represents a framework for training development.

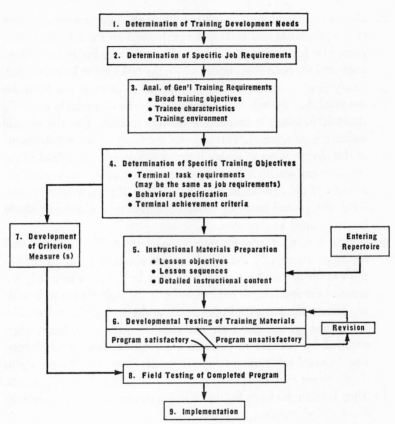

FIGURE 6: *The training development subsystem—showing the sequence of steps in training development.*

The general steps in Figure 6 are listed as follows, along with statements identifying the principal characteristics of each:

1. *Determination of training development needs.* Training development needs arise from efforts to achieve organizational goals. These range from the most general goal of a company, e.g., "to increase profitability"; to goals of intermediate specificity, e.g., "to reduce general training costs"; to highly specific goals, e.g., "to provide for the maintenance or marketing of a newly released item of equipment." Any of the more specific goals can give rise to training development, but they might also give rise to needs for new personnel selection standards or improved work operations.

2. *Determination of specific job requirements.* This is a specification of the job duties and tasks to be performed on the job, the proper procedure for performing these tasks, standards for task performance, and the conditions under which the tasks are to be performed.

3. *Analysis of general training requirements.* Once it has been determined that the organizational goals can be met wholly or partly through training, it becomes necessary to determine the general training requirements. This requires the study of the requirements of the environment in which training would take place and of the attitudes and qualifications of persons to be trained. It may include a study of deficiencies of existing training, if such training exists. Also, the general scope or broad objectives of the training would be determined at this step.

4. *Determination of specific training objectives.* The *terminal task requirements* specify the tasks trainees should be able to accomplish at the end of the course. They may be the same or nearly the same as the specific job requirements, if the trainees are to be able to perform the job duties adequately at the end of the course. The *behavioral specifications* are the abilities, i.e., skills, knowledge, required by persons to perform the terminal task requirements. *The terminal achievement criteria* specify how the trainees are to demonstrate that they have met the terminal task requirements. They furnish the basis for the criterion measure used in evaluating the finished training program.

5. *Instructional materials preparation.* This involves the preparation of *lesson objectives* and arranging lessons in the sequence most effective for learning. Detailed instructional content then can be prepared. Depending on the type of instruction, i.e., programed instruction, lecture, etc., the product of this step may be complete learning materials or an instructional outline, etc. The *entering repertoire* is the specification of abilities and knowledge of persons who will take the training program and helps to determine training content.

6. *Developmental testing of training materials.* In programed instruction, as the instructional materials are prepared, they are tried out on appropriate persons to determine their teaching effectiveness and revised until they meet standards of quality. This step rarely is done in a systematic way for conventional materials.

7. *Development of criterion measures.* The criterion measure is based on the terminal achievement criteria and has as its purpose the determination of whether the completed program meets the training objectives. It may be written concurrently with program development.

8. *Field testing of the completed program.* This involves giving the training course to a sample of trainees from the population for which the course is designed. The criterion measure is used to evaluate the product.

9. *Implementation.* This involves the introduction and integration of the new training into the operating environment where it will be used. It includes gaining the trainer's acceptance of new and unfamiliar techniques in addition to acceptance of specific programs.

Examples of Developmental Procedures: The training development subsystem shown in Figure 6 essentially is a list of the general requirements to be met in training development. The question can be raised as to how closely this framework matches the development requirements as seen by companies which prepare programs in-house. First, it may be helpful to furnish a couple of examples provided by survey respondents. Figure 7 shows the development procedure for the International Business Machines Company in Rochester, Minnesota. The programs they develop are designed primarily to train men to maintain data processing machines. In terms of classification of subject matter described earlier, their programs would be classified as general and specific procedural skills. Another example of program development is shown in Figure 8.

There are a number of differences between the two charts, but when unimportant differences in format are ignored and the terms are translated, many of the differences disappear. The term "output behavior" in Figure 8 can be translated as "terminal behavior" or "training objectives." "Input behavior" which corresponds to the "entering repertoire" of the training development subsystem is not represented in the IBM chart. Neither chart contains the specifications of the organizational goals or the training requirements, and neither makes analysis of job requirements explicit as a separate step although it might be implied as part of the objective-setting step. The IBM chart also

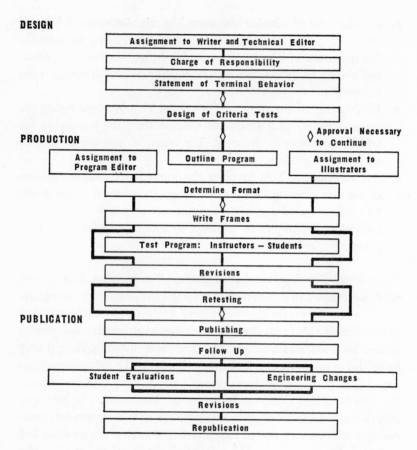

DESIGN

| Assignment to Writer and Technical Editor |
| Charge of Responsibility |
| Statement of Terminal Behavior |
| Design of Criteria Tests |

PRODUCTION ◊ Approval Necessary to Continue

| Assignment to Program Editor | Outline Program | Assignment to Illustrators |
| Determine Format |
| Write Frames |
| Test Program: Instructors — Students |
| Revisions |
| Retesting |

PUBLICATION

| Publishing |
| Follow Up |
| Student Evaluations | Engineering Changes |
| Revisions |
| Republication |

FIGURE 7: *Flow chart for the development of programed courses. (Courtesy of Wayne R. Munns, Manager of Education, Planning-Customer Engineering, Data Processing Division, International Business Machines, Rochester, Minnesota.)*

shows the "production" and "publication" phases as well as the development phase. Otherwise, the two procedures are quite similar to one another and to the training development subsystem in Figure 6.

It is interesting to compare the procedures shown in Figures 7 and 8 with a procedure believed to be quite common in preparing conventional courses. The following example represents the procedure used by one company for the development of a lecture course designed to teach characteristics of new equipment to maintenance personnel:

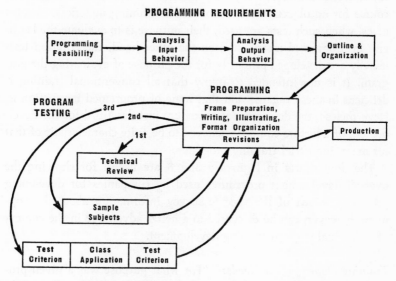

FIGURE 8: *Development sequence for programed courses. (From the notes of a talk by R. W. Walker, The Martin Company, at seminar entitled "Programed Instruction in Company Training and Development" at the American Management Association Headquarters, New York, October 1963.)*

1. An instructor is assigned to develop the course using, as sources of information, equipment manuals, drawings, and operating practices previously developed for the equipment by design engineers and methods agencies. The product of this step is a course outline plus visual aids, e.g., vu-graphs. Approximately three weeks are allowed to write the two-week course.
2. The outline undergoes technical review by the instructor's supervisor.
3. A trial class is conducted by the instructor who wrote the program.
4. The outline is revised if necessary as judged by the instructor who prepared it.
5. The outline is published for use by other instructors.

There are several notable differences between these development procedures and those for programed instruction shown in Figures 6 and 7: (a) It usually is taken for granted that the programed materials will require revisions, whereas revision is indicated as problematical for the conventional course. (b) No provision is made in the conventional course for an objective evaluation of the training materials. In most cases, when such tests are used, their purpose is to evaluate the learners; in programed instruction, on the other hand, the criterion tests usually are developed primarily for the purpose of evaluating the program. It is not intended to imply that all conventional training is deficient in these regards and that none of programed instruction is. Nevertheless, the development procedure just described for the development of a lecture course is believed to be quite characteristic of that for many industrial training programs.

The flow charts in Figures 7 and 8 are useful for showing the over-all development procedures used by companies for developing programs. Much of the specific survey information about development, however, can be discussed to a better advantage in the context of individual steps in training development.

Training Development Needs: "For what purpose was a given program developed?" This question cannot be answered very precisely from the survey data. Nevertheless, there are some general trends which are apparent. Some programs were prepared to meet the acute needs for courses to teach new product information to salesmen or maintenance personnel. Others were written because existing training was judged to be unsatisfactory in some way. Still others were developed to meet the need for new basic training courses. In a large number of cases, however, programs were developed on the basis of the belief that programed instruction was worth considering as a more efficient alternative to existing instruction. The advantages cited by survey respondents to support these decisions already have been discussed.

Requirements for Training: There are several questions to be answered in determining the type of training required. What is the scope required for the training course? What are the characteristics of persons who will take the training course? How many are to be trained over what period of time? What are the features of the environment in which training will take place? What are the characteristics of the subject matter? Is it stable? Is there a need for great uniformity? The answers to these questions provide the principal basis for making an enlightened decision of whether or not to use programed instruction. Nevertheless, it appears that the choice of programed instruction in industry often has been made in the absence of evaluation of specific training requirements. In fact, some trainers seem to approach programed instruction from the point of view that "this technique looks promising, now let me find some course I can apply it to," rather than "we have a training need, let's find the best technique including possibly programed instruction to meet it." While the first point of view is reasonable as an exploratory step in the early history of programed instruction, hopefully the latter point of view will become ascendent as the field matures.

Training Objectives and Job Requirements

The term "training objectives" has not had a uniform meaning among persons who develop training. The present-day viewpoint in programed instruction is that training objectives must be very specific and detailed. Moreover, it often is insisted that they be stated in *action* terms; i.e., they should specify what the person is expected to *do* rather than only to "understand" or "know" upon completion of the course (see 48).[4] Most persons contacted in the telephone interviews made a point of the importance of detailed objectives in describing their development procedures. The source of objectives for courses which deal with bodies of general knowledge, such as mathematics, is usually a consensus of authorities in the field ("consensual" objectives). The majority of commercially available programs deal with subject matter of this type. The objectives for job-oriented programs derive

---

[4] This requirement often is put in terms that the "terminal behavior" of the trainee should be specified. It is believed important to distinguish between terminal *task requirements*, which identify the performance requirements toward which the training is aimed, on the one hand, and terminal *achievement criteria* which represent the *measurement* criteria for judging whether trainees are capable of the desired terminal task performance, on the other. In many cases, the measurement criteria involve direct measurement of the desired performance. For example, in automobile driving courses, efforts often are made to measure driving ability by requiring trainees actually to drive under realistic conditions. Such direct performance measures are desirable when feasible because it is often easy to demonstrate their validity. On the other hand, it is not always possible or desirable for the criteria to have such a direct correspondence to the desired task performance. Paper-and-pencil tests sometimes are used as indirect criteria to indicate potential for future performance, as, for example, in a driver's examination where ability to select descriptions of appropriate driving actions in multiple-choice questions is presumed to predict appropriate driving behavior. A possible source of con-

their validity only from their relevance to specific job requirements (job-derived objectives).

If detailed and accurate objectives for job-oriented programs are to be obtained, they must be derived from detailed and accurate specification of job requirements. In conventional instruction, as has been mentioned before, the reliance is often placed on the instructor to provide the details of the job from his own experience. In many cases, the instructor relies on outlines and assumes that it is unnecessary to document the details of the job for his own teaching purposes. Thus, in such cases, there may not be any complete documentation of the job. For programed instruction, on the other hand, because of the heavy investment in a program, pressures are greater to provide a high standard of quality which in turn creates a necessity for accuracy and completeness of the statement of job requirements upon which the objectives are based. Accordingly, it may be necessary to perform an analysis of the job requirements first if one has not been done.

Program Characteristics

There are data from the survey describing the format characteristics of programs used by companies. Table 7 shows summaries of these data for in-house programs and for programs either purchased on the market or contracted. With respect to program format, there is a clear general trend toward greater use of linear format as compared with intrinsic "branching" format. There is a ratio of about 5 to 1 in favor of this linear format. This is considerably less than the 20 to 1 ratio reported in the schools (80) and may be explained by the relatively greater use of early intrinsic programs (i.e., "TutorTexts") by industry. It is also fairly clear from the data that companies are much

---

fusion comes from the fact that the actions of the trainee in taking the paper-and-pencil test can be described as *performance* just as truly as the actual driving behavior itself.

Thus, when one speaks of performance objectives of training, he should make clear whether he is talking about the actual task (job) performance itself or the performance used to measure the learner's achievement *toward* task (job) performance objectives. The term "terminal behavior" has been somewhat ambiguous in relation to this distinction, but perhaps more commonly it is used to designate terminal *achievement* criteria rather than terminal task performance. For example, it frequently is used to designate the behavior required on terminal frames of self-instructional programs in cases when the behavior is an indirect measure of the task performance toward which the program is directed.

TABLE 7

Characteristics of Programs

Characteristics	Percent Developed* In-House N=152	Percent Purchased* or Contracted N=127
Linear	82.2	66.9
Branching	6.6	22.8
Unspecified	12.5	10.2
Write-in response	68.4	51.2
Multiple-choice response	8.6	18.9
Unspecified	26.3	34.7
Program in book form	79.0	54.3
Machine used with program	27.6	40.2
Unspecified	10.5	7.1

*Percentages do not add to 100 because of overlapping categories.

more likely to use a linear format than intrinsic "branching" format in the programs built in-house. The data for type of response parallel that for program format. That is, the high frequency of write-in responses corresponds to the frequent usage of linear programs. The rather large, unspecified category for type of response may partly reflect the use of other modes of response than multiple choice or write-in, i.e., keypunch, typing, oral responses, etc.

The data in Table 7 conform to the general trend in the field toward the use of programed textbooks rather than machines. Moreover, it can be seen that the trend is toward greater use of programed textbooks for in-house programs. Of the 20 percent of linear programs where machines were reportedly used, one-half consisted in the use of equipment the trainees were being trained to operate, i.e., IBM proof machines, airline reservation machines, typewriters, etc. In other words, in only about 10 percent of the programs in the linear format were special teaching machines used.

Mention should be made at this point of characteristics of industrial programs which reflect problems and needs of particular significance to industry. These were not numerous in the survey results. However, they are mentioned here because they appear to have particular significance for future developments. These special characteristics may be grouped within three classes:

1. *Characteristics which reflect the need to provide the trainee with practice on job tasks.* Examples are use of an airline reservation machine as a training device in a program designed to teach its use; the use of audio tapes for simulated customer contacts in telephone operator training; and the use of audio in conjunction with the IBM proof machine for training bank accounting clerks.

2. *Provisions for adapting programs to fit the needs of persons varying in previous experience.* Groups of employees who are scheduled for industrial training often bring relevant skills and knowledge from past training and job experience. Sometimes, considerable saving of time can be achieved by allowing individuals to skip portions of programs in which they demonstrate mastery. Programs can incorporate features such as "test probes" which make this possible (26, 83).

3. *Provisions for making necessary changes in programs.* When operational practices change, it is often necessary to change the training program. If extensive changes are required, it may be necessary to build a new program. However, program format can be designed in such a manner as to make it possible to change specific frames efficiently. In a program used by one company, for example, a page is allowed for each frame, and the pages are easily changed. In other cases, looseleaf notebooks are used.

Evaluation

It is important to distinguish two types of objective evaluation in the development of programed instruction for industry.

1. *The evaluation of the teaching effectiveness of particular frames.* The criterion ordinarily used here is error rate; a high error rate can be taken as an indication that a program requires improvement. However, a low error rate can be regarded as a necessary but insufficient basis for acceptance of a program. If the error rate were to be based only on unprompted or "criterion" frames, it would be more trustworthy as a basis for evaluation. Even then, however, there may be the problem that performance on such frames is largely a function of short-term memory since they follow prompted frames and answers closely. Short-term memory does not necessarily predict long-term retention (74, 75).

2. *The evaluation of the teaching effectiveness of a program through use of external criteria.* Achievement tests or assessment of job performance often are used to determine how effectively the program meets the course objectives. The companies which do in-house programing vary considerably in the thoroughness and type of external evaluation or field testing.

A few companies do no external evaluation, trusting to a low error rate and/or subjective judgment to provide them assurance of the program's effectiveness. In a report on program development in his company, one trainer states, "We relied on subjective management opinions to determine whether any improvement had been made in our salesmen's training. The consensus of these opinions was that our salesmen were much better trained and had learned much more in the nine weeks of programed instruction than many men who had been with us for nine months" (36). In some cases, unfortunately, there is little doubt that general enthusiasm for programed instruction and programs on the part of trainers serves as a substitute for objective evaluation. One respondent, in fact, remarked that a good program is one that would elicit from a training expert the response, "This is the most exciting program I have ever seen," and that no other evaluation is necessary. The authors' point of view is that objective evaluation of proficiency is vitally necessary. Nevertheless, the importance of trainee-acceptance should not be minimized. Under some circumstances, trainee-acceptance is as important a criterion as proficiency, particularly when trainee attitudes are important factors in the motivation to begin and finish programs.

Among companies which undertake field tests of their programs, there are three main approaches:

1. *Assessment of a program against a criterion examination or other measure.* In the better examples of such evaluations, criterion measures are carefully related to job requirements, and the trials are carried out with representative samples from the populations which will eventually use the programs. In some cases, minimal scores on examinations will be specified. Also, in some cases, the examinations will be given both before and after the program and the evaluation based upon gain scores. A special use of gain scores for evaluating programs is reported by McGuigan (54). In a few

cases, job performance measures are used as criteria, i.e., billing errors for a billing clerk program. In the case of the evaluation of a program for telephone operators (which is described at length at a later point), the performance of the program-taught group is compared with that for a group of employees identified as high performers on the job. The use of job performance criteria is not common, probably due to the fact that the programs usually contribute only part of the skills required for a job, i.e., the number of "total-job" programs is small. This makes it difficult to attribute variations in job performance to the program with any confidence.

2. *Comparison of a program with another training course in terms of a criterion examination.* This usually consists of a comparison of the program with the conventional course which the program is designed to replace. One justification for this is that the results provide a basis for determining whether or not it is worthwhile to replace the conventional course with the program. Another way to think of a comparison study is that the conventionally trained group provides a reference norm or "benchmark" to which the programed group can be compared. Of course, if the conventional course does not meet the objectives, the reference norm it provides is of dubious value.

This kind of comparison can be criticized because of lack of control of the conventional instructional treatment. By contrast, the programed instruction treatment is well controlled and can be replicated. With an instructor in the picture, however, control and replicability are difficult to insure. The result is a comparison of the program with a unique class. The situation can be improved considerably by comparing the program with a sizable sample of classes taught by a number of instructors. In many instances, a program represents an entirely new course rather than a substitute for an older course, and hence no comparisons are possible. Even when an old course exists, a comparison may not be legitimate because of changes in objectives which often result from a careful task analysis done as part of the program development.

3. *Comparison of a program-taught group with a control group which generally receives no training.* This type of evaluation apparently does not occur frequently, yet it is an important type for evaluating programs designed to raise skill level rather than to teach new

skills. For example, a program was developed by Schuster for teaching troubleshooting strategy (81). For its evaluation, it was tried out on a group of technicians from Collins Radio Company, all of whom had previous skill in troubleshooting (82). In the evaluation experiment, two matched groups of technicians were administered a pretest of troubleshooting skills. One group subsequently received the program, the other group no training. Finally, the proficiency measure was administered again to both groups. The program-taught group was slightly superior to the control group in gain on various facets of troubleshooting skill from pretest to posttest, indicating that the program increased their skills. If a control had not been used, the gain of the program-taught group could not be attributed to the program with any confidence. It could have been attributed to the practice they received from taking the pretest or some other experience in between pretest and posttest.

There is a slight variation on the type of evaluation using a control group that would seem to have possible applications for the evaluation of programs designed to increase the level of skills already possessed by trainees, but in addition require the trainee to learn a few new principles or general concepts. An example of this type could be an evaluation of a program designed to improve writing skills. The program presents principles of effective writing, some of which are likely to be quite novel to the learners. There is evidence to indicate that the writing skills of individuals are increased as a result of taking the program. But the question can be raised, for this program and others of the same type, "Was a program of this length required to produce the improvement, or could it have been achieved more economically simply by having learners study a brief list of principles abstracted from the program, plus examples of these?" To answer this question it would be necessary to do an experiment in which the program-taught group is compared with a control group receiving the materials in a briefer form.

Whichever approach to evaluation is followed, attention must be given to providing a suitable criterion measure. In the first place, it must be a valid and reliable measure in relation to the training objectives. Another highly desirable feature in tests used to measure the achievement of training objectives is that the test items identify the

TABLE 8

Summaries of Evaluation Studies
Reported by Survey Respondents

Subject Matter and Trainees	P* vs. C* Comparison	Number of Subjects P	C	Criterion Measure
Billing procedure for billing clerks	Yes	50	50	Job performance (billing errors)
Characteristics and adjustment of complex mechanical system for field engineers. (Described, pp. 703 ff.)	Yes	10	9	90-item comprehensive achievement test
Bank teller procedure for tellers	Yes	39	25	Paper-and-pencil achievement test
Total-job training for telephone operators (outward or toll). (Described in detail pp. 728 ff.)	Yes	64	90	Job performance on five criteria and over-all performance measure
Basic electricity for technicians. (Described, pp. 699 ff.)	Yes	34	30	Two verbal achievement tests: (1) facts and (2) concepts
Union contract understanding for first line supervisors	No	180		Paper-and-pencil achievement test used both for pre- and posttest

* P = program taught; C = conventionally taught

TABLE 8 *(continued)*
Summaries of Evaluation Studies
Reported by Survey Respondents

Proficiency P (%) C		Time (Hours) P	C	Time (Savings)	Remarks
No difference between P and C groups		35	53	34%	P-group required more on-the-job training
88.9 (80-95)**	90.7 (79-98)	16.2	20.1	20%	P-group trainees indicate preference for programed instruction
86.2 (70-100)	82.9 (65-96)	22.5	48.0	53%	P-group trainees judged superior on follow-up training
P-group superior on over-all performance and 4 of 5 criteria		78.3	107.9	27%	Six months after training, P-group equal to average of 50 "best" operators in over-all performance and superior to C-group and "best" operators on 4 out of 5 appraisal criteria
(61-93) (1) 85 (2) 77	(39-87) 61 64	43.1	44.0	2%	Retention loss for both groups after 6 mo.; P-group retains superiority
(5-60) Pretest 43% Posttest 87%	(60-100)	2.5	—	—	6 mo. after training P-group performance 75% of post-program performance

** Ranges in scores

levels of performance that would meet training objectives. This makes it possible to set a minimum attainment score on the test and have confidence that trainees who achieve this score have met the training objectives. The use of job samples as a basis for test items probably is helpful in this regard, since performance standards for job tasks usually can be specified. In cases where it is difficult to preset minimal attainment criteria for tests on rational grounds, it becomes necessary to establish empirical norms for test performance by administering the test to a reference group. For example, in the outward operator program developed for the Bell System, performance of the program-taught trainees was compared with performance of the "best" five operators in each of 10 offices.

Examples of Evaluation: There are several published accounts of evaluation studies (25, 30, 31, 33, 65, 82). It will serve the present purpose, however, to present brief summaries of some of the more succinct results reported in the survey. The cases cited in Table 8 are not necessarily a representative cross section of program evaluations. They are examples from the survey in which relatively complete information about evaluation was furnished.

Many of the points about evaluation can be illustrated by presenting a reasonably detailed description of the evaluation of a particular program developed for training outward (toll or long distance) operators in the Bell System (24, 65). During its development the program was given several trials. These included trials of portions of the program on the contractor's employees, one-day partial trials in a local telephone company office, three- and four-day partial trials in the office of three operating companies near the contractor, and, finally, a major trial of the entire course in ten offices of nine different associated telephone companies.

About half of the finished product consists of what is ordinarily defined as programed instruction. The remainder of the course consists of skill and technique demonstrations, practice and review exercises, and performance evaluations. The entire course consists of the following materials. To be used by the student: 34 Learning Guides (programed books), five Learning or Practice Tapes (including programed audio tapes), Labels, Tickets, Notebook, and other similar materials. To be used by the instructor: one Training Guide (with supplements, five Study Guides, and Evaluation Forms). To be used by supervisors for introduction and administration of the course: Administration Guide.

In the evaluation of the programed course, detailed data were collected on the amount of training time, amount of instructor or supervisor time spent in training, and number of call conditions covered in training. A special performance appraisal was developed for the study, based on a standard series of calls generally comparable for all 10 offices. The appraisal allowed for the scoring of technique, service qualities, key pulsing, completion ticketing, and over-all performance and speed analysis. The performance appraisal was administered at the end of training, after three months, and then after six months. The appraisal also was administered in each office to the five regular operators rated as "best operators" by their supervisors. Before the programed training course was introduced in the 10 trial offices, new operators, who had just completed conventional training, were evaluated with the performance appraisal. Data also were gathered on conventional course length, number of call conditions taught, etc. These data and ratings from the 10 trial offices taken together constitute a basis for comparison with similar data gathered from programed training-taught groups in the same offices. The new operators who had just completed conventional training are designated as the "pre-experimental group" (P), and the programed-taught trainees are designated as the "experimental group" (E).

As a result of the program, training time was reduced 27 percent, while instructor (supervisor) involvement was reduced from 100 percent to 60 percent of total training time. The average number of call conditions taught in the conventional course was 144. In the programed training course, 160 call conditions are taught. Thus, it can be said that not only is the training accomplished in less time at less cost, but it also is more complete.

The performance appraisal results are shown in Figure 9. The average performance of the two groups is shown immediately after training, then three months, and then six months after training. An arrow marks the average performance of the "five best" operators in the 10 offices (a total of 50 operators). Improved performance over time is indicated if the line slants down, except for "speed analysis" which is the opposite. Components of the appraisal criteria are as follows:

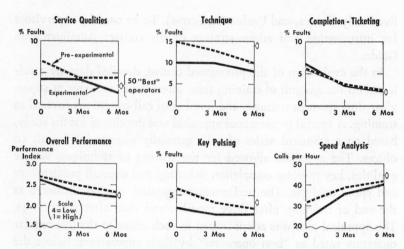

FIGURE 9: *Performance appraisal results for the outward operator training program (adapted from 24).*

1. Technique. Operators are observed for faults associated with handling cords, cord clips, tickets, use of bulletins, and overlapping activities within and between calls.
2. Service qualities. Operators are observed for faults in voice, speech, courtesy, and use of judgment.
3. Key pulsing. Faults are observed: failure to key KP (key pulse), key, etc.
4. Completion ticketing. These include omissions and incorrect steps of procedure.
5. Over-all performance. The supervisor rates each call with respect to over-all operator performance.
6. Speed analysis. The analysis consists of a count of the number of control practice calls completed in a limited time.

All but one of the ratings has to do with accuracy, and together they show that the E group is consistently more accurate than the P group and, in fact, generally more accurate than the "five best." The E group was not as fast as either the P group or the five best, although the differences between the groups narrow at three months and almost completely disappear at six months. (The programed course was strengthened in an attempt to bring up speed without losing accuracy.) Upon completion of the trial, the program was revised and printed in a format convenient to use and which would allow for changes to be made as operating practices change.

In the evaluation study just cited, the evaluation was approached from two different angles: (a) comparison with conventional training and (b) assessment against norms of high-performing job incumbents. First of all, the proficiency of program-taught trainees was compared with the proficiency of conventionally taught trainees. Many of the difficulties of this type of comparison were avoided, since the pre-experimental data were gathered from 10 different offices with different instructors in charge. Then a sample of job performance was taken (the performance appraisal) both of the program-taught group and the 50 "best" operators in the 10 offices.

A question is frequently raised as to the effectiveness of long-term retention provided by programed instruction. In discussing this question, there is an important, and to many an obvious, distinction to be made. Attention may be centered on the *absolute* amount retained, or on the amount retained *compared with* the amount of original learning, i.e., relative retention. In the Holt-Valentine study cited on page 699, for example, the performance of the program-taught group six months after training was superior to that of the lecture-taught group immediately after training. The *relative retention*, however, for the two groups was very similar. That is, the amount of retention loss was about the same in the two cases, but the program-taught group retained its superiority over the lecture-taught group. As far as is known, the *relative retention* produced by programed instruction is comparable to that produced by conventional instruction. However, relatively few systematic studies of retention have been made.

In discussing retention, it is important to take into account the experiences trainees receive between the time they completed training and the time retention is measured. If they are engaged in activities for which the course subject matter is highly relevant, there is likely to be an increase in the level of performance when retention is tested. In the example of outward operator training given above, it can be seen that performance improved on all components of the performance appraisal over a period of six months. Another expectation which is supported by the outward operator data is that the differences between experimental and control groups will diminish as both groups approach the optimum level of performance.

If the training is not relevant to the experience received by trainees in the interval between training and retention testing, a retention loss can be expected. Indeed, looking at it the other way, a retention loss might be taken as one indication that the subject matter training is not sufficiently relevant to job activities. As an example, a considerable retention loss has been found for courses in basic electricity for technicians (25). This should cause companies using these courses to take a hard look at training and job requirements for technicians to determine how job-relevant various topics of basic electricity actually are.

Implementation and Maintenance of Programed Instruction

After a programed course has been developed, the next stage, and one whose importance should not be underestimated, is the introduction of the program into operational use. Since the use of programed instruction in industry is relatively new, there is little evidence to point up appropriate procedures for introducing programs in a systematic way. Nevertheless, it is possible to identify three general problem areas: (a) introducing programed instruction in general, and specific programs in particular, to trainers and management in such a way that they will be accepted and properly used; (b) integrating programed instruction with lectures and other training; and (c) maintaining programs, i.e., making revisions to accommodate changes in methods or practices or to improve them in other ways.

There are several facets to introducing programed instruction into operational use. If the company is using programed instruction for the first time, it becomes necessary to educate management personnel to the new method in order to obtain their support in obtaining proper facilities and making proper arrangements for using programs. For example, because of the self-pacing and individual learning feature, it becomes desirable to schedule training time in a more flexible manner. If upper management understands the needs for such flexible arrangements, the administrative arrangements required may be facilitated. Another facet of the introduction of programed instruction is gaining the trainers' acceptance of features which may run counter to their customary practices. Self-pacing and its implications for more flexible rest periods and variable training times seems especially hard for some to accept. Several of the survey respondents reported that introduction of a new program into operational use was relatively easy in their companies because operational training is under the same administrative control as is the development of programs. Under these conditions, more direct control can be exercised over the use of the course than can be exercised when training and development come under different management.

Limited experience suggests that the following general steps be taken in introducing a course to trainers who have not previously used programed instruction: (a) orient them to the characteristics of programed instruction in general; (b) have them work through the program as a trainee would (if it is not feasible to have them complete the program, at least have them complete a sample); and (c) establish explicit procedures for dealing with administrative problems and procedures (a written guide for the instructor is worthwhile for this purpose).

In training programs which call for conventional lecture courses to follow programed courses immediately or be integrated with programed courses, scheduling problems arise due to the variable training time which is a consequence of the self-pacing feature. If the succeeding course is delayed to accommodate the slowest learner, the faster learners will finish early, creating the question of how they should be occupied. This scheduling difficulty probably arises less often in industry than in public education because industrial training is more often a "one shot" affair. Nevertheless, it does occur, and as programed instruction becomes more often used it may become more of a problem.

Probably it generally would be agreed that any solution to the scheduling problem is far from ideal. One way to handle it has been to give the faster learners supplementary work. Another way is to partially defeat the self-pacing feature and resort to what is sometimes known as "group pacing." In one application of this, for example, arrangements are made to have the learners begin together each of the several sections of the program. Another method is to require home study of the programed material and set deadlines for its completion. Here the variability of learning time is taken up in home study time. It was reported that two companies which bring in engineers from the field for conferences and training mail programed courses to them early enough so that the engineers can complete them before arriving at the training site.

Maintaining programs or keeping them up to date is particularly relevant to industrial and military applications where changes in operating practices and modifications of equipment require changes in training materials. Programs dealing with general knowledge would not ordinarily require these types of changes. Of course, if the changes are too frequent or extensive, there is some doubt that the material should have been programed in the first place. Another facet of maintenance is making improvement in programs after they have been introduced into use. Such changes may come as a result of follow-up studies or improvements in programing techniques.

Most of the survey respondents admitted that they had not yet really faced the problem of program maintenance. A few companies have seen the necessity for creating some relatively foolproof system for keeping abreast of changes and modifying programs appropriately. One company reported that they expected to revise the programs yearly.

The Future of Programed Instruction in Industry

In this chapter, the authors have tried to present their view of how industry has responded to programed instruction. A mixed view it is, too, ranging from those individuals who refuse to use it for a variety of reasons to that relatively exclusively group who either through team effort or adequately monitored contracts are using programed instruction to full advantage.

One need only look back at the history of other innovations in training and see what happened to them in order to make an educated guess as to the future of programed instruction in industry. During and after World War II there was a great wave of enthusiasm for sound motion pictures. The keynote was "more learning in less time." The movement reached large proportions under the impetus of military and industrial mobilization, and its momentum carried it well into the postwar period. A host of studies of the effectiveness of motion pictures was conducted which did, in fact, indicate that well made, relevant films, when used properly, could, indeed, give at least as much, and sometimes more, learning in less time (89). The overhead projector was next, and it, too, appeared in military and industrial classrooms all over the world. And, of course, along with it and the sound film, there appeared a host of "audiovisual aids" such as flannel boards, flip charts, magnetic blackboards, sound filmstrips, mockups, "trick" stages or instructor platforms, etc. About 12 years ago, the latest "panacea" of education and training came on the scene in the form of "educational" television. It has not seemed to catch on particularly well in industry, but has had a respectable showing in some public school and college education. Television, like motion pictures, has been dignified by a long series of research studies which show it to be effective, i.e., as effective as the teacher who presents the lecture on it.

The interesting thing about all of these innovations is that they all have come in more or less as fads and have been hailed by many as a panacea for the ills of training. Obviously none of them has been a panacea, but each of them in time has taken its place in the repertoire of training methods, and the critical factor in its success has been the degree to which it has been *properly* used.

Programed instruction is not a medium like sound motion pictures and television when it is used properly. It is rather an application of a technology of instruction in which the following features are integral:

1. Attention is given to the setting of complete and accurate training objectives.
2. Programs, when properly prepared, go through an empirical development process and are considered complete only when they have been certified to teach the relevant skills with the desired level of proficiency.
3. Accommodation of individual differences in rate of learning is achieved through self-pacing and branching features.
4. The instructional materials which result are self-contained and constant with the result that quality is standardized and a more uniform level of proficiency is assured. In other words, the effect of instructor variation is removed.
5. Assurance is gained that the trainee is responding actively to the relevant materials.

In summary, if industrial users regard programed instruction as a panacea for all training problems or treat the problems of "programing" lightly in any number of ways (such as having instructors convert existing training materials into superficial program format, i.e., small paragraphs with blanks in them), it never will reach its potential and may even fade away. On the other hand, if such users realize that the full exploitation of programed instruction requires the commitment of competent resources in adequate amounts and involves *all five* of the characteristics listed above, it may be expected to flourish and to serve them well.

References

1. Administrative Management. "Programed Text Speeds Training." *Administrative Management* 24: 72-73; No. 7, 1963.
2. American Educational Research Association, 1962 Interim Report of the Joint Committee on Programed Instruction and Teaching Machines. "Criteria for Assessing Programed Instruction Materials." *Journal of Programed Instruction* 2: 57-67; Spring 1963.
3. Baumann, Robert. "Establishing Training Objectives." *American Management Bulletin No. 22.* New York: American Management Association, 1962.
4. Brink, R. O. "Programed Instruction—Industry Training Tool." *Telephony* 164: 19-20; May 25, 1963.
5. Brink, R. O. "Programed Instruction—Factors in Equating Costs." *Telephony* 164: 1-28; June 8, 1963.
6. Buckingham, Walter. "The Impact of Automation on Skills and Employment." *Computers and Automation* 12: 16-21; April 1963.
7. Business Management. "How To Develop Courses for Automated Learning." *Business Management* 23: 34ff; March 1963.
8. Chapman, Robert L. "Programmed Learning and the Use of Teaching Machines—A Revolution in Industrial Training." *Computers and Automation* 10: 21-24; October 1961.
9. Christian, Roger. "Programed Learning: Where It Works, Where It Won't, What It Costs." *Factory* 120: 108ff; March 1962.
10. Christian, Roger. "Guides to Programed Learning." *Harvard Business Review* 40: 36-42; November-December 1962.
11. Cook, Donald. "Industrial Training Problems." *American Management Bulletin No. 22.* New York: American Management Association, 1962.
12. Corrigan, R. E. "Automated Instructional Methods: An Advanced Technology for Industrial and Military Training Applications." *Journal of the American Society of Training Directors* 14: 11-18; April 1960.
13. Dolmatch, Theodore B.; Marting, Elizabeth; and Finley, Robert E.; editors. *Revolution in Training: Programed Instruction in Industry.* New York: American Management Association, 1962.

14. Federal Electric Corporation. *Programed Learning and Federal Electric Corporation.* Paramus, N.J.: Federal Electric Corporation, July 1963.
15. Finn, J. D., and Perrin, D. G. *Teaching Machines and Programed Learning, 1962: A Survey of the Industry.* Occasional Paper No. 3, NEA Technological Development Project. Washington, D.C.: National Education Association, 1962. 11 pp.
16. Gagné, R. M. "Military Training and Principles of Learning." *American Psychologist* 17: 83-91; February 1962.
17. Gagné, R. M., editor. *Psychological Principles in System Development.* New York: Holt, Rinehart and Winston, 1962.
18. Geer, L. N. "A Study of Comparative Methods of Teaching Basic Electricity." *Journal of the American Society of Training Directors* 16: 17-24; December 1962.
19. Glaser, Robert. *Training Research and Education.* New York: John Wiley & Sons, 1965.
20. Glaser, Robert, and Glanzer, Murray. *Training and Training Research.* Contract Nonr-2551(00). Pittsburgh: American Institute for Research, August 1958. pp. 42-43.
21. Glaser, Robert, and Taber, J. I. *Investigations of Characteristics of Programmed Learning Sequences.* Pittsburgh: Department of Psychology, University of Pittsburgh, October 1961.
22. Goldstein, L. S., and Gotkin, Lassar. "A Review of Research: Teaching Machines vs. Programed Textbooks as Presentation Modes." *Journal of Programed Instruction* 1: 29-36; No. 1, 1962.
23. Halley, William C., editor. "Private Tutors for Mechanics." *Dupont Magazine* 57: 24-26; January-February 1963.
24. Holt, H. O. "Development of Self-Instructional Programs for Telephone Company Training." *Telephony* 165: 118ff; November 23, 1963.
25. Holt, H. O., and Valentine, C. G. *An Exploratory Study of the Use of a Self-Instruction Program in Basic Electricity Instruction.* Report to Bell Telephone Laboratories, 1961. [An adaptation of this report is included as a chapter in *Programed Learning: A Critical Evaluation.* (Edited by J. L. Hughes.) Chicago: Educational Methods, 1963. pp. 15-39.]
26. Horn, R. E. *A Typology of Branching Techniques.* Technical Memorandum. New York: Center for Programed Instruction, August 15, 1963.
27. Huffman, H. "Will Teaching Machines Make You Obsolete?" *Business Education World* 40: 11-13ff; February 1960.
28. Hughes, J. L. *The Effectiveness of Programed Instruction.* Technical Report. White Plains, N.Y.: International Business Machines Corporation, January 16, 1961.
29. Hughes, J. L. "Industrial Applications of Teaching Machines." *Journal of the American Society of Training Directors* 15: 30-40; July 1961.
30. Hughes, J. L. *Programed Instruction: A Follow Up Study of 7070 Train-

ing. Technical Report. White Plains, N.Y.: International Business Machines Corporation, October 1961.

31. Hughes, J. L. *A Preliminary Study of the Feasibility of Programed Instruction for Customer Engineering Field Training.* Technical Report. White Plains, N.Y.: International Business Machines Corporation, December 1961.

32. Hughes, J. L. "Effect of Changes in Programed Text Format and Reduction in Classroom Time on the Achievement and Attitude of Industrial Trainees." *Journal of Programed Instruction* 1: 43-54; No. 1, 1962.

33. Hughes, J. L., and McNamara, W. J. "A Comparative Study of Programed and Conventional Instruction in Industry." *Journal of Applied Psychology* 45: 225-31; August 1961.

34. Hughes, J. L., and McNamara, W. J. "The Potential of Programed Instruction." *Personnel* 38: 59-67; November-December 1961.

35. Hughes, J. L., and Schwartz, H. A. *Personality Factors and Trainee Attitude Toward Programed Instruction.* Technical Report. White Plains, N.Y.: International Business Machines Corporation, October 1963.

36. Ivers, Harris S. "Lever Brothers . . . Experimenting with P. I." *NSPI Journal* 2: 13-14; July 1963.

37. Klaus, Phillip. "Video-Sonics Cuts Production Defects." *Aviation Week,* January 4, 1960.

38. Kopstein, Felix F. *Report on Evaluation of Cobal Programed Instruction.* Detroit: Product Planning, Auto-Instructional Systems Division, Burroughs Corporation, January 22, 1963.

39. Leverenz, H. W., and Townsley, M. G. *The Design of Instructional Equipment: Two Views.* Occasional Paper No. 8, NEA Technological Development Project. Washington, D.C.: National Education Association, 1962. 51 pp.

40. Levine, Stanley L., and Silvern, Leonard C. "The Evolution and Revolution of the Teaching Machine." *Journal of the American Society of Training Directors* 14: 4-16; December 1960.

41. Levine, Stanley L., and Silvern, Leonard C. "The Evolution and Revolution of the Teaching Machine." *Journal of the American Society of Training Directors* 15: 14-25; January 1961.

42. Lysaught, Jerome P. "Programed Learning and Teaching Machines in Industrial Training." *Journal of the American Society of Training Directors* 15: 8-13; February 1961.

43. Lysaught, Jerome P. "Programed Learning and Teaching Machines in Industrial Training." *Journal of the American Society of Training Directors* 15: 13-20; June 1961.

44. Lysaught, Jerome P. "Industrial Training Through Programed Learning." *Personnel* 40: 165-69; September 1961.

45. Lysaught, Jerome P., editor. *Programed Learning: Evolving Principles and Industrial Applications.* Ann Arbor, Mich.: Foundation for Research on Human Behavior, 1961.
46. Mager, Robert F. "On Sequencing of Instructional Content." *Psychological Reports* 9: 405-413; October 1961.
47. Mager, Robert F. "Elements of Programed Instruction." *American Management Bulletin No. 22.* New York: American Management Association, 1962.
48. Mager, Robert F. *Preparing Objectives for Programed Instruction.* San Francisco: Fearon Publishers, 1962.
49. Mager, Robert F. *The Psychologist's Role in Automated Instruction.* Palo Alto, Calif.: Varian Associates, February 1963.
50. Mager, Robert F., and Clark, D. Cecil. *The Effects of Normative Feedback in Automated Instruction.* Palo Alto, Calif.: Varian Associates, 1963.
51. Margulies, S., and Eigen, L. D. *Applied Programed Instruction.* New York: John Wiley & Sons, 1962.
52. McCauley, John S. "Nationwide Survey Will Show Amount of Training in Industry." *Journal of the American Society of Training Directors* 15: 42-49; May 1961.
53. McGehee, William, and Thayer, Paul W. *Training in Business and Industry.* New York: John Wiley & Sons, 1961.
54. McGuigan, F. J., and Peters, R. J. *Assessing the Effectiveness of Programed Texts—Methodology and Some Findings.* (In press)
55. Moon, Harold L. "The Two Phases of Programming." *Programmed Instruction.* New York: McGraw-Hill Book Co., 1962.
56. Morse, Richard J. *Programmed Training: An Industrial Tool.* Santa Monica: General Telephone Company of California, n.d.
57. Morse, Richard J. *Programmed Training As We See It.* Presented at a conference on programed instruction, New York City, November 10, 1961.
58. Morton, F. Rand. "Integrating Programed Instruction." *American Management Bulletin No. 22.* New York: American Management Association, 1962.
59. Odiorne, George S. "Training for Profit." *Journal of the American Society of Training Directors* 15: 7-18; July 1961.
60. O'Donnell, L. H. *Programmed Instruction for Industrial Training.* New York: American Society of Mechanical Engineers, n.d.
61. Opinion Research Corporation. *The Potential for Industry in Teaching Machines and Programmed Training.* Princeton, N.J.: Opinion Research Corporation, June 1962.
62. Pask, Gordon. "Automatic Teaching Techniques." *British Communications and Electronics* 4: 210-11; April 1957.

63. Pask, Gordon. "Report on Symposium Papers at Conference on Automata held in Teddingham, England." *Automation Progress*, circa 1957.
64. Pask, Gordon. "Electronic Keyboard Teaching Machines." *Teaching Machines and Programmed Learning.* (Edited by A. A. Lumsdaine and R. Glaser.) Washington, D.C.: National Education Association, 1960.
65. Peterson, R. O., and Yuzuk, R. P. *Research on the Training of Outward Operators: Experimental Comparisons and Course Implementation.* Final Report. Pittsburgh: American Institute for Research, August 1963.
66. Polin, A. Terrence; Morse, Richard J.; and Zenger, John H. "Educational Criteria for Selecting Instructional Programmers from In-Plant Employees." *Journal of the American Society of Training Directors* 16: 12-17; September 1962.
67. Powers, Carl A. *Application of Programed Instruction in a Marketing Organization.* Paper presented at the annual meeting of the American Psychological Association, Philadelphia, Pennsylvania, August 29-September 4, 1963.
68. Pressey, S. L. "A Third and Fourth Contribution Toward the Coming Industrial Revolution in Education." *Teaching Machines and Programmed Learning.* (Edited by A. A. Lumsdaine and R. Glaser.) Washington, D.C.: National Education Association, 1960.
69. Pressey, S. L. "Teaching Machine (and Learning Theory) Crisis." *Journal of Applied Psychology* 47: 1-6; February 1963.
70. Prion, Erich E., and Powell, David R. "A Study of the Training Director's Functions." *Journal of the American Society of Training Directors* 15: 12-17; April 1961.
71. Ramo, Simon. "A New Technique of Education." *Engineering and Science* 21: 17-22; October 1957.
72. Redding, M. Frank. *Revolution in the Textbook Publishing Industry.* Occasional Paper No. 9, NEA Technological Development Project. Washington, D.C.: National Education Association, 1963. 32 pp.
73. Rogers, James, and Bullock, Donald. "The Application of Programmed Instruction in the Computer Field." *Computers and Automation* 12: 22-25; April 1963.
74. Rothkopf, E. Z. "Some Conjectures About Inspection Behavior in Learning from Written Sentences and the Response Mode Problem in Programed Self Instruction." *Journal of Programed Instruction* 2: 31-46; Winter 1963.
75. Rothkopf, E. Z., and Coke, Esther U. "Repetition Interval and Rehearsal Method in Learning Equivalences from Written Sentences." *Journal of Verbal Learning and Verbal Behavior* 2: 406-16; December 1963.
76. Rummler, G. "Programmed Learning for Business." *Michigan Business Review* 15: 16-19; March 1963.

77. Rummler, G., and Yaney, J. P. *A Preliminary Cost Survey on Programed Instruction.* Ann Arbor, Mich.: Center for Programmed Instruction for Business, July 1963.

78. Rust, Grosvenor C. "Transfer Approach to Programmed Training." *Journal of the American Society of Training Directors* 16: 5-54; May 1962.

79. Schelle, Wayne N., and Lippitt, G. L. "Training Director's Attitudes Toward Programed Instruction." *Journal of the American Society of Training Directors* 16: 9-17; November 1962.

80. Schramm, Wilbur. *Programed Instruction, Today and Tomorrow.* New York: Fund for the Advancement of Education, November 1962.

81. Schuster, D. H. *Logical Electronic Trouble-Shooting (A Program).* New York: McGraw-Hill Book Co., 1963.

82. Schuster, D. H., and Smith, R. M. *Training Electronic Technicians in Trouble Shooting via Programed Instruction.* Paper presented to the American Society of Training Directors, Chicago, May 6, 1963.

83. Shettel, H. H.; Clapp, D. J.; and Klaus, D. J. *The Application of a By-Pass Technique to Programed Instruction for Managerial Training.* Pittsburgh: American Institute for Research, July 1963.

84. Silvern, Leonard C. *Methods and Devices for Putting an In-Service Training Program into Effect.* Paper presented to the Institute on In-Service Training and Intramural Communication for Supervisors in School of Library Science, University of Southern California, Los Angeles, December 13, 1960.

85. Silvern, Leonard C. "An Analysis of the Teaching Machine Field and Implications for Home Study Courses." *Home Study Review* 1: 5-22; January 1961.

86. Silvern, Leonard C. "Implications of the Teaching Machine for Firemanship Training." *Fire Engineering* 114: 290; April 1961.

87. Silvern, Leonard C. "The Influence of Teaching Machine Technology on Electronic Systems Maintenance Training." *Institute of Radio Engineers Transactions on Human Factors in Electronics* HFE-2: 78-83; September 1961.

88. Sindler, A. J. "Self-Instructional Analog Computer Training. A Comparative Study of Programed Instruction vs. Conventional Methods." *Journal of the American Society of Training Directors* 15: 14-17; November 1961.

89. Special Devices Center. *Instructional Film Research (Rapid Mass Learning), 1918-1950.* Technical Report No. SDC 269-7-19. Port Washington, N.Y.: Special Devices Center, December 1950.

90. Spectrum. "Programmed Instruction." *Spectrum* 10: 88-95; September-October 1962.

91. Thelen, Herbert A. "Programmed Materials Today: Critique and Proposal." *Elementary School Journal* 63: 189-96; January 1963.

92. Utter, R. F. "Development of Training Aids for Equation Typing." *Sandia Corporation Training Bulletin* 1, July 1962.
93. Gilmer, B. von Haller. "The Third Crisis in Industrial Training." *Journal of the American Society of Training Directors* 16: 4-11; September 1962.
94. Walker, R. W. *The Economics of Programed Instruction.* Paper presented at the annual meeting of the American Psychological Association, Philadelphia, Pennsylvania, September 4, 1963.
95. Waller, T. "The Future of Programed Instruction." *American Management Bulletin No. 22.* New York: American Management Association, 1962.

GLENN L. BRYAN
JOHN A. NAGAY
Office of Naval Research

Use of Programed Instructional Materials in Federal Government Agencies

The reaction of the federal government to a new product is always a matter of considerable interest. The government represents a vast potential market, and adoption of a new product by the government virtually assures its commercial success. This, in turn, permits the manufacturer to produce large product batches which are made available to the nongovernmental purchaser at economical prices. Furthermore, the widespread adoption of a new product by a cost-conscious government may provide convincing evidence to prospective buyers who do not have extensive test and evaluation facilities of their own.

Interest in the government's reaction to a new product is especially keen when it is known that the government itself has great needs which the product is specifically designed to satisfy. Such is certainly the case with respect to training innovations. The federal government's training needs are monumental. Indeed, it is tempting to dwell on the variety of training given by the government, the far-flung nature of the enterprise, and the many different kinds of people that it trains. However, these things are relatively well known. Suffice it to say that the total amounts of training time, money, and effort expended by the government are staggering. It almost goes without saying that any product which reduced these amounts significantly would be big business. Obviously, any new addition to instructional technology which was heralded as a "breakthrough" and promised to result in great all-around savings would be given very serious consideration. Such claims have been made on behalf of programed instruction. Therefore, one would surely expect that various government agencies would be engaged in tryouts and evaluations of programed instructional materials. And, of course, they are.

Purpose

This chapter presents the results of a survey of the extent to which programed instructional materials are being used in the federal government. The results reported include information regarding problems and benefits experienced by those attempting to prepare and implement this new method of instruction. The chapter concludes with observations, speculations, and suggestions by the authors regarding the utilization of programed instruction in the federal government.

Procedure

The information presented here was collected by means of a telephone survey. Calls were made to a sizable sample of individuals responsible for employee development and training. Initial calls were made to the headquarters of each agency. In the typical case, such a call produced a list of names of individuals responsible for training at subordinate levels in the organization who might have the information desired. These people were then called. This usually yielded information regarding local usage of programs and some further leads. The calling process continued during the first several months of 1963, until it seemed reasonable that instances of utilization in that agency would have been uncovered had they existed. In many cases, amplifying information was sought by mail or personal interview.

Scope

No effort was made to collect information regarding research dealing with programed instruction. Questions in this survey were directed to those involved in the actual training operations. Without exception those interviewed were extremely cooperative. Although many deprecated their own knowledge of programed learning, their conversations revealed substantial information regarding the history of the field and its theoretical foundations. Even where programed instruction was not in actual use, serious consideration was being given to it. This consideration took several forms: program tryouts, staff conferences, in-house study groups, briefings, programing institutes, and presentations by paid consultants.

Appendix A lists the 125 organizations contacted in the course of the survey. In interpreting the appendix, it is necessary to keep in mind that large organizations are often listed along with their subordinate units. This simply means that the headquarters is reporting on its own training program, and each subordinate unit is making its own report. In other cases, the headquarters has chosen to report for the total organization. When this occurs, the subsidiary bureaus are listed as having been surveyed even though they were not contacted directly.

Programs Covered

Three hundred and eighty-two different programs were reported by the organizations surveyed. These are listed alphabetically in Appendix B. Despite efforts to restrict the data to programs in actual use, a difficult problem arose because very few programs had been completely checked out and firmly established as a part of a specific curriculum. Rather, most programs were either under development at the time of the survey or were undergoing tryout and modification. The cautious approach would have been to report the few firmly established programs. However, it was decided to relax the criterion of "actual use" and to include all of those programs which were being prepared for tryout and eventual inclusion in some specific training course. Only programs that were frankly experimental or were being tried out in a very casual, exploratory way were excluded.

It is likely that the more than 380 programs uncovered in the course of this survey represent a very conservative estimate of the number of different programs that are being tried out in government training establishments, since frank research programs have been excluded. Secondly, despite efforts to cover all organizations within the government, it is unrealistic to expect that no omissions have occurred.

Topics Covered

The programs listed in Appendix B cover a very wide spectrum of subject matter, ranging from such broad topics as "Philosophy" to such specific topics as "Principles of A-28 Gyro Stabilized Mount." Scientific and technical topics dominate the list. One is led to ask why these topics have been chosen to be programed. One obvious (but nonetheless important) factor influencing the selection of topics is that programs are written to be used. Consequently, programs get themselves written in areas where instruction is given. The composition of the program list reflects the fact that the U.S. government, and particularly the Department of Defense (the largest user of programed instruction), is essentially a technical organization. Other factors which influence the selection of topics to be programed are the interests of the programers. To a large extent they program the topics they know about—or would like to learn about. And, finally, in experimenting with the new medium, it is challenging to try one's hand in a brand new subject matter. Such homely factors as these seem to be responsible for the curious assortment of topics programed. There is very little indication that formal, theoretical considerations had very much to do with the selections. Rather, it seems more common to select a topic on informal grounds and then examine it to see if there are any good reasons why it should not be programed. This technique for selecting topics to be programed has resulted in great diversity which may be partially responsible for the differential success of programed instruction reported by those contacted; this will be discussed later.

Borderline Cases

It was arbitrarily decided not to include language laboratories in the survey, despite the fact that some of them employ features which are characteristic of many teaching machines. Since there are many language laboratories in use within the government, had they been included in the sample, it would have colored the data considerably. An opposite decision was made regarding two other borderline devices: the letter-sorter operator trainer and the Classroom Communicator. The letter-sorter operator trainer employs tactile, visual, and auditory cues and feedback principles for the purpose of training postal employees to work in automated post offices. There are currently three of these devices in use: one in Detroit, one in Flint, and one in Washington, D.C. These machines use films that are especially programed for the particular community that each serves. Some 1,800 postal employees have been trained with these devices. The Classroom Communicator is used with two of the programs listed in Appendix B. This is a device which consists of 30 student response stations connected to an instructor's console. Questions may be asked of the class which are responded to by pressing keys at the student station. Student responses are displayed visually at the instructor's console. In this manner the instructor may assess the class's comprehension of the material being presented and modify his presentation accordingly. In addition, the instructor may announce the correct answer after the class has responded. This feedback provision permits the operation of the device as a sort of teaching machine. Sixteen of these are currently installed at the Naval Air Technical Training Center at Memphis, Tennessee. At the present time, these devices are undergoing tryout in various modes. It is not entirely clear how they may be used by the Technical Training Center in the long run.

Program Length

Each respondent was asked to give descriptive information for each program being used by his organization. One item of information was the program length. As can be seen from Table 1, programs differ markedly with respect to length.

The running times shown in the table range from less than 1 hour to 150 hours, with a median of 6 hours. This does not include the letter-sorter training of the Post Office Department. As mentioned above, it is a borderline case and requires from 300 to 1,200 hours to complete, depending upon the size of the city being served.

There appears to be a general feeling among programing advocates that eventually all material which is suitable for programing will be programed. From this point of view, the small programs that are currently being written are but fragments of larger programs which will evolve as a result of program mergers. However, in many (if not most) cases, no formal procedures have been worked out to guarantee effective program coordination. Hence, although such mergers could occur in principle, it appears somewhat optimistic to expect it to happen in

TABLE 1

Frequency Distribution of Length of Programs
(in Instructional Hours)
$N=245$

Length in Hours	Number of Programs	Length in Hours	Number of Programs	Length in Hours	Number of Programs
1	26	16	2	31	0
2	35	17	0	32	1
3	25	18	4	33	0
4	17	19	1	34	0
5	14	20	6	35	1
6	26	21	1	36	2
7	14	22	0	37	0
8	7	23	0	38	0
9	5	24	1	39	1
10	9	25	2	40	0
11	6	26	0	41	0
12	14	27	0	42	0
13	2	28	0	43	0
14	3	29	1	44	0
15	8	30	2	45	0
				over 45	9

actual practice. Different formats, varied writing styles, and dissimilar objectives are apt to limit the number of cases where two programs actually do merge spontaneously.

Besides, long programs may not be desirable. There is some evidence to indicate that long programs create special problems of their own. For example, they tend to accentuate the differences in completion times when administered in the classroom. It is more difficult to plan group "breaks." And some organizations that are currently using programs which run for entire school days (or more) report motivational problems from the long, unrelieved sessions.

In summary, it seems optimistic to expect short programs to merge into longer programs without specific provision for that to occur. Furthermore, something has to be done to relieve the boredom associated with taking many of the present programs, if it is realistic to think of requiring students to go through them hour after hour and day after day. Although it is not possible to say at the present time what the optimum length programs should be, it does seem that they can be too long.

Sources of Programs

Respondents were asked to indicate the source of each of the programs that they reported. This information is presented in Table 2. As can be seen, the bulk of the programs have been produced by in-house programers. These are employees who have been assigned the responsibility of producing programs for use by their own organizations. They customarily receive special training in program writing. This training is usually given under contract with a commercial program-writing organization. The courses are relatively short, seldom longer than six weeks. The Air Force has about 250 trained programers; the Army has about 80; the Navy has 15. Only a few government in-

TABLE 2

Sources of Programs in Use

Source	N	%
Developed under contract	14	3
Commercially available	46	12
Developed "in-house" by using organization*	322	85
Totals:	382	100

* In-house program development is frequently supplemented by guidance from programing consulting organizations.

house programers are known to exist outside of the Department of Defense (although this situation is likely to change rapidly). The Air Force has indicated that it elected to develop a strong in-house capability because it was so expensive to obtain custom-built programs under contract. It is not possible to determine, at this point, exactly the relative costs of programs prepared in-house and under contract.

Survey respondents thought in-house programing was cheaper, cheaper in an absolute sense and cheaper in the sense that it could be incorporated in the work schedule of the instructors without involving the expenditure of additional funds. However, it is the opinion of the authors that in-house costs can be reckoned in many ways. For this reason, one is often unaware of the full cost of in-house efforts. In any case, some value would have to be placed upon prompt program preparation, and certainly any direct cost comparisons would have to allow for possible differences between various programs in terms of their quality and effectiveness. In all likelihood, if appropriate cost-effectiveness studies were made, the apparent cost advantage of programing in-house would diminish.

In any case, relatively few of the programs in the survey were prepared under contract. However, it is again necessary to stress that many programs produced under research contracts are not listed. If they had been, the category "developed under contract" would have been substantially increased, but probably would not have exceeded the number of commercially obtained programs. Commercial programs account for about an eighth of the programs reported in Table 2. Since most organizations have indicated that they intend to use commercially prepared programs whenever they are available, it seems that there will be a continuing government market for good programs. However, it is interesting to note that only a few of the programs listed in Programs, '62 (1) showed up in this survey. Even making allowance for the fact that many of those programs are grossly unsuited for adult use, there seem to be many currently available commercial programs which are not now being used by any government organization. However, there is at least one area where the part of commercially prepared programs is being vigorously exploited, the area dealing with information about computers. Several of the organizations with large computer facilities use programed courses during the introductory phases of the training for their computer personnel.

At the time of this survey, about 88 percent of the programs used in the government were custom built. The main reason given for this situation was the nonavailability of suitable off-the-shelf programs. One possible explanation for the limited use of off-the-shelf programs is that many government training programs deal with specialized subject matter. That is to say, they deal with topics which have no civilian counterparts. However, examination of the training needs across the broad spectrum of the federal government indicates many topics that are common to the nongovernment market. One big factor in the discrepancy between off-the-shelf programs and custom-built programs was the Air Force's decision to develop a strong in-house capability, which has led to the development of many programs specifically tailored to Air Force needs. In all likelihood some programs have been custom built when a suitable program already existed. Such is the state of information exchange at the present time. However, extensive efforts are now being undertaken to maximize the sharing of information about tested programs within the Department of Defense. Once this becomes operational, a base will exist for extending it beyond the Department of Defense.

Type of Instruction

Those who used programed instruction were asked to indicate how the programs were used. Responses were obtained for 199 programs. Of these, 108 were classified as "sole source," that is, they carried the entire teaching burden for the topics covered. The remaining 91 were used in conjunction with other materials and techniques to cover a particular topic. All cases are classified in terms of the type of training they accomplished in Table 3.

TABLE 3

Type of Training Provided by Programs in Use

Type	Number of Programs
Standard	149
Remedial	12
Refresher	6
Preparatory	20
Self-development	12
Total	199

The term "standard" simply means training in its usual sense—regular training anticipated in the lesson plan to which all trainees are routinely exposed. "Remedial" training is employed in an attempt to salvage the student whose academic performance is submarginal. "Refresher" training refers to training given prior to an established course. It is intended to provide a quick review of materials which have been learned previously. For example, the U.S. Naval Postgraduate School at Monterey, California, requires those officers who have not had formal calculus training for a stated period of time before entering postgraduate training to take a programed refresher course in calculus. The category "preparatory" was used for programs covering material not previously learned and administered prior to an established course.

An example of this is the policy of the Naval Command Systems Support Activity, which requires certain new employees to take a programed course in computers if they had not had previous computer training. In this manner, those individuals partially overcome this deficiency and are better prepared to take classes dealing with the particular computers used there. The "self-development" category contains programs that are not specific to any particular course objective. They are usually voluntary (at least at the outset).

As can be seen, the most common usage of programs is for standard training. In 20 instances, programs were used in preparatory training. Most of these cases involved military training. In such settings, men frequently report for training some days in advance of the convening of a new class. One obvious way to occupy their time profitably is to engage them in pertinent self-instruction. It is somewhat surprising that more of this is not being done.

Where Used

The locale at which programed instruction is administered was thought to be a matter of some interest, and available information of this sort is presented in Table 4. The "classroom" locale refers to those situa-

TABLE 4

Locales at Which Programs
Are Being Used

Locale	Number of Programs
Classroom	154
Homework	30
Correspondence	24
Total	208

tions where programed instruction is administered, usually on a scheduled basis, to individuals during their normal school or working hours in a more or less formal classroom setting. In "homework" situations, individuals are made responsible for their own instruction and complete programs on a self-imposed schedule, either at home or in libraries, study halls, or the like. "Correspondence" is used in the usual sense.

The reader is cautioned against making generalizations from the data in Table 4. There are likely to be many changes in the programed instructional picture within the federal government in the near future which will create drastic shifts in the frequencies reported above. The bulk of programs under development, for example, are intended for use in military training programs and will probably be administered in classroom situations. This will serve to produce an even higher number of classroom-administered programs. As will be discussed later, some of the more knotty administrative problems initiated by the advent of programed instruction derive from the fact that it is self-paced, i.e., the student is free to proceed at his own rate. Perhaps a special kind of teaching facility will have to be developed to handle such problems. Substantial increases in the use of programed formats in correspondence training also seem to be a reasonable trend for the future.

Voluntary or Required

Whether the training accomplished through programed instruction is voluntary or required also suggests something about the uses to which this kind of instruction is put. Such information was available on 215 of the programs in use. Of this number, 171 were required courses and 44 were used on a volunteer basis. Voluntarily used programs tend to be those classified as serving the purposes of self-development and less frequently as preparatory to a more intensive formal course of training. Participation by the student is required where programs are used as scheduled portions of training courses, where they serve a remedial purpose, or where they provide the sole source of training in a specific subject matter. Programs used for refresher training tend to be either voluntary or required, depending on such factors as the age of the trainee or the amount of time that has elapsed since his last period of instruction. It seems likely that as programs progress through tryout to adoption for routine use, the number in the required category will rise sharply.

Attitudes Toward Programed Instruction

During the interviews, questions were asked which were intended to reveal the attitudes of training personnel toward programed instruction and the bases for these attitudes. The majority of those interviewed seemed favorably disposed to programed instruction. They were optimistic about the possibility of its eventual success. These favorable attitudes seemed to stem from the logical appeal of student-centered instruction developed on firm empirical foundations. Many were favorably impressed with published results and informal reports of savings in time achieved by programed instruction. Much of the acceptance appeared to be uncritical. Many of those interviewed indicated that they felt the need for competent, unbiased professional advice.

A few individuals displayed outright hostility to programed instruction. They were inclined to be vehement about their lack of confidence in the claims made on its behalf. Several of the organizations had adopted an official wait-and-see attitude. For the most part, this attitude appeared to reflect an unwillingness to pioneer rather than a strong negative attitude toward programed instruction.

Advantages and Disadvantages

As has been pointed out, most of the programs covered by this survey are still under development. Rather few of them have been used routinely, with sizable numbers of trainees. Consequently, there is a paucity of hard experience within governmental training upon which to base firm conclusions. However, such information of this sort as was obtained is reported below.

Many who have tried programed instruction are discouraged by its cost. At the present time, preparing a program requires a considerable expenditure of man-hours. The Air Force reports that they have averaged 137 programing hours for each instructional hour. In the absence of comparative statistics, the Air Force experience must be taken as an indication of the effort (and, therefore, the cost) of preparing a new program. Since this is a pioneering effort, there are many reasons for believing that the ratio of programing to instructional hours will ultimately be reduced as programers gain experience and facility. In all likelihood, sophisticated programing aids and techniques will be developed to expedite the production of programs and reduce their costs.

Several users complained of the bulkiness of programed materials.

This contributes to high initial reproduction costs as well as to high logistics costs. The bulk itself militates against extensive use of some materials in situations where the availability of space and weight restrictions are critical. Disappointment was also expressed because many programs seem to require extensive (and seemingly endless) revision. It is frustrating to purchase or develop a program at very considerable expense only to find that it is a rough first approximation.

Other problems grow out of the self-pacing features of programed instruction. Since students are allowed to go through the material at their own speed, and since their speeds differ, some finish before the others. This tends to produce administrative and scheduling problems. It also complicates the life of the classroom instructor. As a matter of fact, much remains to be done in working out the role of the instructor who uses programed instruction. As an example, one instructor who typically stopped her class during work periods for group discussion or to clarify a point that was creating student questions found that this technique was no longer suitable.

Colonel Gabriel D. Ofiesh, who organized the Air Training Command's trail-blazing efforts in programed instruction, lists several of the problems presented above along with "problems in sequencing instructional materials, the determination of the most profitable and adaptable subject areas for programming, the selection and training of programmers, and the establishment of criteria for evaluating programmed materials."[1] The latter point is specially important to the federal user who wishes to determine whether a particular program will serve his training purposes. Although it is possible to specify a variety of procedures for evaluating the program, generally speaking, the behavioral objectives, proficiency tests, and agreed-upon procedures are not available. Consequently, the training director who wishes to develop or purchase a program for some particular use finds it necessary to develop extensive evaluation materials. This is a sobering task. More frequently than not, it calls for a sophistication in test development which does not exist within the training organization. A so-called "90-90" standard has been adopted by one user agency. This means that 90 percent of students must achieve 90 percent correct responses on a criterion test before the program is deemed acceptable

[1] Personal communication, September 11, 1963.

for routine use. This kind of dependence upon a criterion test, of course, calls for considerable care and skill in its construction. The situation is no worse, however, for the adoption of programed instruction than it is for any new training technique.

On the brighter side, the experience of the federal government with programed instruction has been generally encouraging. The largest federal effort to produce and evaluate programed instruction is being conducted by the Air Force Air Training Command. To date 46 programs have been completely checked out. In 37 of 46 comparisons the groups who received programed instruction achieved higher criterion test scores than those trained by so-called conventional methods. In 39 of 46 comparisons the experimental group completed their coverage of the topic in less time than did the conventionally trained groups. Other users have not conducted such extensive comparisons so they are limited to more fragmentary bases from which to draw conclusions. Examination of their results leads the authors to believe that other users have had less consistent success than has the Air Training Command. Despite this, there is a general belief that sooner or later programed instruction will be importantly involved in federal training. One organization is even looking forward to using programed instruction to train an occupational group which has heretofore resisted their best training efforts.

At the present time it appears that there are many benefits of programed instruction which are not commonly recognized. Actually, several organizations have indicated that their whole training endeavor has improved as a consequence of "the programing point of view." This is to say that the student-centered, objectives-oriented, tough-minded approach led to improvements in courses that were not programed.

Unrealized Potential

For the most part, the programs being used are of the general sort suggested by Skinner, Pressey, and Crowder. This is not to say that there has not been some moderation in some of the original points of view. And, it is not to say that, for example, mathetics programers have not been trained. But, somehow, one gets the feeling that those currently involved with federal training think of programed instruction primarily in terms of these rather limited early techniques. It is not apparent that they are putting pressure on the research community to come up with new and different approaches.

Not only are they not pressing for more new ideas, they seem to be ignoring some of the vaunted advantages of the old programed techniques and available equipment. Perhaps the most obvious example of this is the fact that none of the agencies contacted was found to be taking particular advantage of devices such as the Autotutor for providing protection for classified information. Many agencies are required to teach sensitive materials. These agencies have all of the problems associated with the control of classified training documents, class notes, and scratch paper. But, no instances have been noted where sensitive material is presented on film in a locked machine and the students' responses are limited to button pushing specifically for the purpose of taking advantage of the security inherent in the use of such a machine. Offhand, it would appear that this method of presentation would afford far more protection for the sensitive material than other instructional methods currently in use.

There also seems to be little attempt to take advantage of the privacy which programed instruction offers. An individual working alone with a program has no need to attempt to cover up his ignorance of the topic under consideration. He can make mistakes without fear of ridicule. He can submit to remedial loops which contain elementary information for which he would be embarrassed to acknowledge a need publicly. He can get feedback which could contain valuable supporting information. There are situations where this type of privacy is extremely important, for example, in the instruction of senior officers and civilians in very high official positions. Their high status makes it difficult for them to benefit from group instruction. Actually the need for privacy is not restricted to top officials. In caste-conscious organizations there are many pressures which inhibit honest questions and restrict class participation by those who do not wish to reveal their ignorance.

In contrast to secrecy and privacy, it might also be pointed out that adequate consideration does not appear to have been given to the use of programed instruction under nonprivate conditions; e.g., team learning. Although one constantly hears complaints of instructor shortages, there is no evidence of team learning efforts. With teacher shortages, it would be reasonable to organize students into small groups, perhaps five, and present material to them in programed instructional format where the students would read the frame together and then, say, take turns in providing the answers. It might even be advisable to weight the criterion test scores of the individual members of each group by the group average. This would presumably motivate individual students to band together to help other members of their group.

It was also rather surprising to discover that the technique developed by Utter (2) for using the typewriter as a teaching machine at the Sandia Corporation has not been more widely adopted for use elsewhere. He uses this technique to teach girls with general typing skills how to type complicated formulas from handwritten notes. The formulas involve many superscripts and subscripts and require skills not normally developed in regular typing classes. Utter prepared a straightforward program which presents a handwritten expression to be converted into type. The handwritten formula appears on the left-hand side of a page inserted in a typewriter. The trainee types the formula, or part of it as directed, on the right-hand side of the page. She then advances the paper in the typewriter so as to expose the "correct" answer. The construction of the typewriter itself prevents the typist from seeing the correct answer until she has advanced the paper. Of course, it is also possible to present explanatory information along with the feedback term to provide further assistance to the trainee if desired. Since the programs may be inexpensively reproduced and typewriters are plentiful, it is somewhat disappointing that this clever technique has not enjoyed greater popularity.

Summary Comments

As one can see, the federal government has begun to utilize programed instruction. At the present time most of this utilization is quite tentative. The experiences of the users have ranged from "success beyond fondest hopes" to "bitter disappointment." However, even those disappointed with programed instruction tended to interpret their results in terms of the limitations of their own situation and not to fundamental shortcomings of the programed techniques. The tendency at the present time is to watch and wait. Most of the training organizations that are getting involved with programed instruction are doing so very cautiously. It is the judgment of the authors of this chapter that programed instruction may not be receiving a fair trial.

Very frequently, a newly fledged program is pitted against an established method of instruction. Usually this means that an early version of a developmental model of a program is thrown into competition with a well-oiled "something" called conventional instruction. Whatever else conventional instruction is, it has evolved over a period of time and is tailor made to the needs of the user. One almost never hears of a *series* of comparative studies which extend over time with the objective of producing a program that is in fact clearly superior to the existing method of instruction. In other words, the comparison is usually done in the name of research instead of development.

Furthermore, the fact that one of the instructional systems is new (and the other is old) confounds the comparison of the two systems in unknown ways. There are some indications that "newness" in and of itself can create negative biases in some conservative organizations. This is sometimes called the "Not Invented Here" phenomenon in federal agencies. Or, of course, it can lead to uncritical acceptance as well.

It would be misleading, however, to suggest that the only reasons for inadequate tests of programs stem from carelessness or inexpertness. Rather, it would appear that the questions being asked are inherently difficult to answer. To inquire regarding the relative effectiveness of programed *versus* conventional instruction may be similar to asking, "Which is faster, a jackrabbit or a racehorse?" Although the question appears to be sensible, one finds that it is quite intractable in its general form. Not only is it necessary to worry about the sampling problems (from populations of jackrabbits and racehorses), but it is also necessary to specify the particular conditions under which the comparison is to be made. This is by no means easy. For example, must the jackrabbit and the racehorse run under the *same* conditions? Should they go the *same* distance? Will the race course require them to jump over six-foot stone walls? Will it lead through the hollow logs or culverts? Should both animals be required to carry the same weight? Trying to set up the conditions to answer questions about the relative speeds of rabbits and horses is an interesting pastime. Clearly, the situation could be arranged to guarantee any desired outcome. Certainly a strong case can be made for the possibility that the results of the comparisons between programed and conventional instruction are at least as dependent upon the *conditions* of the comparisons as they are upon the *merits* of the methods of instruction.

However, one must not be too critical of training personnel for being unwilling to pioneer. It is understandable that they would be hesitant to expend limited training resources and to disrupt established schedules to conduct fair tryouts for every innovation that comes along. If this is a correct estimate of the mood of the training directors, the best guess would be that the use of programed instruction would gradually increase in the federal government if (and when) it yielded tangible benefits. However, there are several things which could alter the situation drastically and bring about a much more rapid expansion of programed learning within the government. One of these is the experience of the Defense Department. The only large-scale tryouts of programed learning materials are in the Air Training Command, and if the preliminary results of the Air Force experience stand the test of time, this, in itself, will create tremendous pressures to push others into the programed instruction area.

Another factor that could change the situation markedly would be a substantial decrease in the cost of programing. Although programing costs have moderated somewhat in the highly competitive programing market, they are still high enough so that they represent too great a risk for many training directors to take. Most of those contacted seemed to be willing to give programed learning a reasonable trial if it could be done at a very modest cost. Perhaps program costs could be reduced substantially through the use of techniques analogous to those of computer programers, and programs might even be produced with computer assistance. Voluntary users' groups could be formed. Members could submit programs to a central clearinghouse from which they would be announced and copies made available to other members of the group. This type of service would be particularly helpful if common formats could be established. Then, portions of programs, analogous to computer subroutines, could be exchanged. This degree of format standardization is more likely to be produced by the manufacturers of present types of teaching machines, since they are much more definitely tied to fixed formats than are their "booklet" brothers.

It would be ironic if this "weakness" of teaching machines turned out to be their greatest strength.

Another occurrence which would alter the predicted gradual increase of programed learning in the federal government is a research breakthrough. Of course, the occurrence of a breakthrough cannot be predicted. However, the climate is right. There is a lot of research activity. Many attractive possibilities have not been examined. The research being done at the present time is more characterized by system and order than by imagination and ingenuity. But, the stage is set, and Pressey, Skinner, and Crowder have been wrung pretty dry. Considerable attention has been devoted to very limited aspects of instructional systems. It is likely that future research in this area will come up with other exciting possibilities. Adaptive devices, job-involved devices, and instructional programs integrated with information retrieval systems all have great potential. They could very well be the vehicles for the long-awaited revolution in instructional technology.

Undoubtedly, the government will take the lead in providing research in these areas. However, with some notable exceptions, the people responsible for dispensing training in the federal government do not seem to be in the mood for blazing new instructional trails. Perhaps the real impetus for programed instruction will have to come from elsewhere.

References

1. Center for Programed Instruction. *Programs, '62.* Washington, D.C.: Government Printing Office, 1962. 383 pp.
2. Utter, R. F. *Development of Training Aids for Equation Typing.* Training Bulletin. Albuquerque, N. Mex.: Sandia Corporation, July 1962.

Appendix A

Federal Government Organizations Surveyed

Agency for International Development
Agriculture, Department of
   Agricultural Research Service
   Agricultural Marketing Service*
   Agricultural Stabilization and Con-
     servation Service*
   Commodity Credit Corporation*
   Commodity Exchange Authority*
   Cooperative State Experiment Station
     Service*
   Economic Research Service*
   Farmer Cooperative Service*
   Farmers Home Administration*
   Federal Crop Insurance Corporations*
   Federal Extension Service*
   Foreign Agricultural Service*
   Forest Service*
   Office of Rural Areas Development*
   Rural Electrification Administration*
   Soil Conservation Service*
   Statistical Reporting Service*
Air Force, Department of
   Directorate of Civilian Personnel
   Director of Personnel Procurement
     and Training
   Logistics Command
   Office of Industrial Relations
   Training Methods Division, Air
     Training Command
Armed Forces Institute of Pathology
Army, Department of
   Air Defense Human Research Unit
   Ammunition and Surveillance School
   Anniston Army Depot
   Army Air Defense School
   Army Adjutant Generals School
   Army Aviation School
   Army Engineers School
   Army Ordnance Center and School
   Army Ordnance Guided Missile
     School
   Aviation Human Research Unit
   Continental Army Command
   DCS Military Operations
   DCS Personnel (Office of Civilian
     Personnel)
   Harry Diamond Laboratories

   HUMRRO Representative, CONARC
   Infantry Human Research Unit
   Signal Center and School
   Supply and Maintenance Command
Atomic Energy Commission
Budget, Bureau of
Central Intelligence Agency
Civil Aeronautics Board
Civil Defense, Office of
Civil Service Commission
Commerce, Department of
District of Columbia Government
Export-Import Bank of Washington
Federal Aviation Agency
Federal Communications Commission
Federal Mediation and Conciliation
   Service
Federal Power Commission
Federal Reserve Board
Federal Trade Commission
General Accounting Office
General Services Administration
Government Printing Office
Health, Education, and Welfare, De-
   partment of
   Food and Drug Administration
   National Institutes of Health
   Office of Education
   Public Health Service
   St. Elizabeth's Hospital
   Social Security Administration
   Vocational Rehabilitation
Housing and Home Finance Agency
Interior, Department of
Interstate Commerce Commission
Justice, Department of
   Federal Bureau of Investigation*
   Bureau of Prisons
   Immigration and Naturalization Serv-
     ice*
Labor, Department of
   Bureau of Employment Security
Library of Congress
Marine Corps Landing Force Develop-
   ment Center
National Aeronautics and Space Agency
National Labor Relations Board

* Not contacted directly.

National Science Foundation
National Security Agency
Navy, Department of
Aviation Training Division, DCNO (Air)
Bureau of Naval Personnel
Bureau of Supplies and Accounts
Bureau of Naval Weapons
Chief of Naval Air Technical Training
Chief of Naval Air Training
Commander, Training Command, U.S. Atlantic Fleet
Naval Command Systems Support Activity
Naval Guided Missiles School, Dam Neck, Virginia
Naval Missile Center, Pt. Mugu
Naval Ordnance Test Station, China Lake*
Naval Training Center, San Diego*
Naval Training Center, Great Lakes*
Naval Training Device Center
Office of Industrial Relations

Office of Naval Intelligence
Naval War College*
U.S. Fleet Anti-Air Warfare Training Center
U.S. Fleet Sonar School, Key West*
Peace Corps
PERT Orientation Training Center
Post Office Department
Securities and Exchange Commission
Selective Service System
Small Business Administration
Smithsonian Institution
State, Department of
Tax Court of the United States
Treasury, Department of
U.S. Coast Guard
Bureau of the Mint*
U.S. Secret Service*
Bureau of Customs*
Bureau of Engraving and Printing*
Bureau of Narcotics*
Internal Revenue Service
United States Tariff Commission
United States Information Agency
Veterans Administration

* Not contacted directly.

Appendix B

Programs in Use

A-28 Camera Mount
A/C Electrical Systems
A/C Electricity
AC Fundamentals of Electricity
ADF (Automatic Direction Finding)
Administrative Specialist 1
Administrative Specialist 2
Adventures in Algebra
Aerodynamics
AF Customs and Courtesies
AF Form 246—Record of Emergency Data
AF Manual on Programmed Learning (Parts 1 & 2)
AF Technical Order Systems
AF Technical Publications System
Airborne Interception
Aircraft Electrical Systems
Aircraft Familiarization
Aircraft Oxygen Systems

Air Force Accounting Structures and Codes
The Air Force Letter
Air Force Organization
Air Force Technical Publications and C&E Maintenance Procedures
Air Force Training Publications
Airman Career Program
Air Police Investigations
Algebra I*
Algebra II
Algebra, Review of
Ammunition Publications
Ammunition Sources and Information
Analysis of Basic Stowger Switch
Analysis of Telephone Circuit Wiring Diagrams
Applied Nuclear Physics
Apprentice Personnel Specialist
Apprentice Procurement Specialist

* In use at more than one agency.

Arithmetic for Computers*
Arithmetic, Review of
Arithmetic Unit
Available Supply Rate
Aviation Physiology
Awards and Decorations
B-47 Fuel Systems
B-52 Aircraft Performance
B-52 Combat Crew Training Program
B-52 Communications
B-52 Ejection and Emergency Procedures
B-52 Electronic Warfare Training
B-52 Gunners' Emergency Procedures
B-52 Release Systems
Basic Aircraft Maintenance
Basic Concepts in Human Development
Basic Electricity for Mechanics
Basic Electronics**
Basic Electronics I and II*
Basic Electricity
Basic Electricity, Alternating Current
Basic Electricity, Direct Current
Basic English for Foreigners
Basic Hydraulic and Pneumatic Principles
Basic Management
Basic Mathematics
Batteries
Basic Navigation
Basic Navigation Equipment
Basic Principles of Military Law
Basic Principles of Jet Engines
Basic Russian
Basic Transistors Text
Batteries and Their Maintenance
Binary Arithmetic
Binary Conversion
Binary Number System
Boarding
Boolean Algebra
The Bombing Pattern and Ballistics Computation
C-124 Compass, E-4 Auto Pilot
Calculus 1
Calculus 2
Camouflage and Evasion Movement
Care and Use of Multimeter
Celestial Navigation
Centigrade and Fahrenheit to Centigrade

Circuit Analysis
Code of Conduct
Colorimetry and Photometry
Communications Security
Communicative Skills
Computer Mathematics*
Computer Programming, Part 1*
Computer Programing, Part 2: Techniques*
Computer Programming, Part 3: Techniques*
Computer Programming, Part 4: Business and Scientific Appl.*
Computing Nuclear Weapons Effects
Concepts of Air Force Maintenance in Accordance with AFM 66-1
Concepts of Symbolic Logic
Control Registers
Control Unit Arithmetic
Cost Reduction and Work Simplification
Course Control Documents**
Course X
Counter-insurgency
Cryptanalysis of Bilateral Substitution
C. W. Doppler Theory
C. C. Circuits
D/C Electricity
DC Fundamentals of Electricity
Dental Orientation
Descriptive Statistics
Detecting & Correcting Malfunctions of 90mm Gun
Development Approach
Diabetes Control
Diazchrome Transparencies Methods & Techniques
Differential Calculus
Dimensional and Electro-Mechanical Standards
Diode Wave-Shaping Circuits
Disaster Action and Buddy Care
Disaster Control Course
Document Indexing
Effective Executive Practices*
Effective Writing* **
Effective Writing Course
Eighth Grade Mathematics
Electronic Warfare Fundamentals and Target Intelligence
Electronics 1

* In use at more than one agency.
** Two different programs have this title.

Elementary Electricity
English 2600*
English 3200*
English Grammar
Equipment Familiarization
Evaluation and Measurement
Exercise Tolerance and Ortho Static Tolerance Tests for Flying Training Medical Examiner
Explaining the Organization of the Air Force
Factors Involved in Load Planning
Federal Personnel System
Filing AF Regulations for Security
First Year Algebra
First Year Electronics*
Fleet Ballistic Missile System SSB(N) 616 Class Submarine and Polaris MK II Missile: A Functional Introduction
Flight Instruments
Flight Planning
Flow Charts
Food Proc. Survival School
Foundations of Trigonometry
Fractions: A Review Course
Fuel, Specialist Conv. Fuel
Fuel, Qualitative and Quantitative Control
Fundamentals of Achievement Testing
Fundamentals of Statistics
Fundamentals of Defensive Combat: Forward Rifle Platoon
General Principles of Test Construction and Construction of Multiple Choice Items
Gyroscopic Principles
H-21 Weight and Balance
How To Instruct
How To Instruct Programmed Learning
How To Study
How To Use a Programmed Text
Human Relations
Hydraulics for Firefighters
Identification of G-Agents
Improving Your Writing
Inertial Navigation
Insignia of Grade, Basic Military Training
Installation Security, Restricted Area Pass

Instructional Control
Interpolation for Determination of Dew Point
Interpretation of Electrical Wiring Diagrams
Interviewing
Introduction to AC&W Radar
Introduction to Algebra*
Introduction to B-52 Fire Control Systems
Introduction to Cryptography
Introduction to Digital Control
Introduction to Electricity
Introduction to Electronics
Introduction to Evaluation
Introduction to Hand Tools
Introduction to Intelligence and USAF Organization
Introduction to ROAD Division
Introduction to Transmitter Principles
Introduction to Transistor Systems
Introductory Algebra*
Introductory Calculus 1
Introductory Calculus 2
Inventory Planning and Procedure
Jet Engine Compressor Section
Jet Engine Mechanic
KC-135 Emergency Procedures
KC-135 Rendezvous Procedures
Language of Algebra: Fields and Ordered Fields
Lesson Analysis
Lesson Planning**
Lesson Plans
Letter Sorter Operator Training
Linear Programming and Its Advantages
Locating Air Force Publications
Logarithms
Logic Circuits
Logistics Planning (spare parts replacement) (procedures, reporting)
Low Altitude Aerial Observation
Machine Grading, Scoring & Test Analysis
Maintenance & Inspection of Missiles
Maintenance Data Collection & Reporting
Maintenance of Brake Systems
Maintenance of Publications Reference Library
Management 1

* In use at more than one agency.
** Two different programs have this title.

Management
Manhour Reporting, AFM 66-1
Maneuvering Board Problems
Map Reading
Map Reading Refresher Course
Marine Corps Map Reading
1st Unit of Mathematical Bases for Management Decision Making. Part I: Matrices and Mathematical Programming
Mathematics and D.C.
MATS Grid Navigation
Mechanical Training on Caliber 38 Revolver
Medical Laboratory Specialist
Memory Unit
Message Structure—Joint Message Form
Message Format—Single Address Message
Meteorology
Methods of Determining Stock and Supply Levels
Methods of Instruction
Methods of Oral Communication
Military Correspondence
Military Explosives
Missile Digital Control Units
Missiles
Model 19, Composite Set
Naval Message Format
Navigation and Weather
Nike Hercules Command Coding
Ninth Grade Basic Mathematics
Nuclear Physics
Nuclear Safety
Number System and Position Location
Objectives of Staff Development Course
Observing, Recording & Encoding Visibility and Obstruction to Vision
Octal Number System
Office Procedures
Office Machine Repair
Ohm's Law
Ohm's Law, Parts 1 and 2
OJT in Advanced Transportation
Organization and Installation Property Book
Organizational Maintenance
Organizational Pattern for AV Seminar
Organizational & Use of AF Technical Manuals

Parallel AC Circuits
Parallel Circuits
Parameters of Ballistic Missile Trajectories
Pattern of AF Instruction
Personnel Management
PERT*
PERT (Time)
Philosophy
Photo Fundamentals
Physics
Planetary Gears
The Platoon in Defense
Powers of Ten
Precision Measuring Equipment Technician
Precision Photo Processing
Pre-Program
Pre-Marksmanship
Preparation of an Air Force Letter
Preventing Electric Shock-Portable Tools
Preventive Dentistry
Principles and Use of the Multimeter
Principles of A-28 Gyro Stabilized Mount
Principles of Automatic Transmissions
Principles of Flight
Principles of Learning**
Principles of Magnetics
Principles of Management
Principles of Missile Guidance
Principles of Navigation and Map Reading
Principles of Pilot Static Systems
Principles of Reconnaissance, Selection, & Occupation of Position
Principles of Servo Tuning
Principles of VOR
Probability and Statistics in Weapon Employment Planning
Programmed Learning
Property Responsibility
Prosthodontic Literature
Protection from the Elements
Civilian Training in AF (Public Law 85507)
Publication Management
Punctuation*
Quality Control of Fuels and Lubricants
Questioning Techniques**

---

* In use at more than one agency.
** Two different programs have this title.

Radar Return (Navigator-Bombardier)
Radiation Detection
Radioactivity
Radio Compass Equipment, AN/ARN-6
Radio Operations
Radio Theory
Radio and Telephone Procedures
Records Maintenance
Records Management
Remedial Mathematics
Resistor Applications No. 1
Retired Serviceman's Family Protection
    Plan
Rotary Wing Aerodynamics
Routine Orders
SAC
Saluting Procedures and Basic Military
    Training
Second Year Algebra
Security
Series Circuits
Seventh Grade Arithmetic
Shop Mathematics
Single Sideband Transmission
The Slide Rule*
Smoke Generator Operations
Social Security
Speech Composition
Standard Publications
Statistical Inference
Stenospeed
Straight Line Instruments
Strategic Air Command
Student Study Guides
Supervisory Techniques
Supply and Stock Levels
Supply Procedures
Survival Techniques and Procedures
T37 Emergency Procedures
Taking Care of Diabetes
Tandem Rotor Engineering
Task Analysis
Technical Training Supervisor
Telescopes
Teletype Machine Sequences
Teletype Message Structure

Testing and Grading
Testing
Textronix 545 Oscilloscope
Theories of Weapon Controlling
Theory of Oscilloscopes*
Theory of Rotary Wing Flight
Thermonatry
Total Active Federal Military Service
Training Materials & Evaluation
Training Technology
Transistor Audio & Video Amplifiers
Transistors
Transistors for Computers and You
Transmitter Theory
Travel and Evasion
Trigonometry**
Trigonometry, A Practical Course
Trouble Shooting Electronic Equipment
Typing Course
UCMJ
Use of AF Tech. Manuals in Airborne
    Communications Career Field
Use of AF Tech. Order Indexes
Use of Bibliographic Note Card File in
    Conducting Research
Use of Electronic Recorder in Teaching
Use of Oral Questions in Teaching
Use of Straight Line Instruments
Use of the Multimeter
Use of the Oscilloscope
Vacuum Tubes; Diodes
Validation Techniques
Vapor Compression Refrigeration Cycle
Veterans Rights
VFR Search and Rescue Procedures
VOR and TACAN
Warning Systems
Water Supply
Wave Propagation and Antenna Theory
Weather Programs
Weight and Balance
Wheatsone Bridge Circuits
I. Your Agency; Its Function, Organ-
    ization, and Relation to Other Com-
    ponents of Government
II. Planning of Research Projects

* In use at more than one agency.
** Two different programs have this **title.**

Directions

ROBERT GLASER
University of Pittsburgh

Toward a Behavioral Science Base for Instructional Design

Over the past decade, the work on teaching machines and programed learning has been one response to education's growing demand for a scientific and technological base. Particularly, it is the response of certain behavioral scientists, primarily experimental psychologists, who have attempted to apply their knowledge and methodology to the design of the teaching process and educational environments. The behavioral scientist, as an educational designer, begins to work as a technologist supplied with a presently meager, but apparently increasing, body of technological principles and practices which is emerging from the interplay between practical attempts at education and relevant research from the sciences which contribute to pedagogical methods. Ideally, he has approached the job of teaching subject matter knowledge in terms of the following tasks.

First, he has analyzed the behavior under consideration and specified some performance which will represent a standard of competence to be attained at the end of a sequence of educational experiences. This performance specification establishes a model or standard around which individual differences will be displayed. The selected performance must be specified in terms of the properties of a representative sample of instances which exemplify it. The stimulus, response, and structural characteristics of these instances of subject matter content

771

and the behavioral repertoires involved will determine what to teach and, correspondingly, how it is to be taught. One cannot be too rigid, however, in sticking to an early specification of this performance because certainly the selection of instructional goals will be influenced by the designer's analysis of the behavior under consideration.

Second, he has specified the characteristics of the students that are to be taught. These characteristics need to be determined either prior to instruction or in the process of early learning. It is necessary to know the extent to which the student has already acquired some of the things to be learned, the extent to which he has the prerequisites for taking the next instructional steps, the extent to which antecedent learning facilitates or interferes with new learning under the conditions the designer has in mind, and the extent to which the student can make the necessary sensory discriminations and can exhibit the motor skills required for initial learning steps.

With information about both the target performance to be attained and the existing preinstructional behavior, the educational designer can proceed from one state to the other. This sets up the third task: he must guide or allow the student to go from one state of development to another and construct the procedures and materials that are to be employed in the educational process. As part of this process, he must take account of motivational effects; this means providing conditions which will result in the maintenance and extension of the competence being taught.

Finally, the educational designer must make provision for assessing and evaluating the nature of the competence achieved by the learner in relation to the performance criteria that have been established.

This description of the process of educational design may sound harshly technological and, indeed, perhaps some elegance has been lost in analysis. But presumably, once the basic techniques are constructed, it is time for the teacher-practitioner to use the tools of his profession with all the artistry and sensitivity he can muster. The components of the above plan of operation for the design of teaching comprise the major sections of this chapter: analyzing the characteristics of subject matter competence, diagnosing preinstructional behavior, carrying out the instructional process, and measuring learning outcomes. The intention of this chapter is to follow the leads of the previous authors in this volume and to point out some of the considerations and questions involved in developing a behavioral science base for the teaching process. These matters are of common interest to experimental psychologists and educational designers since they are relevant to instructional practice and of significance to the science of learning.

Analyzing the Characteristics of Subject Matter Competence

When the experimental psychologist turns his attention from analysis of the behavior involved in standardized, arbitrary tasks used in the laboratory to the identification of the processes involved in learning the nonarbitrary behavior generally taught in society, he runs head on into the problem of the analysis of subject matter tasks. The significance of this problem is highlighted by the fact that task analysis has preoccupied the activities of psychologists when they have turned their attention to training, as they did in the Air Force program under the direction of Arthur W. Melton (19). The concern with task analysis is a reaction to the fact that while the investigator in a laboratory decides upon and constructs an experimental task pertinent to his particular purposes, he is not in a position to do this in the training and educational situation. In the laboratory, by preselecting his task to fit a problem, he has in a sense analyzed its stimulus and response characteristics. However, when working with nonarbitrary behavior, he is faced with the problem of identifying the properties of the behavior involved so that he can proceed to operate in his usual way. As a behavioral scientist he is used to working with specified behavior, and he needs to do so in the instructional situation. The transition from the laboratory to application frequently requires this additional consideration. The recent writings and explorations of Bruner (6, 7), for example, continuously emphasize a concern with subject matter structure, and this most likely develops out of his concern with real-life subject matter.

The significance of subject matter analysis is emphasized when Lane[1], involving himself in the learning of a second language, points

---

[1] In this final chapter, formal references to other chapters in this book are indicated merely by the name of the chapter author.

out that he had the good fortune to discover that, in this subject matter field, much time had been devoted to the systematic specification of the terminal behaviors of instruction. In contrast, when working in the field of English, Markle indicates that a major problem centers around the fact that instructional designers demand better specification of the behavior to be taught by English teachers. She points out that in English, the prescriptive nature of traditional grammar has "apparently settled in prescriptive methods of instruction." Needless to say, the stimulus and response requirements of subject matter properties affect instructional technology and, in turn, detailed analysis of subject matter characteristics will probably demand advances in instructional procedure. Some illustrative influences of subject matter characteristics upon the investigation of learning and instruction will be suggested here.

Component Repertoires and Content Repertoires

A subject matter expert usually can divide his subject into subtopics, primarily on the basis of content interrelationships and subject matter logic and arrangement. In contrast, a psychologist considers subject matter analysis less in terms of content-orientation and more in terms of the behavior of the learner and the kind of stimulus-response situations involved. "Content" and "subtopic repertoires" are terms that can be used to refer to a subject matter oriented analysis. The term "component behavioral repertoire," or merely "component repertoire," can be used to refer to a behavioral analysis. The concern of psychologists with taxonomies (30, 31) reflects initial attempts to develop schemes for describing and analyzing component repertoires.

From the point of view of instruction, the practical requirement for component repertoire analysis is to identify the kind of behavior involved so that the learner can be provided with instructional procedures and environmental conditions which best facilitate the learning of that kind of behavior. The underlying assumption is that the learning of various kinds of component repertoires requires different kinds of teaching procedures, and an important research task is to identify the learning processes and appropriate instructional procedures associated with different component repertoires. This kind of thinking underlies Gagné's "analysis of instructional objectives for the design of instruction" when he lists the following as categories of behavior: response differentiation, association, multiple discrimination, behavior chains, class concepts, principles, and strategies; he then attempts to suggest learning conditions relevant to each category.

A useful taxonomical distinction with respect to component repertoires has been made by Skinner (39) in distinguishing between formal repertoires and thematic repertoires. In formal repertoires there is point-to-point correspondence between stimulus and response, as in imitating, reading, and copying; in thematic or mediated repertoires, responses are controlled by common sets of variables, but without formal correspondences, as in responding appropriately to a question with a meaningful answer. Formal repertoires are the less complex of the two to study and have received most work in operant analysis. In second language learning, Lane indicates that kinds of formal repertoires have been categorized, such as echoic behavior, when both stimulus and response are spoken; transcription, when both stimulus and response are written; textual behavior, when a spoken response is controlled by a written stimulus; and dictation, when the stimulus is spoken and the response is written.

There is much less applicable research on thematic repertoires, although research on mediation is a burgeoning enterprise at present. Much of language learning consists of thematic repertoires involving syntactic sequences, grammatical structures, contextual constraints of the language, etc. Understanding of the behavioral characteristics of these intraverbal sequences requires laboratory research along the lines of such things as the effects of language patterning on recall (32) and the acquisition of syntactic patterns in children (5).

One ramification, then, of the analysis of behavior upon instructional design is the necessity to distinguish between subject matter content and component repertoires. The designing of optimal instruction may be a matter of choosing the proper tactics for categories of behavior implied by the component repertoire characteristics of instructional objectives (16). In this context, disciplines that study subject matter disciplines, like linguistics and logic, should become increasingly useful in providing interaction between subject matter structure and the behavioral structure required for learning. For example, a contrastive analysis of the linguistic requirements of a student's first language and the target second language to be learned can provide details for an instructional prescription.

Process and Objective

The trend toward the behavioral analysis of instructional objectives has led to the term "process" objectives. For example, the recent AAAS curriculum for science in the elementary grades (1) considers process objectives, such as observation, classification, prediction, and inference. The content as such—whether magnetism, sound, light or heat phenomena, or biological events—is of secondary importance in this curriculum. The learning of "processes" is most important. Also, at higher levels of science teaching, there is increasing concern with more than "formal and descriptive knowledge" of the current body of science, and emphasis is placed on such behaviors as generating hypotheses, selecting fruitful hypotheses, testing hypotheses and deciding upon experiments, and the more generalized traits of a scientist such as perseverance and curiosity. The trend toward the statement of so-called process objectives reflects a recognition of the importance of the component repertoire.

It should be pointed out, however, that the word "process" in process objective can be somewhat misleading. A statement of objectives refers to a behavioral state which is some performance by the student; the performance itself, or the results of the performance, can be measured in some way. It is important to distinguish between the terminal behavioral state and the process of attaining that behavioral state which is carried out by an instructional sequence. For example, the terms "formal" and "thematic" repertoire describe certain kinds of behavioral classes, whereas words like "discrimination," "differentiation," and "chaining" refer to learning and instructional processes utilized to attain certain terminal behavioral states. It can be said that a person is discriminating or he is performing chaining behavior, but the instructional process required and the behavioral state attained need to be recognized as different things. Sequential statements of hierarchical subobjectives, as Gagné suggests (15), essentially list behavioral states. The cognitive simulation workers (34, 38), in contrast, are primarily concerned with the process between states. Either state or process description alone is only part of the requirements for instructional design.

Perhaps nowhere in recent years has the confusion between process and state been more rampant than in the recent emphasis on "discovery learning." In both the practical and the research work in this area, there is a confusion between two kinds of events: one event has to do with learning *by* discovery (process), that is, teaching certain objectives by a discovery method; the other event has to do with learning *to* discover (a behavioral state), or teaching for a terminal state which is manifested by the ability to make discoveries.

Transfer and Concept Formation

Subject matter properties very significantly determine the dimensions along which the student must be taught to generalize and transfer his knowledge. Presumably the ability to generalize and transfer is a function of experience with a variety of examples and different subject matter instances. What, however, defines variety, and what defines different instances? For some stimulus dimensions of subject matter, there is little ambiguity about generalization gradients and whether variations are instances of a basic case. However, as a subject matter becomes complex, definition of a range of examples may become difficult, and problems arise concerning whether training in various instances does indeed carry over to new situations. What seems to be required is investigation of stimulus variation and generalization gradients in the dimensions and multidimensions determined by analyses of subject matter. In instruction in critical reading, Markle states that while "the recognition of unsound interferences" might be a behavior that is clear, the stimulus conditions under which the behavior occurs are not clear. What is the population of stimulus material involved? It is obviously material which the student can comprehend, but the teaching objective is that it should extend to new material as the student learns to comprehend this new material.

The influence of the analysis of subject matter dimensions can be made most clearly when one considers the teaching of concepts. Many psychologists would agree that the basic procedure for teaching the ability to use concepts involves teaching the student to generalize within classes and to discriminate between classes. The student must learn to make the same responses to all members falling within a class and to make different responses to members of different classes. Mechner illustrates the procedure involved by the simple case of teaching a child the concepts of red and blue. Discrimination and generalization trials are presented with the colors red and blue. Other properties of the objects are varied randomly so that the student learns to generalize among objects having in common no characteristic other than their color. For example: First, the child is shown successive sets of three objects, two red objects and one not red. Each time these three objects are presented the question is asked, "Which is not red?" This is repeated a number of times with blue objects. In this way discriminations are established between red and not red and blue and not blue. The child might then be presented with two objects, one red and one blue and asked "Which one is red?" or "Which one is blue?" The number of nonred and nonblue objects could then be increased so that only one out of a number of objects is red or blue. In order to carry out training for generalization, objects with a variety of characteristics would be included in the sequence of color discrimination training—large and small objects, dark and light ones, rough and smooth ones, near and far ones, square, triangular, and irregularly shaped ones, etc. This would prevent the responses "red" and "blue" from being attached to stimuli other than the appropriate ones. With the properties of the objects varied, the child would learn to generalize among objects in which the common characteristic is color. In this way the child is presented with a series of progressively graded experiences by which he acquires the concepts of redness and blueness. As Mechner points out, this instructional process becomes complicated when the subject matter properties to be generalized and discriminated are not clear-cut or are very subtle—for instance, such concepts as classic and neoclassic art or early Mozart and late Mozart. A major problem in teaching such subtle and complex concepts is the definition of the subject matter classes. This becomes increasingly problematical when there is disagreement among experts and where there are semantic imprecisions. Sometimes the distinction between classes is not clear to the learner because he does not have the necessary preliminary training required. At other times the confusion is subject matter imprecision itself.

Response and Reinforcement Modes

After reviewing the studies carried out on response mode in programed instruction, Holland suggests that the results indicate that the nature of the learning task determines the preferred response form. For example, when the criterion performance includes a precise response topography, such as writing a new Spanish word, constructed response seems to be the better form. When recognition is the criterion of performance, the response form seems to be unimportant, and for fine stimulus discriminations, alternative response choices may be preferable. In elementary concept learning (44), the ability to transfer was more effective when subjects had to choose the presence or absence of the concept than when they selected it in a multiple-choice arrangement.

The response mode investigations in programed instruction up to the present time have been very feeble attempts to match learning task with appropriate stimulus and response characteristics. The underlying problem is the design of the means of display and response by which the student interacts with his subject matter. Analysis of the properties of the subject matter stimuli in terms of their content, duration, scheduling, and novelty will influence instructional design. Skinner points out that "there are potentially as many different kinds of teaching machines as there are kinds of contingencies of reinforcement." Analysis of the subject matter changes fed back to the student as a result of his interacting with the subject matter provides for the arrangement of appropriate response contingencies. Such feedback need not be so patently artificial as repetitive presentation of the correct answer contingent on every small step. For example, in solving a problem, the response of a student may produce new information, lose information, or introduce a delay in receiving information. In chemical analysis, a response may result in a predictable change, an unpredicted occurrence, or no change at all. The stimulus feedback the student receives is the result of his manipulation of the subject matter and is hence a function of its special properties.

Analysis of subject matter stimulus and response requirements suggests breaking away from the confines of the primarily paper-and-pencil learning environments prevalent in school learning and examining in detail the requirements of the "interface" between the student and his subject matter. The trend in this direction is not toward the restricted sense of usual audiovisual aids; the challenging direction seems to be that taken by such work as is going on in computer-based instructional laboratories (10), for example oscilloscope-screen teaching of graphical representation (27). In such work, more than computer capabilities should be taken into account; the capability of engineering technology to provide ways of interacting and manipulating subject matter is of primary importance (20). This trend is a useful meaning of "mechanizing education": mechanizing is not necessarily doing by machine what was formerly done by people. What is needed is an analysis of the content and component repertoires involved and the instructional functions to be served, followed by the design of appropriate equipment. The adaptation of generally available all-purpose equipment, like slide projectors and tape recorders, will tackle only a small part of the need in this area. Initially, experimental setups should be built which are highly overdesigned in complexity and capability. Research and development with such facilities can help determine the requirements for appropriate hardware demands and tolerances, programing requirements (both computer and instructional), and teaching advantages.

Summary

The analysis of behavioral objectives is an area that cannot be overlooked in research and development on learning leading to effective instructional practice. To emphasize the point, one can resort to testimonial quotes. "So important is the principle of programing that it is often regarded as the main contribution of the teaching machine movement, but the experimental analysis of behavior has much more to contribute to a technology of education." This is from the chapter by Skinner, and while he means somewhat more than only the analysis of behavioral objectives, his point is certainly related. In analyzing English teaching, Markle says, "In the case of the critical and evaluative skills in literature, not the technology of designing frames but the technology of task analysis is crucial." Gagné, with his emphasis on sequential objectives, says "the entire sequence of objectives ... is considered to be the most important set of variables in the instructional process, outweighing as a critical factor more familiar variables like step size, response mode, and others." Crawford, in considering the extensive experiences of HumRRO, says that "perhaps the most important single contribution to the development of training through research has been the determination of methods for the formulation of objectives of instruction" (11, p. 326). The importance of this first component in a plan for the design of teaching cannot be emphasized enough. It has been neglected in psychological research, and, as Crawford says, it is probably the most important element in recent improvement in instruction. It is the first step in the sequence of tasks in instructional design, and without it the succeeding components will be inadequate.

Diagnosing Preinstructional Behavior

Once the subject matter behavior objectives have been analyzed, the instructional designer turns his attention to the characteristics of the learner who is to attain these objectives. This raises the problems involved in diagnosing the preinstructional behavior or the entering repertoire of the learner. For measurement psychologists, this has been a primary concern. For psychologists interested in learning, preinstructional individual differences have, for the most part, been relegated to error variance in experimental design. It is increasingly obvious, however, that a psychology of learning relevant to instructional practice cannot consider individual differences as error variance. Classroom and laboratory studies are constant reminders that individual differences is one of the most important conditions of learning as yet unaccepted in both learning theory and subject matter teaching (see 42).

In research on programed instruction, one is uniformly impressed with the extent of variability in student learning rates (22). Rate of learning, however, is only one relevant dimension of individual differences. It is the dimension which programed instruction has emphasized, and it is probably the easiest one to accommodate (even though it certainly can upset the organization of a school). There are other dimensions of individual differences of equal or more important significance which pertain to the component and content repertoires of the student, i.e., his aptitude pattern, skill level, etc. At least four classes of preinstructional variables are determinants of the course of achievement (50): (a) the extent to which the individual has already learned the responses to be acquired in instruction, e.g., previous achievement of certain of the skills to be taught; (b) the extent to which the individual has acquired the prerequisites for learning the responses to be acquired, e.g., knowing how to add before learning to multiply; (c) learning set variables which consist of antecedent learnings which facilitate or interfere with new learning under certain instructional conditions, e.g., prior experience or information in a particular area; and (d) the ability to make the discriminations necessary to profit from instruction, e.g., aptitude in spatial visualization.

In the instructional process, just as objectives define the target behavior which is accepted as a given to be attained, so must preinstructional behavior also be accepted as a given, if one does not or cannot rigorously control or delimit student behavior up to the point of entry into instruction. The array of concepts involved in the preinstructional measurement of aptitudes, readinesses, and diagnostic measures of achievement must be systematized for theoretical development and for use in instructional design. For example, the long-term prediction by aptitude tests of achievement scores at the end of a course might be supplemented by measures of behavior which predict whether the individual can achieve the next immediate instructional step. "In certain of the new curricula, there are data to suggest that aptitude measures correlate much less with end-of-course achievement than they do with achievement in early units" (12).

While most of the available products in programed instruction show an appalling lack of recognition of differences in entering behavior, recent discussions of programed instruction are very much concerned with it. Markle points out that student variability ranges from no information to misinformation and that the majority of presently available programs in English make no provision for diagnosing and then using this diagnostic information. She says, "There can be little doubt that individualized instruction is a necessity, not a luxury, in English class. The English instructor . . . must begin at many points and go at many paces while covering a multitude of points. . . . The task is impossible." Carroll (9), in discussing implications of language development in children for teaching, says "teachers must ponder the extent to which they can . . . attempt to alter a system of habits which are not only highly practiced, but which also probably serve a supportive role in the child's adjustment to his non-school environment" (p. 342).

Stolurow and Davis consider the relationships between entering behavior, teaching strategies, and achievement outcomes. They suggest research concerned with such questions as: For specified objectives in a given subject matter, how many strategies would a computer-based instructional system need to teach effectively with a given range of student entering behavior? What are the relationships between the characteristics of certain teaching strategies and the nature of subject matter content? How do different strategies effect the ordering and dispersion of the achievement of students in a class? In discussing accommodation to individual differences, Stolurow and Davis point out that in studies that have compared programed textbooks with teaching machines, the pertinent variable does not get manipulated. In the typical machine-versus-book study, the number of teaching programs is the same, and the branching capabilities of the machine are not used, so there is no reason to expect any differences.

If the assessment of preinstructional behavior is considered to be the determination of an entering behavioral repertoire which the instructional process is designed to guide and modify, then research becomes reoriented in a number of areas. In the analysis of readiness, for example, measurement of the fact that readiness factors differ with age and with individuals must be supplemented by analyses of the conditions influencing these differences and the contribution of these differences to learning.

The approach to developmental norms requires reconsideration. When is a child "normally" capable of distinguishing a "b" from a "d" so that it is useful to teach him to learn to read? Prevailing norms necessarily assume prevailing learning conditions; however, new learning environments can change the norms. One approach for research and development in education is to adjust a learning environment to preinstructional behavior capabilities and then to study maturational limitations. A valuable discussion of the question of when to teach what has been presented by Tyler (51).

Research on aptitudes might be reoriented. If designing instructional environments for early ages is considered, it is conceivable that the "curriculum" will not be formal subject matters like mathematics or spelling, but instruction in behaviors which look more like aptitudes. For example, Skinner (41) has been concerned with teaching rhythm behavior, Holland (24) and Bijou (2) with teaching inductive reasoning, and Brinkman (4) with attempts to use programed instruction to influence scores on tests of spatial visualization. It is exciting to hypothesize that if certain of the behaviors generally classed as "aptitudes" are treated as instructional requirements in a sequence of educational progress, then teaching these behaviors, e.g., foreign language aptitude, should enhance subsequent learning and achievement.

With respect to preinstructional repertoires, the important problem is to investigate the relationships between individual differences and learning variables and, more practically, to develop techniques for the accommodation of instruction to individual differences. Work along these lines (21) points out that the identification of pertinent entering behavior can be a complex and subtle task. The determination of entering behavior that facilitates the next learning step requires the solution to difficult problems such as the identification of transfer hierarchies of learning. Furthermore, the identification of the relevant differences in preinstructional behavior when one student learns and another student does not may be extremely difficult to accomplish. Identification in nonspecific terms such as "inadequate aptitude level" or "poor motivation" does not provide the behavioral detail required for the design of an appropriate teaching sequence.

Carrying Out the Instructional Process

Once the content and component repertoires involved in terminal behavior objectives and subobjectives have been described, and once the entering behavior of the student is described, the instructional process can be implemented. For example, if a student is learning to sound out phonemes that correspond to displayed graphemes, and he does not have the pronunciation of phonemes in his repertoire, he must first be taught this. If these responses have already been learned, then instruction concentrates on bringing the pronunciation responses under the control of appropriate graphemes. In subject matter learning, the instructional process can be defined as a way of arranging the student's environment to expedite such kinds of learning which comprise subject matter competence.

At least three kinds of processes seem to be involved: (a) setting up new forms of student behavior, such as new speaking patterns or a new skill like handwriting; (b) setting up new kinds of subject matter stimulus control, for example, learning to read after having learned to speak, so that the already learned response of making speech sounds is attached to particular visual symbols; and (c) maintaining the behavior of the student. This third category is less involved with behavior change and more concerned with increasing the student's likelihood to behave and therefore often falls under the label of motivation. Brief elaboration of these general categories can be made here.

Setting Up New Forms of Response

A very evident characteristic of learning which leads to subject matter mastery is the increasing precision of the student's responses. In learning complex behavior, the student's initial performance is variable and quite crude and rarely meets the criteria of subject matter competence. Effective instructional procedure tolerates the student's initially crude responses and gradually takes him toward mastery. In order to accomplish this, the instructional process must involve the establishment of successively more rigorous standards or criteria for the learner's performance. Increasing competence in new learning is accomplished by gradually contracting the permissible margin of error, that is, contracting performance tolerances. For example, if precise timing and tempo were being taught to a student of music, it would be unrealistic to reward the student only on those rare occasions when he briefly maintained an accurate response. Since the performance of the beginning student will be quite variable, standards should be initially gross and performance criteria changed at a rate which insures continuing progress toward mastery. Each successive range of acceptable performance should include a major portion of the range of variations already in the student's performance so that there will be frequent opportunity for the reinforcement of success. Over the sequence of instruction, the range of observed performance will align itself with the particular range of acceptable performance defined as subject matter competence. In the course of the instructional sequence, a sudden or inappropriate constriction of performance criteria is one environmental change which can lead to extinction and loss of interest.

Setting Up New Kinds of Stimulus Control

While the category just described is interpreted as the operant shaping process and has been quoted as a paradigm in programed instruction, an equally if not more significant process in subject matter learning is the stimulus control of performance. Second language learning, for example, has stressed the importance of the transfer from an initial repertoire to a target repertoire. There is often the difficulty, as in teaching translation, of transferring from one stimulus class to another. The oral response "flower" has to be transferred from the English word "flower" to the German "die Blume." In learning a concept, the responses "apple," "peach," "pear," etc., are transferred as responses to the word "fruit." The restructuring of the student's entering repertoire is the pertinent instructional task, and this involves not only differentiating out new forms of response but also transferring stimulus control. With respect to this, Lane points out that the learning conditions involved in restructuring a student's initial repertoire have a limited resemblance to laboratory research on the control of behavior. He says, "Transitional behavior effected by shifting contingencies of reinforcement, patterns of discriminative stimuli, or both, is little studied and poorly understood in comparison with the shaping, maintenance, and extinction of behavior in initially naïve organisms." The transfer of stimulus control is a major process involved in teaching students to make responses to more precise subject matter discriminations and teaching them to use previously learned skills in response to new stimuli (46).

Maintaining Behavior

The processes just described of setting up new forms of response and new kinds of stimulus control assume only that the behavior of an expert in a given subject matter is characterized by the facility with which it is called out by particular subject matter contexts. A further characteristic of an expert's behavior is that it is apparently self-sustaining. The expert may continue to respond for relatively long periods of time without seeming external support and without support from aids and references that are needed by the novice. Not only is the expert's behavior guided or controlled by the subject matter, but with increasing competence it can be characterized as self-sustaining and highly independent of environmental supports. Research and development into the teaching and learning of such self-sustaining sequences is an important problem—a problem that is related to the behavior-maintaining situations which come under the labels of motivation and curiosity.

Some Conditions Influencing the Instructional Process

If it can be assumed that learning involves the kind of processes just described, attention can be turned to some conditions which influence these processes. The conditions to be described are those suggested by the work of experimental psychologists and by practical attempts at instructional programing. In discussing these conditions, it is useful to emphasize the term "transitional behavior." If an instructional sequence is concerned with modifying student performance in order to get from entering behavior to specified terminal behavior, then transitional behavior is defined as the performance carried out by the student in the course of attaining terminal behavior competence. Conceivably the stimuli involved in terminal behavior are not necessarily the most effective transitional stimuli. While it is sometimes difficult for educators to accept, efficient learning conditions for transitional behavior may be radically different from the eventual conditions under which subject matter competence occurs. As illustration of conditions influencing the instructional process which can be subjected to psychological study, the following shall be considered: sequencing, stimulus and response factors, self-monitoring, interference, and response contingencies.

Sequencing

The sequencing of transitional behavior is a condition of learning which requires detailed analysis. The notion of gradual progression in programed instruction of course is related here. However, more subtle analyses are required. Subject matter scholars frequently point out that their subject is not organized as sequentially as, say, mathematics, and that instruction cannot be so carefully sequenced; in addition, their subject matter requires that many considerations be handled at one time so that the student can perform in an integrated fashion. However, it appears that when one undertakes to lay out details in instructional sequences and establish partial attainments goals, as Markle says, the "all things at once" idea seems to fall. Decisions need to be made, on some basis, about what is to be learned before what. The sequencing requirement cuts across many areas of interest in psychological research, certainly the area of transfer, particularly transfer from the learning of one subobjective to the entering requirements for learning the next subobjective. For example, in experiments with elementary mathematics concepts (42) and with teaching time-telling (21), one is surprised by the very specific nature of transfer in young children. Generalization and transfer to new situations cannot reasonably be assumed, and the learner must be provided with conditions which facilitate generalization. As has been pointed out, the identification of the structure of subconcepts determining the nature of transfer is a central problem in learning theory related to instruction (42).

Sequencing cuts across the notion of a gradual progression of difficulty in learning hierarchies. An analysis of what is meant by "difficulty" and of the variables that influence "learning difficulty" can involve an amazing number of subject matter factors. Silberman's analysis of the factors influencing sequencing in learning to read illustrates the complexity involved. The variables he lists include word frequency, letter frequency, syntactic structure, meaningfulness, redundant patterns, pronounceability, word and sentence length, word familiarity, stimulus similarity, and grapheme-phoneme correspondences.

Sequencing requirements point up at least three general problems in designing instructional sequences: (a) regularity of structure, (b) response availability, and (c) stimulus similarity and dissimilarity. Regularity of structure refers to the structure of concept development. The neglect of this area is very forcefully brought out when one examines most present-day methods of teaching reading. There seems to be little structural regularity in the development of, say, phonemic concepts, or morphemic regularities as the former is taught in the reading program by Buchanan (8) or the latter in the word analysis program by Markle (29).

Response availability refers to the notion that the responses to be learned in the course of an instructional sequence should be available at the time these responses are to be associated with or come under the control of relevant subject matter stimuli. This is an area investigated in studies of verbal learning; for example, Underwood and Schulz (52) concluded that the pronounceability of certain verbal units is a predictor of the extent to which these units were learned in word association experiments. Response availability would seem to be neglected in instructional design. In teaching reading, for example, there is little relationship in language and syntactic patterns between the oral language of children and the material by which they learn to read. It has been suggested that a closer relationship between the two can profit from facilitation involved in response availability. In everyday school practice, experience charts take account of the availability of already strong responses. In Gagné's hierarchial charts on subobjectives (15), an important factor is response availability which facilitates the learning of the next subobjective.

Stimulus similarity and dissimilarity in the sequencing of instruction relates to such procedures as introducing subject matter content in terms of increasing similarity of form or meaning. This means that simple dissimilarities are introduced initially, and as these discriminations become learned, more difficult ones are introduced. In learning grapheme-phoneme correspondences, some programed instructional procedures take account of this by not using all of the letters of the alphabet in early reading instruction (8). It is further possible to use only maximally discriminable letters early in instruction and to reserve difficult letter discriminations until after a sizable reading vocabulary has been built up with the initially learned letters.

Stimulus and Response Factors

In addition to sequencing conditions in the instructional process, it is necessary to decide upon the specific responses that are desired and to determine what subject matter stimuli will be related to them. This matter has already been mentioned in the discussion of objectives and the analysis of behavior. Stimulus and response factors are primarily concerned with the dimensions along which the content of subject matter can be presented to the learner and the dimensions along which he can respond to it. Although some concern with stimulus and response factors has resulted in much work with visual and auditory media, as Silberman points out, the full range of these channels has not been explored. For the most part, the primary contact of the student with his subject matter in general education is through the printed page, with supplementation by audiovisual aids and field and laboratory experiences. Despite all the service that printed materials and traditional aids have provided, it seems appropriate, in the light of present engineering technology, to examine new possibilities for providing interaction between the student and his subject matter environment. It seems possible to be able to present the learner with ways of seeing and manipulating his subject matter that extend and enrich his contact with it and form a learning environment in which subject matter dimensions need not be so drastically reduced as they are when forced into a primarily paper-and-print learning environment. In engineering, the term "man-machine interface" is commonly used to describe the point at which a human comes into contact with a machine, and in engineering psychology much work has gone into the experimental analysis of the appropriate display and response characteristics by which a human can communicate with the machine and provide an optimal man-machine unit or system. The term "student-subject matter interface" can be used to express concerns similar to this in education—at least to the extent that it suggests examination of the display and response characteristics by which a student can interact with a subject matter discipline (20).

In broad outline, a learning environment consists of the display of the subject matter to the student, controls or manipulanda (e.g., a pencil or a teaching machine) by which the student works with the subject matter, and some logic between these two. If the objective of a teaching sequence is the manipulation of symbols—for example, addition and subtraction or phoneme-grapheme correspondences— what combinations of information displays are required and how should students manipulate these symbols in order to learn to generalize and apply their competence to a wide range of future instances? The manipulanda are related to the nature of the student response and also to the kind of manipulation of the subject matter required by subject matter characteristics, the nature of the learning process, and the kind of subject matter competence to be attained. For example, concepts of more or less, of speed and acceleration, of rate of change in functional relationships as related to the terms of an equation, and conceptual models in science may be taught best if the student can operate a display in which the results of manipulating a variable are shown or fed back in a dynamic fashion in terms of its influence on related variables or outcomes. This feedback requirement is an integral part of the display and response logic of an instructional interface. Feedback characteristics are dictated by the kind of logic (both subject matter and teaching logic) that is established between student response to the display and a change in the display as a result of the response.

A major research issue in the development of teaching machines is the problem of interface requirements, feasibility, and effectiveness. Teager (47) indicates the importance of the development of graphical input and output facilities in automated instructional systems that can remove the student from the restrictions of keyboards, limited sets of characters, and one-dimensional inputs. He points out that in the use of modern technology and computer-based instruction, major innovations are required in the form of input and output consoles. Work is proceeding along these lines; Licklider (27), for example, uses oscilloscope displays to teach German and the graphic representation of equations, and Uttal (53) employs an electroluminescent character generator in teaching stenotypy. The work of Licklider is a good illustration of the potential of new technological developments for an instructional interface: in a computer-based arrangement, the student works with a typewriter response unit and an oscillosope display unit. As a means of developing an understanding of the relations between symbolic and graphical representation of mathematical functions, the student types coefficients of an equation on the typewriter, and the oscilloscope screen displays the corresponding curve. This arrangement also permits the student to use the automated context for exploration of the concepts he is learning.

Self-Monitoring

Programed instruction has highlighted the importance of the study of self-monitoring and self-sustaining repertoires. Evans describes a program in which children were taught to write numbers by making only discrimination responses during the course of instruction. Throughout the programed sequence, no numbers were actually constructed by writing; the child responded with multiple-choice discriminations, either by circling a correct matching response or by pushing an appropriate button in a multiple-choice machine. A posttest showed that the children learned to write numbers fairly well. It seems that the learning of appropriate discriminations made it possible for them to monitor their own motor responses.

Markle points out that out from under the eye of the English teacher, the student is no longer subjected to differential reinforcement from the school environment. He must reinforce himself with good writing. The student must be able to make the discriminations that an English teacher would make when confronted with the material. If the discriminations involved are too difficult to be put into a program, the teacher is needed to make them. However, it may be more efficient to train the student to make these discriminations so that he can immediately reinforce himself as his progress demands. Kersh concludes from his studies that it is not difficult to train observers to identify the occurrence of hypothesis-formation behavior in problem solving from verbal reports or written notes. Since it seems possible for people to learn to recognize examples of "forming hypotheses" in the behavior of others, it should be possible for the student to learn to recognize such behavior in himself by appropriate training. Markle writes that Klaus has discussed the possibility of a program on "creative writing." In the procedure suggested, not only are there multiple right answers but also the possibility that the student will come up with an unpredicted response. This response, after it has occurred, can only be reinforced by the instructor's discriminations or by teaching the student the appropriate discriminations so that he is independent of the instructor. Even in present-day programs, the student must make appropriate fine discriminations.

The suggestion, then, is that the process of teaching new responses can be facilitated by first teaching the student to discriminate the desired response in others. Once this is done it becomes possible to teach "self-discrimination" or self-monitoring so that he may become his own observer and evaluator. Self-monitoring as a class of behavior might be strengthened with effective reinforcement for self-observation and self-error detecting.

Interference

In general, it can be stated that interference in learning is a function of competition between a response repertoire and other responses learned prior to or subsequent to it. This response competition results in forgetting and in a decreased rate of acquisition. Competing responses, when they exist in the entering behavior of the student, affect instructional design and necessitate special training sequences. For example, in order to anticipate interference in second-language discrimination training, Lane indicates that confusion matrices can be prepared and contrastive analyses undertaken prior to programing in order to identify sources of interference between entering repertoire and terminal behavior. Inappropriate sequencing also produces sources of interference. The work of Morton in foreign language training (see Lane), for example, suggests that when formal repertoires are learned first, the later introduction of meaningful utterances impairs the performance of the previously learned sound patterns.

Sources of interference in the course of instruction may be reduced by employing what Lane calls "collateral" stimuli as is done in Schaefer's redundancy programing procedure rather than direct controlling stimuli. In this procedure, German vocabulary is learned in the course of transitional behavior by utilizing the context and redundancy of English texts to provide the meaning for a foreign word in a passage of English text (17, 37). The "fading" technique frequently used in the context of operant conditioning and programed instruction is similar to this procedure as a way of transferring stimulus control in order to minimize interference effects.

Practice

Many of the early experiments in programed instruction involved the manipulation of the number of steps in a program so that programs with different numbers of frames but teaching the same things were compared. Holland's chapter indicates that the results obtained from quite a few studies along these lines cannot be unambiguously interpreted. However, they serve to make one aware of how little is known that can be applied about the variable of practice, which is an old and respectable topic in learning. With present techniques for designing programs, the amount of practice and review employed needs to be completely empirically determined and is certainly subject to individual differences. The situation is exemplified by a study in which one-fifth of the frames of a published program were removed; average performance for the original program and the shortened version showed no differences.[2]

A study completed by Reynolds and Glaser (36), in which experimental sequences in junior high school general science were imbedded in a larger general science program, investigated the amount of repetition of stimulus and response and the spacing of review sequences in the learning of technical terms in biology. The results, measured for immediate learning and retention, showed that variations in repetition had only transitory effects, but that spaced review in the course of a programed instructional sequence significantly facilitated retention of the reviewed material. Similar results in a laboratory situation have been reported by Greeno (23) in paired-associate learning with

---

[2] Personal communication, James R. Hawker and Lois S. Lackner, 1964.

massed and distributed repetitions of items. The results suggest that the often-criticized monotony of repetition found in many early programs may in fact be of little value in enhancing retention for certain kinds of subject matter content and may profitably be replaced by a series of short instructional sequences in several related topics, each interspersed with reviews of the preceding material.

The general conclusion is that the entire question of practice, review, and retention with *meaningful* academic subject matter needs to receive more help from experimental psychology and requires extensive investigation in both laboratory and educational contexts.

Response Contingencies

The fact is that practice as such does not change behavior, but that practice conditions which supply consequences of an individual's actions serve to modify his behavior. These response contingencies influence the course of learning. Reinforcing events which are a consequence of behavior fall into one class of response contingency. Other classes, of course, are extinction, punishment, and one that has been generally ignored in psychological study, called correction. The study of the contingent relationships between the behavior of an organism and consequent events is a key area for both basic and applied research in learning relevant to instruction. There are so many things which are not known. Many studies show the powerful influence of various reinforcing operations (e.g., 13, 26); then there are studies like that by Swets and his co-workers (45), where, in a task of categorizing the characteristics of different sounds, the authors conclude that "fairly extensive feedback may be detrimental . . . and provide no support for the hypothesis that efficiency of learning varies directly with the probability of reinforcement." As Lane indicates, such negative findings may be attributed to many sources and need to be analyzed carefully, particularly with respect to the nature of the terminal behavior and the relationship between transitional and terminal behavior. In most available small-step programed instructional sequences, response determination is a programing principle; this results in few response errors. Under these conditions a major mechanism is the occurrence of reinforcing events following an appropriate response, the crucial aspect being the contingency between the relevance of the answer and the critical subject matter content in the frame. The primary questions in programs of this sort are what factors serve as reinforcing events and what operations are involved in the reinforcement process.

Errors and Correction: If correct responses are not so highly determined as they are in a small-step linear program, then the student makes some errors. It is known, at least on a common sense basis, that individuals learn from making errors, but very little is known about the process involved and how to use error behavior efficiently. The area of response contingencies that can be called correction seems to have been neglected, if one looks at the literature. Correction refers to the contingency whereby an incorrect response is followed by a stimulus event which serves to inform the student of the nature of the correct response in such ways as telling him the right answer, showing him how to get the right answer, making him perform the correct response, and so forth. There has been work in "corrective" feedback in motor skill learning; a "correction" trial in animal learning means something different than what is meant here. There has been little work in verbal learning, even though some studies have been appearing recently. Some writers flatly assume that, in verbal learning studies, providing the correct answer following an incorrect response is a reinforcing event in the same way that confirmation following a correct response serves as a reinforcer (3).

How do students learn from their errors? Some investigators, like Kaess and Zeaman (25), when they have studied multiple-choice items with incorrect alternatives in a Pressey punchboard-type situation, conclude that incorrect alternatives increase the probability that the subject will repeat his error. Suppes and Ginsberg (43) report the desirability of overt correction procedures to facilitate learning in children. The suggestion is that there may be differences in the effects of correction between adults and children and also differences as a function of the behavior being learned. In this latter respect, formal repertoires may be learned more efficiently with highly determined correct-response reinforcement; thematic repertoires may profit from the use of corrective feedback.

The chapters by Lewis and Pask and by Evans provide provocative contrasts on the subject of errorful vs. "errorless" learning. Skinner's work has emphasized the minimization of error, and the interesting work of Terrace (48, 49) has questioned discrimination learning the-

ories in which the extinction of responding to an inappropriate stimulus, and hence the occurrence of errors, is a necessary condition for
the formation of discriminations. The general rationale for error minimization in instruction seems to be the following: (a) When errors occur, there is lack of control over the learning process, and opportunity
is provided for the intermittent reinforcement of incorrect responses;
this results in interference effects highly resistant to extinction. (b)
Frustration and emotional effects that are difficult to control are associated with extinction and interference. And (c) richer learning, that is,
richer in associations, takes place when the associative history of the
learner is employed to extend his learning; this is accomplished by
mediators or thematic promptings which make positive use of existing
knowledge and serve to guide learning. Perhaps another reason behind
the drive to minimize errors is the fact mentioned above, that the use
of errors and the possible value of incorrect responses have not been as
widely nor systematically investigated as other response contingencies
in studies of learning related to the educational process.

Lewis and Pask make the case that error responses must be used in
the course of an adaptive teaching procedure. Such a teaching procedure
requires the student to reveal, by making some sort of error, the kind
of instruction he should receive next. If adaptive control is competently
designed, student weaknesses are revealed by his selection of response
alternatives. Where no adaptive procedures are available for dealing
with error, the minimization of error is forced upon a teaching procedure. Error minimization advocates might suggest that the adaptive
system could do better by preventing errors from occurring in the first
place. Lewis and Pask react to this by pointing out that the presence of
error is tacitly acknowledged by the error minimizers when they cue or
prompt in the course of a program to adjust a program to the population of students who are being taught. These nonadaptive programs
remove error factors without allowing them to be manifested in the
form of overt mistakes. This necessarily involves working in the dark,
and hence programs which forestall error often make provisions for far
more error possibilities than any one student is likely to have; they
therefore consist of less-than-challenging tasks. An important area for
learning research relevant to instructional practice is study of the effects of response contingencies, called correction, which follow the
occurrence of incorrect responses.

Effective Reinforcers: A second broad problem that the work on programed sequences has emphasized is the question of what the effective reinforcers in a subject matter learning sequence are and the related practical problem of what reinforcing contingencies can be employed in designing instruction. As is known, reinforcement can be quite subtle. For example, Skinner points out that certain "consequences are used to motivate the beginning reader when a textbook is designed to be 'interesting.' Such reinforcement is not, however, contingent upon accuracy of response in the manner needed to shape skillful behavior" (39, p. 66). Silberman points out that an interesting text may reinforce the behavior involved in obtaining meaning from printed material, but may not differentially reinforce correct phonemic responses. Reinforcing events must be determined on the basis of detailed analysis of appropriate subject matter and component repertoire relationships. Just as one identifies what stimuli feel hot or cold, or pleasant or frightening, one needs to identify what events can serve as reinforcers for students in the course of learning certain subject matters.

Studies in learning and instruction do suggest the effectiveness of certain events as reinforcers. Some illustrative leads can be mentioned: One of the most interesting discoveries about reinforcement especially related to what has been referred to in this chapter as self-sustaining behavior repertoires has been described by Premack (35). Premack points out that of any two responses, the one that occurs more often, when both are available, can reinforce the one that occurs less often, so that, for a child, if playing is a higher strength behavior than eating, it might be used as a reinforcing event for eating behavior, or if certain words occur with a higher probability than others, they might be used as reinforcing stimuli for words that have a lower probability of occurring. Implicit in this kind of analysis of reinforcing stimuli is that the particular event that constitutes a reinforcement is not a situation external to the learner so much as it is the behavior produced by the situation. For example, it may not be the food but the eating which reinforces a hungry person; it may not be so much the achievement of the goal but the behavior produced by obtaining the goal. Thus reinforcers may be defined either in terms of behavior or in terms of stimuli; either definition may serve a particular purpose, and both are useful ways of thinking about the operation of reinforcement. If carrying out a learned performance can be reinforcing, it seems rea-

sonable to hypothesize that in a chain of activities which terminate
in a reinforcing event, each response acts as a reinforcer for previous
responses. However, a response will only act as a reinforcer if it has
a higher probability of occurrence than the behavior it is reinforcing.
This kind of analysis suggests studies that lead to the interesting suggestion (16) that in an instructional sequence which teaches a chain
of operations, e.g., long division, instruction need not proceed in the
order in which the sequence is finally performed; that is, learning the
first operation, A, which is performed in carrying out the chain and
then learning the second operation, B, and then learning C, the third
operation. Since B is a weaker response than A which was first learned,
and C weaker than the others since it is newly learned in the sequence,
the suggestion is that operation C be learned first, then BC (since C
is a higher strength behavior that can reinforce the new response B),
and then operations ABC.

Another apparently powerful reinforcer in learning is overt control
of the physical environment. This has been particularly suggested by
the work of Moore (33) and what he calls a responsive environment.
Reinforcement of this kind seems to be related to the study of behavior
generally labeled as curiosity and exploration to which an increasing
amount of research has been directed within the past decade (14). In
infrahuman studies, research has been aimed at the discovery and identification of variables which serve to elicit and maintain curiosity and
exploratory behavior in the absence of conventional laboratory motives
such as hunger or thirst or other conditions of deprivation. The specific
responses which have been observed are such behaviors as orienting,
approaching, investigating, manipulating, etc. The significant variables
influencing such exploratory responses have been characterized as stimulus objects or patterns that are novel, unfamiliar, complex, surprising,
incongruous, asymmetrical, etc. All these aspects can generally be
described as a change in the stimulus displayed to the individual. Research has indicated that the strength of exploratory behavior which
is elicited is positively related, within limits, to the degree of change
in the stimulus situation provided by the novel, unfamiliar, or incongruous situations introduced into the environment. Too great or too
abrupt a change, however, is disrupting and may preclude exploration.
In complex situations, an individual encounters change by way of his

interaction with or manipulation of the elements involved. Such interaction provides the stimulus change which can elicit curiosity and exploratory behavior.

Investigations have demonstrated that behaviors are learned that lead to a change in the stimulus display. Thus, in addition to stimulus change eliciting exploratory behavior, experiments show that organisms will respond in order to secure novel, unfamiliar stimuli. In general, these findings demonstrate that stimulus change or sensory variation may be employed selectively to reinforce behaviors which result in stimulus change and that this variation in the stimulus situation will serve concomitantly to elicit exploratory behavior. When stimulus change is used as a reinforcing stimulus, it seems reasonable to hypothesize that learning variables which influence acquisition and extinction of other learned behavior will influence the acquisition and extinction of exploratory and curiosity behavior. This suggests that a student's curiosity and explorations may be both elicited and selectively maintained in an instructional environment which provides for appropriate variation and change in both the stimulus characteristics of the subject materials confronting the student and also the responses required of him by these materials.

Looking over the topics and issues covered in this section on conditions influencing the learning process, one may be struck by the fact that there is no *explicit* mention of transfer or meaning and mediation effects as special topics. Transfer phenomena do represent an important class of problems which obviously has been recognized in this discussion, but the suggestion is that perhaps the notion of transfer can be more definitively analyzed in terms of the topics that are discussed. Meaning and mediation effects have been emphasized in programed instruction in terms of thematic prompting and the shaping of thematic repertories. Mediation is an increasingly busy area for experimental psychologists, and its implications for instruction need to be made more explicit. The general implication of the work by experimentalists, which can be profitable for an analysis of instructional operations, is that meaning and mediated behavior can be treated in terms of stimulus and response events which are amenable to learning processes such as discrimination, generalization, chaining, and stimulus control in a manner similar to other kinds of student responses.

Measuring Learning Outcomes

An effective technology of instruction relies heavily upon the detailed measurement of subject matter competence at the beginning, in the course of, and at the end of the educational process. The mastery of the skills and knowledge required to begin an instructional sequence and to continue along its course insures the availability of behavior on which the teacher and the student can rely in subsequent learning. Elsewhere the author (18) has pointed out that the presence of teaching machines and programed instruction has raised into prominence a number of questions concerning the nature and properties of measures of student achievement and the assessment of subject matter competence as it may be defined by recognized subject matter scholars. Achievement measurement can be defined as the assessment of criterion behavior involving the determination of the characteristics of student performance with respect to specified standards. Achievement measurement is distinguished from aptitude measurement in that the instruments used to assess achievement are specifically concerned with the properties of present performance, with emphasis on the meaningfulness of its content. In contrast, aptitude measures derive their meaning from a demonstrated relationship between present performance and the future attainment of specified knowledge and skill. In certain circumstances, of course, this contrast is not quite so clear, for example, when achievement measures are used as predictor variables.

The scores obtained from an achievement test can provide primarily two kinds of information. The first is the degree to which the student has attained criterion performance, for example, whether he can satisfactorily prepare an experimental report or solve certain kinds of word problems in arithmetic. The second is the relative ordering of individuals with respect to their test performance, for example, whether Student A can solve his problems more quickly than Student B. The principal difference between these two kinds of information lies in the standard used as a reference. The standard against which a student's performance is compared in order to obtain the first kind of information is the criterion behavior which defines increasing subject matter competence along a continuum of achievement. Criterion levels of competence can be established at any point in instruction where it is necessary to obtain information as to the adequacy of a student's performance. Behaviorally defined objectives describe the specific tasks a student must be capable of performing in order to achieve a particular knowledge or competence level. The student's score with respect to these tasks provides explicit information as to what he can or cannot do and indicates the correspondence between what the student does and the achievement criteria at that point in his learning. Measures cast in terms of such criterion standards provide information as to the degree of competence obtained by a particular student which is independent of reference to the performance of others.

On the other hand, achievement measures also convey information about the capability of a student compared with the capability of other students. In instances where a student's relative standing is the primary purpose of measurement, reference need not be made to criterion behavior. Educational achievement examinations, for example, are administered frequently for the purpose of ordering students in a class or school, rather than for assessing their attainment of specified curriculum objectives. When such norm-referenced measures are used, a particular student's achievement is evaluated in terms of a comparison between his performance and the performance of other members of the group. Such measures need provide little or no information about the degree of proficiency exhibited by the tested behaviors in terms of what the individual can do. They tell that one student is more or less proficient than another, but do not tell how proficient either of them is with respect to subject matter tasks. In large part, achievement measures currently employed in education are norm referenced, and work needs to be done which will contribute to the development of criterion-referenced tests in order to assess the outcomes of learning.

A further point along these lines relates to the fact that achievement tests are used not only to provide information about the student but also to provide information about the effects of different teaching procedures and instructional designs. It seems likely that tests which are constructed to be sensitive to individual student differences may not be the same kinds of tests which are sensitive to the differences produced by different instructional conditions. Test theory for the most part has been primarily concerned with the development of tests that are maximally sensitive to individual differences. Less work has been concerned with test development for the purpose of curriculum evaluation and curriculum design. This point is further discussed in the article referred to above (18) and more fully in an article by Cronbach

(12) concerned with course improvement through evaluation. Among many provocative statements, Cronbach writes, "I am becoming convinced that some techniques and habits of thought of the evaluation specialist are ill-suited to current curriculum studies. . . . How must we depart from the familiar doctrines and rituals of the testing game?" (p. 672) and "The three purposes—course improvement, decisions about individuals, and administrative regulation—call for measurement procedures having somewhat different qualities" (p. 677). Particularly with respect to instructional design, test data are becoming important indicators of the properties of the learning environment that effected certain behavioral changes. As Lumsdaine indicates, there is a difference between the data obtained in the course of constructing an instructional sequence and the data obtained to prove its final effectiveness. The former kind of data will become increasingly significant as the design of instruction becomes a more rigorous enterprise. Cronbach writes, "Evaluation, used to improve the course while it is still fluid, contributes more to improvement of education than evaluation used to appraise a product already placed on the market" (12, p. 675).

A final point to be made about the measurement of learning outcomes is that such measurement cannot be narrowly conceived. Other effects must be evaluated along with, for example, gains in achievement. To again quote Cronbach:

Outcomes of instruction are multidimensional, and a satisfactory investigation will map out the effects of the course along these dimensions separately. To agglomerate many types of post-course performance into a single score is a mistake, because failure to achieve one objective is masked by success in another direction. Moreover, since a composite score embodies (and usually conceals) judgments about the importance of the various outcomes, only a report that treats the outcomes separately can be useful to educators who have different value hierarchies (12, p. 675).

Trends in Practice

The chapters surveying the use of programed instruction in schools, industry, and government agencies show somewhat different reactions from these three sources. In the federal government, utilization is active but tentative. Hopes have been high enough that disappointments have been inevitable. The guess of Bryan and Nagay is that programed instruction will increase in government agencies if it yields tangible benefits; in this respect they feel that the experience of certain present activities is critical. In industry, Shoemaker and Holt indicate a growth of acceptance that has been greater than in public education or the government (with the exception of the Air Training Command). For many industrial applications, the self-instructional, self-pacing features are highly valued. In elementary and secondary schools, Hanson and Komoski document an important trend—a trend toward increasingly effective individualization of instruction. They write:

There should be no question that programs of the future will be designed and presented for a still greater variety of students to use them in increasingly varied ways. If research into the design and use of programed materials is carried out on a large scale, there is little doubt that the school of the not-too-distant future will be able to boast a curriculum that may be offered in as many different ways as there are pupils in the school. In such a school, each learner will seek and achieve mastery of a subject matter or a skill by proceeding along a path largely of his own choosing, a path that is neither too easy nor too difficult for him to traverse. Ideally the teacher will help the learner to discover a system of learning that suits his own capabilities. In other words, the learner will be taught how to learn; he will be provided with new tools for learning. . . . Both the techniques and the materials of learning will be very different in the schools of tomorrow, and there can be little question that today's programed instruction is helping to lay the foundation for such schools.

To be superimposed on this trend toward the self-resourceful learner is the development of group tuition systems. Lewis and Pask suggest, "The ability of one human to understand the difficulties of another derives from the richly complex ways in which they are capable of sharing common dimensions of experience. . . . But this ability is not peculiar to the teacher-student relationship. Two students can have it equally well, and this raises the possibility of a computer-controlled system which *induces students to teach each other.*"

A recurrent theme in many of the chapters in this book is the emergence of the individual as the entity of instruction. Educators and educational psychologists need to take seriously the fact of individual differences and the platitude of accommodating individual needs. The existence of individual differences must be more strongly reflected in educational design. In 1920, the insightful Pressey was keenly aware of the inefficiencies of the instructional procedures used in schools to adjust to individual differences. Kersh points out that the Winnetka

Plan of almost 40 years ago attempted to do this. He reports that Washburne, who served as the force behind it, gives the following reasons why individualized instruction had not spread more widely by 1940: (a) there were not available adequate tests and texts for individual work, (b) there was a swing away from subject matter emphasis to an emphasis on child-centered learning, and (c) there occurred the development of "compromise plans" of ability grouping and group projects in which each child could presumably participate according to his own abilities.

At present, a fresh start on research and development for instructional procedures and organizational requirements for the individualization of instruction seems possible in light of the following events: (a) increasing study of the relationships between learning and environmental factors affecting individual differences, (b) the renewed emphasis of curriculum groups on subject matter, and (c) the success of certain programed instructional materials when they are used in ways not constrained by fixed classroom groupings.

In the future, the design of instructional procedures will be modified as behavioral science and educational practice begin to be related in a mutually helpful way—a way not atypical of science and practice in other fields. As this occurs, it is hypothesized that four main areas of the educational process will be influenced: (a) the setting of instructional goals will be recast in terms of observable and measurable student behavior including achievements, attitudes, motivations, and interests; (b) the diagnosis of the learner's strengths and weaknesses prior to instruction will become a more definitive process so that it can aid in guiding the student along a curriculum specially suited for him; (c) the techniques and materials employed by the teacher will undergo significant change; and (d) the ways in which the outcomes of education are assessed, both for student evaluation and curriculum improvement, will receive increasingly more attention.

As these changes occur, it is likely that they will result in the following changes in school operation: (a) Obviously, the role of the teacher will be restructured; it seems likely that the teacher will be able to become more concerned with individual student guidance and individual progress in addition to the role of group mentor. (b) The educators' goal of the individualization of student progress based upon student background, aptitude, and achievement will come closer to realization through school reorganization and the adoption of new practices. (c) Instructional materials and devices supplied by industry will come under close scrutiny as to their instructional effectiveness. (d) Mastery of subject matter competence will be easier to attain for a larger number of students, and tests which measure progress toward mastery will become important aids for the quality control of educational excellence.

By and large the educational profession will show an increasing trend toward professionalization so that the teacher will have to be provided with tools and procedures designed on the basis of scientific research and development; the most effective use of these new designs will be influenced by the personal artistry and skill of the practitioner.

Certain other directions seem to be clearly outlined: Programed learning will continue to offer the opportunity for an investigator to obtain detailed records of a controlled reproducible sequence of instructional events in which independent and dependent variables can be manipulated to study the learning process.

The amount of research oriented toward the unsystematic empirical testing of the characteristics of instructional sequences will decrease in favor of research oriented toward theoretical derivation of the characteristics of an effective instructional sequence prior to experimental investigation.

Research on long-term, sustained educational environments will increase along with measurement of the long-range effects of these environments upon retention and transfer.

Research will increase on the application of programed instruction to training in manipulative and psychomotor skills.

Now that some dust has settled on the machine-program distinction, major effort will be devoted to the teaching hardware and automation possibilities in instruction.

Increasing attention will be paid to subject matter competence and mastery, and this will be accompanied by teaching of the heuristics of thinking and discovery.

In the foreseeable future, published instructional materials will be accompanied by manuals describing their teaching philosophy and rationale, their educational objectives, target student population, and evidence of their effectiveness and limitations. This development will be brought about by technical developments in the publication of educational material and by increasing sophistication of the educational consumer in the criteria for evaluating these materials.

There will develop a new professional specialty in education, perhaps called "educational designer," to serve the engineering function between scientific developments and teaching practice.

Increasing effort will be devoted to the determination of the quality and characteristics of ongoing educational systems. Extensive and detailed assessment will be made of educational outcomes so that these measurements can serve as baseline information for the evaluation of innovation.

In 1954, in a talk entitled, "The Science of Learning and the Art of Teaching," subsequently published in Volume I of *Teaching Machines and Programmed Learning* (40), Skinner concluded with the following:

We are on the threshold of an exciting and revolutionary period, in which the scientific study of man will be put to work in man's best interests. Education must play its part. It must accept the fact that a sweeping revision of educational practices is possible and inevitable. When it has done this, we may look forward with confidence to a school system which is aware of the nature of its tasks, secure in its methods, and generously supported by the informed and effective citizens whom education itself will create (p. 113).

The chapters in this book give the impression that educators, subject matter scholars, and behavioral scientists have stepped over the threshold and have been invited to sit down together.

References

1. American Association for the Advancement of Science. *Science—A Process Approach.* Washington, D.C.: the Association, 1963.
2. Bijou, Sidney W. *Systematic Instruction in the Attainment of Right-Left Form Concepts in Young and Retarded Children.* Seattle: University of Washington, 1964. (Mimeo.)
3. Bower, Gordon H. "An Association Model for Response and Training Variables in Paired-Associate Learning." *Psychological Review* 69: 34-53; January 1962.
4. Brinkman, Erwin H. *Educability in Visualization of Objects in Space: A Programmed Instruction Approach.* Doctor's thesis. Ann Arbor: University of Michigan, 1963.
5. Brown, R., and Fraser, G. "The Acquisition of Syntax." *Verbal Behavior and Learning Problems and Processes.* (Edited by C. N. Cofer and Barbara S. Musgrave.) New York: McGraw-Hill Book Co., 1963.

6. Bruner, Jerome S. *The Process of Education.* Cambridge, Mass.: Harvard University Press, 1960. 92 pp.
7. Bruner, Jerome S. "Some Theories of Instruction Illustrated with Reference to Mathematics." *Theories of Learning and Instruction.* (Edited by E. R. Hilgard.) Sixty-Third Yearbook, National Society for the Study of Education. Chicago: University of Chicago Press, 1964. pp. 306-35.
8. Buchanan, Cynthia D. *Programmed Reading.* New York: McGraw-Hill Book Co., 1963.
9. Carroll, John B. "Language Development in Children." *Psycholinguistics: A Book of Readings.* (Edited by Sol Saporta.) New York: Holt, Rinehart and Winston, 1963. pp. 331-45.
10. Coulson, John E., editor. *Programmed Learning and Computer-Based Instruction.* New York: John Wiley & Sons, 1962. 291 pp.
11. Crawford, Meredith P. "Concepts of Training." *Psychological Principles in System Development.* (Edited by Robert M. Gagné.) New York: Holt, Rinehart and Winston, 1962. pp. 301-41.
12. Cronbach, Lee J. "Course Improvement Through Evaluation." *Teachers College Record* 64: 672-83; May 1963.
13. Ferster, Charles B., and Skinner, B. F. *Schedules of Reinforcement.* New York: Appleton-Century-Crofts, 1957. 741 pp.
14. Fowler, Harry. *Curiosity and Exploratory Behavior.* New York: Macmillan Co., 1965. (In press)
15. Gagné, R. M. "The Acquisition of Knowledge." *Psychological Review* 69: 355-65; July 1962.
16. Gilbert, Thomas F. "Mathetics: The Technology of Education." *Journal of Mathetics* 1: 7-73; January 1962.
17. Glaser, Robert. "Some Research Problems in Automated Instruction: Instructional Programming and Subject Matter Structure." *Programmed Learning and Computer-Based Instruction.* (Edited by J. E. Coulson.) New York: John Wiley & Sons, 1962. pp. 67-85.
18. Glaser, Robert. "Instructional Technology and the Measurement of Learning Outcomes: Some Questions." *American Psychologist* 17: 519-21; August 1963.
19. Glaser, Robert. "Implications of Training Research for Education." *Theories of Learning and Instruction.* (Edited by E. R. Hilgard.) Sixty-Third Yearbook, National Society for the Study of Education. Chicago: University of Chicago Press, 1964. pp. 153-81.
20. Glaser, Robert; Ramage, William W.; and Lipson, Joseph I. *The Interface Between Student and Subject Matter.* Pittsburgh: Learning Research and Development Center, University of Pittsburgh, 1964. 177 pp.
21. Glaser, Robert, and Reynolds, James H. "Instructional Objectives and Programmed Instruction: A Case Study." *Defining Educational Objectives.* (Edited by C. M. Lindvall.) Pittsburgh: University of Pittsburgh Press, 1964. pp. 47-76.

22. Glaser, Robert; Reynolds, James H.; and Fullick, Margaret G. *Programmed Instruction in the Intact Classroom.* Pittsburgh: Learning Research and Development Center, University of Pittsburgh, 1963. 48 pp.

23. Greeno, James G. "Paired Associate Learning with Massed and Distributed Repetition of Items." *Journal of Experimental Psychology* 67: 286-95; March 1964.

24. Holland, James G. "New Directions in Teaching-Machine Research." *Programmed Learning and Computer-Based Instruction.* (Edited by J. E. Coulson.) New York: John Wiley & Sons, 1962. pp. 46-57.

25. Kaess, W., and Zeaman, D. "Positive and Negative Knowledge of Results on a Pressey-Type Punchboard." *Journal of Experimental Psychology* 60: 12-17; July 1960.

26. Keller, Fred S., and Schoenfeld, William N. *Principles of Psychology.* New York: Appleton-Century-Crofts, 1950. 431 pp.

27. Licklider, J. C. R. "Preliminary Experiments in Computer-Aided Teaching." *Programmed Learning and Computer-Based Instruction.* (Edited by J. E. Coulson.) New York: John Wiley & Sons, 1962. pp. 217-39.

28. Lumsdaine, A. A., and Glaser, Robert, editors. *Teaching Machines and Programmed Learning.* Washington, D.C.: National Education Association, 1960. 724 pp.

29. Markle, Susan M. *Words: A Programed Course in Vocabulary Development.* Chicago: Science Research Associates, 1962. 224 pp.

30. Melton, Arthur W. "The Science of Learning and the Technology of Educational Methods." *Harvard Educational Review* 29: 96-105; Spring 1959. [Reprinted in *Teaching Machines and Programmed Learning.* (Edited by A. A. Lumsdaine and Robert Glaser.) Washington, D.C.: National Education Association, 1960. pp. 658-60.]

31. Melton, Arthur W., editor. *Categories of Human Learning.* New York: Academic Press, 1964. 356 pp.

32. Miller, G. A., and Selfridge, J. A. "Verbal Context and the Recall of Meaningful Material." *American Journal of Psychology* 63: 176-85; April 1950.

33. Moore, Omar K. "Autotelic Responsive Environments and Exceptional Children." *The Special Child in Century 21.* Seattle, Wash.: Special Child Publications, 1964.

34. Newell, Allen, and Simon, Herbert A. "Computer Simulation of Human Thinking." *Science* 124: 2,011-17; December 22, 1961.

35. Premack, David. "Toward Empirical Behavior Laws: I. Positive Reinforcement." *Psychological Review* 66: 219-33; July 1959.

36. Reynolds, James H., and Glaser, Robert. "Effects of Repetition and Spaced Review upon Retention of a Complex Learning Task." *Journal of Educational Psychology* 55: 297-308; October 1964.

37. Schaefer, Halmuth H. "A Vocabulary Program Using 'Language Redundancy.'" *Journal of Programed Instruction* 2: 9-16; Fall 1963.

38. Simon, Herbert A., and Newell, Allen. "Information Processing in

Computer and Man." *American Scientist* 52: 281-300; September 1962.

39. Skinner, B. F. *Verbal Behavior.* New York: Appleton-Century-Crofts, 1957. 478 pp.

40. Skinner, B. F. "The Science of Learning and the Art of Teaching." *Teaching Machines and Programmed Learning.* (Edited by A. A. Lumsdaine and R. Glaser.) Washington, D.C.: National Education Association, 1960. pp. 99-113.

41. Skinner, B. F. "Teaching Machines." *Scientific American* 205: 90-102; November 1961.

42. Suppes, Patrick. "Modern Learning Theory and the Elementary-School Curriculum." *American Educational Research Journal* 1: 79-93; March 1964.

43. Suppes, Patrick, and Ginsberg, Rose. "Application of a Stimulus Sampling Model to Children's Concept Formation with and Without Overt Correction Response." *Journal of Experimental Psychology* 63: 330-36; April 1962.

44. Suppes, Patrick, and Ginsberg, Rose. "Experimental Studies of Mathematical Concept Formation in Young Children." *Science Education* 46: 234-40; April 1962.

45. Swets, J. A., and others. "Learning To Identify Nonverbal Sounds: An Application of a Computer as a Teaching Machine." *Journal of the Acoustical Society of America* 34: 928-35; July 1962.

46. Taber, Julian I.; Glaser, Robert; and Schaefer, Halmuth H. *Learning and Programmed Instruction.* Reading, Mass.: Addison-Wesley Publishing Co., 1965.

47. Teager, Herbert M. "Systems Considerations in Real-Time Computer Usage." *Programmed Learning and Computer-Based Instruction.* (Edited by J. E. Coulson.) New York: John Wiley & Sons, 1962. pp. 273-80.

48. Terrace, Herbert S. "Discrimination Learning with and Without Errors." *Journal of the Experimental Analysis of Behavior* 6: 1-27; January 1963.

49. Terrace, Herbert S. "Errorless Transfer of Discrimination Across Two Continua." *Journal of the Experimental Analysis of Behavior* 6: 223-32; April 1963.

50. Travers, R. M. W. *Essentials of Learning: An Overview for Students of Education.* New York: Macmillan Co., 1963. 544 pp.

51. Tyler, Fred T. "Issues Related to Readiness To Learn." *Theories of Learning and Instruction.* (Edited by E. R. Hilgard.) Sixty-Third Yearbook, National Society for the Study of Education. Chicago: University of Chicago Press, 1964. pp. 210-39.

52. Underwood, Benton J., and Schulz, Rudolph W. *Meaningfulness and Verbal Learning.* New York: J. B. Lippincott Co., 1960. 430 pp.

53. Uttal, William R. "On Conversational Interaction." *Programmed Learning and Computer-Based Instruction.* (Edited by J. E. Coulson.) New York: John Wiley & Sons, 1962. pp. 171-90.

Subject Index

A

Abstraction (*see* Concept learning)
Acceleration of learning, 668
Achievement measurement
Criterion vs. norm-referenced, 800-802
(*See also* Evaluation)
Adaptive teaching systems, Chapters 5 and 6
Group tuition, 258-62
Research data, 248-62
Selection of programs, 175-77
(*See also* Branching)
Adjunct programing, 67, 146
Administration of programed instruction
In industry, 732-34
In schools, 680-82
Analysis of behavior
Behavioral chains, 465-68
Mathematics, 406-11
With respect to machines, 167-68
(*See also* Objectives)

Aptitude, 8, 189, 202, 782, 783-84
Entering behavior, 172
And instructional method, 182-85
Interaction with instruction, 205-206
Language, 586-87
Art judgment, 575
Artificial intelligence, 219
Representation of learning, 220-25
Association, 43-45, 74-77
Associative strength, 75-76
Attitude toward programed instruction, 392-95, 753-54
Audiolingual method, 613-20
Audiovisual devices
Interest and attention, 10
Second language learning, 617-19
In teaching literature, 573
Television, 11, 656-57
Augmented Roman Alphabet, 510-11

Automation (*see* Machines)
Autotelic, 427-28, 530-31
Awareness, in learning, 419-21

B

Behavioral categories (*see* Taxonomy)
Behavioral outcomes (*see* Terminal behavior)
Branching, 105-107, 138-40, 183, 243, 346, 425, 533
   Decision rules, 186-89
   Studies of, 105-107, 398-99

C

Case method, in science education, 477
Case studies of school program use, 654-77
Chaining, 38, 44-45, 48-49, 526-27, 798
   Backward, 143
Chains, of behavior, 465-76, 500, 526
   Intraverbal responses, 624-28
Classroom Communicator, 747
Classroom teaching
   Automated, 342-46
      CLASS, 343-44
      Effectiveness of, 362-64
      TRAC, 343-45, 347-64
   Lesson plans, 326-27
   Methodology for design of, 346-47
      TRAC procedure, 347-62
   Teacher interaction skills, 339-40
   Unit plan, 324-27
   University of Illinois Committee on School Mathematics, 327-29
   Winnetka Plan, 330-34
Classroom teaching model
   Olson, 334
   Woodruff, 329-30
Coding, 45

Computer-based systems, 779-80
   Speech, 618-19
   (*See also* Machines)
Concept learning, 49-51, 86-89, 461-83, 595, 777-78
   In critical reading, 574
   Illustrative frame sequences, 488-89, 490-501
   In mathematics, 412, 426, 478-79
   Variety of examples, 89
Configurationist theory, in programed instruction, 120-27
Confirmation, 77-78, 524, 610
   Studies of, 384-85
   (*See also* Reinforcement)
Confusion matrices, 597, 604-605
Connectionist theory, in programed instruction, 120-27
Contiguity, 43, 136
Contingencies, 794-99
   In programed items, 78-92
      Blackout technique, 82-84
   Of reinforcement, 6-7, 8, 13
   Teaching program for analyzing, 490-501
   (*See also* Reinforcement)
"Conversational chaining," 136
Correction, 795-96
   (*See also* Error)
Correspondence courses, 670
Cost factors in program development
   Federal agencies, 754-55, 760
   Industrial training, 707
Creative writing, 579-80
Criterion measures
   Sensitivity of, 101
   Standards and norms, 800-802
   (*See also* Evaluation)
Cueing (*see* Prompting)
Curiosity, 798-99
   In science, 459-61
Cybernetics (*see* Artificial intelligence)

D

Decision processes
  In instruction, 175-77, 186-89
  For selecting instructional method, 170-85
Density ratio, 82
Department of Defense (*see* Federal agencies)
Design of instruction, 41-61
  And categories of behavior, 54-56
  Component tasks in, 771-73
  Flow charts, 351-61
  Principles for, Hilgard's list, 323-24
  Requirements for, 335-42
  Review of, 322-34
Dictation, in second language learning, 622-23
Differentiation (*see* Response differentiation)
Discovery learning, 69, 235-36, 350-51, 356-60, 414-17, 421
  In mathematics, 327-28, 429
  As trial-and-error learning, 414
Discrimination, 58, 71-74, 412, 424-25, 461-65, 500, 532
  Applicable to second language, 591-600, 609-13
  Coordination with response differentiation, 609-13
  In critical reading, 574
  In English instruction, 568
  Errorless learning, 422-23
  Multiple, 45-48
  Self-monitoring, 791-92
  And subject matter properties, 476-77
Drill, in language learning, 625

E

Echoic behavior, 613-19
Effectiveness of instruction, measurement of (*see* Evaluation)

Efficiency index, 185, 310
English composition, trends in instruction, 575-80
Entering behavior, 170, 172-73, 308-309, 390-91, 781-84
  In English instruction, 547, 553
    Diagnosis of, 565
  Interaction with outcomes and instruction, 177-80
  Machine design, 182
  Readiness, 531-33
Entry behavior (*see* Entering behavior)
Error
  In adaptive systems, 232-37
  Control of, 136-38
  Effects of, 152
  Feedback, 134-36
  And individual differences, 138-40
  Learning effects, 85-86, 91-92, 149, 795-96
  In multiple choice responding, 137
Error factors, 231
  In learning and teaching, 226-29
Error rate, 82-85, 90-91, 291-92, 722-23
Errorless learning, 412-13, 415, 421, 422-23, 597
Evaluation, Chapter 7, 759-60
  Course improvement vs. individual assessment, 801-802
  Criteria and standards, 272-90
    Checklists, 280-82
    Content appropriateness, 274-75
    Cost practicality, 274
    Criterion vs. norm-referenced tests, 296-97
    Effectiveness, 274-75
    Effects of, 273
    External, 283-86
    Internal and external information, 275-76

(Evaluation, cont'd.)
  Kinds of, 273-86
  Measures, 293-97
  Predictive vs. validating,
    276-77
  Retention, 312
  Savings measures, 311
  Time and achievement,
    309-11
  Time to criterion, 310
  Validating, 277, 283-86
  Design of, 723-28, 731-32
  Design of instruments for,
    295-97
  Item sampling, 296
  Developmental vs. performance
    measures, 290-91
  Experimental design, 297-301
  External criteria, 722-28
  Gain, 299, 300-301
  And Efficiency, 310
  Industrial training, 701, 722-32
    Examples of, 726-27, 728-32
  Laboratory vs. field tests, 298
  Methodological problems,
    308-12
  Product testing vs. general meth-
    od, 269-71
  Programed instruction and con-
    ventional methods, 107-108
  Program effects vs. individual
    differences, 296-97
  Program reviews, 278-80
  Reporting of effects, 301-305
    Joint Committee recommenda-
    tions, 305-308
  Reproducibility, 304-305
  Of transfer, 59-60
  Use in schools, 650-51
  Utilization conditions, 297-99
Experimental design, 372-75
  In evaluation, 297-301
Exploratory behavior, 798-99

F

Fading, 46, 71-77, 165, 243,
    523-24, 627, 793
Federal agencies, program usage
  Advantages and disadvantages,
    754-58
  Functions of, 751-53
  Kinds of programs, 745-47,
    763-67
Feedback, 193-94, 600, 795-96
  Automated classroom, 363
  Personality measures, 173
  Studies of, 384-85
  Tactile, 244
  (*See also* Reinforcement; Error)
Formal and thematic repertoires,
  distinction, 589, 775
Frequency, in reading, 515-16

G

Game theory, relation to teaching,
    177-80
Games, cooperative and competi-
    tive, 232
Generalization, 39, 47, 50, 58, 412,
    461-65, 630
  Applicable to second language
    learning, 600-605
  And subject matter properties,
    476-77
Grammar, types of, 555-60
Grapheme-phoneme correspond-
    ence, 509-12, 521-24, 536
  Stimulus-response matrix,
    520-22
Group teaching, 289, 757-58,
    Chapter 8
  Adaptive teaching systems,
    258-62

H

Hypothesis formation, 338-39,
    454-55
  Studies of, 419-21

I

Identification learning, 45-48
Individual differences, 138-41, 202
  Ability-teaching method interaction, 182-85
  Automated classroom procedure, 362-63
  Branching, 105-107
  In English instruction, 552
  In entering behavior, 781-84
  And errors, 138-40
  Grade level, 386-87
  Machine and program design, 180-82
  Machines, 169-70
  Rate of learning, 141
  In reading, 531-33
  Studies of, 386-91
  (*See also* Entering behavior)
Individualization, 676-77
Individualized instruction, in English, 552, 571-72
Induction (*see* Generalization)
Inductive reasoning, 425-26
  (*See also* Reasoning skills)
Inductive teaching, 484-88
Industrial training
  Developmental procedures, 711-15
  Examples of, 715-18
  Programing styles, 720-22
  Program usage
    Advantages of, 697-702
    Functions of, 693-96
    Future trends, 734-36
    General information, 687-90
    Implementation of, 732-34
    Limitations of, 702-10
  Types of subject matter, 690-93
Inspection behavior, 130
Instruction, compared with performance, 154-55
Instructional outcomes, measurement of (*see* Evaluation)

Instructional process
  Components of, 784-86
  Variables in, 786-99
Instrumentation (*see* Machines)
Intelligence
  Effect on program performance, 387-91, 657
  And instructional method, 182-83
  And rate of learning, 141
Interaction, computer controlled, 258-62
Interface between student and machine, 190, 779-80, 781-91
Interference, 46, 792-93
  In reading, 519-20
Intraverbal responses, 624-28
Intrinsic programing, 147-50, 194

J

Joint Committee on Programed Instruction, Chapter 6

K

Knowledge of results, 135, 183-84, 193-94, 195
  (*See also* Reinforcement)

L

Laboratory instruction, 480-81
Language laboratories, 614
Learner characteristics (*see* Individual differences; Entering behavior)
Learner controlled instruction, 203-204
Learning sets, hierarchy of, 143, 408-409
Length of programs
  Federal agencies, 747-48
  Industrial training, 696-97
Lesson plans, 326-27
Linear programing
  Compared with adaptive systems, 235-37
  Features of, 152-53

Linguistics, and language programing, 624-25
Literature, teaching of, 570-73

M

MAC trainer, 28-29
Machine-man interaction, 215-16
Machines, 5, 653, 758, 790-91
  Adaptive systems, examples of, 241-48
  As aids to performance, 203-204, 246
  Analysis of behavior, 167-68
  CLASS, 197, 343-44
  Comprehension skills, 247-48
  Computer-based systems, examples of, 196-97, 198-201
  Cost practicality, 206-207
  Definition of, 168-69
  Design of, 180-82
  Display function, 195
  Evaluation function, 192-93
  Functions of, 191-95
  Hierarchical control mechanism, 227-29
  History of, 163-66
  Intellectual skills, 247
  Interface, 190, 779-80, 781-91
  Maintenance training, 246-47
  Perceptual skills, 245-46
  PLATO, 192, 193, 196, 198, 204
  Vs. programed text, 107, 109, 205, 382-83, 649
  And programs, 166-67, 169
  Response accommodation, 191-92
  Responsive environment, 536-37, 676-77
  Saki, 242-43, 244
  Second language learning, 617-19
  Selection of program content, 193-94
  SOCRATES, 192, 193, 194, 196, 198-202
  TRAC, 343-45, 347-48, 357,

(Machines, cont'd.)
    362, 363, 364, 365, 366
  Vigilance and signal detection, 245-46
Mands, 630-31
Mathematical behavior, study of, 399-430
Mathematics
  Hierarchies of objectives, 29-30
  Learning of, 48, Chapter 9
Mathetics, 26, 153, 409-10
Meaning, in reading, 524-27
Measurement (*see* Evaluation)
Mechanization (*see* Machines)
Mediation, 46-47, 53, 629, 799
  In reading, 524-27
Military training, 22-23, 26
  Definition of objectives, 28-29
  (*See also* Federal agencies)
Monitoring, in instruction, 187-89
Montessori procedure, 528-29
Motivation, 426-28
  In adaptive teaching systems, 229-32
  Attitude toward programed instruction, 392-95
  Maintaining behavior, 786
Multiple discriminations, 38, 45-48
Multiple tracks (*see* Branching)

O

Objectives, Chapter 2, 293-95
  Amenability to human or automatic instruction, 340-41, 357-58
  Analysis of (*see* Task analysis)
  Attainment compared with transfer, 59-60
  Behavioral categories, 36-39
  Complex processes, 335-36
  Compounded outcomes, 341-42
  Content and process, 348-49
  Effect of definition of, 27-31

(Objectives, cont'd.)
Hierarchies of, 29-30, 349-51, 352-53
Higher education, 28
In industrial training, 713-14, 718-20
Levels of, 330
In mathematical behavior, 402-405
Measurement of, 59-60, 295-97
Military training, 28-29
Operational specification, benefits of, 444
Preparation of, 33 (*See also* Task description)
In second language study, 587
Student awareness of, 30-31
Taxonomy of, 39-41
In teaching literature, 570-73
In terms of process, 776-77
And test items, 41
And transfer, 59-60
In Winnetka Plan, 331-32
(*See also* Terminal behavior)
Oddity problem, 225-26
Operant span, 48
Orthography, learning of, 619, 622

P

Pacing, 234
Performance, compared with instruction, 154-55
Personality measures, type of feedback, 173
Personality traits, in scientific behavior, 457-61, 481-82
PLATO (*see* Machines)
Practice, 793-94
Pressey Punchboard, 86
Principles, learning of, 51-53 (*see also* Strategies, learning of)
Problem solving, 428-30
Hierarchical process, 220-21
Procedural learning, 48-49

Process learning, 54
Programed textbooks, 382, 653
Vs. machines, 382-83, 107-108
Programing, styles of, 144-55
Crowder, 147-50
Gilbert, 153-55
Pressey, 144-47
Skinner, 150-53
Programs
Assessment of (*see* Evaluation)
Availability of, 272
Case studies in schools, 654-77
Characteristics of, 118-20, 173-74
Vs. conventional instruction, 107, 375-81
Defects in science teaching, 501-502
Definition of, 67, 118-20, 287-89, 553-54
Development of
Cost factors, 703-707
Industrial training, 703-707
Format studies, 383-84
History of school use, 651-54
Illustrative frame sequences, 469-74, 484-87, 488-89, 491-99, 534-35
Length of
Federal agencies, 747-48
Industry, 696-97
And machines, 166-67, 169, 649
Organization of, 141-44 (*See also* Sequencing)
Reading, evaluation of, 533-37
Response- and stimulus-centered, 121-27
Second language, summary and description, 626, 641-43
Sources of
Federal agencies, 749-51
Industrial training, 702-703, 710-11
Stimulus content, 130-33
Types in industrial training,

(Programs, cont'd.)
690-93
Usage patterns in schools,
649-50
Project Talent, 551
Prompting, 74-85, 131-33, 136,
152, 183-84, 356, 627-28
And confirmation, 184
And error minimizing, 235
Overprompting, 81-82
Use of pictures in reading,
522-24

Q
Quality control (*see* Evaluation)

R
Rate of learning, 217-18
Individual differences, 141
And IQ, 141
Rate of response, as a reinforcer,
530
Ratings, of instructional effective-
ness, 529
Readiness, 783
In reading, 531-33
(*See also* Entering behavior)
Reading
Critical, 574-75
Whole word and phonic ap-
proaches, 512-15
(*See also* Textual behavior)
Reasoning skills
Diagnostic, 466-76
In science, 452-57
Recall (*see* Retention)
Redundancy, in written and spoken
language, 517-18
Reinforcement, 6, 600, 794-95,
797-99
Autotelic, 530-31
Confirmation, 89-91, 134-36
Contingency, 13, 14, 151
Differential, 70-71
Extrinsic, 529-30

(Reinforcement, cont'd.)
Hypothesis formation, 420-21
Personality traits, 458-61
In reading, 527-31
Response probability, 428, 530,
797-98
Response-produced stimuli, 73-
74
Schedules of, 14
Second language learning, 610
Self, 578
In shaping vocal responses, 605-
608
Stimulus change, 798-99
And subject matter analysis,
778-80
Temporal order, 10
And terminal behavior, 26-27
Response
Appropriate behavior (correct
answer), 18, 27, 78-89
Availability, 43, 788
Constructed vs. multiple choice,
103-104, 423-24
As data for revision, 292-93
Determination, 84-85
Differentiation, 42-43
Applicable to second language
learning, 605-13
Coordination with discrimi-
nation learning, 609-13
In textual behavior, 621
Factors
In instructional design,
789-91
In reading, 520-24
Intraverbal, 624-28
Learning (*see* Response differen-
tiation)
Machine evaluation of, 192-93
Mode, 183, 185, 191-92, 778-80
Studies of, 92-104, 397-98
Monitoring of, 187-89
Multiple choice, 86, 137, 152
Oral (*see* Echoic behavior)

(Response, cont'd.)
  Overt and covert, 93-103, 129
    Time and efficiency, 102-103
  Requirements in programing,
    127-30
  Successive approximation, 785
  Topography, 70-71
    Time and efficiency, 102-103
Responsive environment, 530-31,
    536-37, 798
Retention, 35, 56-57, 312
Rule learning
  Illustrative frame sequence,
    484-87
  (*See also* Principles, learning of;
    Strategies, learning of)
"Ruleg" procedure, 133, 214-15,
    239

S

Savings measures, 311
Schools, program usage
  Case studies, 654-77
  History of, 651-54
  Implementation of, 680-82
Second language learning, evalu-
    ation of research in, 587-89
Self-editing, 143
Self-monitoring, 791-92
Self-organizing systems, 217
Self-pacing, in industrial training,
    699
Self-reinforcement, 578
Sequence learning, 48-49
Sequencing, 47, 141-43, 787-89
  Gradual progression, 67-68, 509
  And intelligence, 390
  Learner determined, 30-31, 142
  In reading
    Analytic vs. synthetic, 512-15
    Factors in, 508-13
    Frequency, 515-16
    Relationship to behavioral anal-
      ysis, 465-76
    Studies of, 385-86

Shaping, 70-74
  Compared with stimulus control,
    142, 151
  Speech response topography,
    605-609
Size of step, 86-89, 141-42, 185,
    607
  Definitions of, 395
  Studies of, 395-97
Skill, hierarchy of, 218-19, 223
SOCRATES (*see* Machines)
Spaced practice, 69-70
Speech
  Correction, 611
  Perception, 601-604, 612, 613
  Synthetic, 601-604
Speedreading, in adaptive systems,
    256
Spelling, 576
Spiral programing, 240
Stimulus
  Change, as a reinforcer, 798-99
  Content, of programs, 130-33
  Control, 585, 785-86
    Compared with shaping, 151
    Transfer of, 71-74
  Factors
    In instructional design,
      789-91
    In reading, 520-24
  Generalization (*see* Generaliza-
    tion)
  Pretraining, 532
  Response-produced, 73-74
  Similarity, 518-20
  Transfer, 627-28
Strategies, learning of, 53-54
  (*See also* Principles, learning of)
Subject matter structure, 9-10
Successive approximation, 70, 785
  Transitional behavior, 787
Syntactical structure, 516-17
Synthetic speech, 612

T

Tactile information, 244

Tacts, 628-30

Task analysis, 23, 34-37, 773-81
  Behavioral categories, 36-39
  And education, 39-41
  Interaction with instruction, 37-39
  In military training, 35-37
  (*See also* Task description)

Task description
  Criteria for, 33-34
  And instructional objectives, 33
  (*See also* Objectives)

Taxonomy
  Of behavior (*see* Objectives; Task analysis)
  Categories of behavior, 41-56
  Educational objectives, 39-41

Teacher, role in use of programed instruction, 650, 675-77, 755

Teaching
  Compared with testing, 7
  Conventional vs. programs, 107, 375-81
  Definition of, 6
  Experimental analysis of, 17
  Improvement of, 8-11
  Strategies, 174
    Selection of, 170-85

Terminal behavior, 23-27, 170-72, 182, 222, 237-41
  Analysis of, in instructional design, 773-81
  Classes of, 25-26
  Component and content repertoires, 774-75
  In English instruction, 547-50, 553, 555-70
  Interaction with entering behavior and instruction, 177-80
  Levels of, 238-39
  In mathematics, 449
  Measurement of, 24-25

(Terminal behavior, cont'd.)
  And problem solving, 237-39
  And reinforcement, 26-27
  In science education, 444-61
  In second language learning
    Formal repertoires, 590-623
    Formal-thematic repertoire distinction, 589
  Vs. terminal achievement criteria, 719-20

Testing, compared with teaching, 7

Tests
  Time and efficiency scores, 102-103
  (*See also* Criterion measures; Evaluation)

Textual behavior, 619-22
  Integration with echoic behavior, 616

Thematic repertoires, in verbal behavior, 623-31

Time for instruction, reduction in, 698

TOTE model, 220

Transcription, in second language learning, 619

Transfer, 56-60, 219, 481-83, 777-78, 799
  And behavioral categories, 57-59
  In discrimination learning, 591-600
  Research with adaptive systems, 248-56
  Of stimulus control, compared with shaping, 142
  Between verbal repertoires, 631-32

Translation, in language learning, 625, 627

Trends, in programed instruction, 802-806

Trial and error, and teaching, 14

U

Unit Plan, 324-27
University of Illinois Committee
on School Mathematics,
327-29, 379-80

V

Vanishing, 46
(*See also* Fading)

W

Winnetka Plan, 330-33

Author Index

A

Alexander, H., 384, 398, 434
Allen, D. W., 114, 384, 387, 389, 436
Allen, L. E., 428, 430
Alter, M., 57, 61, 100, 110, 383, 384, 387, 430, 438
Anastasi, A., 632
Anderson, A. R., 430, 507
Angell, D., 61, 77, 110, 183, 184, 207
Angell, G. W., 90, 110
Annett, J., 135, 156
Ashby, W. R., 180, 207
Asher, J. J., 632
Associated Public School Systems, 430
Austin, G. A., 53, 431
Austwick, K., 158, 430
Ausubel, D. P., 366, 401, 414, 415, 416, 417, 430
Avner, R. A., 207

B

Baker, B. L., 68, 114, 386, 436
Baker, R. L., 268, 319, 544
Barcus, D. L., 632
Barlow, J. A., 136, 157, 346, 384, 398, 399, 431, 434
Barnhart, C., 509, 540
Bassler, O. C., 57, 89, 112
Baumann, R., 736
Beane, D. G., 110, 185, 207, 380, 388, 393, 399, 431
Bear, D. E., 540
Beberman, M., 327, 366, 368, 401, 402
Begle, E., 401, 402
Belton, J. R., 280, 282, 314
Bennett, G. K., 183, 207
Berko, J., 624, 633
Besnard, G. G., 23, 29
Bijou, S. W., 783, 806
Birt, A., 101, 112
Bitzer, D. L., 196, 207, 208, 212

Bloom, B. S., 22, 25, 28, 39, 56, 59, 61, 294, 314, 366
Bloom, L. A., 110
Bloomer, L. A., 514, 540
Bloomfield, L., 509, 510, 540
Bloomfield, M. W., 557, 580
Blough, D. B., 431
Blumenthal, J. C., 563, 564, 580, 683
Blyth, J. W., 378, 431, 633, 636
Bohrson, R. G., 683
Bolles, R. C., 23, 36
Bolt, Beranek and Newman, Inc., 314
Bond, J. H., 345
Bonkowski, R. J., 637
Boring, E. G., 477, 506
Borst, J., 633
Bossone, R. M., 582
Bottiglia, W., 635
Bower, G. H., 806
Bradfield, J. M., 325, 367
Branson, R. K., 580
Braunfeld, P. G., 196, 207, 208, 212
Brethower, D. M., 633, 637
Brickell, H., 680, 682
Briggs, F. A., 580
Briggs, L. J., 23, 29, 61, 110
Brink, R. O., 736
Brinkman, E. H., 783, 806
Broder, L. L., 366
Brooks, N., 614, 633
Brown, J. S., 431
Brown, L. T., 367, 416, 417, 433
Brown, O. R., Jr., 379, 380, 431
Brown, R., 624, 633, 806
Bruner, J. S., 19, 53, 61, 366, 400, 401, 403, 404, 427, 431, 773, 807
Buchanan, C. D., 534, 536, 778, 807
Buckingham, W., 736
Buiten, R. L., 618, 635
Bullock, D., 740

Burk, F., 330, 333
Buros, O. K., 279, 314, 431
Burton, B. B., 103, 110, 183, 208
Burton, W. H., 366
Bushnell, D. D., 185, 197, 208, 366
Buswell, G. T., 336, 366

C

Calvin, A., 654
Cameron, F., 209
Campbell, D. T., 314
Campbell, V. N., 96, 105 ,110, 112, 183, 208, 315, 386, 391, 399, 431
Carlson, M. E., 99, 112
Carlton, S. T., 581
Carpenter, C. R., 208, 212
Carroll, J. B., 278, 314, 512, 513, 540, 581, 587, 588, 604, 615, 618, 619, 629, 633, 638, 782, 807
Carterette, E. C., 517, 540
Cartwright, G. P., 184, 208
Case, H. W., 69, 115, 386, 437
Caulfield, R. L., 268, 314
Chapman, R. L., 736
Charap, M., 211
Chomsky, N., 547, 556, 581
Christian, R., 736
Ciardi, J., 578, 579, 581
Clapp, D. J., 741
Clark, D. C., 739
Clark, J. W., 634, 638
Clayton, M., 648
Cofer, C. N., 633, 806
Cogswell, J. F. A., 197, 208
Cohen, I. S., 15, 19
Coke, E. U., 740
Comenius, 15
Conant, J. B., 9, 19, 477, 506
Cook, D. A., 61, 129, 135, 157, 506, 507, 736
Cook, D. L., 21
Cook, J. O., 78, 111
Cooper, F. S., 633, 636

Corrigan, R. E., 736
Cotterman, T. E., 26, 37, 61
Coulson, J. E., 22, 62, 88, 104, 111,
    112, 113, 157, 158, 159, 161,
    185, 197, 208, 209, 210, 211,
    263, 317, 389, 399, 431, 434,
    436, 437, 541, 636, 640, 807,
    808, 809
Cram, D., 137, 157
Crawford, M. P., 780, 807
Crnkovic, J. K., 367
Cronbach, L. J., 208, 801, 802, 807
Cross, D. V., 601, 602, 633
Crothers, E., 597, 604, 639
Crowder, N. A., 129, 132, 134, 138,
    144, 147-50, 157, 186, 208,
    399
Csanyi, A. P., 72, 111, 408
Cummings, A. Q., 111

D

Davidson, H. P., 532, 540
Davy, R. A., 514, 540
DeCecco, J. P., 156, 157
Deese, J., 62
DellaPiana, G., 417, 432
Denova, C. C., 279, 314
Detambel, M. H., 206, 208
Deterline, W. A., 129, 157, 314
Diack, H., 525, 540
Dick, W., 184, 212, 391, 393, 433
Diederich, P., 549, 581, 658
Dodd, B., 264
Dolmatch, T. B., 118, 157, 736
Donahue, V. M., 68, 112
Downing, J. A., 510, 540
Dressel, P. L., 22, 28, 62
Drooyan, I., 314
Duncker, J., 337, 338, 341, 367
Durkin, D., 533, 540
Durrell, D. D., 540

E

Easley, J. A., 192, 209, 432
Ebbit, W. R., 557, 583
Edgerton, H. A., 314

Edwards, A. L., 432
Edwards, W., 207, 209
Eigen, L. D., 81, 94, 111, 157, 160,
    209, 268, 278, 314, 381, 382,
    383, 384, 386, 387, 388, 393,
    394, 401, 404, 430, 432, 436,
    638, 648, 652, 653, 683, 739
Eldridge, G., 417, 432
Ellis, A. B., 115
Ellis, H. C., 374, 432
Ellson, D. G., 523, 540
Ely, D. P., 315
English, H. B., 164, 209
Epstein, B., 119, 157
Epstein, S., 119, 157
Epstein, W., 516, 540
Ericksen, C., 440
Erlebacher, A., 515, 540
Ervin, S. M., 517, 540, 543
Esbensen, T., 315
Estes, W. K., 157
Evans, J. L., 21, 26, 62, 73, 88, 100,
    111, 112, 129, 133, 157, 263,
    374, 379, 382, 384, 385, 386,
    391, 396, 398, 408, 413, 419,
    424, 432, 523, 526, 530, 540,
    578, 581, 652, 683
Everett, J. B., 654, 659, 680, 683
Everett, R. M., Jr., 540

F

Fant, C. G. M., 634
Farnsworth, P. R., 318
Fay, L. C., 514, 515, 540, 544
Feigenbaum, E. A., 264, 525, 541
Feldhusen, J. F., 101, 112
Feldman, J., 264
Feldman, M., 532, 542
Felds, P. E., 412, 433
Fernandez, G., 673
Ferster, C. B., 401, 433, 459, 506,
    626, 634, 807
Feurzig, W., 197, 212
Fiks, A. I., 634
Filby, Y., 395, 433

Filep, R. T., 317, 431
Finch, G., 209
Findley, J. D., 62
Fine, B., 377, 433
Fine, R., 429
Finley, R. E., 157, 736
Finn, J. D., 16, 19, 209, 573, 581, 737
Flanagan, J. C., 287, 315, 551, 581
Flanders, N. A., 367
Flavell, D., 220, 263
Fletcher, L., 315
Ford, E. A., 669, 683
Fowler, H., 807
Fowler, W., 523, 541
Francis, W. N., 556, 568, 581
Frandsen, A. N., 367
Frase, L. T., 209
Fraser, C., 624
Fraser, G., 806
Freedman, J. L., 600, 636
French, J. W., 581
French, R. S., 23, 28, 62
Fries, C. C., 557, 558, 560, 581
Fry, E. B., 112, 129, 131, 141, 142, 157, 372, 433
Fullick, M. G., 308, 315, 376, 377, 434, 683, 808

G

Gage, N. L., 209, 317, 368, 582, 633
Gagné, R. M., 21, 23, 26, 29, 36, 45, 48, 57, 62, 63, 70, 89, 112, 143, 158, 294, 315, 318, 348, 349, 350, 367, 390, 391, 393, 401, 408, 409, 416, 417, 433, 737, 776, 788, 807
Galanter, E., 158, 161, 220, 264, 275, 278, 315, 317, 435, 437
Gannon, D. R., 63
Garvey, C. J., 634
Gates, A. I., 541
Gavurin, E. I., 68, 112

Geake, R. R., 541
Geer, L. N., 737
Geis, G. L., 268, 292, 315, 634
Gelder, H. M., 209
Gerlach, V. S., 268, 319, 544
Gibson, E. J., 46, 63, 511, 532, 541
Gilbert, T. F., 21, 26, 35, 38, 39, 43, 45, 46, 47, 48 49, 50, 52, 56, 63, 133, 143, 144, 153-55, 158, 346, 375, 396, 397, 398, 401, 403, 409, 410, 417, 421, 427, 428, 433, 585, 634, 807
Gildmer, G. G., 210
Gilmer, B. von H., 742
Gilpin, J., 315, 384, 398, 434, 617, 634
Ginsberg, R., 90, 116, 418, 419, 439, 795, 809
Ginzberg, E., 507
Glanzer, M., 26, 63, 737
Glaser, R., 21, 22, 23, 26, 57, 62, 63, 65, 67, 69, 70, 72, 88, 92, 100, 105, 111, 112, 114, 115, 116, 117, 119, 133, 134, 157, 158, 160, 208, 210, 263, 268, 283, 285, 287, 294, 296, 308, 311, 315, 317, 346, 374, 376, 377, 379, 382, 383, 395, 396, 427, 432, 433, 434, 435, 436, 438, 523, 541, 545, 565, 581, 634, 638, 648, 653, 683, 684, 737, 740, 793, 807, 808, 809
Gleser, G. C., 208
Goldbeck, R. A., 96, 103, 110, 112, 183, 208, 315
Goldberg, I., 21, 63, 134, 158
Golden, W. M., 209
Goldsmith, M., 264, 265
Goldstein, G. D., 265, 266
Goldstein, L. S., 28, 111, 383, 434, 565, 581, 649, 684, 737
Goodman, R., 209
Goodnow, J. J., 53, 431
Gorn, S., 222, 263
Goss, A. E., 541

Gotkin, L. G., 209, 268, 315, 374, 383, 434, 565, 581, 649, 684, 737
Gray, G., 684
Gray, W. S., 368
Green, E. J., 21, 63, 112
Greenhill, L. P., 212
Greenman, M. H., 514, 541
Greeno, J. G., 793, 808
Groesberg, S., 117
Gropper, G. L., 158, 183, 209, 293, 316
Grubb, R. E., 434
Gruber, H. E., 264
Guthrie, E. R., 136
Guthrie, P. M., 112
Guttman, N., 434

H

Hagaman, N., 367
Hall, R. A., Jr., 523, 541
Halley, W. C., 737
Hammock, J., 296, 316
Hammond, P. C., 626, 634
Hanna, L. A., 367
Hanson, L. F., 272, 316, 648
Hanson, N. R., 337, 367
Harakas, T., 105, 112
Harlow, H. F., 63, 215, 226, 263, 264
Harms, L. S., 622, 623, 634
Harris, C. C., 626, 634
Harris, C. W., 515, 540
Harris, T. L., 514, 541
Harrison, R. H., 435
Hartman, T. F., 99, 112
Hatch, R. S., 122, 158
Haugh, O. M., 157
Hawker, J. R., 793
Hayes, A. S., 608, 634
Hayman, J. L., Jr., 183, 210, 544, 632, 684
Heath, R. W., 316
Hebb, D. O., 121, 158
Heidbreder, E., 434

Helwig, J., 19
Hendershot, C. H., 272, 316, 576, 582
Hendrickson, L. N., 532, 542
Hendrix, G., 327, 367, 434
Herrnstein, R. J., 477, 506
Hickey, A. E., 195, 209
Hilgard, E. R., 158, 323-24, 367, 807, 809
Hill, S. A., 405, 439
Hively, W., 113, 268, 308, 316, 407, 424, 434, 509, 521, 524, 542
Hobbs, N., 211, 212
Holland, A. L., 64, 73, 113, 611, 613, 635
Holland, J. G., 113, 122, 138, 158, 160, 268, 316, 375, 401, 424, 425, 426, 434, 635, 783, 808
Holt, H. O., 699, 731, 737
Holz, W. C., 109, 113
Homme, L. E., 21, 62, 88, 100, 111, 112, 133, 157, 263, 346, 374, 379, 382, 383, 396, 408, 428, 432, 434, 435, 653, 683
Hook, J. N., 582
Horn, R. E., 737
Horvath, R. W., 435
Hovland, C. I., 264, 298, 308, 316, 435
Hough, J. B., 113
Huffman, H., 737
Hughes, J. L., 435, 737
Hull, C. L., 435, 461, 506
Hunt, E. B., 220, 264
Husky, H. D., 194, 209
Hutchens, R. M., 12, 19

I

Inhelder, B., 403, 404, 735
Irion, A. L., 64
Isard, S., 582
Israel, M. L., 75, 76, 113, 627, 635
Ivers, H. S., 738

J

Jackson, W., 635
Jacobi, G. T., 265, 266
Jacobs, M., 308, 320
Jacobs, P. I., 269, 280, 316, 318
James, W., 8, 19
Jeffrey, W. E., 532, 542
Jenkins, H. M., 435
Jensen, A. R., 158
Jevons, W. S., 209
Johnson, E. A., 367
Johnson, J. T., 632
Jonckheere, A. R., 251, 256, 264
Jones, J. C., 264
Jones, L. B., 684
Jones, M. J., 517, 540
Judd, C. H., 524, 542

K

Kaess, W., 90, 100, 104, 113, 795, 808
Kalin, R., 381, 435
Kalish, H. I., 434
Katz, M., 316
Kay, H., 130, 135, 158
Keislar, E. R., 99, 114, 378, 381, 394, 396, 435, 522, 526, 530, 542, 543, 610, 637
Keller, F. S., 412, 436, 461, 506, 542, 635, 808
Kelly, B. C., 514, 515, 542
Kendler, H. H., 158, 519, 542
Kendler, T. S., 111, 519, 542
Kersh, B. Y., 367, 436
King, S., 384, 430
Kitzhaber, A. R., 547, 553, 556, 560, 570, 576, 577, 582
Kjeldergaard, P. M., 542
Klaus, D. J., 21, 63, 64, 119, 158, 159, 280, 315, 316, 575, 579, 741
Klaus, P., 738
Koch, S., 159, 264

Komoski, P. K., 381, 382, 386, 387, 393, 404, 432, 652, 653, 683, 684
Koppitz, W. J., 196, 209
Kopstein, F. F., 114, 738
Kormondy, E. J., 97, 101, 114
Kosowski, I., 545
Krathwohl, D., 294
Krumboltz, J. D., 91, 114

L

Lackner, L. S., 793
Lambert, P., 97, 101, 114, 388, 398, 436
Lane, H. L., 43, 591, 601, 602, 605, 613, 618, 633, 635
Lawrence, W., 635
Leeds, D., 97
Legg, O., 376, 377, 384, 436
Lenneberg, E. H., 630, 635
Lermontoff, A., 616, 622, 631, 636
Leverenz, H. W., 738
Levin, G. R., 68, 114, 386, 436
Levin, H., 510, 532, 542
Levin, S. L., 738
Levine, S. L., 436
Lewin, K., 123
Lewis, B. N., 260, 264, 265
Lewis, J. S., 582
Liberman, A. M., 603, 604, 612, 613, 633, 636
Lichtenberger, W. W., 196, 208
Licklider, J. C. R., 185, 197, 203, 209, 210, 626, 636, 791, 808
Liedke, O. K., 636
Lindvall, C. M., 294, 315, 316, 807
Lippert, H., 116, 211, 524, 545
Lippitt, G. L., 741
Lisker, L., 636
Little, J. K., 182, 210
Llewellyn, J. E., 112
Loban, W., 582
Long, E. R., 424, 542
Long, L., 220, 266
Lorge, I., 545

Lumsdaine, A. A., 36, 61, 64, 67, 77, 107, 110, 112, 114, 115, 119, 131, 136, 157, 158, 159, 160, 183, 184, 207, 208, 209, 210, 211, 269, 283, 285, 287, 292, 293, 298, 299, 308, 316, 317, 319, 385, 395, 433, 436, 438, 582, 634, 638, 648, 684, 740, 808, 809
Lyman, J., 398, 437
Lysaught, J. P., 158, 159, 160, 582, 738

M

McCann, J., 26, 30
McCauley, J. S., 739
McCracken, G., 542
McDonald, F. J., 114, 384, 387, 389, 436
McGehee, W., 739
McGeoch, J. S., 64
MacGowan, J., 662, 665
McGuigan, F. J., 723, 739
McGuire, W. J., 43, 64
McIntire, R. W., 530, 543
McKnight, B. A., 439
McNamara, W. J., 738
McNemar, Q., 318
McNeil, J. D., 99, 114, 182, 210, 522, 526, 530, 542, 543
Mace, L., 526, 530, 542, 610, 637
Mackinnon, A. R., 542
Mager, R. F., 21, 22, 23, 24, 26, 29, 30, 33, 36, 40, 64, 142, 159, 239, 264, 294, 318, 739
Maher, A., 211
Maier, M. H., 268, 316, 318
Maltzman, I., 367
Margulies, S., 81, 94, 111, 157, 158, 160, 436, 507, 739
Markle, S. M., 118, 159, 278, 286, 289, 318, 543, 582, 788, 808
Marshall, G. R., 117
Martin, R. M., 221, 264
Marting, E., 157, 736

Marty, F., 636
Massy, M., 97
Matthews, J., 64, 73, 113, 611, 613, 635
May, M. A., 299, 317
Mayer, E., 637
Mayzner, M. S., 543
Mead, G. H., 264
Mechner, F., 21, 61, 135, 157, 506, 507
Meckel, H. C., 562, 567, 571, 573, 577, 582
Mednick, S. A., 600, 636
Meierhenry, W. C., 158, 159, 314, 432, 580, 582
Melaragno, R. J., 91, 115
Mellan, I., 210
Melton, A. W., 773, 808
Meyer, S. R., 90, 115, 131, 159
Michael, R. E., 367
Mildenberger, K. W., 636
Miles, M. B., 582
Miller, D. M., 97, 101, 114, 388, 398, 436
Miller, G. A., 220, 228, 264, 517, 543, 559, 582, 624, 636, 808
Miller, R. B., 23, 26, 32, 33, 35, 40, 56, 64, 318
Miller, W. R., 517, 540, 543
Minsky, M., 264
Moon, H., 398, 437, 739
Moore, D. J., 635
Moore, J. W., 115, 116
Moore, O. K., 401, 427, 430, 436, 460, 507, 530, 531, 536, 676, 677, 684, 798, 808
Moraud, M., 616, 626, 636
Moren, R. I., 617, 631, 638
Morris, D., 264
Morrison, B. A., 99, 112
Morse, R. J., 739, 740
Morton, F. R., 129, 159, 615, 617, 622, 626, 627, 631, 633, 634, 636, 637, 638, 639, 739, 792
Mostofsky, D., 600, 633, 637

Mowrer, O. H., 43, 65
Muehl, S., 532, 542, 543
Mueller, K. A., 614, 620, 637
Mueller, T., 616, 625, 637
Muses, C. A., 265
Musgrave, B. S., 633, 806

N

Najam, E. W., 637
Newcombe, T. M., 634
Newell, A., 264, 265, 436, 808
Newman, S. E., 518, 543
Newmark, L., 557, 580
Noble, C. E., 63
Nordberg, H. O., 325, 367
Nostrand, H., 587, 637

O

Odell, W. C., 325, 367
Odiorne, G. S., 739
O'Donnell, L. H., 739
Ofiesh, G. D., 118, 158, 159, 314,
     432, 580, 582, 755
Oinas, F. N., 639
Olson, W. C., 323, 334, 367
Ordahl, G., 163, 210
Ordahl, L. E., 163, 210
Osgood, C. E., 518, 543
Osser, H., 511, 541

P

Page, D., 401, 402, 404
Paradise, N. E., 21, 112, 390, 433
Parker, W. R., 571-72
Parry, S., 576, 583
Pask, G., 198, 210, 222, 247, 251,
     260, 264, 265, 739, 740
Paulson, C. F., 318
Pennington, D. F., 159, 395, 436
Perrin, D. G., 16, 19, 209, 737
Peters, R. J., 739
Peterson, R. O., 740
Piaget, J., 220, 225, 263, 265, 401,
     410, 411, 435, 437, 461, 507
Pick, A., 511, 541
Pimsleur, P., 587, 610, 611, 637
Plumlee, L. B., 393, 437

Polin, A. T., 740
Pollock, W. T., 210
Polya, G., 428, 437
Popp, H., 521, 523, 524, 542, 543
Popplewell, C. M., 264
Porter, D., 113, 182, 210, 523, 543,
     578, 583, 619, 638, 652, 653,
     684
Potter, G. L., 367
Powell, D. R., 740
Powers, C. A., 740
Premack, D., 160, 401, 428, 437,
     530, 543, 797, 808
Pressey, S. L., 7, 19, 67, 86, 115,
     129, 132, 137, 141, 144-47,
     160, 163, 164, 165, 166, 210,
     437, 694, 740
Pribram, K. H., 220, 264
Price, J. E., 115
Primoff, E., 65
Prion, E. E., 740

Q

Quackenbush, J. F., 650
Quine, W. V. O., 265

R

Ramo, S., 740
Raygor, A. L., 544
Read, E. A., 367
Redding, M. F., 740
Reed, J. E., 183, 210, 544, 684
Reid, J. M., 566, 572
Reid, R. L., 265
Reiff, G. D., 605, 638
Resnick, L. B., 115, 336, 368, 526,
     544
Revsin, B., 113
Rickover, H. G., 19
Rigney, J. W., 186, 210, 388, 437
Rinsland, H. D., 544
Rivlin, H. N., 368
Roberts, P., 564, 566, 583
Robinson, J., 109, 113
Rock, I., 76, 115
Rocklyn, E. H., 616, 617, 631, 638

Rocky Mountain School Study Committee, 280
Roe, A., 69, 97, 103, 115, 374, 377, 382, 386, 391, 393, 398, 399, 437
Roe, K. V., 69, 115, 386, 437
Rogers, J., 740
Rogers, M., 526
Rogovin, S., 544, 564, 565, 583
Roosinck, P. A., 544
Rosenbloom, P., 402
Roshal, S. M., 114
Rotberg, J. C., 65
Rothkopf, E. Z., 115, 130, 160, 265, 268, 275, 280, 283, 285, 287, 311, 318, 544, 740
Rubinoff, M., 265
Rummler, G., 740, 741
Rushton, E., 654, 655
Russell, B., 266, 440
Russell, D. H., 541
Rust, G. C., 741
Ryans, D. G., 319

S

Saltz, E., 43, 65
Saltzman, I. J., 278, 319, 638
Sapon, S. M., 587, 604, 615, 622, 624, 626, 634, 638
Saporta, S., 557, 581, 583, 624, 639, 807
Schaefer, H. H., 22, 23, 65, 77, 116, 132, 160, 627, 628, 639, 793, 808, 809
Scharf, E. S., 91, 116
Schelle, W. N., 741
Scherer, G. A. C., 614, 615, 620, 639
Schlosberg, H., 422, 437
Schneider, B. A., 635
Schoenfeld, W. N., 412, 436, 506, 542, 635, 808
Schramm, W., 272, 283, 319, 372, 426, 437, 659, 663, 684, 741
Schulz, R. W., 43, 45, 516, 545, 788, 809

Schuster, D. H., 725, 741
Schutz, R. E., 268, 319, 544
Schwartz, H. A., 738
Seashore, H. G., 183, 207
Seeman, W., 160
Selfridge, J. A., 517, 543, 624, 628, 636, 808
Selfridge, L. E., 434
Shaw, J. C., 264, 436
Shay, C. B., 106, 116, 387, 397, 438
Sheffield, F. D., 298, 308, 316
Shettel, H. H., 140, 160, 319, 741
Shibutani, T., 266
Shinkman, P. G., 635
Shrader, W. B., 211
Sidman, M., 438
Sidowski, J. B., 116
Silberman, H. F., 88, 104, 111, 116, 185, 208, 292, 319, 344, 391, 399, 438, 526, 529, 544
Silverman, R. E., 100, 110, 268, 275, 319, 383, 438
Silvern, L. C., 436, 738, 741
Simon, H. A., 264, 429, 436, 438, 525, 541, 808
Simon, P. A., 429, 438
Sindler, A. J., 741
Singer, M. G., 238, 266
Sisk, J. C., 582
Skinner, B. F., 19, 20, 21, 42, 65, 67, 73, 77, 93, 113, 116, 123, 128, 130, 144, 150-53, 160, 163, 164, 165, 166, 183, 192, 198, 210, 211, 284, 319, 371, 373, 374, 375, 382, 385, 386, 387, 395, 397, 398, 399, 400, 401, 402, 403, 404, 406, 412, 413, 415, 422, 423, 427, 429, 433, 438, 456, 459, 461, 482, 506, 507, 525, 528, 544, 561, 577, 579, 583, 624, 625, 639, 652, 654, 775, 783, 795, 797, 806, 807, 809
Skinner, H., 163

Slack, C. W., 159, 395, 436
Sledd, J., 557, 583
Smallwood, R. D., 211, 224, 225,
    266
Smedslund, J., 438
Smith, D. E. P., 541, 627, 641
Smith, L. M., 184, 211, 439
Smith, M. D., 379, 384, 399, 439,
    636
Smith, N. H., 381, 391, 393, 439
Smith, R. M., 741
Smith, W. I., 115, 116
Smoke, K. L., 439
Snyder, M. S., 527, 544
Socrates, 15
Solomon, R. L., 422, 437
Spalding, R. B., 532, 544
Spalding, W. R., 532, 544
Sparks, P. E., 514, 515, 544
Spiel, O., 235, 266
Spitzer, M. E., 111
Squire, J. R., 571, 573, 583
Staats, A. W., 529, 544, 545
Standing, E. M., 545
Stanley, J. C., 314
Stake, R. E., 211
Steinberg, E. R., 583
Stendler, C. B., 368
Stevens, S. S., 116, 636, 639
Stolurow, L. M., 21, 23, 26, 37, 38,
    65, 100, 116, 133, 142, 155,
    161, 184, 186, 196, 206, 208,
    211, 212, 268, 316, 318, 319,
    368, 374, 382, 390, 391, 398,
    439, 524, 545
Stone, C. R., 545
Strickland, R. G., 368, 516, 545
Stutz, R., 671, 672
Suchman, J. R., 368, 439
Sullivan, M. W., 563, 564, 565,
    566, 583
Summers, E. G., 544
Suppes, P., 116, 401, 405, 418, 419,
    439, 595, 597, 604, 639, 795,
    809

Sweet, R. J., 608, 639
Sweet, W. E., 608, 622, 626, 639,
    640
Swets, J. A., 77, 117, 597, 598,
    640, 794, 809

T

Taba, H., 368
Taber, J. I., 22, 23, 65, 72, 92, 111,
    116, 117, 523, 545, 737, 809
Taylor, L. R., 518, 543
Teager, H. M., 207, 211, 790, 809
Terrace, H. S., 71, 92, 117, 422,
    423, 439, 795, 809
Terrell, G., 264
Thayer, P. W., 739
Thelen, H. A., 741
Thomas, C. A., 161, 213, 266
Thorndike, E. L., 16, 20, 122, 123,
    161, 163, 211, 545
Thornley, D. G., 264
Tobias, S., 100, 117
Tolman, E. C., 122, 123, 161
Tosti, D., 440
Townsley, M. G., 738
Tracey, W. R., 280, 319
Training Psychology Branch, Aero-
    space Medical Laboratory, 23,
    65
Travers, R. M. W., 322, 323, 368,
    809
Traxler, A. E., 318
Tresselt, M. E., 543
Tucker, J. A., 132, 161
Tyler, F. T., 783, 809
Tyler, R. W., 22, 25, 28, 39, 65,
    294, 319

U

Underwood, B. J., 43, 45, 65, 440,
    516, 545, 788
Uttal, W. R., 134, 161, 193, 196,
    211, 640, 791, 809
Utter, R. F., 742, 758, 761

V

Valdman, A., 616, 617, 626, 641
Valentine, C. G., 699, 731, 737
Valentine, J. A., 211
Vallance, T. R., 211
Van Atta, E. L., 97, 101, 114
Van Riper, C. G., 627, 641
Verplanck, W. S., 419, 420, 421, 440
Vogel, M., 368
Vygotsky, L. S., 220, 225, 263, 266

W

Wahler, T. G., 658, 684
Walcutt, C., 543
Walker, C. C., 100, 116, 398, 439
Walker, R. W., 742
Walker, V. R., 669, 683
Wallen, N. E., 322, 323, 368
Waller, T., 742
Walters, R. H., 545
Wark, D. M., 544
Washburne, C., 323, 330, 333, 368, 804
Watson, J., 510, 532, 542
Wechkin, S., 522, 545
Weiner, M., 100, 117
Weir, R., 597, 604, 639
Weisman, R. G., 91, 114
Welch, D., 661, 662, 684
Welch, L., 220, 266
Weltman, G., 97
Wepman, J. M., 522, 545
Wertheimer, M., 264, 368, 614, 615, 620, 639
Wesman, A. G., 183, 207

Whipple, G. M., 368
Whitehead, A. N., 266, 440
Wiener, N., 212
Wiley, D. E., 97, 101, 114, 388, 398, 436
Williams, A. P. O., 212
Williams, C. A., 582
Williams, C. M., 159
Williams, J., 93, 102, 105, 117
Wills, H., 414, 440
Wittrock, M. C., 117, 367, 368, 436
Wolfe, M., 69, 70, 117
Woodruff, A. W., 323, 329-30, 342, 368
Woodworth, R. S., 253, 266
Woolman, M., 513, 545
Wooton, W., 314
Wyckoff, L. B., 422, 440

Y

Yaney, J. P., 741
Young, R. K., 65
Yovitis, M. C., 266
Yovits, G. T., 265
Yuzuk, R. P., 740

Z

Zacharias, J., 507
Zeaman, D., 90, 100, 104, 113, 161, 795, 808
Zenger, J. H., 750
Zimmerman, D. W., 545
Zinovieff, A., 638
Zuckerman, C. B., 117
Zuckerman, J. V., 308, 320